BIRMINGHAM LIBRARIES
DISCARD

A CRICKETER'S COMPANION

BIRMINGHAM LIBRARIES
DISCARD

A CRICKETER'S COMPANION

EDITED BY
CHRISTOPHER MARTIN-JENKINS

SMALLMEAD
PRESS

Produced exclusively for Smallmead Press by
Lennard Books
Mackerye End
Harpenden
Herts AL5 5DR

A catalogue reference is available
from the British Library

ISBN 1 85291 112 3

First published in this edition 1992
© Lennard Associates Ltd

All rights reserved. No part of this book may be transmitted
in any form or by any means, electronic or mechanical,
including photocopying, recording or by any information
storage or retrieval system, without permission in writing
from the publisher and copyright holders

Jacket design by Pocknell & Co
Designed by Cooper Wilson
in association with Forest Publication Services
Printed and bound in Great Britain by
Butler & Tanner Ltd,
Frome and London

CONTENTS

INTRODUCTION

Chapter 3

FAR PAVILIONS

Chapter 4

CRICKET WATCHING

Chapter 10

FICTION DEPARTMENT

SOURCES AND ACKNOWLEDGEMENTS

INTRODUCTION

Christopher Martin-Jenkins

If God grants me an old age I suppose there may come a period of life when time seems to hang heavy but it is hard to envisage it. In industrious middle age the happy problem is to make time for all the things life has to offer and not the least amongst them is reading.

If you have had time to get this far I hope you will *make* time to go further because there is pleasure ahead if you do in what is not quite a conventional cricketing anthology. There have been so many of them that another perhaps needs justification. It is simply this: so much has been written about cricket, and so much of it is worthy but unread, that there is good reason occasionally to unearth the gems that have been blushing unseen. This is, I hope, an anthology of the excellent but unfamiliar.

Of course, someone once read and appreciated all the pieces and excerpts in this volume or they would not have been published in the first place, but most have been forgotten inside unopened books on dusty shelves and each, I hope you may agree, deserves a little further exposure to the light. The great advantage of an anthology is that those for whom time is forever fleeing can enjoy a short read on a train or a 'plane, or before the eyelids drop, without losing the thread. Few threads, in fact, bind this volume, unless it is simply a common enthusiasm for the game.

You would have to be very enthusiastic indeed, for example, to field for three days in a *club* match, as the men of Essendon in Victoria did in 1898 in the game which A.A. Thomson, that felicitous writer, recalls in the opening piece. Chasing a mere 1095 to win, Essendon had to do without three men, all marked in the extraordinary scorecard as 'absent 0'. Who could blame them?

A total of 1000-plus had not yet been achieved in a single Test innings and unless we revert to timeless Tests it probably never will, but there is undoubtedly a fascination in days when the batsmen are totally in command, so long as they do not happen too often. Two of the more memorable days of cricket I have watched and reported on in recent years were the first of the 1989 Trent Bridge Test, when Mark Taylor and Geoff Marsh batted through the entire day for Australia (after Marsh had been perilously close to becoming Devon Malcolm's first Test victim early in the morning) and the one at The Oval in 1990 when

Neil Fairbrother made over 300 in a day for Lancashire against Surrey. Some found the match boring. As a *match* it was, but I confess I rather enjoyed seeing what a lot of county cricket must have been like between the two world wars.

Neville Cardus described another such run-glut in *Good Days*. Having put on 388 together in the 1934 Leeds Test, Bradman and Ponsford shared a second-wicket stand of 451 in the timeless (Ashes-deciding) Oval Test which followed. It is a fascinating account with shrewd observations of field placings, proper strictures about England's fielding (Ponsford was eventually dropped six times in his innings of 266) and a correct prediction that Australia would not ask England to follow on – even if their first innings reached 700, which it did.

Looking at other reports of the match I note that 420 overs were bowled in four days, an average of 105 a day despite the fact that England's attack comprised Verity plus four fast bowlers (Bowes, Allen, Clark and medium-pace Hammond). I also see that, in his summary of that 1934 series in the same volume, Cardus wrote: 'England never found a unified team. Performances in county cricket were constantly proved to possess no value. English county cricket is deplorably slack; there is too much of it week by week. The visit of the Australians exposed weakness of technique and weakness of point of view of the game.'

Who did not conclude much the same after Australia's four-nil defeat of England in 1989?

That word *slack* is especially pejorative when it describes a cricketer or his team, but so often it seems to be true that one player appears slack, the other slick; one set of players to be merely going through the motions, while the other team, the winning one invariably, seems to be fuelled by enthusiasm. Certainly, zest for the game is a precious quality, exemplified by men like John Wisden, whose life was cricket, succinctly portrayed herein by Alan Hill; or Godfrey Evans, whose 'tigerish satisfaction' when whipping off the bails Henry Blofeld recalls so vividly; or W.G. himself, so confident of his strength and ability that he indulged himself fully at dinner with the Oxford undergraduates in 1886, not least in the champagne deliberately offered in a Machiavellian plan to 'nobble' him, before making a hundred and taking all ten wickets the following day.

Many a cricket enthusiast is largely or even wholly a spectator. Robert Lynd conveys their pleasure memorably in his description of a day at Lord's on which 'the wind came from the east in sunny mouthfuls'. There is, too, a vicarious pleasure in being present at a cricket ground when great deeds are performed, and Cyril Foley puts that extraordinary innings by Alletson, the Notts professional, perfectly into its context in an extract from *Autumn Foliage*. Why did Alletson play like Jessop and Botham fashioned into one on one amazing afternoon and never again? Foley calculates that by scoring 115 out of 120 in seven overs, Alletson scored at 278 runs an hour!

Another famous hitter was C.I. Thornton, which makes Lord Granville's submission that Thornton 'was never very keen on my being in with him' the most splendidly boastful in the book. Granville, it transpires (for it is not generally known!) used to hit so hard that 'the pace was soon too warm for him'. Notably one day when they batted together against 'Bexley, or Bexhill, or whatever its name was.' There is a vagueness about the facts which perhaps only a senior aristocrat would be allowed to get away with!

The noble Lord is more modest when he ascribes an innings of 11 in *two days* by the notorious blocker Jupp of Dorking to his own failure to catch an edge early in his innings, low down at point off the corner of the bat as Jupp aimed to square-leg.

Which brings me to technicalities. That master of the art and science of cricket captaincy, Mike Brearley, would be especially interested in a remarkable exposition by 'Gryllus' on 'Captaincy Technological'. It contains a great deal of wisdom but I rather hope that the author has at least half a tongue in his cheek when he claims that to the good captain 'the pitch simply gets up and talks to him, saying how it will play now and how it will play in a couple of hours or more'. The most intuitive of captains often read pitches wrongly.

Another great theoriser on cricket, Trevor Bailey, gave a characteristically honest account of the Lord's Test matches in which he played in his *Wickets, Catches and the Odd Run*, concluding of his own bowling (having made 97 in 150 minutes) against New Zealand in 1949 that 'my bowling was well below international standard. . . as I had not yet acquired sufficient control'. He can say it about himself as well as about others! His attempt, however, to play down the significance of his famous partnership with Willie Watson in 1953 fails despite itself: its epic qualities remain intact.

There is so much else worth recommending: J.C. Squire underlining the fascinations uncovered by Lucas and Ashley-Cooper in the Hambledon Cricket Chronicle; Ron Yeomans on the compulsions which drive cricket collectors; 'A Country Vicar' describing some matches on Corfu which precisely agree with my own experiences there; 'Traddles', the little boy cricketer most of us have met; and some engaging fiction too.

I must detain you no further. After all,

> 'Time driveth onward fast,
> And in a little while our lips are dumb.'

Chapter 1

GREAT MATCHES

A.A. Thomson

Half-a-century ago I used to spend my Saturday's penny on a quarter of sweets called Hundreds-and-Thousands, which were magnificent in quantity and, for the young in heart and stomach, pretty sound in quality, too. I am irresistibly reminded of these things when I think of the interesting match played between Melbourne University and Essendon in the year 1898. Since then many records have been woven into the warp and woof of time by the eternal Webber, but this game, as they say, still presents some notable features. Some people, for instance, complain of five-day Test matches: this game extended over the best part of three weeks. They did not play all day every day, you understand: the match took place on three successive Saturdays and the following Wednesday, and by that time the season was practically over. Players and umpires were all two weeks and four days older and it must have seemed a good deal longer.

Melbourne University batted first and made 1094. I will repeat that. One thousand and ninety-four. The relevant *Wisden* called this the highest total on record. So it was at the time. It was beaten 29 years later, oddly enough in Melbourne, when Victoria totted up 1107 against the visibly ageing bowlers of New South Wales. With electronic batsmen like Mr Ponsford, you never knew what would happen. All the same 1094 seems to me a pretty fair score. And there was no nonsense about 75-yard boundaries. The circumference of the ground, we are told, was 554 yards. Thus, using a simple mathematical formula and hoping that the arena was reasonably round, we may reckon that the average boundary was about 88 yards from the pitch. Hard pounding, gentlemen, hard pounding.

The first two wickets fell for a mere 156, but after that there was quite a stand. L. Miller pushed along to 205 and E.C. Osborne was well past his century. They raised the total to 453 and were, you might say, practically set, when Miller, like the delectable Arthur Wood in similar circumstances, lost his head in a crisis and was caught at the wicket. One of the shortest stands of the innings followed: it was only 83. Osborne went on serenely towards his 190, but his new partner, O'Hara, had a meagre time. You can imagine Osborne greedily 'hogging' the bowling, hitting up 70 while O'Hara made 7. As I see it, this so exasperated O'Hara, probably a wild Irish character to start with, that he hit his own wicket down in sheer frustration and achieved the distinction of being the only man on the side to make under 20.

The nervous 990s

Two further respectable stands brought the score to 828 for six and then entered the last of the five century-makers. His name was Bullivant and having come in at the end of the second day, he showed a disposition to stay there all the third. He soon lost Feilchenfeld, who had made 176, but life went inexorably on until 968 for eight. At that point the tempo slowed down. With the total standing at 998, it kept on standing. The batsmen were in the nervous nine-hundred-and-nineties and were taking no chances. There was no relaxation, no throwing of caution to the winds. Bullivants never forget. Maiden over after maiden over was sent down. The batsmen were fixtures. The bowlers were somnambulists. Even the wicket-keeper dozed off; a ball slipped past him for four byes and the tension was eased. There was a cheerful stand for the tenth wicket and the end came when the last man was caught at 1094 by a colleague from his own side, fielding as substitute. Now the labourers' task was o'er and the morning and the evening were the third day.

The bowling analysis is an epic in itself. Never in the field of human conflict have so many been put on for the loss of so few. Eleven men had a go and 263.3 overs were sent down, one of them by the wicket-keeper. You would think that, once he had been prevailed upon to take off his pads, he might at least have been allowed more than one over. Perhaps he would have improved. There were only five wides in the whole of the innings and there is no actual proof that he bowled all of them in his one lone over. No, I suspect that jealousy was at work. There is a parallel in W.G. Grace's observation during the 1896 Manchester Test to Lilley after that splendid wicket-keeper had doffed his gloves to take a turn with the ball. He did not gate-crash history as sensationally as that earlier England wicket-keeper, Alfred Lyttelton, who in the 1884 Test at The Oval took four for 19, with lobs, almost, you might say, before the batsmen noticed he had got his pads off. But Lilley did his best. His first over yielded 14 runs and a wide, but soon after that he got a wicket and Lilley could never think why the Old Man took him off. 'Put those gloves on, Dick,' said W.G. 'You must have been bowling with the wrong arm.' Yes, jealousy. The Essendon wicket-keeper passes from our ken a much-wronged man.

Two Christians, one Hymn

The heroes of the bowling were the brothers H. and C. Christian. Their combined figures (H. and C.) were: 90 overs, 25 maidens, 2 wickets, 380 runs. Did the Bedser twins ever display such Christian endurance? I have set down H. and C. as brothers, though, of course, they may have been father and son; indeed, as the thousand-mark approached and time faded into eternity, they may have felt like grandfather and grandson. H. Christian's individual tally was: 52 overs, 23 maidens, 1 wicket, 243 runs. He may have imagined that these noble figures would remain a record for all time. It is sad to think that, had he lived till 1951 – and he need only have been about 70 – he would have seen this record shattered by that remarkable bowler, J.J. Warr, who in Tests in the 1950–51 tour of Australia had the following awe-inspiring analysis:

73 overs (584 balls), 6 maidens, 1 wicket, 281 runs.

I have heard Mr Warr express indignation towards a critic who questioned the number of runs. 'No,' said he austerely, 'I remember the figure exactly. Hymns Ancient and Modern, No.281. *Art thou weary, art thou languid, art thou sore distressed?*'

The record, however, of 11 bowlers in one innings, five of whom each had over a hundred runs hit off him, remains unassailable to this day. These bowling heroes were not so heroic with the bat. There can be few single-innings matches that have been lost by over a thousand runs. This was one. Our heroes' total against their opponents' 1094 was only 76. Two men reached 20, W. Griffiths, who had already proved his mettle by taking two wickets for 137, and C. Dalton, who had bowled only 10 overs and must have been fresher. The saddest part of the story is that the match ended with the fall of the seventh wicket and the tail of the score-sheet reads:

W. Smith, absent 0

C. Sampford, absent 0

J. Gaunt, absent 0

What happened to these missing persons? Had they gone on strike? Had they fallen into a state of coma? Had they just come to dislike cricket? The man I feel sorriest for is C. Christian, who at the moment when his comrades deserted the stricken field, was 13 not out. You can just imagine him musing in the pavilion afterwards, in his mild, wistful Australian way: 'There was I, well set, and only 1019 to get to win. If I'd only had somebody to stay with me we'd have got 'em, too right, we would.' He probably ended by thinking 13 an unlucky number.

OVAL TEST MATCH

Neville Cardus

First Day

AUSTRALIA FIRST INNINGS

W.A. Brown, b. Clark	10
W.H. Ponsford, not out	205
D.G. Bradman, c. Ames, b. Bowes	244
S.J. McCabe, not out	1
Extras (b. 1, l.b. 8, w.2, n.b. 4)	15

Total (for 2 wickets)   475

To bat.—W.M. Woodfull, A.F. Kippax, A.G. Chipperfield, W.A. Oldfield, C.V. Grimmett, H.I. Ebeling, and W.J. O'Reilly.

Fall of the wickets:

1	2
21	472

On a beautiful Oval wicket in hot sunshine Bradman and Ponsford exceeded their own stand of 388 made at Leeds a few weeks ago; this time these two great batsmen came together when Australia had lost one wicket for 21, and not until five minutes before half-past six did the broken English attack take another wicket. The Australian score was then 472. For five and a quarter hours Bradman and Ponsford repeated the double concerto of Leeds, but this time Bradman was even more remarkable in his technique than ever, while Ponsford for a long time looked vulnerable but elusive to English fast bowlers – when at certain intervals these fast bowlers really did bowl fast.

Bradman and Ponsford scored at an average speed of eighty runs an hour, which is quicker than English batsmen ever travel all day in a Test match. Beautiful strokes delighted the eye continually. Yet such is patriotism that many weary voices were heard to complain during the afternoon of boredom; also the view was expressed that 'timeless' cricket was monstrous and not sport. Maybe a 'timeless' Test is not a cricket match according to English ideas, but so far Bradman and Ponsford have done nothing to offend against the most lofty notions of the game, whether played in one-day, two-day, three-day, or any other form.

Eighty runs an hour in first-class cricket can be achieved only by brilliant batsmanship. If the 'timeless' Test does end in boredom the responsibility will not be Bradman's or Ponsford's, but the groundsman's. He is the spoil-sport, and, of course, he is helpless; the money bags must be filled. Cricket, like all things of the earth, is open to the corruptibility of filthy lucre. As to today's 'boredom' and 'monstrousness', would we have heard about these afflictions had Hammond and Sutcliffe batted all day and made 451 together in five hours and a quarter? We should have been told in noble numbers that cricket had received honour and much glory and that the expected dreariness of a 'timeless' match had been blown away in a great, refreshing wind of true batsmanship!

Little can be said in these notes about Bradman and Ponsford that was not said a month ago, after the Leeds partnership. Consider the wonder of the two stands achieved consecutively. If I were a writer of boys' fiction, I would not dare to make my two heroes score 388 together in one Test match and 451 together in the next. The critics would tell me to keep my imagination within reasonable bounds and respect what Aristotle said about the improbable – that is, if critics ever do review boys' books, except at Christmas, and if ever critics nowadays do quote Aristotle.

The partnership did not avoid human fallibility, or at least Ponsford did not. He began by flicking speculatively at Allen's fourth and fifth balls; he gave a tolerably easy chance at fine short-leg to Wyatt when he was 57, off Allen. He was guilty of a bad edged stroke at 68 off Bowes through the slips, which Woolley's great height made into a chance to an outstretched right hand; he was again missed by Wyatt when 113 from a hard hit to mid-off (Verity the bowler); and two runs later he drew back to a short rising ball from Allen and cut it to second slip, where Woolley could not hold it. A rare palaver was made about Woolley's inability to bring off two superb catches; apparently he has not yet been awarded that certificate of immunity from blame for missed catches which has been in the possession of Hammond and others for several summers. Woolley should not have fielded second slip to the fast bowling; Hammond is wasted at first slip, a place scarcely visited by the ball on a hard wicket nowadays – why, I cannot tell. Ponsford gave no more than two palpable chances; the slash through the slips at 68 was of the swift order that Mr Fender can catch, now that he is in the press box, with an even greater ease and celerity than he exhibited when he was fielding for Surrey in his best years.

It is poor sportsmanship to harp on two or three or four mistakes in a stand of five hours, with runs coming all the time at a decisive speed and with a rare skill and culture. Bradman was flawless; he gave no sign that in his extensive machine there was any seat of error. His first stroke was a mis-hit along the ground through the slips off the middle of the bat; this was his only miscalculation. When he was 77 he chopped a ball from Hammond and put his arm over his eyes in self-criticism; at 97 he achieved another chop – quite safe, of course. (And a stroke not perfect was indeed an achievement for Bradman today.) He began with a calmness and quietness which were sinister. Tamed was the imp of mischief that pricked him to wayward and lovely and dangerous hazards in June. At the right moment in the cricket match of the year Bradman called back the Bradman of 1930, only here we had a Bradman richer by four years in experience. He did nothing all day that was not fine. After tea he slashed two strokes at off-side balls from Allen and did not hit anything but space. And because of that we were certain Allen was bowling splendidly for a time.

Whenever Bradman did not hit a ball for runs we congratulated our bowlers gratefully and fulsomely. Bradman made his first fifty in 95 minutes; his second fifty in 80 minutes; his third fifty in 50 minutes; his fourth fifty in an hour. He played all his strokes like a cricketer who had before going to the wicket mapped out his innings to the nicest detail; the cool generalship of Bradman's 244 was as impressive as the incomparable skill. He was not disturbed by the fast bumper when it came along from time to time; he cracked it severely once or twice, and at 120 he ducked to Bowes like a man bowing with ironical politeness. But Ponsford many times decided to let the fast ball bury and suffocate itself in his substantial hindquarters; this means of evading an issue looked comic, and it served Ponsford's purpose and helped to irritate many people who voluntarily suffered the long 'boredom'. (As though a day's play that sees only two or three men out were a thing 'never done' in English county cricket; the new thing about today's 'tedium' was the rate of scoring!)

Bradman's innings was ended by an attempt at a hook off a bumping ball. The pavilion roared him home tumultuously. Ponsford will begin again on Monday morning. A tremendous effort will have to come from England's bowlers and fieldsmen to prevent an Australian total of 700. The terrible thought overwhelmed me this afternoon that in a 'timeless' match it is unlikely that Australia will ask England to follow on; the wicket will last a long time, but Australia will probably not care to risk a fourth innings on it. And so the labours of England's bowlers have only begun.

On the whole, Clark was the most hostile of England's bowlers. The cruel wicket detracted from his powers. And many of us could not help feeling that something was wrong with the setting of his field. When he bowled at half-past twelve there was a huge gap between fine-leg and mid-on; not until Australia were 330 for one was there any obstacle to the view of Walden, the square-leg umpire. Clark all day should have bowled to a field containing three men close up on the leg side and a short mid-on. There is no reason in fair sport why Clark's field against Australia on a docile wicket should ever vary from the field he is entitled to when he plays, say, against Lancashire at Northampton, where the pitch is usually lively. A left-handed swinging bowler loses half his deadliness if he is deprived of his proper field or if it is set with a tentativeness that is bound to embarrass him.

The case against fast leg-theory depends on the high-kicking ball persistently exploited. If a fast bowler is not bumping over after over by malice prepense, he is free to set his field in whatever way he is prompted by invention, speculation, or even desperation. Bumping balls today were extremely few; there might have been more had the wicket been less comfortable than it was. But surely the fact that a wicket has been tamed to quiescence gives the fast bowler an unquestionable right to use his strength to get the ball higher than the middle of the bat, since in circumstances so favourable to the batsman the bowler may do his utmost without fear of imperilling anybody's head. At no period of cricket has a fast bowler been expected to pitch the ball where it can be played; at no period until the present has anybody challenged the bowler's liberty to set his field exactly where he wants it.

Allen was good and indifferent by turns, but always plucky. Bowes suffered from his usual fluctuations – medium to fast according to some hidden periodic law deep down in him. England badly missed leg-spin or the ball that asks awkward questions while it is coming through the air.

THE CUP FROM THE PRU

Mihir Bose

. . . After the 1973 England–West Indies one-day international at Headingley a group met in the small bar below the main Leeds complex and the TCCB sounded the Pru out. Would they be interested in sponsoring a World Cup? It would make a nice move: three years of one-day internationals followed by a world one-day international. The Pru were interested and though the original TCCB price was considered to be steep, eventually the company proved willing.

It was ideal: cricket's first World Cup, followed by cricket's most established international contest: England v. Australia. And English cricket, at last learning some of the PR tricks that were the hallmark of cricket's sponsors, began to exude remarkable confidence. For the first time, after repeatedly turning down the idea, Lord's had acquired an efficient PR department. On 9 and 10 October 1974 Lord's held a seminar for the various interested parties: advertising and PR executives, television, press and county secretaries and officials.

Donald Carr, the TCCB Secretary, fairly bubbled with enthusiasm for the coming summer. 'It is the most interesting programme the country has ever known. As regards the World Cup, sponsorship and television should at least cover all the expenses of the competition. Receipts should produce a satisfactory and substantial profit to be distributed among the member countries of the International Cricket Conference.' A.B. Quick, the Essex Chairman, told the somewhat surprised audience that even though not a ball had yet been bowled in the 1975 season, it was already a success: promotional income, from sponsorship and television, should be £750,000, which would leave a tidy sum in hand. Within days of the seminar the Prudential confirmed that they would sponsor the World Cup to the tune of £100,000.

There were to be only two minor hiccoughs before the Prudential Cup began on 4 June. The first concerned the draw and took place in that dreadful summer of 1974. It was announced by Billy Griffith, in a room opposite the Long Room, and known at Lord's as the Writing Room, the traditional place for a press conference at the headquarters. I was sitting next to an Australian journalist and he could hardly contain himself as he heard the draw: Group A: England, India, New Zealand and East Africa; Group B: West Indies, Australia, Pakistan and Sri Lanka. It was, perhaps, bad luck that the draw was announced just a few days after England had bowled out India for 42 in eighty-seven minutes to win a Test by an innings and 285 runs.

Australian journalists were convinced that the draw was 'fixed' and after incessant questioning Billy Griffith, much nettled, conceded that England and Australia had been seeded. A few weeks later, when Pakistan annihilated England in the Prudential one-day internationals,

Group A looked ridiculously easy; even non-Australians were beginning to suspect that Lord's, albeit clumsily, had tried to provide England with the best possible chance of qualifying for the finals, or at least the semi-finals. An England v. West Indies or Australia final was of course the dream ticket but in the process they had produced two groups so badly unbalanced that there were serious doubts about the competition.

These were dramatically increased when five days before the competition began, the second day of the County Championship match between Derbyshire and Lancashire was abandoned because of a freak snowstorm that swept the Buxton ground. Mid-winter could not have looked more desolate. However when the day of the first Prudential matches dawned, sunshine bathed the country, and it developed into a heat wave that lasted for much of the summer. It was late September before the rains returned – to the relief of some. By then the first World Cup had passed into cricket history as one of the most brilliant fortnights the game had known.

The first Saturday of the competition saw relatively easy victories for England and New Zealand in Group A and Australia and the West Indies in Group B. Though England beat India by a massive 202 runs – the biggest victory in the history of one-day internationals – the talking point was the strange batting tactics employed by Sunil Gavaskar. In near perfect weather, before a crowd of 20,000, England batted first; Amiss forced the second ball of the second over from Ghavri off his legs for four, and England were away.

The Indians, captained by their off-spinner Venkatraghavan, dropped Bedi on the grounds that his subtlety was likely to prove expensive, and played a hand of average seamers. But though Venkat was reasonably inexpensive – 41 runs in 12 overs – the seamers were mercilessly plundered. Amiss, who owed his cricket renaissance to the invaluable practice that the Indian bowlers had provided in 1972, now put on an exhilarating display: 98 at lunch in a score of 150 for 1.

He finally scored 137 off 140 balls in an innings that was technically flawless and remarkably calm. Apart from Greig, who made 4, all the English batsmen made runs; Old and Denness put on 89 in the last ten overs, 63 of these coming in the last thirty balls. By the time the 60th over was completed, England had reached a colossal 334 for 4, exactly the same number of runs that they had scored on the first day of the previous summer's Test against India at the same ground, when they went on to reach 629.

For all practical purposes the match was over, but India's response mattered, not only for morale but because should they finish level on points the run-rate would make a difference. But Gavaskar, it seems, had decided that the match was over – and in front of the huge crowd, many of them colourful Indian spectators, he decided to convert a match into a virtual net. In 60 overs he made 36 not out, as India crawled to 132 for 3. He disgusted his own supporters, was disowned by his captain and manager, was later reprimanded by his board – and quite confounded everyone else. To this day he has never provided any sensible explanation, though in 1982, after yet another massive one-day defeat at the hands of England, he could joke about it. The Indian manager, Raj Singh, had spoken of the six-hitting exploits of the great C.K. Nayadu, and Gavaskar responding said, 'Well, you have heard how C.K. could win matches with his batting; you know how I can lose matches by mine.' The most plausible explanation is that Gavaskar had lost form; he could neither score nor get out and suffered a sort of brainstorm – years later he would once or twice give his wicket away in Tests by playing in the most reckless one-day fashion.

The New Zealand–East Africa match produced an easy victory for the Kiwis by 80 runs, the principal feature of this being the 171 not out made by Glenn Turner, a batsman who had arrived in England in the late Sixties as a correct but methodical batsman and used the experience of domestic English one-day cricket to learn how to play his strokes entertainingly. The East Africans were making up numbers in the competition and it showed; they lost by ten wickets to India, and by 196 runs to England. Composed mainly of people of expatriate Indian or Pakistani stock they might have done better had they selected some of their younger, possibly better players, or even East Africans like Basharat Hassan, Owen-Thomas and Solanky, playing in county cricket. They were probably not helped by their supporters, whose enthusiasm rather outweighed their knowledge. They seemed to be more interested in their batsmen hitting fours, though they were not always sure who was at the crease.

The West Indies' victory over Sri Lanka was just as easy. Julien took four for 20, Boyce three for 22 and Roberts two for 16, bowling out Sri Lanka for 86. Only three batsmen reached double figures, Tissera the highest of them with 14. By half-past three the match was over as the West Indies hit the 87 required for the loss of only Fredericks's wicket. Because of the early finish the West Indians took the field again to amuse the crowd for an exhibition twenty-overs match.

The only match that provided some contest was the Australia–Pakistan clash at Headingley. Pakistan's triumphs in the 1974 Prudential Trophy had fostered dreams of winning the cup and as the organisers shrewdly arranged the match at Leeds, the Yorkshire Pakistanis thronged Headingley. For the first time since 1966, the gates were closed with 22,000 inside. Australia with a left-hand, right-hand opening combination (the New South Wales pair Alan Turner and Rick McCosker) made a sound start. But though both the Chappell brothers made useful runs, at 128 for 4 Pakistan seemed to be in with a chance. However, Ross Edwards held Australia together and when, to everyone's surprise, at 199 for six Pakistan brought on their leg-spinner Wasim Raja, Australia plundered runs: 79 in the last ten overs.

An Australian total of 278 always seemed too much for Pakistan, the more so when Lillee reduced them to 27 for two. But Majid, mixing luck with brilliance, and Asif, kept Pakistan in the chase till Majid fell to Mallett for 68. Then Lillee returned to bowl Asif for 53 and blow away the tail, finishing with five for 34; Australia won by 73 runs.

The second-round group matches – four days later – produced some of the most sensational cricket ever seen in the one-day game. Again all the fun was to be had in Group B, while Group A produced limp victories: England, thanks to 131 from Fletcher, defeated New Zealand by 80 runs. India got some consolation by beating East Africa by 10 wickets, in front of only 720 paying spectators. Madan Lal, who had conceded 64 runs for one wicket against England, took three for 15 and Gavaskar in 29 overs and five balls made 65, underlining the gulf between Indian and East African cricket.

On paper there should have been a similar gulf between Sri Lanka and Australia. Sri Lanka, fearful of a quick despatch, as in the West Indies match, won the toss and put the Australians in. This did not seem to do them much good, for Alan Turner started scoring freely, and Australia soon were racing away to a great score. The Sri Lankan bowling was friendly, the fielding eccentric and after 60 overs Australia reached 328 for five; Turner 101, McCosker 73, with fifties from Greg Chappell and Doug Walters. The Oval crowd had barely begun to debate how long these amateurs would last against Thomson and Lillee when, in the words of Thomson (as told to David Frith), 'it all clicked just right'.

Thomson and Lillee had smashed England during the previous winter's Ashes tour, and the pair were welcomed with that mixture of awe and faint disbelief that England reserves for fast bowlers who have destroyed the country's batting. Most of the interest centred on Thomson who seemed to be the living embodiment of the most cherished English myth, that Australia could always whistle up a champion from their unknown outbacks. In fact, before the 1974–75 tour Alec Bedser, chairman of the selectors, had expressed, albeit jocularly, just such a fear.

In the first match against Pakistan Thomson had lived up to his tag of wild and unpredictable by bowling five no-balls, including a wide that went for four. The crowd had booed him and he had given them the Harvey Smith two-finger salute. Then, at the nets preceding the Sri Lanka match, Thomson's no-ball problems had worsened, leading to much press speculation. But new, better-fitting boots eventually solved the problem.

At The Oval on that June day the Sri Lankans seemed to be making the most unexpected and spirited response to the Australians. They scored 23 runs in the first five overs, at tea, after 25 overs, they were 115 for 2, and by the 32nd over, the 150 was on the board with Wettimuny past his 50 and Mendis, playing quite beautifully, on 32. Then Chappell called on Thomson again. Do something. Anything. Thomson had solved his no-ball problems and the Australians, who under Ian Chappell began to specialise in this, decided to gee him up. Thomson later described to David Frith what happened.

'They knew I was keyed up and out to prove everything, that I was a hundred per cent again. Anyway, I hit this bloke Mendis on the head. They're only little fellas, so you couldn't call it a bouncer exactly. He fell down face-first, and when they brought him around, his captain's saying "You'll be all right" or something or other. But Mendis just says, "Oh my God! I'm going!" [Mendis vehemently denies saying this.] He went out: he wasn't coming back! They took him to hospital. But the real trouble came when I hit Wettimuny on the foot. He was waltzing round and he wanted to go too. That was enough for him. I'd already hit him on the chest. As I walked past him at the end of the over I said to him, "Look, it's not broken, you weak bastard," I said. "I'll give you a tip," I said. "If you are down there next over, it will be!"'

Wettimuny had already begun to feel shivers down his spine. Thomson appeared to be swearing and grinning at the same time, and sure enough, in the next over the ball landed on the same spot and Wettimuny's instep again took the full force. Now came the infamy. Thomson recalls:

'The ball had come straight back up to the pitch to me, and as I collected it, the boys are yelling out, "Throw down the stumps, two-up, throw down the stumps!" I'm saying to myself, "No, no, I can't do that, no," all in a split-second. Then I thought, "Bugger it," and I threw the ball and knocked the stumps over. I jumped up and shouted an appeal, but no other bastards moved. They all sat or stood there with their arms folded! They'd done me stone cold on purpose.'

Perhaps so, but now The Oval was indignant. Whenever Thomson bowled he was booed. As it happened Wettimuny's runner was in his ground, though Wettimuny was carried from the field to hospital. However, Tissera (52) and the captain Tennekoon (48) fought on to take gallant Sri Lanka on to 276 for four – a defeat by 52 runs. Faced with a prospect as daunting as India's against England, they had shown what could be done with spirit and a will to try and win – whatever the odds.

The Thomson–Sri Lankan story did not end there. All the World Cup players were staying in the same Kensington hotel and next morning, as Thomson came down for breakfast, he found himself surrounded by Sri Lankans, some of them sporting bandages. But instead of a knife in the back, as Thomson expected, they just wanted to offer breakfast. Suddenly Thomson discovered he had no appetite. Frith, Thomson's biographer, reckons that Thomson might have faced charges. A policeman overheard an exchange at the hospital between one of the injured batsmen and a medical attendant:

'What happened to you?'

'I was hit playing cricket.'

'Where?'

'At The Oval.'

'Who did it?'

'Thomson!'

At this point the policeman asked, 'Do you wish to prefer charges?' but the Sri Lankans did not pursue the matter, though in the macabre humour that Ian Chappell had, he called Thomson "Our ambassador to Sri Lanka" at a Lord's Taverners dinner.

Meanwhile, 110 miles away, at Edgbaston, there were equally exciting things going on at the match between the West Indies and Pakistan – though here the excitement had everything to do with cricket, and nothing to do with blood sports; this match would later earn the description, 'little short of a cricket miracle'. Pakistan, without their captain Asif, were captained by Majid, who set a fine example by scoring 60. Zaheer made 31, Mushtaq 55, Wasim Raja 58 and Pakistan a good 266 for seven. In fact, at various times their batsmen had played with such command that they had looked like getting considerably more. When Sarfraz took the first three West Indian wickets to make them 36 for three, it looked like Pakistan's day. Lloyd and Kanhai engineered a partial recovery but by the time the eighth wicket fell the West Indies were only 166, 101 behind. At this point Deryck Murray, one of the few West Indians to play with the necessary discipline, found a useful partner in Holder. Even so when in the 46th over Sarfraz had Holder caught by Pervez for 16, the West Indians were still 64 runs short of victory. It was seven o'clock, the 20,000-odd at the ground were thinking of wending their way homewards, when the miracle happened.

Murray found an ideal partner in Roberts and they slowly began to take the game away from the Pakistanis. With five overs left, 23 were wanted, and, crucially, Sarfraz's quota of 12 overs had been exhausted. The source of the crowd noise now told the story. The Pakistanis were becoming quieter, the West Indians, just beginning to glimpse an incredible victory, more exuberant. With three overs left, West Indies were 251 for nine: 16 wanted. With nine balls left, 10 runs were wanted, and Murray survived a possible run-out when a straight throw would have meant the end. The Pakistani fielders were getting rattled, and they had no real one-day bowlers left. With five runs wanted Wasim Raja, a leg-spinner, bowled the last over. It was an unlikely card to play – and it proved no trump. Roberts got two off a leg-bye, with the help of an overthrow, another two, then the final, winning, single. It had been the most memorable victory in the history of the game, the most crushing defeat.

Later, the West Indians would see this as the turning-point in their World Cup campaign. Clive Lloyd, who had earlier been very upset about an umpiring decision, now found himself celebrating:

'In all my days of playing cricket, I have never known such elation in a dressing room. Some years later, when we won a similarly close World Series Cricket match in Australia, there was great jubilation but it wasn't quite as emotional. Men with years of cricket experience were jumping up and down and hugging each other. Several were sobbing uncontrollably.'

It was only in the final group matches that Group A came alive. England, already home and dry, easily beat East Africa by 196 runs. If this seemed almost a practice match, the one between India and New Zealand was for real. Both sides had one victory, and this was the decider. Despite the modest bowling resources of both sides, both sets of batsmen struggled to make runs. India did not get going till Abid Ali, at No. 7, made 70 and took them to 230. A lot depended on Turner, and his 114 not out guided New Zealand to a four-wicket victory in the last over but one. It was not a very smooth win but New Zealand always seemed just ahead.

With both the West Indies and Australia having qualified for the finals, their group match meant nothing – except in psychological terms. And for all the ballyhoo before the match, the crowd of mainly West Indians with a smattering of Australian exiles from Earl's Court, did not see a great match. Australia, put into bat, lost a wicket without a run on board, and were always struggling. Their 192 owed a great deal to Edwards's 58 and Marsh's 52. The West Indian reply answered one question: what will the heirs of Weekes and Walcott do when Lillee and Thomson drop them short? Fredericks was hooking and cutting from the first ball, and Kallicharran was quite magical. In ten balls from Lillee Kallicharran hit 4, 4, 4, 4, 4, 1, 4, 6, 0, 4: 35 runs. Lillee conceded 66 runs in ten overs and by the time Kallicharran was out, he had made 78, and victory was a formality.

The West Indies easily brushed aside the New Zealanders in the semi-finals, beating them by five wickets. Apart from a brief period before lunch when they were 92 for 1, the Kiwis never looked like offering much of a challenge. The England–Australia semi-final was better balanced. For the first time in the series the pitch was grassy and the Headingley weather characteristically overcast. Australia won the toss, put England in, and while the country waited for the confrontation between Lillee–Thomson and the English batsmen, Gary Gilmour, an unconsidered all-rounder from New South Wales, stole the honours.

Bowling left-arm over the wicket he was lively, could swing both in and away from the batsman, and exploited the conditions well by keeping to a full length. With the first ball of his second over, and the score on 2, he had Amiss lbw for 2 and England were on the slide. Gilmour bowled his 12 overs in one spell and removed the first five in the order and Knott: he had taken six for 14, and England were 36 for six. England did not look like reaching 50 but Denness held on to make 27, Arnold, the next highest scorer made 18 not out, and England, 52 for 8 at lunch, reached 93.

Australia seemed to be coasting at 17 for no wicket but then Arnold had Turner l.b.w., Snow had both the Chappells and Old took three wickets. Australia were 39 for 6 when Gilmour joined Walters. Not a man who believed in leaving things half done, Gilmour began to play his shots and with the experienced Walters to guide him, they put on 55 runs to win the match by four wickets. Both captains criticised the pitch – Denness understandably more than Ian Chappell – but that was hardly surprising given that 19 batsmen had scored only 187, and a 120-overs match had finished after only 65 had been bowled.

Nothing like this marred the final which was just what the advertising executives would have ordered: brilliant sunshine, a lovely mid-summer's day, capacity crowds, and two great teams. Had England been one of them, the final would have been ideal, but by the end of this match even that seemed unimportant. It was the longest day of the year, 21 June, and a glorious one for cricket. The West Indies came to the final as the shortest of short-priced favourites. They had been made favourites even before the competition began; now with their impressive wins behind them they seemed unstoppable. Their win against Pakistan had been critical. Lloyd himself would later see that victory as the moment the West Indians were convinced they could win the cup.

In that match he felt he had been given wrongly caught behind – a decision that had so upset him that he had thrown his bat round the dressing room. When, eventually, the West Indians won, Lloyd, unable to control himself, had raced from the dressing room out into the section of the pavilion reserved for members, shouting, 'That will teach you . . . you cheats.' Later, much calmer, Lloyd would feel that, 'That was a very important win. After that I believe the team as a whole knew that it would not be stopped and would win the cup. It was the type of performance which helped erase the age-old feeling that the West Indies were no good fighting from behind.'

In the final, as Lloyd walked out to bat, the West Indies once again had to fight. Chappell had won the toss, put the West Indians in and through a piece of luck (Fredericks hooked Lillee for six but in completing the stroke overbalanced on to his wicket), and good cricket reduced the West Indians to 50 for 3. Australia had done everything right and though Lloyd soon hooked Lillee for a six, on 26 he offered a catch to Ross Edwards at mid-wicket. Edwards dived but could not hold it and Lloyd was convinced that, somehow, this was going to be his day.

The pitch held nothing for the bowlers; the Australians had no spinners, just a pack of quick to medium-pacers, and Lloyd's bat – having got rid of its croak – began to trumpet some extraordinary shots. While the grey-haired Kanhai, who in his younger days himself played like this, dropped anchor – he did not score for eleven overs – Lloyd took Australia apart. In 82 balls he made 102 with two sixes (both off the back foot) and 12 fours. He and Kanhai had put on 149 in 36 overs when there was another controversial Lloyd dismissal. Lloyd chased a ball going down the leg side from Gilmour and in trying to glance it got an edge. Umpire Bird heard the snick, saw the deviation but was not sure it carried. As West Indians and Australians offered conflicting advice Bird walked towards umpire Spenser and when he confirmed it, gave Lloyd out. At 199 for four with Richards, Boyce, Julien and Murray to come a total in excess of 300 looked on. But Gilmour removed Richards for five, and the patient Kanhai for 55; 209 for six. But Nos. 7, 8 and 9, Boyce, Julien, and Murray took the West Indies to 291 for 8 – not overwhelming but commanding.

Australia lost McCosker early, but Turner and Ian Chappell, driving and placing the faster bowlers with astonishing ease, soon picked up momentum. However the need to score at just under five an over began to pressurise the Australians. They went for runs that were not there, or somewhat marginal. Richards, having done nothing with the bat, figured in two run-outs, twice throwing down the stumps from side-on, running out Turner at 40, and Greg Chappell at 15; he also made the throw that enabled Lloyd to run out Ian Chappell for 62. Then Lloyd bowled Walters for 35, and slowly Australia, losing more wickets, began to fall behind the required run-rate.

For much of the day Mike Brearley had sat at the Nursery End with Peter Walker and others, luxuriating in the cricket atmosphere that only the West Indians bring to the game: a wonderful mixture of exuberance and exhortation. Now, as Thomson came out to join Lillee at 233 for nine, Brearley went to sit by the boundary rope, confident the end was near. It had been a good final, but a twist was still to come. For Lillee was confident Australia could get the runs and Lillee and Thomson began to push the ones and twos and slowly runs came. Suddenly Lillee drove Holder in the air, neatly to Kallicharran at cover. The match was over, Brearley and his friends picked up their beer cans and scorecards, the West Indians raced on to the ground. Umpire Bird lost his white cap, the spare ball and received a sharp blow that made him feel dizzy, Thomson lost his sweater. (In the group match between these two countries Bird had another white cap stolen which he subsequently saw being worn by a London bus conductor who proudly claimed he had got it from 'Umpire Dickie Bird'.)

But nobody had noticed that Spenser had ruled Holder's delivery a no-ball, Kallicharran shied at the stumps and missed, and the ball was lost. The crowd from the Tavern, anticipating victory, advanced on to the ground. Thomson shouted to Lillee, Lillee bawled at Thomson – eventually they began running. Thomson recalls:

'We ran a fair few runs but the umpire was going to give us two. I said, "Hey, how much are you giving us for that?" and Tom Spenser says, "Two" – real abrupt. "Pig's arse!" I shouted. "We've been running up and down here all afternoon. Who are you kidding?" I really got into him. Then I think he changed it.'

Spenser awarded three runs. And still Lillee and Thomson went on picking up more. They had put on 41, just 17 short, when at 8.43 p.m. Thomson lost a ball from Holder against the background of the bricks of the pavilion. He started to run anyway, Murray got the ball and, underarm, threw down the stumps. Thomson was run out and West Indies were World Cup champions. Thomson felt 'a numb feeling, because we were not all that used to losing. I sat in the dressing room there and felt really annoyed, what a bastard: we played wrongly.'

But if he was exhausted, and hated losing, the West Indians celebrated – and with them the cricket world. It had been, as Mike Brearley was to write later, 'a miraculous day, in cricketing terms: perfect weather, perfect pitch and a superb game'. A crowd of 26,000 had watched the final – 158,000 the entire tournament – and cricket's official verdict was provided by the editor of *Wisden* who, reviewing the match, wrote in the 1976 *Wisden*:

'From 11 a.m. till 8.43 p.m. the cricketers of the Caribbean had been locked in a succession of thrills with cricketers from the Southern Cross. It might not be termed first-class cricket, but the game has never produced better entertainment in one day . . . It was the longest day of the year; the longest day in cricket history and one that those who were there and the millions who watched it on television will never forget.'

VERITY'S TEST MATCH

Robert Lynd

When the second Test Match came to an end at Lord's on Monday, amid a happy delirium of excitement, it was difficult to believe that the game had ever seemed dull – at times even deadly dull. It was difficult to believe that on Friday morning half the spectators had been talking contemptuously of the English batting, that on Saturday afternoon half the spectators had been talking contemptuously of the English bowling, and that through part of the game the majority of the spectators had been talking contemptuously of the English fielding. For somehow, to the surprise of everybody, the game had turned out to be as sensationally exhilarating as even the most sensation-loving spectator could desire, and the despised English batsmen, bowlers, and fielders had managed to beat the Australians by an innings and 38 runs. No doubt, the weather had something to do with it. Contrary to what one would expect, there is nothing like rain for making Test cricket worth watching. Still Verity, with his record of 15 wickets for 104 runs, played at least as brilliantly as the weather. He made such tricky use of the tricky English climate as only a bowler of genius could do. As a result, he walked straight into history – not, perhaps, Thucydidean history, but Wisden history – on Monday.

When the game began on Friday, everything was perfect but the cricket. The sun was shining, the June-green trees were tossing in the wind, the field with its thirteen white players and its lime-white-coated umpires was lovely as only Lord's can be, every spectator was happy at being present on so great an occasion, and the wicket, everybody said, was ideal. It was evident from the start, however, that we were in for some of the tedium of a war of attrition. This would not have mattered if Sutcliffe had not played as if he were either hypnotised by Australian prestige or blinded by the sun. He, the indomitable, the man of iron nerve, played with such caution that again and again he did not seem to know what he was trying to do. As Mr Robertson–Glasgow said of him, he stood at the wicket and 'scraped about like an anxious bird'. He infected the spectators with his anxiety, and the only astonishing thing was that he remained at the wicket for nearly two hours for his 20 runs.

Walters, in the meantime, in his green county cap, was grace itself at the other end. After a slow beginning, when he played the ball as if he were not on a cricket-pitch, but on a putting-green, he let himself go like a master at the bowling. Grimmett, who bowls so slowly that he does not even trouble to take off his cap and leave it with the umpire during his overs, set traps for him such as had tempted him to destruction at Nottingham. Wall bowled ball after ball at his wicket after the longest run-up ever taken by a bowler. Big Bill O'Reilly, lanky and with thinning fair hair on his crown, had a turn at him. McCabe, who looks rather like Low when he takes his cap off, wasted his energies in over after over. But Walters, without ever becoming contemptuous, was always at his ease, and kept the wickedly keen Australian fielders busy racing for the ball. For a time it looked as though he were the only hope of preventing an English rout. Sutcliffe was out l.b.w. after an innings in which almost the only incident was the ball's losing itself in his pad above the knee. 'W.G. once ran eleven when that happened,' said a spectator behind me. Hammond came after him and sent a schoolgirl catch to Chipperfield, the bowler, when he had scored two. Hendren, who had superstitiously refused to take advantage of the democratic revolution at Lord's, which permitted the professionals and amateurs to use the same dressing-room, was given a reception that showed that he was the most popular man on the field, but it was to an accompaniment of sad hand-clapping that he walked back to the Pavilion when he had made only 13. England had now lost three wickets for 99 runs on a wicket said to be perfect.

Wyatt, whose thumb-guard was twice sent flying into the air, kept his end up steadily till Walters was caught, having made 82 runs, and the score stood at 130 for four wickets – a disastrous-looking situation with Walters gone.

It was Wyatt, Leyland, and Ames who pulled the game together during the rest of the afternoon. The crowd gradually lost its sense of impending defeat, as Leyland and Ames began to run dangerous singles, and Leyland's left-handedness kept the fielders on the run. There was a shout of joy when Leyland swept a no-ball right among the spectators for six. But it was a day of few striking incidents, few conspicuous personalities. At the end of the day, when England had scored 293 for five wickets, the crowd had a rather dull sense of an impending draw.

The second day's play was, in parts, a little soporific. I do not know why anybody pays to be present at a Test match if he wants to sleep, but it should be put on record that on Saturday both on the grass and in the stands several spectators were to be seen sleeping. To be sure, those who remained awake had the pleasure of seeing centuries completed by Leyland and Ames, and the appearance of the figure 100 in the scoreboard has always a curiously elevating effect on the spirits. At the same time, the English batting was not quite so exciting as the Australian fielding. It must have been pretty sound, however, to knock up a score of 440 against such fielding. To the expert – if not to the inexpert – eye, it was even beautiful.

It was later in the afternoon, however, that the cricket achieved a beauty that could not have been missed even by a spectator who understood neither the technique nor the rules of the game. While Bradman batted, a livelier emerald twinkled in the grass for every man, woman, and child present. He put into his play all the high spirits of cricket. He is a player who can often be seen talking laughingly to the wicket-keeper between one ball and the next, and there was a boyish glee in the way in which he whipped and flicked the ball into every corner of the field as he wished. It is always good to see a boundary hit smashingly. To see three boundaries in succession hit smashingly as Bradman hit three boundaries off Verity on Saturday is like draughts of bubbling wine to the spectator. There is nobody else living who can intoxicate a crowd on the cricket-field like this. How beautiful is incaution when it is linked with masterly skill! But how dangerous! I confess that, though I hoped England would win, my heart sank when Bradman was caught and bowled by Verity at 36, and the flashing bat was to flash no more for the day.

Then came the wet weekend, turning the pitch into a Slough of Despond for the Australians. So soaked was it that on one occasion Hendren, when stepping across it, pulled up the legs of his trousers like a Victorian lady holding up her skirts to cross a puddled street. In vain did the Australian batsmen pat it and remove this thing and that from its surface. Verity, meditative as an economist at Geneva, cunning as Ulysses, had exactly the pitch that his left hand of the many wiles needed, and he bowled all day long as if to men who had been stupefied by drugs. Aesthetically, he is one of the most delightful of bowlers. As an in-expert, I am all in favour of fast bowling, but there is such grace in Verity's movement as he runs slowly up to the wicket and sends the ball spinning to its goal that one could watch him for ever – at least, if it had always been raining during the previous weekend. By the end of the Australian first innings, when eight wickets had fallen for only 92 runs more than the Saturday score of 192, he had taken six of the eight. And how exciting it had become when Australia needed only a few runs to save the follow-on! One watched every ball in the hope or fear of catastrophe. This was dramatic cricket at its best. No wonder the spectators went wild with joy when Wall was given out l.b.w. and the players trooped back into the Pavilion.

As for the second Australian innings, it was played by men who seemed to realise that they might as well have stayed playing cards in the Pavilion. Woodfull, slow as Learoyd, stood his ground nobly for a time – a great cricketer, though one gets tired after a time of looking at the Rock of Gibraltar. No-one else but Chipperfield looked as if he knew what to do with Verity's bowling. Occasionally, a batsman would hit out at it, like an exasperated man striking at a wasp with a tennis-racquet; and, when he did so, sure as fate the ball would go on wings into a fielder's hands. Bradman took a careful look at it for a time, and then decided that he was the equal and indeed the superior of the English climate. He sent one ball high as a shrilling swift into the air and almost scored a boundary. That convinced him that the spirit of don't-give-a-damn could beat even Verity. He struck out nobly again, mistimed his stroke, and the ball shot high above his head and was lost for a time in the ether. The only danger of its being missed when it came back was that so many English fielders were waiting for it that they might collide and knock each other over. Wisely, all but Ames stepped aside, and Bradman was gone to a shout of joy that must have reached Australia. It was now all over. The spectators became uproarious as one wicket fell after another and dejected batsmen made their way through the slough back to the Pavilion. Australia was undoubtedly on the run. The team, possibly, is at least as good as the English team, but it had been routed by Verity plus the English climate. On such an occasion, who wants the better team to win? No one but an imaginary sportsman. There were very few of these angelic characters present at Lord's on Monday.

THE FASTEST HUNDRED

Richard Streeton

Fender's famed hundred so nearly failed to happen on three counts. He was not due originally to play in the match with Northamptonshire, who in 1920 were hardly the strongest of sides. Then, as soon as he went in to bat, he was dropped at cover-point. Finally, if Fender had been leading Surrey in this game, he would, he thought later, have declared sooner than Wilkinson did, without waiting for his own hundred, or for Peach, his partner, to reach his double hundred. Fender's unselfish approach to his own cricket led him to disapprove of personal milestones 'getting in the way', as he termed it. Fender became angry with R.W.V. Robins on this issue in a match at the 1928 Bournemouth Festival. Robins ignored a request from Fender to stop bowling leg-side full tosses to help Leslie Townsend (Derbyshire) reach his thousand runs and complete the double. 'You've got to leave a chap feeling he got his record properly,' was Fender's view. 'With the last pair at the wicket, I went on myself in place of Robins. I didn't try to get Townsend's partner out, but I did my best against Townsend himself and he still got what he wanted.'

Fender admitted that this question of records and landmarks was difficult for captains. He remembered arguments with Lionel Tennyson and Charles Bray when next he saw them after he felt they had transgressed in this context: Tennyson for continuing in the rain to let Bradman reach his thousand in May at Southampton in 1930; Bray for 'allowing' the no-ball to be discovered that ensured the record 555 to Holmes and Sutcliffe at Leyton in 1932. Fender often found his attitude brought him criticism but that the player concerned would be less indignant than the newspapers or public. There were regrets in the press, for instance, when Fender declared Surrey's innings closed against Northamptonshire in 1921 with Sandham 292 not out. Sandham himself readily understood that a first day score of 616 for five was enough for Surrey. Similarly, Hendren laughed when Surrey took the new ball and he was dismissed for 199 at The Oval in 1926, but a section of the crowd barracked Fender. A disgruntled Middlesex supporter sitting in the pavilion seats called out: 'That's why you're not England captain, Fender.'

The Surrey team list for Northampton, published in several newspapers on Wednesday, 25 August 1920, did not include Fender, but among the names was D.J. Knight, who six days earlier had been injured at Hastings. It might have been Surrey's first intention for Fender to rest before the show-down with Middlesex at the week-end, or he might have had a business engagement. His plans seemed to have changed when Knight withdrew at fairly short notice. Certainly Fender travelled separately and the match had started when he reached the County Ground. This explained why a substitute held the catch to claim an early Northamptonshire wicket. Northamptonshire were dismissed for 306 and they owed much to an innings of 128 by 'Fanny' Walden, who was only five feet two inches and better known as a masterly dribbler for Tottenham Hotspur and England. Bad light ended play a few minutes early, with Surrey 12 for the loss of Hobbs, prompting the *Sporting Life* to comment that Surrey had 'a stiff task ahead of them this morning'. What that unknown pundit felt shortly after tea, when Surrey declared at 619 for five, was never disclosed.

Northamptonshire must have been fairly satisfied thirty minutes before lunch next day when Surrey were 160 for four. Wilkinson, Shepherd and Sandham had all fallen to the straight-forward medium pace of 'Dick' Woolley, elder and right-handed brother of Frank. Peach and Ducat were together at the interval, but Northamptonshire still had no idea what Wordsworth's 'ruthless destiny' had in store. These two went on to make 288 for the fifth wicket in about two and a quarter hours, and the bowling was slaughtered. Fender's innings that followed, therefore, was carnage among the dead and dying, but all the same it was a remarkable example of ferocious hitting. Fender and Peach shared a sixth-wicket stand of 171 in 42 minutes before Surrey declared. It converted to an hourly scoring rate of 244, something unapproached in first-class cricket before or since by any partnership lasting longer than half an hour. When the end came Fender was 113 not out and Peach 200 not out and it is only by a statistical chance, of course, that Fender superseded Peach as the day's main hero. For Fender the flogging of tired Northamptonshire bowling happened to bring a world record, but there were other more significant bouts of hitting in his career. For Peach in his first full season as an all-rounder, this maiden hundred was to remain the greatest occasion of his life as a batsman.

Fender's record, however, must remain the prime topic. He hit five sixes and either 18 or 17 fours, it being impossible to compile an authentic breakdown, stroke by stroke, of Fender's innings. The Surrey scorebook disappeared in the war: only the Northamptonshire one has survived and some appalling discrepancies mar its pages. The famous Leo Bullimer was the Northamptonshire scorer in this game. He was 44 and not yet half-way through his 51-year stint as the county's scorer. Bullimer's customary neatness and distinctive copperplate writing are apparent in the photograph of the relevant score-sheet. He scored with a pen; one six has been inked over heavily, as if he first wrote a four, perhaps, but otherwise not an amendment or second thought. Yet, to give only a few inaccuracies from the batting shown, Fender's strokes totalled 112 and not 113; Peach's runs totalled 188 and not 200; Ducat's 142 and not 149; and Wilkinson's 40 and not 43. These mistakes alone made Surrey's score 596 and not 619. Bullimer's scoring was normally reliable and it has to be assumed that the profusion of runs on this occasion proved too much for him.

There have been several worthy attempts by statisticians in recent years to reconstruct Fender's innings and though such matters by no means have universal interest they have a place in this account. Easily the most reasoned interpretation, ball by ball, of what happened has been put together by Mr L.T. Newell, an expert on Northamptonshire's statistics and a man familiar with Bullimer's methods. Though inconsistencies exist in the bowling analyses for this match, they were not as glaring as the errors in the batting records. It was from the bowling figures that Mr Newell worked, over by over, when he assembled the most likely sequence of Fender's hits. He published some of his deductions first in *Cricket News* on 30 July 1977, and both the article and other facts generously passed on by Mr Newell have been of the utmost help to the author. Five players from the match were still alive when this chapter was first drafted and in addition several spectators helped with eyewitness accounts.

As Fender walked out to bat just after four o'clock he flailed the air with his bat, one-handed. He was capless and had neither a sweater nor the neckerchief he often wore. To those who had not seen him before Fender looked both awkward and menacing. He faced almost every ball with the bat already raised to his shoulder, which was not a normal trait of his batsmanship. It confirmed a suspicion gleaned that this hundred came about during a light-hearted slog that could have ended abruptly at any moment. All through, a great deal of trust was placed in the eye, and the ball was usually hit in the air and in all directions. The day was sunny and warm; after lunch the crowd had grown to between 3,000 and 5,000, evenly spread around the edges of the field. There was no delay in returning the ball, as boundary followed boundary. Northamptonshire, whose four main bowlers were all medium to medium-fast, averaged around 24 overs an hour throughout the Surrey innings and they used none of the defensive or delaying tactics that their latter-day successors would have done. The County Ground varied little from its present size and shape, with tempting spaces for the pull and square drive, and the pitch was lifeless. Nearly everything, in fact, was conducive to fast scoring and both score-boards failed to keep up with what happened next.

This can best be looked at first through the local evening newspapers. There were two in Northampton at this time – they have since merged – both providing a lengthy run-of-play report until about five o'clock. It was a pity that Fender was still batting as their deadline approached. There had been so much eventful cricket already that afternoon that space was running out, even with a daily quota of some 1,500 words. Here, verbatim, is how the *Northampton Daily Chronicle* described Fender's innings:

'Fender should have had a very brief stay for after a single he skied one to a great height that Freeman dropped at cover-point. But he, too, started to revel in the bowling, and making use of his long reach, he hit away to some purpose. Eighteen were scored in one of Murdin's overs, and Fender to vary matters sent the ball alongside the ladies' stand for six. He had another life when Humfrey failed to judge a chance in the country, but he laughed at risks and proceeded to give a dazzling display of fireworks.

'The big amateur now completely filled the picture. He drove Thomas for two 6's in one over which yielded 18 – 17 to Fender, and from the other end he took 19 out of 20 in an over off Murdin, including another six. When an adjournment was made for tea he had hit 93 in half an hour, the score then reading 574 for five.

'Fender on his return treated the bowling absolutely mercilessly, and hoisted his century with a six and having been at the crease barely thirty-five minutes.

'The Surrey captain waited until Peach had reached his 200 before applying the closure, which he did at five o'clock with the score at 619 for five.'

• • • • • •

The rival *Northampton Daily Echo* report was shorter and other than that Fender reached 50 in twenty minutes added nothing significant. There were, however, variations in minor detail, the main one concerning the tea score. This was given as 574 in the *Chronicle* with Fender 93, and as 572 in the *Echo* with Fender 91. These differences were perpetuated next morning in the national newspapers, who did not have their own men at the match. From several recognisable phrases there was no doubt that both Northampton reporters, and possibly one other journalist, filed stories to the London agencies and newspapers after their own work was finished. There was obviously no collusion between these reporters and it was possible that they took their facts from different scorers. The Northampton press-box layout made this feasible: three separate cubicles, the scorers in the middle one, flanked on both sides by press. A sliding partition allowed reporters to communicate with the scorer immediately next to them. By tea-time the scorers might have had different tallies: one at least, we suspect, had already lost his way.

In the next day's London newspapers, and in the rewrites carried by the Northamptonshire weeklies, Fender's time for 50 had shrunk from 20 minutes to 19 and his half-hour's batting before tea had become 29 minutes. The *Daily Mirror* used a stock picture of Fender from its library and settled on 91 in half an hour in their caption and 93 in 29 minutes in their match report. These differences remain trivial, of course, other than when dealing in retrospect with an historic innings. Fortunately for posterity there seemed unanimity that Fender reached three figures in 35 minutes, even though few people at the time, and certainly the majority of the press, failed to appreciate that Fender's time *was* a world record. Cricket statistics were not as thorough then as they have become since. None of the newspapers in headlines or text categorically seized on the basic fact that cricket's fastest hundred had been scored.

Only the *Daily Sketch* specifically mentioned this and they buried it in the depths of their story. They added that Jessop's best was the 101 he made in 40 minutes at Harrogate in 1897, thereby implying that this was the previous fastest hundred, as indeed it was. Broadly speaking the newspapers shirked the issue and the *Morning Post* epitomised the widespread cautiousness by saying that Fender's batting 'must approach a record in important cricket'. The *Daily Mail* showed its lack of awareness when it said about Fender's hundred: 'It was an astonishing piece of forceful cricket but by no means a record,' and went on to remind people of Alletson's 189 in 90 minutes in 1911 and Jessop's 191 in the same time in 1907. (Alletson took approximately 66 minutes over his first hundred runs and Jessop 42 minutes.)

Fender agrees that it was not appreciated at the time that he had achieved a world record. He did not keep the bat he used and felt certain he would have done if he had known. In several interviews in later years Fender further confused researchers by saying that he only batted 23 minutes before tea. He would say that he looked at a clock as he went out to bat and it showed seven minutes past four. It was never clarified whether this was the same clock being used by either the scorers or the umpires, nor whether tea was taken promptly. There was no point in pursuing this particular memory further, but it did provide one more puzzling aspect. So did Bullimer, once again, because the scorebook had Fender timed in at 4.01 and Ducat out at 4.05!

Fender was on firmer ground, probably, when he also said that he might have reached his hundred even more quickly but had held back after tea to let Peach get his double hundred. Wilkinson told Fender at tea he would declare when Fender reached his hundred. Peach was 175 not out at tea and by then had his sights set on his own milestone. Fender seems to have tried to give Peach the strike after the interval as he took two singles in each of the first two overs before reaching his hundred in the third over. Fender always maintained that Peach reached 200 first, but the scorebook did not bear this out. It also seems improbable that the evening newspapers would have been wrong on this sequence of events.

Fender went from 97 to 103 with a six against Murdin and scored 15 of the 16 runs this over cost. 'Merry' Murdin bowled from one end throughout the Fender-Peach stand and must have needed to draw heavily on the qualities which led to his nickname. Murdin was faster than Woolley and his stock ball tended to move towards the slips. The over by Murdin mentioned by the *Chronicle* as costing 20 runs was the penultimate over before tea. Fender did not often play back, but the first ball of this over brought him the only six in his life that he struck while playing back defensively. 'I had anticipated a bumper, but the ball never rose; I went through hard with the stroke and it cleared the bowler's head and skimmed low all the way into the football field.' Murdin was the bowler when Fender was missed at cover by Freeman, who lost a high, swirling chance in the sun. 'Ned' Freeman was substituting for Walden, who was resting a bruised leg, and was himself a footballer with Northampton Town. Fender's reported chance in the deep field at 34 might not actually have gone to hand. Neither Fender nor Stuart Humfrey, who later became a well-known ophthalmic surgeon, remembered it.

For those who wish the fullest possible detail: Fender and Peach faced only 89 balls between them under Mr Newell's reconstruction. Fender arrived to play the last ball of an over by Thomas, who could swing the ball both ways and later in his career came close to being chosen for Australia in 1928–29. Fender took a single from his first ball and Murdin and Thomas then each bowled five complete overs before tea. Afterwards, before Surrey declared, Murdin bowled a further 2.4 overs and Woolley bowled two overs at the other end. Extras conceded during the stand before tea make it impossible to deduce precisely the proportion of bowling for each batsman. All that can be calculated is that Fender before tea received a minimum of 33 balls, and a maximum of 39 balls, and scored 93 runs. After the interval he received 13 balls and scored 20 runs, his hundred coming from the seventh ball he faced in this period.

In total, therefore, Fender needed somewhere between 40 and 46 balls for his hundred and he played between 46 and 52 balls in all. Chris Old took 72 balls when in 1977, playing for Yorkshire against Warwickshire, he gained second place to Fender on the list of fastest hundreds. Another rapid modern hundred came from Robin Hobbs in 1975 for Essex against the Australians. Hobbs was timed at 44 minutes and he received 45 balls. Without decrying these efforts it must be said that both Old and Hobbs scored many of their runs against innocuous slow bowling deliberately tossed up. The ultimate speed in which a first-class hundred could be made remains open to argument, but Fender's record would not seem unassailable, as Old's time of 37 minutes showed.

There have been two instances of hundreds scored in 18 minutes in minor cricket, according to Mr E.K. Gross, who for 30 years has been an accepted authority on records outside the first-class sphere. These were believed to be the quickest hundreds ever made in a properly conducted match at any level, but Mr Gross warned there were gaps, inevitably, in this area of knowledge. He knew of a case in South Africa of a man scoring 250 in an hour, but the time for reaching 100 was not recorded. The 18-minute hundreds came from L.C. Quinlan in Australia in 1909–10, playing for Trinity v. Mercantile at Cairns, NSW, and from G.J. Bryan at Maresfield Park, Sussex, in 1925 for the Royal Engineers v. Royal Corps of Signals. It would be possible in theory for a first-class hundred to be reached in 18 minutes, but seems unlikely without collusion from the fielding side.

Just over an hour remained for play after Surrey declared and North-amptonshire were 59 for two by the close to bring the total runs scored that Thursday to 666. The wicket remained docile and it was ten to five on the Friday before Northamptonshire were all out for 430 and Surrey went on to win by eight wickets. The match aggregate of 1475 runs has remained a record for the County Championship. John Moss, of Nottinghamshire, one of the umpires, was probably the only man present at Northampton to have seen more runs scored previously in a three-day game. In 1904 he had stood in the Worcestershire v. Oxford University match at Worcester, which brought 1492 runs.

THE GREATEST GAME I EVER PLAYED IN

Pelham Warner

It is not a little curious that two of the most exciting games of cricket I have ever taken part in should have been against the South Africans. On the first occasion I was playing for Middlesex, and on the second for the team sent out to South Africa by the Marylebone Club. The result of the Middlesex and South African game was a tie, and that of the MCC v. South Africa a victory for our opponents by one wicket. On paper the first match would appear to be the more exciting, but the second was of greater importance to the general public of the two countries and to the individual cricketers in the two elevens, and was at least as full of thrilling moments. I have therefore selected MCC v. South Africa as the most exciting game in my cricket career.[1] In both matches

---

[1] In many ways, of course, that wonderful game at Lord's in 1920 with which I wound up my playing career, was my greatest cricketing experience. But, although it was a great game in every sense, the end was not so exciting as that recounted here, and, in any case, it was too *personal* an experience to justify my claiming it as the 'greatest game I ever played in'.

I happened to be acting as captain, and, therefore, am not likely to forget either, and especially the second, in which every stroke, I had almost said every ball, in that long three days' battle is still fresh and vividly painted on my memory.

And now for my 'greatest game.' To begin with, I will give the names of the two elevens who were drawn up face to face on the red-dust Wanderers' ground at Johannesburg on 2 January 1906. I give the order of going in. MCC – P.F. Warner, F.L. Fane, Denton, Capt. E.G. Wynyard, Hayes, J.N. Crawford, Relf (A.E.), Haigh, Board, Lees, and Blythe. *South Africa* – L.J. Tancred, W.A. Shalders, M. Hathorn, G.C. White, S.J. Snooke, J.H. Sinclair, G.A. Faulkner, A.D. Nourse, Vogler, R.O. Schwarz, and P.W. Sherwell (captain).

Marylebone won the toss and made 184: three wickets fell for 15 runs, and only Crawford batted really well.

One hundred and eighty-four was generally considered to be far too small a total, but South Africa replied with 91. Lees, Blythe, and Crawford bowled splendidly, and everything came off for us. Indeed it was a triumph for our bowling and fielding. Lees and Blythe went on over after over sending down the most perfect-length deliveries, from which scoring was extremely difficult. The batsmen played carefully and patiently to tire the arms of our bowlers. But they refused to be tired. When the six-foot-four-inch Jimmy Sinclair – all arms and legs to look at him from a distance, though a closer view reveals a magnificent breadth of beam and shoulder – was seen walking slowly to the wicket a great shout went from the ten thousand spectators who by this time were sitting five and six deep round the cycle track beneath the giant gum trees. Here at last is one who will knock these amazingly accurate professionals off their length.

There is a hush, so intense that one feels that one would hear a pin drop, as he prepares to face Lees. The long-striding bowler sent in a fast and rather short-pitched ball. Up goes the bat, looking like a walking-stick in those brown and sinewy hands, there is a dead silence for the fraction of a second, 'Catch it, Walter,' shouts someone, and Jimmy is on his way to the pavilion. And so things go our way. Seven are out for 44 runs. Then Vogler, so like the George Hirst of twenty-five years ago in build, and with the same pronounced energy as the famous Yorkshireman, whether batting, bowling, or fielding, makes a drive or two off Blythe, and Crawford takes Blythe's place. He catches the ball eagerly, and the next moment Vogler's leg-stump is down on the red sand, laid low by a beautiful-length break-back. At six o'clock South Africa had eight men out for 71 runs, and the crowd passed out of the ground talking eagerly and enthusiastically about the day's cricket – as well it might, for there had not been a single dull moment.

On the second morning the South African innings was soon over for 91, Nourse carrying out his bat for 18. He was in for an hour and twenty minutes – a sure proof of the quality of the bowling – and showed fine defence, and a grit and stubbornness which, as the sequel showed, was to contribute very materially to our ultimate undoing.

With a lead of 92 runs, at one time in our second innings we had 160 runs on the board with only five men out; but the tail went down before Faulkner.

South Africa was left with 284 runs to win and at the drawing of stumps had made 68 runs for two wickets – Tancred and Hathorn. Next morning everything went right for us at first. Shalders was run out, Snooke leg before wicket, Sinclair splendidly caught at long-on by Fane, who ran some distance and took a hard drive high up on the left side, and Faulkner run out. This run out deserves a detailed description, as it was so characteristic of Board, our wicket-keeper. Point was standing a good deal deeper than the legitimate position requires, when White played a ball a little to the right of where point would have been standing in the ordinary way. He called Faulkner for a run, and Board dashing after the ball threw the wicket down in brilliant style, and Faulkner was out by feet. Six wickets were now down for 105 runs, and the game looked to be ours.

Then Nourse and White added 121 runs in two hours and a quarter before Relf bowled White with a fine ball. During this long stand the cricket all round was of the highest class, the fielding being superb and a stern duel going on between batsmen and bowlers. When he had made 11 Nourse gave an extremely difficult chance to extra-slip, but it would have been a marvellous catch had it come off, and indeed the fieldsman deserved great credit for getting his hand to the ball, which was travelling very high and wide on his left side.

White was in four hours for his 81 and never looked like getting out. The position of his side and the admirable bowling compelled him to play a purely defensive game; and it was his superb defence and judgment that helped to wear down our bowling.

The score was 226 when White left. Vogler was clean bowled by Hayes four runs later, and at 239 Schwarz was caught and bowled; and with 45 runs to get and one wicket to fall the odds would have been almost anything on MCC if the last man in the South African side had been of the calibre of the usual eleventh man. But Sherwell is a capital bat, and from the first ball he received, which he hit for four, appeared perfectly at his ease.

Runs came faster than at any other period of the innings, the bowlers, whether it was owing to the excitement or to the long physical strain they had undergone under a hot sun on a hard grassless ground, losing something in their length and direction; and as each run was scored the crowd roared with delight as the idea began to dawn on it that after all, perhaps, South Africa might win. When eight runs were wanted, Crawford sent down a very fast ball which Sherwell snicked between first and second slip, and the spectators literally yelled with joy at this lucky escape.

Nourse then made a three on the leg-side off Relf, and the game was a tie. The fielders were now brought in round the batsmen, and three balls were bowled by Relf to Sherwell, who played two and left the third alone. Then Relf sent down a full pitch on the leg-side, and Sherwell seized the opportunity and hit it to the boundary.

Nourse played a magnificent game. His back play was exceptionally strong, and he had a beautiful half-drive, half-cut behind point, while he was also very strong on the leg-side. He scarcely ever drove straight, but made most of his runs just in front or just behind point, and on the leg-side. His level-headedness and sterling cricket won the match for South Africa.

Sherwell deserves just as much praise as Nourse, and no one could have played more calmly and coolly. Everything depended on him.

If he failed the match was lost to his side, and the way he rose to the occasion and snatched a victory from the game of defeat stamped him as a big-hearted cricketer. One envied him his feelings at the end of the match. He had led his men with discretion and judgment in the way of placing the field and changing the bowling, and then, when an extraordinary effort was demanded of him, he emerged with flying colours. No captain ever inaugurated his reign of office with a more striking or happier result; for up to this date, 4 January 1906, a South African team had never got the better of an English eleven in what is now commonly called a Test match. 'Twas, indeed, 'a famous victory', achieved by magnificent and splendid pluck in the face of grave difficulties, and in all my experience of cricket I have never seen a side fight a better rearguard action. With six wickets down for 105 runs in face of a necessary 284 to win the match, the last few men on the South African side might well have been excused had they failed; but, so far from doing so, they stuck to their ground with that grit and courage which we are so fond of saying are inherent in the

British race, and though naturally the first person to regret the result, one could not but appreciate the splendid qualities which brought victory to our opponents.

And we too, I think, deserved as much praise as our conquerors; for, handicapped on the last day by the absence of Haigh, owing to sudden indisposition, we fought with splendid determination, the fielding being so close and keen that scarcely half a dozen runs were given away, and the bowlers working with such courage and goodwill that it took South Africa just on five hours to get the 284 runs.

Never have I witnessed anything like the scene at the finish. Men were shrieking hysterically. Some were actually crying, and hats and sticks were flying everywhere. When the winning hit had been made the crowd 'tackled' Nourse and Sherwell and carried them into the pavilion, while, for half an hour after it was all over, thousands lingered on, and the whole of the South African eleven had to come forward on to the balcony of the committee room.

And so we were beaten, but defeat in such a struggle was glorious, for the first Test match will be talked of in South Africa as long as cricket is played there.

MCC

P. F. Warner c Snooke, b Schwarz	6	b Vogler	51
F. L. Fane c Schwarz, b Faulkner	1	b Snooke	3
Denton c Faulkner, b Schwarz	0	b Faulkner	34
Capt. E.G. Wynyard st Sherwell, b Schwarz	29	b Vogler	0
Hayes c and b Vogler	20	c Schwarz, b Snooke	3
J. N. Crawford c Nourse, b Sinclair	44	b Nourse	43
Relf b White	8	c Sherwell, b Faulkner	17
Haigh b Faulkner	23	l.b.w., b Nourse	0
Board not out	9	l.b.w., b Faulkner	7
Lees st Sherwell, b White	11	not out	1
Blythe b Sinclair	17	b Faulkner	0
B 6, l-b 9, n-b 1	16	B 23, l-b 8	31
	184		190

SOUTH AFRICA

L. J. Tancred c Board, b Lees	3	c Warner, b Blythe	10
W. A. Shalders c Hiagh, b Blythe	4	run out	38
M. Hathorn b Lees	5	c Crawford, b Lees	4
G. C. White c Blythe, b Lees	8	b Relf	81
S. J. Snooke c Board, b Blythe	19	l.b.w., b Lees	9
J. H. Sinclair c and b Lees	0	c Fane, b Lees	5
G. A. Faulkner b Blythe	4	run out	6
A. D. Nourse not out	18	not out	93
Vogler b Crawford	14	b Hayes	2
R. O. Schwarz c Relf, b Crawford ...	5	c and b Relf	2
P. W. Sherwell l.b.w., b Lees	1	not out	22
B 9, l-b 1	10	B 6, l-b 2, n-b 7	15
	91		**287**

BOWLING ANALYSIS

SOUTH AFRICA

	O.	M.	R.	W.		O.	M.	R.	W.
Schwarz	21	5	72	3	...	8	1	24	0
Faulkner	22	7	35	2	...	12.5	5	26	4
Sinclair	11	1	36	2	...	5	1	25	0
Vogler	3	0	10	1	...	11	3	24	2
White	5	1	13	2	...	4	0	15	0
Nourse	1	0	2	0	...	6	4	7	2
Snooke						12	4	38	2

MCC

	O.	M.	R.	W.		O.	M.	R.	W.
Lees	23.1	10	34	5	...	33	10	74	3
Blythe	16	5	33	3	...	28	12	50	1
Crawford	7	1	14	2	...	17	4	49	0
Haigh					...	1	0	9	0
Relf					...	21.5	7	47	2
Wynyard					...	3	0	15	0
Hayes					...	9	1	28	1

A GREAT ONE-DAY MATCH

Jim Laker

For as long as I watch one-day cricket I cannot seriously believe I shall see a more dramatic day's cricket than the Gillette Cup semi-final played at Old Trafford between Lancashire and Gloucestershire on 28 July 1971. Apart from an hour's delay through rain at lunchtime continuous play extended from 11 a.m. to 8.50 p.m. in front of a crowd officially estimated at 23,520 who paid receipts of £9,738. I am sure the latter figure is a correct one but remain unconvinced of the attendance figure which would never take into account the hundreds of 'free-loaders' coming in over the top.

The vast crowd was still streaming in and jockeying for position as Tony Brown won the toss for Gloucester and decided to bat on a perfect pitch of easy pace. Nobody was more anxious to do well than David Green, formerly of Lancashire, who in the company of Ron Nicholls weathered the early attack of Lever and Shuttleworth. An opening stand of 57 gave Gloucester the necessary base before Green was run out. Nicholls battled on for an admirable 50 but it was the mighty Procter who held the stage; a string of superb drives brought him nine fours and a six in his 65 before Farouk Engineer took a brilliant catch to dismiss him. The score was then 150 for three and Gloucester were ahead on points. Not for the first time Lancashire turned to the burly Jack Simmons to provide an answer. His immaculate off-spin brought his side back into the game; he bowled his 12 overs for only 25 runs and a couple of wickets. At 210 for six the odds now favoured Lancashire and despite an aggressive 29 not out from Mike Bissex, a final score of 229 left me feeling that the visitors were 30 or 40 runs short and a score of 230 was well within Lancashire's compass on a pitch unaffected by the rain and offering no help to the bowlers.

As is their wont Lancashire looked for a solid start from David Lloyd and Barry Wood and this they duly supplied. Although the first 50 had taken 17 overs, and 11 runs later Lloyd fell to Tony Brown, Harry Pilling and Barry Wood saw them safely into three figures and it seemed the game was theirs for the taking. John Mortimore had different ideas. After the departure of Wood and Pilling, the Gloucester off-spinner, in a fine accurate spell, clean bowled Clive Lloyd and induced Farouk Engineer to hit his wicket. With Davey accounting for Sullivan, Lancashire had slumped to 163 for six and the game again was wide open. This enormous and vibrant crowd who previously had been cherishing and cheering every run went quiet. The clock had crept past the 7.30 p.m. mark and the light was gradually worsening, umpires Bird and Jepson consulted and play went on. The new batsmen in charge were 'Skipper' Bond and Jack Simmons and they badly needed to right the ship. With typical Lancastrian common sense and no trace of panic they went about their task skilfully and professionally and the colour gradually began to come back into the faces of the Lancashire supporters. These two added 40 runs, defying all the bowling changes made by Tony Brown, until Mortimore broke through again and bowled Simmons to make it 203 for seven. Twenty-seven were wanted, three wickets in hand and six overs left. By this time it seemed impossible that the game could be finished that day. It was now very, very dark, the pavilion light casting shadows on the enclosure and in the background Old Trafford station had been ablaze with lights for some time. The umpires only needed a nod from Jack Bond for the play to be suspended when down the pavilion steps appeared David Hughes unnoticed for more than one reason. The focus was on Bond. Would he now decide to call it a day? He goes on record as saying that his first thought was to ensure that this noisy excitable crowd would not be deprived of a finish that day. It would be a terrible anticlimax to come back the following day and complete the final 20 minutes or so in front of 10 men and a dog. Jack Bond is an extremely honest man and I believe his thinking would be along those lines. Perhaps it was also supported by the fact that Gloucester had already been in the field for well over three hours and the strain was beginning to tell. Of the six overs left Procter and Davey could bowl four of them and after a night's rest may well be a different proposition in the morning. Any lingering doubts he had were dispelled by the confidence of David Hughes who maintains that he purposely sat in a dark corner of the dressing room 'to become accustomed to the light'! His reply to Bond's instructions to look for the singles was 'if I can see them, skipper, I think I can hit them'.

In view of what followed it must have been the understatement of the year. Most people will forget that Hughes came within a whisker of being bowled first ball by John Mortimore and batted through a fine over from Davey who was extremely difficult to pick up at all. In this light their only chance was to attack the slow off-spin of John Mortimore and what followed must go down as one of the most remarkable overs of all time. The unfortunate Mortimore was hammered for 24 runs in his next over in a wonderful exhibition of shrewd and skilful hitting by David Hughes. There was no wild slogging or hitting across the line and it seemed it was almost premeditated execution. By dint of excellent footwork the first ball was hit over extra cover safely for four and the second deposited in the crowd at long on for a mighty straight six. The crowd was going wild, up and down in their seats as Hughes, running like a hare put the third ball through the off side for two and the fourth wide of mid-on for two more. The cover drive off the fifth ball for another four was the shot of the match and nobody could have bettered it. To crown it all the last ball was hit high and handsomely for six over mid-on and unbelievably the scores were level. Appropriately it was left to Bond to nudge Procter wide of gully for a single and the crowd erupted. The entire playing area was invaded, Lancashire had won a famous victory with David Hughes so rightly adjudged Man of the Match. The same people who had been queuing for a seat at 8 o'clock that morning were rushing to get the last bus home from the ground after 10 o'clock that night.

Jack Bond asserts that it took weeks to get over it, and no doubt David Hughes is still accepting drinks as a result of his memorable achievement!

In acclaiming Lancashire's great day one cannot help but sympathise with Gloucester and John Mortimore, in particular. I can think of no reason for John to reproach himself or believe that he was responsible for his side's defeat. The fatal over did not include a solitary bad ball, although one could possibly argue that he might pushed the ball through quickly on a fuller length around the leg stump. This has never been John Mortimore's method. Praise be that he always goes down in my book as an attacking bowler and did he not previously account for Lloyd, Engineer and Simmons in this manner? For three minutes in that match he was unlucky to run across a man totally inspired who produced half a dozen shots worthy of being ranked with the greatest of our time and when that happens, no matter who the bowler is, there is precious little that anyone can do about it.

One of the least publicised facts about this game and one which I am sure in retrospect had a profound bearing on the result concerned the final period of play. The Gloucester side in fact must have achieved some kind of record with an unbroken spell of four hours in the field. There would be a public outcry if any side were asked to field from start of play at 11.30 a.m. right the way through until the tea interval which, of course, is the equivalent of Gloucester's marathon effort in the field. A 20-minute break in that final period would have allowed them vital breathing space, a chance coolly to reassess the situation and break the Lancashire concentration, all of which must have been very much in their favour.

If the players unanimously agreed that it was some time before they recovered from their efforts, the same may also be said of the TV commentary team. For some time our producer in charge of BBC1 cricket, David Kenning, had the happy knack of selecting the best of the one-day matches but on this occasion he was, for once, thwarted by the weather. Believing that the thrills and excitement of the semi-final would come from the other game between two evenly-matched sides, Kent and Warwickshire, he took himself off to Canterbury along with Peter West and Richie Benaud and posted me North to Old Trafford to complement the main coverage. Only as an afterthought did he book Tony Lewis to help me out and make his television début as a commentator. The inevitable of course happened – Old Trafford was bathed in sunshine most of the day, and Canterbury was awash with overnight rain. A little after 10 a.m. Tony and I took up our position in the commentary box and apart from a short break, when a shower held up play, recorded just about every ball bowled until we finally descended the scaffolding shortly after 9 p.m. For obvious reasons we sat cross-legged over the last three hours! Soon after 8 p.m. we had a call from the Controller of BBC1, Paul Fox, asking if there was any chance of the game still being in progress at 8.50p.m. Peering through the gloom, I replied that there was no chance unless the game was transferred over the road to the floodlights at the other Old Trafford. As everyone knows play did go on and at 8.50p.m. I received a message that on a 10-second count down, the game would be taken live into the National News. Thus cricket history was made and no one-day game that I have ever witnessed was more deserving of the immense publicity that surrounded it.

Chapter 2

GREAT
CHAMPIONS

Alan Hill

The nightmare wicket resembled the thinning locks of an elderly gentleman's head and its preparation was akin to the urgent brushwork with which he tries to conceal his balding crown. The place where the ball pitched was covered with grotesque tufts of rough grass wetted and rolled down with equally futile results.

The outfield was a wasteland of ridges and furrows. John Lillywhite said that the only comparison between the ground and a billiard table was that both had pockets. This was hallowed Lord's, far from its immaculate self, in the middle of the last century. Upon the swamp-like pastures W.G. Grace, not then 20, demonstrated his genius by scoring 134 out of 201 for the Gentlemen against the Players in 1868.

Eighteen years earlier John Wisden (the 'Little Wonder' of Sussex) had proved too 'fast and ripping' for the batsmen of the South at Lord's. Playing as the given man for the North, he took all 10 second innings wickets, all clean bowled. It was said that he 'kept his break from the off from one to two feet throughout the innings'. Wisden is one of the five Sussex players – the others are G.H. Bland, James Lillywhite, George Cox senior and Ian Thomson – to take 10 wickets in an innings.

Wisden, tiny and frail in physique as a youngster although he stepped up into the welterweight class in later years, seems ill-cast as a cricketing hero. He was only five feet four inches tall and in his heyday he tipped the scales at a little over seven stone. Yet he excited the praise of his fellow professionals, including William Caffyn, one of a contingent of famous 19th-century players.

Caffyn, a great favourite at The Oval where he was known as the 'Surrey Pet', said of Wisden: 'He was the best fast bowler I ever saw for so small a man. He was a remarkably good-natured little fellow, with a most comical expression of face. He was a grand bowler with, I think, the easiest delivery I ever saw, and a great command of pitch. As a batsman he was first-rate, with a beautifully straight bat.'

At Harrow, where the School was never beaten by Eton during his four years as professional bowler and cricket tutor, the Sussex man gained further acclaim. One observer said: 'He has a perfect delivery, with a short but rapid run, a graceful and easy sweep of the arm, moderate pace, hardly a loose ball, and always on the spot.'

John Wisden was born at Brighton on 5 September 1826. His

career spanned 18 years until an injury playing racquets coupled with encroaching rheumatism forced him to concentrate his efforts on promoting the game. He first played for Sussex in 1845 and he quickly soared to prominence. Against Kent at Hove in 1848 he took 15 wickets with slow underhand lobs.

One of his most resolute batting feats in a career which produced over 4000 runs as well as 2707 wickets was achieved in the first county match played at Bramall Lane, Sheffield. In August 1855, Sussex beat Yorkshire by an innings and 117 runs. Wisden, opening the innings, scored 148 – his highest score – out of 292 to quell the home attack, which included Isaac Hodgson, the first of Yorkshire's illustrious slow left-arm bowlers.

Centuries were rare on the fiery wickets of Wisden's time, but he also hit a hundred against Kent in 1850. The innings included four sixes and these were scored against Edgar Willsher, a formidable left-arm bowler with a spiteful, lifting delivery.

Wisden, dapper and neat in his straw hat which he adopted in preference to the white topper worn by older players, reached his zenith as a bowler between 1848 and 1859. In this period he averaged 225 wickets a season. His roundarm deliveries, with his fast shooter invariably rattling the stumps, wreaked havoc in the summer of 1851. Wisden took an incredible 455 wickets in 43 matches.

In 1859 Wisden was a member of George Parr's powerful England team which travelled to North America on the first overseas tour. The English professionals, after a terrible voyage across the Atlantic, did not lose a game and even local teams of 22 were overwhelmed. In eight matches Wisden took 64 wickets. The tour ended with an innings victory over the XXII of the United States and Canada in a snowstorm at Rochester. Wisden's match tally was 29 wickets (16–17 and 13–43) and his figures included a double hat-trick – six wickets in six balls.

Before the rise of county cricket William Clarke and John Wisden and another Sussex man, James Dean, quickened the pulse of the game in England with their all-star touring elevens which attracted enormous crowds. Clarke had a reputation as a dictator – 'his services to cricket were marred by over-tenacity in asserting his rights, real or otherwise,' commented a contemporary writer. The consequence was that Wisden and Dean formed their own United England team as a rival group to Clarke's All-England men.

In 1855 Wisden began his prosperous reign as a London businessman and sporting promoter. He was first associated with Fred Lillywhite as the proprietor of a cricket outfitters and cigar depot in New Coventry

Street, off Leicester Square. One of his sporting products was the celebrated 'catapulta', a curious device 'borrowed from the Romans', who used it as a siege engine. It was designed to bowl at any length a batsman selected. The device was used in practice at Harrow School and models were sold at Lord's for eleven guineas each.

Wisden later moved to nearby Cranbourne Square where he published his famous almanack for the first time in 1864. It coincided with the first appearance of W.G. Grace in major cricket. The annual was initially a primitive affair, consisting of only 112 pages (compared with around 1,300 pages today) and including mainly scores. In its first 20 years there were two other substantial cricket annuals and *Wisden* was slow to build up its popularity. The rarity of the first issue would seem to indicate low sales. In 1870 the almanack underwent its first major overhaul and, in 1887, with the introduction of the Pardon family to the editorship, it established a format which was to last for 50 years. The enthusiasm and devotion of succeeding editors, notably the late Norman Preston, have ensured its place among sporting best-sellers.

John Wisden, the 'thoroughly upright man, fast friend and generous employer', died of cancer at the age of 57 on 5 April 1884. The worthy almanack is his most enduring legacy to cricket. As a collector's piece, browser's pleasure and work of reference, it is in itself a 'little wonder'.

A 'W.G.' STORY

Major C.H.B. Pridham

(Freely quoted from Lord George Scott's interesting book *The Fleeting Opportunity*.)

In June 1886, W.G. Grace was down to play for the MCC v. Oxford University. When it was first rumoured at Oxford that W.G. was going to play, his reputation was so great that the minds of several of the University eleven were filled with consternation. One of them said: 'W.G. is coming down to play for the MCC and we shall never get him out. What can we do?' Another replied, and with some reason: 'We shall never get him out unless we can make him drunk'!! Due consideration had evidently not been taken into account that a bottle, or even two bottles, of champagne would have no more effect on his mighty frame than a liqueur glass of Kummel would have on a bunker on a golf course. However, J.H.

Brain, who had played for Gloucestershire and knew the Champion well, generously decided to give a dinner party on the night of the first day's play; and every alluring arrangement was made to induce the strong personality of W.G. to fall to the general wishes of the undergraduates. Hopes ran high when the great man accepted the invitation.

It was 21 June. Oxford won the toss, and, handicapped by the absence of several Blues, who were in for Schools, scored 142 runs. W.G. Grace and E.J.C. Studd then opened the innings for MCC. Those who had never before seen W.G. batting wondered, as he advanced towards the wicket, if he really was so wonderful a cricketer as he was said to be. His physique was splendid. He looked huge, and his large, dark beard gave him at first sight a dominating appearance, though possibly slightly lacking in agility on account of his size. Although his actual zenith had probably been ten years earlier, when he was slimmer and more active, he was not only champion in 1886, but he was universally recognised as such for many years to come.

He looked extremely bright and happy as he asked for guard and described a line on the ground parallel to the pitch with one of the bails. When facing the bowling his methods appeared to be simple. He gave a considerable uplift to his bat in a beeline from the bowler's arm to his wicket. The bowling obviously gave him no trouble, and it was delightful to see how, when playing back, he put such power into his strokes that, if the fielders failed to stop the ball it generally went to the boundary. The Parks' wicket was a lively one, and the most impressive part of his play was the way he treated the bumping balls. When a ball got up high on his off-stump or outside it, instead of leaving it alone he appeared to tap it down on the ground, generally to the boundary, as if he could place each delivery as he liked.

The opening pair were not out for 90 runs at the end of the first day's play, W.G.'s share of them being 50, made by what appeared to be faultless cricket. One who was there said that he was much struck by the charming manner with which W.G. treated the young men. He went out of his way to encourage and reassure all the keen young cricketers present. The dinner as a party was a great success. There was plenty of champagne going round, and all – including W.G. – thoroughly enjoyed the evening.

Next morning he went to the nets to have a few 'sighting shots' before continuing his innings. The number of those watching him was considerable, and all were full of interest. Now, there was a keen cricketer in his third year at Oxford who, incidentally, was playing for MCC in this match. This was E.A. Nepean, who bowled what at first sight appeared to be simple deliveries, which, apart from an occasional slight off-break, turned very considerably from leg even on a fast wicket, when they came fast off the pitch. For some unexplained reason, Nepean's bowling was almost ridiculed until the following year, when he bowled for both Oxford and the Gentlemen v. Players at Lord's. On this occasion he was determined to bowl to the Champion at the nets, and actually clean bowled him with one of his leg-breaks. This was really encouraging, and the fiction spread like wildfire: 'W.G. dined rather too well last night and can't see the ball at all this morning!' It was even asserted that he had been bowled out *three times* at the nets. When play began, however, it was soon obvious that no Oxford bowler was likely to get past W.G.'s bat. Centuries at that time were by no means common in the Parks, and when his score was 104 he was *given out l.b.w.* (modern critics of W.G. kindly note) to Page, the Oxford captain. He had hit 15 fours and one six. The MCC total score was 260.

Hopes were now centred on Oxford's second innings. Two freshmen with great public school reputations were being tried for the first time. The innings began to the bowling of W.G. and Walter Wright (the Kent professional), whilst M.C. Kemp kept wicket. W.G. actually secured *all 10 wickets for 49 runs* (his analysis was: 36.2–17–49–10, overs of four balls), and he looked supremely happy, as he had every reason to be, when the MCC won by an innings and 28 runs. During Oxford's first innings he was bowling when Hine Haycock caught a fine catch on the boundary at square-leg. During their second innings, when Brain looked like making many runs, he was brilliantly caught on the same boundary by the same fielder. W.G. remarked in high glee: 'I haven't had a man who could do it like that for me since poor old G.F.' G.F. Grace, his less famous younger brother but a fine all-rounder, died in September 1880, only three weeks after he had played for England v. Australia, at The Oval, together with both W.G. and E.M. Grace.

W.G.'s bowling on this occasion is thus described: 'With rather a low action, he seemed to put the ball towards the wicket rather than to bowl in the conventional manner. It looked easy for a quick-footed batsman, but he did what he liked with the batsmen that day, and this was probably where the snare lay. W.G. was said at that time to be the best change bowler in England. Given a fast wicket, he probably required a full-sized ground even more than most slow bowlers. And although he might be hit hard and even frequently, his knowledge of the game and complete control of length enabled him to detect and attack any weak spot in the batsman's armour. He took 2876 wickets in first-class matches during his long career – a number only exceeded by six other bowlers in the history of the game, all of them professionals. In this particular match, the hospitable wiles of the undergraduates had conspicuously failed – in fact they had only succeeded in producing from the intended victim the almost unprecedented feat of a century and all 10 wickets on the same day. The moral was that W.G. was impervious to the lures of a festive board.

The only other instances of a player taking all 10 wickets as well as scoring a century are credited to V.E. Walker, for England v. Surrey, at The Oval in 1859, and to W.G.'s elder brother, E.M. Grace, for MCC v. Gentlemen of Kent, at Canterbury in 1862. E.M. scored 192, carrying his bat through the innings and taking 15 wickets in a 12-a-side match; with one man absent in the second innings he took the remaining 10 wickets. It is interesting to note that, although 38 instances have occurred since 1886 of a bowler taking all 10 wickets in a first-class match, not one of the bowlers concerned has as yet equalled W.G.'s feat of scoring a century in the same match. Even in club cricket the double feat is extremely rare, but in 1929 R.G. Seldon, for Devon Dumplings v. Somerset Stragglers in a two-day match at Exeter, took all 10 wickets (hitting the stumps seven times) for 70 runs, and scored 100 not out on the same day.

To return to W.G. That night, after the game was over, another dinner party was given by another hospitable undergraduate – H. Acland Hood. One of the guests was a popular and well-known character at Oxford. When introduced to W.G., he asked: 'Did you see the cricket in the Parks today?' To which the reply was: 'Yes, I did.' The individual in question knew nothing about cricket, and had probably never heard of W.G. Grace – either as a cricketer or as anything else. At a time when W.G. was probably the best-known and most easily recognised man in England, this, in itself, is a remarkable incident.

The recorder of the above story, Lord George Scott (who scored 100 for Oxford v. Cambridge in 1887 as a last choice to fill the vacancy caused by an injury to Wreford Brown, and whose average for Oxford v. Cambridge in three years, five innings, was 61), also gives the following details concerning W.G.'s hundredth century, in 1895: 'I had the impression that he considered his bat was to be used entirely as a weapon of offence. It was almost unknown for him to leave a ball alone. In 1895, when he was 47 years old and admittedly many years past his zenith on account of his great size and weight, he was nevertheless still the Champion when conditions were easier for a batsman than they had been 20 years before. That year he played for

Gloucestershire v. Somerset, at Bristol, on 16, 17 May. On this occasion the Rev. A.P. Wickham was keeping wicket for Somerset, and W.G. scored 288 out of a total of 474 in 5 hours and 20 minutes, without making a single mistake. A.P. Wickham wrote to a friend afterwards as follows: "I had the advantage of watching that innings from the closest quarters, and have no hesitation in describing it as the most marvellous performance with the bat that I have ever seen. I can never forget the way Tyler's good-length slows, converted by W.G. into half-volleys pitching about a foot outside the off-stump, were driven, rather than pulled, over mid-on's head, and pitched over the ropes. If these strokes had been counted as sixes (as they would now be), he would have nearly topped the 300. He only allowed *four balls* to pass his bat; one was on the leg-side and the other three were low ones on the off-side. But no matter how high the ball leaped – and Sammy Woods who had 40 overs at him, could 'prance' a bit – W.G.'s bat dropped on to them. Some of them went for fours, and others for a safe one or two to the man on the boundary, while those aimed at his head generally found the ropes on the leg-side!'"

Partly owing to his immensely powerful build, W.G. could stand great punishment when hit by fast bowling on his body. In 1896 he played in the opening match of an Australian tour for Lord Sheffield's Eleven, at Sheffield Park, Brighton. The wicket was fiery, and E. Jones, one of the fastest bowlers of all time, hit him several times on the chest. A few days after this match W.G. showed his chest to a friend in the pavilion on the county ground at Bristol, who saw what looked like six or seven black puddings around his heart.

W.G. said: 'Although I am forty-eight in a couple of months, I don't mind how fast they send them down to me. They can chuck them if they like; the faster they are the better. It's the slow ones I don't like. I never did. I know how they ought to be played, but I was never quick-footed enough to get bang out to them.'

It is probable that he derived his supreme batting efficiency from his remarkable physique and immense power, which in turn made it impossible for him to be quick-footed to the same degree as Jessop, who could dash into the middle of a cricket pitch to any ball. Nevertheless, W.G. was, as a batsman, far nearer perfection than any man in the Victorian era; and there has never been anybody in the same category against fast bowling, for in his zenith he was a terror to all fast bowlers, even on bumping wickets. W.G. was such a glorious figure on a cricket ground that when one arrived at Lord's and saw him at the wicket, it seemed almost too good to be true, especially when he proceeded to smite the ball in all directions. At the same time, when necessary, he could show wonderful and exceptional patience.

Fifty years ago bearded cricketers were by no means uncommon, including such celebrities as Alfred Shaw, Barlow, Blackham, Boyle, Bonnor and others; but the beard of W.G. outshone those of all others by its voluminous magnificence. Many years ago, when the pavilion at Lord's was packed during the first day of a match between England and Australia, very many country members of the MCC had come up full of interest to see this great match. Walter Forbes and my brother Henry were sitting in the pavilion watching the Australians batting, when a germ of mischief took possession of their brains. Henry after looking at his match card, said: 'I think I can make out the names of most of the English eleven, but I wonder who that stout man with the large beard fielding at point is?' A man sitting immediately in front began visibly to fidget; so Walter Forbes said: 'I think that must be Abel.' The man in front could resist no longer, and turning round said: 'That, sir, is Doctor W.G. Grace.' Whilst thanking him for this valuable piece of information, Walter inwardly regretted that fat trout could seldom be induced to rise to his lures with such avidity.

These are a few instances connected with a man who for many years was magnificent, both in appearance and performance, on practically every well-known cricket ground in England and Australia. There are still some who played a great deal with him and know much more about his play than I do, but all agree that W.G. Grace was incontestably the champion of the game of cricket during the reign of Queen Victoria, and, taking into consideration the great number of wickets which fell to his bowling, there has surely never been one more deserving of the title, a fact which the late A. Stuart Wortley skilfully brought out in his masterpiece now hanging in the pavilion at Lord's.

DENIS COMPTON

Ralph Barker

Since Hobbs, and with all possible respect to the greatness of Hammond, we have never seen an England batsman so thoroughly equipped for every sort of situation on every sort of pitch.

E.W. SWANTON

The pace and hostility of Lindwall and Miller in 1948 was something that few English cricket followers had seen before. Not many of them could remember the Gregory and McDonald of 1921, and Larwood had seldom developed the venom in England that he attained in the 1932–33 tour of Australia.

There is no doubt that speed in itself is intimidating. It requires a physical effort on the part of the batsman to measure up to it. When it is allied to frequent use of the bouncer, flying at great pace at the batsman's head, it requires a radical adjustment in the batsman's approach to his innings. Such adjustments are not made easily.

It was in the speed and certainty with which he made this adjustment that Compton stood out among English cricketers in the summer of 1948. It was in this, rather than in his merits purely as a batsman, that he earned the comment that he had surpassed Hammond and bore comparison only with Hobbs. While one could imagine forms of attack which might hamper Hammond and seriously inconvenience Bradman, one felt that Hobbs, alone among English batsmen in finding a ready answer to the invention of the googly, would as a young man have dealt with any bowling threat that could be devised. The same was true of Compton. Allied to a perfect technique was this gift for improvisation. Nothing could take him by surprise. He was never caught out without his music.

Over the whole of his career one would not put Compton in front of Hutton, or Hammond. But in the years immediately after the Second World War he earned himself a place in English cricket that is above comparison, relative only to that of Victor Trumper amongst Australians. He reached his peak in 1947, a year in which he scored 22 centuries – 18 in England and four in succession in Australia. By the end of that year his knee was already giving trouble, but it did not stop him playing football, nor did it prevent him from reaching the summit of achievement in 1948.

The announcement of the team for the third Test at Old Trafford that year caused a sensation. The selectors – A.J. Holmes, J.C. Clay and R.W.V. Robins – had dropped Len Hutton.

Bradman on his farewell tour had brought a team that seemed invincible, and England had already lost the first two Tests. In the second Test at Lord's, Hutton had played the worst innings of his career. He was dropped at slip by Lindwall off Johnston before he had scored, and then, apparently unsettled by a succession of bumpers, he had slashed wildly at several rising balls outside the off stump. When his rash, unworthy innings came to its humiliating end, the crowd showed their puzzled disappointment by allowing him to walk back to the pavilion in silence. Yet they never contemplated the dropping of the man who with Compton represented England's best chance of renascence.

The selectors believed that Hutton's lack of confidence against Lindwall and Miller was affecting the other batsmen in the side. Unfairly, as it now seems, he was blamed not only for his own failures but for the failures of others. For the climactic Third Test, which England had to win to keep any chance of regaining the Ashes, and to draw if they were to save the series, Hutton was left out.

If England could not resist the Australians with Hutton in the side, what chance had they got without him? Were they, perhaps, in a desperate attempt to force a win, putting the emphasis on attack? Hardly. Wright, Laker and Wardle were all omitted and the bowling comprised Bedser, Pollard and Young, plus Yardley and Edrich.

The value of Washbrook and Edrich to the England side in this period is stressed elsewhere. It is no disrespect to them to say that Hutton and Compton were in a different class from all other England batsmen. The load on Compton's shoulders would be doubled. Emmett and Crapp came in for Hutton and a fourth bowler. There was much to be said in their favour. There was nothing more to be done but to wish them well.

Thirty-five thousand people were there on Thursday 8 July to see Yardley win the toss and elect to bat. On this slightly green wicket it needed courage to bat first against Lindwall and Miller. In the event, Miller was not called upon and the opening assault came from Lindwall and Johnston. Twenty-two runs came in half an hour, and then Washbrook went to drive a swinging full-toss from Johnston that started outside the leg stump and yorked him middle and off. Six runs later Emmett, losing sight of a bouncer from Lindwall that rose awkwardly, turned his head away and held out his bat one-handed in front of him. Barnes at very close short-leg took the catch. His presence there was a constant embarrassment to the England batsmen. Some felt he was closer than the umpires should have allowed.

Edrich began uncertainly, but with the utmost determination, as though survival were his sole end. Four low scores in this series, coupled with the dropping of Hutton, had convinced him that if he didn't play an innings today it would be his turn next. Such was the psychological effect of the selectors' action.

Twenty-eight for two was a bad start, but Compton was next, and while this pair were together there was still hope of a good score.

Compton at once began to play with assurance, while Edrich looked more settled, but they were facing Lindwall at his most dangerous. The ball hummed through the humid Manchester air, first the out-swinger, then the fast yorker. Compton met both confidently, while Edrich hung on grimly. Lindwall, anxious to unsettle them, began a series of bumpers. Edrich ducked, but one bumper, hurled at great pace, hit Compton on the arm.

In Lindwall's next over Compton went back to fend off another bouncer when umpire Dai Davies called 'no ball'. Compton, changing his mind, tried to swing it down to long-leg. He was late with his shot and just got a top edge. The ball flew upwards and struck him on the forehead, just above the eye. Stunned and blinded, he dropped his bat and reeled towards the off side, hands covering his face. Bradman, Barnes and Tallon rushed to his aid. The ball had hit him with such force that it ballooned more than half-way to the fine-leg boundary before falling to the ground. A staggering Compton was led from the field, blood pouring from a cut on the forehead. It looked as though he might be out of the game.

The mutterings of the crowd showed what they thought of it. Sir Pelham Warner, recalling the strong objections of the Australians to bodyline, as they had called it, commented on the suspicion that they were now using this form of attack. 'To condemn uncompromisingly a form of bowling,' wrote Sir Pelham, 'and later to give any suspicion that it is being used again, if only occasionally, is, to put it mildly, not only illogical to a degree but greatly weakens the arguments in favour of the original protest.' Sir Pelham, as joint manager during the bodyline tour, might be dismissed as a hostile witness. But not, surely, Bill O'Reilly. 'There were several occasions,' wrote O'Reilly, 'when the only difference I could see between our bowling and that of Jardine's team was the disposition of the field.'

There were no protests from the England players. Although not relishing the experience, they accepted that the 'scalper' was a legitimate weapon and longed for the day when some English fast bowler would come along to redress the balance. But the bouncers in this game were grossly overdone, and there was no mistaking the animosity that crept in as a result.

After a delay of 10 minutes, at 32 for two and with one batsman knocked out, Jack Crapp came in to play his first innings in Test cricket. To tone with this appalling situation, the sun disappeared, ominous clouds hung over the stands, and the wind blew chill. But great hopes were vested in the left-handed Crapp, who came fresh from a century against the Australians for Gloucestershire earlier in the week. He and Edrich fought their way through to lunch, when the score was 57 for two. Edrich had batted an hour and a half for 14 and Crapp an hour for 11. England were resisting strongly but the advantage of winning the toss was gone.

During the interval Compton had two stitches in his cut forehead. It was announced that he was resting and would bat again *if needed*. This got just about the best laugh of the series.

After lunch Edrich and Crapp batted with more confidence, Crapp particularly showing his liking for the slows of Ian Johnson, driving him for a six and three fours. Meanwhile, at slip, Lindwall was seen to be limbering up. A glance at the scoreboard disclosed the reason. The new ball was due. Before the war it would have been taken after 200 runs. Now it came after 55 overs, at three o'clock on the first day, with the score at 87. Surely the second new ball had never appeared at such a low score.

Nine runs later Crapp attempted no stroke to a Lindwall out-swinger (an in-swinger to him) and was l.b.w. Dollery played over a Johnston yorker, and England were 97 for four.

Compton had wanted to go in at the fall of Crapp's wicket, but Yardley would not allow it. 'Go and have a net first, Denis,' he said. 'Then, if you're are all right, you can go in after me.' Compton duly went and had his net, facing Pollard and Young. After a few minutes he pronounced himself OK. 'I can see them all right,' he told them. 'Now for Lindwall.'

He did not have to wait long. Half an hour after Yardley went in, Edrich was caught behind the wicket off Lindwall: 119 for five, last man 32. Edrich had batted 3 hours and 10 minutes, and for much of the time he had been struggling and out of touch, but he had played an invaluable innings, holding up the Australian attack while Compton rested and received first aid.

Compton, a patch of plaster showing white above his left eye, went back to the wicket to face Lindwall. The crowd applauded him emotionally all the way to the wicket. But they feared that after such a stunning blow he could not have recovered so soon. The pace of Lindwall would be too much for him. But Compton, showing no trace of nerves, at once began to play calmly and easily, seeming to see Lindwall early and to have plenty of time to deal with all he could offer. Yardley, too, looked safer than any of his predecessors, playing Lindwall mostly off the back foot. There followed a period of confident, rational play which lasted till tea.

Immediately after tea Yardley played an indecisive stroke off Toshack, mis-hit, and was caught at mid-wicket. In capered the perky figure of Godfrey Evans. There was nothing even vaguely comical about Evans when he was keeping wicket. Transformed by cap and gloves, he was the picture of militant efficiency. But remove the cap, and put a bat in his hands, and he was a natural jester. It was hard for any captain to keep up the tension with Evans at the wicket, and for the next 75 minutes Evans played a succession of bold strokes that would have been unwise in another player, interspersed with occasional lucky snicks to long-leg which delighted the crowd. Meanwhile Compton, taking full advantage of the relaxed atmosphere, reached his 50. He had come in to bat that morning at 12.15 and it was now twenty to six. A lot had happened to him in that time.

Immediately after reaching his 50 Compton got a thick edge to a Lindwall out-swinger and gave a wide, low catch which looked like passing safely between wicket-keeper and first slip. Tallon dived and got his right hand to the ball but it didn't stick. It was a wonderful try and hardly deserved to be called a chance, but it stood out as the first mistake made by Compton so far.

This pair scored at the rate of a run a minute, adding 75 runs and taking the score to 216 before Evans swung once too often at Lindwall and gave a catch. He had scored 34. His gay impudence had done much to restore England's belief in herself and the possibility of victory.

Compton and Bedser addressed themselves to the task of playing out time. They looked safe enough until, with the last ball of the day, Johnston bowled an in-swinger which Compton glanced down the leg side, and Tallon very nearly got across to make the catch. It was a narrow escape for England. Compton was not out 64 and Bedser not out 4, and England were 231 for seven. They seemed set for no more than a moderate score, but if Compton and Bedser could survive the third new ball, which Bradman had held back for the following morning, England might still make 300. Both the Ashes and the rubber could still be saved.

Tallon needed no excuses for the two 'chances' he was alleged to have missed. Both would have been miraculous catches. But he was in fact suffering from extremely tender palms, caused by the barrage of Lindwall bumpers earlier in the day.

Compton went back to his hotel that night with a splitting headache, and next morning, forehead still patched and the whole area around his eye black and discoloured, he was a sorry figure. 'How do you feel this morning?' asked Arthur Mailey, who was staying at the same hotel. Compton winked with his good eye and grinned. 'I might feel better when I get in the middle.'

It was a dull, cloudy, hazy morning, but 30,000 people were there at the start to see Compton and Bedser face Lindwall and Johnston and the new ball. Bradman saw to it that Lindwall bowled to the end occupied by Bedser, bringing the field in to cut off the singles, but the wicket was comfortably paced now, and Lindwall couldn't quite attain his extreme speed of the day before. Bedser played his first two overs confidently, while Compton began at once to use his strokes off Johnston, taking two twos for a cut and a leg glance. The first eight overs produced only 10 runs, but then Bedser got Lindwall away to the square-leg boundary for the first four of the day.

When he had scored 73 Compton played another fine leg-glance which Tallon got a glove to, but the ball trickled away for 1. Another sharp single and Compton made the score 250. England had been batting 400 minutes. With the weather unsettled and Australia facing the fourth innings, it was beginning to look like a reasonable score.

Bradman rested Lindwall and tried Toshack, left arm over the wicket. At once Compton drove him for two characteristic fours behind extra-cover, the blade turned at the last moment. He took 10 runs off the over, making his own score 84. This burst of scoring worried Bradman so much that he brought Lindwall back after only one over's rest. Perhaps the fact that Bedser was facing the bowling influenced him. Lindwall worked up to something near top pace in this over, and Bedser was several times beaten for speed. Twice he snicked the ball dangerously in the air, but each time it flew over the slips' heads for 4. The second of these edgy shots put up the 50 partnership. Toshack was brought back, and bowled a maiden to Bedser.

All this time Johnston had been operating from the opposite end, but now Bradman switched to Ian Johnson. Bedser looked far less comfortable against Johnson's flighted off-spinners, but when Johnson dropped short he carted him to the leg boundary, and the score still moved ahead steadily, 43 coming in the first hour's play. For Compton the field was spread wide, encouraging the single, while for Bedser everyone closed in. Any firm shot or snick from Bedser that did not go straight to hand went for four, and an edged boundary off Toshack took him into the thirties.

The deep-set field for Compton, however, restricted him almost entirely to singles. Thus his score crept run by run to 97. In an effort to disturb him, Bradman brought Bill Johnston on for Johnson, and set an attacking field. But just after one o'clock Toshack at last over-pitched one and Compton drove it past deep mid-on for four. This shot not only completed his century but put up the 300. He had batted for just under four hours without a false stroke, except for the three narrow escapes that could barely be called chances to Tallon. Compton had always done well at Old Trafford and the crowd rose to him.

Only when Compton was at the wicket had there been any look of freedom and permanence about England's batting. When he returned to the crease 20 minutes before tea on the first day, with the score at 119 for five, England had looked unlikely to make 200. Now with any luck they would make 350.

Typically, Compton in this sublime moment moved suddenly, naturally and inevitably to the ridiculous. Immediately after reaching his 100 he called for a short run, which Bedser refused. Compton, spurting forward, and now required to go sharply into reverse, slipped and fell. For a moment he looked certain to be run out, then he turned and made a dive for the crease. Dishevelled and without his bat, he literally scrambled home. It was in this youthful fallibility that Compton especially endeared himself to lovers of cricket.

Recovering his composure at once, as though such alarms were part of a normal day's work (which for Compton they were), he off-drove Toshack for another four, and back came Lindwall for a final burst at top speed before lunch. This perhaps was the fastest sustained piece of bowling ever projected by Lindwall. Often he would put in one really fast ball, but rarely bowl two or three overs at a time at full pace. But now, with England gradually moving into a commanding position, Lindwall threw himself into the attack, urged by Bradman, who felt that if Lindwall could get but one wicket before lunch the end of England's innings must be near. Thus it was quite safe for Lindwall to burn himself out in one frenzied effort.

The last over before lunch was the fastest of all. Three times Compton was morally bowled as he moved into line defensively and was beaten for pace. Once he was struck on the knuckles, then he ducked to the inevitable bouncer. The tussle between these two great cricketers, fought from the beginning without sentiment but in a good spirit notwithstanding Compton's injury, was thrilling to see. When the players came in to lunch, with Compton at the back of the field, still undefeated, it was Lindwall who stood aside at the gate applauding Compton and motioning him to precede the Australian team.

Directly after lunch the impersonal antagonism between Lindwall and Compton was renewed. Compton on-drove Lindwall's first ball sweetly for four, then cut the next one to the rails wide of third man. Lindwall responded with a lightning bouncer. Johnston was the other bowler, and Compton late-cut him for another four. This Test match, which had begun in a kind of vacuum without Hutton, and developed an atmosphere of unreality as Compton was temporarily removed and strangers like Crapp and Dollery took his place, was now alive with drama and tension. England's score had passed the stage of respectability and was swelling rapidly. The clouds still threatened rain. If England could pull back the deficit by winning this Test, the selectors would surely restore Hutton and at least two of Wright, Wardle and Laker, and the series would be wide open.

Compton was so contained and imperturbable a player that it is unlikely that this electric atmosphere had any bearing on what followed. As with so many tragedies, the basic situation looked innocuous. Johnston bowled, Compton tapped the ball quietly into the covers, and as Loxton and Bradman moved in rapidly to gather the ball, Compton and Bedser showed no inclination to go for a run. Bedser, who had backed up as Johnston bowled, turned round to watch the fielders, his back to Compton, sliding his bat into the crease. As he did so he saw that Bradman and Loxton, in their anxiety to cut off a run, had collided. The ball trickled past them, and Compton called for a run.

Compton, two or three yards out of his crease, could make it. Bedser, having returned to his own crease, and being unprepared to run, had a more difficult task. He set off, head down, but meanwhile Loxton, recovering quickly, had the ball in his hand. In an instant he measured the batsmen's chances and saw that Compton would get in but that a good throw would beat Bedser. He hurled the ball over the bails at Tallon, and Bedser was run out by yards.

A partnership that had lasted 2½ hours and added 121 runs was thus denied the distinction of being the highest ever for the eighth wicket for England against Australia. Four more runs would have done it. England were 337 for eight. Bedser, who had not scored since lunch, had made 37.

The red-headed Pollard appeared in place of Bedser, to a thunderous reception from his home crowd. Compton did his best to keep the bowling, but Bradman's tactics were plain. For Compton the field was spread so wide that Tallon, standing back for the fast bowlers, was the nearest man to the bat. No one else was within 50 yards of the wicket.

The field was the same for Ian Johnson when he replaced Lindwall, except that Tallon stood up.

Under these circumstances it was difficult for Compton to score at all, except in singles. He could not pierce the deep field off the slower bowlers, and every fielder was alert to cut off a second run. At length he called Pollard for an intended two but Loxton raced in and the batsmen had to be content with one. Pollard faced Johnson. Now the field was brought right in. Some of the Australians were almost sitting on the bat. Closest of all, at forward short-leg, was Barnes. Pollard determined to shift him.

Johnson tossed up one of his flighted off-spinners, on a length, near a half-volley. Pollard lunged at it cross-batted in a typical tail-ender's pulled-drive. It was a dangerous shot, but Pollard had a good eye. He felt the satisfying little recoil as the ball exploded from the barrel of the bat.

The ball had time to travel no more than two or three yards before it struck its target amidships. Pollard, chagrined for the moment at the loss of a certain four runs, watched Barnes sink like a stricken ship. To confirm that Barnes had taken the full force of the shot, the ball fell dully at his feet. He tried to get up, but could not do so unaided. After several minutes, three policemen appeared and carried him off.

Pollard, of course, had not thought in terms of shifting Barnes quite so literally. He had never expected to score a bull's-eye. But, however unwittingly, he had removed one of the biggest obstacles to an England victory.

England were past 350 when Toshack bowled Pollard, and 11 runs later, at 363, Young was caught by Bradman off Johnson. Most of the last 25 runs came from Compton. He had made 145 not out. 'For five hours twenty minutes,' said Wisden, 'he carried his side's responsibilities, and nothing earned more admiration than the manner in which he withstood some lightning overs of extreme hostility by Lindwall.' To come back and weather these frequent squally interludes from Lindwall after a stupefying blow to the head must surely make this innings Compton's greatest. He had turned the certainty of defeat and the loss of the Ashes at 119 for five into the prospect of victory in this Test and rehabilitation in the series. For the first time since the war the initiative lay with England.

It remains to record how England and Denis Compton were cheated of the fruits of this wonderful innings. Without Barnes, Australia were dismissed for 221, their first batting failure of the series, and then Washbrook and Edrich played brilliantly against Lindwall and a revitalised Miller, who, with defeat threatening, bowled some of the fastest overs of his life. At the end of the third day, Saturday, England were 174 for three – 316 ahead with seven wickets to fall. Then, on Monday, came the rain. There was no more play until after lunch on the final day, when, on a lifeless wicket, Morris and Bradman played out time.

Against this powerful Australian side, regarded as one of the two greatest ever, England had the better of the fourth Test up to the last day, and there is no telling what the psychological effect might have been if we could have won at Manchester. It remains one of the great 'ifs' of cricket. It is quite conceivable that England might have gone to The Oval all square. That they would have been vanquished nevertheless is fairly certain. England were without Washbrook through injury, and the Australian fast attack was irresistible. But what a finish it would have made to the series!

ENGLAND v AUSTRALIA
Manchester: July 8, 9, 10, 12 and 13, 1948

ENGLAND

C. Washbrook	b Johnston	11	not out	85
G.M.Emmett	c Barnes b Lindwall	10	c Tallon b Lindwall	0
W.J.Edrich	c Tallon b Lindwall	32	run out	53
D.C.S. Compton	not out	145	c Miller b Toshack	0
J.F.Crapp	lbw Lindwall	37	not out	19
H.E.Dollery	b Johnston	1		
N.W.D. Yardley	c Johnson b Toshack	22		
T.G.Evans	C Johnston b Lindwall	32		
A.V.Bedser	run out	37		
R.Pollard	b Toshack	3		
J.A.Young	c Bradman b Johnston	4		
	B 7, l–b 17, n–b 3	27	B 9, l-b, w 1	17
		363	(3 wkts dec.)	**174**

AUSTRALIA

A.R.Morris	c Compton b Bedser	51	not out	54
I.W.Johnson	c Evans b Bedser	1	c Crapp b Young ...	6
D.G.Bradman	lbw Pollard	7	not out	30
A.L.Hassett	c Washbrook b Young ...	38		
K.R.Miller	lbw Pollard	31		
S.G.Barnes	retired hurt	1		
S.J.Loxton	b Pollard	36		
D.Tallon	c Evans b Edrich	18		
R.R.Lindwall	c Washbrook b Bedser	23		
W.A.Johnston	c Crapp b Bedser	3		
E.R.H.Toshack	not out	0		
	B₅, l-b₄, n-b₃	12	N-b 2	2

B$_5$, l-b$_4$, n-b$_3$ 12   N-b 2 2

221   (1wkt) 92

	O.	M.	R.	W.	O.	M.	R.	W.
AUSTRALIA								
Lindwall 40	8	99	4	14	4	37	1	
Johnston 45.5	13	67	3	14	3	34	1	
Loxton 7	0	18	0	8	1	29	0	
Toshack 41	20	75	2	12	5	26	1	
Johnson 38	16	77	0	7	3	16	0	
Miller				14	7	15	0	
ENGLAND								
Bedser 36	12	81	4	19	12	27	0	
Pollard 32	9	53	3	10	8	6	0	
Edrich 7	3	27	1	2	0	8	0	
Yardley 4	0	12	0					
Young 14	5	36	1	21	12	31	1	
Compton				9	3	18	0	

FALL OF WICKETS

	Eng.	Aus.	Eng.	Aus.
Wkt.	1st.	1st.	2nd.	2nd.
1st	22	3	1	10
2nd	28	13	125	
3rd	96	82	129	
4th	97	135		
5th	119	139		
6th	141	172		
7th	216	208		
8th	337	219		
9th	352	221		

Match Drawn

THE FIRST OFF-SPINNER: LAMBORN
'THE LITTLE FARMER'

G. D. Martineau

A young cricketer learning to bowl is at once anxious to know how he may make the ball break. He is fascinated by the idea of that sudden turn which can deceive a batsman and make him alter the direction of his stroke at the last moment.

The reply that length must be mastered first, as spin is useless without it, is invariably received with a gloomy look, and soon one may see the youthful wrist pudgily contorted in an attempt to produce guileful deliveries.

If he is a right-handed bowler, the first break he achieves is usually from the off. Under modern laws and conditions, the spin obviously comes more easily from that side, and quite a natural grip of the ball may achieve it without loss of control. Endeavours to turn it from the leg result at first in weird miscalculations, and may even imperil those standing behind the experimentalist.

In underarm days the position was reversed. The old bowlers found the leg-break a simpler device to master than the off-break.

This was so much the case that the first off-spinner came as a shock and a surprise to everybody.

The innovator was Lamborn (not Lambert, as John Nyren called him), and the name may have been derived, as so often happened in the country, from an ancient and hereditary occupation; for he tended his father's sheep.

It was while he was so employed that he beguiled the hours by setting up a hurdle and bowling away at it.

Lamborn was known as 'The Little Farmer', and he had what John Nyren described as 'the most extraordinary delivery I ever saw'. He goes on to say that 'the ball was delivered quite low, and with a twist; not like that of the generality of right-handed bowlers, but just the reverse way, that is, if bowling to a right-handed hitter, his ball would twist from the off-stump into the leg. He was the first I remember who introduced this deceitful and teasing style of delivering the ball.'

But Lamborn, who had thus stumbled by accident on a new form of attack, had very little idea how to turn it to advantage. The care of sheep is apt to induce a rather ovine cast of mind, and he lacked the initiative as a bowler displayed by a somewhat earlier shepherd of the Bethlehem Club. 'The Farmer's comprehension,' we are told, 'did not equal the speed of lightning,' – and, instead of pitching the ball on or outside the off-stump, he bowled it dead straight, with the result that, having beaten the batsman, it either hit him on the shins or missed the leg-stump.

He was bowling one day to the Duke of Dorset when this occurred, whereupon 'the plainspoken little bumpkin, in his eagerness and delight, and forgetting the style in which we were always accustomed to impress our aristocratical playmates with our acknowledgment of their rank and station, bawled out – "Ah, it was *tedious* near you. Sir!" The familiarity of the tone and the genuine Hampshire dialect in which it was spoken set the whole ground laughing.'

It was left to the General, old Nyren, to instruct Lamborn how best to make use of his peculiar gift. Under that shrewd coaching, he directed his deliveries, so that, for a time, they proved deadly.

'When All England played the Hambledon Club, the Little Farmer was appointed one of our bowlers; and, egad! this new trick of his so bothered the Kent and Surrey men, that they tumbled out one after another, as if they had been picked off by a rifle corps. For a long time they could not tell what to make of that cursed twist of his.'

Today it is the ball that goes away from the bat which causes most trouble, but in a padless age, when the straight bat had only just come in, and batsmen were still disposed to stand some way from the wicket, it is easy to understand the deadliness of the first off-spinner.

Lamborn's name appears in matches for only five seasons, the first being 1777, and there is a general vagueness about his Christian name, birthplace, age, and date of death which are doubtless characteristic of the man himself. He was 'a very civil and inoffensive young fellow', one of those who made his mark and went his quiet way to pastures new, leaving batsmen to revise their footwork and devise still more vexed questions for the morrow.

GODFREY EVANS

Henry Blofeld

When I was ten years old I gave up a potentially erratic career as a leg-spinner and donned a pair of wicket-keeping gloves because one of the regular wicket-keepers in the first game at my school was injured. I suppose I must have shown some sort of aptitude for I was allowed to continue and I did my best to learn all I could about the art. By the end of the summer term in 1950, the greatest man on earth as far as I was concerned was Godfrey Evans. He had replaced Denis Compton by the length of a street.

My mother and father took me to watch one day's play of the second Test match at Lord's, England versus West Indies, in 1950. I was mesmerised by Evans, and from that moment on, I spent all my waking life trying to imitate the great man. I can still see in my mind's eye on that far distant day at Lord's the blur of movement as he ran to meet a bad throw-in and take it on the full toss. Then there was the thrilling, ear-splitting appeal for a catch behind with the ball thrown far in the air in his moment of triumph. There was, too, the tigerish satisfaction of the appeal to the square-leg umpire as the bails were whipped off and the umpire was asked to give his views on a possible stumping. Evans was like a coiled spring all the time. But probably the single movement which fascinated me more than any other was the way in which, when he was standing back and took the ball in those gloves with exciting red rubber faces, he despatched it to gulley in the same movement as he accepted it into his hands. It was all done with such an infectious flourish. I am sure I was unable to appreciate fully the tremendous skills necessary to stand up to the stumps to Alec Bedser, especially when he went across to leg to take that in-swinger, but it was magnetic and I was unable to take my eyes off my hero for a single second. When my mother and father suggested an early lunch a major family row ensued.

All I ever wanted to do after that day was to own a pair of red-faced wicket-keeping gloves, which seemed to me to be the last word in just about everything. Of course, if I was going to imitate Godfrey Evans, first I had to look like him. The problem now was that I and approximately 70 other little boys at Mr Fox's establishment in Sunningdale had had it drummed into our heads that swank was wholly unacceptable. We had to be modest in everything, and what was good enough for Godfrey Evans was most palpably not good enough for little show-offs aged ten. On my 11th birthday I was given a copy of Evans's biography, *Behind the Stumps*, which I devoured at breakneck speed. I became word perfect when it came to the tips to young wicket-keepers. There was a photograph of a leg-side stumping and then of a diving catch which made anything of Michelangelo's look like the answer to question one. I lay awake at nights, though, wondering why ear-splitting appeals and throwing the ball far into the air when appealing for a catch behind should be regarded by those in charge of my welfare as the unacceptable face of professionalism.

Then, too, they did not care much for the one aspect of Evans's keeping that I was pretty good at. After hours, days and weeks of practice, I felt I had really come to terms with taking the ball in my gloves and sending it sideways to gulley all in the same satisfying movement. I suppose polite young wicket-keepers were probably expected to under-arm the ball back to the bowler when he was at the end of his follow-through. But after a time, Charlie Sheepshanks, who ran the cricket, was prepared to turn a blind eye when I threw the ball away to gulley.

Evans's batting also brought me a great delight and joy as he impishly slogged fast and slow bowling alike to all parts of the field. And then there was the wonderful occasion when I sat with my ear glued to a wireless – they were most definitely not radios in those days – when he almost scored 100 before lunch in a Test match against India at Lord's in 1952. In fact, he was 98 or 96 at the interval, and although he reached three figures immediately afterwards, I remember taking it as a personal insult that the umpires would not allow just one more over before going in.

To those who tried to tell me that while it was one thing to model one's wicket-keeping on Godfrey Evans, to try to adopt his batting style was quite another, I would point angrily to the Adelaide Test on the Australian tour of 1946–47. In England's second innings, Evans batted for over an hour and a half before he scored a run, making it possible for Denis Compton to score his second century of the match and England to dig themselves out of a pretty nasty hole.

I don't think I have experienced such vicarious nervousness as I did when I went into the classroom having just heard that Evans had struck his firt ball mightily for four. For the next 50 minutes it was sheer agony, and then a frantic scramble back to the wireless when the class ended. Yes, we heard that Compton was still batting, but who was with him? With my heart in my mouth I waited for the score – even in those days commentators did not give the score often enough – praying fervently that England were still only five wickets down. If Evens was out, it made me slightly vindictive towards those who taught me. But then it was joy unconfined, almost deliruium, when a batsman, preferably an Australian, got an inside edge and there was Evans standing back, diving far to the left down the leg-side and bringing off a catch that the commentators could only describe as miraculous.

I collected every newspaper cutting about Evans I could lay my hands on. I devoured tour books and I would endlessly re-read the bits about his brilliant diving catches down the leg-side or in front of slip. Then there was that photograph of all photographs when on the last morning at Melbourne, I think it was, Evans flashed away full length to his right to pick up an authentic leg-glance which Neil Harvey had played against Frank Tyson. Harvey was 92 and that catch virtually guaranteed victory for England. I still have my copy of A.G. 'Johnny' Moyes' book about that series, *Fight for the Ashes*, and my heart still beats just a little bit quicker when I come to the well-worn page which describes that piece of sheer brilliance. Evans claimed 219 dismissals in Test cricket and he also made 2439 runs, with two hundreds, but these figures do not tell a millionth of the man. For me, there will never be a greater or more perfect wicket-keeper.

Oh yes, and I got those red-faced gloves eventually – when my hands were big enough to fit them. And I have to pinch myself almost daily to believe that these days I rub shoulders with Godfrey Evans and even have the temerity to call him 'Godders'. He is as good a friend and companion as he was a wicket-keeper.

J.T. TYLDESLEY

Neville Cardus

In July 1895 a young cricketer, playing for Lancashire against a strong Gloucestershire XI, batted with an assurance that moved W.G. Grace, in his position at point, to paternal interest and approval. 'Eh, eh,' commented his high voice, 'he's a good lad, and when he learns to play with a straight bat he'll do.' The young cricketer, though he never learned to play with the straight bat (it wasn't in his line), became one of the greatest professional batsmen we have ever had. 'What's his name?' asked Old Trafford on that July day. 'Ty'desley, Tyl-des-ley, Ty'd-dle-sley?' The progress of this cricketer to a popularity with the Old Trafford crowd far beyond that ever known by any other Lancashire player was marked by the changes in the name the crowd knew him by, each change denoting a more and more intimate notion of him. First it was 'Ty'd'sley', then 'J.T.T.', and finally 'John Tommy'. He became one of the county's common possessions – institutional. 'Mornin', Johnny,' somebody would say to him as he stood at his place on the boundary, and when he let it be understood by a glance over the shoulder that Familiarity had not gone out to the winds over his head, then Familiarity preened itself and said to the multitude around: 'Nice feller'.

A lot of people, it seemed, knew him very well – met him on the train from Monton every morning and even went to the same barber's. He really was everybody's business. Mature men, working at grey cloths in George Street on hot afternoons, used to ask, on hearing Lancashire's score was 157 for five: 'How's Johnny gone on?' A great man does not come to this kind of easy familiarity with average folk unless there is nature as well as art in his achievement. Nobody on the sixpenny side ever shouted right from his heart, 'Hello, Charlie!' at C.B. Fry, or 'Hello, Willie!' at W.G. Quaife. Art or high skill refined these cricketers out of the tracks of simple comprehension. Tyldesley was even cleverer than these two batsmen, but his play had in it no austerities, no alienating refinements. His was batsmanship of a sort the average man would cultivate if he could. Technically, of course, Tyldesley's cricket touched an excellence rare even amongst the masters; it is the spirit of his play that is being discussed at the moment, and that was democratic enough – his was batsmanship 'a fellow could understand'.

A bat, indeed, can look an entirely different instrument in different hands. With Grace it was a rod of correction, for to him bad bowling was a deviation from moral order; Ranjitsinhji turned a bat into a wand, passing it before the eyes of the foe till they followed him in a trance along his processional way; George Hirst's bat looked like a stout cudgel belabouring all men not born in Yorkshire; Macartney used his bat all for our bedazzlement, as Sergeant Troy used his blade for the bedazzlement of Bathsheba – it was a bat that seemed everywhere at once, yet nowhere specially. And for Tyldesley a bat was an honest broadsword – a broadsword drawn in no service but the service of Lancashire. This last sentence is not intended as a rhetorical flourish. If we are not to go wrong over the character of Tyldesley we need to know that for him batsmanship was first and last a means to a workmanlike end, which was Lancashire's welfare. The brilliance of his play often blinded one to Tyldesley the canny utilitarian. Art for art's sake was not his cry; his play took the senses by assault, inflamed the imagination, but certain it is he never set himself deliberately to do it. To say the truth, we are at liberty to remark of this wonderful cricketer, who was perhaps the most skilful, the most audaciously inventive batsman of his time, that his philosophy is contained in: 'Be good in service and let who will be clever.' He shed glory over the field unwittingly. A bird that is attending to the hard utilitarian job of building a nest will move us to the artist's delight by poise of swift curving flight. And an innings by Tyldesley, though moving on wings and enrapturing the senses, was always attending to the utilitarian job of building the Lancashire nest. What was an innings of a hundred to Tyldesley if victory did not come to Lancashire along with it? – the man was mocked; the taste of ashes was in his mouth. This, of course, is not the way of the artist. *He* can thrive on an individual achievement because of the wonder in it. He lights his fire that he and others may just be ravished by colour and fine flame: he does not insist that it should be capable of boiling the pot. Tyldesley was certainly not an artist in this deliberate and proud, selfish way. Remember his dourness as he stood over his bat ready for the bowler's attack. He was the image of antagonism, vigilant and shrewd. Tyldesley never seemed, even in his most sparkling innings, to be toying with the bowlers in the manner of the virtuoso, merely to amuse himself and us; he most plainly was checkmating them by courage and opportunism. If he was audacious that was because audacity 'paid' – offence was his best means of defence. He improvised strokes never seen before on the cricket field, not out of the artist's love of doing things in a new way, but because inimical circumstances could not be thrust aside by the old expedients. When he tried a fresh stroke he asked if it 'worked' – like a born pragmatist – not if it was 'artistic'. We all recollect his slash stroke, that upper-cut over the slip's heads. It was not beautiful to see, but immensely fruitful of runs. Had it happened in an innings by Spooner it would have looked like a flaw in a delicate piece of porcelain. But how in keeping the stroke was with the punitive game of Tyldesley!

Again, take his on-driving: he had no objections to lofting the ball, so long as it was lofted warily and profitably. The batsman who is an artist before he is a cricketer has a fastidiousness which is set all on edge, so to say, at the very sight of a stroke 'off the carpet'. Tyldesley had no such compunction. Nor is his lofty on-driving to be taken as evidence that after all he was more than the canny utilitarian, that he liked now and then to live dangerously for the good of his spirit. No; when Tyldesley sent the ball into the air he knew exactly what he was doing; he was not snapping fingers at Providence, nor indulging in quixotry. It is doubtful whether Tyldesley ever hit into the air during a big match out of sheer high spirits. Perhaps the field was set inconveniently for ground hits; very well then, they must go over the heads of the scouts. He could place the ball almost to a nicety. So with his famous cut from the middle stump. Surely, you might object, this stroke was a piece of coxcombry – a display of skill for skill's sake, or, at any rate, a display of skill intended to astound us. Why should it have been? The cut was Tyldesley's master-stroke; he had it under perfect control. 'But,' you may still object, 'why from the middle stump? – nothing canny about an adventure like that.' You may be sure Tyldesley did not cut from the middle stump without a good workmanlike reason. Bowlers knew that he would cut to ribbons anything on the off-side at all short, and they would in consequence keep on or near Tyldesley's wicket. Was Tyldesley then going to let his cut go into disuse? Was his most productive hit to run to waste? Why should he not cut a short ball on the middle stump? Let him only get into position for it – and his foot-play was quicker than the eye could follow – and it was much the same as a ball on the off-side, made for cutting. Of course if he missed it the chances were that he would be out. Well, he weighed the chances against his marvellous ability at the cut, and the risk was not palpably greater than the risk a cricketer takes in playing any straight ball – either defensively or offensively.

Macartney used to cut from the middle stump – but for a different reason than Tyldesley's. Macartney would exploit the hit even when it was in his power to make another and safer and even more profitable stroke. For Macartney, though a good antagonist, was a better artist; the spoils of war became in time cheap and tawdry to him. Often did one see disillusion on his face at the end of an opulent innings. Then would he find the challenge of the best bowler irksome: he would throw discretion to the winds in a way that a sound tactician like Tyldesley never did. To refresh his spirit, to save himself from the stale and the flat, he was ready to risk the profitable – to indulge in some impossibly fanciful play of the bat. In this hot quixotic mood his wicket would go to the simplest ball. 'Macartney gets himself out,' was a common saying. How rarely one heard that much said of Tyldesley. A bowler had to work for the wicket of Tyldesley. You might baffle him by skill, inveigle him into a false step; never could you hope that he would give himself away. He wore the happy-go-lucky colours of the care-free soldier of fortune, but they were as borrowed plumes: in the flesh Tyldesley was a stern Ironside, with a Cause – the cause of Lancashire – so sacred that it demanded that a man cast the vanities of art and self-glorification to the wind. This most dazzling of all Lancashire batsmen was, forsooth, a Puritan – a conscript of conscience even, trusting in Lancashire but keeping his powder dry!

There lived not a bowler in his time that did not suffer the scourge intolerable from Tyldesley's bat. Rarely was he to be found not 'ware and waking – on a sticky wicket he was as formidable as on a dry one. At The Oval, or at Edgbaston, his happy hunting-ground, the bowler all too soon would behold Tyldesley's wicket as a wicket a long way distant, his bat a sword of fire guarding it. 'Heaven help me!' the sweaty toiler would appeal to the sky. 'If only he would let one go! I don't ask for his wicket – I've been flogged out of vanity like that – but merciful power can surely grant me a maiden over now and then.' Maiden over, indeed, with Tyldesley in form! He would plunder the six most virgin deliveries you ever saw. It was hard even to pitch a decent length to him. For he knew, unlike the modern batsman, that length is not absolute, but relative to a batsman's reach. And though Tyldesley was a little man, his feet had the dancing master's lightness and rapidity of motion. He covered a larger floor space as he made his hits than any batsman playing today – not even excepting Hobbs. What a disdain he must have in these times for the excuse of timid batsmen that they must needs cultivate patience till bad bowling comes to them! How long would Tyldesley have required to wait for half-volleys from J.T. Hearne, Trumble, Blythe, Noble and the rest? He turned the well-pitched bowling of these masters into the length a punishing hit asks for by swift foot-play. He would jump a yard out of his ground to make a half-volley; he would dart back to the wicket's base to make a long-hop. Two old cricketers once discussed an innings by Tyldesley after the day's cricket was over in something like this language: 'Tha's a reight bowler, Tom. What's thi analysis today – after Johnny'd done wi' thi?' 'Nay, Bill, be fair – tha can't deny I bowl'd well. It wer' t' wicket were too good; I couldn't get any spin on th' ball.' 'Spin, eh? I likes that. Spin on th' ball? Why, I never saw thi hit th' floor all th' afternoon.'

He was in possession of all known strokes, and, as we have seen, he improvised strokes of his own when circumstances challenged him to do so. His square cut was powerful, and the action of it has been vividly described by C.B. Fry: 'He threw the bat at the ball without letting go of the handle.' Many a day-dreaming point – they needed a point, very deep, to Tyldesley – has been seen hopping agitatedly after the advent of the Tyldesley cut. Sometimes he went on his toe-points to make this stroke. His driving was accomplished by a vehement swing of the bat and a most gallant follow-through. There was no saying whether forward or back play was the mark of his style, he combined the two so thoroughly. He was perhaps the best batsman of all time on a bad wicket. P.F. Warner is never tired of singing the praises of Tyldesley's innings of 62 made on a 'glue-pot' at Melbourne in 1904. England's total was then 103, and Relf was the only other batsman to get double figures.

A great batsman is to be estimated, of course, not merely by his scores, or even by his technique, but also by taking into account the quality of the bowling he had to tackle in his day, and the quality of the grounds he mainly played on. When Tyldesley came to greatness English bowling was in a classic period; he had to face men like Lohmann, Richardson, Peel, J.T. Hearne, Noble, Jones. But not only did he take his whack out of some of the best of our classical bowlers; he was also one of the first batsmen to master the new 'googly' bowling. He passed, in fact, through all the manifold changes in fashion which came over bowling between 1903 and 1919. And whether it was J.T. Hearne or R.O. Schwarz, Rhodes or D.W. Carr, Tyldesley was always the same brilliant and punitive Tyldesley. Then let us bear in mind as we do honour to his genius that half of Tyldesley's cricket was played at Old Trafford, where in his time the wickets were not above suspicion. What would Tyldesley's record have been had he played mainly on the hard, beautiful wickets of Kennington Oval? But Tyldesley himself never would worry his head over the averages and records, nor need we. His service was all for England and his county – given in happy devoted heart. Think of him as eternally brilliant if you like, but also think of him as eternally modest – if you would have a notion of the real Tyldesley in mind. The man is by nature as discreet and modest as few geniuses ever are, and that modesty and discretion, as one has tried to show, came out even in his most flashing play. Once, in the days when cricketers were asked by a London newspaper to write reports, Tyldesley was the historian of the Lancashire XI. And he wrote his accounts very much in this style: 'Yesterday we had the good luck to get Worcestershire out cheaply, thanks to some good bowling by Mr Brearley and Dean. When we went in the wicket was faster, and Mr MacLaren and Mr Spooner, batting finely, gave us a good start. Sharp did well too, and Mr Poidevin had the misfortune to play on after a promising beginning. I also managed to get a few.' And turning to the scores you would read:

A.C. MacLaren b. Wilson	41
R.H. Spooner c. Arnold, b. Wilson ...	31
Tyldesley, not out	200
L.O.S. Poidevin b. Arnold	16
Sharp b.Burrows	20
Extras	10

Total (for 4 wickets) 318

The real Tyldesley peeped out in his cricket writings – and he never played an innings that was untrue to his nature.

HAROLD GIMBLETT

Major C.H.B. Pridham

At noon on a day in June 1932, there assembled in the pavilion dressing room at Wellington School, Somerset Stragglers to the number of *ten*. One of these – usually referred to as Ned – created a mild sensation by his unwonted punctuality. Not only did he arrive in good time, but also with a solution to the 'one short' problem, producing a schoolboy – one of his *protégés* – to complete the side. The latter (in his red and black school cap), going in to bat at No. 6, calmly collected 142 runs in 75 minutes – a surprising performance in one so youthful, and a substitute at that!

A year later – on 29 June 1933, to be exact – eleven of us converged from far and wide to oppose a team of locals on the breezy ground at Watchet. The homesters, batting first, had lost four wickets for 30-odd, when the aforesaid youth – opposed this time to Straggler bowling – proceeded to the wicket. With E. Ross (his mentor), E.R. Nesfield, A.S. Bligh, J.C.P. Madden–Gaskell and Co. available to dish up an attack, our bowling was up to average strength; but forthwith the boy began to 'make hay' of them all. Ball after ball was flashed away, to be retrieved laboriously from hedges, ditches, and adjacent fields – several long fielders seemed to be continually engaged in scaling fences. Huge hits soared into the sky to vie with the bursting shells of an anti-aircraft battery at practice on the downs. Never can Straggler bowling have suffered from less respect. He had long since passed the century – how far none but Trump and his score-book could truly tell – when suddenly this astonishing product of local talent disappeared off the field of play, and vanished into the pavilion. Persuasion on the part of the captain was necessary before the young batsman could be prevailed upon to return and complete his innings. This was done; though whether of his set purpose, or due to the somewhat obvious cunning of Gaskell's notorious deliveries, will never be known: for the very next ball was gently pushed into short-leg's hands.

Thus ended an amazing innings of 168 runs scored in 80 minutes, or thereabouts. The total of his side amounted to 278, one other player alone exceeding 30. Most of us were so disgusted, or amused, as scarcely to realise the greatness of H. Gimblett's display. As an earnest of future fame it did not seem to strike anybody.

The sequel we learnt last summer. Only chosen, rather reluctantly, to fill a vacancy in the County XI at the last moment, he had to bat at No. 8. Never was opportunity better seized – perhaps the rustic field of Frome inspired him. Six wickets had gone for 107 before the fast bowling of Nichols, of Essex and England – hardly an occasion for care-free confidence on a public début. So boldly did he play his natural game as to score 99 runs in five minutes under the hour, without a chance! Followed a nerve-racking interlude – he lost the bowling, it seems – while the century-completing run eluded him; 100 was reached at last, in 63 minutes – the fastest *first innings* century in cricket history – thus securing the Lawrence £100 Trophy, only previously won (in equal time) by that greatest of all left-handed hitters – Frank Woolley.

FIVE CRICKETERS OF THE YEAR

Wisden's Almanack for 1935

WILLIAM HAROLD PONSFORD, about whose performances alone could be written far more than the space at disposal for these biographies permits, can in the course of a busy career point to many remarkable achievements. Indeed, as a modern run-getter he easily held pride of place until his fellow-countryman Don Bradman appeared as a more brilliant star in the cricket firmament. Ponsford was born on October 19, 1900 at North Fitzroy, Melbourne, and all his important cricket is associated with Victoria and Australia. Quite early in life he took a leading position, being Cricket captain for two years of the Alfred Crescent School. After that he assisted Fitzroy Metropolitan, a team just about equal in strength to a second-rate club eleven in England. Two years' play on matting wickets enabled him to perfect his footwork and timing and, from about 1917 he played for St. Kilda for something like fifteen years. Going there with a good reputation he went straight into the first eleven. Then in the Australian season of 1922–23 he played his first game in the Sheffield Shield Competition, turning out for Victoria against South Australia at Adelaide and scoring 108.

Before this he had received some coaching from Les Cody, a former well-known New South Wales batsman and secretary of the Fitzroy Cricket Club, and Ponsford very generously says that he owed a great deal of his subsequent success to Cody. An uncle at Fitzroy also gave him much valuable advice on the art of batting.

The fact that he put together a three-figure innings on the occasion of his opening appearance in Sheffield Shield Cricket did not come as a surprise to those who had closely watched his gradual improvement in a less exalted sphere, and before his 108 against South Australia he astonished not merely Australia but England as well by scoring 429 against Tasmania at Melbourne. That huge innings paved the way to his introduction into the highest grade of Inter-State cricket. It was at once obvious that a batsman of more than ordinary ability had arisen, and in the following season of Inter-State cricket Ponsford made 529 runs in seven innings (once not out), with an average of 88.16, his scores being 45, 24, 81, 159, 110, 110 not out and 0.

This fine work meant that he was to all intents and purposes a certainty for Australia in the following season when the MCC team under A.E.R. Gilligan was in Australia, and he more than justified himself by scoring 110 on the occasion of his first appearance in a Test match. The only other Australian batsmen to have accomplished this performance up to that time were Charles Bannerman, H. Graham, R.A. Duff, R.J. Hartigan and H.L. Collins. Ponsford followed this by making 128 in the Second Test Match, and he finished third in the batting averages for Test matches with figures of 46.80. He also hit up a hundred in Inter-State games and, all things considered, more than maintained his form. His early promise had been fulfilled; but he had not yet begun his wonderful association with Woodfull as an opening batsman. Compared with his previous years, the season of 1925–26 was a comparatively poor one for Ponsford for he made only one hundred in State cricket and that in the last game played by Victoria. However, there never existed any doubt about him being destined for a tour in England, and in 1926 he paid his first visit to this country. Although not registering a century in either of the two Tests in which he took part – he was troubled a good deal with illness that summer – he made four hundreds during the tour, and in first-class matches finished fourth with an aggregate of 901 runs and an average of nearly 41.

To be quite frank spectators in England were a little disappointed in him. They had heard of his doings in Australia and expected much more. However, he more than recovered his form on returning to Australia where in the season of 1926–27 he put together scores of 214, 151, 352, 108, and 116 in consecutive matches, having an aggregate of 1,091 runs and an average of 126 for Victoria. He wound up with 131 in Macartney's benefit match, and altogether had by far his best season. A year later he set up a world record – since beaten by Bradman – with a score of 437 against Queensland, for which he was at the wickets more than ten hours. Other Inter-State matches brought him scores of 336 against South Australia, 202 and 133, his aggregate being 1,217 runs and his average just over 152. When, in 1928–29 the MCC team under A.P.F. Chapman was in Australia he had another poor season. He appeared in only two Test matches, scoring 13 runs in three innings. A broken bone in his left hand caused by a slightly rising ball from Larwood kept him out of cricket for the rest of that season, but before the injury that stopped his activities he played an innings of 275 not out for Victoria. He came to England again in 1930 when he was third in the Test match averages with 55 and fourth in the batting averages for first-class matches with an average of just over 49. He hit up the hundreds, including 110 in the fifth Test match at the Oval. He batted much better than he had done four years previously but, generally speaking, his great days as a prolific run-getter seemed to be over.

Still, he was thought by the Selectors to be quite good enough to come to England again last summer when, on his third and last visit to this country, he showed English critics his best form. Scoring 181 and 266 in consecutive Test matches, he took part with Bradman in two remarkable stands which produced 388 for the fourth wicket at Headingley and 451 for the second wicket at The Oval. Curiously enough he was out hit-wicket on each occasion, just as he had been in the first hundred he ever made in Sheffield Shield matches. His aggregate for the Test matches was 569 runs with an average of just under 95, and he headed the list, while in first-class matches he was second only to Bradman, his aggregate being 1,784 runs and average over 77. In addition to the hundreds he made in Test cricket he scored 281 not out against the M.C.C. at Lord's, 229 not out against Cambridge University at Cambridge and 125 against Surrey at The Oval so that he finished up in England in a blaze of triumph.

It is, perhaps, scarcely too much to say that English bowlers last summer thought he was every bit as difficult to get rid of as Bradman. Never a graceful or elegant batsman, Ponsford could with greater emphasis be called sound and workmanlike. He seemed in 1934 to hit the ball much harder than when he was here in 1926 and 1930, while his placing improved out of all knowledge. A delivery overpitched to any degree, he almost invariably punished to the full, while he could cut and turn the ball to leg with great certainty. Opinions probably will always differ as to his ability to deal properly with fast bowling. There have been occasions, and the writer has himself seen them, when his batting against Larwood in particular was absurdly ineffective, and yet at other times – one remembers him in the last Test match at The Oval in 1930 – he has scored off rising balls on the leg side in wonderful style. Still, when all is said and done, one would incline to the idea that he does not care for the fast rising ball on the leg stump. Far too often last season he turned his back to it and got hit, and his one real weakness in batting has always been a tendency to step too far across to the off side and get bowled leg stump. All the same Ponsford, who announced his retirement from big cricket shortly after his return to Australia, can look back upon his career with the greatest personal satisfaction. In the course of roughly twelve years he has accomplished many remarkable performances and his name will go down to history as one of the most consistent run-getters in the game. If tending towards the end to lose some of his pace he was, for a long time, splendid in the deep field and, like nearly all Australians, could throw beautifully.

OTHER DEATHS IN 1919:
CAFFYN, WILLIAM

Wisden's Almanack for 1920

CAFFYN, WILLIAM. Many cricket memories were revived by the announcement that the veteran Surrey player, William Caffyn, died at his home, at Reigate, on Thursday, August 28. Born on Feb. in 1828, he had lived to the great age of 91. His fame rests mainly was the fact that he was the best all-round man in the Surrey eleven that, with the late F. P. Miller as captain, used to meet – and twice beat – the full strength of England at Kennington Oval. Of that brilliant band the one survivor now left is Mr E. Dowson – only ten years Caffyn's junior, but quite hale and hearty. Many other amateurs who played with Caffyn in his prime are still living, but of the great professionals who used to make the match at Lord's between the All England and United Elevens one of the events of the season, only George Wootton, the Notts bowler, remains with us.

Caffyn played his first match for Surrey in 1849, and in the following year – there were very few county fixtures in those days – he headed the batting. From that time he never looked back, becoming more and more prominent as the fame of Surrey cricket grew. He was the leading bowler in the team, as well as the finest batsman. About 1857 he reached his highest point, and right on to 1863 his powers showed no decline. Then came the end of his real career in English cricket. In the autumn of 1863 he paid his second visit to Australia as a member of George Parr's team – he had gone out two years before with H. H. Stephenson's side – and at the close of the tour he stayed behind in the Colonies, accepting a position as coach. While in Australia he played in inter-Colonial matches, but though he did much to develop young talent he scarcely, judging from the scores, added to his own reputation. He was back in England in 1872, and played several times for Surrey that year and in 1873, but it was too late to start over again. His day was done, and, though Surrey were far from strong, he could not keep his place in the eleven. His long stay in Australia lost him the chance of a benefit match at the Oval, but to the end of his life the Surrey Club paid him an annuity of £39.

'On the evidence of all who played side by side with him in his great days, Caffyn was a very fine batsman, free and attractive in style and master of a cut that only Tom Humphrey surpassed in brilliancy. Had he lived in these days he would no doubt have made big scores, for he needed a good wicket. The Oval and Fenner's at Cambridge were the grounds that suited him best. On the rough wickets at Lord's he was admittedly far inferior to George Parr, Carpenter, Richard Daft, and the first Tom Hayward. Still even at Lord's against Jackson he was on two occasions seen at his best. As regards his bowling, one is rather doubtful. Right hand medium pace, he belonged to the purely round arm school – he had just settled in Australia when the law was altered – and modern wickets would very likely have been too good for him. Still on the best wickets of his own time he did wonderful things for Surrey and the United All-England Eleven. As an all-round fieldsman he had scarcely a superior. – S.H.P.

Lord Cobham – the Hon. C.G. Lyttelton in his cricket days, and incidentally one of the most brilliant batsmen in England – who played several times against Caffyn in Gentlemen v. Players matches, and also in matches between Cambridge University and Surrey, has very kindly sent the following notes on the veteran as he knew him. –

'My recollections of Caffyn date back sixty years, when I was captain of the Eton Eleven and Caffyn was our "coach" for a few weeks. He was rather a small man, well and compactly built and very active. I do not think he was a born coach, or that he troubled himself to give much oral instruction, but his bowling, which was slow to medium, straight, and of a good length gave us excellent practice, and much could be learnt from watching his batting which was sound, graceful, and often brilliant.

'Until he left England in 1863, Caffyn was always a good man on a side. He never ceased to be a dangerous bat and he was as consistent a scorer as most of his contemporaries. He could hit hard all round, but his most notable hit was his cut, which denoted great strength and flexibility of wrist. I well remember, in a country match, his cutting an over-pitched ball of mine through a big drum, supposed to be at a safe distance from the wicket. It was said that when facing the great Jackson at Lord's, he was apt to show some "softness" and want of nerve, but then Jackson on a characteristic Lord's wicket was a "terror" such as is never seen in these days. Once, at all events, in the 1857 North and South match at Lord's, Caffyn made 90 against Jackson, which long ranked amongst historical innings, with those of R. Hankey, C. G. Lane and others.

'Caffyn was a good bowler, but never I think quite in the first rank. His bowling had no cunning or "devil" in it and on present day wickets it could probably be "pulled" or "hooked" without much difficulty. Nevertheless he took plenty of wickets, and runs did not come easily or rapidly from him, as his analysis shows. He was a good and active field.

'At Eton, and as long as I played cricket with him, I always thought of Caffyn as a well-mannered man and pleasant to deal with, and this impression seems to me to be borne out by his book – "71 Not Out" – which is written in a modest and kindly spirit, free from jealousy or depreciation of others.'

Mr E. Dowson, now, as already stated, the only survivor of F.P. Miller's famous Surrey eleven, writes: –

'He was a neat, good-looking, dapper little man. As regards his bowling he bowled a medium pace ball, not difficult to look at, but he nearly always obtained his share of wickets. Curiously enough we were always glad when he had a good innings, as the more runs he made the better he bowled. His batting was always worth watching as he could hit all round, and his cutting was brilliant, especially balls off the bails. He used to get hundreds, which were very few in those days. In my opinion he would have been one of the first chosen in a Test Match. He also was a good field. I must relate one case when he was really frightened. In a match v. Yorkshire at Sheffield a storm came on which deluged the ground. The captains, Mr F.P. Miller and Mr W. Prest, both agreed that there could be no more cricket. Poor Caffyn had dressed and got out of the ground when some of the roughs brought him back with his bag, swearing they were not going to be done out of seeing more cricket as they had paid their 3d. Chaffing then commenced and we said we were not afraid to go on. They gathered round Mr Prest, saying "Are you not ashamed of yourself?" He replied "Yes, that I was born here and amongst such a lot!" The wickets were again pitched and I should imagine never on a wetter ground. The water spluttered in your face as you fielded the ball. However, Mr Prest was so angry that he came in and won the match himself, hitting the bowling all over the place.'

Mr Herbert C. Troughton writes: –

'I saw Caffyn pretty frequently during the years 1859–1863. I thought him an extremely brilliant bat. He had not the defence of Carpenter or Hayward, but he was, in my opinion, far more interesting to watch, as when he made runs, he always made them quickly; he – at least whenever I saw him – acted upon what is supposed to have been the immortal Yardley's maxim – "Get runs or get out." He was rather impetuous and was apt to get himself out by adopting hitting tactics before he had got set. Caffyn had many strokes, and all of them stylish. With perhaps the exception of Lord Cobham, better known as the Hon. C.G. Lyttelton, he was the hardest cutter I have ever seen, and his hitting to deep square leg was brilliant in the extreme. His driving powers, too, especially to the on were quite out of the common, and he had one stroke which he and W. Mortlock alone, so far as I remember, have ever regularly put in force – a huge hit between deep square leg and long on, rather nearer long-on than square leg, a stroke that earned him hundreds of runs. As a bowler he was most excellent and did many brilliant things. He seemed to love bowling, and when he did not go on first, his joy, when he was put on, was unmistakable. He had an easy and very graceful delivery, and could bowl equally well, either round or over the wicket. If the wicket gave him ever so little help he could be deadly in the extreme. He generally failed at Lord's, where Jackson's expresses were not to his liking. Indeed though I saw him at Lord's in some eight matches I can only remember his coming off in one match and that was for South v. North in 1861 when he played a beautiful first innings of sixty-five, and supplemented this with an excellent 25 in his second innings, Jackson's bowling, for once at Lord's, having no terrors for him.'

TOM GRAVENEY

Frank Keating

I seldom have nightmares. Say a couple a year. But enough to re-establish my stark fear of heights. Extremely scary. I always wake only a split second before I hit the deck – splat! There's a still fevered moment or two for a shaking hand to fumble for the light switch and a smoke. Then, with relief and realisation dawning that I'm both in the land of the living and my pungent pit, I will inhale deeply, smile to myself and, content again, think of . . . Clem Attlee, a former Prime Minister, and George Emmett, a former Gloucestershire bat. And thoughts of George soon turn to recollections of Tom. Ah, Tom. Dear Tom. *Our* Tom.

You need an explanation: in 1946, at the age of eight, I was unaccountably sent the 30 miles from Stonehouse in Gloucestershire to a boarding prep school near Hereford. Now, in spite of his aberration on private education, in all other matters my father, bless him, was as trenchant a socialist as you could ever meet. And you didn't meet many in that true-blue neck of the Randwick Woods unless you bumped into Bert Cole, Ben Parkin, Bill Maddocks or my Uncle John planning the revolution in the Woolpack Inn. Anyway, it so came to pass that, between them, they had won the seat for Labour in the 1945 landslide election. Word of this stunning reverse of the established order seeped even over the county border at about the very same time that I had turned up in Hereford as the most midget, meek and miserable mother's boy even such as Dotheboys had seen. The bigger boys bullied and we namby newts cowered and cringed by day and, at nights, wept and then wet the bed.

Many and varying were the forms of torture. You had done well if you survived a day with only a ear twisted off in the boot room, or a bottom blackened with a scrubbing brush and Cherry Blossom. Most horrendous was 'The Tower', so awful that even the leading sadists only summoned the courage once or twice a year. I heard the dreaded, awful, conspiracy, 'Keating for The Tower tonight; pass it round', whispered through the school on three occasions. The school's church tower was more squat Saxon than tall and fluted Norman. But it was high enough to be absolutely petrifying when you were dangling over its edge held, only by the ankles, by two other boys. The rest of the school would watch the fun from below. I'm still surprised no child ever fell to his death. I am certain it is the reason for my recurring nightmares and my fear of heights. (I can never look out of an aeroplane till it is in the clouds.)

On two occasions I was 'towered' for 'family connections' – that is, every other short-trousered prig in the place was, of course, a Conservative, so when I boasted about my father's and uncle's political affiliations, I did so with my heart in my mouth. I cannot remember exactly why, but I was possibly sent to The Tower when the Labour Party nationalised steel and when they 'sold out' the Indian Empire to 'the wogs'. I was hung as a martyr for Clem Attlee's great radicalism.

The third time was altogether different. In the midsummer of 1948, the triumphant march of Bradman's Australian cricketers had the English selectors in all sorts of panic. For the third Test match at Old Trafford, out of the blue, they selected two Gloucestershire players. I would have got away with it had the only selection been Jack Crapp, our doughty left-hander who had scored a century against the tourists in the county fixture at Bristol. But the wee sprog, George Emmett, was another matter altogether, for he was chosen to replace Len Hutton, revered both in the school and the land as a national institution. So my one-man Gloucester gloat at Emmett's selection had its comeuppance at once. In a seething fury the word went round, 'Keating for The Tower tonight.' I was hung as a martyr for Georgie Emmett. (When he failed in both innings there were threats that I should be 'done' again.)

Here is the point of these rambling recollections: if George Emmett had not been picked for that one solitary Test match, it is quite possible that the world would never have seen Tom Graveney bat. After Bristol Grammar School and National Service in the Army, young Graveney had seemed to have fluffed his apprenticeship as a Gloucestershire cricketer. At the time of that Manchester Test match, which began on 8 July 1948, his 'career' seemed to have ended before it began. On his first-class début he had made a duck, and followed that with just over 200 runs in 20-odd innings. He was seriously thinking of re-signing for the Army, which he had enjoyed, and taking a PT instructors' course. Certainly he had been demoted to the Gloucester Second XI, and looked unlikely for re-engagement.

Then Crapp and Emmett were selected for England. Graveney was hastily despatched to Bournemouth for the First XI fixture with Hampshire. He made a precocious and calm 47 against the spinners, Knott and Bailey, on a spiteful wicket. In the following match against Somerset at Bristol he scored an undefeated 81. By the time I got home for the holidays, my Stonehouse chums, Peter Beard and Robin Bassett, were filling me in with details of his century against the Combined Services at Gloucester Wagon Works. It had, they said, been amazingly wizard-prang.

The Cheltenham Festival – nine full days of cricket – couldn't come quick enough. Sometimes we'd catch that chippy little chuffer, the 'Railcar', and change at Gloucester. Other mornings would have us in front of the queue outside Woolworth's in Stroud for the Western National double-decker, over the top past Painswick's yews and the Prinknash Pottery. We had our greaseproofed-paper sandwiches, a shilling extra for a bottle of Tizer and a pound of plums, a bat and tennis ball for tea-time, and our autograph books. The first time I saw him, Tom made a silky half-century – all coltish, gangly, upright youthfulness, with a high, twirly, backlift and a stirring, bold, flourishing signature in the follow-through – and he came back to the 'gym', blushing at the applause, and signed my book before he went in to lunch. 'T.W. Graveney', neat, joined-up, surprisingly adult.

Next Easter term, I began to feel less of an outsider at school when Dad sent me a present of my first *Wisden*. Even the bully boys asked, nicely, to borrow it. I would show them the Gloucestershire Notes, and the last sentence about the batting – 'A pleasant feature of the season was the form of a newcomer, T.W. Graveney, a product of Bristol club cricket, who showed graceful right-handed stroke play'.

By Cheltenham that August, the young man was actually leading our parade. That in itself was a triumph. Schoolboy romantics do not readily forsake their first heroes. And there had been lots of them about in 'Glorse'. True, Charlie Barnett had gone, off to the Lancashire League; and, sure, we missed the Chalford autocrat's hook of nose and stroke; he smacked bumpers, thwack! as if he was smacking down plaice on the wet slabs outside his fishmongers in 'Zoiren' or 'Chelt'. Then there was the aforementioned Jack and Georgie. Crapp was the calm and watchful leftie; we were never in real trouble till he was out. Unperturbable, he would push his ones and twos to keep the numbers rolling in gentle rhythms, but then, of a sudden, he would break out and hit the thing with a clean, wicked ferocity, then lean placid on his sword, the handle supporting his buttocks like a shooting stick, and he would cross his arms and legs and wait, serene, while the ball was retrieved from miles away. 'Good ol' Jack! Give 'em another one, Jack!' we shouted. But he seldom did it twice in succession. Or even twice in a session.

Emmett was in direct contrast. A tiny man with a nutbrown face and whipcord wrists. He had the twinkling feet of an Astaire, and the same sort of hairstyle. His on-drive singed every blade of grass between the bowler and mid-wicket. His cap was a very faded blue because he wore it everywhere – even in bed I bet, we giggled – and there was always a groan of real sadness when he got himself out. Emmett, and especially Crapp, I learned many years later, were the wise and generous mentors and mother-hens to the young chick Graveney.

In Tom's earliest days, Billy Neale also nursed him in the middle orders. He was a farmer, from Grace country, down Thornbury way. He had gone to school, at Cirencester Grammar, with the county's previous emperor and champion, Wally Hammond, and had always been, they said, the one to understand the moods and melancholy of that great, smouldering genius. They would walk together for hours in the orchards of Neale's Breadstone Farm, talking of this and that; after which Wally was refreshed again. Tom's first captain must have been an influence as well: B.O. Allen was Clifton and Cambridge and once got a double century against Hampshire; he looked as fierce as our Latin master and we never dared ask him for an autograph. He went forth to toss for innings in a brown trilby, like they said Hammond used to do, and he blew his nose with a whopping, red-spotted snuff hankie. And like Charlie Barnett, he used to ride to hounds in winter.

There were other tyros, too, with Tom: Milton was to become a dear favourite; the *Yearbook* started calling him 'Clement' and then 'Charlie' before settling, by public demand, on Arthur. He had the soccer player's bow legs – he remains the last 'double' international – and was the most versatile and thrilling fieldsman I ever saw. And Martin Young, suave and smarmy-haired and always beautifully turned out; his bat always looked pine-fresh new. Arrogant, he had South African connections.

Our bowlers would take up another book: we all tried to copy George Lambert's action – he was faster than Lindwall, for sure. His new ball mucker was Colin Scott, who used to work at the Co-op and had great ten-to-two Underwood feet, and occasionally specialised in sixers. There was Sam Cook (whom the *Yearbook* called 'Cecil' *always*), who was left-arm and reliable and the much-loved apprentice to the very sorcerer himself, our wizard of tweak, Tom Goddard, whose 2979 career bag of wickets has only been bettered by four others in the whole history of the game. Stumper was Andy Wilson, a tiny tot with massive appeal in every way. He once took ten catches in a match. After all his years keeping to Goddard and Cook, he took bets that he would be the only batsman in the whole land to read Ramadhin's wrong 'un when the West Indies came to Cheltenham in 1950. Both innings Andy shouldered arms to let the little long-sleeved mesmerist's first ball go by outside the off-stump. Both times he was clean bowled. Gloucester were routed that day. Only Graveney made double figures, all blushing uncertainty and middle-of-the-bat, and a man next to me said, 'Our Tom'll be servin' England this side o'twelvemonth'.

And he was. When Denis Compton was injured, Freddie Brown blooded him against the South Africans at Old Trafford in 1951, and on a real sticky he made 15 against Athol Rowan – 'every run full of cultured promise', said John Arlott on the wireless. Tom served England for the next ten years. When George was still King he was taking 175 from the Indians at Bombay; when Lindwall and Miller were still lethal he matched Hutton, stroke for stroke, in a partnership of 168 at Lord's; and a couple of years later he collected a century at Sydney with three successive boundaries; onwards a summer or two, and his massively flamboyant 258 nailed down forever the wispy mystique of Ramadhin and Valentine, after May and Cowdrey had done the tedious, pad-prod spadework earlier in the month.

Yet while these, and even the shortest innings, were a delight, word was going about that he lacked the cruel competitive edge to take a game and an attack by the throat; he was getting out when the very critical need was just to stay in. He was, horror! playing Festival cricket instead of Test match cricket. Never the twain must meet, and he was dropped for, as someone said, 'being happy only to present his ability, but not to enforce it ruthlessly'.

He had moved from Gloucestershire now. But so had we. And wherever I was in the world, I daresay I wasn't the only Gloucester man to sneak a look first at the Worcester scores to see how Tom had done. For it was soon apparent that there, under the old Norman shadow that matched the mellow architecture of his strokes, his batsmanship had actually become even better. It was still joyous and free of care, but now it was more stable, more serene, more *certain*. The England selectors, of course, seemed oblivious to the fact, and though century followed century and Championship followed Championship, not even the wildest betting man would have wagered on a recall by England. But at last they had to. After his four years in the pleasant backwaters of the shires came an almost tangible rumbling of public demand for Graveney's Test match place to be restored, following another woeful England start to the West Indian series of 1966. They turned to Tom, now in his 40th year.

And at Lord's too! The full-house standing ovation started as he made his way through the Long Room once again. Hall and Griffith and Sobers and Gibbs . . . he returned to grandstand applause after a magnificent 96. 'It's like a dream come true,' he said as he went back up the stairs, eyes moist with tears. In the next match, at Trent Bridge, England were 13 for three, Hall's Larry Holmes and Griffith's Joe Frazier both murderously, cruelly, hostile. Graveney and Cowdrey alone had the technique and fearlessness to stand unflinchingly firm. Tom finished with 109, and many still shake their heads in wonder and insist it must have been his very best innings.

But there were still more gems in the old man's kitty. A superlative 165 followed at The Oval; then, next summer, a charming 118 runs against the West Indies. 'Any art gallery in the world would have bought that innings,' wrote Henry Blofeld, who was there. He overflowed with fluent strokes and quite outplayed the 1968 Australians, as he did the Pakistanis in the winter, when Karachi saw his last Test match century. When the West Indies rejoined battle next summer he scored 75 in the first Test then, on the free Sunday of the match, played in his own benefit game at Luton. It was against the rules and Lord's banned him for three Tests – in effect forever. But Our Tom of Gloucester had become Worcester's Tom, then England's, then the world's.

As this book is a cricket writers' book, it would be nice to quote the retirement panegyric offered to Graveney after his final Test. It can do more justice than I can to a fine cricketer and a fine man. It was written by one of the very best of writers, J.M. Kilburn, who was for 40 diligent and creative years the correspondent of the *Yorkshire Post*: 'Graveney may have disappointed some cricketers by playing in Graveney's way, but he has adorned cricket. In an age preoccupied with accountancy he has given the game warmth and colour and inspiration beyond the tally of the scorebook. He has been of the orchard rather than the forest, blossom susceptible to frost but breathing in the sunshine . . . Taking enjoyment as it came, he has given enjoyment that will warm the winters of memory.'

Yet it might never have happened had George Emmett not been picked for his solitary Test match in the midsummer of 1948. The very same day that Tom was despatched to Bournemouth and I was dangled, head first, from the top of a church tower in Hereford.

COUNTY CRICKET FROM 1860 TO 1871

Richard Daft

There were not many county matches played during the early part of my career; but in a few years there were almost as many played every season as there are at present. About 1865, Notts, Surrey, and Cambridgeshire were all very strong; and Yorkshire, Kent, and Sussex were each able to put good elevens in the field. Notts had at this time some wonderfully good young players coming on, who bade fair to equal the old ones, some of whom were now beginning to show signs of falling off.

We had a grand bowler in J.C. Shaw – the best left-hand, in my opinion, we ever had. He came a great pace from the pitch, with a good deal of break, and a slow ball he kept dropping in now and then very often obtained a wicket. But when Jemmy finished bowling he had finished altogether; for he was a very indifferent fielder, and was about the worst man with the bat I ever came in contact with. In plain words, he was never worth four runs against any bowling in his life. I, however, well remember a match when he saved his county from signal defeat by remaining with me at the wickets for an hour and forty minutes.

This was at Clifton, when we were playing Gloucestershire. Dr W.G. Grace mentions this match in his most interesting book, and, alluding to Jemmy's performance, observes that he had on the previous night 'not gone to bed at orthodox hours'. As a matter of fact, he never went to bed at all. On the morning of the third day of the match, I went to breakfast at the house of a friend in Bristol, who, when I arrived, told me he was afraid we should have to bat a man short this day, for he had heard that old Jemmy Shaw had, the previous evening, got quarrelling at cards with some of his friends at the place where they were staying, and, after breaking all the glasses in the room, had rushed out of the house without his coat, saying he would 'go and do for himself', and had not been heard of since.

I was much annoyed at hearing this, and considerably alarmed too, for my thoughts at once turned to the Suspension Bridge. Some hours later, however, I met Mr Frank Townsend, who relieved me by telling me that, when walking across the Downs a short time before, he had seen an object lying under a tree, which, on going up to examine it, proved to be nothing less than Jemmy Shaw, fast asleep. I had been not out myself over night, and on this morning was required, I believe, something like 70 runs to save the follow-on when Jemmy came in last man. He had kept out of my way as much as possible, being sure of a sound rating for his conduct of the previous night; but this lecture I thought it advisable to postpone until after the innings was over.

Well, Jemmy, to the amazement of all on the ground, remained at the wicket till the innings was saved. I got the greater part of the runs myself, being 90-odd not out at the finish; Jemmy making nine only. I never in the whole course of my life saw such an exhibition of batting as his was that day. Sometimes he was down on his knees, then he would come out to drive a ball which would miraculously fly over the head of long-slip. I kept going to him between the overs to tell him to be careful, but every time I did so he coolly told me that *he* was all right, and that *he* shouldn't get out; seeming to imply that it was my wicket that would go down, if either did. But directly the requisite number of runs was obtained he collapsed.

During the whole of the day he kept looking very shyly at me, expecting the deferred lecture with regard to his nocturnal adventure; and at last I made his mind easy by saying: 'It's lucky for you, Jemmy, that we saved the match to-day; and as I never saw you play half so well before, I should strongly advise you never to go to the expense of a bed again, but should always, if I were you, sleep in the open air.'

Jemmy had as good an appetite as most men. Once on the second or third day of a match at Birmingham, he was very seedy and unable to bowl. I expressed some surprise at this to Carpenter, as he had seemed perfectly well the day before. 'You wouldn't feel much surprised if you had seen what he had to eat last night,' Bob replied; 'for he came into the hotel "elevated" about nine o'clock, and sat down and ate eleven eggs, and finished off with cold beef and cold peas, which,' Carpenter continued, 'the old fool kept pelting at me as I sat at another table writing letters.' This account, I suspect, was somewhat exaggerated; but I have often seen Jemmy perform some extraordinary feats in the eating line since then.

Jemmy possessed at one time a favourite dog – a greyhound. This dog was the terror of the inhabitants of Sutton, where he resided; and his marauding visits to the neighbours' larders were many and frequent. Jemmy used to tell a good tale about this dog. He said that on one occasion he had a beefsteak kept hot for his own dinner on the oven in the house. The dog was lying fast asleep on the hearthrug, and as Jemmy wanted to leave the room for only a minute or two, he thought he might safely do so, taking care not to wake the dog. He declared he was not two minutes out of the room, but when he returned there was no beefsteak to be seen, and there lay the dog, to all appearances, as fast asleep as when his master had left the apartment. Indeed, he had committed the theft so cleverly that Jemmy, though deprived of his dinner, could not find it in his heart to give him the thrashing he so richly deserved.

Charles Brampton was a good bat, and did useful service for his county for many years, always going in first at one time.

George Wootton was a fine left-hand bowler, and being at his best at the same time as Jemmy Shaw, we had now perhaps what no other county had at this period; viz., two as good left-hand bowlers as could then be found.

Biddulph was our wicket-keeper; and one of the best in England, besides being a very useful bat. One match I recollect well which he won for us. It was against Surrey, at The Oval, in 1874: and here again J.C. Shaw was called upon to distinguish himself. We required 15 runs to win when Jemmy went to the wicket (last man, of course), Biddulph, at the other end, having made four or five runs. I remember I sat in the pavilion with a telegraph form in front of me, which I was writing out to send to George Parr, at Radcliffe. I had already written, 'Surrey won by – runs,' and waited for the end. But here, as at Clifton, Jemmy was equal to the occasion, and though he only made one run himself, he kept his end up till the required number were made by his partner; which having been done, Jemmy was seized by some of the delighted supporters of Notts, and carried to the pavilion shoulder high.

The last time I played with Jemmy was in a little match in Derbyshire. After the game was over, we were entertained at dinner by the opposite team, after which some singing and music were indulged in. When several pieces on the piano had been given someone having been erroneously informed that Jemmy Shaw was an accomplished pianist, called on him for a solo, which call was unanimously echoed by all in the room, accompanied by much rapping on the tables and cheering. This was rather rough on Jemmy, who had probably never struck a note on a piano in his life. 'Whatever am I to do?' he whispered to me (I was sitting next to him). So to get him out of his difficulty, I rose and informed the company that Mr Shaw would have been most happy to have obliged them, but as the piano in the room was not a *left-handed* one, he greatly regretted his inability to do so.

I remember a laughable incident that occurred once when we went to play at The Oval. Biddulph was ill, and unable to go, and after some deliberation the committee decided to play little Frank Moore in his place. Frank was then (and is now, for that matter) little more than five feet in height, and made a queer figure when he walked down from the pavilion padded and gloved to take the wicket, of course, getting between two of the biggest men in the eleven.

Mr Johnson, our secretary, had asked me to look out some nice quiet lodgings for Frank, as he had never been in London before. This I had some difficulty in doing, for whether the lodging-house keepers thought Frank was a suspicious-looking character, or whatever was the reason, I cannot say, but at the first half-dozen places at which we called they 'declined him with thanks'. At last I succeeded in safely planting him at a place a few hundred yards' distance from the ground. At lunch-time on the first day Frank was not out, and when the bell rang after the forty minutes' interval he was nowhere to be seen. The second bell rang, and still there was no Frank.

I then ran round to the different refreshment places on the ground, but could hear no tidings of him. The Surrey players began to walk into the field, and I despaired of his turning up at all, when all at once I thought of his lodgings, and, after begging a few minutes' grace from the Surrey captain, to that place I rushed off. 'Is Mr Moore here?' I called out at the open door as soon as I got there, when a little squeaking voice replied from an inner room: 'Yes, all right, Mr Daft, here I am.' I walked into this apartment, and was for some seconds thunderstruck with what I saw. On the table were the remains of a beefsteak, and there, in an armchair, his coat and waistcoat off, smoking a long churchwarden pipe, sat the man for whom some thousands of spectators were waiting at The Oval. He had thought the luncheon interval was an hour, whereas it was but forty minutes. 'Confound you,' I shouted, 'what the deuce are you doing here? The players have all been in the field ever so long, and you have forfeited your innings.'

Frank did not wait to hear any more, but snatching up his coat and waistcoat he flew down the street like a wild man, taking with him in his excitement his churchwarden pipe, and with this in one hand and his coat and waistcoat in the other, and having no hat on, he cut a most remarkable figure. The people in the streets must have thought him an escaped lunatic. He arrived on the ground only just in time, and to see him putting on his pads was a sight not to be forgotten, for he was quite out of 'wind' with running, and after every buckle he fastened he looked up to see if the fielders were still on the ground, or whether they had become tired of waiting, and had claimed his wicket.

Not long ago, I was playing at Captain Oates' house (Langford Hall), and Frank (as umpire) was appealed to for me for leg-before, and gave the decision in my favour, although both the bowler and wicket-keeper declared I was well out. After the innings was over, someone asked Frank if it had not been a near thing. 'Yes, sir,' answered he; 'it was just about the heighteenth of a hinch off being out, that's all.' Although Franky is such a little bit of a fellow, his wife, he tells me, is a very fine woman; and he also relates how she once took a child's ticket for him when travelling by rail, and passed him off for 'under age'.

After playing our match at Captain Oates' house it has been our invariable custom to drive from Langford to Newark, to dine at the 'Clinton Arms,' and there to spend a few hours before returning home. After dining Frank always disappears until train time, when he appears, generally emanating strong odours of spirits. When asked where he has been he always says: 'Well, you know, Mr Daft, I've a lot of *relations* lives in Newark; there's my "huncle" in this street and my "haunt" in that, and my second cousin somewhere else, and if I wasn't to go and see them and have a drink with 'em all round, they'd be ever so offended.' As a matter of fact, I don't think Frank has a single relation within miles of the place.

After one of these matches, as we were returning home in the railway carriage, someone seized Frank's hat and threw it across the compartment to a companion, and in this way it was passed round several times. The window, however, being open, the hat was accidentally thrown out. Of course a subscription for a new hat for Frank was at once started, and half-a-sovereign was quickly collected. Considering that Frank's hat was a very old one, probably not being worth more than eighteen-pence, he came off handsomely by the accident. Next year, when we went to Langford, I noticed Frank wore what was evidently the very oldest hat he possessed, hoping no doubt that on our return in the evening it would be thrown away and another half-sovereign awarded him; but this, unfortunately for him, did not take place.

Poor little Frank! He has, I believe, always been greatly attached to me. He used to bowl at me on the Forest when I was a boy, and years before I took part in first-class cricket. He was always a favourite with me, and always will be.

Another young player came into note about this time; he was first played for his batting, but afterwards turned out to be one of the finest bowlers of his own or any other time. This player was Alfred Shaw, whose name, for years to come, was to be a household word wherever cricket was played. He had always wonderful command over the ball, and never seemed to tire. His many remarkable performances in this department of the game are far too numerous to mention here. He once achieved a great feat when we played Lancashire at Manchester, and I won the only bet, I believe, I ever made over a county cricket match during my career. We were dining after the day's play, and on the following morning Lancashire had to go in for the second time to get comparatively few runs. A Lancashire gentleman called down the table to me and asked how many wickets they were going to beat us by the next day. 'Oh! I don't know,' I replied; 'it's not a hundred to one that you will beat us at all.' 'I'll lay you £5 to 5/-, we do,' said he. 'Done!' I replied, and the bet was made. The next morning, so splendidly did Shaw bowl that the whole of the Lancashire Eleven were out without obtaining the required runs. I ordered a case of champagne at our hotel for our team, in honour of so great a victory.

William Oscroft was another of our crack bats at that time, as he continued to be for many years. He was one of the finest leg-hitters we ever had, hitting like Carpenter, high and square. His hitting all round was a treat to behold whenever he was well set. He gave me a fright at the Clifton Suspension Bridge many years ago. I have always a great objection to looking down from a great height, and when crossing the bridge in question took care to keep well away from the side. Oscroft knowing this, and probably to let me see that he felt no such fear himself, took a run and vaulting on the rail sat across it as though on a horse, swaying himself about in the (to me) most alarming manner; and the more frightened I became the better he enjoyed it. Oscroft succeeded me as captain of the Notts Eleven after I left off playing, and was himself succeeded by Alfred Shaw some years after.

Tom Bignall was another fine batsman. His leg-hitting at one time was little inferior to that of George Parr, being a similar kind of stroke, low down and 'fine'. For years he and Fred Wild were the two first men to go to the wickets for Notts. I once played old Tom the following trick.

At the time of which I write, I always carried a box of cigars in my cricket bag, and often fancied that I ran through many more than I either smoked or gave away; and at last got to know by a side wind that Tom Bignall was in the habit of helping himself to one whenever he felt inclined. One day I purchased some explosive cigars and put them in the box in my bag, and during the day Tom was seen blowing away at a weed as usual. Someone who was in the joke asked him where he had got it from, to which he replied, with a wink: 'Hush! not a word. One of Richard's! A real foreigner!' He was in the dressing-room when the explosion took place, and never having heard of such cigars before, he was frightened very nearly out of his wits. There was a skylight in the roof of the room (which was not a lofty one), and through this he tried to throw the cigar, but missing his aim, it came down again right on the top of his head. He was not hurt, however; and I am pleased to say that my cigar-box received no more visits from him from that time forward. I met Tom a short time ago, and asked him if he remembered the circumstance which I have just related, and he assured me it was still quite fresh in his memory, and would always continue to be so.

'THE BISHOP' – A GREAT EDWARDIAN ECCENTRIC

Gordon Strong

The Rev. Archdale Palmer Wickham kept wicket for Somerset CCC from 1891 to 1907. Known to his family as Archie and to his team-mates as 'The Bishop', he remains one of the most colourful characters of the golden age of cricket.

Behind the stumps at the county ground, his legs wide apart and his gloved hands upon his knees with a stance so low that his Harlequin cap just appeared above the bails, he chose to wear black-topped pads, grey flannels and a black cummerbund. This dress, combined with a heavy 'soup strainer' moustache and side whiskers, guaranteed comment even in an era when eccentricity was commonplace.

His career follows the classic path of the Edwardian amateur: captain of the First XI at Marlborough, awarded his Blue at Oxford, claiming A.P. Lucas and the Hon. Ivo Bligh among his dismissals, and on taking a position as curate in Norwich he played for the Norfolk XI before joining Somerset at the age of 36. A Kent newspaper wrote of him:

'When he played for Norfolk he made a great reputation and might be considered the finest wicket-keeper in England. The way he stumped Leslie Watson in the first innings from a ball on the leg side was simply grand'.

Consistent and courageous

For Somerset he took 90 catches and made 56 stumpings. During a match in 1902 he dismissed six batsmen. But he is most remembered for his consistent and courageous taking of the ball during mammoth run totals inflicted upon the county at the end of the last century. He still holds the record for the highest first-class total without byes when Hampshire scored 672 for seven declared at Taunton in 1899 and he was behind the stumps in 1895 when Archie MacLaren scored 424. He is even mentioned in the *Guinness Book of Records*, for a performance in 1895 when in a total of 474 by Gloucestershire he conceded only four byes. This total included a score of 288 by W.G. Grace, the great man's hundredth century. Wickham never tired of recalling this feat, and once held Jack Hobbs spellbound with a description of the way the Doctor despatched the bouncers of S.M.J. Woods. 'He put them in where he liked,' he told Hobbs.

Like most 'keepers he was a tail-end batsman, managing only a career highest of 28, but he once knocked off the winning runs in an exciting finish to a match against Sussex in 1894.

Wickham was vicar at Martock, a town 20 miles from Taunton, during his sojourn with the county, and on match days a bell would be rung from the top of the house to summon the pony and trap that conveyed him to the county ground.

It appears he must have lived in some style, with his wife and three children and a staff of many servants to cater for the guests at his many tennis parties that were held in the summer, and the vicar regularly enjoyed his game of billiards and a hand of whist. The story is told that he once wagered the prize ducks that he kept on the lawn on the outcome of a hand of cards and subsequently losing, the winner of the prize insisted that the plump birds be driven along the high street to his own residence, and all this is in the early hours of the morning!

His playing days over, he moved to East Brent, married for the second time and devoted much of his time to another great passion, collecting butterflies and moths. He visited Shapwick and Loxely Woods and other corners of Somerset in pursuit of these winged creatures and often at night the villagers could see his lantern glowing on the slopes of Brent Knoll as he waited for his prey. So magnificent was his collection that a room at the vicarage was used exclusively to house it and the many display cases were given to the British Museum at his death.

The cricketers, however, did not desert him. Harold Gimblett came over to coach his son Peter, and during the Weston Festival week many of the players would stay at the vicarage. R.C. Robertson–Glasgow, a relative by marriage, and his former captain Sammy Woods were frequent visitors.

It is hard to imagine two more diverse characters than the boozy, bulky Australian and the teetotal clergyman. Woods loved the social life and above all he loved to sing. A charming scene was described to me of Archie and Sammy singing snatches of Gilbert and Sullivan airs to my grandmother's piano accompaniment, with a falsetto added by R.C. Robertson–Glasgow and an irascible dog! After diverting the company in this manner they would retire to the billiard room and play into the night. Rev. Wickham was not averse to a trick or two during the game and his favourite ploy was to ring for buttered toast and grease the cue ball before his opponent's shot!

Somerset honoured Archie in 1924 by making him the county's president. He had followed the side the length and breadth of England since he had retired from playing and he returned to the county ground as much a character. As a spectator on the boundary he was not above asking a fielder to move if he obscured his view of the wicket, and once the deckchair in which he was sitting was demolished by a towering six from the bat of Arthur Wellard. The fielding side immediately left the game and ran to his assistance only to find the clergyman a highly bemused figure amidst the wreckage.

Archie lived out his life very much as the patriarchal vicar of a small Somerset parish. He even bought an orange T-Ford car, a sight that astonished the villagers who were quick to remove themselves from the roadway when confronted with his wife's furious driving.

He died in 1935, well loved by all who knew him, and a stained glass window was put into the church to commemorate his life. Among the Christian symbols can plainly be seen a set of stumps, a ball and a pair of wicket-keeping gloves. Wickham stands head held high amongst the personalities that have given Somerset cricket the traditional rural flavour that it retains to this day.

ZAHEER ABBAS

Patrick Murphy

If the year 1982 remains a memorable one for Glenn Turner, it will linger equally long in the memory of Zaheer Abbas. For Zaheer became the third non-English batsman to reach the target of a hundred centuries and, to his great delight, he managed it during a Test.

Earlier in the year, he had told me how much he envied Geoffrey Boycott's achievement of making his hundredth hundred in a Test match; Zaheer admitted his sights were set on getting there in a Test against England, the opponents for whom he had the greatest respect. He cautiously agreed, too, that the Lord's Test would be perfect, as appropriate for Zaheer as Headingley was for Boycott in 1977. It was not to be. Zaheer had to wait until December, but at least he got there in a Test match and – even more typically – with a double century.

He had started the Pakistan season on 96 hundreds, still fretting over missing out during the English summer. Due to a combination of illness, lack of opportunity and good English bowling during the Test series, Zaheer had managed only six first-class centuries during the 1982 English season. He was quickly into his stride in Pakistan: a hundred in each innings for the eighth time put him one ahead of Hammond and he came to Lahore and the first Test against India on 99 centuries. On a typically slow wicket, with only Kapil Dev bowling above medium pace, Zaheer resumed his love affair with the Indian bowlers. He had slaughtered them in 1978 and continued the carnage throughout this latest six-Test series, scoring three more hundreds.

Just after lunch on the second day, Zaheer came to his hundred. At the other end, the equally graceful Mohsin Khan had been comprehensively overshadowed by his dominant partner. Madan Lal provided the delivery that sent Zaheer into the record books for the umpteenth time and the stroke was one of his specialities – a flick off his pads through midwicket for three runs. Typically, he took a fresh guard and went on to score 215.

Such is his hunger for runs and fondness for batting records that he had been on course for a hundred hundreds for several years – all of them made with charm and distinction. Zaheer is that precious commodity: an unashamed seeker of records, yet a lovely player incapable of being dull. Spectators of differing loyalties shelve their partiality when Zaheer Abbas comes in to bat – they want him to stay in almost as much as he does.

He was the first Asian to reach the target, an achievement that meant a great deal to him: 'I have always wanted to be respected in the cricket world and by its historians in later years. I want to be like Don Bradman and Jack Hobbs, to be talked about long after I've finished.' Zaheer combines the typical Asian batting subtleties with the mental approach of a Boycott – he is a wristy, elegant player who flourishes the bat on the follow-through. His on-side play is almost faultless and his driving square on the off-side a joy. Slow left-arm bowlers are meat and drink to him. Sunil Gavaskar remembers how he continually pierced Bishen Bedi's field of six men on the offside and Derek Underwood remembers suffering the same treatment with seven men on the off. Says Underwood: 'He's so wristy that he deflects the ball at the moment of impact and guides it into places where there are no fielders.' Underwood needs no reminding that Zaheer averages 81 against Kent.

He is unashamedly a big-innings man, cashing in on flat wickets because he knows that on the next day the bowler will have the advantages and that his defence is not his strong point. He has made 274 and 240 in Tests in England and if the wicket was lifeless on both occasions, nevertheless Zaheer batted charmingly. He makes a conscious effort to carry on past the hundred mark, and admires Boycott for the same approach. Ten years of county cricket have tightened up his technique; when he first played for Gloucestershire, he played away from his body rather too often and kept the slips and wicket-keepers occupied up and down the land when the ball seamed around. In recent years he has got closer to the ball, and he now plays it down off his toes to gully with practised ease.

His fondness for long innings puts a strain on his slight physique: during his two centuries at The Oval in 1976, he lay on the floor during the intervals to harbour his resources and then screwed himself up to a pitch of concentration just before going out again to the middle. It seemed to work – he scored 372 without being dismissed in the game. In an English summer, Zaheer will eat porridge and drink Guinness to build up his strength, in the process laying himself open to some ribald comments in the Gloucestershire dressing-room.

A friendly, soft-spoken man, Zaheer is grateful to his father for fuelling his ambition: 'One day he took me to the railway station at Karachi and pointed to all the sweating masses in the overcrowded third-class compartments. He then showed me the air-conditioned first-class compartments and told me that would be my reward if I worked hard. He didn't realise that I would get there by playing cricket!' He promised his father that he would give up cricket if he failed on the 1971 tour of England, but an innings of 274 in the first Test silenced the paternal doubts.

Since that day in June 1971, Zaheer has scored six more hundreds for Pakistan, a poor return for such a prolific, talented player. His Test average (44) compares unfavourably with his overall one of 54; he averages just 17 against the West Indians, who have usually managed to rattle him with fast bowling. Zaheer agrees his Test record is a little disappointing and suggests that it is harder to score hundreds in Test cricket because of the predominance of fast bowling: 'It's very difficult to score against men like Holding, Croft and Willis. The standard of batting is deteriorating because of the quality of quick bowling.' Certainly Zaheer is at his weakest against authentic quick bowling, as Bob Willis agrees: 'On bouncy wickets, the place to bowl at him is his nose – he doesn't fancy that at all.' David Graveney, Zaheer's county captain, says he noticed a change in his attitude to fast men after he returned from two years with World Series Cricket: 'He had been subjected to high pace aimed purely at his body. His courage was tested and he had to learn to stick it out. As a result, certain bad habits have stayed – he now shows more of this chest to the fast bowler in order to get quickly into a hooking position. Before Packer came along, he was never out of position between 1975 and 1977.'

If the wicket does not favour the fast bowlers, Zaheer is a very difficult man to contain. The England bowlers did very well to restrict him during the 1982 series on wickets that would normally suit Zaheer's style. The England captain, Bob Willis, worked out a way to block his shots: 'We had a square cover and a normal cover, just ten yards apart, to combat that wristy stroke of his that goes square. The place to bowl at him is about a foot outside his off-stump to encourage him to play his strokes. He rarely hits you to mid-off, he prefers to take his right leg back towards leg stump and work you squarer. He murders you if you bowl straight – he'll just whip you away through legside.' The plan worked and a frustrated Zaheer never got past 75, despite majestic displays in the county games.

It seems Zaheer Abbas will never achieve greatness. He still remains a slightly 'iffy' player: if batting was just a matter of playing slow bowlers and seamers, he would be supreme. Against sheer speed, he will always give the bowler a chance. For all that, he remains a splendid batsman, a man who thankfully eschews the bored attitude of someone like Barry Richards and who never gets tired of charming runs out of tired bowling. He tells me with feeling: 'If only I could bat all the time! You know, I hate fielding – someone once said to me, "we've come here to see you bat and not field", as I stood at third man. I couldn't help agreeing with him!' There speaks a batsman with the right priorities.

W.G. QUAIFE

H.B.H.

Parsons, with a despairing turn of the head, saw the ball cleanly held at second slip, turned suddenly, and with a step at once defiant and dismal, walked quietly to the pavilion.

The man sitting by me waited for the perfunctory applause to die down, took a quick glance at his scorecard, and turned to his neighbour.

'Willie,' he murmured.

His companion nodded, took out his pipe, and filled it. They both smiled. Not a smile of anticipation or of satisfaction, but a half-nervous, half-paternal smile, which broadened warm-heartedly as a little figure appeared from the pavilion rails. It was almost as though he had come from between the rails, for until he was clear of them he was not completely distinguishable. The applause spread and widened. He looked rather like those match-stick men we used to draw at school.

The small fellow, using his bat as a walking stick, halfway to the wicket suddenly tucked it under his arm, pulled his cap a fraction forward and looked up at the sun. Before he reached the wicket he hitched his shirt a little under his right arm. He spoke to no-one. Although he had to pass his partner-to-be, there was no sign of recognition. Looking down at the wicket, he twisted his bat methodically and took guard.

Then in incredibly short time he completed a series of sartorial exercises. His cap, the hair behind his left ear, an infinitesimal hitch to his diminutive trousers, and finally the never-omitted rubbing of the left elbow. In much less time than these lines take to read were these rites performed.

Suddenly he became marble – or is it porcelain?

The fieldsmen closed in slightly and half-apologetically, although long field shortened his distance by thirty yards. Then a curious thing happened.

Around the ground there was hardly a man or woman, player or spectator, who did not feel the chords of sympathy tauten. W.G. Quaife, probably never nervous except when facing a Brearley or Kortright, Bradley or Gregory, became the centre of concern – all were anxious; an anxiety of affection rather than fear, of compassion rather than danger, and this, before a ball was bowled.

Then came the ball – the Lilliputian lifted his bat, and with the stroke, all qualms vanished. The delicate mechanism was in order. From that first ball, minds were at rest.

In facile little curves, but in stately measure, his game was played. Chester once said that the back view of Chapman batting reminded him of the Rock of Gibraltar. To bowl at Quaife must surely have appeared as bowling to a fourth stump. Yet those curves and motions of his, almost as streamlined as those of the little Rother he knew so well – provide one with a new angle on cricket. Size does not matter. It is a game for all.

I think from the first Quaife realised and admitted the handicap provided by those diminutive legs of his. With every ball bowled to his partner, he was half-way up the pitch in anticipation of the stroke and in a twinkling flash he was either forward or backward to the wicket. His running somehow suggested Sullivan's Savoyard music.

Never off the ground

The more runs he made the more tidy he became. He rebuttoned his sleeves, he adjusted his gloves – but though I saw him in half a hundred games, never did he touch his pads except for some major repair. Neither did he scavenge the pitch, the blade of his bat was never used to beat down an unruly spot. Perhaps he thought it is too small a weapon to be effective; and there is evidence to show that he regarded this bat of his merely as a supernumerary to run-getting. That, so to speak, he could do almost as well without it. Yet such was his mastery, that the orange-stick he wielded, at times sent the ball streamlining through the covers as though the pitch were a polished dance-floor. For Willie was brought up in the school taught never to lift the ball. He had no use for the stroke which does not make the ball contact the earth within, at most, twice his own length. And his aggression was always in reverse. The speed of the bowler was the gauge for the hit. The gun-shot delivery was deflected only. The subtle slow was as subtly placed. I doubt if there was one season in which Willie was 'c and b' three times.

But it was the medium-paced ball that he loved. Here the batsman and the bowler combine to make the runs, for here pace means place: and it was placing that was the outstanding feature of the Little 'Un's play. I am sure when set he gave the field regular turns. 'Is there an opening here?' he said, in effect. 'Let's try it out.' And so it went on. But having exploited a breakthrough must not however, be taken to signify that the stroke would be repeated – yet. He would collect weak points, and should the field be altered or rearranged, patiently he would begin all over again.

As a partner he was not ideal. An enterprising batsman at the other end had to realise certain eccentricities. When his partner made a stroke I have always felt that Willie in that split-second was calculating what he would have done with a similar ball and having settled the question (albeit he was on the move up the pitch) was rather surprised to find himself at the other end, and that the score figure was changing.

There is a lovely little story told of him in a match between Warwickshire and Hampshire, which has the merit of being confirmed by that great batsman, Major Poore. I do not think it has ever been printed. Warwickshire badly needed runs, and the captain indirectly notified the ingoing batsman that Willie should be got out. The newcomer did his job well. Turning a ball to fine leg, he called Quaife, hesitated, halted, and then waved Willie back. The little man was half-way up the pitch when the wicket-keeper had the ball returned. But that worthy knew the game and Willie too well. He realised Hampshire's best ally was batting. He fumbled the ball, and holding it close to the wicket remarked, with a shake of the head, 'No! we don't run little 'uns out!'

The Little 'Un – therein lies Quaife's charm as it did with Bobby Abel. He was the perpetual youngster. He was the eternal boy shaping to play well – sometimes too well – playing to stay with the eager intensity of a junior at the nets.

'ENDREN, 'EARNE AND 'AIG

Alan Gibson

It is an odd thing, but I cannot remember much about my first visit to Lord's. I know I was staying with Uncle Dick and Auntie Mollie at

Hendon. I often would spend short holidays with them – special treats – in the early Thirties. They were both cricket enthusiasts, and would take me with them to Lord's on a Saturday, the *speciallest* treat of all. I was already watching first-class cricket regularly at Leyton, and can remember a good deal about many of the matches I saw there. But the pictures of Lord's are vaguer. I would have guessed that my first match was Middlesex v. Nottinghamshire – I can see Uncle Dick scanning his scorecard with a professional air, and saying disappointedly, 'Oh, Sam Staples isn't playing'; or it might have been Middlesex v. Lancashire, a match in which a Lancastrian called Hodgson (a fast bowler) took a splendid catch in the deep, only a few yards away from us. We usually arrived early, and took seats in front of the Tavern, though on one occasion at least – perhaps there was an especially large crowd, or Uncle Dick had had a rise in pay – we ascended to the Mound Stand. Yet I have studied the scores in *Wisden* for the conceivable seasons, and no detailed memories are stirred.

'Patsy by nature'

But I retain strong impressions of some of the Middlesex players of those years. The strongest – very properly, for a small boy – is of Hendren. He was small, he was nimble, he could catch them in the deep as well as the slips, he could hit the ball like a thunderbolt: everyone knew him as Patsy ('He was baptised Elias and the crowds would have none of it', wrote Cardus, 'for he is Patsy not only by name but by nature'). Once the Middlesex players were throwing catches to one another, at the fall of a wicket. They were fairly languid catches, for it was a hot day. Hendren caught a gentle one near the ground, and in the same movement flicked it smartly backwards to his captain, Haig, who was standing, arms folded, a few yards behind him. It took Haig in the tummy. How we laughed!

Hendren was not one of those cricketers whose apparently brimming good humour on the field was matched by moroseness off it (we can all think of one or two of those). He was a man of wisdom as well as gaiety, what our ancestors used to call a 'thorough' man, the same wherever you sliced him.

Uncle Dick and Auntie Mollie were both Northerners, as I was myself, but like everyone else they yielded to Hendren, and cheered when he made a big score, even if it was against Yorkshire or Lancashire. They had plenty to cheer. I know that a comparison of the statistics of different periods is a vague guide, but he scored over 57,000 runs, average nearly 51, in a career lasting from 1907 to 1938 (not much accomplished before the first war) with 170 centuries. Only Hobbs and Woolley have scored more runs, and only Hobbs has scored more centuries. It is true that Hendren took some time to get going in Test cricket. This was partly because he was hesitant early in his innings, not a good quality against Gregory and MacDonald. He began the 1921 Test series with 0, 7, 0 and 10. But he would hook the fast bowlers fearlessly when his eye was in, and had the footwork to run down the pitch to the spinners, and at the end of his 51 Tests he had scored 3500 runs, average 48.

We did not – Auntie Mollie and Uncle Dick and I – think so much of Haig, or even Hearne, who after Hendren was the best Middlesex batsman. In the case of Hearne, this was understandable. He was near the end of a long and distinguished career, which had been much handicapped by ill health. He had become a slow, and even dull, batsman, at least to small boys. I have a recollection of even the Lord's boys urging him to get out, so that Hendren could come in. We were unjust to the elegant Hearne, but even Robertson–Glasgow, in a laudatory article, was constrained to write of him, 'So smooth and contained was his method that few spectators, with all respect to them and their shillings, could know how wonderful was the art presented to them.' I was not one of the few, though Uncle Dick, anxious to be knowledgeable, made explanatory comments. Hearne scored 37,000 runs, average nearly 40, so he could not have been too bad; and also took 1,800 wickets, mostly with leg-breaks, though we did not think of him as a bowler by the time I saw him.

H's at The Oval

The joke has often been repeated that the Lord was being mischievous when, in the 1900s, he granted Surrey a succession of cricketers whose name began with the letter H. All the talk at The Oval was of 'Ayward, 'Obbs, 'Ayes, 'Olland and 'Itch. But Middlesex (where the aitches are not, apart from the pavilion, much more common than at the Elephant and Castle) were doing well in the early Thirties with 'Endren, 'Earne, 'Ulme, 'Art and 'Aig. Auntie Mollie, who was careful to pronounce her aitches, did not like Haig much. 'Too much of a toff', she said, and certainly he looked one as he strode down the pavilion steps (the professionals used to come out from their own dressing-room, tucked away to the side, a comfortable distance from the pavilion. They need not have done so, but they thought it was not worth the bother of walking round).

Robertson–Glasgow writes more affectionately of Haig than of

Hearne. No doubt the men had more in common. Haig was captain of Middlesex from 1929 to 1932, in which years they came nearer to the bottom than the top. He was in one respect a good captain, fond of a chancy declaration. Sussex felt that one season he deprived them of the championship when he made a rash one against Lancashire. In another respect he was a bad one, because once he had started bowling (fast-medium with the occasional out-swinger) he could not bear to take himself off. He played for England against Australia in 1921 – but a great many cricketers played for England in that series. I think Hendren did quite right to smack him in the tummy.

THE 'DEMON BOWLER' OF NOTTS

R.D. Woodall

Born 150 years ago on 21 May 1833 John Jackson was probably the most formidable cricketer who played for Nottinghamshire in the 19th century. Jackson, a native of Bungay in Suffolk, was the best fast bowler of his day. When he was very young, his parents moved from Suffolk into Nottinghamshire to live near Newark. Sport was in his blood and he is said to have run barefoot after the hounds in the hunting field. He learned how to play cricket well at Southwell and his skill as a cricketer attracted the attention of local gentry who were the backbone of English teams of the day. He got work as a professional first with a Newark team. Later, after experience as a professional at Edinburgh and Ipswich, Jackson was engaged to serve in the Nottinghamshire Eleven.

In the ten years he was with the Nottinghamshire team his name was a household word and Jackson was subject of some of the best cartoons by John Leech for *Punch*, then very much an organ of humour for the better-off. Leech was good at showing the expressions of village cricketers and the extent of their injuries after they came up against the lightning deliveries Jackson was famous for.

Jackson first appeared at Lord's in a match between North and South in 1856. In 1857 he was recognised as the most prominent bowler in England, when in the North versus South match he took eight wickets for 20 runs. By then, those who came up against him had a fair idea of what to expect. In 1858, when helping in the Kent versus England match, Jackson excelled himself by taking nine wickets for 27 runs at Lord's. In another match at Canterbury he took 13 wickets for 90 runs.

In Jackson's day scores were rarely very high and his highest batting score in first-class cricket was 100 in the Nottinghamshire versus Kent match of 1863.

Between 1857 and 1864 Jackson played in 13 matches for the Players versus the Gentlemen and in a match at Lord's in 1861 he and another famous player of the day, Edgar Willsher, bowled unchanged through both innings of the Gentlemen.

In Jackson's day international cricket was in its infancy and it was regarded almost as a revolutionary step when English teams began to play teams from other countries. In 1859 Jackson was a member of the first English team which went to North America. It achieved phenomenal success in playing American teams and helped to create a body of goodwill which survived the American Civil War.

Although matches with United States teams were impossible during the period of the Civil War between 1861 and 1865, matches in Australia were not. Jackson was a member of George Parr's All England Eleven, when it went to Australia in the winter of 1863. Jackson was still in his prime when his career as a cricketer was virtually finished by a leg injury he received playing for Nottinghamshire against Yorkshire.

From then on his story was really a tragic one. Unlike many professionals of today who have businesses to fall back on in bad times, he had not. From 1870 he lived mainly in Liverpool. From 1870 till 1872 he was the professional at Princes Park and in 1871 acted as caterer, groundsman and bowler to the Liverpool club. His injury prevented a successful comeback. In 1874 he received £300 from his Notts benefit match, but he drank it all away and by 1875 Jackson was working in a Liverpool warehouse.

Six feet tall and weighing over 15 stone, in his heyday he was a first class round-arm bowler with an easy action and a tremendous pace which earned him rightly the nickname of the 'Demon Bowler'. Had he lived in the 1920s or 1930s his figure, like that of Jack Hobbs or Herbert Sutcliffe, would have been on the cigarette cards.

Few came to help him in his old age, when he was in dire poverty. His genius was unknown to the generation of players, nationally famous, when he died in Liverpool Workhouse Infirmary on 4 November 1901. But for the injury which incapacitated him, Jackson might well have gone on playing successfully for a number of years more and ended his days as a successful instructor in a school, training the players of the future.

MR C. I. THORNTON

W.A. Bettesworth

There were many famous hitters in Mr Thornton's time, but he was à king among them all. There is no one like him to-day; there never was anybody like him. The remark made in *Lillywhite* of 1874, that he was 'the grandest hitter ever seen' is as true now as it was then. One of the chief differences between his hitting and that of other men was that whereas he never played a long innings without making several wonderful hits, they would sometimes score a hundred runs without making any hit which attracted especial attention. In 1898 a record of the longest hits appeared in James Lillywhite's *Cricketers' Annual*. It is headed by a hit of 175 yards by Mr W. Fellows on the Christchurch ground at Oxford, in 1856[a], and is followed by hits given as 168 yards 2 ft. and 162 yards[b]. These were made by Mr Thornton during practice at Brighton, and the distance was there and then measured by the Rev. James Pycroft, the well-known author of the *Cricket Field*. Most of Mr Thornton's other famous hits were measured immediately after they were made, and the distance ranges from 152 yards to 140[c]. It is noticeable that in the list given in *Lillywhite* Mr Thornton's name appears six times and Bonnor's name three times. Bonnor's longest authenticated hit was 147 yards at Mitcham[d]. This was measured by James Southerton and others.

Mr Thornton was not able to play first-class cricket regularly after he left the University, for he went into business[e]. He has for some years been chairman of a large timber firm in the City. He was perhaps at his

---

a. – The hit was made off a ball delivered by Charles Rogers, and the distance was measured by Edwin Martin, who played for Kent from 1845 to 1851. The genuineness of the feat has been questioned, but both Mr (afterwards the Rev.) Walter Fellows and his brother, Mr Harvey Fellows, assured me that it was authentic. Martin, who measured the drive, was at the time ground-keeper of the Christ Church ground.

b. – These two hits were made in 1871.

c. – Mr Thornton hit a ball 152 yards off Mr W.M. Rose when playing for South v. North at Canterbury in 1871; the distance was measured by Mr W. de Chair Baker. In the match between Orleans Club and the Australians at Twickenham in 1878 he made a hit the same distance off H.F. Boyle; the hit was measured with a chain by Rylott and Wild. Whilst batting for Gentlemen of South v. Players of South at the Oval in 1871, he hit a ball from Southerton over the old Rackets Court, a distance of 140 yards from hit to pitch.

d. – In May, 1880. During practice at Melbourne, Bonnor has been credited with hits of 160 yards and 150 yards.

e. – Mr Thornton played in 18 matches for Kent between 1867 and 1872, and in 29 for Middlesex between 1875 and 1885. In addition he appeared for the Gentlemen against the Players, for Gentlemen of the South, and in other representative matches, including several at Scarborough and Cambridge.

best as a cricketer between 1873 and 1880, although he seldom had an opportunity of playing in first-class cricket during that period; but at intervals he found time to play and also to make good scores until about 1888. His connection with the Scarborough Festival was commemorated in 1894 by the presentation of a splendid silver cup, which he highly values[f]. He represented Kent as often as he could, and he also assisted the Gentlemen against the Players. For about eight years he, with his cousin, Mr P.M. Thornton, hunted in Leicestershire, and for five or six years in the Vale of Aylesbury.

An idea of the way in which Mr Thornton used to hit may be gained from the following extracts from the *Ceylon Mail* of 7 March 1891. They refer to two hits made by him during a match at Colombo in which he played. (*i.*) 'The ball flew far out of bounds, pitched half-way to the Galle Face Cottage, and was stopped by the wall of the compound – six and much enthusiasm.' (*ii.*) 'The batsman lifted the ball right into the compound of the house adjoining the church, amid great cheering, for six.'

Mr Thornton went to Eton in 1861, but it was not until 1866 that he was chosen for the eleven[g]. 'I think I should have been in the eleven in 1865,' he said, 'but I knocked the bowling of the professional about, and he did not like it at all. The usual way of coming to the front at Eton, at any rate in my time, was to keep on getting runs in the lower games until you attracted the attention of someone in authority who would place you in the Upper Club, where you could get some practice. If you happened to come off in one of the first-class games you might be put into the eleven. I remember that I made 40 or 50 the first time I played for Eton; it was in a match against Christchurch College, Oxford.'

'You made a good score in your first match against Harrow?'

'I think it was 46 not out[h]. It was Cobden's first year for Harrow, and he bowled most of us out; we were very badly beaten[i]. He and F.L. Shand, fast left hand, were the two best boy bowlers I ever met[j]. I saw

---

f. – The cup – a silver loving-cup – exhibits a representation of the Scarborough ground with Mr Thornton at the wicket. The Scarborough Festival was originated by Mr Thornton.

g. – Mr Thornton played for Eton in 1866–67–68, and for Cambridge in 1869–70–71–72; he captained the College in 1868 and the University in 1872.

h. – Mr Thornton's scores against Harrow were 46 not out and 7, 35 and 47, and 44 and 13; against Winchester he made 47, 1, and 16 and 1.

i. – Mr F.C. Cobden took eight Eton wickets for 47 runs (five for 37 and three for 10), and Harrow won by an innings and 136 runs. The Eton totals were 124 and 42.

j. – Mr Shand played for Harrow in 1872 and 1873. In his two matches against Eton he took fourteen wickets for 210 runs, or 15 runs each.

Cobden early this year (1905) and we were talking about the Oxford and Cambridge match of 1870, in which he took the last three Oxford wickets in the second innings with successive balls, when only three runs were required to tie. It has always been a subject of controversy as to the exact history of the last over bowled by Cobden, the reason for this being that everybody was so excited that when the question was discussed in after years various accounts were given. But Cobden tells me that he is perfectly sure that F.H. Hill, who carried his bat, hit the first ball of the over – there were only four balls to the over – so hard that it would have gone to the boundary, and the match would have been over. But Bourne, fielding at mid-off, made a fine effort, and stopped it cleverly with one hand, although it was impossible to save the single. Bourne caught S.E. Butler off the next ball, and then Cobden bowled T.H. Belcher and W.A. Stewart with the last two balls of the over'[k].

'In your first University match you made the two highest scores for Cambridge?'

'Yes, 50 and 36. It was very wet weather, I remember, and the scoring on both sides was low[l]. A.F. Walter, the present proprietor (1905) of the *Times*, was the Oxford fast bowler, and in our second innings he took five wickets for 35. I was one of the victims[m]. I remember that I began hitting directly I got to the wickets, and that I drove a ball through the side of one of the carriages.'

'Had you a preference for any particular kind of bowling?'

'I liked slow bowling better than fast, and bowling which broke into you better than that which broke away. You had more time with slow bowling than with fast and were not so likely to make a mistake. But I never liked old Barratt – one of the very slowest left-hand bowlers

---

k. – Mr Henry Perkins, in a footnote to this match in his 'Scores of the Oxford and Cambridge Cricket Matches from 1829,' says: – 'The finish of this match was most extraordinary. Oxford, in their second innings, had three wickets to go down, and wanted 3 runs to tie and 4 to win, with one batsman well set. Mr Hill received the first ball from Mr Cobden's over, and hit it so hard that it would have gone to the boundary, but Mr Bourne, with one hand, so nearly stopped it that one run only resulted. Mr Bourne caught Mr Butler off the next, and Mr Cobden bowled the last two batsmen first ball.' It will be seen that this account tallies exactly with Mr Cobden's recollection as told by Mr Thornton. The 1870 match is always spoken of as 'Cobden's Match', and, in consequence, the fine performance by Mr E.E. Harrison Ward in Oxford's second innings is generally overlooked: Mr Ward bowled 32 overs for 29 runs and six wickets. – Mr Cobden's analysis was 27 overs, 35 runs and four wickets.

l. – Mr Thornton's scores in his four University matches were 50 and 36, 17 and 11, 4 and 12, and 20. Five of the seven innings were played on muddy ground.

m. – Mr Walter died at Bearwood, Wokingham, on 22 February 1910. He was pardonably proud of the bowling feat mentioned; for his victims were Messrs J.W. Dale, H.A. Richardson, W. Yardley, C.I. Thornton, and C.A. Absolom.

I ever met – for there was no one who had so much twist on the ball. But other men used to hit him pretty often. I remember that the first time I ever played against him I had to go in after Russy Walker for the South against the North. Russy, who had backed his runs against Jupp's, had only to make five to be level with him, but the first ball broke in and bowled him. Like everybody else I was immensely amused. Then I went in and was stumped first ball'[n].

'You used to bowl underhand?'

'Fast underhand. The reporters described them as "sneaks"[o]. Occasionally I met with success, and the first time I ever bowled at the Oval Humphrey, Jupp and W.C.C. Lane fell to me, as far as I remember[p]. In another match at the Oval the crowd became very angry because I bowled three of their favourites, Jupp, Humphrey and Pooley, and they began to shout "Take the ——— off." Willsher, the famous old Kent bowler, then walked to the ring and said to them, "Look here. If you can't behave yourselves in a respectable way we shall not play any more. See?" They saw, and became quiet, but I wonder what a crowd would say nowadays if a player of the visiting side were to talk to them like that.'

'How long is it since you played in a cricket match?'

'The last time I played was in a little match in 1902 at George Bulteel's place at Slough. It was a nice warm day, the wicket was uncommonly good, the bowling moderate, and the ground very small. I think I made about fifty runs. I remember that after the match someone asked me to give one of my bats for the *Daily Express* Fund which was being raised on behalf of the Cricketers' Benevolent Society. So I said that I had only the old one that I had been using that day, and that as I should not want it any more they could have it. A Mr Gladstone, of Sunbury, bought it there and then for the fund for £1 17s. 6d.'

---

n. – The match was played at Prince's in May, 1872. The score contains the following entries: – H. Jupp c Carpenter, b Barratt, 5; R.D. Walker Esq. b Barratt, 0; C.I. Thornton Esq. st Pinder, b Barratt, 0. Barratt took eight wickets for 60 runs in a total of 186.

o. – Playing for his own Eleven against King's School, at Canterbury, in 1870, Mr Thornton bowled *down* all the 10 wickets in an innings.

p. – This was in the match between Surrey and Cambridge University, in June, 1870. Mr Thornton bowled 88 balls for 36 runs and four wickets – those of Tom and Dick Humphrey, Mr W.C.C. Lane, and Jupp. Strange to say, Mr Thornton again bowled the brothers Humphrey in the first innings in the match between Gentlemen of the South and Players of the South, at the Oval, in June, 1871. Mr Thornton's analysis on that occasion was 116 balls, 38 runs, 4 wickets. In the second innings (398) of the same match he took three wickets for 83 runs. The bowling on each side was opened with fast underhand, Mr Thornton doing so for the Gentlemen and H.H. Stephenson for the Players.

'On which of your innings do you look back with the greatest pleasure?'

'My innings of 107 at Scarborough in twenty-nine hits in 1886 for Gentlemen of England against I Zingari. I was in for a little over an hour, and the runs were made out of about 133[q]. In club cricket the innings which I enjoyed the most was played at Rickling Green. We had to make about 250 to win in two hours and won with ten minutes to spare. My score was 173 not out, and Arthur Appleby and Jack Dale were the other two men who made runs[r]. I remember that I was talking to my cousin, J.C. Partridge, just before the innings about the chances of making the runs, and I said that it was ten to one against us. The result was that I laid him five pounds to half a sovereign that we did not make the runs, and of course I had to pay up.'

'How is it that one so seldom hears of Rickling Green now?'

'Well, it is a long way from London, a few miles from Bishop's Stortford, and the only reason why so many good matches were played there in former days was that Sir Walter Gilbey used to interest himself in the game, and we always used to stay at his place at Elsenham. But country house cricket was very much to the fore in my days. I remember once playing at Lord Sondes' place[s], when Lord Harris was bowling roundarm in the most erratic manner. He was pitching the ball shorter and shorter, and as I was at point I judiciously stepped back a little. Presently he said, "Stand in nearer." "Not I, while you are bowling short like that," I replied. So he said, "Well, let Ned Knight go there." "All right," was my reply, and Knight took my place and went in close. The very next ball was hit tremendously hard on to his knee-cap and he had to be carried off the ground. During these matches a band used to play, and once when I was batting, and feeling like making a large score, I went to Lord Sondes and asked him to stop the band. "It's impossible to play while the music is going on," I said. The band was stopped at once. And I was bowled in the very next over.'

'Will you tell me something about the great hitters that you have seen?'

---

[q]. – On this occasion Mr Thornton scored 107 out of 133 in 70 minutes. He made eight sixes, twelve fours, two twos and seven singles, obtaining the following hits: – 6 1 6 4 6 2 1 1 4 6 4 6 1 4 4 4 1 6 4 4 4 6 1 6 4 4 1 4 2. Mr A.G. Steel was among the bowlers.

[r]. – Mr Thornton made 173 out of 250 in 110 minutes, making seven hits out of the ground. The match was Orleans Club v. Ricking Green, at Rickling Green, in 1883.

[s]. – Lees Court, Faversham. Earl Sondes was, as the Hon. G.W. Milles, a member of the Eton Eleven of 1842. He died in 1894, and was succeeded in the title by Viscount Throwley, who played occasionally for Kent.

'I think I should place Bonnor and Lyons first among them. Bonnor is said to have made longer hits than Lyons, but as far as I can understand they were never measured, and it is very difficult to guess distances, as I have often seen in the case of my own hits, some of them when measured proving to be much longer than they seemed, while others were not so long. But I saw Bonnor hit A.P. Lucas out of the ground at Scarborough three or four times, and they were all very big hits[t]. Alfred Lubbock could hit about as hard as most people, and I once saw him drive W.H. Wathen[u] out of the Chislehurst ground over the lodge gate in the Empress Eugenie's park – a very big hit indeed. Jessop can hit more balls than anyone I have seen, but perhaps he can hardly be classed as a hitter pure and simple. I've seen W.G. make some tremendous hits when he has been letting himself go; I once saw him hit A.G. Steel to square leg out of the ground at Scarborough, and nobody had ever done this before[v]. The ball was breaking away a little and he had a go at it, just happening to catch it full. Among other men who could hit with immense power were George Ulyett, Percy McDonnell, W.J. Ford and C.E. Green. I don't think that men nowadays hit as hard as these.'

Mr Thornton has played cricket in many parts of the world. He never went on a tour, although, naturally enough, he was asked to go to Australia several times. Indeed, he was once offered £3,000 if he would go there with one of the English teams, but he played cricket for the love of the game and not for profit. 'I have practised at Bombay, Hongkong, Colombo[w], Sydney, Melbourne, and many other places,' he said. 'I remember that at Hongkong I had two nigger professionals to bowl to me on a bit of matting. They bowled exceedingly well, and I had quite as much exercise as I wanted, for the weather was about as hot as it could be. There are a lot of black professionals at Colombo, and they are excellent practice bowlers, although their action is very much like a throw. I remember that when I was practising at Sydney I was interviewed by a reporter for the *Australian Star*, with most entertaining results. The reporter drew largely on his imagination, and

t. – Bonnor hit Mr A.P. Lucas for 20 runs (6, 4, 4, 6) off a four-ball over in the match between I Zingari and the Australians at Scarborough in September 1882.
u. – Mr Wathen played for the famous West Kent Club for many years, several times for the Gentlemen of Kent, and once Philip Norman has described his bowling as 'slow, with a low round-hand delivery, perhaps hardly as accurate as it might have been.' He was educated first at Brighton College and afterwards at Rugby – not at Blackheath Proprietary School, as generally stated.
v. – In the match between Gentlemen of England and I Zingari in 1886.
w. – Whilst practising at Colombo in 1891 Mr Thornton drove a ball 150 yards from hit to pitch.

among other items of interest that he gave to the readers of the paper was the information that although "he played for Kent in his earliest days, he subsequently transferred his allegiance to Nottinghamshire, proving his usefulness in both districts." Which was news to me.'

'In one of the matches at Scarborough,' said Mr Thornton, 'Stoddart, W.G. and I had all failed to make a good score[x]. It was just about the time when amateur photography came into vogue, and we were asked to pose dozens of times. At last when we were standing in a group for about the twentieth time W.G. said, "Well, it strikes me we've been photographed more times than we've made runs." I met W.G. recently (1905), just after I had seen a photograph of him and George Edwardes in golfing costume. They had been playing a match at golf. I told W.G. that he was getting to be a man of some importance in the world, and asked him his opinion about golf. "Well," he said, "I've come to the conclusion that golf is a good excuse for a walk and a nice chat."'

It is well known that Bonnor, the Australian, was not the man to hide his light under a bushel if he could help it, and when he made a fine hit he liked to dwell upon its points. Mr Thornton tells a good story which bears on this. 'When we were going to play the Australians at Norbury Park'[y], he said, 'Bonnor, who had been over in Jersey, told us that while he was there he had hit a ball over a fence and a garden into a river – about two hundred yards altogether. I said, "Well, I don't know what we shall do about it tomorrow, as there is a lake at Norbury about a hundred and fifty yards off, and if you get set you will fill it up, and we shall have no balls left to play with."'

It may be stated that Mr Thornton did not wear pads even when he was opposed to the very fastest bowling. Nor did he use a glove until towards the close of his career as a first-class cricketer, and then only on his right hand[z].

. . . . . .

Note by Mr Thornton, 12 April, 1910: 'I remember that, in addition to

---

x. – This was played in the Yorkshire v. MCC and Ground match in September, 1887. – 'W.G.' made 17, Mr Thornton 14, and Mr Stoddart 12.

y. – Australians v. Mr C.I. Thornton's XI., at Norbury Park, in May, 1888. Bonnor scored 3 and 9 not out.

z. – The following account of a first experience of Mr Thornton's batting is told by Mr C.J. Butcher, the Assistant Editor of the *Field*. 'I had gone to Canterbury with Charles Box, who was then the Editor of the *Field*. We saw Mr Thornton go to the wickets. He missed the first ball, threw his bat at the second, which was very wide, drove the third high over the trees – a magnificent hit – and was bowled by the fourth. Charles Box turned to me and groaned, "And they call this cricket!" But I saw Mr Thornton play many wonderful innings afterwards.'

Barratt, E.M. Grace was a slow bowler whom I did not like. I don't think he ever got me out, but once the ball only missed the wicket by a hair's breadth – he very seldom went on to bowl when I was in. He kept his hand very near the ground, but the ball did not rise high in the air in the way that it does with so many modern lob bowlers. I consider that he and Walter Humphreys and Rose were the best lob bowlers I ever met.'

HESKETH PRICHARD

Eric Parker

Hesketh Prichard will be remembered first and foremost as a bowler, and it was to make himself into a bowler that he set himself first – as has been mentioned in another chapter. And it was as a bowler that he first played for Fettes, in the summer of 1892, when he was fifteen. He got eight wickets for 88 in the first three school matches, but did not get into the Eleven until the following summer, when his figures were 40 wickets for 471, or an average of 11.77. The next year he headed the school bowling averages, with 46 wickets for 463 runs, or an average of 10. In that year he was described in the *Fettesian* as –

'The best bowler we have had for a long time. Fast right hand, with a good break back on a bowler's wicket. At present is hardly steady enough, and he wants experience. Unfortunately he is leaving, but he ought to do something in the future.'

And in that year he was asked, but was unable, to play for Scotland against South Africa. He left, as we have seen, on his own decision, at the age of seventeen and a half, when he had another year – the best year of a schoolboy's life – before him.

County club cricket was all that fell to his lot in the few years after leaving Fettes, for he was occupied with more serious business. He played in June 1896 in a match for Young Players v. Sussex Club and Ground. In the following year he would have been definitely invited to play for Sussex, but the invitation was at first indefinite and sent as a message, and somehow miscarried. The real beginning of his county cricket career sprang from his friendship with Sir Arthur Conan Doyle, who suggested him as a bowler, first to W.G. Grace, then managing the newly formed London County Cricket Club, and afterwards to Major E.G. Wynyard, captain of the Hampshire County Cricket team. For London County he took many wickets; W.G. Grace had a great opinion of him, and liked to have him on his side whenever possible. It was under Grace's captaincy that he played in a match at Bristol, in aid of the funds for the Prevention of Cruelty to Children, against a team got up by the Gloucestershire captain, C.L. Townsend. The match was played under special rules, each side to bat for two and a half hours. Grace's side made 250 for 7 wickets, Grace and Prichard putting on 100 runs and being not out; then Townsend's side went in, with Grace bowling at one end and Prichard at the other, and W. Troup, the Gloucestershire player, made the winning hit off the last ball of the match.

He played his first match for Hampshire in 1900 against Somerset, at Bath, when he had the distinction of clean bowling that accomplished batsman L.C.H. Palairet, and took 3 wickets for 34.

In 1901, occupied with getting out his book, *Through the Heart of Patagonia*, he did not play county cricket, but in 1902 he played in all the twelve county matches for Hampshire, and was second in the county bowling averages, with 38 wickets at an average of 20.78. This was a year in which he had two very remarkable matches: one against Sussex, when he bowled C.B. Fry, then at his best, and took six wickets for 39 runs; the other against Derbyshire, when on a perfect Southampton wicket – and what that means first-class county bowlers know – he actually took seven wickets for 47 runs. This Major Wynyard, who was his captain at the time, considers to have been on the whole Prichard's best performance during the years he played cricket with him, for everything was in the batsman's favour, and only a naturally great bowler who could also use his head could have got wickets under such conditions.

In 1903 he took 45 wickets for 19.95 apiece, and for the first time was chosen to represent the Gentlemen against the Players at Lord's. In this match he was unlucky; there was a strong wind blowing, and the bowler at one end had to bowl against it. MacLaren, who captained the Gentlemen chose Walter Brearley to bowl with the wind, and Prichard had the uphill task of bowling against it.

But his turn was to come. The next season, 1904, was Hesketh Prichard's great year. Perhaps his most remarkable bowling performance was in a match not for his county, but for MCC v. Kent, when in the Kent second innings he began by taking five wickets without having a run scored off him, and in all got six wickets for 23. He headed the Hampshire bowling averages, playing in thirteen matches, and he took over 100 wickets in the season, his analyses for Hampshire and for all matches being as follows:

	Overs	Maidens	Runs	Wickets	Average
Hampshire	... 526.2	... 132	... 1520	... 62	... 24.51
All matches	... 762.4	... 179	... 2324	... 106	... 21.92

His real triumph was, however, in the Gentlemen and Players' match at Lord's. He was chosen, of course, as a bowler, but it was not only as a bowler, but as a batsman, that he had a share – perhaps as great a share as anyone's on the side – in winning the match. The Players won the toss, and in their first innings made 327, Prichard taking three wickets for 102. The Gentlemen, losing one wicket for 4 runs on the first evening, on the following day, Tuesday, had actually nine wickets down for 112 with Hesketh Prichard to come in. He joined Jackson, his captain, and while he kept up his wicket, Jackson scored, till the pair had added 59 runs, Prichard's share being not out 10. This left the Gentlemen with a score of 171, 156 runs behind on the first innings. In the second innings the Players made 255, Prichard bowling at a great pace and taking five wickets for 80 runs. But even so the Gentlemen were left with 412 runs to make on the fourth innings of the match – and how many of those in the game on either side thought that it was possible they could make them? Ranjitsinhji and Jackson, however, for the fourth wicket took the score from 108 to 302, and with 6 wickets to fall 110 runs were wanted, with 100 minutes to get them in. But McDonell, one of the six, had badly damaged his hand, and when the eighth wicket fell at 400, 12 more runs were still wanted, A.O. Jones being not out 51 and practically only Hesketh Prichard able to bat. He came out and took up his stand, with the Players edging up so close to him that Lilley, the wicket-keeper, actually put Hayward, who as cover-point was in a couple of yards of the bat, further away. Prichard, doubtless, could have appealed to the umpire, for fieldsmen standing so close are unquestionably interfering with the batsman's play; but he stood there unheeding, and stopped ball after ball, glancing one to leg, and another through slips for two. For this second hit they could have run three, but Jones wanted the bowling, and when he got it cut the first ball and drove the second, each to the boundary, so that at a quarter to seven the Gentlemen had won by two wickets.

This was a great win for the side, and Hesketh Prichard's share in it was eight wickets for 182 runs, and two not out innings for the last wicket, which enabled his partner to add nearly 50 runs to the score in the first innings, and to make the winning hit in the second. It was one of the most memorable finishes ever seen at Lord's, and if you try to explain two such innings played by a cricketer who was in the side only for his bowling, you come back in the end simply to character. Many better bats would have failed under such a test – and yet if you admit that, can you call them better bats? Captain Wynyard, at all events, thought much more highly of Hesketh Prichard's batting than many other judges of cricket, and he would point to these two innings to back his opinion.

'Cricket such as this,' wrote one of the chroniclers of the match, 'raises the national pastime to a higher standard, in which nerve and brains co-operate with mere physical or mechanical attributes;' and we find other critics, in the same way, more deeply impressed with Hesketh Prichard's batting in this match than with his bowling.

'Prichard carried out his bat for 10,' wrote 'Astral', 'and I have witnessed many a century that was not worth half so much. It will be a libel after this to say that Prichard is chosen only for his bowling.' And again, describing the last few overs of the match: 'Twenty minutes to go and 12 runs to get, with Hesketh Prichard as the last resource, for McDonell was suffering from a broken finger. It was a nerve-destroying situation for any batsman, but Prichard came out with his usual merry smile, planted his long legs at the crease, and prepared for cavalry.' And the feat of keeping up his wicket with the fieldsmen crowding round him delighted the big crowd. The *Star* reporter wrote that 'the way "H.P." defended his wicket was worthy of high praise, and he returned to the pavilion undefeated by the professional bowlers. He has a queer style, but we liked his innings much better than any three-decker novel, and the crowd were of the same opinion.'

This capacity of his for keeping up his wicket when runs were wanted came to be appreciated – or rather, even, looked forward to – by the crowd, who enjoyed his innings none the less because he obviously enjoyed it himself. In the following year, playing for the Gentlemen of England against the Australians, he was twice set the same task of keeping in rather than getting runs, and a writer in *To-day* described the close of the first innings:

'Captain Wynyard took Jessop's place, I believe, as a player in the English team. It was Hesketh Prichard, however, who was really

Jessop's substitute, and set the benches under the awnings and in the stands roaring. Hesketh Prichard is a golden-haired giant, who can tell stories or bowl with something of the tempestuous delight of a fighter at a fair. He bats, however, more like a child scooping out sand with a wooden spade. On Thursday the Australians could break no hole in his infantile defences. He stood there throwing back his little spadefuls of sand, and letting a great laugh out of him on two occasions on which he came by a run. Twice, too, the ball missed the middle of his bat. It just grazed the edge, and veered past the wicket-keeper, carried by its own force the length of the boundary. Hesketh Prichard, seeing his score mounting up, threw his huge, capless head back, and joined in the roars of delight that went like a storm round the field. Such a munificence of good nature I have never seen before on the playing-field.'

The curious fact is that in reality Hesketh Prichard was an exceptionally hard hitter. He always hit hard in country house matches, and in 1912 – as an example of what he could do – playing for Hants against Surrey, he went in last and made 36, hitting the Surrey bowlers all over, and out of, the ground.

In 1905 he played for the third successive season for the Gentlemen against the Players at Lord's, and got two valuable wickets, besides making the useful score of 17. For Hampshire he played in five matches, and against Derbyshire had a wonderful record. In the first innings he took five wickets for 46, but Derbyshire made 278 against Hampshire's 263. Hampshire in the second innings made 261, leaving Derbyshire to make 247 to win; and then got them out on a wicket that was still good for 58, Hesketh Prichard bowling 17.5 overs for 32 runs and eight wickets. His record for the match was thus 13 wickets for 6 runs apiece, and a note on the game by the Derbyshire captain, A.E. Lawton, gives an idea of the quality of his cricket:

'If anyone wishes a new kind of lion-rampant for his coat of arms, let him photograph Hesketh Prichard when he bowls as he did to-day. We don't mind him turning from the off, or even swerving, but when he bowls very fast, with a perfect length, pitches the ball on the leg stump and knocks the off out of the ground, there is nothing for it but to bow politely and depart.'

For Hampshire he was again head of the bowling averages, and his analysis for all matches was as under:

Overs	Maidens	Runs	Wickets	Average
250.1 ...	... 35	... 952	... 39	... 24.41

But the main part of his cricket for the year was played before the English season opened. In January he sailed for the West Indies as a member of Lord Brackley's team, and though he joined the team a little later than the rest, owing to work he had to do at home, and was also incapacitated during part of the tour by an attack of malaria, he was extremely successful as a bowler, some of his figures being five wickets for 22, six for 19, four for 17, and six for 17, and his total for the tour amounting to 38 wickets at an average of 14.73 runs.

In 1906 he played in only two matches for Hampshire, but in 1907 he was chosen by the Committee of the MCC – perhaps as high a compliment as could be paid to any cricketer – to captain the MCC team visiting America. The side included Major E.G. Wynyard, Gregor McGregor (the Middlesex captain), J.W.H.T. Douglas (the future England captain), G.H. Simpson–Hayward, K.O. Goldie, L.P. Collins, L.G.A. Collins, F.H. Browning, R.O. Schwarz, and S.J. Snooke, and was probably the strongest team that has ever crossed the Atlantic, with the exception of that which was captained by K.S. Ranjitsinhji in 1899. The tour was in every way successful. Hesketh Prichard himself did some remarkable bowling, getting five wickets for 15 against the Philadelphia Colts, and seven wickets for 20 against the Gentlemen of Philadelphia, both at Philadelphia. But the actual cricket was not less important than the good fellowship of the tour. It was spoiled by not a single unpleasant incident, and throughout the time the team was in America the matches were distinguished by good humour and sportsmanship which reflected the qualities of the MCC captain. Major E.G. Wynyard (who was also a member of Lord Brackley's West Indian team) has very kindly written for me an appreciation of this task of captaincy:

'Cricket tours are a much more arduous undertaking for the captain of the side than is usually realised. In addition to all details of management which fall on the captain, unless a manager is especially appointed, which is not the case in American or Canadian tours, a great deal of speech-making has to be done, and this is, of course, the duty of the captain. I think, speaking with a very varied experience, that no one was so eminently successful as Hesketh Prichard was; his speeches were delightful, tactful, and very humorous. Always he had to reply to some very capable after-dinner speaker, and always his speeches were up to the very highest standard which obtains in Canada and in the United States.'

That, as all will realise who know how the Americans study the art of after-dinner speaking, must be regarded as a very considerable tribute. The sequel came in 1908. In that year Hesketh Prichard was asked by the MCC to get up a team to play the Philadelphians at Lord's. And on the evening of the first day of the match, when the Philadelphians were the guests of the MCC at dinner, it was Hesketh Prichard's happy gift of friendliness which turned everyone's feelings into the right channel. Such meetings have a habit of beginning in an atmosphere of stiff formality, and that was the *aura* of the reception-room when he arrived, to infuse the whole gathering with something of his own infectious cheerfulness. As Mr Walter Long (Lord Long of Wraxall) wrote to him after the dinner: 'You made all the difference between success and failure, and I am deeply grateful to you.'

JACKSON

Alan Gibson

Colonel the Honourable Sir Francis Stanley Jackson, PC, GCIE, as he had become by the time he died more than seventy-six years later, was born at Chapel Allerton, near Leeds, on 21 November 1870. On the same day, in South Australia, Joe Darling was born, who never, so far as I know, held any titles or formal honours, but who was to be one of Australia's greatest cricket captains, as Jackson was to be one of England's.

Jackson showed promise as a cricketer from his earliest years, as so many Yorkshire boys do. At his preparatory school, Lockers Park in Hertfordshire, he was fortunate in having a cricket-loving headmaster, Mr Draper. The head once promised a bottle of ginger beer to the bowler every time he was bowled out. The small Jackson proceeded to earn eighteen bottles of ginger beer. It was at Harrow, however, that he first made his impact on a wider public. He was in the eleven from 1887 to 1889, and captain in his last year. He did not achieve very much against Eton on the first occasion, and in 1888 his father, then a member of Salisbury's Cabinet, offered him a sovereign for each wicket he took, and a shilling for each run he made. He scored 21 and 59, and took 11 wickets for 68.

His father was not so rash again. His son's comment was that he had been glad to be successful, as 'it would do father so much good'.

Harrow won that match by 156 runs, after being 26 behind on the first innings, and Jackson's performance has been commemorated in one of the best of E.E. Bowen's Harrow songs:

> Ten score to make, or yield her!
> Shall Eton save the match?
> Bowl, bowler! Go it, fielder!
> Catch, wicket-keeper, catch!
> Our vain attempts controlling
> They drive the leather – no!
> *A gentleman's a-bowling,*
> And down the wickets go.

Harrow won again in 1889, Jackson taking five wickets and scoring 68. He went to Cambridge, where he was expected to get his blue as a freshman without any difficulty. As is not unusual in such circumstances, however, he began nervously and had several failures. At this, S.M.J. Woods, his captain, took him aside and said: 'If you are worrying about your blue, you can have it at once' – or, one suspects, words to that effect. It was a characteristic gesture by Woods, and it brought a characteristic response from Jackson. His place in the Cambridge side was thenceforwards never in doubt. He was captain in 1892, heading the averages for both batting and bowling. In the University match that year he took eight for 147, and scored 34 and 35. In 1893, he was re-elected captain, an honour even more unusual then than now, and though his bowling fell off slightly he averaged 43 with the bat and made top score in each Cambridge innings. In three of Jackson's four years Cambridge won, and in 1892 they were beaten in a remarkable match, in which 1100 runs were scored, and approximately 47,000 people watched the three days of cricket. *O tempora, O mores!*

'I remember,' writes 'A Country Vicar', 'the game in which I was first impressed by the complete mastery of his batsmanship. It was a college match – between Trinity and Jesus on Jesus Close. The game – a two-day fixture – was regarded as a contest between the two strongest college elevens of 1893.' Trinity, behind on the first innings, needed 253 to win, and began badly. 'Then F.S. Jackson and K.S. Ranjitsinhji made a remarkable stand, adding 136. 'Ranji' was never a slow scorer, but his share of those runs was 47, which shows the nature of Jackson's hitting! It was magnificent. He used every stroke; but the one which dwells most vividly in my memory was an on-drive, out of the ground, which pitched on the creeper-clad wall of the College buildings.' E.H.D. Sewell has a similar memory of the same period. 'I was standing slip,' he writes, 'to our star bowler at Chepauk, Madras, in November, 1892, and saw [Jackson] hit a six over the trees on the square-leg boundary.... I've seen some 'sixers', including one over the long-leg boundary by Constantine at Lord's, but never the equal of this one at Madras for easy, effortless acquisition. The ball seemed to be persuaded over those trees, not hit.' On this tour of India, under Lord Hawke, Jackson took 69 wickets at 10 runs apiece, and tied for first place in the batting averages.

His captaincy of Cambridge at Lord's in 1893 caused a storm. Cambridge scored 182, and Oxford were 95 for nine. The follow-on was then imposed compulsorily if a side was more than 80 runs behind. Cambridge did not want to bat last, and Jackson instructed C.M. Wells to bowl wides deliberately, to prevent Oxford from following on. As a result of this, and a similar incident in another University match three years later, a bad law was changed, and the follow-on made optional. Why had not one of the Oxford batsmen thwarted Jackson's plan by knocking down his wicket? This question is often asked by Cambridge men, and perhaps I may be forgiven for recalling the remark of one veteran Oxford blue, who said that 'only a Cambridge man could ask it'!

Although still at Cambridge, Jackson was picked for the first Test against the Australian side of 1893, captained by J. McC. Blackham, who is still remembered as one of the very great wicket-keepers. Jackson went in at 31 for 2, Stoddart and William Gunn out, and put on 137 for the third wicket with Shrewsbury. His score was 91. Thus early was the pattern of Jackson's greatest innings becoming clear: it was not just the runs he made, but that so often he made them when they were most needed, and others were failing. Exactly the same could be said of his bowling: his career figures are not specially impressive, but they cannot show just how often he took a wicket at a critical moment.

In the second Test of 1893, W.G. Grace, who was captaining England, said to Jackson: 'With all these batsmen I don't know where to put you.'

'Anywhere will do.'

'Then number seven.'

'Thanks. That's my lucky number. I was the seventh child!' (He had one older brother and five older sisters.) At number seven, Jackson scored his first Test century. 'Mold came in last when I was 99. He nearly ran me out, so in desperation I jumped in and drove Giffen high to the seats, reaching 103. Then the bewildered Mold did run me out.' England won this match, the only one of the three Tests to be finished, by an innings and 43 runs. Jackson did not play in the third Test, preferring to assist Yorkshire in a vital match at Brighton. Yorkshire needed to win that match to make sure of the championship, and duly did so: it was their first championship, unless one goes back to 1870 and before, when the 'championship' was so informal as scarcely to deserve the name. Nevertheless the incident, which was not an isolated one at this period, throws a useful light on the relative importance attached to Test matches then and now.

Before we leave this section of his career, it should also be recorded that it was Jackson who gave Ranjitsinhji his blue – and who had overlooked him the previous year! Ranji was actually in his fourth year before he received the honour, and though we have often been assured it had nothing to do with the fact that he was an Indian, one may be permitted a tinge of doubt. It may not have been that any colour bar was involved: a Frenchman might have been equally handicapped in trying to convince people that he was good at so English a game. Perhaps Jackson's Indian experiences in 1892–3 helped him to realise that those of other than English stock could be fine cricketers. Jackson had seen Ranji bat the previous year, but had not been impressed. He would often comment ruefully on his mistake in later years. For myself, I imagine that Ranji's hopes were not furthered by the fact that he spent two years at Fitzwilliam Hall before moving to Trinity in 1892. To be at a 'fashionable' college still helps sometimes, and may have done so even more then.

In 1894 Jackson joined with his former Cambridge captain, Woods, in one of the most remarkable feats ever achieved in the Gentlemen v. Players series. He and Woods bowled unchanged throughout the two innings, with these figures:

	First Innings				Second Innings			
	O.	M.	R.	W.	O.	M.	R.	W.
Woods	24.2	8	61	4	24.4	6	63	2
Jackson	24	8	36	5	24	7	41	7

Jackson also made 63, the highest score of the match, which was won by the Gentlemen by an innings and 37 runs before four o'clock on the second day. Since this fixture has now fallen into desuetude, it is perhaps right to offer a reminder that in its day – and the 1890s were emphatically its day – it was considered, by most cricketers, quite as important as any Test match.

Jackson would have been a sure choice for Stoddart's Australian team in the winter of 1894–5, but now that his Cambridge days were over he never had the time to travel abroad in the winter. All his Test cricket was played in this country. What a loss this was to England – and to Australia! His Test career continued in 1896, when G.H.S. Trott's Australians visited us, and he did not miss a Test match at home from then until he retired. He played in twenty Tests in all, all against Australia, scoring 1415 runs at an average of nearly 49 (which would have been a splendid figure even in the run-soaked Twenties and Thirties), and taking 33 wickets for 24 apiece. In all first-class matches, he scored 16,251 runs, average 33, and took 834 wickets at an average of 19. As with two other famous Yorkshire cricketers, Sutcliffe and Leyland, his batting average for Test cricket was much higher than that for more run-of-the-mill affairs.

In 1896, a low-scoring series, Jackson made 44 and 45 in his two best innings. He also scored 51 against the Australians on a bad wicket at Lord's in the MCC match – the match when Pougher of Leicestershire put in such a remarkable spell of bowling, and the Australians were all out for 18. Jackson seemed to have a habit of being around when Australia made low scores. In 1902, for Yorkshire, he and Hirst had them all out in a famous match at Leeds for 23. Jackson took five for 12, including the last four wickets (Hopkins, Kelly, Jones and Howell) in five balls. He was in the field that same year when Hirst and Rhodes bowled Australia out in the first Test at Edgbaston for 36. Nineteen hundred and two was also the year of his best bowling performance for Yorkshire, when he took eight for 13 against Lancashire. He was a fast-medium bowler, who varied his pace skilfully and sometimes brought the ball back sharply from the off. Many people speak of the ease and beauty of his action.

In the meantime, the 1899 Australians had come and won the rubber. After the first Test, in which Jackson failed, W.G. Grace was dropped, and MacLaren was appointed captain. This has always been a puzzling episode. Jackson was senior to MacLaren, both at Harrow and in the England side. Furthermore, though MacLaren had twice toured Australia, he had been out of first-class cricket that season. C.B. Fry, who was at the meeting of the selection committee, says that 'it was quite forgotten that by order of seniority and on the score of at least equal merit, F.S. Jackson ought to have had the reversion of the captaincy (upon W.G.'s retirement) even if Archie MacLaren was brought in to raise the batting strength. It was true that Archie possessed a full knowledge of the Australian personnel owing to his recent experience in Australia, but I do not believe that any of those present at the selection committee realised that in bringing him in in place of W.G. they were going over the head of F.S. Jackson. I did not.' This seems scarcely credible, though selection committees have been known to do curious things! (Is it not alleged that a selector once handed in his considered team without noticing that it did not contain a wicket-keeper?) But whatever actually happened, the consequences for England were unhappy. While it is easy to speak with the advantage of hindsight, one may doubt whether the 1899 rubber, and, even more, that of 1902, would have been lost with Jackson at the helm. Jackson's superior qualities – not necessarily as a man or a cricketer, but for that particular job – were recognised with happy results in 1905; but after he retired from first-class cricket in 1907, MacLaren was recalled, and in 1909 the rubber was lost again, against an Australian side which seemed rather less strong than that of four years before.

Whatever may be said about the inadequacy of statistics as a guide, they do give us some sort of yardstick by which to judge players of the past (and, after all, matches are won by statistics – i.e. by the side that makes most runs!). The qualities that make a captain, however, are imponderable. I do not judge MacLaren to have been a very good captain, partly because his supporters instinctively take up a defensive attitude when the question is raised, partly because he was apparently inclined, on the morning of a Test match, to survey his team and say 'Look what the selectors have given me this time!' or words to that effect. There is also the question of his playing Tate instead of Hirst in the decisive Manchester Test of 1902. I will not rehearse all that story again, but if Fry's account of it is accurate, MacLaren's behaviour seems to me appalling.

Jackson's outstanding merits as a captain have never, I think, been queried, least of all by those who played under him. He was a natural leader. Sometimes he was criticised for tactical decisions, as we shall see when we come to the 1905 series, but of what Test captain can that not be said? His success as a captain is the more remarkable in that he did not get very much practice at it, Lord Hawke retaining his command of Yorkshire throughout Jackson's career. Sir Pelham Warner, the gentlest of critics, says that Jackson 'had to wait some time' for the England captaincy, which does delicately imply that he might have been given it earlier! He was, in fact, offered it in 1903, when Warner himself gained the reversion.

In 1899 Jackson had a successful series, after his failures in the first Test, and in the final Test scored his second century against Australia, 118 out of 185 for the first wicket with Hayward (who went on to 137); but he does not seem to have been particularly fond of opening.

In the great rubber of 1902, Jackson was England's most reliable batsman. In the first Test he scored 53, supporting Tyldesley in a crisis when early wickets had fallen (this was the series when both Fry and Ranjitsinhji averaged less than 4). In the second Test, after two wickets had fallen for 0, he scored 55 not out, helping MacLaren to put on 102 before the game was washed out. In the third Test he failed as a batsman, though he took four wickets, the three in the second innings being those of Trumper, Hill (both when going very strongly) and Noble. In the fourth Test he scored 128 out of 262 in England's first innings, going in at number six after Palairet, Abel, MacLaren and Ranjitsinhji were all out, 15 runs between them. In the fifth Test he scored 49 in England's second innings, and his batting, in the view of many who were there, did as much to win that match as Jessop's, especially in the pre-lunch period on the last day, before Jessop had really got going. On this occasion he batted at number five, and the first four in the order – MacLaren, Palairet, Tyldesley, Hayward – scored 13 between them. Had it not been for Jackson's resistance, Jessop would never have had the chance to play his glorious innings.

In only one season, 1898, could he play for Yorkshire regularly, but all told he scored more than ten thousand runs, and took more than five hundred wickets, for his county.

He was a strong, well-built man, standing nearly six feet high, with (by the standards of those days) a not unduly lavish golden-brown moustache. Fry says he was 'exceptionally good-looking in the Anglo-Saxon Guards officer way'. He was famous for his impeccable turn-out on the field. He had, says Hubert Preston in the 1948 *Wisden*, 'exceptional courage which amounted to belief in his own abilities'. It is this theme to which those who knew him constantly recur. P.F. Warner: 'He never underrated bowlers, nor did he overrate them; he merely played each ball on its merits.' This recalls the dictum attributed to W.G.: 'There is no crisis in cricket: there is only the next ball.' E.H.D. Sewell: 'All that Jackson did on the cricket field he did so easily that it seemed to be the only thing to do.' Wilfred Rhodes: 'He . . . possessed the gift of a fine temperament, with plenty of confidence and pluck, and always appeared at his best on great occasions, especially when fighting with his back to the wall.' Canon F.H. Gillingham: 'He always seemed to have that extra reserve of strength to compete with any cricket crisis, however severe.' Sir Home Gordon: 'It was his unexampled coolness that was so astounding; an unruffled calm arising from justified confidence in what he himself could do. His concentration was abnormal. . . . I think it must be no exaggeration to say that no one ever saw Jackson hesitate.' C.B. Fry makes the same point, but one passage he wrote on Jackson is worth quoting in full:

'Not only has he an extraordinary number of different strokes of all kinds, but he has a quite notable ability of adapting these strokes without altering them, except in the matter of timing, to all kinds of bowling and to all kinds of wickets. Many batsmen, and good ones, have one game for fast wickets and another for slow, one for good-length bowling and another for bad-length bowling. F.S. Jackson has one game of a most comprehensive and elastic kind which he plays with consummate confidence always, and which he brings into effective relation with all conditions of play. Perhaps, among modern batsmen, there is no one who maintains what may be described as perpetual uniformity of style on every kind of wicket and against every kind of bowling as he does, with the possible exception of Victor Trumper.

'Probably the secret of this uniformity is nothing more nor less than a settled habit of watching the ball from the bowler's hand to the pitch, and from the pitch on to the bat, and of taking every ball as it comes absolutely and entirely on its independent merits; and then – of just playing it quite naturally. Such a method brings the easy and the difficult into the same plane, provided the batsman has versatility and what, for want of a better name, we call genius.'

It is interesting, incidentally, that *Wisden* for 1906 criticises Trumper for trying to play the same free game as he had done in 1902, even though it was not bringing results. This criticism seems a little odd, for one would have thought that a dashing game on wet wickets, such as Trumper employed so successfully in a very wet season in 1902, would have been even more successful on the comparatively dry wickets of 1905. But then no rules, no generalisations can ever be applied to Trumper. He will always be the most enchanting, and the most maddening, cricketer of them all. (It is interesting, too, that Warner says of Trumper 'batting seemed simply a part of himself', which is just the kind of thing people also said of Jackson.)

Nineteen hundred and five was Jackson's last cricketing year. He played only one or two matches in 1906 and 1907, and first-class cricket never saw him again. Nevertheless it was very appropriate for a man who was something of a perfectionist that he should retire at the height of his ability and success, needing no apologists as his powers faded.

It need hardly be said of such a man that his usefulness did not end with his retirement from first-class cricket. In 1915 he entered parliament as the Unionist member for the Howdenshire division of Yorkshire, and represented it for eleven years. One day in the House of Commons Winston Churchill, who had been his fag at Harrow (it must have made an interesting combination), introduced him to Lloyd George. Lloyd George swiftly said: 'I have been looking all my life for the man who gave Winston Churchill a hiding at school.'

This is not the place to discuss F.S. Jackson's political career at length. He was not, perhaps, of the same political stature as his distinguished father (Lord Allerton, as he became). At the same time, he showed himself a very capable parliamentarian, and it is entirely untrue that, as I once heard alleged, he was the original of the famous (and no doubt mythical) back-bencher, whose one speech in many years of service in the Commons was 'Will somebody please shut that damned window?' In fact, when he wanted to make his maiden speech, the debate went unfavourably for a while, and the Speaker passed him a note: 'I have dropped you in the batting order; it's a sticky wicket.' Then, later, when things were going well: 'Get your pads on: you're next in.' This story is recounted by Hubert Preston in the 1948 *Wisden*, but I confess I have my doubts of it. The House of Commons gives no maiden speaker, least of all so distinguished a maiden, a troublesome passage – unless he sets out to ask for trouble.

Jackson became Financial Secretary to the War Office in 1922, and in 1923 was chairman of the organisation of the Unionist party (as it was then known). In 1927, he went to India as Governor of Bengal, where he behaved with exactly the calm and courage one would expect in the face of an attempted assassination. His long friendship with Ranjitsinhji must have been of value to him in this job. He acquired the 'Colonel' in his title through service in the Boer War (with the Royal Lancasters, of all regiments!) and in the Great War, when he raised and commanded a West Yorkshire battalion. He was still, in a sense, in the front line in 1940, when his London home was bombed.

After retiring from cricket, he took up golf. It is told that he spent the whole of one winter practising strokes in front of a mirror, with the aid of the best advice and the best textbooks, before he ever struck a ball. When he did so, in a very short time he was playing off a handicap of one. This would be typical both of his character, and his natural ability for any kind of ball game.

He was President of MCC in 1921, chairman of the England selection committee in 1934 (a very difficult year in which to be a selector), and ultimately succeeded Lord Hawke as President of Yorkshire. In 1943 he presided over the very useful committee appointed by MCC to consider the rebuilding of first-class cricket in the post-war years.

He died on 9 March 1947. I think it is no exaggeration to say that he was one of the very best cricketers – perhaps *the* best all-rounder, saving W.G. – ever to represent England, as well as being a great gentleman. His work in other fields was more important than anything he did for cricket; for cricket, when all is said and done, is only a game. But it is a good game, it is worth serving, and he had every right to take pride in the season of his apotheosis, 1905, henceforth always to be known to cricketers as 'Jackson's year'.

THE THREE WS

Ivo Tennant

By 1953 the 'Three Ws' were in their prime. Opinion differs to this day as to which was the finest batsman. Between 1949 and 1960 they scored Test hundreds between them and their overall figures are similar. Walcott scored 3798 runs in 44 Tests, averaging 56.68; Weekes 4455 in 48 Tests at 58.61; Worrell 3860 in 51 Tests at 49.48. Yet figures and the fact that each came from Barbados was about all they had in common. Walcott lacked in polish and charm, and at times was reserved to the point of being suspicious; Weekes was small, crude and humorous; Worrell gazelle-like with his nicely barbed Bajan sense of humour.

Walcott, who initially played for West Indies as a wicket-keeper, was probably the most difficult of the three to bowl at on a good pitch, particularly in the Caribbean. He could strike the ball with tremendous power off either front or back foot. He was also somewhat self-centred. When, in 1950, West Indies made their memorable total of 730 for three against Cambridge University, Weekes was in line for the fastest century of the season. Worrell continually gave him the strike. Weekes claimed Walcott would not have done that: he would have kept the bowling for himself. Weekes was a compact back-foot player, perhaps the most complete batsman of the three. Like Walcott, he pulverised good and bad bowling alike on true pitches and he became, through his Lancashire League experience, as competent on a bad pitch as any West Indian with the possible exception of Headley. Worrell by contrast was full of grace and deft touches, not so sound against pace which perhaps was why he scored fewer runs in the Caribbean than the other two, but the best of the three when the ball wobbled about. Walcott considered Worrell to have more natural ability than he possessed. Worrell, of course, had an advantage over the other two in that he could bowl.

Jeffrey Stollmeyer, who saw the best of each of them, makes this comparison of Weekes and Worrell, whom Weekes considered to be his best friend, in *Everything under the Sun*:

'I considered Worrell the sounder in defence, Weekes the greater attacking force; Worrell the more graceful, Weekes the more devastating; Worrell the more effective on soft wickets, Weekes the more so on hard wickets. Worrell gives the bowler less to work on, Weekes has the wider range of strokes. Both are good starters but Weekes is the more businesslike; Worrell appeared to be enjoying an afternoon's sport; whereas Weekes was on the job six hours a day. Due possibly to his wider stroke range, Weekes took more chances than did Worrell and the latter was probably, all told, the sounder in principle but this did not extend outside the realms of actual batsmanship for Worrell was not as capable a runner as Weekes was, nor was he as meticulous over the little accessories that make the complete batsman.

'Both men were delightful characters on and off the field, cheerful and humorous. They were both match-winning characters. Worrell, in addition to his batting, bowled left-handed either at a pace well above medium or slow-length stuff. Indeed, he was quite equal to the task of opening our Test attack in 1950, and whenever he bowled his slows he kept the runs down. In the gully or at short leg Worrell took many brilliant catches which, together with his quickness of eye and footwork, were indicative of amazingly quick reflexes. He was the complete cricketer.'

Stollmeyer goes on to praise Weekes's slip fielding.

By 1953 Worrell had tightened up his defence as a result of playing on English pitches. He was the most orthodox of the 'Three Ws' despite having been largely self-taught. He would not, for example, attempt to cover-drive an off-spinner who was extracting turn. Generally he would watch the ball on to the face of the bat and play it late, hitting it as swiftly as Walcott without resorting to brute force. When Worrell and Walcott were batting during their record partnership of 574, Worrell reproved his partner for hitting the ball too hard. The fielders, he pointed out, were not having to run.

Worrell's batting average was lower than those of Walcott and Weekes probably for two reasons: they retired at a younger age and they were also probably more concerned than he was with amassing big scores and records. Worrell felt that a batsman should not be judged on the number of centuries he scored. When Worrell went out to bat he was usually in a relaxed frame of mind, often as not having been asleep in the dressing-room. He would wash his eyes out, wander to the crease, greet the wicket-keeper and then enjoy himself.

The 'Three Ws' were friends, certainly; but there were some jealousies beneath the bond. Before and after their playing days Walcott and Worrell did not get on. Worrell had resented Walcott being made vice-captain instead of him for the 1957 tour of England; Walcott in turn seemed to resent Worrell's fame in later life. As batsmen, though, there was markedly little rivalry between the three.

THE TRUTH ABOUT TRUEMAN

Brian Statham

Half the people of the North seem to be convinced that Freddie Trueman and I are rivals. I suppose that logically that's a fair enough assumption – we are both fast bowlers, we come from those cat-and-dog counties Yorkshire and Lancashire.

Yet, in fact, nothing is further from the truth. We are the best of pals, and I don't give tuppence how many wickets he takes. Admittedly, if he's knocking them over at one end, I might go a little bit harder myself to see if I can chip in with a couple. But that's just a normal reaction. I would do that whoever was bowling with me.

But the popular picture of two surly fast bowlers, envying each other's success and not speaking to each other, is a million miles off beam. I don't care if Fred picks up all ten when we are playing for England, as long as I am satisfied in myself that I have bowled as well as I can.

As for not speaking . . . we jabber away like a couple of old women over a pot of tea. And, in all the time we have been playing and touring together, we have never had a cross word.

I should think Fred feels the same way about bowling with me. We are both much more interested in the result of the match than in our own achievements. I have seen him with a 'ton' (a hundred runs) against his name overnight, and the only effect it has had is for him to come out and do his darnedest to improve matters next morning.

Fred, with his hands-on-hips postures and his glares, has a reputation for being a temperamental character. And rightly so.

Compared with his earlier days, he is a well-mannered angel. But he still has flashes of temper and occasional outbursts of language that would burn the hair off a coconut. I don't take any notice. They don't mean anything – at least, not anything lasting.

He's a likeable chap with a heart as big as a soup-plate. If he likes you he would do anything for you – except one thing. He won't lend anybody money. That's his principle and he stands firmly by it. He wouldn't even lend money to me, and I suppose we are closer than any other two players in the England dressing-room.

I have always enjoyed bowling with Fred, and I reckon myself lucky to have been in harness with him for such a long time (we first came together in the West Indies on the tour of 1953–4). It's a help when you know the bowler at the other end is trying as hard as you are.

Yet, terrific fighter that he is, his bowling still depends to a certain extent on that fiery temperament of his. He can be a thoroughly nasty proposition sometimes in even the easiest of conditions. It depends on his mood.

And the batsmen themselves have a certain amount of control over how he bowls to them. If they play him well and firmly, then Fred looks upon it as an honourable duel, even going so far as to give grudging credit.

But if they play at him and miss a lot, then woe betide them! Batsmen not batting well, Fred expects to see go. And if the luck runs with them and they stay, then Fred becomes thoroughly angry and gets stuck into them. That is his attitude to the game.

You never get to know anybody properly in this game of cricket until you have lived with them for a while. Fred and I found we hit it off so well together – we shared rooms on the last trip to the West Indies – because we are similar in some ways, unlikely as that may seem to spectators watching from a distance.

He is a restless sort of person, not fond of going to bed early. I am like that, too. When we had to bed down early during the Tests we would read to all hours of the night.

Yes, we share much common ground, and we like bowling together, but we have got our differences, too. For instance, we quite often differ on how we think we can get a batsman out. Fred might go for a leg-stick attack while I fancy the off-side. It doesn't mean that either of us is wrong, merely that we approach our problem differently. After all, I have yet to meet the batsman who is infallible on any stump.

Again, it will surprise those who still class Fred as something of a wild bowler (so wrongly!) that he is a deep thinker about the game. He has a prodigious memory for batsmen's weaknesses, details of matches and even scores.

And on Yorkshire cricket history he is a regular one-man brains trust. He can tell you details of their championship-winning sides from the year dot, when players retired, their runs, wickets, and anything you like to ask.

Fred Trueman now is a complete fast bowler. His erratic days are behind him and his control now is better than most. He does most of his work through the air, swinging the ball considerably. He cuts one back off the seam occasionally, but he is essentially an out-swing bowler.

He describes himself as a middle-and-leg bowler, which I presume means that he starts his swing on the middle- and leg-stumps. His bowling, in fact, is a complete contrast to my own, for my target is invariably the off-stump, with the ball doing little or nothing through the air but moving either way off the seam. In addition, Freddie is inclined to pitch a shorter length than I do.

But he has more or less perfected a good flat yorker, which is good theory – get them on the back foot and then throw in the yorker.

Yet to talk of Fred in terms of theory is not right. He is essentially a human, full-blooded cricketer, full of moods, whims and brilliance.

Typical of him was the incident at Johannesburg in 1960, when we were playing together in a private tour that was full of good fun and good cricket. The number-one requirement of that trip was to provide entertainment. And, as you might guess, Fred did his bit to the full.

When this gag was dreamed up, he was batting with Tom Graveney. During the tea-break, Tom came up to Fred and told him that Jackie McGlew, who usually bowled leg-breaks, was coming on to bowl after tea. As McGlew had received as many bouncers from Fred as any man, it was reckoned it would be a good gag if he bowled one at Fred.

Said Tom: 'Jackie says it will be second ball after tea, so watch out for it. It will go down the leg-side and you are to swish your bat after it has gone by – as if it is too fast for you.'

'O.K.,' said Fred. 'Anything for a laugh.'

Sure enough, second ball after tea, McGlew, who had been bowling slow off a six-yard run, suddenly turned and marched miles back in this giant Wanderers ground. The crowd hummed, and then this tiny figure turned and hurtled back towards the stumps to let go a bumper, the genuine article.

The only thing wrong with the plan was that the ball, instead of whistling harmlessly down the leg-side, was pitched on the middle stump and came close to nailing our Fred, as he nearly ducked into the line of it.

I have never seen such indignation in one man in all my life. His hands were jabbed on his hips, and he bristled up the wicket at McGlew. The crowd loved it.

Fred was outraged when he got back to the pavilion. He was absolutely certain McGlew had laid a trap for him. I talked a long long time to him, pointing out that it was an accident and that a chap like McGlew wouldn't be able to control the direction of a bouncer.

Even in the end I don't think Fred was completely convinced.

You will hear a lot of nonsense talked about Fred Trueman. He has been found guilty of far more things than he ever did. He has taken the blame and never squealed back.

Unlike most of the critics, I know him. And I could not wish for a better friend.

Chapter 3

FAR PAVILIONS

ORIENT LINE

The CRICKETER

Reproduced from a special menu card used on the "Orontes," in which the Australian Test Team returned to Australia.

WINTER HOLIDAYS

AUSTRALIA & BACK

£140

'A Country Vicar'

In April 1895, I was playing cricket in Corfu. 'It is the fairest island that exists,' wrote John Addington Symonds, 'and . . . I wonder how Gladstone had it in his heart to resign this garden of the Mediterranean to the Greeks. . . . You live in a perpetual Claude Lorraine picture of the most tranquil beauty.'

Never was truer word written; and no one regretted more the end of the British occupation than the Corfiots themselves.

The one surviving relic of the old country, when I was there, was the cricket. It still flourished. There was a men's club; and all the little boys who could procure, or manufacture, a bat and ball played the noble game. In addition they used the English terms, though their language was mainly Greek. 'Innings', 'run', 'catch', 'bowl', 'stump', 'score': one heard the familiar words coming from the lips of dark-skinned urchins who could not speak English at all.

I do not know why I should have taken a cricket-bag to Corfu. Eric and I journeyed thither in February, and our object was to shoot in Albania. But my old bag went with us; and, when our shooting was over, we found the 'Golden Island' so pleasant that we stayed on for another month.

One day an English warship – HMS *Collingwood* – anchored outside Corfu Harbour. Immediately a deputation from the men's club called at our hotel. If they could arrange a cricket match, between the Island and the ship, would I play for Corfu? I said I would.

Barren waste

The fixture was made. The day of the match arrived. I made my way to the ground. *The ground!* I have played on some bad wickets, but that was the worst! It was on the Great Square, near the citadel – a barren waste, almost destitute of grass. The wickets were pitched on a footpath, since that was considered the smoothest spot. There was no matting – simply the bare earth, worn by the passage of feet into countless little hills and holes and plentifully sprinkled with small stones.

The Corfu captain – an Englishman resident in the island, engaged in business – welcomed me with great stateliness and inquired what position I usually occupied in the field.

I said I would gladly field anywhere he liked, but that I frequently kept wicket.

He announced firmly that he meant to occupy that post himself:

without actually saying so, he led me to believe he was extraordinarily good there. 'Do you bowl?' he concluded.

I said I tried to do so.

'What style?' he asked. 'Fast – slow? Roundarm – overarm? – Which?'

I mentioned my humble lobs. I added the information that, on occasion, I also attempted overarm.

He snuffed me out again. He already had a lob-bowler – an excellent one; but would I send down one or two of my overarms for his inspection.

I acquiesced with meekness. He took up his position behind the nearer wicket, and waved me to the further one. 'We shall not do the pitch any harm!' he said.

I felt that was indeed impossible, but I was too tactful to say so. And I felt a certain slight antipathy towards the captain.

I had not bowled a ball for over six months, but my first one happened to be straight, and it hurried along off the sun-baked footpath. It just missed the bails. The captain took it full on the end of his thumb. I regret to record the fact that it dislocated that member.

The captain seemed a little vexed and a good deal hurt. He uttered frequent exclamations of pain and annoyance in three languages – Greek, Italian, and simple English. I pulled the joint in again and expressed my profound sorrow for the occurrence. I also improvised a bandage for his thumb and a sling for his arm.

Then the Naval men arrived – six or seven officers in their eleven – and, after mutual introductions, the unfortunate incident was described in detail. Our own players were also filtering in, and each one was regaled with the same sad story. The captain was most voluble.

The tale appeared to me to grow somewhat with repetition. I caught little scraps of the recital – '. . . pace terrific' – '. . . comes off the ground like lightning,' '. . . never more surprised in my life' – '. . . a real fast bowler' – '. . . most alarming!' The sailors seemed to eye me with some apprehension.

The match began. We lost the toss and went out to field, amid the applause of a considerable crowd: Corfu had gathered in force. The captain, who had decided to umpire, but to retain command of his team, threw the ball to me. I felt something was expected of me, and I endeavoured to rise to the occasion. I shared the attack with the lob-bowler (so-called). He was a Greek, with a fine, long, high-sounding name, like Ossopiledonpelion, or Palaeocastrizza, or Polatianó, or Popocatepetl – I believe it began with a P. He played in a bright red shirt and very tight, white trousers. He bowled the fastest 'daisy-cutters' I have ever seen delivered! They zigzagged about on the adamantine, uneven wicket in a manner frankly terrifying. Often they beat batsman, wicketkeeper and long-stop, and each time that happened it meant two or three byes. My own deliveries sometimes defeated two people, but my scarlet-shirted colleague was long-stopping at that end, and he was almost invincible. His shins must have been made of iron. At the smallest provocation he would hurl the ball at the wicket. I hated that habit of his, for he had a devastating power of throwing, and the wicketkeeper – a poor, craven creature – would always skip out of the way and leave the matter to me. To do the 'terrible Greek' full justice, however, he usually hit the stumps.

We got our opponents out for 40: 'Mr Extras' was easily the top-scorer. Then we amassed 55.

Tip and run

But the British Navy was not done with. Time was growing short, so they played 'tip and run'. Often they ran without any 'tip'. Unfortunately Popocatepetl's aim deteriorated and overthrows were frequent. They scored 44 for 6 and declared, leaving us 20 minutes in which to make 30. Of course we accepted that challenge and 'went for' the runs. We did it – on the stroke of time – with one wicket to spare.

It was a great match – a Homeric contest – worthy of Greek and Trojan (I mean British) heroes. Though the good ship *Collingwood* finally went under, it was with colours bravely flying. Though Corfu just scrambled home as winners, it was by the most infinitesimal margin. Honours were fairly divided.

I played in two other 'matches', but they were inferior to the first. The *Collingwood* had gone, so there were no genuine opponents. We had to arrange sides – improvise a more or less imaginary opposition. Once, I remember, I played against Popocatepetl and I believe he got me given out l.b.w. I wondered then, and I wonder still, when a ball pitches nine times, how many bounds must be in a straight line between wicket and wicket? All the nine or only one? And, if one, is it the first or the last which counts? It is a question for the MCC!

But I captured many wickets. I maintained my reputation.

For the period of one month I was considered a great bowler! A fast bowler! A dangerous bowler! A Demon Bowler! Another Spofforth!

And all on account of one ball, which the Corfu captain took on the end of his thumb!

LONDON

R.A. Fitzgerald

A hot night's journey was in store for the Nine leaving Toronto at 11.30 p.m. on Saturday evening, they arrived at London on Sunday morning, September 8, at 7 a.m.

'The Nine' involves an explanation. Sing, ye Muses, the charms that detained the three. Who were the three Graces, and who were the three absentees? Suffice it to record that the amorous Appleby, the Ojibbeway and San Francisco had applied for leave to spend the Sabbath in the same pew with three of the loveliest ladies of Toronto, and leave was granted on condition of their turning up in time for the morrow's match.

The morning of Sunday, September 8, was sultry and oppressive. The Nine crawled into the Tecompsee Hotel languid and dusty after the night's journey. The hotel was not up, the rooms were not ready, there was only one bath in the house, and it was not very clear where or when that one bath might be available. A fiend in human guise suggested a stroll to the Sulphur baths. It did not sound savoury, but by this time the nostrils were seasoned to oil. We were now in the kingdom of Paraffin. We had struck oil long before arriving at London, it struck us as very beastly, but then it must be remembered we had no share beyond the smell in this flourishing department of trade. Oil is cheap, not to say nasty; we had long been acquainted with its marvellous properties, we had detected it in every room and smelt it in every passage from Quebec to London. It was brought home to us here, or rather we were brought to its home.

The bread tasted of oil, the beer was impregnated with oil, the ice was oily, the attendants were oily. We thought a sulphur bath would at least be free from the all pervading element; but no! there was oil on the troubled waters of the sulphur bath! The stroll was a half hour's walk through wide streets, at that early hour, without signs of life. It was not the cool, nor was it the fragrant hour of morn. The sulphur bath is extremely cold, we dipped our toes in it, but could not be persuaded to venture further. The oil was preferable to the sulphurous exhalation. The Thames is not a magnificent river. The stream was very low and its colour creamy. Westminster Bridge is not a gorgeous structure. We passed St Paul's Cathedral on our return to the hotel. We were not tempted to linger in its precincts. London is a loyal town, it has its Pall Mall and Piccadilly, and later in the day we were pleased to find it had its loungers. It is called the Forest City. The neighbourhood is indeed lovely. It is the centre of a rich agricultural district. The Middlesex farmers rank amongst the best in Canada. Already preparations are being made for an Autumn exhibition of agricultural produce. London was founded about the year 1824, by General Simcoe. It does not show any signs of such antiquity. It appears to have started into life within the last ten years and to be now growing fast. The visitors were very hospitably entertained by several of the leading residents. Amongst them must be mentioned Mr Beecher, QC, Messrs Harris and Griffin. The attendance during the match was very gratifying, and a more appreciative circle had never yet been formed. It might have been a match in the Midland Counties of the Old Country. So to the cricket.

Monday, Sept. 9. – The Three did not turn up in time. The ground, as usual, deserves a remark. We walked over it before we were aware that we had passed the wickets. These were marked out on a small plateau, the only one visible, in dangerous vicinity to a long range of wooden buildings, afterwards discovered to be 'The Barracks'. Rifle pits abounded on all sides. The barracks at some recent period must have sustained a siege. However a fair wicket was obtained, dead from thunder showers and evidently not a run getting one. The first question that arose was 'How many' to allow for a swipe into the bedrooms of the barracks. Was it a lost ball in the scullery? Might the long-stop lean against the palings? These little questions were soon amicably adjusted. It was agreed that no Scotchman should stand long-stop, the temptation to scratch his back being too tempting to resist. The Captain (of course) won the toss and in the absence of one of 'the gentlemen in waiting', W.G. and Hornby went to the wickets. The sun was now shining and the ominous clouds that had copiously discharged their contents up to twelve o'clock rolled away. Messrs Gillean and Wright bowling, both fast and straight. Nothing occurred till the fifth over, when 'Mr Grace was caught by Henley, but it proved to be a ground ball'. The crowd was delighted 'as the umpire decided not out'. It may as well be stated that a hit to the fence scored 3, and over the fence 4. The Monkey was bowled in the tenth over of Gillean for 14. Hadow, the Unlucky, went in. To quote again, 'He made a fine cut for 1 which was well fielded by Mr Despard, of the Bank of Montreal, at long leg.' His stumps were then scattered by Wright. Mr G had made a few, but not without luck, he 'gave a splendid chance to Wright, as he sent the ball straight up, but it was beautifully muffled,' 44 for two wickets. Alfred succeeded and runs came quicker. A change was now made. Ebberts taking Wright's place. 'His delivery was from the shoulder, and he bowls a swift destructive ball.' Alfred was printed 'Tubbock' in the scores. 'Mr Tubbock was run out for 9,' his own fault; 52

for three wickets, of which Gilbert owned 30. George went in and 'slipped a ball for 1'; Gilbert was now sent home for a lucky score of 31, very well caught off a good hit at deep square leg by Hyman. The 'Gentlemen in waiting' had now arrived, and C.J. Ottoway went in. Runs were hard to get. The Honourable George 'was driven to his tent by Gillean, his wicket being entirely flattened out'; 56 for 5 wickets. The Ojibbeway only made 1. The other 'Gentleman in W.' took his place, love had less effect upon him for he made 12. Shooters made short work of the rest. The Unaffected only arrived in time to carry his bat out for 1. The innings closed for 89. The bowling of Messrs Gillean and Wright was admirable, the fielding was creditable, the long-stopping of Mr Fradd to the swift bowling was excellent. The Londoners were much pleased at the small score obtained by the visitors. It was the smallest hitherto obtained by them. It may be attributed to the bowling on a dead wicket being fast and straight, as well as to the accurate fielding, the 'return' being very noticeable, and making it difficult to achieve the second run for a hard hit. The Cockneys went in at 4 p.m. and at 5.30 were all out for 55. Hyman played resolutely, with some luck, as he was badly missed twice; he hit well to leg and faced the Tormentor, who bowled superbly, with great spirit. Eleven Londoners laid an egg a piece, and being market day it led to some merriment amongst the farmers' wives, six of them made 1 run apiece, 10 wickets fell for 43, and the remaining twelve contributed a dozen. If it was difficult to the Twelve, it was impossible for the Twenty-two to score. It was calculated that at least seven thousand spectators were on the ground, and the receipts must have amply rewarded the outlay.

Sept. 10. – The return match was resumed at noon. Very heavy storms had saturated the ground during the night, so that the chances of the Twenty-two dismissing the Twelve for another short innings improved. W.G. and Ottoway went to the wickets, W.G. not very fit and the Ojibbeway languid after his exercise at the ball of the previous evening. W.G. had wisely declined the hop and should have been fit to run for the Derby. Gillean and Ebberts commenced the bowling. The O. was given out l.b.w. having made 6, while W.G. made 2. This does not often occur. The Monkey went in and caused much amusement by stealing runs, and with Gilbert's aid the score rapidly mounted. Dr Bray has a curious corkscrew motion of the arm and provoked some laughter at his bowling. W.G. at last hit a ball over the fence, Which was only thirty-five yards from the wicket; the first hit out, which showed how dead the ground was as well as how true the bowling. It was soon repeated, however.

The Monkey was the next to go, bowled by a shooter of Whelan's; his 21 consisted of one three, one two, and sixteen singles, 98 for two wickets. Alfred to the wicket, and W.G. again hit over the fence. At two o'clock luncheon was called, 112 for two wickets being telegraphed, of which W.G. laid claim to 64. He had been badly missed at square leg. On resuming play Gilbert was the first to leave, caught at long on for a score of 76, 130 for three wickets. His score consisted of one five, four fours, three threes, eleven twos, and singles. Hadow maintained his ill luck, being bowled for nought; four wickets for 131. Alfred only secured 8. The Captain had intimated that it was desirable not to prolong the innings if possible, and consequently there was a little slogging which soon terminated the innings. George obtained 10, and the small offerings thankfully received raised the score to 161, of which the large number of 24 was given by extras. No time was lost and the Twenty-two were very busy in putting pads on and taking them off, until time was called. The result of this process was that 10 wickets were disposed of for 45 runs. This unfortunately necessitated another morning for the conclusion, and as time was pressing the third day's play commenced punctually at eleven.

Sept. 11. – The remaining eleven wickets gave little trouble. Hyman and Henley were very free with Rosa, but Appleby was ticklish at all times and allowed no liberties. The cockneys improved on their first journey by 10 runs. Total 65.

This was not a bad win – 130 runs to the good. The batting of the Canadians was again tested by the slow and fast ordeal of Rose and Appleby, and the same remark applies to the Middlesex lads as to their neighbours. They did not do themselves justice; the same unwillingness to open the shoulder, the same preconceived dread of the straight long hop. The Twenty-two were fair specimens of the youth of Canada, and their bowling was quite first class. The ground militated against a good display of cricket, the dead wicket equalising the good and indifferent player to a great degree. The Barracks, where luncheon was provided, are a pitiable sight. Rats and vermin had long since left them, as much too comfortless. They are rotting surely if slowly. The absence of the soldiers is as much deplored here as elsewhere. Mixing as we did with every class and listening to varied expressions of opinion, it is worthy of mention that we never heard the departure of the Red Man mentioned except with disapprobation. We do not pretend to analyse the policy, we only record facts. The ladies, as may well be supposed, are to a man, as they say in Ireland, against the withdrawal.

ENGLAND v LONDON

ENGLAND

ENGLAND		1st inn		2nd inn
W.G.Grace, c Hyman, b Gillean	31	c Cook, b Henley		76
A.N.Hornby, b Gillean	14	b Whelan		21
W.H.Hadow, b Wright	2	b Henley		0
A. Lubbock, run out	5	c Neville, b Whelan		8
Hon.G.Harris, b Ebberts	1	c Ebberts, b Saunders		10
C.K.Franceis, b Ebberts	12	b Gillean		3
C.J.Ottaway b Gillean	1	leg b w, b Gillean		6
E.Lubbock, c Wells, b Ebbert	9	b Saunders		6
W.M.Rose, b Ebberts	2	c Eberts, b Saunders		0
F.Pickering, b Gillean	5	c Danks, b Saunders		1
A.Appleby, not out	1	not out		4
R.A.Fitz-Gerald, b Gillean	0	c Ebberts, b Gillean		2
B 5, l-b 1	6	B 12,l-b 3, w b 9		24
Total	—89	Total		—161

LONDON		1st inn.		2nd inn
Street, c Pickering, b Rose	0	c Grace, b Rose		2
Dayrill, b Appleby	1	c Hadow, b Rose		3
Neville, c Harris, b Grace	0	leg b w, b Grace		4
Wells, c Grace, b Rose	7	c Grace, b Appleby		0
Whelan, b Appleby	9	c Hornby, b Grace		0
Henley, c Ottaway, b Rose	2	b Appleby		9
Goldie, b Appleby	0	b Appleby		2
Hyman, run out	18	b Appleby		9
Wright, c Ottaway, b Rose	0	c Grace, b Rose		0
Bray, b Appleby	1	absent		0
Shaw, b Rose	1	c Francis, b Grace		0
Patterson, c Grace, b Rose	1	b Appleby		0
Rae, b Appleby	0	b Grace		7
Saunders, c Fitz-Gerald, b Rose	0	c Grace b Rose		0
Cooke, leg b w, b Rose	0	b Rose		4
Ebberts, b Appleby	1	b Rose		9
Bradbeer, c A.Lubbock, b Rose	1	b Rose		3
Fradd, c E.Lubbock, b Rose	0	absent		0
Despard, c E.Lubbock, b Rose	0	b Appleby		0
Danks, c A.Lubbock, b Rose	2	c Grace, b Rose		1
M'Lean, b Appleby	7	c Grace, b Rose		2
Gillean, not out	0	not out		0
B 1, l-b 1, w b 2	4	B1, l-b 1		2
Total	—55	Total		—65

Matrimony is at a discount, and a street full of marriageable girls taunts the bachelor on the way to church in every town. The young Canadian is too busy to love – or at least to flirt. The Red Man was always ready for either emergency. There are no picnics, no strolls in the forest, no lunch at the barracks, no nothings that often led to something in the good old time.

The Londoners were not in any way behind Toronto in their desire to make the visit of the Twelve memorable. They had not been many hours at the Tecompsee Hotel before an elegant card was left upon the Captain, bearing the following not strange device:-

---

CRICKET CLUB BALL.

IN HONOUR OF THE ENGLISH CRICKETERS.

The Members of the London Cricket Club request the
pleasure of Mr. Fitzgerald's and Gentlemen Players of
England company at the City Hall on Monday evening the 9th
September, at half past eight o'clock.

Lady Patronesses.

Mrs Walker.	Mrs W.R. Meredith.	Mrs Hyman.
Mrs Street.	Mrs B. Waterman.	Mrs E.S. Birrell.
	Mrs H. Waterman.	

R.R. BROUGH,
Hon. Sec.

It is needless to say that the Twelve accepted, and a capital dance it was. A few friends had followed the fortunes of the rovers. Amongst them one young being, who had come from a considerable distance for another dance with Alfred the Great. Her name will not transpire; nor may she, perhaps, know herself who she is under the tender soubriquet of 'The Fly'. It is a touching little story. Alfred caught a fly in one of the pauses of his wild waltz, and the lady had begged him to give it to her as a memento – imprisoning the helpless souvenir in her locket – a fly-leaf in a love-story, which we may fairly claim as original.

It was during the London match that the little difference between Stiff and Strong, the reporters, took place. London was very hospitable, and the reporters fell in for their share of the general greeting. Hence the adventure in which Strong and the lamp-post were the central figures. The Tecompsee Hotel was not equal to the Rossyn. Mosquitoes were abundant here; we cannot say the same for the provisions, although the landlord was very civil.

On the night of the ball an awful thunderstorm gathered over the town; it broke in a deluge of rain, accompanied by lightning, which defies description. Sheets of electric light illumined the dark sky, revealing vistas of the surrounding forest, and forming a display of the elements at war, such as is never witnessed in Europe. Earth, air, and water are on a grander scale; the elements have more elbow-room for their effects apparently – at any rate they leave that impression. Fires destroy whole towns; hurricanes sweep every sail off the waters; everything partakes of the wholesale on the great continent. The human body does not increase in proportion to the room allotted it to grow in; on the contrary, it rather decreeases in size.

Mr Becher, QC, entertained several of the Twelve each evening of their stay; his house is situated overlooking the Thames, and it might almost be in Richmond Park; forest glades in every direction; forest trees of no mean dimensions. The humming-birds hovered over the flowers in his garden, evidently tended by fair hands, and bright with thoughts of English homes. Several birds of beautiful plumage were seen here. The vicinity of the forest city is very attractive – seen, as we saw it, in its summer garb. Mr Harris was equally attentive to others of the Twelve, and the visit, though short, was prolific of friendship. The match concluded in time for the Captain to take up a challenge presented by two fair ladies of London. They were the champion croquet players of the district, and the Captain and W.G., with some trembling, took up the mallet. Victory inclined to the visitors, not without a good struggle; the Captain's object in visiting America was not to be beaten at any game; it will be seen hereafter whether he succeeded. It is satisfactory, also, to record the success of the junior croquet game, in which Alfred the Great and George, by good luck, managed to get home first in an encounter with two young ladies just out of the schoolroom. But the scream of the approaching engine warns us to take our tickets for Hamilton. The platform was crowded with kind friends, and we were off at last with the warmest wishes for our success in the States.

IN DARKEST BURMA

Brigadier G.P.L. Weston

The end of the Japanese War found a Brigade of a famous Indian Division garrisoning, and attempting to maintain order in the province of Tenasserim in darkest Burma. Here there is no real cold weather and the annual rainfall would submerge all but the mightiest of England's pavilions.

Cricket possibilities were small and we had practically no sports gear but we had two priceless assets – unlimited Jap labour, 19,000 to boot, and a very, very heavy roller. The choosing of a site for a wicket proved something of a problem as the only possible area in Thaton, where Brigade Headquarters was situated, had already been purloined for a light aircraft landing strip. A compromise was finally achieved, twelve yards of flattish ground provided a net at Thaton and the Baluch Regiment, who had also won a roller, set about preparing a ground at Kyaikto some 40 miles north.

The Japs were mobilised and harnessed in incredible numbers to the roller. Others moved in an endless procession carrying empty petrol tins, which they filled with water at a stream, which ran a hundred yards or so from the net site, and deposited the accumulation of water on the pitch. Tent walls provided very adequate nets. The same scenes of furious activity raged at Kyaikto, the venue of the forthcoming contest on Sunday, 9 December.

Our equipment was like the curate's egg. The best features were one good Imperial Driver, with the handle bound by 4 × 2 (born 1936, still going strong), one box and *The Cap*. For ballista we had one very whiskery cricket ball and two hockey balls. Pads were cunningly

SOUTH OF THE BILIN

Major N. M. Mischler, c Wilde b Waddell 16	lbw Sawan	0
Lt. D. E. Boyle, c Waddell Lt. D. E. Boyle, b Wilde 15	not out......................................	23
Brig. G. P. L. Weston Brig. G. c. Martinnant b Bridget 30	c Waddell b Wilde.....................	16
Major P. Edwards, b Wilde 10	c and b Sawan	0
Brig. M. R. Smeeton, c Hardinge b Sawan 6	b Sawan	0
Lt.-Col. K. Dunlop, c Bridget b Daani Ram 0	c Waddell b Sawan	0
S./Sgt. Braganza, b Sawan 10	st Hardinge b Wilde.....................	1
Major J. R. B. Kean, b Sawan 5	b Sawan	8
Capt. D. Bayley, c Waddell b Sawan 0		
Sepoy Madurai, not out..................................... 6		
Cpl. Shaw b Wilde 4	b Sawan	14
Extras 7	Extras	–

Total 109	Total (for 8 wkts. dec.)	62
Sawan, 4 for 13; Wilde, 3 for 18; Bridget 1 for 24; Waddell, 1 for 9; Daani Ram, 1 for 13.	Sawan, 6 for 21; Wilde, 2 for 10.	

constructed by the farrier of a Mule Company using bamboo and saddle numnahs, batting gloves were *non est* – but we had one fine left-hand wicket-keeping glove. Bamboos were successfully fashioned into stumps and bails.

Practice was undertaken with a will and nets were held every evening from 4.30 to 6 p.m., when darkness stopped play. The Brigade Gurkha Defence Platoon provided the outfielders, their enthusiasm was unbounded and their determination to field the ball proved most alarming – a soccer tendency to head the ball or take a flying kick at it in mid-air being among the more disturbing features. A ball once retrieved was hurled at once with roars of laughter at either the luckless batsman or at the next bowler when about to deliver the ball. The wicket surprisingly proved to be an excellent one, it was crushed into submission and all players survived safely for the great day, though three postings at the eleventh hour caused a final desperate search for substitutes.

Two days before the match a great coup was achieved – the purchase of three brand-new cricket balls from far-off Rangoon. Here indeed was class with a new ball for both innings and the doubtful hope, which was never realised, of one side scoring 200 runs and being able to demand the new ball.

On the fateful Sunday the team were early afoot and were safely ferried by the Japs across the Bilin River from where Jeeps carried us to Kyaikto. No half-day cricket for us, this was the real thing with play starting at 11 o'clock and continuing, if necessary, until darkness set in.

NORTH OF THE BILIN

Capt. F. J. Whelan, c and b Mischler	2	b Smeeton	1
Capt. J. A. Bridget, b Smeeton	4	c Boyle b Mischler	0
Fitter Sawan, c Edwards b Smeeton	0	b Kean	13
Capt. N. R. Waddell, b Smeeton	0	c Boyle b Mischler	3
Lt. J. R. Wilde, c Bayley b Mischler	8	b Smeeton	3
Maj. L. B. H. Von Hardinge, c and b Mischler	5	b Kean	3
Jem Daani Ram, b Bayley	5	not out	3
Maj. J. P. Randle, b Mischler	0	c Kean b Weston	2
Capt. A. E. B. Martinnant, not out	6	b Weston	13
Sap. Joseph, c Weston b Boyle	13	b Mischler	0
Sub.-Maj. Fateh Mohd, st Edwards b Boyle	0	c and b Kean	6
Extras	2	Extras	5
Total	45	Total	53

Mischler, 4 for 12; Smeeton, 3 for 8; Boyle, 2 for 8; Bayley 1 for 13.

Mischler, 3 for 8; Smeeton, 2 for 6; Kean 3 for 9; Weston, 2 for 6.

The Baluch had prepared a delightful ground, some even spoke in scorn of Canterbury. We had a pavilion; easy chairs under the shade of some adjoining trees; a scorer's box and two score boards with telephonic communication to the scorers. Most important of all there was plenty of gin and fresh limes. The only point on which we cavilled was the length of the boundaries, which were almost out of sight, and running between the wickets is no fun in Burma even in December. Runs would have been worth at least double on an ordinary ground.

The captains inspected the wicket, with professional thumb pressing. South of Bilin won the toss and decided to bat. Our star, Mischler, of Public Schools and Cambridge fame, who scored over 1200 runs with an average of 87 for St Paul's in 1938, opened with easy elegance and was at once dropped at square-leg only to be well caught there a few runs later. With our score standing at 47 for one, despite the disaster to our star, the opposition became distinctly worried.

It, however, proved unnecessary and lunch was insisted on with the very professional flourish of 97 for 9 – despite the fielding captain's assertion that it only required one more ball to complete our downfall. Perhaps our fall from grace was accelerated by the lordly manner in which our captain, who wore *The Cap*, insisted on the removal of a sleepy Pi Dog from behind the bowler's arm – this was regarded as unprecedented swank and galvanised the bowlers into furious and successful action.

An excellent lunch of cold bird and fruit salad sat very heavy on the visitors' tummies and they were thankful for the respite which the last pair provided by carrying the score to 109. North of the Bilin fared badly against Mischler's and Smeeton's fast swingers (or did rank and discipline help!) and lost five wickets for 11 runs. Hitting out masterfully they saved the follow on and then proceeded to take six of their opponents wickets for 10 runs, including that of Mischler for a duck, with a comfortable first innings lead of 63 now only 73 with but four wickets to fall, and with our bowlers nobbled by attentive waiters with double gins. South of the Bilin was definitely uneasy. However our opponents flattered only to deceive and with the pitch showing signs of wear we ended up comfortable winners by 74 runs.

One final point must not go unmentioned, North of Bilin's wicket-keeper had protected his most susceptible area with a cut-down Japanese fencing mask, worn outside the trousers, and early on a bull's eye rang its vindication over the field.

SEVENTH MATCH:
BAU v. QUEENSLAND

P.A. Snow

The *Sydney Referee* reported:

Fijians at Brisbane.

Curiosity to see the Fijians in the field drew a very fair attendance to the Exhibition Ground on New Year's Day when a Brisbane eleven commenced a match against them. Bare bodies to the waist and bare legs, hatless and bootless, the dusky representatives from across the Pacific presented a quaint appearance. Active men, over the average size, muscular and well-proportioned, their skins shining with the coconut-oil dressing, they showed alertness in the field that made a fitting object lesson to the representative men in the Brisbane team who, by the way, are not yet recovered from their disgust at their poor fielding in Sydney. Ever ready and stooping, the Fijians looked not unlike emus, the black fibrous adornment hanging from the waist adding to the resemblance. There was a keenness about everything they did, and withal delight in it, the white shining teeth showing so often the laugh when one of them did anything noteworthy and gained the plaudits of the crowd. As fieldsmen here they rank very high; as bowlers, save Ratu Pope, they were nothing out of the ordinary. The exception referred to, Ratu Pope, was the favourite with the crowd. He has a high overarm delivery. Although bowled almost too much, it appeared that Pope (pronounced Popay) never sent in a loose over and throughout was treated with respect. He is a cousin of Ratu Kadavulevu, both being grandsons of the late King Cakobau. A peculiarity of the Fijian language is that the letter 'd' is pronounced 'nd' and 'b' as 'mb', 'c' is very like 'th' and 'e' is spoken of as 'a'. These are only some of the peculiarities. Kadavulevu therefore is pronounced Kandavoolevoo, Meleti is called Malaitey, Rabonu becomes Rambonoo, Sokidi is spoken of as Sokindi, Liceni is pronounced Lithaney, and so on.

With such a capital exhibition of ground fielding one expected something above the ordinary in batting but what a disappointment. Marsden certainly shaped well, as he also did with the gloves, and Pope showed that he is a good bat as well as a bowler, till a good break from Hayes shifted the off bail. Ratu Kadavulevu was given out caught at the wicket in the first over, a decision that he made no secret that he disagreed with as he averred that he never touched the ball, and the other umpire stated that he was not out. With four down for 10, the situation changed for bowling to instruction. The bowlers sent down some easy ones which were hit in all directions to the delight of the dark-skinned visitors. Easy catches were not even tried for, stumpings and run-outs were not attempted and boundaries allowed when they could easily have been prevented. Naturally the interest waned when the desire of the fielding side became so unmistakably evident that they did not want to get the batsmen out. And yet the public were entertained to some extent by the batting of the visitors which was of the slogging variety. The batting of the Brisbane team was not sensational though Hayes and Evans made an excellent stand. The former showed fine defence and executed some pretty leg-glances. He had a life when six, this being the only blemish in his innings. Evans looked safe for the century when splendidly caught near the back by Esala, a feat that well earned the hearty applause.

The match was continued on Saturday in most unfavourable weather. Heavy rain had made the wicket soft and passing showers throughout the afternoon made matters uncomfortable for both players and spectators. Evans decided to go in again and the second innings of the Brisbane team was declared with seven down for 165. Save Hutcheon, none of the batsmen could do much on the wicket. The North Brisbane hitter, however, revelled in it and executed some clinking shots and was not out 71 when the innings was closed. Ratu Pope was again the best bowler for the Fijians who, as on the first day, fielded brilliantly. Fiji's second innings with the bat yielded 88 for seven wickets when stumps were drawn. Marsden batted very brightly for 16 but splendid defence was shown by Rabonu who, going in first, was sixth out for 39 out of 72. He was partial to the leg glance.'

Marsden reports: 'The weather was unfortunately very wet on the second day of the match after Queensland had occupied the wickets most of the first day and had totalled 274 runs on a perfect wicket with their full inter-state side. Pope again proved what a fine bowler he is by taking seven wickets for 106 runs, bowling with plenty of pace and spin. We replied with 152 runs, and, on Queensland going to the wickets a second time, they closed with seven wickets down for 165 runs, leaving the Fijians about one hour or so to get 287 runs to win. In trying to hit first-class bowling on a bad wicket, the islanders very nearly came to grief, seven of our wickets falling for 88 runs at call of time, the match thus ending in a drawn game in favour of Queensland.

The fielding and catching of the Fijians in this match was little short of phenomenal and it was very gratifying to read the large headlines in the papers the following morning – 'Wonderful Native Fieldsmen' – and the *Brisbane Courier*, the leading morning paper, described the work of the team in the following words:

'Much had been heard of the prowess of the natives as fieldsmen and bowlers, and events proved that the reports which had heralded their advent had not been exaggerated. It is not too much to say that finer ground fielding has never been seen in Queensland than that of the Fijians yesterday. The excellence was uniform and it is difficult to individualise any of them in this respect. The field on the off in particular was brilliant and the hottest drives were fielded with exceptionally fine precision, while the returns were so fast and accurate that the metropolitan men dared not take any risks between the wickets.'

Speaking of the native bowling, the same paper goes on to remark:

'The accuracy of the attack was indeed a surprise to all, and even such a vigorous batsman as Evans (the Queensland captain) was kept quiet and he had to fight hard for every run. The Fijians' trundlers will not pitch up balls to hit but plug away with a splendid length combined with a fair amount of pace. The pick of their bowlers is Ratu Pope, and were he a Queenslander, he would be immediately selected to represent the State. Small wonder was it that the Queenslanders began very moderately and it was only a fine partnership between Hayes and Evans that saved them.'

QUEENSLAND

First Innings		Second Innings	
G. Brown b Pope	26	c Meleti, b Pope	16
W. A. Armstrong b Samu	21	st Marsden, b Samu	16
S. J. Redgrave c and b Pope	18	c and b Siqila	0
W. J. Lewis c Kadavulevu, b Pope	7	c Vulatolu, b Samu	5
J. S. Hutcheon c Rabonu, b Pope	28	not out	71
T. B. Faunce b Pope	0	c Siqila, b Pope	19
W. B. Hayes c Liceni, b Pope	85	c Rabonu, b Pope	18
W. T. Evans c Esala, b Samu	32	b Sokidi	8
W. B. Bruce Ibw, b Pope	11	not out	4
B. Cook not out	15		
C. B. Barston b Samu	0		
Byes, 4; leg byes, 7	11	Byes 7	7
	274	For 7 wickets declared	**165**

BOWLING

First Innings	O.	M.	R.	W.	Second Innings	O.	M.	R.	W.
Samu	18.2	3	74	3		9	2	45	2
Pope	32	9	106	7		14	3	55	3
Siqila	7	1	31	0		7	0	34	1
Liceni	13	2	44	0		2	0	15	0
Sokidi	4	1	8	0		3	1	9	1

Fall of wickets: First Innings—43, 47, 67, 75, 131, 133, 240, 258, 258, 274. Second Innings—29, 55, 57, 57, 100, 113, 135.

THE FIJIANS

First Innings		Second Innings	
Ratu P. Kadavulevu c Evans, b Barston	0	c Hayes, b Cook	0
Ratu M. Rabonu c Faunce, b Hayes	1	b Redgrave	39
Meleti Raimuria b Barston	1	c Redgrave, b Lewis	3
Lt. E. J. Marsden b Barston	11	c Hutcheon, b Redgrave	16
Ratu Pope E. S. Cakobau b Hayes	1	b Armstrong	2
Liceni Taukei b Hayes	19	b Barston	4
Sokidi Valutu c Cook, b Redgrave	16	c Redgrave, b Barston	9
Esala Matou c Brown, b Bruce	41	not out	2
Epeneri Vulatolu c Hayes, b Bruce	52	c Faunce, b Evans	4
Jone Siqila b Bruce	3		
Samu Bainivanua not out	3		
Byes, 4	4	Byes, 8; leg byes, 1	9
	152	For 7 wickets	88

BOWLING

First Innings	O.	M.	R.	W.	Second Innings	O.	M.	R.	W.
Barston	7	2	13	3		5	1	14	2
Hayes	7	1	21	3		2	1	4	0
Redgrave	8	0	49	1		6	0	23	2
Armstrong	10	1	51	1		3	2	12	1
Bruce	3	0	14	3					
Cook						5	2	6	1
Lewis						6	1	16	1
Evans						2.5	0	4	1

CRICKET IN INDIA

R. Wilkinson

It may be of interest to readers in England to know some details of the many various ways we poor exiles in India play our spasmodic games of cricket. Having had twelve years' experience of cricket in several corners of the Indian Empire, I will give some of my own personal reminiscences of the game and the way it is played.

To begin with, cricket is impossible in the Upper Plains of India between April and November owing to the intense heat and rainy season. In the Punjab and United Provinces and Bengal, it is never played between April and November, as the shade temperatures, varying from 90 degrees to 120 degrees, prohibit play. In some parts of Central India it is played regularly from July onwards, as the temperature is lower on account of several of the cricketing stations being situated some 2000 feet above sea level on a large plateau. In the hills cricket is playable between April and November. In the plains the best months for the game are November to March, when all-day matches are possible. Some stations, however, in the warmer months, play from 7 a.m. to 10 a.m. and 2 p.m. to 5 p.m., resting in the middle of the day. Except in the biggest towns and stations, grounds are mostly small and outfields rough.

Coming direct from four years of play in a Public School XI, on one of the best and biggest school grounds in England, which is renowned for its perfect, quick-drying, hard wickets, I started play in November on a ground at Moradabad, a small station in the United Provinces. Here we were compelled to use matting, owing to the excessive dryness and crumbling nature of the ground. The matting was yellow in colour, and was pitched on a parched yellow-green ground, very rough in the outfield. The boundary was not more than fifty yards, and an ordinary lift was an easy six. We had an excellent pavilion, and among the players was another ex-Public School captain, who had had a record average for his School the previous year at home. We found it quite easy, when once set, to make a century in three-quarters of an hour, owing to the short boundaries and not too strong bowling. Matting is easy to bat on, and heart-breaking to bowl on, though several bowlers can get a large amount of turn on the ball. Once the ball is hit fairly hard, it travels along the hard ground and reaches the boundary with ease, and one is thus tempted to hit more often, and become an impatient player. Also, even in November and December, and the other cold months, an innings of 50 or over is a considerable strain in many ways. One is compelled to bat in a solar topee before 4 p.m., and it is often heavy and cumbersome. It is also difficult to bat on matting in spiked soles, so rubber soles must be worn, and they are more tiring.

Within half an hour of play starting on a ground like the above, the ball becomes the colour of everything else – that is, a muddy, earthen colour – and all the polish and surface has by then got rubbed off, and the ball gets cut in many places by sharp stones in the outfield. Thus when fielding in the deep, a ball often comes along and jumps over your hands at the last minute or picks up a small stone, and you grip ball, stone and all, to your natural discomfort.

At Allahabad there used to be one of the best grass wickets in India, quite a change from the ordinary, and the outfield was also considerably better, and I played some enjoyable knocks on this park-like ground, surrounded by trees. At Meerut also there is rather a similar ground, and on most of these cantonment grounds there is a square of about 30 to 40 yards in very good condition, and often a little higher than the rest of the ground, but the outfield has generally to look after itself, owing to lack of water.

The ground at Naini Tal up in the hills is probably one of the most difficult grounds to play on in the East. The whole 'field' of play is grey gravel, and on the ground, which is about 400 yards long by 300 broad, are played hockey, tennis, polo, football, and cricket. For the latter a strip of yellow matting is laid down, but as the gravel is rather yielding on the surface the matting often wears loose and rucks up. Within fifteen minutes the surface of the ball is quite cut up, and it becomes the colour of everything else in the neighbourhood. Behind the wicket at one end, just over the screen, is a public road, with figures, horses, etc., moving past in a constant stream, and taking your eye off the ball; at the other end is also a road backed by a very dark wooded hill. The whole ground is in a sort of cup, with high hills on three sides towering hundreds of feet above you. This makes the catching in the outfield extraordinarily difficult to judge, and the higher a catch goes (thereby giving you a sight of the ball against the sky and not against a wooded hill) the easier it is to judge. A long, low catch in the country is very difficult to bring off successfully. On the matting surface at Naini Tal many batting reputations have gone temporarily, but I have seen a well-known bowler there break a foot both ways, owing to the softer surface under the matting, which affords a certain amount of 'bite'.

On a ground at Lucknow in the Mohammad Bagh Club I have seen 180 knocked up in an hour by two batsmen hitting at everything. Here, again, the boundary is very short, and the club roof and windows are very easy targets! On a regimental ground at Allahabad, I once played with the pitch so close to a road that the road was included in the outfield!

The ground in the Eden Gardens at Calcutta is said to be a very difficult batsman's wicket, and tall scores are few. In Central India cricket is of quite a different kind. The lower temperatures at Mhow, Indore, etc., make cricket possible throughout the 'rains', i.e., from July onwards. The soil is black cotton, very soft and yielding, and with deep holes and fissures every now and then. The playing area is usually a 40-yard square, or 30 yards by five, of hardened, rolled mud, with matting laid down on it. The space round the wicket is therefore often fast and earth-coloured, and the out-field is quite green and bumpy, and treacherous for foothold, as the feet often sink into the ground an inch or so. This makes running and ground fielding very difficult, and one cannot get off the mark with any speed. A high lofted drive will stop dead in the ground, and perhaps bury itself, and the ball won't travel. A strip of white canvas cloth is usually sewn over the batting area at each end of the matting, giving the whole thing a curious appearance. Of course, on a ground like the above, play is not possible in very wet weather, but only during a break. Only the other day I played on a ground with only a 30 yards boundary!

Screens are seldom of any practical use in India. They are almost invariably too low, and seldom cover the bowler's arm; one gets used to them, and takes no notice. Clubs cannot often afford the best balls nowadays, as a 'Duke's' would be ruined in half an hour, therefore mostly country-made balls are used. These are exceptionally hard, both on the bat and the hand, and as our bats are usually out of regular use, and get hardened by the weather, the resulting shock on the muscles of the hand is often painful. Sometimes after a long knock I have been unable to write, hold a knife, or play the piano owing to stricture of the muscles of the palm of the hand.

Undoubtedly the most enjoyable cricket I have played in the East was at Port Blair, in the Andaman Islands. This outpost of the Empire possesses a really excellent ground, the nearest approach to an English one in the East. Like Naini Tal, there is a flat space cleared for all games, but the cricket pitch, and forty yards round it, is kept inviolate from the inroads of golf, hockey, or football. The whole area is beautiful with springy, thick turf, which flourishes owing to the heavy rainfall (eight months in the year). No matting is necessary, as the grass wicket is splendid. The boundary can be made 80 to 100 yards all round, the light is excellent, the balls last well, and a pleasant sea breeze blows straight off the harbour across the ground, and the blue sea and swaying coconuts form a picturesque background.

Though the settlement is small, one can always raise two elevens, but of very mixed calibre. During the three years of my stay there I only found six players of Public School 1st XI standard, and one Indian of a very high class, and also left-handed. A detachment of a British infantry regiment usually provided half a dozen players, very much 'of sorts', but of undoubted keenness, and the boys in the Bazaar were quite good and keen. Owing to the somewhat trying humid climate (it is never less than 82 degrees in the shade), we only played from 2.30 to 6 p.m. once a week.

This meant that each side was only allowed about 1¾ hours each to bat, and if one wanted to make runs, one had to hurry and retire at 50 to give others a chance. A quick 50 was an exhausting proceeding, as one got entirely wet through, and often the rubber handle of the bat became impossible to hold without applying rosin. Occasionally all-day matches were played with teams of visiting ships, but they were too exhausting. The Tommies provided several humorous interludes; some had no idea of the game at all, and when I asked one where he would like to field, he chose 'Half-back, please, sir!' The scorer one day was ignorant of the bowlers, names, so he wrote down one bowler as 'Diddums', and the other as 'Diddums II'. We had to provide our own umpires on the 'next man-in' principle, and few were cognisant with the l.b.w. rule, and stood in the most extraordinary positions.

Thus it can well be seen that cricket in India is played under many varying circumstances. The heat, the physical effort of running your own and your partner's efforts, the excessive glare, the heavy helmet, the necessity (or desire) to score quickly and knock the cover off the ball over the (apparently) easy boundary, the colour of the ball, and any amount of minor details, all combine to make the cricketer (who spends his time up country) lose his form. So when those who play regularly at Home on good, green, grass, grounds, on a perfect summer day, in perfect surroundings, wonder why we exiles from India cannot at once find our form on return to England, perhaps the above will help them to realise the disadvantages under which we labour. We learn to take liberties with weak bowling; we tend to become impatient to avoid fatigue and heat; and our best 'sixers' in India almost invariably find a safe place in the hands of the man in the 'country' at home. The billiard-table wickets at home usually find us late for the ball, and the higher standard of bowling all round shows up our batting weakness. After years of the

East, too, our fielding declines, and we find it difficult to get down to the ball on the carpet. Net practices are few and far between, and often we only use our bats once in three months, and possibly once in three years, so what chance have we of retaining our form? From November 1913 to November 1918, I only played eight innings. In an up-country station in the winter it is possible to play tennis on Monday, hockey on Tuesday, golf on Wednesday, football on Thursday, racquets on Friday, and cricket on Saturday! Therefore, we don't specialise in any one game if we are all-rounders, and cricket is not played sufficiently regularly to enable us to do so, and we don't like to lose the chance and benefit of the other games.

EUROPEAN CRICKET IN INDIA

Cecil Headlam

With a drawn match against the North of India at Cawnpore, Mr K.J. Key's team of Oxonians brought their tour in India to a conclusion. That the tour had been an intensely interesting and enjoyable one for those who took part in it goes without saying. But the record of achievements shows that, from a cricket point of view also, it had been extraordinarily successful. The record stood at 19 matches played, 12 won, two lost, and five drawn.

This is good enough, but when it is added that the Test Match v. the Gentlemen of India was won by six wickets, that all the five drawn games were overwhelmingly in favour of the Authentics – moral victories – and that the two games lost were lost within ten days of landing, when the bowlers were soft and stiff and four of the best men were absent or disabled, it must be granted that the record is very good indeed. It was certainly unfortunate that the match against the Parsees was put down for so early a date, for I am confident that on their form any time during the last two months the Authentics, with their full side, would have accounted pretty easily for the Parsee combination. But the fact remains that the Parsees beat them handsomely, as did also, but by a narrow margin, a weak team representing the Bombay Presidency. It has been the invariable fate of visiting teams to lose their first matches in Bombay, and it is to be hoped that in future any touring team will benefit by the experience of Mr Vernon's, Lord Hawke's, and Mr Key's elevens, and take their Bombay games at the end instead of the commencement of their tour; otherwise, against a keen side in full practice like the Parsees, they are bound to give a false impression of their powers.

Time saved the Hindus, and rain the men of Aligarh, from practically certain defeat. For once they got hard and fit, and received the welcome aid of a left-hand bowler in Powys-Keck, there was no holding the 'Tics. Out of their last 15 matches they won 12 – six in single innings – and drew three. Those whose knowledge of cricket extends only to the paper records of players in the first-class County Championship regarded the bowling of the Authentics as hopelessly weak. But Williams has done some fine performances for Berkshire and for Oxford, and those who knew him were justified in believing that he would do well in India. As a matter of fact, he did not do quite so well as I had anticipated, but he succeeded in taking over a hundred wickets. He was, however, more expensive than Simpson-Hayward, who from beginning to end shared with him the brunt of the bowling. One had foretold a rich harvest of wickets for the Worcestershire lobster, who is not really so much a lobster as an under-hand flicker, and his original style of delivery, when once he got his hand in, proved extraordinarily deadly. A glance at the averages will show that he bested a hundred-odd batsmen for a remarkably small number of runs. On certain days and wickets he was peculiarly deadly, and on two occasions he succeeded in performing the hat-trick.

But perhaps the most consistent and successful bowler was Powys-Keck, who joined the team for the fifth match at Bangalore, and whose fast left-handed deliveries seemed to turn the scale of fortune in our favour. Not only did the great swerve which this really good natural bowler imparts to the ball again and again out the best of the opposing batsmen, but his style of bowling lent a needed variation to the attack, and thereby greatly improved it. These three shared the burden of bowling. The other bowlers were only occasionally requisitioned, for Clayton, who would undoubtedly have proved a very successful change, and who secured seven wickets for 60 in the first innings of the first match, was disabled during the Parsee match, and could not play again till the last three matches. I have referred before to the cruel stroke of fortune which befel him. Blood poisoning from a scratch, infected by Bombay dust, and not even neglected, kept him out of the field for many trying weeks; but in the few innings he was able to play he scored with a brilliant consistency which showed how valuable a batsman the side had lost.

In Bombay he skippered the Authentics in the absence of Key, and an admirable skipper he made. Key himself was unfortunately unable to join his team before they reached Calcutta, nearly half-way through their tour. His presence immediately made itself felt. He played some very fine innings, notably his 96 at Calcutta, his 51 at Lahore, and his 116 at Cawnpore. He almost always won the toss, he never missed a catch, and he gave every single member of his team a bowl, including himself. What more could the most exacting ask of an ideal captain? When Clayton was ill, and Key had not arrived, Hollins acted as deputy-assistant-adjutant-skipper. His success with the bat throughout the tour was beyond all anticipation. Playing with far greater freedom than he had usually shown at home, whether for Oxford or Lancashire, he made big scores with amazing consistency. Strokes behind the wicket were the chief features of his game; his cutting and slipping, leg-hitting and leg-gliding being safe and brilliant always. He put century after century to his credit, and gained the distinction of being the first English visitor to score 1000 runs in India. Hornby, in the last match, followed his example, and also completed his 1000 runs.

Hornby's fast bowling was not so deadly as one might have expected it to be, probably because he was for the greater part of the tour suffering from the after-effects of fever. But the same cause makes his batting performances all the more creditable. At the beginning of the tour, when we were short-handed and he very weak with fever, he got valuable runs every time. As he got stronger he naturally played a more vigorous game, but though he can hit well and hook splendidly, he watches the ball like a cat a mouse, and his defence is extremely good. His 113 at Rawal Pindi, and his 70 not out against the Gentlemen of India, were about as good innings on difficult wickets as you could wish to see. Simpson-Hayward played many useful innings in the first half of the tour, but it was not till later that he played himself into really first-rate form as a bat. Then he suddenly made the fine score of 203 not out at Peshawar, and from that time onwards he could not go wrong. Raphael, on the other hand, after scoring consistently well during the earlier stages of the tour – notably, a splendid century against the Parsees – fell off somewhat when runs were less needed. Tomkinson, though he never made a large score, made a regular and very useful 30 or 40. Disabled after the first innings he played in Bombay, Chinnery marked his reappearance in the team with a splendid 98. Then he fell off for a time, and took some while to play himself into form. For the last three or four weeks, however, the Middlesex amateur was in fine fettle. He got runs every time, and got them always by the most brilliant and delightful cricket. It is a thousand pities that he does not play regularly for his county.

On a tour of this kind there are always some batsmen who play above their form and others who play below it. Williams started off with a good century at Bombay, but after that, probably on account of the amount of hard work in the bowling line which fell to his share, he struck a bad patch, and hardly made a run. Headlam, too, was clean out of form and luck with the bat, but he did a lot of hard work with the gloves. The casual nature of the umpires on tours of this kind makes wicket-keeping a more than usually thankless job, but the fact that in 31 innings the number of byes averaged little over five is sufficient testimony to his watchfulness. Aspinall showed good form with bat as well as gloves when he played, and Ridley started well, but did not fulfil the promise he gave with both bat and ball in the earlier games. Kershaw, on the other hand, though inconsistent, nearly always made runs when they were most wanted, the Oxonian half-back having a happy gift of hitting up an invaluable 30 when the ground was bad and the wickets falling.

It was prophesied that the fielding of the team would be brilliant, as befitted Oxonians, and there have been no two opinions on that subject in India.

'The batting and bowling figures,' said *The Englishman*, 'are worthy of all praise, while the fielding throughout was proportionately even better, and Cecil Headlam kept wicket in irreproachable style, and with conspicuous success from start to finish . . . The way the eleven worked together was a treat to see. If special praise must be accorded to individuals we have no hesitation in bestowing it upon Headlam at the wicket, and a splendid trio – Hollins, Chinnery, and Hornby – at cover, extra-cover, and mid-off respectively.'

'In the field,' wrote *The Asian*, 'the side, as a side, was even stronger than in batting. The pick-up was clean and smart, and the return to the wicket prompt and accurate almost without exception, and when the fields-men once got accustomed to the light, very few catches were missed. It was the keen combination which was chiefly noticeable after what is usually seen out here, but Chinnery, Hollins, Hornby, and Simpson-Hayward were also individually excellent. In Headlam the Authentics possessed a first-class wicket-keeper, quiet and effective, and the way in which his hands lasted all through the tour was wonderful. Aspinall was also very smart, but only kept in comparatively few of the matches.'

In that important department of the game then the Authentics were first-class, or more than first-class, throughout. Our victories were in a large measure due to the fact that we never grew slack in the field, whilst, when the match was felt to be in jeopardy, the fielding was keen, close, and brilliant in the extreme. The ground-fielding was excellent, and extraordinarily few catches were dropped. That fact speaks volumes for the keenness of a team on tour through India.

RECORDS OF THE TOUR.

Matches won, 12; lost, 2; drawn 5. Total, 19.
Highest score for Authentics, 696, v. Peshawar.
Highest score against Authentics, 412, v. Bombay Presidency.
Lowest score for Authentics, 85, v. Madras Presidency.
Lowest score against Authentics, 31, v. Trichinopoly.

ARABS EAST OF SUEZ

J.H. Fingleton

Up to the Sunday of the third Test at Sydney, the Arabs had never played east of Suez. Now it can be said that they have never been beaten east of Suez and it is a record, possibly, on which they will rest.

With the Founder, President, captain and sole selector, E.W. Swanton, resting with his caravan in Sydney, it seemed a natural thought that the Arabs should appear for the first time in Australia. Naturally and unnaturally (in a cricket sense), they have appeared in many countries.

Off to play the Forces in West Germany once, the Arabs were momentarily shaken when they were met at the border by a translator in Arabic. But E.W.S's Arabs are a pretty hardy lot – not over-blessed with respect for the authority of the Head Sheikh at times – and there was a most enthusiastic response when a game against I Zingari of Australia was mooted for Sunday, 13 January.

The same enthusiasm waned a little as the time approached and particularly when it was known that Martin Donnelly, Ian Craig, Jim Burke and Ted White, all former internationals, were to play for I.Z. And Gamini Goonesena. Arab G.O. Allen, unfortunately, had a sciatic twinge, a relic of his former nomadic days, and couldn't be cajoled out of his tent. But Bill Hayward did a magnificent organisational job and the Arabs turned out in resplendent force. A very proud day, indeed, for Jim Swanton. At the school masthead flew the Arab flag, brought to Australia by Frank Mennim, and it consoled them not inconsiderably when it was known that IZ, the night before, had enjoyed their annual dinner.

The epic game was at Cranbrook School, Bellevue Hill – a beautiful ground with a pitch good enough for a Test and with magnificent views across the harbour. The Arab captain, whose caravan in all climes is suitably majestic, might well have won the toss had not Headmaster Gethin Hewan, a prominent IZ man, not pointed out that his Rolls had come to rest on the school tennis courts and there was already action pending against the builders for damage to the aforesaid courts.

So E.W.S was not quite poised for the toss which he lost. He quickly recovered his usual aplomb, however, when he took a sighting, *à la Benaud*, on first slip and, much against the will of first slip, had *The Times* correspondent move a fraction to starboard. The Arabs, not the easiest side to handle, quickly sense sand in their sugar.

Potter opened with a wide. Having lulled air-ace John Waddy, also a Member of Parliament, into a false sense of security he then knocked his stumps back next ball with an absolute 'blinder'. Hayward took a glorious catch at gully slip, like his old Cambridge days, and IZ were 1 for 2. At this stage, Potter, who had both wickets, said he was very short of a net and asked for his sweater. He asked in vain.

Hayward deceived Craig; then Burke, Donnelly who batted in his usual grand manner, and Goonesena left before Hewan deceived the Arabs who were beginning to have oasis-like visions of their strength. Hewan drove in the noble manner. He gave the impression he was on the first tee at nearby Royal Sydney Golf Club, where he repeatedly takes out the championship.

S.C. Griffith seemed to have more polish – and solidity – about his 'keeping than either of the two MCC men at this stage. Roger Kimpton took over after lunch and was a suitable substitute.

Kimpton had flown 500 miles from Melbourne for this game (and flew back immediately it was over) and Geoffrey Keighley had flown his own plane from southern New South Wales. When it came to calling runs, Jack Fingleton thought Keighley was still up in the clouds.

The Arabs began in a straggly manner but Griffith (Billy) was in tremendous form, stroking as of old. Colin Ingleby-Mackenzie thought this was the most perfect pitch he had ever batted on. He certainly made the most of it – a really perfect innings. Kimpton had the misfortune to be thrown out from 22 yards but Hayward, one tremendous 6, deserved to do well after all his yeoman work to arrange the game and he and Potter – who could not have batted better had he had more nets – got the Arabs home in an exciting finish against the clock and Goonesena. Jose and Mennim, after the game, regretted they had not been called upon to bat in the crisis.

The Founder played some nice strokes and showed that even in crossing legs while awaiting the bowler, there is still an old-world grace in the game. His innings was cut short by an excessive use of the feet. It was almost as if he had read the *Daily Telegraph* Correspondent deploring the lack of footwork among modern batsmen . . . walking four yards down the pitch, he kept walking.

A grand day, full of fun and much good cricket. Much pleased, the Arabs folded their tents and went to Bill Hayward's for tiffin. *Never beaten east of Suez!*

Scores: I Zingari of Australia: J. Waddy, b Potter, O; W.B. Douglass, c Hayward b Potter, 1; I.D. Craig, b Hayward, 3; J.W. Burke, b Keighley, 45; M.P. Donnelly, b Jose, 20; G. Goonesena, c MacLachlan b Keighley, 14; G.E. Hewan, not out, 44; N.J. Ranken, b Hayward, 1; J. Newton, retired, 23; E.S. White, not out, 5; extras, 12; total (8 wkts dec), 168. Did not bat: P.S. Davey and H. Siddeley.
Bowling: Potter, 11–1–74–2; Hayward, 11–1–39–2; Jose, 5–1–17–1; Keighley, 2–0 5–2; MacLachlan, 2–0–10–0; Swanton, 1–0 11–0.

The Arabs: J.H. Fingleton, run out, 3; W.G. Keighley, b White, 3; S.C. Griffith, c Davey, b Waddy, 23; A.C.D. Ingleby-Mackenzie, c Rankin, b Goonesena, 60; R.C.M. Kimpton, b Burke, 3; H.G. MacLachlan, c Craig, b Goonesena, 6; W.I.D. Hayward, not out, 35; J.C. Woodcock lbw b White, 6; E.W. Swanton, st Davey b Goonesena, 4; I.C. Potter, not out, 21; extras, 8; total (for 8 wkts), 172.
Did not bat: A. D. Jose and F. Mennim.
Bowling: Siddeley, 3–0–6–0; White, 13–3 43–2; Waddy, 7–0–44–1; Burke, 5–1–19–1: Goonesena, 9–0–54–3.
The Arabs won by 3 wickets.

WATER MARTINS IN EGYPT

Hubert Martineau

The first English XI to go out to Egypt was an IZ side and their last visit there was in 1912. When I was asked by Jock Hartley in 1927 to play for the Free Foresters in Alexandria and Cairo, it never occurred to me that I should be taking a side of my own out there for many springs to come, but that is how things turned out. The arrangements were completed between then and the end of 1928, and 1929 saw the beginning of the series.

I selected my side with great care and found myself in the happy predicament of suffering from an *embarras de choix*. I could have picked several good elevens as well as just the one. In the end, my choice fell on:

Colonel Alec Johnston
Captain Isherwood
S.A. Block
R.D. Skeene
R. Scott
F.O.G. Lloyd
C.H.A. Wood
T. Akers-Douglas
C.H. Knott
C.K. Hill-Wood

It was something of an event for a team like this to go abroad under its own steam, so to speak, and *The Times* thought the enterprise of sufficient interest to give coverage not only to our matches against All Egypt sides, which amounted to Test matches, but to every day's play we had out there between 1929 and 1939.

We crossed the Channel on 28 March 1929, went by train to Genoa, where we picked up a boat, and eventually arrived in Alexandria for our first game. The change in climate, atmosphere, and way of life took a few days to get used to, and we had a number of cases of 'Gippie tummy', but these were soon got over. As I had been out in Egypt in April for many years, I knew a lot of the residents there, as well as Service people, so I felt very pleasantly at home.

We got off to a fine start on 2 April against the Alexandria Cricket Club on their own ground. This was composed of sand, with a matting wicket, which was very, very fast. All the grounds in Egypt were similar to this one until 1937, when they were turfed over. John Knott, who went in seventh, made 151, and the speed of his scoring was terrific: he knocked up 100 in 60 minutes, and his remaining 51 only took him 17. His partner, Skeene, made 116, and they brought the score up to 409: altogether, the partnership produced 220 runs, achieved by an amazingly free-and-easy way of hitting.

I think that 'free-and-easy' also describes the spirit in which we tried to play. We were out there to enjoy ourselves, to give pleasure to our opponents and to entertain the spectators, should there be any. On the first day there was only a sprinkling, as I imagine that few people expected to see anything out of the ordinary in the way of cricket, but they soon found out their mistake. By the end of the tour, when we played against All Egypt sides, there was as much fervour and excitement as at Test matches at home.

The Water Martins eventually declared at 457 for six in the first innings against Alexandria. I put on Hill-Wood and Lloyd to open the bowling next morning, and Hill-Wood got an immense pace off the wicket with his fast left-handers. Knott took a spectacular catch at the square-leg boundary, and the day's play ended with Alexandria 141 for 6, 316 runs behind us.

On the third and last day we had them all out for 231, but they did very much better in the follow-on, knocking up 300 for 3. One of these wickets fell to me, thanks to another remarkable catch by Knott. The match ended in a draw.

Block and Knott were outstanding in the field. Block saved many a boundary by brilliant fielding at third man, and his speed and accuracy in returning the ball were a joy to watch and an example to be copied. I think we surprised our opponents and sent a buzz round Egypt, particularly amongst those against whom we should be playing later.

Brigadier John Turner, who had once played for Middlesex, enlivened one match by an unintentional comic turn that no one present will forget. His particular strident way of appealing came out with immense force and volume, and he was the possessor of an admirable set of false teeth, so it was only a question of time before the inevitable happened. Seeing a likely l.b.w, he shot out his appeal and his false teeth simultaneously. Unfortunately, I cannot now remember whether the added dental emphasis carried the day and caused his appeal to be upheld!

Our second match, against the Gezira Sporting Club of Cairo, was a tougher and more laborious affair. There had been a certain amount of celebrating during the three nights and two days between the matches, and an uncomfortably hot wind scarcely provided a tonic. Brigadier Turner, who was captaining the GSC, won the toss and elected to bat. Hill-Wood and Isherwood opened the attack, but the pitch lacked the speed which we had enjoyed so much at Alexandria. However, Hill-Wood secured the first wicket at 12, and Isherwood took the second at 44. Runs came slowly, averaging some 8 a wicket, and we had them all out shortly after luncheon for 104. This total would have been a great deal more if our standard of fielding and returning had not been so strong.

Johnston and Isherwood batted first for us, but Alec was out for 6 and Isherwood for 10. It fell to my Nos 5 and 6 – Knott and Skeene – to make most of our runs against some really deadly bowling. Its quality may be judged from the fact that it took Skeene an hour to make the first 13 runs out of his eventual 50, but we finally reached 189 for nine. I then decided to declare, leaving Gezira to go in again on the following morning.

The weather next day was blessedly cool, and Hill-Wood and Isherwood kept the scoring down so well that Gezira only secured their first run in the fifth over! Their No.2 bat, Ryder, was caught off me by Hill-Wood in the slips, and it was not till their sixth man, Mitchell, arrived at the crease that they really got going. He knocked up 99, mainly in partnership with de la Mare, who himself, made 102. These two fine batsmen were the saving of their side, but the rate of scoring had remained very slow, and we found ourselves left with only 1¾ hours in which to make the 235 runs necessary to win.

Alec Johnston and Block went in, determined to set about the bowling, but both the bowling and the fielding were pretty hot, and by the fall of the fourth wicket we had only reached 75. It then became the task of Isherwood and Akers-Douglas to try to save the game, which they just succeeded in doing, though it was a very narrow squeak. By close of play we had made 145 for 9, and the match ended in a draw. It was an extremely interesting game, since, at various times in the course of it, each side seemed to be in a strong position, and we had to play a very different kind of cricket from that in Alexandria at the beginning of the week.

Between matches, as I have already indicated, we were most generously entertained, and met many delightful, warm-hearted people, as well as a number of characters. One, who was both, was Oswald Finney, who left Rugby to join the staff of Peel & Co., cotton brokers in Alexandria. After a while, he started up on his own in what he described as a 'chummery' in a block of flats. His prosperity was such that he was able to buy the whole block, bit by bit, and turn into it one large residence for himself. He retained the original lifts, imported a magnificent marble staircase from Italy, and installed a ballroom that held some 600 people. Oswald and his very charming wife, who was a great favourite of all of us, gave two balls every year during our visits, and we came to regard them as the high-spots of our stay. He left Egypt to go on a voyage to South Africa for his health, and, alas, never returned. Everyone who enjoyed his hospitality and that of his wife, José, will always remember them with great affection.

We were put up in Alexandria either by residents or by regiments who had friends in our eleven. Two members of the side stayed with the Royal Warwicks, commanded at that time by Lieutenant-Colonel Bernard Montgomery, and were not wholly appreciative of the runs before breakfast, which they could not decently avoid. In Cairo, Shepheard's kindly put up two of us, and residents extended their hospitality to the rest. I stayed first with the Army No.2, and then with Dick Moore, a wonderful man, who was Secretary of the Sudan and an ex-Middlesex cricketer. Later on, I stayed with Keown Boyd, who was in charge of the equivalent of the Home Office and made a fortune with the Distillers and Dyers after his retirement. There was certainly no dearth of entertainment, by day or night, what with dinners, dances, and the Cairo Embassy Club, and, as I look back on it, I am amazed by our stamina.

The All Egypt XI, against whom we played in our third match, contained many of the players whom we had got to know in our two previous matches. The game took place on the slower Gezira pitch. I won the toss and sent in Alec Johnston and Isherwood as openers. With the bowling well pitched and accurate, the scoring was slow, but we had no great difficulty in dealing with it, and reached 200 for five, followed by 201 for six, by three o'clock in the afternoon. Knott and Block made 183 between them, almost equally divided: Knott remained unconquered for 90, in which there were three sixes and 12 fours. At the tea interval, when we were 310 for eight, I decided to declare, with Hill-Wood also not out and Lloyd still to bat.

All Egypt started off confidently against Hill-Wood and myself, Skeene caught their first batsman, Mellor, off Hill-Wood, and, one run later, Hill-Wood caught their second batsman off me. After that, it became difficult to make much impression on them and they had reached 100 for four when stumps were drawn at the end of the first day's play.

Unfortunately, Knott had suffered an injury and was unable to play when the match was resumed next morning in cold and dull weather. So we called on the services of Abdou. He was the professional at the Gezira Club, a delightful and very popular man, who became a superb player at any game he took up. A great bowler on the mat, he possessed a most venomous leg-cutter (as it is called today), which would pitch on your leg stump and then hit either the middle or the off stick. I cannot, however, pretend that he was anything of a batsman. He was mad about cricket, and this was the first of several occasions when he found himself roped in as a temporary honorary Water Martin.

On resumption, All Egypt's progress was as dull as the weather, and it took them a good twenty minutes to raise their score from 100 to 120. After the 150 mark was reached, a rot set in and they were all out for 194. Though this meant that the Water Martins were leading by 116 runs, I thought it more courteous not to force the follow-on, and we went in for our second innings.

Alec Johnston made 24 and was then run out – or, rather, his runner was run out for him. It was not in his nature to regard such an occurrence entirely philosophically, and, ever after, members of my side were somewhat apprehensive when called on to act as 'runner for Alec'. John Knott recently told me that he felt this attitude to be uncharitable, though he was forced to admit that the responsibility involved held, even for him, its alarming aspects.

However, despite this unfortunate start, we did show All Egypt how we *could* score, and knocked up 170 runs in 90 minutes, which was not bad going. I declared at this total, with four wickets down, so as to let the home side have a go at bashing us about. They needed 287 to win, which I reckoned to be a bit beyond them.

Hill-Wood and I opened the bowling as before, and it was not long before Hill-Wood accepted one catch off me, and Wood another. The only batsman who made anything like a decent score was Mitchell, who got his half-century before being caught by Block off Hill-Wood. Subsequent wickets fell for precious few runs and, though the match was finally drawn, we had definitely gained a moral victory.

Chapter 4

CRICKET WATCHING

THE GENTLEMEN OF
ENGLAND BATTING

Robert Lynd

No-one can reverence the sun and look without thrills at a cricket match on a bright day. On Thursday, a day on which the wind came from the east in sunny mouthfuls, I went to Lord's, where the Gentlemen of England were playing against the Australians. Here I found a great crowd of City men with black stove-pipes on their heads, looking very intent and very respectable. Their clothes, however, had lost all their neatness with the dust that had been blowing about in the streets. The city men looked foolish, indeed, compared with the tradespeople who were scattered among them, and who had an air of greater comfort in their tweed suits and round hats.

So terribly was the sun burning down that only a few of us persisted in smoking. Most of the spectators sat with wrinkled temples, as though all their efforts were needed to keep their eyes fixed on the brightness of the field and on the game. The grass was by this time of an exhausted green colour, and, when I arrived, beautiful white and lithe figures were running this way and that way over its surface.

The Gentlemen of England were batting. They had just lost their second wicket, and Beldam was carrying his bat back to the pavillion. MacLaren came out in his place, large and airy, and undisturbed by the clapping of the spectators. He did not earn many cheers, however. Cotter was bowling from the east, and MacLaren seemed to regard him with something of the fascinated amazement with which they say a rabbit watches a stoat. Cotter, indeed – a compact, hard man, with jutting hips and a strong neck – cannot be an altogether pleasant enemy. Before he bowls he takes a long race up towards the wicket, ducking like a water-hen as he runs, and juggling with his wrist in the oddest way. Then, at the right moment, he lets the ball loose in a violent hurl, and if it pauses on this side of the end of the world it is the fault of the wicket-keeper or the boundary railings.

Newland, the wicket-keeper, a little fellow clothed as though in the leg-guards and gloves of a giant, stood far back from the batsman while Cotter was bowling. One might have caricatured him as a shivering schoolboy, determined to be plucky, and standing with his mouth open and groaning inwardly, as he saw the little dark devil of a ball speeding towards him, and suddenly realised all that he had let himself in for. One felt that he must be mediating upon the wisdom of turning tail and flying for his life towards the pavilion. Only behind some barrier could he have watched the coming of the little dark devil with equanimity. No wonder that it sometimes beat past the combined picket of his arms and legs, and tore on, as if with a grin, to the boundary. No wonder that MacLaren, posted still nearer Cotter, fell, a confused mass of good attitudes, before so swift and terrible an onset. Yet to have frightened MacLaren out before he had made a run, was all the glory Cotter had to his credit at the end of the day.

Warner – 'Plum' the ungilded youth of England call him – stood as immune from all this hurricane bowling as Ulysses, amid the general wreckage, from the splashing rocks of Polyphemus. A small, innocent match of a man, full of wiles in the art of cutting, he swung his bat with ease and – as if he were capable of malice! – with an almost malicious pleasure, as the ball slid over the grass towards him. One could not but admire so impudent a coolness. His bat, from its size, one might have judged to be almost as heavy as himself, and yet he handled it with as brave an assurance as if it had been no weightier than a broom, and he sweeping away ridiculous dust with it. He seemed as if, whenever he chose, he could whisk the ball off to the boundary, and have four more runs placed by his number on the marking-board.

Captain Wynyard at first showed no such housemaidenish ease in dealing with the Australian bowling. Large and alert and graceful at the wicket, he held his bat in close to his legs, and faced the bowlers with crafty suspiciousness. Sometimes, indeed, when the ball came tumbling towards his pads, he would swing his bat in a Berserker rage; but the ball would juke past him untouched, and leave him stooping with one knee on the ground in baffled amazement. He seemed suddenly to realise that his wicket was in a state of close siege, and that he must venture upon nothing but the most diminutive sorties. His tactics changed accordingly. Ball after ball he allowed to slip by him, or merely sent back to the bowler with a click. Every now and again, however, he found an opportunity for more interesting things. Seeing no one standing at mid-wicket, he would nudge a ball into the unguarded place, and be off with a cry towards the opposite wicket. This business of stealing runs became, after a while, a moderately exciting affair. One waited for Captain Wynyard's cry and his scurry up the pitch as a child waits with tense patience for the coming of the seventh wave with its thunders. Later in the day, however, Captain Wynyard became weary of the part of a timid boy robbing an orchard under the gardener's nose. He began, as in former days, to gather his runs in with something of the boldness and great-mindedness of an old chieftain out on a cattle-lifting expedition. Before he resigned his policy of cunning, however, he cost Mr Phillips, one of the umpires, a bad fall; for Evans, hearing Captain Wynyard calling upon him to take part in one of these hairbreadth affairs of his, dashed up the pitch in so blind a frenzy that he was unable to stop until he had leaped against the body of Mr Phillips, and left him lying, a tumbled thing, with his legs in the air, like a house-painter fallen in a fit. This was a windfall, however, to a crowd that of all crowds is the readiest for laughter – the seriously-clad and sunny-faced crowd that sits gossiping and with its half-brains working at cricket matches.

Captain Wynyard took Jessop's place, I believe, as a player in the English team. It was Hesketh-Prichard, however, who was really Jessop's substitute, and set the benches under the awnings and in the stands roaring. Hesketh-Prichard is a golden-haired giant, who can tell stories or bowl with something of the tempestuous delight of a fighter at a fair. He bats, however, more like a child scooping out sand with a wooden spade. No one seems to realise what a darling child's game he is playing at more clearly than himself. On Thursday the Australians could break no hole in his infantile defences. He stood there, throwing back his little spadefuls of sand, and letting a great laugh out of him on the two occasions upon which he came by a run. Twice, too, the ball missed the middle of his bat. It just grazed the edge and, veering past the wicket-keeper, was carried by its own force to the boundary. Hesketh-Prichard, seeing his score mounting up, threw his huge, capless head back, and joined in the roars of delight that went like a storm round the field. Such a munificence of good nature I had never seen before on the playing-field. I felt quite angry with Brearley for letting himself be stumped the moment after and bringing the innings of the Gentlemen to an end. But it was near six o'clock. So I left my seat and came home.

SOMETHING FELL FROM HEAVEN

Peter Roebuck

Gradually the ball descended, obeying Newton's law. No snow on it, for the day was warm. The batsman waited and watched. Eventually he smote at it vigorously, with all the might he could muster. But he was deceived; the ball had not yet arrived.

As he completed his lusty swing, the ball bounced and trickled toward the stumps. A bail was dislodged before the agonised batsman could retrieve his dignity. Another victim for Teer, another fool rushing in. As the disconsolate batsman trudged to the pavilion he muttered under his breath (as Agatha Christie victims mutter mysterious dying words), 'Something fell from heaven.'

Norman Teer bowls donkey-drops. He's been at it a long time, and with considerable success. He launches the ball far into the skies, then relaxes, awaiting the outcome. Something usually happens. His proud boast is to be 'the highest bowler in Somerset', though he concedes that Joel Garner is the tallest.

His deliveries, sent into orbit from 24 yards, after a brief skip or two, soar at least 15 feet into the air. Once in a while he slips in a quicker ball which only rises to twice the height of man. When it bounces, *if it* bounces, his donkey-drop will spin a little. That's an unnecessary touch. Probably Nureyev could sing, too, but who needs it?

In Gambia his deliveries often bounced over the batsman's head. Horrified Gambians were dumfounded by this yo-yo style of bowling, and fell in droves.

Beyond wisdom

From this you may gather that Norman Teer is an original, a remnant from more generous cricketing days. Every ball is a challenge, miserly efforts at run-saving are ignored. It's wickets that matter. Once in a while, say in a 30-over game, Norman's figures of five overs, three for 53, appear a bit of a luxury. But, then, like most bowlers of his kind, Norman is captain, selector and organiser. In these roles he usually manages to conclude that he should bowl, if not all the time, at least a good deal of it. He took well over 100 wickets in 1980, including several bags of 'seven for' and 'six for'. One does not ask 'seven for what?' or 'six for what?'!

With these numerous wickets, a northern dialect, a balding patch and an air of immensely serious intent, one might imagine that Norman's deliveries contain a measure of guile, a touch or two of the wisdom gathered over the years by this sprightly 65-year-old. Not so. Norman is beyond wisdom. His philosophy is simple. 'They can't resist 'em, y'know,' he confides to uninitiated team-mates.

And they can't. Norman arrives at the crease, orders his troops to disappear in various directions (mostly leading to the leg-side boundary) and measures his skip. Up floats the ball. Each delivery is a potential incident. A six, a four, a brilliant stop, or a wicket. 'Dots' are few and far between. Maidens come about once a year (I'm told the position is similar in Cardiff).

At Paulton, in a match reduced to 12 overs, things were going badly. The ball was wet and no-one could grip it. Zaheer was playing for the Acorns. He had a bowl, but his over cost him 12 runs. So Norman came on into the wind. Norman hates bowling in the face of even a gentle breeze. His first ball climbed as high as usual. The batsman advanced to dispatch it. He swung the bat, but missed the ball. It slowly rolled towards the stumps. Recovering his wits, the batsman rushed back to his crease and put his foot behind the barely-moving ball. Norman, ever keen for wickets, appealed for l.b.w. The umpire ruled in his favour. The batsman was stunned, shouting down the pitch that 'the ruddy ball wouldn't even have reached the ruddy wicket'. But he went his weary way in the end.

Things do happen when Norman is bowling. On another famous occasion, this time in Tavistock, Norman was being hit to the leg-side boundary rather frequently by an aggressive left-hander. Norman thereupon sent all his fieldsmen to the affected area (as sandbags are sent to help stem floods). Our left-hander, espying the field, shrewdly decided to drive the ball to the cover boundary. He succeeded only in destroying his stumps, sending pieces of wood flying in all directions. Once again fielders fell about in helpless mirth as a furious batsman retraced his steps trying to think of a convincing story to tell his captain.

If these incidents suggest that Norman Teer plays in a low standard of cricket, they are misleading. His club (*his* Club) the Mendip Acorns has included Zaheer, Underwood, Vivian Richards and Don Shepherd amongst its numbers. To resist Norman's bait is not merely a matter of ability; it requires humility. It is the devil tempting Jesus on the hill. Pride demands that he must be hit for six, for how can one be a man and yet collect gentle singles off these sky-scrapers.

No, no red-blooded man could resist the challenge. Let the voice of caution be still awhile, let the boundary fielders be alert. Alas, the boundary is well staffed, and it is not so easy to hit such slow balls for six. And, thus, numerous self-respecting batsmen succumb, falling into the trap as knowingly as lemmings fall into the sea.

Norman derives enormous pleasure from watching opponents fall prey to his wiles. He loves his cricket in all its variations; the more improbable the venue, the more outlandish the game, the better. He has organised many overseas tours for his club – 25 in the past 12 years. Sierra Leone, the West Indies, Malta, and the Far East have all been visited. Not bad for an apparently innocuous tyre salesman.

That frail, Diary of a Nobody appearance is deceptive. Norman is a talented organiser. His tourists have included opera singers, academics, bookmakers and mechanics. The tyre business is a side-show, an excuse to spend a day by the phone arranging another tour. His only concession to the exigencies of business is to encourage Acorns to buy Teer's tyres (Teer's tyre pressure, it is called), just as Al Capone encouraged clients to buy his liquor.

Nor is Norman as shy as he looks. Startled Acorns often emerge from a 'plane to be greeted by dignitaries, steel bands and dancing girls. In Barbados Dr Eric Glair, by all acounts a formidable man, met the Acorns. 'Morning, Eric,' ventured our intrepid leader. Mr Teer has the hide of a hippo and the nerve of an unhelmeted batsman. He needs it, to bowl like that.

Acorns' cricket is deadly serious, particularly on tour. Humour arises from a haphazard series of events, or an improbable combination of individuals (for Acorns teams include examples of all shapes, hues, ages and abilities). It is not forced, the cricket is not for fun. Often the humour is unconscious.

There is nothing *necessarily* funny about Norman Teer and Derek Underwood bowling in harness. Yet in the West Indies in 1971 they were a hugely popular pairing. Quite what Deadly Derek made of it all one can only speculate. It was not long before local radio stations were providing running descriptions of the game, with commentators in danger of falling from their lofty perches as hilarity increased.

By the end of the tour people were coming from miles around to study this extraordinary bowler. Norman was a hero. Not that he was impressed in the slightest by all this fuss. He wheeled away with a lot of flight and bit of guile, watching with a perplexed air as the ball soared over the boundary, or explaining the subtleties of each wicket with the aplomb of Trueman in his prime.

For all the cheerful optimism of his bowling, Norman is immensely competitive. Woe betide any fielder who misses a chance off his bowling. Any ball hit in the air brings forth the view that the nearest beggar should have caught it. Possibly Norman does not select enough beggars. Once, amidst the usual tirade of hooks, cuts, drives and sweeps, a batsman popped up a ball into the vacant short-leg position. Captain Teer sidled up to me at the completion of the over and said, 'I knew I should have put someone there.' Volunteers for the forward short-leg position to

Norman Teer might have been few and far between in a team of VCs, I suspect.

As a cricketer Norman is, you may agree, colourful and imaginative. He is also not beyond a little deviousness. It is darkly whispered that Acorns teams are chosen so as to include plenty of batting and a scarcity of bowling. As the team gathers, Norman (the man who selected the team) sometimes peers around his players and discovers, to his dismay, that he has no opening bowlers. 'Better open up myself,' he concludes. Once this ploy worked well. Bowling the first over to a proficient batsman, Norman sent all his fielders to the boundary and served up a juicy, slow longhop. The opener duly smote it fiercely back to the bowler. It landed in our hero's stomach, knocking him to the ground. He clung to the ball, rising in triumph as he dusted himself, to explain, 'I knew he'd do that'.

Amidst all the batsman Norman often discovers, to his evident astonishment, that 'though our batting is strong, we don't appear to have a second opener'. Whereupon he straps on his pads, cuts and carves successfully until Cyril or Archie, well used to Teer's ways, judge their President to be l.b.w.

Despite advancing years, I expect Norman will contine for a long while. 'Just one more tour,' he repeats from time to time, much as Frank Sinatra would say, 'Just one more concert.' Anyhow, he still has one ambition left. To travel to a game on a camel. The Acorns tour Bahrain in 1981. Watch this space.

AWOL FROM OLD TRAFFORD

Geoffrey Green

I first saw the Australians in 1926. It was the fifth Test match at The Oval. My father, brother and I queued down the Vauxhall Road to get in and cleverly found ourselves a bench behind the bowler's arm at the Vauxhall end.

'Horseshoe' Collins won the toss for the enemy to take strike and once Harold Larwood and Maurice Tate had tried for a breakthrough without success, Wilfred Rhodes, the 'old man' in his late forties, was given the ball. Almost at once he castled the 'unbowlable' Bill Woodfall on his off-stump. Shortly he had Victor Richardson picked up by George Geary at deep mid-off. When at last he was rested Rhodes's figures were

9–8–1–2. England won that Test and with it the Ashes for the first time since before the First World War.

A quarter of a century later – 1953 to be precise – that same young boy had become a cricket correspondent. Instead of a bench in the open his perch was now in the Press Box to one side of the pavilion. Once again England won the Ashes, regaining the prize at home, indeed, for the first time since that earlier magical 1926.

Much had happened in those years between. For one thing I now wore long trousers instead of shorts. For another I had become a friend of Neville Cardus, the guru, the Poet Laureate of the game. Often we dined at his National Liberal Club at Charing Cross. On one such festive occasion he told me a story I should have marked well and inwardly digested. But I did not and later almost paid for it.

It was a cautionary tale and concerned a three-day Test against South Africa at Headingley in 1929. After two days it all seemed over. With seven wickets gone in their second innings, a mere 24 runs ahead and no batting apparently left to support 'Tubby' Owen Smith, South Africa looked to be down for the count. Cardus decided to leave Leeds that evening and return to London. Almost inevitably, it happened of course. Next day in Whitehall he saw an evening bill poster which screamed in large letters 'South Africa's Great Recovery'.

Sipping his wine, Cardus unfolded his predicament. 'I was in a mess. What could I do? The *Manchester Guardian* would be awaiting my 'on the spot' hot report. Here I was 200 miles from the scene and behind my back Owen Smith, hitting a brilliant 129 in two hours and inspiring a record South African last-wicket stand, had played the innings of his life. In the end England, needing 184 to win, had scraped home by five wickets and might even have lost but for an innings of 95 not out by Frank Woolley.

Wild imagination
'I rushed to my club and consulted the tape messages reporting the bare details of a sensational day's play. From those useful details and statistics I composed a column of "eyewitness" descriptive writing. I likened Owen Smith to the young Victor Trumper: I had schoolgirls watching the play with bated breath through telescopes: small boys could scarcely keep their analyses straight for the trembling of hands. The boundary line became a tightrope as the outcome balanced perilously. I followed blindly where my wild imagination led.

'The irony of it all came a fortnight later when I bumped into H.G. Deane, the South African skipper, at the fourth Test at Old Trafford. He congratulated me warmly on my *Guardian* report of that last day at Leeds. "You must have had the glasses on Owen Smith all the time . . ." '

Where is justice, where is truth? Who is to know. All I know is that half a dozen cricket journalists and myself later fell into the same trap. Our trip-wire happened to be the fourth Test against Australia at Old Trafford in 1953.

After five interrupted days broken by Manchester rain, England completed their first innings at tea-time on the last afternoon. Thanks to a typically stubborn innings by Trevor Bailey a bridge was built almost up to the Australian opening total. With only two hours of play left and the match no more than half-way done, we worldly-wise ones wrote it all off as a dead-duck draw, 'phoned our various offices and caught an early evening express for London rather than the dreary midnight stopper.

Preening ourselves on our shrewd foresight, we settled comfortably into the restaurant car and anointed ourselves with liquid refreshment. When the train stopped at Crewe, a stranger came aboard and sat down at the next table. Soon he fell into conversation suddenly to drop a bomb into the happy proceedings.

'I wonder how that Test ended?' he said. 'Oh! A stone cold draw,' we replied as another glass of liquid gold beguiled the tonsils. 'A stone cold draw!' exploded the stranger. 'I'll tell you something. I live near Crewe station and it was only with the greatest willpower that I dragged myself away from the TV to catch this train. Australia were 35 for eight in their second innings and Wardle had them in a spin.'

That was it. *We* were now in a spin. There was no stop between Crewe and Euston. We were utterly helpless. England could have won and here we were hurtling away from the eye of the storm. The next two or three hours were the worst of my life. AWOL: dereliction of duty. I could almost hear the blazing words exploding from an enraged editor.

At last it was Euston. I fell out of the train into the arms of a West Indies reporter. 'What was the Test result?' I croaked. 'It was a draw, man. But a near thing, man. Australia ended 35 for eight in their second knock, man.' I flew to the office in a taxi and shame-faced rewrote my copy for the second edition with the help of the tape machine details of the finish.

No-one congratulated me on anything: just a stony silence. But for days my life became one big lie as friends asked me whether Wardle *really* bemused the Aussies or whether they had light-heartedly thrown away their wickets. Experience told me they *never* did that. Nor did I ever again leave any event before the finish. Even I was not green enough to be caught a second time . . .

ALLETSON'S INNINGS

Cyril P. Foley

I was fortunate enough to be present on the Hove ground when Alletson, the Notts professional, played his world's record innings in 1911, or at least, to be strictly accurate, I saw the hurricane part of it. Nature had endowed Alletson with perhaps the most perfect proportions of any man I ever set eyes on. About six feet two inches in height, he walked with that springy tread so characteristic of the Zulus. No pen picture of him could be more applicable than Mr Rudyard Kipling's description of the son of the border thief, in his *Ballad of East and West*, which runs: 'He trod the ling like a buck in spring, and he looked like a lance at rest.' But Nature, as if to say: 'Let that suffice' had bestowed no other generous gifts upon him. He proved himself later on to be singularly devoid of judgment.

Alletson had gone in No.9 when Notts were only nine runs ahead of Sussex, and had three wickets to fall, in their second innings. He had scored 47 before lunch in 50 minutes, and had taken some ten minutes to score the 3 runs necessary to complete his 50 on resumption. Therefore when I arrived at 2.30 his score was 50-odd. He was in with the last man, W. Riley, who eventually made 10 not out. Now 50 in an hour is quite a reasonable rate of scoring, and nothing more, but from 2.25 to 2.55 he gave an exhibition of hitting which has never been, nor ever will be, approached. I say this with the greatest confidence. In the first 15 minutes of this half-hour he made 50 more runs, doubling his score and completing his century. But this was a slow rate of progression compared with what followed, for he then proceeded to treat the bowlers in a most ferocious manner, hitting the attack to all parts of the field (and very often out of it) with equal impartiality. In the second 15 minutes he actually added 89 more runs, so that in the 30 minutes' cricket that I was lucky enough to see he scored no fewer than 139 runs! That means that he *himself* was, for half an hour, scoring at the rate of 278 runs per hour. Words fail me.

He finished up by making 115 out of 120 off seven overs, hitting Killick for 22 in one over, and 34 (4, 6, 6, 4, 4, 4, 6) in another, there being two no-balls, and scored 34 off two overs from Leach, or *90 in four overs.*

And indeed had it not been for some unavoidable delays he would have made even more runs than he actually did in that last half-hour. In the first place, when he started hitting balls out of the ground, the new ones which the umpires were carrying in their pockets (for the 200 and 400) could not, in fairness to the batsman, be used, and fresh ones, with the shine off them, had to be sought for in the pavilion. Also time was wasted in trying to prise one ball out of the new stand into whose soft wood Alletson had driven it, no chisel being available. Alletson is the only person who has ever driven literally *into* a stand.

Had all this not occurred I see no reason why he should not have scored say 180 runs in that half-hour, instead of 139. One ball was recovered down by the sea which is, I suppose, a mile away. An old gentleman noticing a very small boy playing with a practically new ball on the sands asked him where he had obtained it. He said he had picked it up in the street outside the ground. One ball was lost for good and all. Alletson hit eight sixes, 23 fours (140 runs by boundaries) and only 17 singles! The fieldsmen and umpires had a very anxious half-hour, but by skilful agility managed to avoid contact with the ball, and no-one was killed or indeed seriously injured.

After these fireworks, his appearance at Lord's against Middlesex was eagerly anticipated. An enormous crowd assembled to see him. He certainly made a fair score, including a gigantic on-drive over the clock, but was otherwise disappointing. From then onwards he retired into his shell and absolutely refused to hit. Later in the season I went to see him at The Oval, and happened to sit in the Nottinghamshire dressing-room next to A.O. Jones, the Notts skipper. 'Jonah' was in despair. He said to me: 'The man can't be normal. I've told him that I will play him in every match all through the season even if he makes recurrent cyphers, *as long as he'll hit*, but he just won't do it. You'll see for yourself presently.' And I did. In came Alletson with a huge crowd on tiptoe with excitement and made the most scratchy 11 runs possible. Never once did he attempt to hit the ball.

As he was not a bowler he had to be dropped out of the side. Considering that cricket was his means of livelihood, his conduct, in the face of what his captain had told him, was so extraordinary as to be quite inexplicable. All the same he did enough in one single innings to establish his name for ever in the records of English cricket.

THE VILLAGE GAME

Edmund Blunden

A thunderstorm is stooping over the old cricket ground in my memory. It is not a date that I can identify, and I do not know who the awaited opponents of our team are – an Estate, a Brewery, the Constabulary, some sort of Rovers, more likely just another village side. It is the forenoon, and that inky cloud is working round the hill, as black almost as the spinney of firs on the boundary, imported trees which I always suspect of being aloof in their hearts from the scene and its animations. I feel oily splashing drops and doubt if we shall have the promised encounter in the afternoon. The summer seems to have fallen into low spirits, and there is nobody about except the rooks and pigeons – we have heard all they have to say – and a crying woodpecker down under the oak at the river. The storm drifts, the cloud-edges are effaced; but the rain patters steadily on the metal roof of the mowing shed, the gutters gurgle, all the trees are grey with the shower. Past the far side of the field a figure with a sack for hood drives his cycle apace, never turning his eyes this way for a moment; and no one from the vicarage steps out to see if there is any prospect of play.

Yet the hours pass, and after all the rain has wearied, and stopped. The smoky-looking day may remain thus, neither better nor worse, and the turf is good. A bicycle is being pushed through the meadow gate by a cricketer in flannels under his mackintosh, and one by one they all assemble. An unlocking of padlocks and shifting of benches in the pavilion, a thump of bats and stumps being hauled out of the dark corners. The creases are marked, and the offer of a bowling screen rejected. Our boys put catapults back in their jackets and affect to know personally the visitors now arriving, pointing out one or two with awe – that one who hits sixes, and that one with the spectacles who never scores less than seventy. There are not many cricket caps on show, and some of the players are observed to feel safest with braces and ties on.

Sawdust wanted! The fielding side have spread themselves about the soaked ground, and all is otherwise ready – even the two batsmen have gone out to their creases, casting rather unhappy looks on their companions in the pavilion, who sit down in a row and brood. It is odd, this serious game; perhaps it is the greyness of the day that causes it to take this mood. Sawdust! A bucket is being carried forth by the groundsman, whose squat shoulders and beard look like the picture of Hudibras; he tips out his two little mounds of sawdust, and marches off to his shed, as who should say, 'That is the end of the match for me. That *is* the match.' The one-armed bowler measures his run, dips the ball into the sawdust, and with three or four sharp steps whizzes it at the opposed batsman; it passes with a wet smack into the gloves of the man behind the stumps. All the fieldsmen attend gravely. This bowler has pace. But no smile.

But the ball won't turn and after a time the batsman lose their reverence and risk sending it over the head of the little man at point; the score is hoisted, and the bowlers are changed. It is mainly that schoolboy who is the cause of this. His score in the book is inspected, it adds up to 18 already. He looks too delicate to perform among these rugged elders, but he is calm enough. At last a large hand and circling arm send him a ball which sails up very much like the one before which he carted over peering faces into the long wet grass; it falls shorter, hits him on the boot. He knows his offence, and the umpire does not let him off; but his innings has gone far enough. There are several batsmen to follow him, and already the total is one which in these games of strong trundlers may serve – 50 up. The boy who has seen to this matter and accepted the punishment for his single error so immediately goes walking away there, with his hands stuck into his green jacket, as if on Robinson Crusoe's island, to the far parts of the field. He seems to have this cricket business in his pocket. When he was questioned just now as he put his pads away 'what the bowling was like,' he answered slowly and peacefully, 'The fellow from the lower end turns them a little from the off.'

The circuit of the field which falls away to the stream is wide enough for him to be still strolling and watching the blue moths among the sorrel when the downfall of the last of his team-mates arrives. It was not so easy out there as he found it. These men with the ball have a terrible natural skill. Perhaps it is not mere talk, that they can drop it on a threepenny bit placed between the wickets. They can probably hit a rat with a turnip in the light of their lantern before he knows that he is in the way.

But here is the second part of the game, and the relaxation of the interval dies into another period of silent close watching. Only about 75 runs are necessary, but those who are to try for them do not look exactly merry at the prospect. The church clock tolls out again, five o'clock; it always comes to the hour slower, speaks it in a lower tone than that brisk silver-voiced one at the grange. In the pavilion a faint notion goes that 'if we can't get the runs we may make a draw of it'; but half-past six under the circumstances is a good way off. Once again in the sulky light against the gloomy trees the bowlers appear the dangerous persons of the drama as they strike their heels in, start their run and slam the ball at their opponents; the stiff farmer and the patient gardener, though their chins express refusal to be less than British, do not quite treat their bats as natural extensions of themselves. As their admirers the boys look at their narrow escapes, there are inevitable gaspings. Meanwhile someone looks away from the torture for a moment and directs attention to two youths in the next field: youths who ought to have been playing here, and who are credited with ability equal to any bowler's attack in the world; and these are on their way unconcernedly to bream swims with rods and baskets and landing nets. A case of defection, too sad to be dwelt upon, but it all goes with this slow grey day.

The home team is in trouble. The curate from whom (on the old principle 'omne ignotum pro magnifico') at least a few wristy educated shots were expected on his first appearance here, has just had his bails flicked off, very hard luck; and the side is half out. The scoreboard is not our study now. Moreover, Mr Warrener won't get his innings; he has received a message from his master, General Goble, who surely could not have sent for him at this (familiar) crisis except on account of some truly grave emergency. A boy, however, is walking out to the captain of the fielding side, to supplicate for leave to bat instead of the confidential Warrener. The captain grins, pulls the boy's ear and says yes. The boy comes back with an attempt to be neutral about it, 'It's all in the day's work,' but he feels alarmed, and things all round are grey.

Bert Pilgrim, who has a rich curly head of bronze hair, goes and confronts the bowlers. He takes a bat which is so chewed up – the only spare one too – that only he (it suits him) uses it in a match. He does not use it long, but he operates it much as when he tries his strength at the Flower Show with the maul which drives a block up a tall post, to ring a bell and return the penny if bumped hard enough. He gets one boundary off the dodging umpire's backside and a six in the homely equipage of the old woman selling popcorn, liquorice straps and still lemonade. The score is not improved enough in spite of all this, and Bert comes back again rather grumpy because a very old gentleman, as he sees age, has wrought his downfall with the very kind of bowling he prays for to his heathen gods. The ancient, belted in several faded colours round a massive central contour, first took leave to bowl a few gentle ones up and down aside from the wicket, while the batsman affected indifference. Such was the fashion of those unhaggling days, though it was going. Then to the game again. The ball was coming up so mildly, but it evaded Bert's punitive swing, he glared round, the bails fell, he said something. And another one.

The end is in sight; some restless man begins putting away the tackle lying about – and the boy who bats in place of Mr Warrender finds himself going in. 'Just you stay there.' But 'over' was called. In his neat shoes polished like his locks for the match, the boy stands prepared to run any number of runs. 'Poggy' at the far end puts his bat to the ball – the boy is called: 'no, yes, go back, come on' – and with a little pause of compassion and shame the bowler, ball in hand, breaks the wicket at the boy's end. He pats him on the shoulder, which is Fame enough. The match is finished, stumps are pulled up; players withdraw from the place, leaving two sawdust patches and some tracks of trampled mud for the alighting rook to investigate. And at last the western sky glows into a little colour, like the streaks on the honeysuckle by the glistening hedge which the players and their friends pass on their way to strong tea and plum cake in their homes. We shall not be very well pleased to find the match reported in next week's *Messenger*.

So runs this once-upon-a-time in my memory, which as I admitted I do not acquit of growing old along with me; yet perhaps it has not given an altogether wrong evidence on this subject. The cricket was all rather a grave affair. I suppose it was the weather mostly that made it so, and any one from abroad who knows the prevailing summer gloom surrounding a landing at Dover may concur. But the game gave me some sense of being rather a continuation of rural labours than a sport and pastime. It was carried through as earnestly as, say, measuring the hops in a bin, or bringing a team of horses over the bridge with that queer thing a car steering along from the other direction; where there was skill, it was applied with the same attentiveness as the skill of grafting a tree. Perhaps it was the weather, I say to myself again, and there must have come another day, and come many a time, when the laughing sky was reflected in the light-hearted frolics and gaieties of my old country cricketers. Not even thus can I find a way from their habit of cricket, a hard game. They were too firmly fixed within necessities of toil and shrewdness, duty and plainness, to be easily renewed in a short interlude as children of the sun. Their cricket was of another mood from that which would be played on the same ground a few days later by those whose tradition was polished entertainment, the social round, the glorious indolence of a 'modest competence' or a small fortune.

TAKING HOLIDAY

W. Pett Ridge

There were great players to be seen at St John's Wood, folk whose names will always be associated with what Nyren's book calls 'the elegant and manly game of Crickett', and occasionally I meet them there now; they come along rather slowly, depending a good deal on a walking-stick, and they take the steps up to the pavilion with a certain deliberation. C.I. Thornton awakens thoughts of big hitting of the past – with one of the Fords and Bonner as rivals in powerfulness – and Mr Wright and Captain Wynyard. The rule at Lord's is that you talk to your neighbour or you listen to him, and the second course I have always found the more profitable. The powers of memory there are astonishing. An elderly man who looks as though his mind is concentrating on the next meal, and nothing else, will suddenly, on some hint, arouse himself, and tell you with detail of an innings played here in '75.

• • • • • •

The description of veteran is applied early enough to a cricketer; at forty the general impression conveyed by those who write about the game is that the player of that age is approaching senility; if at forty-five he should do anything commendable in bowling or batting, profound surprise is exhibited. With such a brief time allowed, it is small wonder that names are quickly forgotten, heard only when reminiscences start at Lord's or at The Oval. There you can hear of the Palairets of Somerset and the Lucases of Essex, and other cricketing families, admired and envied; you listen to good talk of the Graces, and some familiar anecdote concerning W.G. and his antipathy to baths, and once-popular names are flung to and fro. But in his summer day the cricketer has his share of fame. Newspaper posters are devoted to him, conversation in evening trains has no other topic, his exploits are studied even by the middle-aged before any attention is given to 'Advice to Investors'. The autograph collector had scarcely begun his hunting in the last century, but generations to come will study the books of signatures handed down to them and grandfather's aid will have to be called in to sort out the

Hearnes and distinguish the Woolleys. The autumn of a professional's life is certainly better than it was. In the eighties and the nineties there seemed no alternative for him but to act as landlord of The Bird in Hand; now he becomes an honoured coach at a public school with, it can be assumed, a good round sum on deposit account, and the local bank manager always glad to have a chat with him.

Lord Northcliffe asked me to find out how the crowd was made up at a London cricket match; it astonished him to observe that so many people had so much leisure. I had to tell him that the Londoner can always spare the time to watch other people engaged in arduous exercise, and, moreover, there were members of all classes with little other occupation than that of counting the hours. Also, folk could snatch a holiday by candour or ingenuity when bat and ball proved an attraction. As to The Oval and how the minor patrons found the money, I could ascertain no information. One could only suspect that they borrowed from each other.

WANTED FOR MURDER

Terence Rattigan

'The "dullest ever" series between England and Australia has ended fittingly in a dreary, water-logged draw.' So you will have read, no doubt, as also the fairly widely held critical verdict that Test cricket, as a crowd-drawing spectacle, is as good as dead.

If you should also have read the theatrical critics – but why should you, when you don't have to? – you will also have learned that the present London Theatre Season has been the 'worst in living memory' and that 'panic reigns in Shaftesbury Avenue' because plays are so bad today that audiences 'simply can't be drawn to see them'.

Now I suppose if I were as young as some of your readers I would be seriously alarmed by these judgments. My two favourite pastimes, watching Test cricket and going to the Theatre, would both seem to have had it, and the future would be quite unlivable. I would take to drink and, happily, die of it.

But, also happily (anyway in this case) I am not young, and I can assure my fellow cricket and theatre lovers alike that the expert writers on both subjects have been regularly pronouncing their irrevocable death sentences for as long as I can remember, and that is for well over forty years.

In 1921 Test cricket was killed by Warren Armstrong's 'determination to win at all costs', and by England's 'appalling mediocrity'. A couple of years later the West-end theatre was killed by '2 L.O.' and by 'the dearth of good new plays'. At very regular intervals since they have both died a number of times through some sad and irremediable concatenation of circumstances.

In 1930 Bradman killed Test cricket by making too many runs. In 1931 talking films killed the Theatre, by giving the people more entertainment for less money. Body line killed Test cricket again the following year. Somerset Maugham killed the Theatre again the year after that by writing two failures and retiring. In 1934 Bradman killed Test cricket by making too many runs once more. (And in 1938 too, come to think of it.) Meanwhile the Theatre had been completely and finally destroyed by the war-scare, and the war; and after the war by Mr Baird's interesting invention, which later finally destroyed Test cricket too.

The obituaries in fact have been innumerable but the two 'fabulous invalids' seem to have somehow tottered on. Until 1964, anyway, when, I admit, they have been both, for the first time that I can remember, clearly pronounced dead in the self-same year.

This coincidence induces an analogy between Cricket and the Theatre which, though patently inexact, has always, to me, had a kernel of truth.

At about the same time that Dexter was taking guard on Saturday evening at The Oval, while thirty thousand spectators watched in an electric hush of expectation (hadn't they read their morning papers, the idiots? Didn't they know that the game had been killed the day before by Lawry? And the day before that, by England's inept batting?). Laurence Olivier, in another arena, but in Dexter's county, was just about finishing his own innings in *Othello*; and with:

'I kissed thee ere I killed thee; no way but this,

Killing myself to die upon a kiss'

was about to score his anticipated but still breathlessly awaited hundred between lunch and tea. (In fact his Othello, when on form, I would rate as slightly better than three hundred and nine runs, in a Test, in a day. Forgive me, Sir Donald – but there it is.)

One wonders how many of those theatre critics who have firmly buried the British Theatre, 1964, have tried to get a seat for *Othello* at Chichester, 1964. I did, and succeeded only by a calculated blend of toadyism, patience and corruption. The same methods got me into the Final Test 1964, but only just – the corruption and toadyism had to be rather more, the patience only little less. (And Test cricket was buried, remember, at Old Trafford.)

Now does this prove anything at all, except that the critics are almost always wrong? As I have said, only the very young and very gullible need reassurance there. Yes, I think it provides evidence for a belief I nurture about cricket – a belief unpopular with sports masters and possibly with your readers – that cricket is no more a team game than *Othello* is a team play. Test cricket, like great drama, needs a star.

True that I cajoled my way into The Oval in the *hope* of seeing a great drama. A Final Test, with the rubber still at stake, might well have provided one. But would I have cajoled quite as eagerly if Dexter and O'Neill hadn't been in the cast?

True, too, that I slimed my way into the Chichester Festival Theatre in the *certainty* of seeing a great drama. *Othello* is nearly my favourite play, and with McKenzie playing it opposite Trueman as Desdemona it would still give me pleasure. (Rather a lot, come to think of it.) But would I have slimed quite so eagerly if Olivier had been standing down that evening with a slipped disc? – And believe me, in that performance, he can easily slip almost anything.

The answer to both questions is surely a resounding 'No'. We queue to see great stars. For group acting we may wander to our local rep. For team cricket we may meander to our county ground (and in neither place do we always get what we have come to see). But for Test cricket, and for Shakespeare's drama we demand our dram of genius.

Unhappily neither Dexter nor O'Neill made his anticipated ton at The Oval and 'Oh the pity of it, Iago! Oh, Iago, the pity of it!' (which, incidentally, is a line that no plodding club cricketer of a playwright could ever dream up and shows Shakespeare's genius as clearly as a Wally Hammond off-drive) but the 'glorious uncertainty' of cricket has always included the strong possibility of seeing our idols ingloriously dismissed. Even Olivier is capable of an injudicious slash at a rising ball, notable, he tells me, when, in *Othello*, he tries to take the 'Pontic Sea' speech in one breath, as Kean apparently did. Then he too can return to the pavilion to a muted and disappointed ripple of applause.

Besides genius doesn't need a long innings to display itself. As a yelling ten-year-old boundary ball-returner I saw Macartney make a mere nineteen at Taunton in 1921. Genius shone unmistakably for those twenty minutes, and I remember every stroke (or think I do). Those I tried to copy I was instantly and correctly caned for, but my worship of cricket genius has flourished happily since that day.

But as long as there is a Dexter and an Olivier, an O'Neill and a Gielgud, I honestly don't think that either Test cricket or the British Theatre has much to worry about.

THREE YEARS AGO

'Avon'

It is almost three years since Jane and I went to Nottingham. To Midlanders this means since we went to the Test match. Test matches and visits to Lord's were the only events that were allowed to rank with our sojournings at Edgbaston.

This particular Test was, as usual, the first of the rubber, and was an event of some importance. Four English youngsters, Hutton, Edrich, Compton and Wright, already hailed as successors to such giants as Hobbs, Sutcliffe, Woolley and Hendren, were facing the Australians for the first time. The visitors, although lacking the craft of Grimmett, counted on Ward and a much-improved Fleetwood-Smith to balance this loss; whilst we viewed the averages of Badcock and Hassett, 63 and 88, with grave misgiving.

A car was essential if we were to reach Nottingham from our Warwickshire backwater in anything like time to get on the ground, so we naturally took steps to commandeer our nearest car acquaintance. This somewhat disreputable Ford belonged to Claude, Jane's brother. The subsequent news that the Ford was a casualty as the result of an impact with a juggernaut of a lorry, was an appalling setback. A family conclave took place, whereat Jane, Claude, John (Jane's other brother) and I went into conference. We decided that a car must be hired and John undertook this responsibility. Jane and I were to contribute the lunch, and Claude was to bring his binoculars. The meeting then dispersed until Friday.

The task of preparing and packing the lunch got Jane up at six o'clock. She volunteered the depressing news that it was raining – hard. I quelled such gloomy ideas by remarking that early rain invariably preceded a glorious day and anyway it would make play interesting. By seven we were ready, equipped with hamper, rugs, mackintoshes, umbrellas, camera and sun-glasses. Our fears that we might not get our morning papers before the starting hour proved groundless. We had read *The Times* cricket pages, enjoyed Neville Cardus in the *Manchester*

Guardian, and almost completed *The Times* crossword puzzle before there was any sign of the other half of the party. Eventually a screech of brakes and a creak of springs drew our attention to what otherwise would have been overlooked. For the vehicle John had acquired was the smallest of all small cars and exceedingly old and decrepit.

John and Claude seemed to overflow into every available cranny. We surveyed the small area of back seat, the lunch basket, the rest of the paraphernalia, Jane, and finally myself, six feet four and broad in proportion. At one point it seemed that I was in danger of being jettisoned in favour of the luncheon basket, so I promptly squeezed in, repeating firmly to myself that a Test match was worth any amount of physical discomfort. My weight gave an ominous list to the chassis, which the others did not appear to notice. Jane, who mercifully is small and slight, fitted herself in where I wasn't.

On the way John amused himself by coaxing the last ounce of speed out of the overloaded midget; Claude shouted directions gleaned from an AA map on his lap; Jane gave us weather reports every few minutes, while I occupied myself in keeping the hamper on an even keel. The nearer we drew to Nottingham the brighter grew the skies. As the car threaded its way through the labyrinthine parking ground, the sun made its first wan appearance. During the long walk to the ground we readily absorbed the festive atmosphere. We revelled in the jostling crowds, the endless queues, the bunting, the ubiquitous hawkers, the 'To the Test Match' notices.

The hour of waiting was packed with interest. The nets in front of us were the focal point of attention. There, most of the Australians and a few of the English team were busy loosening up. With mounting excitement, we recognised each personality. The subsequent minutes were most absorbing and at the end of them we felt we knew Bradman, Farnes, Paynter, Yardley, Badcock, Fleetwood-Smith and Wright as well as we knew Hollies, Mayer, or Ord. And, at last, we had seen Bradman bat, a pleasure again to be denied us, for Hammond had won the toss. The nets and motor-roller disappeared, and the appearance of Chester and Robinson, sedate and dignified, hushed the crowd.

It was indeed a memorable day's cricket, still unclouded by the fog of war. We can still hear the crack of Barnett's bat against ball, the gasp of the crowd at Bradman's dropped catch, the tense quiet preceding the thunder of applause that greeted Barnett's hundred, the sympathetic laughter aroused by Fleetwood-Smith's pantomime after failing to hold a hot return. We can still see O'Reilly pounding to the wicket in tireless aggression, Hutton facing the attack with typical imperturbability, Compton charming us with his young elegance, and Bradman racing indefatigably along the boundary.

We rose with the rest of the crowd to Paynter and Compton as they returned to the pavilion, and realised with a slight pang (then as now) that it would be a long time before we saw such a day's cricket again.

CRICKET

B. Bennison

The first county cricket match I saw was between Lancashire, my native county, and the Australians, in 1888. It opened to me a world of wonders and told of my greatest adventure. For I watched and feasted with a ghost of a stricken conscience at my elbow – I should have been at school instead of Old Trafford. But gladly did I pay each and all the penalties that inevitably followed playing truant. I had found the home of giants that had seemed impossibly remote from actuality, for there was spread before me, magically, incredibly, what I decided were the greatest cricketers ever: my county's captain, A.N. Hornby, Johnny Briggs, Richard Barlow and the Rev. J.R. Napier; and from Australia had come black-bearded Blackham to challenge comparison with our very own Pilling as wicket-keeper. There were mighty-hitting Percy McDonnell, stone-walling Bannerman and C.T.B. Turner and the lightning bowler, Jones. Every ball, every stroke, every run, every wicket were my own special concern.

And a miracle happened. Lancashire won by some twenty-odd runs. Briggs at one end bowled so as to make the ball talk; Napier at the other pounded away, the fighting parson to the spit. And the apparently impossible having been made possible, I was lifted over the rails and carried by the rush of a multitude of loud-shouting folk to the front of the pavilion, where, the while full-grown men bawled for Hornby and Briggs and Napier, and each and every member of the county team, I piped shrilly.

And now, as I write, after all the long, crowded, changing years that have since gone, I live anew that glorious, never-to-be-forgotten day. It was the day of my marriage to cricket, and had much, if not all, to do with the shaping of my life. I have lived long and worked for every sport – cricket, as all men-making games, my passion, if not my religion. In service I am old, and there are moments when perhaps, like the rest of the veterans, I remark, and even bewail, the comparatively few outstanding cricketers as compared with the days of my youth. But I am not of those who deplore the decadence of cricket, even to the extent of prophesying its death.

That the game as a whole has not the impelling distinctiveness and the bite it once had, may not be denied. But cricket is neither dead nor near to dying; for that which is instinctive of breed and race is eternal. Although we may regret a decreasing number of towering personalities, the game, as a game, is unalterable. I would draw swords with those who say that cricket, whether played by country or county, is no longer inseparable from the life of the people; and I have small patience with those who are for ever reminding the younger generation that there will never be another W.G. Grace, nor the stalwarts of his era. It is surely enough that W.G. Grace, in every regard, stood alone. He was the game's bible, as he was its greatest magnet. For a lifetime he was, and meant, everything to us and all cricketing nations. Physically huge, more than generously bearded, comically capped, it was as if it were pre-ordained that he should overshadow all his contemporaries.

We did not go to see this and that match as a match, whether having to do with country or county, we went to see W.G.

'The greatest cricketer ever, unquestionably,' declared Sir John Le Sage, under whose editorship I served on the staff of the *Daily Telegraph*. 'But,' he added, with a roguish twinkle in his gimlet eye, 'he was perhaps the most handsomely paid of any public servant.' Which dig was by way of recalling the *Daily Telegraph* shilling fund as a mark of appreciation of the Grand Old Man's hundred hundreds. The better part of £10,000 was subscribed. 'And believe me,' invited Le Sage, 'Grace so carefully counted the number of shillings as they were acknowledged in the columns of the paper, that he knew, to the last bob, what would be handed over to him.'

· · · · · ·

John Berry Hobbs, with his near to two hundred centuries, arrived too late. Hobbs will go down into history as an unsurpassed batsman. His unparalleled performances are so fresh that they call for no recapitulation. Indeed, it is scarcely believable that he is no longer England's number one batsman. He retired when he was by no means past his prime. But Hobbs may well be content; his innings was a long and glorious and noble one.

The Oval cannot be the same again without Hobbs, of course not. But much the same was said when Bobby Abel, as 'the Governor', stepped down, and Tom Hayward bade farewell, and when Tom Richardson, the greatest fast bowler of his, or any, age (and I well mind the demon Spofforth), had delivered his last ball, and the inimitable Strudwick had ceased to keep wicket. And those of the older Surrey guard for ever sighed for another George Lohmann, a Tom Hayward, a Lockwood, a Brockwell, and others who, under the captaincy of Jack Shuter, made up the most powerful Surrey team of all.

Reminiscences, however, make for joys and sorrows. In my callow days I did swear that Johnny Briggs was a heaven-sent bowler; and of a truth he was. And A.N. Hornby was at once a martinet and the most remarkable of the game's leaders. There was bearded Dickie Barlow, to whom we gave a licence to stone-wall the day long, so that we might revel in the shade which he gave to the dazzle and daring and dictatorship of Hornby. There was, when free, A.G. Steel, capable of bowling out any side; there was Frank Sugg, a hurricane hitter, and a joy to behold in the long field; and Arthur Mold, whom Jim Phillips, the old Australian Middlesex professional, declared was a chucker, to the loud and righteous indignation of the county. And Dick Pilling, of the high priests of stumpers; and Scotch Alec Watson. How we missed them as, one by one, they dropped out; but there came Archie MacLaren to succeed Hornby, and establish himself as an immensely gifted leader of men. A complete cricketer, when a boy at Harrow, was MacLaren, a batsman of superlative quality. And Johnny Tyldesley, Reggie Spooner, Sydney Barnes, and others came to more than fill up the gaps and set the loftiest standard of excellence. That those who have followed have not conformed to those standards permits neither of wonder nor excuse for repining. In striking comparisons, we are all too apt to lose a sense of values.

The last match I saw between Lancashire and Yorkshire was dull, even wearisome to many of us; there was no bubble in it. But there was delight in the remembrance of other times, the days when there crossed the border into the County Palatine, George Ulyett, often to be teased and lured to destruction by Johnny Briggs; and there were Bobby Peel, Tunnicliffe, J.T. Brown, George Hirst, Wilfred Rhodes, with Lord Hawke on Yorkshire's bridge. If there was no sitting on the splice then, there was abundant reason – the fight of it, the intimacy of the gamble, the humour, the humanity of it all. There was no such cricket in the land, and we were unashamed partisans, every one of us. It is probable that when I last saw the rival counties I was cursed by retrospection; but I confess that I came away from Old Trafford doubtful whether Lancashire and Yorkshire matches were so severely personal as in what I am pleased to call 'my time', or as they were not so many years ago.

When motoring from Scotland I broke my journey to London at Ilkley. With bag and baggage, I sought hotel accommodation for the night. 'Has tha heard?' asked the porter, deaf to my requests to be shown my room. 'Tha wouldna credit it. It's awful. I can't believe it. If it doesn't beat cock-fighting, I don't know what does.' And wild-eyed, he prattled on to set me speculating upon the extent of some near-by catastrophe. 'Well,' I inquired, 'what has happened?' 'You don't mean to say you haven't heard. Why, we've lost, when we had no more than a handful of runs to make.' And away he went, leaving me to fend for myself. The dreadful news, I discovered, was that Yorkshire had lost to Lancashire; and in the matter of that porter, the hotel was as good as closed.

• • • • • •

There are two innings that stand out as the greatest I have been privileged to witness – Ranjitsinhji's 154 not out, in the second innings against Australia, at Manchester in 1896, and Gilbert Jessop's 104 out of 139 in 75 minutes in the concluding Test of the 1902 tour.

Ranji was all the batsmen. For sheer brilliance his batting has never been equalled. Of every known and, if the paradox is permissible, unknown stroke, he was master. Nothing in the art of batsmanship bore relationship to his glide on the leg side. It was a stroke of which he was the inventor. By an almost imperceptible flick of the wrist he would change the course of any ball to fine leg. The shot involved enormous risk. As it was done by Ranji, it seemed to be the natural thing for him to do. His sense of timing was uncanny. Clem Hill summed up the Indian prince exactly when he declared, 'He is not a batsman; he is a juggler.'

Ranji's innings was not the only masterpiece in this particular Test. Tom Richardson put up what I consider to have been the most prodigious bowling performance of his wonderful career. As a feat of endurance alone it was beyond the capacity of any other man to have accomplished. This is what the lion-hearted fellow did. On a perfect wicket, against a batting side of immense power, he bowled no fewer than 68 overs at a pace and of such length as he alone could have maintained; in the second innings he sent down 42 consecutive overs. For three hours he bowled continuously. Altogether, he took 13 wickets at a cost of a little over 16 runs each. No figures can convey an adequate idea of what this lovable man of Surrey did. With everything against him – sun, heat, wicket – he forced the batsman to fight for every single run. No faster bowler, no greater or so natural a bowler ever lived, than black-haired, big and smiling Tom Richardson.

It did not seem possible, despite his unexampled bowling, that England would escape defeat. For this is how the match shaped itself. In response to the Australians' total of 412, England had to follow on 181 behind. Then it was that Ranji, who in his first knock had scored 62, rose in all his glory. The expresses of Ernest Jones were as nothing to him. The higher the ball he made to jump and kick, the more readily did Ranji score. His bat was as a magician's wand. He drove and cut and glided. There was no finality to his strokes. He stood bolt upright to Jones, a thing no other batsman would have dared to do for fear of serious personal injury. But the unerring eye of Ranji, his quick-footedness and supple wrists were such that, of all the mad, rising balls, he missed only one; and though it split the soft part of his ear, he held to his mastery. It was an innings that deserved to win any match. Unhappily for England, it did not. England lost, in a dramatic finish, by three wickets. But what did the result really matter? We had been entranced by a prince of batsmen.

But if Ranji, at Old Trafford, had robbed us of words to express our admiration of his batsmanship, Jessop stirred us to the very depths six years later. We went to The Oval for the last Test in 1902, still tingling by what had happened at Manchester a few weeks before, when, thanks to the inspired bowling of Lockwood, who took 11 wickets for seven runs each, England were left with 174 runs to win. The first four batsmen between them scored 89, and to all appearances the match was as good as won. We reckoned without Hughie Trumble, however, and his never-say-die fellows. Dick Lilley was out to a catch in a thousand by Clem Hill, fielding on the boundary, and when Tate (father of Maurice), the last man, came in, eight runs were still wanted by England to win. Tate got four, and was then bowled by Saunders. So it was that Australia not only won by three runs, but, having been victorious in the two matches of the series that had been finished, had made sure of the rubber.

At The Oval in 1902, Joe Darling had the good fortune to win the toss, and to have first knock on a wicket that was full of runs. Australia, however, scored no more than 324 after batting all day, which was a total smaller than was to have been expected. There was rain during the night, and as a result, a batsman's wicket was changed to one that emphatically favoured the bowler. In the conditions, England did quite well to make 183. Going in a second time, Australia were put out for 121, which meant that England were set the apparently hopeless task of scoring 263 to win. We had given up the ghost, when Archie MacLaren, Lionel Palairet, Tom Hayward and Johnny Tyldesley had been dismissed for 40.

Then came Jessop, to recover all that had been lost. Exploiting his natural bent to the full, he hammered away, though not after the manner of a mere slugger. There was high skill in each and every shot he made. He chanced nothing, and yet he chanced everything. And when the end came to his now-or-never innings, we rose to him as one man. The Australians were dumbfounded. They had had many a quiet wager that Jessop would never make 100 or near to 100 against them. Although he scored at such a rate (104 in 75 minutes), let it not be forgotten, he did not give a chance. He thumped the ball to all parts of the field; he gave to each ball whatever length he cared, the while George Hirst kept his end up like a Trojan. A cricketing miracle had been performed. When Jessop at last fell, he left Hirst in possession, and there were only Lilley and Rhodes to bring up the rear with 49 runs still wanted for victory: 15 runs were still required when Lilley was caught by Darling in the deep field.

Hirst and Rhodes, like true Yorkshiremen, took the bit between their teeth, and got the runs to give England the match by one wicket. But it was Jessop's match, and it marked the greatest achievement of his wonderful career. And it came near to being the finish of a well-known London critic: with the getting of the last run, he collapsed. 'But,' he allowed, when he came to, 'it was worth it.'

HOW'S THAT?

C.H. Freame

I've got a friend named Spencer who takes a special delight in anything in the nature of puzzles and problems. That is to say, he tackles 'Torquemada' in *The Observer* every week and is a bit of a dab at the more difficult kind of acrostics. Well, he affects to be superior to all other forms of sport, but he takes what he says is a purely academic interest in cricket because he contends that it is the only game where brains count for much. Mind you, he absolutely refuses to play the game, but he frequently goes to Lord's and other places to watch a first-class match and returns and demonstrates to me by theory how the batsmen, bowlers and captains all showed a general lack of intelligence and knowledge of tactics, and proceeds to show how, if he had been in the place of the people named, the game would have had quite a different result. Of course, I try to pour scorn on his theories, but at an argument I'm a poor thing compared with him, and, to tell the truth, I've always got a sneaking feeling that he's right.

Well, he and I were seated with two other friends in the Mound Stand on a lovely July day last year, watching India, in the persons of 'Duleep' and 'Pat', making hay of the 'Professor's' attack, when Spencer disturbed our beatific contentment with the following:

'I suppose,' he said, with his maddening air of superiority, 'it's most unreasonable to expect you fellows to tell me what should happen in a case like this?'

We looked at him in irritation.

'Not now,' I begged, 'bottle it up till the tea interval. Have a fruit drop?'

I passed the bag to him, but he waved it aside and continued inexorably.

'We will assume,' he said, 'that a match is being played by two sides, both holding the letter of the law to be more important than the spirit thereof. The opening pair on one side are making a good stand, and the fall of a wicket seems unlikely. The batsman who is in next, No. 3, the 'star' bat of the side, after sitting with his pads on expectantly, has pushed off for the purpose of having what is, I believe, described as a 'quick one'.

By this time we had realised the futility of attempting to stem the flow and had reluctantly detached our minds from the game.

'A number of the other players,' continued Spencer, 'have been taking a little quiet practice in a net in a corner of the ground, and, having returned, are now standing in a group in the pavilion doorway, watching their opening pair get on with the good work. One of them, the wicket-keeper, an atrocious bat, having taken last knock in the net, still has his pads on. Suddenly a wicket falls and enquiries are immediately made as to the whereabouts of No.3, who after a minute or two is located in the bar. Before he can get to the dressing-room and collect his bat and gloves, however, the other players notice the fielding captain approach the umpire and the latter, after a glance towards the pavilion and a moment of indecision, raises his index finger. Seizing a bat and a pair of gloves, the wicket-keeper proceeds towards the wicket, to be told on arrival, as he had expected, that he was out under law 45, which allows only two minutes for a batsman to come in. However, from previous experience of this team, the fielding skipper knows perfectly well that this particular player invariably goes in last, and, suspecting what has happened, protests to the umpire that the 'star' player, No.3, should really be out. The umpire is naturally in a dilemma, but after consulting with his colleague at the other end, adheres to his original decision and states that as the wicket-keeper is the batsman who has come in, he must be the one to be given out. Now the question which arises is, 'Was the umpire right?'

Spencer leaned back complacently and folded his arms, while we pondered.

'Surely,' I said eventually, 'the umpire was right. He couldn't give a man out before he came in.'

'Why not?' asked Spencer, 'a side can be given out in the case where on the umpire calling 'play' the side refusing to play shall lose the game.'

'But,' someone objected, 'there was no refusal to play here.'

'True,' allowed Spencer, amiably.

'Well, I think No.3 ought to have been given out,' said another.

'But why?' asked Spencer, 'a team can change its batting order if it likes.'

'Well,' I suggested, 'perhaps the umpire should have consulted the captain of the batting side to see whether the change was authorised.'

A perfect stranger, who had apparently been following Spencer's narrative, leaned over our shoulders and suggested that No.3 should be given out under the law which states that the umpires are the sole judges of fair and unfair play, to which Spencer immediately replied that the law in question could not be included among those under which a batsman could be given out. Another perfect stranger said he wished we'd all shut our beastly row. He didn't see why people couldn't watch in silence instead of kicking up hell's delight and spoiling everybody else's enjoyment.

Spencer, like the Ancient Mariner, 'fixed him with his glittering eye,' and seemed about to make some cutting retort, but we silenced him abruptly, and, thus reproved, turned our attention to the game, discovering that 'Duleep' had run into the nineties. We retrieved the fruit-drop bag from the floor and sucked jubilantly as he proceeded towards three figures, while Spencer was heard to murmur that he thought 'someone ought to write to the M.C.C. about it'.

THE ASIDE OF CRICKET

'Taverner'

A.W. Carr hit the first six I ever saw. He went down on one knee at
Lord's to J.W. Hearne, and landed the ball cleverly in the tiny balcony
beneath the Tavern score-box. Even now, the scene appears to me as
vividly as a cinema still. I sit in the Mound Stand with freckles and
plastered red hair, clenching nougat; his broad white beam lies dead
square to my line of vision, a little tremulous but magnificent in
triumph. On that day, I realised that cricket is a national possession,
as the theatre was to Elizabethans. It is a drama in which the spectator
is an indispensable actor, one of the Crowd.

For a six is significant out of all proportion to the extra number of
runs it signifies. It is the aside of cricket; it reminds the spectators that
they are an organism of the game, just as the meanest flower reminded
Wordsworth that he was a vital organism of Nature. The man who
throws the ball back becomes for a brief space a microcosm of anxious
humanity, like the man who ascends the stage to help the conjuror. He
carries our honour in his hand; if he reaches the wickets on the third or
fourth bounce, we are reprieved. It was an act of profound insight to
award a special bonus for the stroke that precipitates this crisis. No other
game has, I fancy, made a similar dispensation; the nearest equivalent is
the *dedans* in Real Tennis.

Then again, there is something destructive about a six; and it is healthy to
work off one's very natural passion for destruction in a harmless manner.
Certainly the most memorable sixes are those which one actually sees hit
their targets. I must have been at a match one day when Ames (so we read in
the evening train) broke the window of a passing motor-car; but the climax
was hidden from us by the wall of the ground, and I cannot even recall
the stroke. On the other hand, I vividly recall the same cricketer hitting
a uniformed constable first bounce in the car-park at Dover; Wellard
exploding a vegetable marrow beyond the wire netting at Yeovil; and
a remarkable piece of iconoclasm by (of all people) Iddon, who drove a
ball so high at The Oval that, descending, it pierced the corrugated iron
covering of the pavilion stalls, and sat in its hole above the members, as
contentedly as an egg in a cup. Most sixes, I suppose, travel straight over
the bowler, or perhaps beyond square-leg; it would be interesting to know
the actual statistics. But I once saw Woolley at Dover (an inspiring ground)

lean back to a high bumper from Bowes and scatter the old gentlemen in the little horse-box stand at cover. And a story goes that L.N. Constantine, receiving a fast full pitch at the Pavilion end at Lord's, swivelled and hit it straight-batted over the Press Box at very fine leg.

Trott over the top
In dissatisfied moods, I sometimes ponder on the sixes I should most like to have seen. Albert Trott, of course, cleared the Sanctuary itself, and is reported to have thereby ruined his cricket for evermore. But the price was not too high. N.M. Ford is supposed to have scored a direct hit on an occupied perambulator in the Oxford Parks, miraculously without consequence. And who was the batsman who pinpointed a window at Charterhouse and drove two consecutive balls through the same pane? Ordinary window-breakers are fairly frequent; but has anyone ever damaged the clock? There is a tragic tale of a six which struck a sleeping cleric in the mouth and became so deeply embedded in his false teeth that a new ball had to be called for, and the old ball and the teeth were consigned to a common grave. That was a divine snook, like the peal of ordnance which burnt down the old Globe Theatre, and the legendary shot which ricochetted over the ropes off the umpire's head! Especially, though, I should like to have witnessed those two sixes achieved by C.S. Marriott, off the refreshed Somerset opening bowlers at Frome. The strategy of these has been expounded to me in detail by the batsman. But I should like to know.

On an old scorecard I have disinterred, Sixes I Have Seen Hit garnish the Matches at Lord's, 1934, like a round robin. Woolley (7) is easily first; then come P.G.H. Fender (5), Hendren and Santall (4), and Wellard, R.E.S. Wyatt(!) and Ducat (3). Carr, my original, remains among the ones. I don't think I ever saw him play again. But he will always be, to me, one of the great figures of the game. Surely there is something symbolic in the picture which lies engraved on my memory. For Cricket is not one of those invertebrate goddesses, like Croquet and Golf, that dare not unbend for fear lest, having no marrows, they might never straighten themselves out again. Cricket is a Romantic divinity; and vulgarity is an essential perquisite of all Romanticism. Man, himself a romantic animal, depends on the continual attendance of three million microbes to keep him from disintegration; and the trousers of Mr Carr are as essential to the intricate mystery of Cricket as was Sir Toby Belch to the harmony of *Twelfth Night*, or the Wife of Bath to the stately tapestry of *The Canterbury Tales*.

PLACE AUX DAMES

'A Country Vicar'

It is a little unfortunate that there is no feminine form of the noble word, cricketer. A huntress can ride with a hunter. A hero may pair off with a heroine. Authoresses are as numerous as authors, if not more so. But the dictionary has no distinctive title for her who wields the willow or bowls the ball. One is forced to fall back on compound-words, such as lady-cricketer (which sounds affected), or woman-cricketer (hardly polite), or female-cricketer (quite rude). Yet what else can one say?

The want will have to be supplied, since the fair sex is taking enthusiastically to the game. At least one great daily newspaper is already devoting a column a week, during the summer months, to matches played by *les dames*. And, no doubt, there will be more and more cricketresses (my own word!) as the years roll by.

Do not think, though, that these modern players are, in any sense, unique. They have had their parallels in history. Is not roundarm bowling said to have been invented by a woman: and did not 'the Champion' – the one and only 'W.G.' – owe something to the early coaching of his mother? For many years the fair sex have played the game, more or less. James Lillywhite's *Cricketers' Annual* for 1890 actually contains a photograph entitled, 'The Original English Lady Cricketers'. They wear striped caps, perched high on their hair: their collars are striped, and they have stripes on their skirts. There appear to have been two elevens, which were to play exhibition matches in many of the large towns. I suppose they did so, though I never saw them.

But, as I look back over my own life, I can recall some Amazons of cricket.

First and foremost, my nurse!

No-one in common everyday life could have been more kind and gentle. But her character seemed completely altered when she held a cricket ball and prepared to bowl to me. Like Nebuchadnezzar, the form of her visage was changed. Her face turned grim. She would take four or five quick steps and, with intense vigour, trundle the hard ball straight, seemingly, at my legs – bare and unprotected, save for thin, white socks. It was terrifying! Did she secretly dislike my constant appeals for a game of cricket and work off her spleen thus? Or had she stern views as to the necessity of teaching courage to a small boy, and think battering and bruises the most salutary method? I cannot say: I only know that for a very brief period I had grave doubts as to whether cricket was altogether an unmixed joy!

Ann, as a cricketer, remains in my memory as almost another 'Brown of Brighton', who bowled underhand so fast that, on one occasion (tradition asserts), an historic delivery defeated the wicket-keeper and two long-stops, penetrated an overcoat held up by a spectator on the boundary, passed through a stout wooden fence, and killed an unfortunate dog on the further side. Perhaps tradition has a tendency to exaggerate.

. . . .

Matilda Mitchell was a bowler of another type.

I suppose we were much of an age; and, in early years, I had an absolute horror of her. The poor thing suffered from an unpleasant complaint, supposed to be ringworm; in consequence she was completely bald! I can remember the school treat at which Matilda – a keen player of all games and entirely regardless of appearance – in the heat of a summer afternoon and 'blind-man's-buff', cast aside her hat and revealed a white and shining head, like a giant hen's egg or an immense billiard-ball! Not a single hair appeared on that glittering dome! A dreadful sight!

For some years I was haunted by the fear, whenever we met, that Matilda Mitchell might again become oblivious of how she looked. As much as possible I avoided her; but she rather liked me, and, at school treats, always wished to play on my side at round-games. Her preference brought one comforting thought: so long as I held her hand tight, she could not, with fine, careless rapture, sweep off her head-covering and expose her nakedness! Not with the hand I held: I saw to that! The other I could not control, and that fact caused me acute anxiety. But all went well; so far as I remember I was never again forced to behold her shining crown.

Then, like all our village maidens, she left the parish for domestic service. I forgot her very existence until, at the the end of my first year at Cambridge, our squire's wife asked me to form a Selection Committee of one and choose a team of girls to play the Amazons of a neighbouring parish at cricket. There were practices two or three times a week; and I endeavoured to form a just appreciation of the ladies' skill, quite regardless of graceful figures and pretty faces. Not altogether easy!

It was on one of these occasions, when the day of the match was drawing near, that I was told Matilda Mitchell had come home and wished to play; also, it was stated, she could bowl overarm. And there stood the horror of my childhood, smiling, blushing, quite grown-up, and comely in appearance. But her head – what of her head? It gave me a thrill of dreadful anticipation when, with the gesture of the distant past, she tossed her hat away and revealed . . . *a mop of clustering curls*! Was it a wig? I think not. I believe her hair had grown.

And Matilda *could* bowl! Very slow stuff, but she kept a fine length, and did not mind being hit.

The Squire's wife, prompted by me, arranged with our opponents that each side should be captained by a man, who might keep wicket, but must go in last and bat with a broom-stick. I wanted to 'keep' to Matilda; I believed that. If the chances of stumping were not allowed to go begging, we could win!

We did – thanks to Matilda. She took the bulk of the wickets, made top-score, and emerged from the game a kind of feminine 'W.G.'!

I suppose by this time she is a grandmother!

. . . . . .

The best girl-bowler I ever saw was neither Ann nor Matilda.

I had a very dear friend, who was a first-class cricketer: we played a good deal together in days gone by. But I knew nothing of his family until he took a little house in our neighbourhood and invited me to go over to luncheon. 'And after lunch,' he said, 'Toby shall give you some batting-practice.'

I had no idea who 'Toby' was – a boy, I imagined. But, when 'Toby' appeared, I saw a girl – twelve years old, perhaps, with bare legs and bare feet, dark, gleaming eyes, and a mane of tawny hair.

'You'll want my pads and gloves,' said my friend: 'Toby's pretty fast.'

She was! And, as she bowled from a distance of only eighteen yards, the ball was on to one unexpectedly soon. Also she had a natural leg-break, and she nipped off the pitch almost like a Sidney Barnes. It was a curious experience to be kept playing for all one was worth by a little bare-legged girl, with dancing, eager eyes and a white arm whirling over amid a wealth of flowing, rippling tresses. She made a charming picture.

'Bowl him out, Toby,' cried my friend. 'He's Cambridge!'

Toby did her best. And I – for the honour of the Light Blue – was forced to try and repel the Oxford attack. I think I succeeded. I believe that particular University match ended in an even draw.

A pity Toby was not a boy: she might have become a great bowler. Being a girl, she finally gave up cricket.

. . . • . . •

All this is long ago; but I still see some feminine cricket. My parish is cricket-mad. The men play: the boys play: the members of the Women's Institute play: the Girl Guides play.

The last-named started the game when my wife, Angela, was their captain. I was called in to coach them. They were very keen: they improved rapidly: the only want was genuine opponents. And these were found, at last – a company of Rangers, much older, bigger, stronger than our Guides, said they would take us on. Or, rather, their commander – a noble lady – said so.

The preparations for that match were immense. Every week-day evening for a fortnight, weather permitting, we practised. No Test team was ever more carefully chosen. Who should play, who should be left out, who was to open our innings, who should lead the attack, the various positions in the field; all were studied. The one bone of contention, at the Vicarage, was caused by Angela's modesty as to her own powers. I said her place in the batting-order was No. 1; she maintained it was No. 11. I said she should bowl; she argued against me. Persistent self-effacement is sometimes annoying.

The afternoon came. Angela carried out the first duty of a captain and won the toss; but, despite all my reasoning, wrote her own name last. However, we started in grand style. Our first pair put up 40 runs before a wicket fell. Kitty, the churchwarden's daughter, stayed on and made 54 of the best. Everyone else got a few; and, when Angela declared our innings closed, the score was 120 for seven.

It was an excellent declaration. Our opponents had not quite time to make the runs, though there was a moment when it almost seemed as though they might. They had a young woman who could both cut and place the ball to leg, and she rattled up 40 very quickly. Then the wickets began to fall, and the excitement became intense. Angela performed prodigies of valour at silly point. Kitty followed up her admirable batting by some deadly bowling. Should we win, or not? The spectators roared or shrieked their applause, in accordance with their sex: the match was on our ground, and we are nothing if not partisans, though we try to appreciate the good play of visiting sides. The Rangers' last hope really departed when their captain carelessly strayed outside the crease when our wicket-keeper had the ball in her hand: I was compelled to give the noble lady out. But the enemy died game. They only failed to save the match by five minutes. They played most gallantly and scored 93.

It was a great victory; but it had one unfortunate effect. The heads of the Girl Guides were completely turned. They imagined that, having beaten a team of Rangers, they could play the boys with some hope of success. I, when consulted on the point, agreed that they could – provided the boys played left-handed and with broomsticks. The girls were sure the only handicap necessary was that the boys should bowl underhand.

A match, on the girls' terms, was arranged. Angela was not responsible for the contest: she only acquiesced in the matter when she found how disappointed her little company would be if she positively forbade it. 'After all,' she said, 'they will merely be playing against their own brothers, and boys are very chivalrous!'

It was unfortunate that there were two boys who could bowl underhand really fast! They proceeded to do so: they 'wanged them in'. And the girls very quickly tumbled out. Kitty defended her wicket for quite a long time. Angela had no chance of doing so, since again she put herself in last; she could only carry her bat for 1. I believe the total was 35: which was not, in the circumstances, such a bad score.

What was still more unfortunate was that the girls could not part the boys' opening pair. They had no Toby – no Matilda Mitchell not even an Ann! All the bowlers were slow underhand. They had laboriously learned to keep a length, but were soon knocked off it. The two young gentlemen at the wicket were thoroughly enjoying themselves: grinning broadly, they ran out to every ball and hit it hard. Angela was forced to relinquish her position at silly-point and stand square. Long on and deep square leg were run almost off their feet, though they stuck to their work nobly, chasing the ball and throwing it in with undiminished ardour. (Don't imagine that no girl can throw! Some can!) Three of the weaker spirits, however, wilted. One small fieldsmaiden stopped a lusty drive with her shin and retired, bathed in tears, to the pavilion. Another, ashen of face, sought Angela, with the announcement: 'Please, Madam,' (Girl Guides address their captain thus), '*I feel sick!*' She, too, was allowed to leave the field. This sickness, apparently, was catching: a second sufferer reported impending calamity.

The score reached 50–75–100–125, and not a catch went to hand. With only eight weary fielders left, it became increasingly difficult to check the run-getting. Then rain – blessed rain! – fell, and I (as umpire) was justified in ending the farce by drawing stumps.

Angela was so thankful all her team were still alive that she had no regrets. She said it would be a lesson to them. It was: the Girl Guides have not played the boys, on practically level terms, again. They are content to meet their own sex.

· · · · · · ·

There is a moral to this sad story. Feminine cricketers, as a rule, have their limitations.

Cricket *may be* a suitable game for women and girls. I do not say it is (I am a little doubtful on the point); but I do not presume to affirm that it is not. The ladies know what they like; and, if they choose to attempt the use of bat and ball, I am always ready to umpire for them. I would even play, if they would let me.

Here and there some Diana may actually be the equal of the majority of men. I regard such divine beings as the exceptions which prove what I take to be the rule.

True, I have not yet had the pleasure of watching the skilled performers whose names appear in the columns devoted to 'Women's Cricket' in the daily press. In the near future I hope to attend one of their Cricket Weeks. But, at present, I cannot imagine that 'Ladies v. Gentlemen' will ever take the place, in public interest, of the time-honoured Gentlemen v. Players, though, I admit, one can never tell! Women are very wonderful!

At least, these enthusiasts deserve a special word which accurately describes them.

ONE DAY – A MEMORY

G.D. Martineau

'*One of those heavenly days that cannot die*'. – Wordsworth.

To visit Brighton, and that on a Bank Holiday, may well make Wordsworth's line sound incongruous, and indeed my arrival at that resort was inauspicious. I had extricated myself from the platform, and was noting mentally that inferiority complexes might be cured by a study of the local denizens, when I was accosted by two unknown young women. Sweeping down on me with pointing fingers, they exclaimed: 'You are Mr Lobby Ludd of the News Chronicle!'

'By the beard of Grace!' I roared, for I was on my way to Hove, 'I would rather be Ned Ludd of Leicester! He at least had worthy inspirations. You have put shame upon my appearance.'

'Ow! wot a pitee!' said one. 'I did think we'd got 'im.'

I nursed my wrath as far as the Central Cricket Ground, but there I forgot it in surprise, for it was only just after eleven, yet play was in progress and the seats crowded.

The power of Middlesex

Studying the score-card, I gave a sympathetic sigh for Sussex. They had made 296 on Saturday, but what hope had they against the assembled might of Middlesex? Of their opponents, only three had not represented England in Test matches, while Sussex, on their recent form, were one of the weakest sides in the first-class Championship.

I was still reflecting in this vein when there was a click, and little Cornford had caught Compton brilliantly on the leg-side for 31. That made three for 124, but Edrich was there with 48 to his credit, and Hulme, Robins and Allen were to come. I strolled pavilionwards, but had not gone far when Hulme touched a ball from Nye, and John Langridge made one of his easy-looking catches at first slip. Four for 124.

From my position on the flank I considered Nye, whom I had always regarded as too erratic to make a good fast bowler. He took a long run, with giant strides and seemed almost to throw the ball. Edrich completed his fifty and then played outside a fast one, which hit his leg stump. That made five for 127, and at the same total Nye had Sims caught at the wicket. There was some unorthodox resistance by Robins and a little more on Faulkner School principles by Peebles, both ended by Jim Cornford, and Middlesex were all out for 178, giving Sussex a lead of 118.

This was good, but I feared the Middlesex bowling. The opening attack was of practically Test match standard, and the same might be said of the spin bowlers to follow. Nemesis seemed to wait upon the surprising advantage we had gained.

Allen did a lot of waving his arms about and bowled some practice balls while Parks and Langridge walked to the wickets. This was not the record-breaking Jim Parks of the 1937 season: he played Allen's first ball into the hands of Gray at short-leg, and there we were with a batsman gone and the score, as Dickens once wrote, 'as blank as our faces'. Cruel luck followed, for the other Parks, after making fifteen runs with courage rather than finish, hooked at a short one from Allen and took it in the face. Some time after he had retired the scoreboard announced 'hit wicket', and the pavilion was instantly filled with argument. Harry Parks was reported to have dropped the bat on the wicket and indignant voices claimed that he had not done it in playing the stroke. I believe the expression 'in playing the ball' is always interpreted by umpires as covering any movement made as a result of the stroke. While speculation proceeded, John Langridge and R.G. Stainton put up a stout defence and were still together at 1.30, with 83 on the board.

The temperature was rather more than this when I went in search of lunch, so I asked whether there was any ice to cool the warm cider at the bar. No, there was none, and a 'lounge and snack-counter' in Hove could only show me a dish of water that had been ice an hour earlier. Had they any fruit beyond the cardboard apples in the glass case? A lady upholstered in white concrete announced that the only remaining banana was up in her bedroom, whence, regardless of my urgent protests, it was brought down and placed inescapably before me.

Langridge and Stainton aided my digestive process after lunch by quickening the pace, but the menace of the hour, which had seemed to be receding, loomed suddenly close; Stainton, hooking at Allen, was caught by Sims, and John Langridge was l.b.w. to Smith.

Still there seemed no immediate threat of doom. Sussex, now leading by 255, had six wickets in hand. Another 150 should see us strongly placed. A further piece of seeming good fortune had come to balance Harry Parks's ill-luck. Allen, who had spent much time and raised a simoom in endeavouring to improve his footholds, fell apparently into his own pit, and did something to his knee. (We wished him no such bad fortune, but felt that this made it all square.) His end was taken by Gray, whom at the time I did not greatly fear, while Fate sat back and smiled the smile of a villain.

H.T. Bartlett struck Peebles mightily for six, but not long afterwards played forward and was bowled by Gray. Then James Langridge, who had made 28, was fetched right out of his ground by Peebles and stumped without need of appeal. This was at 169, and then came Gray's wicked over: A.J. Holmes was bowled for 2, Cornford (W.) second ball for 0, and Nye taken in the slips off the next one! Jim Cornford spoilt the hat-trick by leaving the last ball of the over alone, and there was nothing for Hammond to do but open his shoulders to Peebles, whom he hit for six and four. One run later Gray had Jim Cornford l.b.w. Middlesex had 300 runs to win.

It seemed as though they would have little trouble in getting them. Accidents like that first innings seldom happen twice, and I had my first glimpse of Edrich in the kind of form which has given him a place against Australia. Nothing could check his scoring. Ones turned into twos by fast running, fierce hooks, and well-placed drives sent up 65 by tea. It was the same afterwards. There seemed to be no reason for anyone ever to get out when Robertson, overshadowed but apparently secure, played a ball from Jim Cornford on to his stumps.

By then the score was 125 and it bounded to 152 before Edrich, on the threshold of a great century, gave John Langridge his favourite slip-catch off Nye. Immediately the tempo changed. The cheers for Edrich had hardly died away when Sussex, on the toes of sudden hope, had got a third wicket – Compton's – and Price and Hulme were hotly beset up to the close, when Middlesex wanted another 110.

It was a day of blazing heat, a day of fine, fighting cricket – the desperate valour of Sussex against the inexorable power of Middlesex. The ground was packed; the inevitable barracker raised laughter less by the wit of his sallies than by the impact of his irony on an atmosphere charged with the tension of changing fortunes. (By chance I discovered him: he was lying flat on his stomach and watching from under the bowling-screen!) At Brighton station a poster announced that Lobby Ludd had been found.

I could not go to Hove again, so it was not until the following afternoon that I learnt of the Middlesex victory by three wickets – a farewell note, carrying the tragic echo of one day's dramatic splendour.

•   •   •   •   •   •

The issue of The Cricketer, *in which this article first appeared, was dated 2 September 1939.*

Chapter 5

TECHNICAL MYSTERIES

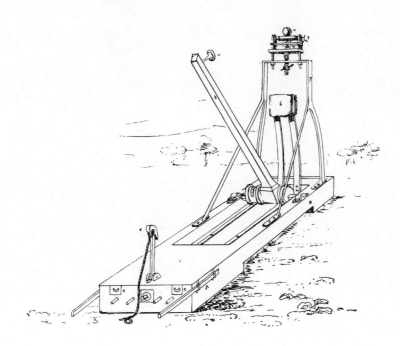

'Gryllus'

Leadership of a cricket eleven is a peculiar gift, so rare that any player possessing it in marked degree is *ipso facto* worthy of his place in a team whether or not he be a skilful player. Very few teams are so fortunate as to have a leader who possesses both the technical and personal equipment for the task. The combination of these two qualifications is extremely rare, often lacking in most likely persons, and sometimes present in those from whom it is least expected. For convenience we shall consider technical and personal functions separately, though of course their combination is essential to successful captaincy.

The technical aspects of captaincy, those which have to do exclusively with the actual conduct of the game in the field, may perhaps be best envisaged if we consider first, in a negative way, the manner in which captains should *not*, but often do, act. It is of prime importance that a captain should get firmly fixed in his head the truth that the functions of a leader in the field are positive, and not negative, active rather than passive. He should divorce from his mind all notions that he is a Sovereign Pontiff, or Lord of Appeal, whose weighty and considered judgment is available and at the disposal of the team should occasion arise or when all else fails. But an impression is forced upon spectators, from time to time, that just this notion, or something very like it, prevails in the minds of a majority of captains. A routine appears to be established both in attack and defence, and should the exigencies of the situation cry out that a change of bowling or of batting order be made, or that a declaration is desirable, a respectful deputation, led by the oldest member of the side, waits upon the captain for his sanction that so momentous a departure from custom be made. This is possibly an exaggeration, but the prevalent notion of a captain's duty thus implied is not unduly exaggerated. It is this Lord of Appeal frame of mind – this notion that a team can play itself without leadership until something goes wrong – which is the antithesis of true leadership.

A cricket captain's business is analogous rather to that of a chess player than to that of a Law Lord. He must not wait for problems to come to him, but must constantly devise schemes and surprises and problems to keep the opposition at sea. This rule applies particularly to the attack, but there is no part of the game which should be governed by routine. To a captain who knows how to get the most out of his material and his opportunities, every match has unique features and calls for separate consideration, and during the match the situation changes every hour and maybe every ten minutes.

There is neither rhyme nor reason in the habit of arriving at the ground with the 'order of going in', as unalterable as the laws of the Medes and Persians, secreted in a coat pocket – the result of earnest deliberation half-way through the preceding week. Ten overs bowled on a hot day are not always the best preparation for a first-wicket batsman, yet on a very cold day they may be his chief qualification for the place – so that he may hold the fort whilst others thaw their frozen limbs in the pavilion. There is no 'proper place' for a hitter, especially in afternoon cricket, when it is so often desirable to press home the advantage of a good start by scoring runs quickly and making an early declaration. All orders of going in should be provisional only, and adherence to the original list should be an exception rather than a rule.

Routine is also undesirable in the disposition of attack, in the changing of bowlers, in the setting of the field, and in the various methods which are used to dislodge the opposition. Special circumstances call for special treatment, and as no two matches are alike, circumstances are always special. The relative importance of time, or of a bowler's cost in runs, is always changing. Dispositions which are sound at one time or in one set of circumstances are suicidal in another. The clock, and the score, and the psychological situation, cannot be ignored with impunity, and no set plan can allow for these important factors. Some leaders would seem to be unaware of the elementary truth that the sun changes its relative position during the course of an afternoon, or even of the fact that it has not position and influence at all! The direction of a strong wind or its effects, and the difference between the light and heavy roller, are things not even dreamed of it in their philosophy. Of course, no disgrace attaches to incapacity in these connections. The captain without 'cricket sense' must not, any more than the poor bridge player, be regarded as a criminal. He cannot help it, and the fault is rather with those who persuade him to undertake the task. But it is a pity that good teams are sometimes handicapped, and their potentialities but half realised, on this account.

It is easy to say that instead of twiddling their thumbs and waiting for the professional to ask for a rest, many captains might with advantage occupy their minds with the positive and dynamic aspects of leadership, so that it may be evident to the otherwise somnolent spectators that an enterprising plan of action is actually in operation, and that this plan is not merely the repetition of that which has done service throughout the season under all conditions, but is conceived with regard to the particular requirements of the moment and the day. It is easy to insist that *any* such positive plan, however modest and however lacking in the inspiration of genius, is infinitely better and more effective than the endless repetition of a set plan. But it is emphatically *not* easy for those without a 'cricket sense' of fairly keen development to fulfil the positive requirements of cricket leadership.

The chief desideratum – immediate awareness of all that appertains to technique and situation – is more in the nature of a natural gift than an acquired virtue. To those who have it more is added, whilst those who lack it seem to lose what little they have. Some enjoy a cricket sense as second nature, whilst many worthy fellows torture their brains incessantly with little or no fruitful result. The most noticeable failings are to be found along this line of suppressed initiative, which in a game like cricket spells absence of control. It is like disposing of a hand at bridge with every care not to perpetrate a revoke, but otherwise playing the cards from left to right. So much mental energy is required in attending to things which should require no thought, that there is no surplus left for initiative. The mischief lies less in what poor captains *do* than in what they leave undone, and in their tendency to allow a team to play itself. Even a team of 'aces' will not always be successful in these circumstances.

It need not be imagined that the ideal technical leader thinks harder, or is more conscientious, or even more enterprising than his opposite. He is not. He is simply more sensitive, and has quicker mental reflexes conditioned by the atmosphere of cricket. When he examines the wicket before play, for example, he does not have to burst his brains 'studying a problem'. The pitch simply gets up and talks to him, saying how it will play now and how it will play in a couple of hours or more, just as a hand of cards will tell its own story to a man with card sense. He visualises at once who to put in first if he wins the toss, which roller to use if his side is to bat first, which bowlers to use and at which end if he elects to field. He is not necessarily thoughtful, but simply incapable of forgetting the roller, of ignoring the sun, or the wind, or the speech of the earth. The idiosyncrasies of opposing players do not requires discernment to observe that there is grass on the ground. He does not have to look for suggestions, but has simply to choose from the suggestions which press themselves upon him, and to reconcile the myriad influences which point in this direction or in that. He may note with satisfaction that the sun shines full in the face of an opposing batsman facing the fast bowler, but he could not possibly fail to feel that the same sun gives equal trouble to his slips.

He has no problem of seeking, but only of choosing. He does not have to scratch a puzzled head when bowling changes are necessary. Changes of every kind have been suggesting themselves to him since the first over, and hitherto he had merely refused the ideas which press constantly upon him. At every minute he lives the whole game. If his side is batting, the notion of declaring the innings does not come to him as an afterthought, but has been in his mind ever since the first ball was bowled. The clock and the speed of scoring are never absent from his mind. The time is always ticking on his pulses, and the score writes itself in his brain as it proceeds. When a wicket falls he is never surprised or disconcerted, for he discounts all accidents in advance, be they favourable or the reverse, and has his plans and alternatives already formed for all contingencies. His sins and failings are always of commission, never of omission. He may choose badly, but he never forgets, is never caught unawares. If his best bowler is tired out in trying to break a partnership, and has no vigour left for later stages, it is because the captain took the risk, never because he did not realise what he was doing. At all moments of the game, each bowler's potentialities impinge automatically upon his mind. Each one is always 'asking to be put on', and 'asking to be taken off', for a hundred and one reasons. He simply chooses, and his success lies in the soundness of his choice, in the discrimination which gives greatest weight to the most important factors, rather than inspiration. He gets *all* the inspirations all the time, without effort, and is merely called upon to judge between them.

It would be idle to enumerate the manifold technical problems which present themselves continually to a cricket captain. They are legion. If we analyse the matter, we find that every man, in the course of an average day in his life, is confronted with, and successfully surmounts, a myriad technical problems. Even jumping on an omnibus, when analysed, contains quite a few problems of technique, as does walking itself. All these things are so familiar to us, however, that they do not present themselves as problems. Sensitive adjustment to our environment has made them automatic, requiring no thought. Failing such adjustment, we should all be helpless in the face of a veritable multitude of difficult problems. We should find ourselves, in short, in the position of a cricket captain who is lacking in 'cricket sense'. All the things which should come as naturally as breathing would present difficulties and involve reflection, so that there would be little time or energy left for the exercise of judgment and choice. We should be splitting our heads over the things which should require no thought at all, such as the desirability of eating food or taking sleep.

Thus the technical leader with cricket sense starts out with this colossal advantage, that he is so attuned to the environment of cricket that all initial problems, together with the various but obvious means of their solution, present themselves, and demand no process of cerebration on his part. Strangely enough, a minority of cricketers, though skilful enough in play, have not made this adjustment to the game in its directive aspects, and are thus ill-suited to the functions of control. Their unawareness is almost unbelievable to me with cricket sense, who are apt to regard them, often mistakenly, as extremely stupid. They are probably far from stupid in other respects, but those of them who undertake to lead their teams in the field are apt to find their task difficult and thankless, and would be well advised to think twice before they take on so tall an order.

PLAYING THE GAME

Lord Granville Gordon

Cricket is another matter. It was once even a good game, but has, of course, been ruined by sensationalism and science. I could name two players who have done more to ruin interest in the game than all the rest together, and they both play in one team. Their cricket policy is so simple as to need little explanation: all balls off the wicket left severely alone, the legs being thrown across the wicket in case of accidents; all straight balls steadily blocked; all half volleys gently returned along the ground; all long hops gingerly placed. Any fool with his share of callousness can, with sufficient practice, block away on a perfect wicket, but he is playing through the fine summer afternoons to the 'Dead March' from *Saul*, not to a British Public, and if C.I. Thornton, in his day, or Jessop of Gloucestershire, had been next man in, that Public would cheer his downfall to the echo. I cannot always advocate playing to the mob, but in this case the mob shows the right taste.

As a mild personal reminiscence, I recollect playing at Kettering for a twenty-two of the Midland Counties against an All-England eleven, and I also remember that on that occasion I fielded point. The All-England eleven won the toss, and in came Jupp. These were the early days of the great block system: Jupp was at the wicket for two days and made

– eleven runs. He was demoralised early in his career that innings by my having just missed him at point when he tried to play a ball to square-leg. It caught the corner of his bat and came straight to point, but low down and unexpected, and so I missed. I think that Jupp did not deliberately try to hit another ball that innings. The memory of that match is rather mournful, by the way, as it was the last in which poor old G.F. Grace played, and a terrible smash he got in the forearm from a sharp return. He was perfectly well at the time, but subsequently caught a chill and was a dead man within a week.

The best cricket I ever played was with C.I. Thornton, in the days of the old Orleans club. We were playing an eleven of Bexley, or Bexhill, or whatever its name was, which included six men who played for Surrey. The great Australian team had just arrived, and Thornton had secured Spofforth, then unsurpassed as a bowler, and Murdoch, also then in his first form. It had been very wet weather, and the wicket was essentially the bowler's. I remember keeping wicket, and also that all our opponents were out for seven runs. In we went, and when I mention that I was in third or fourth wicket down and was the not-out man, with a duck, the reader will form his own conclusions as to the quality of the run getting. In fact, we were dismissed for 20. In went the other eleven again and scored 42. We therefore wanted 30 runs to win. Murdoch and Thornton opened the defence, and the first ball bowled Murdoch. I came next. Now, I beg leave to state that I cite this occasion merely as a curiosity in my cricket log, for I was always too fond of hitting to make anything of a cricketer. On this occasion, however, I knocked up the requisite 30 runs, while 'Buns' Thornton simply kept his end up and scored nothing. He was never very keen on my being in with him, because if by any luck I stayed there, the pace was soon too warm for him.

I have hinted at a couple of cricketers who, in my humble opinion, went far towards destroying the spectacular interest of cricket. Picture a match between Middlesex and Notts on a hot summer's day, with the latter eleven, in the person of its champions, well set at the wickets. Heat and monotony would reign supreme, and there might now and again be a feeble, half-ironical cheer from the dozing crowd when an immeasurable batsman played a half volley somewhat firmly, a ball that Thornton or Jessop would, without an effort, have lifted over the Pavilion. Is it quite certain that these distinguished blockers are always of great service to their side? They are certainly the first men to be beaten on a sticky wicket, when the bowler gets spin and sting on the ball. All that then results from that graceful forward stroke is that the ball flies off the edge of the bat into the hands of one of the fielders. I once, at The Oval, saw Gunn bowled round his legs without any attempt to play the ball, and the crowd yelled itself hoarse with delight. Your hitter, on the other hand, takes just one step, makes a well-pitched ball into an innocuous half-volley, and bangs it. Such scurvy treatment annoys the bowler, so he sends the next a bit short. Back steps the hitter and pulls it round to leg. The bowler regards this as heterodox. Yet the captains and secretaries of county teams, and cricket caterers generally, have to consider their public, and to make certain of drawing the biggest gate round London, you would have to include in your team three Thorntons (in his form of twenty years ago), three Jessops, three Rhodes, and two Haighs.

THREE TYPES OF BATSMEN

A.C. MacLaren

Batting has undergone many changes lately, the pull and hook strokes so common now being considered very bad play once, but I think E.M. Grace was one of the first, if not the first, to upset this theory, pulling and lifting to any position in the field where no fieldsman stood, or what is termed placing his hits.

A really genuine pull off a not very bad ball often has the effect of upsetting a bowler, which will enable the batsman to score at a much greater rate in most instances than he would have done if he had played correct cricket. Batsmen may be classed under the following three heads – (A) The careful or patient batsman, (B) the forcing batsman, and (C) the combination of A and B. The style of A is the most common: he plays absolutely correct cricket, too correct at times for fieldsmen and spectators alike; he never takes any sort of a liberty with a bowler, but waits for loose balls, and when pitted against men like J. T. Hearne and Mead, who rarely send down one bad ball in fifty, then his rate of scoring is worse than slow; but he is of the utmost value to his side for he is taking the edge off the bowling for those who come after him.

These are methods adopted by the majority of the Australians today, and with many players of A's stamp in a match of three days there is little chance of a finish on anything but a bowler's wicket. This is the type of batsman who should be sent out to Australia if we are to win our matches in that country, stamina and patience being of far greater value than brilliance, but patience is at times overdone by the Australians even in their own country, judging from the reports of recent inter-colonial matches to hand. In the event of nothing being left to play for but a draw, then A is for the time being the best man on the side and will be the means of saving many a game, but there are other occasions when he takes so long to obtain his runs that had he got out earlier his side would have secured their runs quicker and would have won the match instead of just not having the time to get the runs, or as often happens, just failing to get rid of one's opponents in time for a win.

There is one more occasion when A is of the utmost value, and that is when his captain wins the toss and knows the wicket will play badly for an hour and then recover; on such an occasion he cannot afford to put in his opponents unless they are a weak lot, so he decides to take first innings, trusting in A's ability to stop there when runs are of not so much value as is the killing of time. Should A defy the bowlers for an hour without scoring even, he has nevertheless by his defence added perhaps 150 to the total of his side. Matches have often been won owing to an innings such as described above, and these sort of batsmen don't get too much credit as a rule from the crowd. In selecting a team for Australia I would rather have one man of A's to every five of B's type.

The man bowlers fear

Next comes B, whose style is of the forcing order. He doesn't care two straws for any bowler, however good, but is determined to make runs so long as he is allowed to remain at the wickets. Very delightful it is, too, to watch him hitting them in the middle of the bat, and when it is his day out then there is no denying him: good-length balls are treated as half-volleys, sometimes being pulled to leg, at other times lifted to the rails: he is at it all the time and often completely changes what looks like a certain defeat into a handsome win. How the bowlers fear this man for he sometimes demoralises them and he is also the cause of captains not knowing what to do at times.

B is a batsman who gets himself out: in other words he is seldom clean beaten in attempting to keep his wicket intact rather than score. As a rule he is caught in the outfield, stumped, or his sticks sent flying in attempting to score off a ball which, in nine cases out of ten, had he contented himself with playing, he would have had no difficulty in keeping out of his wicket, but then there are other good balls that ought to have been treated with respect but have been slapped to the rails. He always has this consolation when defeated. B is very useful when a rot sets in, as he is the one man to hit a bowler off his length and make it plain sailing for his comrades to follow.

There is a very great difference between hitting and slogging. The scientific hitter is always on the *qui vive* for every opportunity, and is watching the bowler as a cat does a mouse; after he has despatched an over-tossed ball for four, he does not necessarily make up his mind to treat the next one in like manner; rather does he expect one a trifle shorter which he hooks round to the leg for four and often upsets a bowler to such an extent that he doesn't know where to put them down. Now the slogger, after a boundary hit, will often make the very same stroke to a ball pitched shorter than the previous one, with the result that it goes beautifully high and is easily caught. Consequently, marching orders to the pavilion. Indeed the blind slogger is always ready to fall headlong into any trap laid for him, and the only occasion on which he shines is when he either has the most awful good luck on his side, or else is batting against two bowlers who are bigger fools than he is.

The all-round batsman
Lastly comes the flyer, or rather the batsman from the tip of his nose to the heel of his foot; he can play any game just as occasion demands, in fact adapts himself to circumstances. On seeing a really good wicket he plays his natural game, which sends up the tens fast enough, for his many strokes will always make the runs come quick without necessarily forcing the pace, good length balls often being got away to the boundary without any apparent effort: he has his eye on all the men round him, making mental notes of every change in the field, and keeps on placing his drives and cuts as only the artist can. When the century goes up and the game is safe for his side as far as being beaten is concerned, he then forces the game, and scores even faster than before, knowing that his opponents will take some considerable time to get out and that the sooner his side has enough on the board to enable them to get at their opponents the better: he never thinks of that accursed average that very occasionally has the effect of losing a match, but is all out for his side and never for himself.

The condition of the wicket is of no consequence for he at times will transform himself into a hitter, the only game to play, when the wicket is absolutely made for a bowler, and when it is in a soft state, without assisting either batsman or bowler, he will combine defence and hitting. This is the customer on whom reliance can always be placed. Seldom if ever out of form, there are times when a rest is necessary, but not being able to get a day off, much less a match, he naturally becomes stale and is bound to go off for a trifle at a time. Writing of losing form reminds me that many batsmen, when they arrive at this unfortunate stage, make the mistake as a rule of playing too carefully, all the time thinking of how they are going to keep the ball out of the wicket rather than to what part of the field they are going to hit it.

WICKET-KEEPING

Pelham Warner

I do not think my best friend would call me a wicket-keeper. I have kept wicket, *in a first-class match, too*, MCC v. Yorkshire at Lord's in May 1901, and in a total of 57 for four wickets let no byes and missed no catches – I did not have one! – and playing for the village of Leeds in Kent against the County Police a stalwart sergeant remarked: 'I should feel a deal happier, Mr Warner, if you weren't behind those stumps'; but not withstanding such feats as these I do not feel competent to write on the subject. The late A.A. Lilley, the England, Players, and Warwickshire wicket-keeper, however, very kindly gave me his views, and as he kept wicket for England from 1896 to 1909, taking part in no fewer than *thirty-five Test matches*, there could be no greater authority. I have also been fortunate enough to obtain the views of J.C. Hubble, the excellent Kent wicket-keeper of the period between 1910–1924.

Why I Became A Wicket-Keeper
A.A. Lilley

My earliest club cricket was in connection with the Bournville Cricket and Athletic Club. I was then employed at the works of Messrs Cadbury Bros, and this club was formed by the foremen of the various departments in the works. Mr George Cadbury engaged J.E. Shilton, the Warwickshire professional, to coach the young players, and the latter used to come up in the evenings for this purpose. On one occasion when we were practising under the guidance of Shilton, the regular wicket-keeper of the club happened to be absent, and so Shilton asked me to occupy this position for that evening. I had not previously acted in this capacity, having been played for bowling and batting, but after Shilton had given me a few hints as to the correct attitude to assume and the proper way of taking the ball, I soon became at home, and as he saw I had some natural aptitude for the position, I became from that evening the regular wicket-keeper for the club. It was therefore quite an accident that I first acquired my knowledge of or liking for wicket-keeping; and had the club's usual player been present upon that particular evening, it is quite possible that I might never have had the opportunity that subsequently meant so much to me.

Methods of standing – How to take the ball – and hints to young players

In taking up position behind the wicket, the young player must always remember that whatever attitude he assumes he must always preserve free and easy movement. This is most important, and must be regarded as fundamentally necessary and to be zealously regarded. The necessity of free movement must indeed never be lost sight of, and I keep this particularly in mind in making the following suggestions.

In taking up position the wicket-keeper should stand with the middle of the left foot in a line with the legstump. The right foot should then be extended only far enough to make the position a perfectly easy one. In extending the right foot it should be slightly drawn back so that the toe of this foot should come in a line with the ball of the left foot. This will give additional 'play' and greater freedom in movements of the right arm, and at the same time provide additional facilities in following the ball. When stooping, the utmost care should be taken that the feet are placed flat upon the turf, so as to provide as substantial a grip of the ground as possible. It affords a quicker and steadier start in making a rapid movement in order to take a ball on the leg-side or wide on the off-side; whereas, if he were on his toes he would be likely to overbalance in attempting to make either of these movements. He should not indeed move on to his toes for *any* action. It will naturally have the tendency to make a player overbalance himself, and so seriously handicap him in taking the ball properly. It has also a tendency to make him 'grab' at the ball, which should be carefully avoided, as not only does it make the catch more difficult to take, but is also very destructive to the hands. The hands, of course, should 'give' immediately on coming in contact with the ball, in order to break the pace of it, and that can only be done when the position allows the ball to be properly taken, which, of course, cannot be done when the body is in any way overbalanced, and causes the ball to be grabbed at. It will thus be seen how essential is free movement: in fact, free and easy movement of the feet is more essential to a wicket-keeper than a batsman, so it can easily be understood how impossible it is to impress this too strongly.

Wicket-Keeping
J.C. Hubble

The art of wicket-keeping is to make a difficult job look easy. It is delightful work when this can be done.

The necessities are a keen eye, steady nerve and a quick mentality.

Balance of body is the principal attribute and to attain this 'stance' is of the utmost importance.

The two feet should be firmly planted on the ground *flat* with perhaps the right toe three inches behind the left, and then move up and down with the feet flat.

As most of the work and chances are just outside the off-stump make the centre of the stance there, perhaps with an inswinging bowler it may be advisable at times to move a bit more to the leg-side.

The ball should be taken with the fingers pointed downwards.

There is no object in getting too low in the stance and most important of all do not get on your toes – this is fatal as it naturally leads to continually transferring the balance from toes to flat feet and is the cause of such things as snatching, bruised fingers, missed chances, and so on; in fact this stance will never lead to good wicket-keeping. I emphasise this point as I find unfortunately this stance is common, due no doubt to a misapprehension that unless one is perched like a frog behind the wicket one is not trying one's best.

As length is to bowling, and a straight bat to batting, so is stance to wicket-keeping.

· · · · · · ·

By general consent J. McC. Blackham, the Australian, was the prince of wicket-keepers, and may, indeed, be said to have been the originator of the practice which has been prevalent for so many years of dispensing with a long-stop even to the fastest bowling. Like Lilley, Blackham had done no wicket-keeping until he was seventeen years old, which goes to prove the oft-repeated saying that a wicket-keeper is born, not made. His keeping to 'the demon' Spofforth with the 1878 Australian team was a revelation, and had an enormous influence on our cricket. With his ever-varying pace and flight Spofforth was a most difficult bowler to keep wicket to, and those who saw the combination of the two aver that the game has produced no greater spectacle.

G. MacGregor, Lilley, and Pilling, the Lancashire professional, must have run even Blackham close. Pilling was very good indeed, and the combination of S.M.J. Woods and MacGregor was almost as fine as that of Spofforth and Blackham. Who, too, that saw it could ever forget that marvellous right-handed catch low down on the off-side by MacGregor, who was standing up, off Kortright's terrific bowling in the Gentlemen and Players match at Lord's in 1893?

K.S. Ranjitsinhji says that MacGregor holds the record for tranquillity at the wicket. 'He is sphinx-like in his calm fixity.' The wicket-keeper has all sorts of returns to take – long hops, full pitches, half-volleys, wide returns, and straight returns. MacGregor had a wonderful knack of gathering them one and all and getting them into the wicket. The wicket-keeper sees much of the game, and MacGregor, by a quiet hint, obtained many a wicket for a bowler. 'You're bowling about two feet too short, Jack,' or 'Albert, a yard shorter,' often improved the analyses of J.T. Hearne and Albert Trott. The late Middlesex captain knew much about cricket. He had no fads, and pronounced judgment on merit. He was a great man for Middlesex.

AVERAGE KEEPING

Major Philip Trevor

By all cricketers the system of average keeping – the keeping of a player's batting average – is condemned. To this rule there is practically no exception. If you have the misfortune to be a bad speaker, and the greater misfortune to be condemned to speak at a cricket dinner, you can always assure for yourself one burst of applause, be your oratory never so lame and halting. Bring pantomime to your aid if necessary, but let it be understood somehow that you disapprove of keeping a batting average, and every glass on the table will dance and sing to you in sympathy. It does not matter that five minutes before those glasses danced and sang when the young gentleman who won the prize given for the possession of the best batting average walked up to the chairman to receive it at his hands.

Talk about the keeping of averages to a man or to a collection of men in a pavilion, read what he or they say in print, lure a suspect to your smoking-room and try to make him confidential over a pipe. There is only one result, and that result is condemnation of the practice. Yet the laws of supply and demand are practically the laws of cause and effect, and in every newspaper which deals even cursorily with cricket the publication of the averages is a feature of its practice or policy.

Is it a case of the wicked press defying the wishes of cricketers and doing violence to their feelings? Or are those cricketers very deceitful people, and do they really love the existence of that which they affect to deplore?

The First Lord of the Admiralty in Mr Gilbert's play, *HMS Pinafore*, rebukes the captain of the ship in an immortal sentence:

'Always remember, Captain Corcoran, that the British sailor is any man's equal. (Loud cheers.) (Aside) Except my own.'

Perhaps we mean, therefore, that no batting averages should be kept – except our own. I say batting averages designedly, because we are not especially eager to have our bowling averages recorded in black and white. We prefer to produce them through the generous medium of our own memories.

It is idle to hope that we shall ever be without the printing of the batting average of the individual, so long as first-class cricket exists as an institution. The twentieth century has opened with a passion for the personal and a passion for arithmetic. The printing of the table of batting averages ministers to both passions, and we are likely in future to have a daily, rather than a weekly, meal of this sort. The system appeals to the form-at-a-glance craze which deludes a hustling age.

The thoughtful cricketer, of course, knows that a man's batting average is not a reliable guide to his real form even in three cases out of ten. And when a man plays solely, or even primarily, for his average, whatever guide it is to his form, it is no guide at all to his value.

A cricket match in England is limited to three days' play, and that fact is always overlooked when the first two men go in to bat and the match begins. They are fresh, they have presumably the best of the wicket, and the bowler seldom 'finds himself' at the very start. They are not disheartened by the failure of comrades or terrorised by the success of a bowler. Each man entirely suits himself and is, in a majority of cases, influenced mainly by a determination to stay at the wicket at all costs.

The case of the man who is number seven or eight on the batting list is very different. The best that can happen to him is that he will occasionally have only tired bowlers to flog and dispirited fieldsmen to consider. He may, of course, improve his average by being 'not out'. But such are not the normal conditions in which he bats. He generally has to bat to order. He has to play to the score, to the situation, and to the clock. The early men have wasted precious time perhaps. The fifth-wicket man has to repair their errors and at the same time to run the risk of paying the penalty of his own. We so often hear of the awful stroke from which (in an attempt to do more than he ought to have been required to do) this man was caught at cover point or mid off. We do not hear of the half vollies and long hops which the more splendid batsmen who went in first omitted to punish. Had they with all their skill been content to run the minimum of risk in the first instance, the later men, possessed of less skill, would not have been forced to run the maximum of risk. A free-hitting batsman is very valuable when you only ask him to make runs at the rate of fifty an hour; when, through the selfish supineness of greater batsmen, you ask him to make them at the rate of a hundred an hour, you are demanding what you would scarcely dare to demand (if you realised the situation) of a Jessop or a Ranjitsinhji. Yet this demand is made in almost every first-class match.

Is the batting average of a man compelled so often to perform in these conditions a fair guide either to his form or to his utility? I think not. Briefly and roughly I should say that the batting averages of the extra-cautious players who are wont to go in first flatter them, and that the batting average of the men who are wont to go in late do not do them justice.

The arithmetical form of the cricket chronicle necessarily overlooks the all-important consideration of context, and I wish that the people who fire statistical volleys at us from time to time would be a little more careful in selecting their ammunition. The hard chunks of bare fact which they particularly favour do not hit some of us with any effect. Will not someone who takes a delight in this statistical work give us the result of his labours in a rather more instructive form?

Here, for instance, is a rough plan. Let him select a dozen batsmen at the beginning of a season, and let us be told at the end of it exactly how they performed in all circumstances. When the batsman makes more than two hundred runs (not out) on the third day of a match on a perfect wicket, when no-one is trying, let the fact be noted.

Or let him confine himself to one man. In the summer of 1906 Hayward made more runs than had ever been made by any individual batsman in first class matches during a single cricket season. I, for one, should read a detailed disquisition on his batting, match by match, with the greatest interest, if only the author did his best to follow the rule laid down by the great master of our language. If he did nothing extenuate nor set down aught in malice, we might have as a result the most valuable treatise on a batting average yet written. Perhaps we might be appalled at the extremes which we should be called upon to consider. We might hardly realise that the man who laboured so heavily and so ordinarily at the end of the season to accomplish a mere arithmetical feat was the man who in the middle of it scored four centuries in two consecutive matches during a week's cricket, in which few (if any) other batsmen really distinguished themselves at all.

But we need not go to first-class cricket for an illustration of the value or otherwise of a man's batting average as a guide to intrinsic merit. With a certain state of affairs every club cricketer is familiar. Two new members join our club. One has an average of forty-odd for the side for which he last played, the other an average of something under ten. It is the rule and not the exception for us to be surprised at these figures, the absolute accuracy of which (as matters of fact) we have no reason to doubt. Match after match we fail to understand how the presumably greater player managed to acquire that average; and to suggest that he is five times as good a batsman as the lesser player is ludicrous to a degree. Yet, if arithmetic as applied to cricket, has any value at all, something of the kind should not be an unfair inference. I do not suppose that in any class of cricket we ever watch a player at all regularly without being surprised when we learn later what is his batting average. We always expect it to be either less or more – one might say considerably less or considerably more. Yet it occurs to few of us that the medium of comparison which we so frequently employ is untrustworthy.

But there is one kind of batting average which does give valuable indications of form and capacity. I refer to the collective batting average, which shows runs per hour and runs per wicket. In 1906 Kent won the County Championship in a manner and by methods practically unparalleled in the history of the competition. Their men discarded a cricket maxim, the expediency of which had so far been unchallenged: 'First make the game safe, and, having done so, begin to try to win.' Kent, after the middle of June, began to win from the start of every game; and when the season ended their average rate of run-getting was about 80 an hour. And this was so in spite of the fact that Mr Burnup, their greatest run-getter, playing to order, nearly always scored slowly.

In this particular, it may be parenthetically observed, Mr Burnup did violence to his own feelings, but of the wisdom of the policy enjoined on him there was no doubt. The contrast provided by him and Mr Hutchings when they were batting together was in itself disconcerting to their opponents, and the score mounted rapidly all the while. Only a point or two separated the batting average of Mr Burnup from that of Mr Hutchings when the season ended, and in each case the average was a true one. Both men played entirely for their sides, and their tactics were invariably part and parcel of a preconceived plan in which the reputation of the individual was never considered. Their regardlessness of the personal element was shared by the other members of the team, and the result was a collective success which, the more closely it is scrutinised, the more does it deserve commendation. It was not merely good sportsmanship; it was mighty good policy too.

Of the collective batting average showing runs per hour, I hope we shall hear a good deal more. In our country where there is a time limit for cricket matches, it is of the highest importance. But it should, in order to be a reliable guide to form, be earned as Kent earned it. Kent, I have said, scored on an average at the rate of 80 runs an hour. But they did not score 40 runs an hour one day and 120 runs an hour another. A habit of that kind only perplexes the captain of the side who indulge in it; nor is such a habit mainly dependent on the state of the wicket or the bowling of the opposition.

When the Kent captain won the toss it was not too much to expect that the side would score well over 300 runs and give their opponents a little more than an hour's batting before stumps were drawn for the day. It was their practically regular rate of scoring, inexorably maintained, that disconcerted bowler after bowler who had to bowl against the victorious Kentish batsmen. I have alluded by name to Mr Burnup and Mr Hutchings, but reading the batting averages of the other members of the eleven in the light of their context, one is struck by the fact that they are all practically true indications of form. There are, of course, exceptions among them to this rule, but the collection of these averages in the shape which I have mentioned gives an absolutely accurate description of the real state of affairs, so far as the work of the eleven is concerned. And that, after all, is the one thing which matters.

Of the bowling average it is necessary to say very little, because it is common knowledge that in first-class and second-class cricket, at any rate, where the bowler bowls much, his bowling average in nine cases out of ten undervalues in figures the merit of his performances, Except in the occasional contingency of being run out, the batsman has only himself to blame for his want of success, and even then he has only one enemy in disguise. The poor bowler has always ten such enemies, and the occasional brilliant catch that is caught does only a little to compensate him for the dozen easy catches given which are not caught.

Apart from that consideration, the good bowler in first-class cricket has very often to bowl when both nature and the tactics of the batsmen demand that he should not bowl. The maxim which insists that any change is better than no change is not a maxim which is applicable to the first-class cricket field. Occasionally the captain of an eleven, such as the Yorkshire eleven, can afford to put a fine bowler on to bowl only when the surroundings are favourable to him, but this state of affairs is so exceptional as not to affect the general contention.

Roughly, then, we may take the bowling average of a bowler who has bowled much in good matches all through a season, and, when we have reduced the runs per wicket by about thirty per cent., we shall get a fair idea (so far as such a thing is possible) of his comparative value. The pride of his heart might in that case lift him up and tempt him to be as purely personal in his efforts as are members of a certain class of batsmen. But as there is no chance of our doing anything of the kind (being, as we are, slaves to rigid arithmetic), there is not the least harm in publishing the bowling averages. They cannot exalt, and they may chasten the individuals to whom they refer.

THE DAY WHEN NEITHER UMPIRE KNEW WHO WAS OUT

R.C. Robertson-Glasgow

'To walk or not to walk, that is the question.' It was the question, anyhow, which popped up in the third Test between South Africa and England at Cape Town. Briefly, there was a South African batsman whom most people in the vicinity, except the umpire, considered to have been caught at slip off his gloves; and there was an England batsman who was caught behind the wicket in the opinion of those well qualified to have an opinion, and, when given 'not out', he disagreed with the umpire and walked off towards the pavilion amid tremendous applause. It is no longer a current topic – just history; but I still think that the umpire's decision (like the Editor's so often) should be final. Over a space of years a batsman's or a bowler's luck in the matter of umpires' decisions surely works out about even. So, when the batsman is given 'out' he should go; when he is given 'not out' he should stay.

Unexpected gift
I was interested to note that the President of the MCC Mr G.O. Allen – in his day a very fine all-rounder for England, Middlesex, and Cambridge

University – when interviewed on this point, said that in his time if he was given 'not out' when he knew he was 'out' he used to welcome the unexpected gift and went on batting: though he never attained to the dictatorial heights of one of the greatest batsmen that the game has known, who, from time to time, when the bowler appealed against him, told the umpire: 'You can't give that out.' And the umpire, knowing he couldn't, didn't.

There are several ways in which a batsman can increase the already considerable uncertainty of an umpire over an l.b.w. decision. If the bowler appeals, the batsman can gaze upwards like some watcher of the skies when a new planet swims into his ken; or he can rub himself on the chest as indication of impossible altitude: or he can look meaningly at his bat; or he can suddenly appear to be standing halfway between the crease and the square-leg umpire. These methods are worth trying even in first-class cricket.

Perhaps the most entertaining umpiring is to be found in junior school games: those games in which a violent throw by long-stop is apt to hit the back of the neck of the wicket-keeper, who is offering untaken advice to the bowler. In such games – the umpires being usually the next two men in – keenness of eyesight and hearing is apt to be conquered by the desire to be batting. Many instances of judicial immorality come back to me across the years. I recall a batsman who had been given out l.b.w. off the middle of the bat saying to the offending umpire: 'Just you wait till the end of this innings.' I recall instances of 'run out' when the victim was at least five yards past the wicket-keeper at the time the wicket was broken. Most clearly of all there returns the memory of the young umpire who, when appealed to for a resounding catch at the wicket, said in loud, clear tones: 'Sorry, I wasn't looking.' I have often thought how such an admission would go down in a Test match.

Terrific finish

Then there were those matches against other junior schools, when the umpires were adult and so presumably equal to their work. But there were exceptions. It was an 'away' First Eleven match against a school whose benign headmaster allowed us to wander for some minutes in his strawberry beds. This match had a terrific finish.

We made 75, and their last man came in with the total at 74; and it was I that was bowling – the last over of the match. I shaved his wicket with five consecutive balls. The sixth was snicked into and out of the wicket-keeper's hands. A draw, I thought. But no; our umpire, a young schoolmaster who wasn't going to give up easily, allowed a seventh ball, and an eighth. This eighth ball hit the now pallid batsman on the right leg, plumb in front. 'Out,' said our umpire, almost before he was asked. Whereat the other umpire, one of the staff of our hosts, walked slowly to our umpire and said: 'Do you know that was the *eighth* ball of the over?' 'Sorry,' said our young umpire, I must have put two pebbles in the wrong pocket.'

To return to first-class cricket. I only once saw two umpires completely unable to come to a decision. The match was Surrey v. Oxford University at The Oval in the early 1920's. The batsmen were Tom Raikes and myself. The facts began very simply. I, facing the pavilion, played a ball past mid-on into the deep, near where a few elderly spectators with Albert chains were taking forty winks.

Philosophic doubt

We ran the first run with ease. Then I asked my partner, Tom, if he felt like another. 'Yes,' he said; so he set off towards the pavilion, and I towards the old Vauxhall end. We were about level, when Tom was seized with philosophic doubt and turned back towards the Vauxhall end. For some reason I followed him. We reached the crease almost level. Twice during our outing I saw the ball flash across the wicket. Eccentric fielding; then, as if desiring another race, we both set out for the Pavilion end. At length, to the shouts of a now thoroughly interested house, the ball reached wicket-keeper Strudwick. He appealed. Neither umpire knew who was out; so much running had gone on. But Tom Raikes solved the problem by marching away with the remark: 'That's all right; I've got an unfinished beer in the pavilion.'

And they say cricket is dull.

A New Thing

Alec Kennedy showed me a new thing in cricket the other day; it is a leg-break bowled with a googly action; that is, the ball has every appearance of one that is meant to deceive the batsman into thinking that it is a leg-break, and actually it is, but not simply. For the whole thing is a fallacy within a fallacy, a logical refinement. He tells me that he invented it some years ago in South Africa, and a certain county captain was so intrigued by its subtlety that he retired into a convenient shed for two weeks to acquire it. He re-emerged in possession of the art, and bowled two of them in a match. He could do no more; for this monument of trickery has one disadvantage. No man can bowl more than six of them without spraining his wrist. A sad thing, very sad.

ON MAKING A PAIR – OR, RATHER, FOUR!

R.W.V. Robins

I suppose there can be no worse fate for a batsman, whether he be of Test standard or merely the village number 11, than to make the long walk back to the pavilion having failed to score a single run. There have been instances, of course, of famous and heroic noughts being achieved (I avoid the use of the word 'scored'), but on the whole, a nought is a blemish and not something to be remembered with much pride. Most of us indeed have scored so many ducks that to remember one or other becomes well nigh impossible. But a failure to 'get off the mark' in both innings is far more memorable just as it is infinitely more rare. Looking back over my own career, I find my memory lets me down badly over most of my noughts in first-class cricket, but the four times I claimed the dubious distinction of making a pair, culminating in a 'King Pair' on the best wicket in England, still remain extremely vivid.

My first pair was against Yorkshire at Fenner's in 1928. It was my final year at the University and we had a strong and flexible side. However, on this occasion we failed miserably in the first innings, totalling but 30 runs between us and I fear that my innings proved to be a typical instance of my natural impetuosity: I was caught off Emmott Robinson, trying my favourite shot – the 'up and over'! As usual it finished in a Garry Owen. Rain ruined the match and by the time I came in for my second innings it appeared to be a certain draw.

As I walked to the wicket, I was met by Wilfred Rhodes: 'Ever made a pair, Mr Robins?' he asked. I replied that I hadn't. 'Ay, right, we'll see that Maurice gives you one off the mark.' I reached the crease and looked up to see Rhodes and Leyland conferring at the bowler's end. Cover was being ostentatiously pushed back and the field generally relaxed. Wilfred himself had been at short leg for most of the match and he again moved in there as Maurice prepared to bowl. However, while I concentrated on the bowling, Wilfred ran round to second slip where he held a comfortable catch as I tried to push the ball into the covers. 'You tried to hit t'ball too hard!' he called as I scythed my way back to the pavilion.

My first full year in county cricket was 1929. I had a wonderful year, getting over 1000 runs while Ian Peebles and I, bowling leg-spin at both ends, took nearly 300 wickets between us. The South Africans were here that year and played Middlesex very early on in the season, which seemed a good time to catch the selectors' eye. However, my confidence slipped when I was out for a duck in the first innings. When the time came to bat again I realised that a place in the team for the first Test might rest upon a good showing in this innings. I therefore came out full of determination to face the bowling of Quinn, a fastish left-hander – but not fast enough to push Jock Cameron away from his favourite position over the stumps. Jock was a great wicket-keeper, in fact one of the swiftest and most workmanlike I ever saw. I watched Quinn carefully for a while, but soon tiring of this I attempted a lusty swing only to miss and have the bails removed by Cameron who immediately appealed for a stumping. I was pretty confident that I had got my right foot back in time, so turning to Umpire Bill Bestwick at square leg, I called out 'Was I out?' Bill did not raise his finger -- he just indicated the pavilion with his thumb. 'Young fellow,' he called back, 'your name's Walker' – so I walked!

In the 'High Summer' of post-war cricket, 1947, I gained my only pair in a county game – against Derbyshire at Derby. In the first innings I was caught at second slip off 'Dusty' Rhodes, and on arriving back at the pavilion gate I was greeted by a small autograph hunter, whom I refused, not feeling on top of the world! The boy's only reply was a loud 'Quack' as he ran off into the crowd.

In the second innings, Eddie Gothard, the captain of Derbyshire, who had only taken one wicket in county cricket before our match, had dismissed Alan Fairbairn and Bill Edrich in successive balls. As I was on the hat-trick, the field was closed in round the bat and I saw Stan Worthington being brought in at very short-leg, so I decided that, despite the ball, I would aim high and hard over the bowler's head – which I did. However, Eddie must have seen me coming as he dropped my first ball short on the leg side and I edged the ball on to my pad and was well taken at short-leg by Stan Worthington. I stalked furiously towards the pavilion not daring to look around; but as I reached the gate I heard a loud 'Quack – Quack,' and looked up sharply to see my intrepid autograph hunter beaming at me from a safe distance!

My first pair was at Fenner's in 1928 and my last, a 'King Pair,' was also at Fenner's, in 1951 – surely some sort of record on what is reputedly the country's best wicket. I was playing against Cambridge for the Free Foresters and drove up with Gubby Allen who invariably made runs in this particular fixture. I often argued that the wicket at Fenner's was much too easy-paced, which he would always deny.

In this game I came in to join Gubby with the score at about 156 for six and managed to be comprehensively bowled first ball by John Wait. As I walked off the ground I was met by George Unwin, who played occasionally for Essex, as he prepared to face the hat-trick. 'Bad luck,' he said. 'That looked like a pretty good one.' My reply was that it was a half-volley and I played all round it, but thanked him for the sympathy. As I walked to the wicket in the second innings I could not ever remember having faced a 'King Pair' in first-class cricket, so it was with the utmost determination I prepared to do battle with John Warr at his most hostile. However it did not do me much good. John's first ball flattened my stumps (I didn't bother to look round to see which ones!) And I can still hear his shout to this day. My partner, again the Treasurer of MCC who was about 50 not out at the time, told me that I had taken it like a man, as I passed him – but the incoming batsman, George Unwin, facing yet another hat-trick was not nearly so sympathetic. 'I'm getting a bit bored with this,' he muttered. 'Don't worry,' I replied, 'the bowling's pie! Just play down the line and you can't miss.' He finished with 7 not out. I gave him the confidence he needed.

MASTERS OF A FADING ART

Cecil Headlam

One of the most noticeable features of modern cricket is the almost complete disappearance of lob-bowling, not only in good cricket or first-class games, but even on the village green. Already before the war Lobsters were becoming defunct. Since the war I have seen only a few surviving, and no new exponents of that interesting and occasionally so effective type of bowling. This is the more remarkable because a good lob-bowler always used to be reckoned a very valuable asset on a side. Even in this year Warwick Armstrong has written, in his *Art of Cricket*, that 'a lob-bowler can be very useful on a sun-baked wicket'.

Underhand deliveries, in fact, constituted a change of type and trajectory so complete that they frequently broke up a prolonged stand or brought to a hurried conclusion the innings of a side which appeared certain of a mammoth score. Even good batsmen, who did not happen to be skilled to play them, were liable to be completely bamboozled by the despised donkey-drops, and, in their presence, would rapidly degenerate into hesitating and feeble performers, or else, succumbing to the temptation to hit them wildly out of the ground, soon retired to a catch in the deep.

To the lubristic batsman there appeared something contemptible in the slow lobbing up of the ball. He was wont to feel that it was incumbent upon him to hit such feeble stuff over the ropes once an over at least. But the big break which can be imparted to such deliveries was often enough his undoing. If he was inclined to lose his head he would pick the wrong one. He would endeavour to drive the ball on the half-volley, and the off twist would slant the ball into the hands of the fieldsmen massed on the on-side, or a leg-break would beat the bat and get him stumped. To a lob-bowler a batsman of this temperament or lack of experience was a gift.

For there is but one good and certain way of playing lobs. Either run out and hit the ball full pitch, or stay at home and treat it with respect. If you decide to run out, run out till you can reach the ball full pitch, without hesitation and undeterred by fear of the wicket-keeper. It is just as easy for him to stump you by a foot as by a yard, and equally disastrous for you. Reaching the ball full pitch, it is not necessary to endeavour to hit it out of sight. It will usually pay better to play it along the ground, even for a single. If, however, you judge that you cannot get to the ball so as to hit it whilst still in the air, then stay within your crease, and play the Lobster with just the same respect as you would a left-handed bowler on a sticky wicket. Never attempt to hit a lob on the half-volley; seldom, or never, play forward to it.

This being the correct and only way for the ordinary batsman to play lobs, it follows that it is very instructive for a young player to have lobs bowled at him. They teach him to use his feet, to exercise self-control and judgment, and to make those rapid decisions as to length and flight which precede all movement of feet and hands and wrists, and to which these should conform.

Underhand, or rather underarm, bowling was, of course, originally the only kind of bowling allowed. Fast underarm bowling has long been a lost art. Slow underarm is the genuine lob which modern cricketers know, and of which William Clark was one of the earliest and greatest exponents.

Masters of temptation

The chief aim of the lob-bowler is to tempt batsman to hit in the hope of getting him caught or stumped. With this object he must bowl balls with a great deal of break on – balls which do not stay too long in the air, which come fast off the pitch, and which, if hit, are likely to go upwards. It is obvious that a bowler of this kind is liable to prove expensive; a hitter may succumb to his wiles, but unless he does so quickly, the score will have mounted rapidly. Much, however, will depend upon whether the fieldsmen understand and work in unison with the bowler. That a lob-bowler is not necessarily expensive may be proved by the analysis of such a successful lob-bowler as Mr W.M. Rose. On the tour in Canada in 1875, described by R.A. Fitzgerald in his *Wickets in the West*, Rose, bowling at the opposite end to the fast left-hander, Arthur Appleby, took 71 wickets at an average cost of 5.59 runs apiece.

Other lob-bowlers of that era were Lord Harris, V.E. Walker, E.M. Grace, Osbert Mordaunt, W.B. Money, R.C. Tinley, E.T. Drake, and Armitage. Notable Lobsters in my time have been J.B. Wood, Gerald Winter, H.C. Bradby, A.J. Thornton, Major E.G. Wynyard, D.L.A. Jephson, and G.H. Simpson-Hayward. Scotland has produced two very fine lob bowlers in Cluny Macpherson and H.J. Stevenson. Amongst professionals, Walter Humphreys stands out by virtue of his long career and brilliant successes for Sussex as the most eminent lob-bowler of the latter part of the last century. Humphreys managed to get a wonderful amount of break upon the ball, either way, even on a fast, true wicket. His fine performances are recorded in a long succession of *Wisden's Annuals*.

Lobs are likely to be particularly effective against three classes of batsmen – the nervous, the slogging, and those who do not know or do not practise the method of playing them. On big occasions, such as the Gentlemen v. Players matches or the Varsity match, when tension is highest and batsmen most liable to be affected by nerves, they have sometimes proved startlingly destructive. In the Varsity match of 1875, when Cambridge wanted four runs to win and had two wickets to fall, the Oxford captain, A.W. Ridley, a very good lob-bowler, had the courage and wisdom to put himself on. He secured both wickets, taking the last with one which came straight on. In 1892 J.B. Wood, the Oxford Lobster, played havoc with a strong Cambridge side. In the same match D.L.A. Jephson was playing, but did not bowl. His greatest triumph was in a match of similar importance in 1899, when he obtained six wickets for 21 in the first innings of the Gentlemen v. Players match at Lord's.

Simpson-Hayward won the match for the Gentlemen at The Oval in 1903, finishing off the last innings with five wickets for 17 runs, at a time when a close finish had seemed a certainty.

Apart from 'nerves', lobs are less likely to be successful against very cautious players of the stay-at-home variety. During the last few years batsmen have taken to playing very much more within the crease than they used to do, and they have devoted much attention to on-side play. Whilst they have developed skill in hooking, pulling and placing on the leg-side, they are much less easily induced to run out and hit. It is, perhaps, for these reasons that the day of the lob-bowler has, at any rate temporarily, passed.

I think his day will come again. For even a bad lob-bowler will sometimes prove a useful change, unless indeed he is so bad to serve up nothing but full-pitches and long-hops. For a lob-bowler, like every other kind of bowler, must aim first and above all at control of pitch. He must study the art of changing pace as well as pitch. He must, like every other kind of bowler, a full pitch to leg is often with him an intentional and commendable device. In the case of a stodgy batsman, who cannot be induced to run out or to hit, a full pitch designed to fall upon the bails is a favourite trick of the Lobster. It is a very difficult ball to play, but also a very difficult ball to bowl. Simpson-Hayward used to manage it with very great skill.

Mysterious diversions

As a variation to a donkey-drop upon the bails a lob-bowler can do what no other bowler can – he can deliberately bowl a shooter. This ball, contemptuously termed a 'daisy-cutter' or 'sneak', is trundled along the ground from the bowler's hand. It seldom makes its appearance in good club cricket or first-class games. For, as its nickname implies, it is held to be not quite the thing in select cricket circles. Why, I hardly know. True, it would be a bore, if bowled continually. But as a diversion, it may be a difficult ball to play, and I do not quite understand why it is regarded as hardly fair. If it hops along the ground instead of shooting, it may arrive at the batsman's end in the guise of a good-length ball, and one which is difficult to time, because each time that it comes in contact with the ground its pace is altered. If it does not hop, but pursues its course as a proper 'grub', it arrives a shooter, and must be firmly blocked ere it pass the line of the left foot.

Another ball in the Lobster's repertory is the ball with the top spin which comes on straight and fast, or with only just enough break on to beat the bat. By using this ball judiciously, after a series of big breaks, he is very likely to dislodge a cautious batsman lbw. It is not an easy ball to bowl. For as Major Stevenson puts it in his article on lob-bowling contributed to Mr Lacey's little pamphlet on *Cricket Coaching*, 'the difficulty for a lob-bowler, after a little, is not to put a big break on, but to take it off'. A ball of this kind, coming straight and fast off the wicket when the batsman expected it to break, was bowled with deadly effect by Simpson-Hayward, who devised an ingenious plan for hiding it. I do not think Humphreys used it, at any rate with much effect.

As an under-arm bowler Simpson-Hayward was in a class by himself. For he delivered the ball as none before or since has been able to do, flicking it off his finger and thumb instead of letting it loose from his hand, and thereby imparting to it an onward spin which caused it to come off the ground at the pace of a medium overhand bowler. Incidentally this gave him the great advantage that, like a googly bowler, a fast wicket suited him even better than a slow.

What makes a lob-bowler so good a change, always worth trying when overarm bowlers are collared and batsmen set, is his low trajectory. Some of the best bowlers of this kind I have known, Major E.G. Wynyard, of Hampshire, and H.C. Bradby, of Rugby and Oxford, for instance, accentuated this peculiarity to the utmost by stooping almost to the ground as they delivered the ball. William Clarke, on the other hand, is said to have had a high delivery. But, other things being equal, one would imagine that the crouching position would help a lob-bowler to avoid the fault of causing the ball to hang too long in the air, a fault which renders it easy for the batsman to strike it before it pitches. It would also make the ball more deceptive when deliberately tossed high, so as to fall shorter than at first it appears about to do.

It is a low trajectory, as Major Stevenson has pointed out to me, that renders it so much more difficult to keep wicket to lobs than is usually recognised. The wicket-keeper frequently gets no sight of the ball until after it has passed the batsman, or only the most momentary glimpse.

A good wicket-keeper and good catchers in the deep field are essential to the success of an under-hand bowler. But apart from support at the wicket and in the deep, a lob-bowler can add enormously both to the cheapness and the size of his 'bag' if he is himself an active and courageous fieldsman to his own bowling.

It takes some courage to face a batsman when he is dancing down the wicket with the intention of knocking the cover off a ball that has been lobbed up to him. It takes a good pair of hands and an eye quick to recognise what stroke is about to be made, if the Lobster is to bring off a c & b or save a single from a ball so struck. But he has by the very nature of his action this advantage over ordinary bowlers, that he does not bowl himself over. He is on his toes after the delivery of the ball, and if he is active and alert he can follow up or anticipate the stroke of the opposing batsman. By far the quickest and keenest fieldsmen to their own bowling I have ever seen were C.M. Wells and H.J. Stevenson. Both, it may be noticed, were great Rugby football players. The latter has been known to bring off a catch somewhere near long leg off his own lobs.

THE ANGLER

J. Barton King
Introductory Note by John A. Lester

Bart King was without question the finest all-around cricketer ever produced in America, and his playing career almost exactly corresponded with the Augustan age of Philadelphia cricket. He was not only the best cricketer, but also, because of his warm heart, ready wit, and ever-renewed stock of cricket stories, factual and fictional, he had hosts of friends on both sides of the Atlantic, and was the best-known cricket figure in our history. Yet up to now no written statement has ever come from him in explanation of his methods as a bowler.

It was during our campaign against the English counties in 1897 that King first demonstrated the effectiveness of the fast right-hand inswinger. We count ourselves fortunate in being able to present his own account of what he always liked to call his 'angler'. What he says will be clarified by this brief introduction.

Nature endowed this man completely with the physical equipment that a fast bowler covets. He stood six feet one inch, weighed 178 pounds, and never in his life has carried superfluous flesh. The physical characteristic that impressed Bart's friends most deeply, however, was not his powerful shoulders or the long and loosely hung arms and lean hips. It was rather the power in the wrists and fingers. This hand power had been developed and was maintained by special exercises of his own. With his wrist held tight Bart could send a new cricket ball to the second story window with a snip of two fingers and a thumb. He kept a religious vigil over his physical condition; in consequence he possessed amazing endurance, and extended his career as a fast bowler over nearly twenty-five years. He was a keen student of bowling technique; experimented widely before adopting his own; but having selected his own methods, used them with that supreme confidence that was his outstanding characteristic.

The incident that most aptly illustrates both this self-confidence and also the control with which King was sending down his 'angler' in the early years of this century is, as far as I know, unique in cricket history. It occurred in a match when nine wickets were down. When the last batsman came to the wicket, Bart dismissed his fielders and bowled him first ball. E.J. Metcalfe, favorably known in Philadelphia as captain of the visiting Incogniti in 1920 and again in 1924, tells the story with several inaccuracies in *The Cricketer* for 10 August 1940, and evidently dismisses it as a fable. George Brooking, whose brother Bob, the Peripatetic Philadelphian, was playing for Belmont in the match, and was one of the fielders called in, gets it straighter in his *Cricket Memories*. Since I have recently checked the essential facts in consultation with King himself, they will be set down here.

About 1910 the most famous figure in baseball was the great but eccentric picher, 'Rube' Waddell, of the Philadelphia Athletics. It was after watching the Rube in an exhibition game strike a man out after calling in all seven fielders in front of the catcher that King began to think of doing something like that in cricket.

The opportunity came when King's club, Belmont, was playing an eleven from Trenton. The Trenton captain had missed his his train, and arrived on the grounds at Elmwood just as King bowled out the ninth Trenton batsman. As the captain walked to the wicket Bart overheard him apologising for coming late, and adding that his team wouldn't be in a mess like this if he had only caught his train. It was the kind of remark no wise batsman would make in King's hearing.

Bart said nothing. He looked the captain over with an appraising eye, then called his fielders together and sent them to the clubhouse. Walking back, and turning to begin his run before delivering the ball, he noticed Edward Leech, the Belmont wicket-keeper, still at his place behind the stumps.

'Why Eddie, Eddie, whatever are you doing there? I won't need you, Eddie; join the rest.'

So there remained on the field at Elmwood two batsman, two umpires, one bowler, and that was all. King would have to hit the wicket or the ball would go for four byes; a snick or any kind of hit would go for four runs. The visiting captain protested, and appealed to the umpires. They went into a huddle as they well might. It was a situation that had never come up in cricket anywhere in the world. They decided, and rightly, that Mr King was well within the law so long as he did not have *more than eleven* men on the field.

Bart, always happiest in a dramatic moment, again paused before taking his run, and then called to the pavilion that on second thought he did need one other man on the field. The player walked out, and King placed him very exactly in a novel position, twenty yards back of the wicket and four paces to leg, that is, to the right, as the bowler faced him. The batsman at King's end was puzzled and inquired: 'For heaven's sake, if you don't need a wicket-keeper, what on earth is that man doing there?'

'He's not a wicket-keeper,' said Bart; 'he's not even a fielder. You see I've given the umpires enough trouble already. That man's there for just one thing, to pick up the ball after the game is over and return it to the umpires.' Then King hit the captain's leg wicket with a fast angler. 'You know,' he told me recently in recalling the incident, 'what pleased me best was not to see the bails jumping, but that I grazed the leg peg just fine enough to take the ball to the man I meant to get it. He didn't have to move a step.'

King performed another extraordinary feat at Haverford, playing against the Irish Gentlemen in 1909, when he shattered the defenses of all *eleven* men opposed to him. He bowled G.A. Morrow, the best bat on the side and the eventual not-out, with a no-ball, and then went on in the second innings to do the hat-trick. Certainly these two performances, taken conjointly, are unparalleled in cricket on this side of the Atlantic.

It was a remark like that of the Trenton captain that gave King another chance to provide entertainment for himself and his mates, this time on board ship as we were returning from the tour of England described in the previous chapter by Percy Clark. A little amateur hypnotist who had attached himself to the party was overheard to say that the Philadelphia cricketers were stout fellows, but there wasn't one of them he couldn't lay low with a few passes. At dinner that night, in Reginald's hearing, Bart let it be known that he couldn't be hypnotised, he would challenge anyone on board to try; and it was soon agreed that Reginald would give a demonstration in the smoking room.

Soon after dinner he began making his passes, Bart facing him with a grim countenance and a mouth tightly closed.

Suddenly King swayed, collapsed in a backward fall, and struck his head violently on the marble floor. His eyes seemed to be glazed and a white froth began to ooze from the corners of his mouth. Before entering the lists he had harbored behind each gum a nubbin of soap scooped out of his Williams shaving stick.

A bystander who knew not King and his ways had already run for a doctor, and it was Dr John William White, the distinguished Philadelphia surgeon, who entered the smoking room. He knelt to listen to the breathing, to look intently into the eyes. Dr White knew King, and what kind of patient he was dealing with. He was perhaps ready for the two quick winks that came from the corpse's left eye. But what superb and rapid diagnosis! He snapped and pocketed his watch, stood up and announced gravely, 'This man is dead.' He turned to one of Bart's confidants, 'Go to the bridge and inform the captain; no one else is to leave the room.'

The captain was a sportsman. Being fully informed of the incident from beginning to end, he sent down two of the younger officers, who put the trembling little hypnotist in irons and led him away to the ship's brig. There he cooled his heels for an hour, while we brushed King down and drank Reginald's health. Then Bart went magnanimously below and rescued the prisoner.

J.B. King's earliest appearance in first-class cricket was against Blackham's Australians in 1893, and his last first-class cricket was played against S.E. Gregory's Australians in 1912. In the course of these twenty years he was a member of all three of the elevens that represented Philadelphia against the first-class counties in England.

We can best appreciate the part he played in the Philadelphia attack from 1893 to 1912 from an actual count of the wickets he took. Of the first-class wickets that fell to our bowlers in these twenty years, whether at home or abroad, Bart King took 42 per cent.

The Angler And How I Bowled It
J. Barton King

We must always remember that the ball that curves is just an adjunct to the stock in trade of a good bowler. It is a very valuable weapon; but first the bowler must be able to hit the wicket with a good-length ball, to turn it from the pitch, and at times to send it down with a deceptive change of pace. When the bowler has equipped himself with these skills he may try to develop the swing. If he *always* curves, a good batsman will find him just as easy to play as the man who bowls perfectly straight.

Writers on cricket have various theories as to what makes the cricket ball curve in the air. I was never a theorist in bowling because I observed

that what made the ball swing for one bowler might not do the same
for another. A man's physique determines his curve just as surely as it
determines his style of batting. In the right-hand outcurve bowled so
effectively by P.H. Clark, and in the left-hand incurve of Cope Morton,
Harry Brown, and Paul O'Neill – the three best swinging left-handers
in Philadelphia – it was physique that was determinant. Their methods
naturally differed.

Hence I am not writing this as a word of advice to the man who wishes
to bowl a swinger, but simply making a statement about what seemed
to make the ball turn in the air for me, in the way I wanted it to turn.
Every seasoned bowler will understand that I arrived at my methods by
experiment – by finding out through a longish process of trial and error
what worked best for me.

I was a pitcher before I was a bowler, and, like Albert Trott, I learned
a good deal from my baseball experience. Fifty years ago right-hand
outcurve pitching was like throwing an off-break. So that it is rather
amazing to me to find my good friend Pelham Warner in his excellent
Badminton *Cricket* doubting that Rhodes was right when he maintained
that it is possible to make the ball both spin and curve. Every baseball
player knows that the old outcurve pitched right-handed will break back
if it pitches on level turf. That old curve, pitched with an off-break grip
was called the 'roundhouse', because it was a true arc of a circle, and
started curving when it left the hand.

It was soon found to be ineffective because the batsman could see its
direction too soon. Today you can watch big-league baseball all through
a summer and never see a roundhouse pitched. Fifty years ago pitchers
were beginning to learn to throw what is called the 'hook', that is, a ball
that travels with very little curve until the last ten or twelve feet, when
it shoots out for the right-hand pitcher and in for the left-hander. And
it was fifty years ago that I began to experiment in order to develop
the same kind of ball in cricket, that is, a ball that would keep back,
store up as it were, its tendency to swing, and let it go in the last ten or
fifteen feet of its flight.

Finding that under certain unpredictable conditions the ball would
respond, and suddenly swing in at an angle or tangent to the flat
trajectory of my fast ball, I christened this infant my 'angler'. But first
I had to discard entirely the grip and the spin that used to produce the
old roundhouse. I found a new shiny cricket ball was favorable to a sharp
hook but not necessary for it. I found I could hook or angle an old ball
as effectively as a new one when conditions were right. My next problem

was to examine these conditions, and by trial and error to identify those in my favor.

Some of them were beyond my control – for instance wind and weather. But I could study them and use those which helped most. When I began bowling I liked best a following wind just strong enough to flutter the left corner of my shirt collar. Although later, when I felt completely co-ordinated and physically fit, I could swing the ball with a wind coming from any quarter, I preferred it coming from the batsman's off, and if I could make it to order, I would have a gusty wind sweeping up the gulley to the right of second slip.

But still on some days I observed that the ball would swing more than on others; and, being by now convinced that I had in the angler a new and effective ball for occasional use, I began to make a careful study of what in my bodily action produced it.

The fundamental essential I found to be complete relaxation and co-ordination – an absence of any tension in arms, legs, or shoulders. This was necessary because my angler required a whole-souled follow-through of body and arm that would carry me well on down the wicket. When conditions were favorable I had the feeling that I was hurling myself after the ball toward the wicket.

In bowling the hooked or angled curve I found the second essential to be the height of the action and the grip used. I delivered the angler from full height straight above my head, indeed at times from slightly over the left shoulder. I held the ball consistently with the seam just between the first and second fingers, with the thumb opposed. The third finger was just in contact with the ball, and the fourth finger idle. It required only a very slight adjustment of this grip to make the ball go straight without any curve, or to give it enough spin for a slight off-break.

As to the control of the angler, I found it to lie in the wrist and the fingers. A strong yet flexible wrist, and long powerful fingers are desirable in every curve bowler; I found them quite essential for the control of the angler. Indeed the wrist and the first two fingers are the controlling factors in putting this ball where it should be. I felt the ball last, not with the side, but with the tips of the two fingers, and discovered that a delicate control of its flight depended on the final pressure. This finger pressure came at the end of a sharp downward flick of the wrist.

I would like to repeat at the end of these remarks what I said at the beginning – that the perfected angler is of value only as an adjunct to the stock-in-trade of the good bowler. If it had gone down every time, the best English batsmen would have soon been on top of it. To be effective it must come as a surprise, and hence the bowler must spare no pains in developing a delivery which can send down a straight ball, an off-break or an angler without any difference of action perceptible to the batsman.

This principle of surprise and variety of attack applies to the sum total of the side's available bowling. My effectiveness was to a large extent conditioned on what was coming down from the other end. What success I had against English and Australian batsmen with my inswinger was due in good measure to the bowling of P.H. Clark and H.V. Hordern at the other end; Clark's sharp outcurve and Hordern's googlies were both excellent foils for my angler.

Chapter 6

CRICKET
GROUNDS

J.C. Squire

No two names could more suitably be found together on *The Hamble-don Cricket Chronicle*, 1772–1796, than those of Mr Ashley-Cooper and Mr Lucas. The former, whose recent productions include a new edition of Pycroft and an exhaustive record of the Eton and Harrow matches, is the most indefatigable of living historians of the game, and Mr Lucas himself compiled, years ago, a book with *The Hambledon Men* as its title. This work, which is in print at the Oxford University Press, is the most delightful of cricket miscellanies, and includes *inter alia*, John Nyren's 'The Young Cricketer's Tutor' and 'The Cricketers of my Time'. It should certainly be read in conjunction with the new volume.

Mr Ashley-Cooper's book is in large measure a summary of facts. He deals with the period 1772–1796, which saw the Club in its prime and in its decline. He gives certain match scores not in *Scores and Biographies*, a match summary for those years during which the little Hampshire village constantly met and defeated All England, a list of officers of the Club, a membership roll, and brief biographies of the Hambledon players. The chief justification for his volume is, however, that two Hambledon documents of great interest are reproduced in it for the first time. Mr Ashley-Cooper has had access to two manuscript volumes, a minute-book and a statement of accounts, chiefly kept by Richard Nyren and the two Bonhams. These volumes are an important supplement to the history of the game in the eighteenth century.

The Hambledon Club was founded about 1750, and by 1756 was very strong. Its years of great glory were those from 1772 to 1787, when the MCC was founded, largely on the initiative of the Hambledon president for the year. The minute-book ends in 1796, just before the death of the elder Nyren, who was secretary. The entries in the MS books are mostly brief, and Mr Ashley-Cooper allows most of them to stand without annotation. They usually deal, as is natural, with the social and business aspects of the Club, but sidelights are thrown on the cricket. On 25 May 1773, it was ordered 'That Mr Richards do endeavour to find out the Expence of A Machine to Convey the Cricketers to distant parts and report the same next meeting.' 'Machine' sounds odd, but Nyren throws light on it. He records: –

'When a match was to be played at a distance, the whole eleven, with umpire and scorer, were conveyed in one caravan, built for their accommodation. Upon one occasion, the vehicle having been overturned, and the whole cargo unshipped, Buck (Peter Stewart) remained at his post, and refused to come out, desiring that they would right the vessel with him in it; for that "one good turn deserved another". This repartee was admired for a week.'

On 26 June 1781, it was 'ordered that eleven Hats be procured for the Cricketers and a black one for the Waiter', and on 16 July 1791, there was a discussion on a point of law. 'The Umpire said: "I really think the Ball hit the Ground, but I cannot be positive."' It wasn't quite the right way to put it, though not quite so bad as the recorded pronouncement of a later and equally candid umpire: 'I didn't see it, but it's out.' Apparently the decision, if it was a decision was made in an England and Hampshire match on Windmill Down; it is significant that it was referred to a Committee of the MCC, including Sir Horace Mann and Col. Lenox (afterwards Duke of Richmond), for it was the establishment and growth of the MCC in the London area that led to the fall of the Hambledon Club from its proud position.

The few actual references to the play in the minutes are supplemented by notes on the matches which Mr Ashley-Cooper supplies. We find it recorded of the match against England in 1772 that 'Lumpy had the honour of bowling out Small, which had not been done for some years.' According to the *Reading Mercury* of the time, a match in the next year, 1773, attracted 20,000 spectators. This may rather surprise the pessimists who think it is a new and portentous thing that great crowds should go to watch cricket; and that other tribe who imagine that betting on games is a product of modern debasement may be presented with the *Reading Mercury's* statement regarding a match at Lord's in 1791: 'It is supposed there was more money depending on this match than on any one ever played before.' Money was laid on the old cricket matches as it is on the new boxing matches; there were wagers bound up with the challenges as well as individual bets, and the best amateurs were glad to make an income out of the game. The graceful Lord Frederick Beauclerk, who was not only a lord but a clergyman, derived a regular income from his bets which would make a modern 'paid amateur' green with envy. In 1772 it was arranged, according to a contemporary, 'that eleven women from Hants shall play, some time this month, with twice the number of Hampton gentlemen, for £500; and what is not a little singular, the odds, it is asserted, are already considerably in favour of the female professors of that noble exercise.'

The cricket, as I have observed, comes in but incidentally in the minutes and accounts. The elections and subscriptions occupy a great deal of attention. The mere records of these provide a skeleton history of the club's decline. As time goes on subscriptions (which were heavy) were more difficult to collect, and members were more inclined to resign after paying them. Marylebone was more convenient than Hambledon for gentlemen who did not actually reside there, and more profitable for professionals; the number of matches also declined. A list of gentlemen subscribers in 1795 gives forty-three names; opposite five of these, for the wars were on, is the inscription 'Gone to sea', and opposite one the comment 'Gone to the Devil'. However, so long as the Club lasted it kept cheerful. Nobody examining its records could suggest that it took its pleasures sadly. Wine and song, as we know from Nyren, were the principal features of its gatherings. Remembering the glees they sang at the 'Bat and Ball' on Broad Halfpenny, he quotes: –

> 'I have been there, and still would go;
> 'Twas like a little Heaven below!'

The extract, I believe, is from Dr Watts; who perhaps might have found the little Heaven something too convivial. Port and sherry were the staple drinks; to an entry regarding thirty-eight bottles of the one and nine of the other Mr Ashley-Cooper appends the sufficient footnote: 'Hampshire beat Surrey on Windmill Down by 127 runs.' Nyren, advertising his tent for the matches, begged leave 'to inform the lovers of Cricket that all sorts of Liquors and cold Provision may be found at his Booth on the Down', and the members of the Club shared the tastes of their supporters. What could be more succinct that these two entries for 1781 and 1782?

'August 15. – Present at the Boys' Match, Hambledon against Petersfield and Buriton. Mr Jervoise, Rev. Mr Cooley, Mr Richards, and Mr Leeke, and a fine Haunch of Venison.

September 5, 1782. – At Extra meeting to eat Venison and drink Bonham's and Fitzherbert's Claret.'

It is small wonder that it was ultimately ordered 'that the last Meeting of the Hambledon Club be in future of a Moon Light Night'.

Amongst the names in the members' list is one 'B. Shelley', who is supposed to be old Sir Bysshe, and a John Shakespear, father of the Shakespear who had a brief partnership with Lord Byron in a celebrated Eton and Harrow match. But the oddest name we encounter here has literary associations of another kind. There seems something ominous about it, for it appears in the next to the last entry in the club minutes. The two last entries (1796) run: –

'August 29. – [Three members and twelve non-subscribers (including "Mr Thos Pain, Authour of the rights of Man") present. No business noted.]
   September 21. – No gentlemen.'

We are not told who brought Tom Paine. Had it been a year earlier we might have presumed his host to have been William Powlett, the famous Radical hunting squire, who was known as Pontius Pilot; but he resigned membership in 1795.

   Nobody will ever know how the Hambledon men would have fared against their successors, and we can only dimly apprehend what their bowling was like. The old men who lived during the transition from underhand to roundarm (which they called 'throwing') never surrendered the position. They lived in a period of experimentation. We have, recorded here, the names of the first man who systematically bowled a length, and the first who systematically played forward; these things did not happen by accident or without discussion; those who imagine that cricket theory was born with the 19th century are grossly mistaken. As for the Hambledon wickets, the care taken about sowing and rolling them suggests that they may well have been as good as the best village wickets today, though modern methods of preparation were unknown. Six days' cricket a week they did not play, and there was no question of a 'Gasworks End'. Change is incessant and we also may make history. I doubt if Broad Halfpenny was ever, as was the Worcestershire County ground, a few years ago, sown in error with turnip seed; and it may be taken for certain that a full history of the Hambledon Club would afford no parallel to the case of the spectator at Leyton who dislocated his jaw by yawning at the slowness of the Essex batting.

BIG HITS AT CANTERBURY

Gerald Brodribb

Cricket 'Festivals' are very much a feature of the game, and there is none more famous than the one at Canterbury, which dates back as far as 1842, right into the middle ages of cricket. In 1847 the venue of the Canterbury Festival was changed to a ground belonging to and bordering the 12th century hospital of St Lawrence; it has been played there ever since, and this ground became the headquarters of the Kent County Cricket Club.

The playing area of the St Lawrence ground is large, and hits for six require a good carry. If a batsman is batting at the Nackington Road end, that is to say facing the pavilion, he must produce a hit of almost exactly 100 yards to reach the pavilion rails. I believe that no-one has ever hit a ball clean over the top of the pavilion, but there are records of a few hits which have landed on the roof with its rose-red tiles 'half as old as time'; this means a big hit, as the roof is about 105 yards away, and is nearly 40 feet high; W.J. Fairservice tells me he remembers J.H. Sinclair hitting a ball off his bowling on to the roof; and in 1925 A.P.F. Chapman in scoring 33 v. Sussex drove a ball right on to the roof; and it rolled down and bounced off to be caught by Colonel A.C. Watson fielding at mid-on. K.L. Hutchings once drove a ball to the upper balcony of the pavilion, and the ball struck his mother, fortunately without damage. During his famous innings of 101 not out v. Kent in 1939 Jim Smith landed one of his seven sixes on to the lead roof below the pavilion clock. Another good hit was by J. Ryder, the Australian, who in 1926 drove a ball and it was 'caught' by Macartney in the Players' Box on the first storey.

If the ball is driven to the off-side of straight, and I take as a central wicket the line between the pavilion gate and the sight screen, the tree between the pavilion and the stand on its right (as you face it) is a good target, and Watt, in scoring 25 v. Hampshire in 1936, put a ball among its topmost branches. To the left of the pavilion is a huge concrete double-decker stand, whose roof must be nearly 40 feet high. It was erected in 1926, and no-one in a county match has yet cleared it (though Viscount Lyttelton in a club match once did so, and actually landed the ball on his own car); Ames, Hammond and C.H. Knott are among those few who have put a ball into the top seats. Before this concrete stand was built, there was a low wooden stand, and it was over this stand that Colonel A.C. Watson made a famous hit out of the ground into the gardens by the Oast House, a carry of at least 140 yards.

A hit to mid-wicket needs 77 yards to carry the boundary and hits have been made into the cars parked on the embankment some 20 yards beyond it. In 1931 G.F. Earle hit three sixes in four balls from A.P. Freeman, and some of these went among the cars. For a left-hander batting at the same end there are less obvious targets, but the boundary to square-leg is only 79 yards, and Frank Woolley (86) once made a huge on-drive off W.J. Whitty in the Australians v. Kent match of 1912, and the ball went in the direction of the Blythe War Memorial, and apparently bounced down through the entrance gates to the very door of the 'Bat and Ball' Inn; it sounds a very big hit.

It would be good to know the exact whereabouts of the four hits in one four-ball over which C.I. Thornton made when playing for Kent v. MCC in 1869. Lord Harris states that they were made towards the pavilion, and 'one or two perhaps' of them may have gone right out of the ground, and all certainly 'over the ring'.

Lord Harris goes on to say that he considers that C.I. Thornton's greatest hit at Canterbury was made from the other end. This was a hit off W.M. Rose (MCC) in 1871; it was measured by the secretary at 152 yards and landed in Nackington Road.

From the square in its present position a straight hit of 125 yards would pitch into the Nackington Road, but if the hit is wider to the on-side the carry to the road would have to be greater. One of the most famous drives at Canterbury is Colonel A.C. Watson's over the President's Tent in 1925; it was the same innings in which he hit a ball to the Oast House – as already mentioned. From this hit over the tent the ball was lost, and found only during the winter in a bush beside the road. It is the nearest rival to Thornton's great hit. In his innings of 101 not out v. Kent in 1939 in the same direction, Jim Smith made one drive considered 'almost as big as Watson's'; three of his sixes went right over the tents, and another of his hits went into the top of the lime tree, but counted only four. The foot of this lime tree, which stands so remarkably within the playing area, is 80 yards distant from the wicket. Watson's drive went over the top of the tree, and Constantine in 1928 also made a more ballooned hit which went over the top. R. Relf in scoring his first century, a score of 210 v. Kent in 1907, made several huge drives over the tree off E.W. Dillon's bowling. At its furthest point, the boundary line behind the tree is 96 yards from the wicket, so a hit over the tents beyond is very considerable; a hit over the screen, which is 93 yards away, is also rare.

Big hits to the off-side are even more rare, but there is a target in the direction of extra cover in the double-decker stand with a scoreboard mounted on it. The front edge of this stand is as distant as the most distant tents, namely 96 yards, so a hit into this stand is far from easy, except perhaps for a left-hander.

LORD'S

Trevor Bailey

Lord's has always been my favourite Test ground. First, it has usually been lucky for me, in that if I did not score runs I normally grabbed a few wickets, or vice versa. Second, a Lord's Test is not just another international match, it is the major cricketing occasion of the summer and an annual reunion for former players. Third, the Lord's Test is the best attended of all Tests in England and I have always thrived on a big audience – the bigger the better. Finally, Lord's is the headquarters of the game and over two centuries has gradually built up its own very special atmosphere.

My first of seven Lord's Tests was against New Zealand in 1949 and, in view of my later reputation, it is, perhaps, justifiable to quote what *Wisden* had to say about that particular innings. I went in at number seven with the score 112 for five to partner Denis Compton, when the pitch was starting to ease and Cowie had tired.

'The change in England's fortunes came when Bailey joined Compton. Fortunate to receive two loose balls down the legside which he turned for four apiece immediately he went in, Bailey showed complete confidence and for a long time he overshadowed Compton. Bailey continued to punish anything loose, mainly by going down on one knee and sweeping the ball hard to the square-leg boundary. Ten fours came in his first fifty made in sixty-seven minutes. With his side in danger, Compton concentrated on wearing down the attack, and not until England were out of trouble did he take the slightest risk. Then he brought into play his wide range of strokes and scored much faster than his partner. Bailey was unlucky to miss his first Test hundred, for which, with only seven wanted, he cut a ball on to the wicket-keeper's foot, whence it rebounded into the hands of second slip. His splendid innings lasted for two and a half hours and contained sixteen fours.'

In contrast, my bowling was not only unsuccessful but also well below international standard. In 33 unimpressive overs I failed to take a wicket – indeed, seldom looked like taking one – and conceded 136 runs. Martin Donnelly, who made a brilliant double-century, displayed, not for the first nor the last time, an understandable partiality for my bowling as I had not yet acquired sufficient control.

My most worrying Lord's Test was against South Africa in 1955, in which Fred Titmus and Peter Heine made their international débuts. Peter May captained England at Lord's for the first time and we won by 71 runs, despite having been bowled out in our first innings for 133. Brian Statham did the damage, bowling unchanged for 29 consecutive overs and taking seven for 39. My personal worry had nothing to do with the cricket.

As usual I had driven up from my Westcliff home. We had won the toss, decided to bat, and found, as so often happens at Lord's, that the pitch was distinctly lively. We had lost a number of wickets and I was padded up when Billy Griffith, Secretary of MCC, came into our dressing-room at about one o'clock and asked me to take a phone call from my wife.

Greta would never have phoned me during a Test unless something was very wrong. My immediate reaction was that her mother had died, so I was totally unprepared when she informed me that Kim, my eldest son, had been knocked down outside our house when he had run across the road to his grandfather from behind a parked car. Greta had picked him up out of the gutter. The car driver, who had no chance to avoid him, happened to be a specialist and took him straight to the hospital where the injuries turned out not to be serious – indeed, he came home the following day.

The reason for the phone call was that Greta realised that somebody at the hospital would have tipped off the local paper, who in turn would have phoned the London Evenings. This meant that I would have heard about the accident in the worst possible way. Greta assured me that there was no point in my returning until close of play, as Kim was in no danger and there was nothing I could do.

Upset and shaken by the unexpected news, I had the added problem of informing my mother, who was at the match, before the placards shouting 'Son of Test Cricketer at Lord's Knocked Down by Car' appeared in the ground. It was, by now, the luncheon interval. When playing cricket I never drank anything but soft drinks at lunch when batting and either a half of bitter or a pint of ginger beer shandy when bowling. On this occasion I broke all the rules and swallowed four brandies. It was one of the few occasions I have gone to the crease unable to concentrate and I did not last long.

When I arrived home I immediately went with Greta to see Kim who was conscious, but drowsy, in the children's ward. What did surprise me was the request of a photographer outside the hospital when I was about to leave. He wanted to take a picture of my son with me inside the children's ward at 8.30 p.m.

My best remembered Lord's Test, but not my best Test, was against the Australians in 1953. It caught the imagination of the general public and because of the situation it gained a fame which was in excess of what it deserved and became something of a legend. It is interesting to note that the length of my stand with Willie Watson has also been greatly exaggerated. What really happened, and why all the fuss?

This Test was a delicately balanced affair throughout and illustrates the fascination the game at this level can provide. For five days, fortune continually swung from side to side – collapse and rally, fine batting, bowling and fielding. Australia's 346 and 368 and England's 372 meant that we required 343 for victory when we commenced our second innings on the fourth day with an hour to go.

It had been decided that if a wicket fell after six o'clock I should take on the role of nightwatchman. This turned out to be somewhat ironic in retrospect as I found myself padded up from six o'clock onwards in my normal position as number six. Our first three wickets fell for only 12 runs and I watched with apprehension as Compton and Watson negotiated an uncomfortable half hour, in which the latter might have been caught at leg slip off Ring. Len Hutton could not hide his disappointment as he unbuckled his pads in the dressing-room, knowing that with three of his best batsmen back in the pavilion our chances of saving, let alone winning the match, were remote, while the chances of our gaining two wins from the next three meetings against opponents who were certainly as good if not better than ourselves was fairly non-existent.

On the final day I travelled up to London with Greta by train and read various newspapers which had all written us off. This rather rankled. It was not that I anticipated the eventual outcome, but with Denis and Willie still at the crease I felt we ought to make them fight hard, even though the pitch was taking spin and Brown, Evans, Wardle and Statham were essentially attacking batsmen and unlikely to remain too long.

After a few anxious moments, Denis and Willie settled down and it came as something of a surprise when the former was l.b.w. to what might be described as a genuine shooter.

When I joined Willie my sole objective was still to be there at lunch. My approach was to assume that every ball was potentially lethal and had to be stopped. Having survived for about half an hour, Willie and I had a short conference and decided that, without making it obvious, I would take as much of the leg-spin as possible, because the rough was making things very difficult outside his off stump for my left-handed partner.

At lunch Willie had reached his half-century and I was in double figures, so we returned to the pavilion reasonably satisfied, though realising that there was a very long way to go and that the most difficult time was likely to be mid-afternoon when Lindwall and Miller would take the new ball.

In the dressing-room I ate my normal hearty lunch which included some of my partner's, who did not believe in eating during an innings. Much to our surprise and delight, Johnston and Davidson shared the attack on the resumption of play, which gave us the opportunity to become reaccustomed to pace bowling before the all-out assault just before three o'clock. Benaud and Johnston bowled cutters for a few overs before the new ball was taken, but by this time we had had a dress rehearsal and had settled back into the groove.

It was noticeable that by three o'clock the crowd and the tension had increased. This was the crucial period and we were very happy when we returned to the pavilion for tea with the scoreboard reading 183 for four. For the first time I really believed that we could avoid defeat and I have seldom enjoyed a cup of tea quite so much. At no stage during that day did we ever consider going for the win and at no time was it necessary for Hassett to set run-saving fields. Both of us concentrated on defence, but like most batsmen gratefully accepted any runs which were available. Willie also happened to be a very fine runner between the wickets, a natural mover who never seemed to be hurrying but covered the ground far faster than most people, which meant we picked up plenty of singles.

In the final session, Hassett switched his bowlers around. Willie completed a splendid century and was eventually caught off Doug Ring, whom we considered the most dangerous bowler and probably should have been used more. The time was 5.50, the total 236 for five, when I was joined by Freddie Brown. We decided that if Ray Lindwall was brought back as we expected, I should take as much of him as possible. Instead Hassett decided on spin from both ends, possibly because the spinners bowled their overs more quickly and the days of 20 overs in the final hour had not yet been introduced. At six o'clock I attempted a cover slash off Benaud, in the circumstances a stupid shot, and was caught out for 71. With only half an hour to go we should, by this time, have saved the game without difficulty, but those last 30 minutes seemed to last for hours, especially as Freddie and Godfrey Evans had decided quite correctly that their best chance was to play their shots.

When Greta and I reached Westcliff, we found we had been sent some champagne and with the help of a couple of friends we celebrated quietly and effectively what had definitely been a day to remember.

In terms of all-round value, my next Test at Lord's against Australia was far superior to my performance in 1953, but nobody remembers it, while my stand with Willie Watson caught the imagination and has gone down in cricket history. This was due to a number of reasons: Australia won by 185 runs because we failed with the bat on two occasions, subsequent performances by Laker, and to a lesser degree Lock, were to dwarf everything else in the series, and later the Australians were partially to disintegrate as a side. Nevertheless, at Lord's I achieved more than was normally expected of me as the all-rounder in a team which contained five specialist batsmen, a wicket-keeper and four specialist bowlers. In the Australian first innings of 285 I took two wickets (McDonald, their top scorer, and Harvey) and held two catches off Laker in the leg trap. I was second highest scorer in our first innings of 171, then took four wickets in their second innings and had the satisfaction of catching Harvey at leg slip off Fred Trueman, which was certainly one of the five best catches I have ever taken. On the final day I joined Peter May with the total at 91 for four. Although there was neither the time nor the ability to make the 372 required to win, there was just a faint hope that we might hold out for another draw, but it was not to be and I was caught just before lunch for 18.

By the mid-1950s, Lord's had acquired a reputation for helping seam bowlers and it was noticeable that Middlesex finished most of their home matches. In these circumstances the selection of the West Indies side for the 1957 Lord's Test made no sense at the time, and still does not. They went into that match with only one pace bowler, Gilchrist, had Frank Worrell at just above medium sharing the new ball, and included four spinners – Ramadhin, Valentine, Smith and Sobers – plus Goddard at medium pace. In sharp contrast, England chose a strong batting line-up, three seamers plus Wardle, plus Close who never even bowled.

Selectors have often made mistakes, especially when they have plenty of players to choose from – it is never easy to compare the form displayed by different players in different teams. However, when selectors on tour blunder in this fashion it is much harder to understand, although it does happen. It puts me in mind of that classic England blunder in Australia in 1962–63 at Sydney, when England with three spinners available included only Fred Titmus, who took seven wickets, while Bob Simpson, not the most devastating slow bowler, took five wickets for Australia. As a result of this misreading of the pitch by the selectors, England lost a match they could have won.

Back at Lord's, we beat a strong West Indies batting side, which included the 'Three Ws' and had Smith coming in at seven, by an innings. They managed only 127 at their first attempt and I had the satisfaction of picking up seven wickets for 44. We amassed 424, of which my contribution was exactly one. Thanks largely to a magnificent 90 from Everton Weekes, who was hampered by a broken finger, the tourists did better in their second innings but I felt more than satisfied with four wickets, including those of Walcott, Weekes and Sobers. I have always liked Lord's, though never to quite the extent I did on that occasion.

THE NEW PAVILION

Graham White

After the war we are going to have a new pavilion. This statement has little news value, I fear, for to my certain knowledge we have been going to have a new pavilion for the last twenty-five years.

The old one was built as far back as 1890 – a squat wooden affair with a red-tiled roof, two poky little dressing-rooms, and a small main room in which the two teams were supposed to forgather for tea. Usually, the visitors sat down to tea while the home team took theirs outside and gossiped to them through the windows. It was easier that way.

There was no room at all for the tennis section, who had to be content with a primitive wooden shack on the far side of the ground. For the pavilion was built in the days when cricket was cricket, and male tennis players pure anathema to the wielders of the willow.

By 1919, however, a more enlightened stage had been reached, and when the tennis committee broached the subject of a combined pavilion, many of us were all in favour of the idea.

'The old place is pretty well finished, anyway,' we said. 'We'll rip it down and put up a roomy affair, with modern dressing-rooms and showers. We'll have a bar, too, and put down a decent floor for dances on Saturday evenings. What with the bar and the dances, the place'll pay for itself in no time.'

At least, that's how some of us talked. There was a noticeable lack of enthusiasm among the older players, who appeared to be quite satisfied with the place as it was. Which, we agreed, was ridiculous; a club must progress or perish. And things had got to the stage when the younger among us were ashamed to show visiting teams to their quarters.

In 1922 we pressed the matter at the annual general meeting. There was a general acceptance of the fact that 'something ought to be done about it', and a determination on the part of the younger members that something should be done, and before very long, too.

'Mark my words,' Johnson remarked to me as we walked home that evening, 'You won't know the place when we get the new place finished. I'm fed up with rushing off five miles away for a dance, and having to go home first, because you can't get a decent clean-up in the pavilion. Next year, we'll have dances on the spot. And, Lord, how some of us are going to loathe it.'

He was referring, of course, to the older brigade, whose idea of a pleasant evening was a loaded pipe, an empty pavilion and a fund of ancient anecdotes. It was difficult to understand why, but they seemed to have become quite attached to the old place – even to the smell, a mixture of linseed oil, disinfectant, blanco, and stale tobacco fumes, that pervaded it.

And there they would sit beneath the faded photographs of W.G. and the teams of 1897 and 1904, talking, talking, talking, until the light faded and Dan, the groundsman, went around making significant noises with the shutters, one eye on the clock and the other on the tap-room door of the 'Rose and Crown', just across the way.

At the next general meeting plans were produced. They were favourably received by all but the old brigade, who hemmed and hawed, said they supposed it would be all right, but, of course, the question of cost must be considered. Perhaps it would be better to wait awhile until we were financially stronger, and in the meantime bring the old place up-to-date a bit.

Figures couldn't be ignored, and to our dismay they carried the day. That spring, three feet were added to the length of each dressing-room, new enamel washing bowls were bought, the leaky roof was repaired, and a bar, measuring four feet by two, was installed in the corner of the main room.

And the old men went on talking and smoking, and Dan, appointed bar-tender, murmured, 'Well, 'arf of mild if you insist, sir,' and no longer cast envious eyes at the 'Rose and Crown'.

Out of curiosity, Johnson and I stopped for a drink one evening, after the game. Not for long, though. Reasonable argument is one thing, but we could hardly be expected to listen long to a series of dogmatic assertions to the effect that modern cricket had gone to the dogs. And some of the old fogeys had never even seen Hobbs and Sutcliffe.

It was about two years later that the tennis section broached the subject again. Their membership had swollen considerably, and the shack was rapidly becoming impossible. Again, the situation was reviewed, and since the membership of the cricket section had also increased, it was decided that the original plans would need revision. And Johnson, with commendable thoughtfulness, suggested an extra room where the 'old 'uns' or anyone else for that matter, could forgather for a chat if they wanted to. As he said, even some of the youngsters wouldn't want to dance all the time: one had to preserve some sense of proportion.

Not that the old 'uns didn't constitute something of a nuisance. More and more frequently we found our plans for the evening put clean out of joint through becoming involved in their endless arguments, and I remember making a resolve that if I ever became as old as some of them, I would take a lesson from them and endeavour to see both sides of the question.

The new plans were produced at the next general meeting. To tell the truth, Johnson and I were a little disappointed in them. We couldn't put our finger on the trouble, but certainly the new lay-out didn't seem anything like as attractive as it had when we originally discussed it . . . At any rate, there was nothing in it to provoke the wild enthusiasm displayed by young Tompkins, and one or two more of the younger set. An unfortunate type of youngster, Tompkins. Altogether too cocksure, and, what was worse, he had little or no consideration for his elders. What he and his crowd appeared to want was a miniature Palais de Danse, which could be used as a cricket pavilion when it wasn't wanted for other purposes.

They had the full support of the tennis section, however, and as the plans were passed it really looked as though the old pavilion was doomed at last.

And then the secretary resigned through ill-health and left the district.

The new secretary was handed the plans and said he'd get the whole thing under way as soon as he'd got the ordinary club business well in hand. Pending this, a bath was installed in the visitors' dressing-room, and the place was further modernised by the addition of the teams of 1922 and 1925. In the winter of 1926 the shack belonging to the tennis section became a total wreck in a gale, and a new and larger building was erected pending the building of the new pavilion.

I imagine they must have been a good deal more comfortable in their new quarters, for there was a considerable lessening in the agitation for the new pavilion, except from young Tompkins and his crowd.

I have a suspicion that this was the reason the new secretary didn't hurry himself very much. He was a fellow of some character, not at all the sort of person to be stampeded into action by a bunch of young hot-heads like Tompkins and his friends. Not that we minded the hot-headedness so much; it was Tompkins's ignorance and bigotry we found it so hard to stomach. I mean, for a youngster like that to air the opinion that Hobbs and Sutcliffe were greatly over-rated, as he did over a drink one night, was just a little too much.

I could see Johnson massing his big guns for attack, and it was perhaps as well that Tompkins remembered an appointment, and dashed off.

'Funny thing,' observed Johnson when he had gone, 'that the lads who are keenest on this new pavilion business are usually the ones who spend the least time in the old one.'

The secretary agreed, and said that as a matter of fact he couldn't see so very much wrong with the old place. And when we come to think of it, we couldn't either. Now that most of the old guard had faded away, it didn't seem such a bad show, somehow. At all events, it was no hardship to sit around the little bar, after the youngsters had gone, and listen to the good talk provided by those who really had something to talk about. If the truth were known, several of us found ourselves looking forward to the destruction of the old place with rather mixed feelings.

And then something happened to give it another lease of life. The man who owned the ground informed us that he had received an attractive offer for the freehold from a firm of builders. He had definitely decided to sell, but if we were prepared to offer the same price as the builders . . . There was only one course open to us; shelve the plans for the new pavilion, and buy the ground.

We paid for it in eight years, which, considering the stiff price asked, was pretty good. And immediately the outcry for the new pavilion was resumed. Mainly by the tennis section members, but it was supported by a crowd of our junior members, headed by a youngster named Marsham. Tompkins didn't seem quite so keen as he had been. For one thing, he didn't hit it off very well with Marsham; he told us one night that Marsham was far too up-and-coming for his liking, which, coming from him, was pretty good. His complete failure to realise the humour of the situation gave Johnson and me many a chuckle as we helped old Dan to put the shutters up that night.

The doom of the old pavilion appeared to be finally sealed, however, when the 1939 General Meeting had to be transferred to the back parlour of the 'Rose and Crown'. It was raining in torrents, and the roof, rotten with age, leaked like a sieve.

Arrangements were made to rip the place down, and get the new one completed by the autumn. In September came the war, and it really began to look as though the old pavilion would have a further indefinite respite.

But now it is no more. A month or two back a bomb dropped just outside the back door. It wasn't a very big bomb, but it was altogether too much for the old pavilion. When we went round to the ground the next morning all that remained were small pieces of splintered wood and broken tiles, which were scattered all over the field. The only thing instantly recognisable was the photograph of W.G. The frame was split to pieces, the glass splintered, but W.G. remained intact, wearing an expression of outraged truculence I swear was never there before.

So we really are going to have a new pavilion after the war. I have just seen the newest plans, and there is no doubt it will be a credit to the club. A double-decker pavilion with a dance-hall upstairs, showers and sunken baths, a glittering bar with chromium stools, and a tea-room to hold 75 people. I imagine it will be the finest pavilion in the southern counties.

And, as Johnson so truly predicted some twenty years ago – Lord, how some of us are going to loathe it!

'SEE YOU AT SCARBOROUGH'

A.A. Thomson

Richard Brinsley Sheridan, the wittiest writer in English between Swift and Shaw, wrote a musical called *A Trip to Scarborough*. It was a jolly romp, full of humour and charm. Almost exactly a hundred years later there came into being Scarborough's Cricket Festival, also a light-hearted romp and also rich in the charm of its setting and the down-to-earth humours of its cricketing characters. The background is Yorkshire and a Yorkshire festival could never be half-hearted.

The scene itself has an air of ritual, the flags, the bunting, the Mayor's and the President's marquees and the band playing, as I remember for more than half a century, selections from Gilbert and Sullivan. Lord

Londesborough was its earliest high patron, C.I. Thornton (who will be for ever 'Buns') was its first father figure and H.D.G. ('Shrimp') Leverson-Gower was its next. Its present organiser is Tom Pearce (whom heaven preserve) whose monumental industry does not interfere with his genial outlook. Of the indisputably great, from W.G. to Jessop, from Trumper to Hobbs, from May to Sobers, there are none among cricket's shining ones who have not played at Scarborough.

There have been variations through the years, but the usual matches of the Festival of the Nine Days – it has almost a religious significance, and why not? – have been: (a) Thornton's (or Leveson-Gower's or Pearce's) XI v. the touring side; (b) Gentlemen v. Players and (c) Yorkshire v. MCC (which is virtually a Rest of England side).

In Sir Pelham Warner's history, *Gentlemen v. Players*, he always includes the Scarborough match, if only because of the high status of both elevens. Since Gentlemen were abolished, a match has been played between an England XI and the Rest of the World, under Rothman's sponsorship; such a match, and a fine one at that, is being played as you read this.

It is an old saying that in Yorkshire we 'don't play cricket for fun'. This was never wholly true and at Scarborough we even cautiously relax. The Championship has been won or even (occasionally) lost. We can relax and ask our friends from counties less blessed to join in the revels. The cricket is gay and sparkling and individual gifts which have endured the rigours and disciplines of county cricket's trench warfare are allowed to flourish in freedom, like bright autumn flowers.

Dedicated to freedom, the Festival became the spiritual home of big hitting and C.I. Thornton, with a kind of diabolical bonhomie, was its pioneer. He was the first of three to hit a ball over the houses in Trafalgar Square, which is not a square but a road of tall Regency houses, running along the south of the ground. (For years his lady dined out on this incident. 'Right over in Trafalgar Square, my dear, but, oddly enough, "Buns" has never said whether he was playing at Lord's or the Oval.')

Another enormous hit was by Cecil Pepper, playing for the Australian Forces after the 1939–45 war. When you reverently survey Mr Pepper, the distinguished umpire, looking in his short, white Australian coat, like the most disinguished dental consultant in Wimpole Street, you would scarcely suspect him of such violence. The third strike came in between these other two and came from Maurice Leyland, though with absolutely typical modesty, he made no claim. 'Nay,' said Maurice, 'it just hit top roof-ridge and bounced over.'

With ordinary sixes Scarborough has been positively sprayed. Richie Benaud in 1953 hit eleven in one innings and since 1961, when Vic Wilson scored a direct hit on the pressbox window, correspondents have cowered under repeated bombardments from Mr F.S. Trueman, whose Scarborough sixes are so many they should be filed and taxed.

As a boy of eleven I saw the match in which F.S. Jackson, England's triumphant captain, won the toss against Darling's Australians for the sixth time. Darling, stripped to the buff, wanted Jackson to wrestle with him for choice of innings, but when Jackson nominated the burly George Hirst as his champion, Darling shrugged, tossed and lost again. Jackson made 123 in an innings, brilliant even for him.

Armstrong's Australians of 1921 went through England with fire and sword, but lost one match to MacLaren's golden boys at Eastbourne. One match did you say? No, sir, two matches. At Scarborough, C.I. Thornton's XI, mostly by superb batting by Sandham and devastating bowling by Woolley, beat them by 33.

And Scarborough's most moving sight was that of George Hirst, bidding farewell from the pavilion balcony. His voice was firm: '. . . From an unselfish point of view cricket is the best game. *What can you have better than a nice green field, with the wickets set up, and to go out and do the best for your side?*'

If there was 'a nice green field', it is on the North Marine Road at Scarborough.

THE CHARM OF CHELTENHAM

Frank Keating

After the Centennial comes the Festival for Festivals. Hard on the heels of many county cricket team's celebrations of the centenary of their founding there follows, like night the day, some more champagne to mark the hundredth anniversaries of their great cricket festivals.

Everyone has his favourite. Canterbury might be yours, oozing middle-class proprieties and boozing pink gins, its tented village as prim and neat as Underwood's action . . . or perhaps Scarborough, more holiday relaxed, beery men in braces, with breezes bracing keen and outfield racing green . . . or Weston, where the tide runs out so far and the cider runs out by teatime. . . .

It was my lovely lot to be lumbered with Cheltenham. This August's

Festival was its hundredth. Gloucestershire had played one annual match on the stately College ground since 1872, but in 1878 two successive games were played and, overnight, it became 'The week'. In our village near Stroud wives would simply tell their neighbours, and we children our chums, that 'we're taking our holidays for "The Cricket"' and that would be 'nuff said.

Barnett the fish

It meant weeks of anticipation; it meant Mum's new frock from Mullins of Stonehouse; it meant studying the scores in the *News Chron.* each morning to see whether this year's visiting giants were in form or not; it meant getting up early on the day to cut the sandwiches and prepare the thermos, then getting higgledy-piggledy and in a rush to Stroud to catch the Western National double-decker over the top past Painswick. The bus dropped you right outside the ground, but some preferred the little Great Western Railway railcar that chuffed cheerily all day between Chalford and Cheltenham: that meant a longer walk from St James' station but, if Uncle or Dad had a mind to, you could steer them up to the top of the Promenade hoping against hope that you might see Gloucester's opening batsman Charlie Barnett giving orders in his fish shop before going down to the ground to change.

In that first 'Week' in 1878, W.G. Grace apparently did not middle much, but he took 13 wickets in the opening match against Sussex and eight against Yorkshire. The organising inspiration in those days was James Lillywhite, who was coach to the College and publisher of *Criketers' Companion* which long rivalled *Wisden*. He was paid £120 by the county committee for setting up the Festival – which included a civic banquet in honour of W.G. and his men at the Plough Hotel at which '103 persons sat down to a splendid repast'.

Earlier that summer Lillywhite had invited tenders 'for enclosing the railings around the ground with canvas sheeting'. I would not be surprised if they are using the same stuff now. A few weeks ago I found myself driving, late at night, past those famous railings on the hospital side of the ground – the hospital where they say a chipped brick under the eaves was purposely not repaired by a builder long ago because he wanted to leave a lasting memorial to one of Gilbert Jessop's mighty swipes.

Anyway ... there I was that night this August. The College had broken up and, though the railings were not yet covered, the skeletal bones of scaffolding for the temporary stands were taking shape. They stood eerie, quiet and outlined against the starry sky.

'What beck'ning ghost, along the moonlight shade
Invites my steps, and points to yonder glade?'

Alexander Pope had but one ghost. Suddenly a lot were beckoning me.
Dressed all in white, but of hale and ruddy face and arms of teak.
I stopped the car and puffed my pipe. I walked. Then leaned against
the railings . . . perhaps I touched the very railing I had gripped in awe
when I joined the massive queue – the largest congregation I had been in
up to then – that snaked around the field from almost dawn in August
1947.

It was my first visit. Exactly 31 years ago to the week, before the days
of gold awards and silver-plated cups, the county reached the old-time
equivalent of a cup final – when the accidental arrangement of fixtures
allowed the two front-runners in the county Championship virtually
to play-off for the title. It was winner take all when 'Glorse' lost to
Middlesex at the end of that golden summer. I know, because I was
there. Aged eight.

People still speak of the match today. At this year's Festival you met
men in beer tents who would recite Gloucester's last innings scorecard.
Needing 169, they only managed 100. Bill Edrich's 50 was the game's
top score, and then Jim Sims and Jack Young bowled too well. Tom
Goddard's 15 wickets were not enough.

The catch of the year

The highlight was a boundary catch by an occasional first eleven
player called Clifford Monks who sprinted, memory says, some fifty
yards to catch Walter Robins one-handed and at full tilt. Memory
also insists that the ball would have hit me on the head had he not
caught it. Still the finest catch I saw. When Monks died 27 years
later the *Gloucestershire Echo's* headline was 'The Man Who Made
The Catch'.

With respect to Mike Procter, Zaheer and Sadiq (those well known
natives of Dean and Dursley and Downend) what a lovely *Western* side
it was that asterisked my youth at Cheltenham: doughty Jack Crapp,
hunched and plodding and faithful; George Emmett, all twinkle toes
and timing; the one and only C.J.B. who smacked first-over bumpers,
thwack! as if he were slapping down plaice at his aforementioned
fishmongers. Then there was farmer Billy Neale from Grace country,
and the magisterial B.O. Allen, soon to be succeeded as captain by the

first baronet I ever saw, Sir Derrick Bailey, of the loping gait and long silk neckerchief.

For some reason I loved the bowlers best: George Lambert of the lovely action we all tried to copy, and his new-ball mucker, great trier Colin Scott. Tom Goddard was my first idol. Huge tent of a shirt billowing out behind him. Huge hands, huge heart, he would wheel and deal for wickets all day. My dad said he once played darts with him in a Gloucester pub on market day.

Goddard's demands for l.b.w. would reverberate round the ring from Cleeve to Birdlip. 'Eh, Ta-am, whadabou' a bloke atop o' Leckhampton 'ill then?' we would shout as he set his field. Once Basil Allen had to leave the field and put Goddard in charge. Over and over he bowled on, though it was not a day for spinners. Finally Goddard, completely whacked, complained to a fielding colleague, 'Why don't the bugger take I off?' He had forgotten he was skipper for the day.

Tom has been dead a dozen years now. His partner, the sorcerer's apprentice in wiles and guiles those thirty odd years ago, was Cecil Cook, who we all called Sam. He is still with us as an umpire. We were very fond of gentle Sam. Cook, a trainee plumber, had arrived unannounced at the County Ground for the first net practice after the war. He asked which was Mr Hammond, then spoke up boldly, 'I'm Cook from Tetbury, sir, slow left hand, sir.'

The great W.R. threw him a ball, faced him for a few, then announced, 'You'll play for England one day'. And he did, almost within the twelvemonth. He took nought for 127, conceding over seven runs an over, against South Africa in the first Test of 1947, was never remotely considered again, but touchingly continued to wear his brocaded international blazer to the day he retired 18 years later. Some say he bought a new one for himself every Christmas. And why not?

Mention of Hammond, whom, alas, I never saw wield willow . . . this August's centenary at Cheltenham marked the half-centenary of one of his finest weeks: in 1928 that champion scored 139 and 143 v. Surrey, took 10 catches, and bowled Jack Hobbs; then took 15 for 128 and scored 80 against Worcestershire in the next match.

Andy's double first

Our wicketkeeper was Andy Wilson, tiny tot with a massive appeal in every sort of way. After all his years keeping to Goddard and Cook, he took bets that he would be the only batsman in the land to read

Ramadhin's wrong 'un when the West Indies came to Cheltenham in 1950. Both times Andy shouldered arms, first ball, to the little long-sleeved mesmerist. Both times he was clean bowled.

That was another match that closed the gates at the College. I was in the ground in time. By then new horses were leading our parade. Another T. W. to succeed Goddard: for in that match young Tom Graveney, all blushing silkiness, made top score. And just before the start the announcer said, 'T. W. Goddard is indisposed and his place will be taken by J.B. Mortimore.' 'J. B. Ooo?' we all aahed. We soon knew. He bowled Clyde Walcott and Bob Christiani. But Glorse were trounced. They were the first black men I had ever seen. But from that day forth black has always been beautiful to me.

By then, too, we had The Bomber. Can any county have loved a man as Gloucester loved its Bomber Wells? (Unless, later, it was Nottinghamshire?) A fat little man with a waddle and a wink and a wide, wide grin, he was to us children a handsome a Pied Piper as we ever did see. I'm a friend of Bomber now – and still find it hard to believe. A brilliant after-dinner speaker, Bomber has written a long memoir of those long-ago summers. I wish a publisher would have the nerve to publish it.

And on and on ... the county's thunderous new foreign trio led them into this year's hundredth Cheltenham festival; but because of their natures and the way they play Gloucester looks on them now as its very own natives. No-one, not even Hammond, can have been held in more affectionate awe than 'Proccy'; the same mellow drives we thought our Graveney had patented are now sketched as smooth by 'Zed'; Sadiq sometimes sparkles as Emmett did ... and anyway still the West is served by the likes of this summer's adored and deserving beneficiaries – that bucolic charmer from Bideford, David Shepherd, and the handsome likewise from Tavistock, Jack Davey.

Then there's the sturdy Andy Stovold; young David Graveney, nephew of Tom; Alastair Hignell, following B.O. Allen's tread from Cambridge; John Childs from Devon; the preserving, guileful Brian Brain; and Jim Foat, who fields as only Derek Randall can ... or rather, come to think of it, as Clifford Monks did, long, so long ago. ...

But this year, at the hundredth Cheltenham Week, those beckoning ghosts played best of all for me. For they played at Cheltenham in my Golden Age, you see. And a Golden Age is any age you care to make it.

KENNINGTON OVAL

H. H. Montgomery

The earliest mention I can find of any event connected with The Oval is in 1818. The *Times* of 12 May says, 'Yesterday, about three o'clock, the body of another man was found drowned in the creek, near Kennington Oval, within 100-yards of the place where the body of Mr Tinkler, late landlord of the 'White Horse', Brixton Hill, was found. The body was carried to the 'Clayton Arms', in Clayton Street, where the other body lay, and was shortly afterwards recognised to be a porter in the employ of a shop-keeper in the neighbourhood, who, it is supposed, was drowned on Friday night in the creek, as he was returning home to his employers with a truck full of empty bottles. The truck was found next morning shattered to pieces, and all the bottles broken. Amongst the many sufferers from the flood we have to notice Mr Perry, the brewer; Mr Fenton, a brick-maker; and Mr Martin, the market-gardener; who has lost to the amount of £100, all his garden being flooded.'

The river Effra, which ran on the south side of The Oval, must have overflowed its banks and caused this destruction. The Effra now is safely stowed away in a large drain made in 1880, to obviate any further annoyance: but the river has sent up to the surface of the earth a substitute. The high terraced banks, which are so much appreciated by sight-seers in The Oval, are composed of the soil dug out of the place where the river now runs. It was a great boon to the Contractors to have a place so near to shoot their earth, and they consented, in return for this favour, to make the banks in The Oval, which are now concrete terraces, and turf them free of charge. If ever there was a mutual benefit to two contracting parties, this was one: and if ever there was needed a reason to bless the Effra on its departure it is afforded every time the inhabitants of Kennington have obtained a good seat for a great match.

Let us now imagine that we are entering The Oval in the year 1845. In the spring of that year an interesting ceremony was performed in the month of March (according to an entry in the diary of the late Mr Briant, of the 'Horns'). The first sod was laid of the present Cricket Ground. The year before it was, and had long been, a market garden, of the same shape, of which the Duchy of Cornwall were landlords.

In 1844, the 'Bee-Hive' Ground, in Walworth, was taken for building purposes, and the Montpelier Club obtained the lease of The Oval. The late Mr Baker, of Kennington Road, a very fine all-round Cricketer entered into negotiations with the Duchy, as the owners would not transact business at that time with a Club as such. A lease was obtained for 31 years, at £120 per annum, and the taxes amounted to about £20 more. Then 3½ acres of the ground were turfed; and the remaining 9 acres were sown. Mr Houghton came forward, as President of the Montpelier Club, and became proprietor of the ground, whilst eight gentlemen of the Montpelier Club guaranteed the rent in case of any failure in getting the money in other ways. The first Secretary was Mr W. Denison, a well-known man in Cricketing circles in those days. It must be confessed, however, that the first few years were by no means prosperous for Cricket here. First, the old Montpelier Club suffered. They played matches here for about two years, but Houghton by degress tried to confine them to one corner of the ground: the result was that they left The Oval and took a ground where Coldharbour Lane now stands. Here they played for a year or two, but finally the Club was merged in the County Club and broke up.

In these early years the South London Club also played their matches upon The Oval.

One question is worth answering. Has The Oval been ever in danger of being built upon? Yes: about the year 1851, Mr Driver, the solicitor to the Duchy, was bringing a bill into Parliament to enable the Duchy to build two half crescents, but the Prince Consort, who was administering the estate for the young Prince, was strongly in favour of keeping The Oval an open space. He argued that as the old Kennington Common had been taken for a public Park, so that the cricketers could no longer use it, it was only right that another space should be found as near as possible, where South Londoners might enjoy the game: and he further declared that The Oval should be available for Cricket at a light rental so long as the people of South London wished to uphold Cricket.

I have said that neither Houghton nor Denison were very successful. Denison was also connected with Clarke's itinerant eleven and ran himself into difficulties with them so that he was not often to be seen in The Oval. In other respects he was a good cricketer: Lord Bessborough says (in a letter written to me), 'The best bowler in the Montpelier Club was Denison, the first man who had the pluck to bowl roundarm slows in good matches. He played for me several times, among other matches, at Canterbury for the Gentlemen of England. He was a *Times* Reporter on legal and Parliamentary subjects; he also wrote for the Press on Cricket, and was the first Secretary of the Surrey Club.' But owing to unfortunate circumstances he was not able to do his duty properly as Secretary, and the work fell upon Houghton who was hardly the man for his post. The President discovered in a short time that the ground did not pay its expenses, and he introduced other amusements which earned him somewhat of a bad name. Among other things he announced a Walking Match of 1000 miles in 1000 hours. A pedestrian named Manx tried to perform the feat, and finally retired before he had concluded the match, after walking for some little time in poultices. The Houghton started a Poultry Show in The Oval, and caused annoyance to a great many people; but he was in some sense proprietor of the ground, and it was difficult to see how to make him resign his place.

This brings us to the origin and growth of the Surrey Club. A Meeting of the old Montpelier members was held in 1844: among the names of those present I find C.H. Hoare, W. Baker, T. Lewis, C. Coltson, J. Burrup, jnr., W. Pickering, W. Houghton, N. Felix and W. Denison. Old Mr Ward (a household name among Cricketers in those days) presided, and it was agreed to found a County Club. In the autumn of the same year (1844) a dinner was given at the 'Horns' to collect members and start the Club in good earnest. The Hon. F. Ponsonby (now Lord Bessborough) came over expressly from Ireland to be present and to take the chair: and about 70 members of the Montpelier Club enrolled themselves in the County Club.

The first match ever played on the ground was between Mitcham and the Montpelier Club in 1845: the wickets were pitched across the ground; and strange to say the match resulted in a tie. The first of few years were not very successful. In 1846, Fuller Pilch, of immortal memory, came and offered his services to Surrey. But the leading members of the Club nobly determined to raise their County into note by the help of men who were born in Surrey and they refused to play Pilch. The Hon. Frederick Ponsonby said at the time that if they only persevered, Surrey one day would be a match for any County. Mr Napper of Dorking went even further and declared that one day Surrey should beat England. Both these prophecies were verified within a very few years. But let me continue my narrative: The Oval was in those days surrounded by a ditch and a quickset hedge. For a year or two the Club did not prosper much: There were internal jealousies, and dissensions, and dissatisfaction with the management, and above all, the money was not plentiful. At the beginning of one season, Mr Denison (the Secretary) announced that the debt amounted to £70 before any of the yearly expenses were considered: and that it seemed impossible to play any first-class matches, that many of the members were retiring from the Club. The meeting almost decided to break up the Club; and

I suppose, had such a vote been carried, The Oval would have been at once built over and some very happy memories of Kennington would never have existed at all. It is to the present Lord Bessborough that we owe the continuance of Cricket upon The Oval. He was Vice-President at the time, and suggested that the £70 should be paid off by allowing six gentlemen to become Life Members by paying down £12 a piece. A gentleman present next said, 'Who would pay £12 to be Life Member of a bankrupt Club?' 'I will,' said Old Mr Cressingham, one of the oldest members: and 'I will' said five others, of whom Mr Ponsonby was one. Lord Bessborough, in writing of this memorable meeting, adds – 'Looking back to that distant day I fear I have been a bad bargain to the Club by becoming a Life Member for £12.' But we may add upon the other side. – 'Had you not spoken up on the occasion it would have been a still worse bargain for the Club.'

Mr J. Burrup, who became Secretary in 1847, saw that the only way to save the ground was to get rid of the proprietor, Mr Houghton. But how could this be done if Houghton was unwilling to depart? Mr Burrup brought forward and carried a motion that the Club should play no matches at all upon The Oval: and then Houghton was driven to part with his right to the field. The lease now fell into the hands of the Surrey Club who have kept it ever since. The new lease given to the Club was granted by the Duchy of Cornwall in the names of C.H. Hoare, A. Marshall and H. Marshall, for a term of 7, 14 or 21 years. The arrangements in those early days were, that players were paid £3 a match if they were beaten, and £4 if they won. Entrance to the ground was never more than 6d.

In 1849, 1850, 1851, Surrey won every County Match, and in 1852, the County beat England. Perhaps it will interest some of my readers to see the score of the first match that was ever played between Surrey and Nottinghamshire.

Surrey won their first match against Notts by 75 runs. Mr J. Burrup says that in all those years they were victorious with Day and Sherman as their first bowlers and Martingell as change.

SURREY v. NOTTINGHAMSHIRE.
AT THE OVAL, JULY 17th and 18th, 1851.

SURREY.

FIRST INNINGS.		SECOND INNINGS.	
Julius Cæsar b Nixon	0	... st Brown, b Tinley	0
T. Sherman run out	6	... st Brown, b W. Clarke	0
G. Brockwell b Grundy	14	... b W. Clarke	2
W. Caffyn c S. Parr, b W. Clarke	29	... st Brown, b A. Clarke	14
W. Martingell b Nixon	1	... 1bw, b Tilney	23
N. Felix, Esq. c Guy, b Nixon	4	... b Grundy	10
J. Chester b W. Clarke	42	... c Brown, b Tinley	14
T. Lockyer c G. Parr, b Grundy	15	... run out	20
C. H. Hoare Esq., b Grundy	5	... b Grundy	15
J. Heath not out	0	... 1bw, b Grundy	1
D. Day b Grundy	1	... not out	1
Bye 0, leg byes 4	4	... No ball 1, bye 1, 1-bye 4	6
	121		106

NOTTINGHAMSHIRE.

FIRST INNINGS.		SECOND INNINGS.	
F. Tinley c Cæsar, b Day	5	... c Felix, b Sherman	0
J. Guy b Sherman,	0	... b Martingell	15
George Parr b Day	1	... b Sherman	23
Butler Parr b Sherman	4	... c Hoare, b Sherman	16
J. Grundy b Day	6	... c and b Sherman	13
Samuel Parr b Day	10	... b Sherman	3
C. Brown b Sherman	13	... b Sherman	7
George Butler not out	3	... run out	5
T. Nixon c Felix, b Day	1	... c and b Martingell	9
Alfred Clarke b Day	0	... not out	0
W. Clarke b Day	0	... c Lockyer, b Sherman	4
Leg byes 2, wides 3	5	... Byes 3, leg byes 6	9
	48		104

YORKSHIRE

Laurence Meynell

Yorkshire's one and only Lord Hawke had a dictum, 'catches win matches', and no doubt there is much truth in it; but a lot of other countries, turning curious eyes towards their great northern rival, must often have been jealous not so much of their ability to hold catches as of the conjurer's ease with which they produced out of the hat an apparently unending succession of first-class bowling talent.

Yorkshire has always had bowlers. It would seem to be a case of *'le roi est mort, vive le roi'*, for no sooner does one great Yorkshire bowler quit the stage after his 15, 18 or maybe 22 years of distinguished service than another steps out of the wings to take his place.

Consider as it were the genealogy of the thing: in the early days George Freeman and the irrepressible Tom Emmett; then Bates and Harrison,[1] now not so well remembered, perhaps, but out-standing in their day; then that wonderful sequence of slow left-handers, Peel, Peate and the immortal Wilfrid Rhodes; and we have yet to mention F. S. Jackson, Macaulay and Kilner; nor has anything been said of Bill Bowes or Schofield Haigh. To this list of names add those of Hedley Verity (one of the greatest of them all), Robinson[2] and Booth, and if here be not opulence of riches where shall we presume to look for it?

What is so outstanding is the abundance of the reserves from which all this great wealth of cricketing talent springs.

It has been said that if you put your head down any pit shaft in the county and call out, 'Send me up a sound opening bat, a useful left-hand spin bowler, and a good all-rounder to go in at about six or seven', the required men, or something uncommonly like them, will come up in the next cage.

Certain it is that time after time England has called upon Yorkshire for the cream of the county side (not infrequently for four or even five of them) and yet Yorkshire has always seemed to be able to field a team which took a lot of beating in spite of the absence of all the stars.

If Yorkshire cricket has been rich in playing talent it has certainly never been lacking in characters. There have certainly been times, too

---

[1] Harrison, a fast bowler, took 100 wickets in his first season for under 14 runs each.
[2] Who took 129 wickets in the first post-second-war season.

many of them perhaps, when Yorkshire tenacity and single-mindedness of purpose have thrown over the grounds at Bramall Lane or Headingley an unmistakable, and to one spectator at any rate, an unpalatable, atmosphere of dourness. An air not so much of 'do or die' but of die far sooner than commit the solecism of doing anything; and there have been occasions, I would be willing to wager, when if you dared to raise up your voice in either of those temples of cricket with the lighthearted suggestion that 'after all, it's only a game', you would be lucky to escape with mere ejection rather than a public lynching on the spot.

All of which is to be deprecated; nor has it always been so, for the Yorkshire nature has inherent in it besides tenacity and single-mindedness a sort of perky, pawky cheerfulness which has a habit of breaking out even on the most solemn occasions.

This has been so from the days of Tom Emmett right down to Emmott Robinson of our own period. What a pair they would have made together! Each of them had some faint flavour of the music-hall about him (Robinson always made me think of Little Tich), and quite apart from cricketing ability, each was invaluable to his side by reason of an illogical cheerfulness which was always capable of producing a heartening quip at the dullest and blackest moment.

Emmott Robinson last played for his county in 1931; Tom Emmett (curious that similarity of unusual names) figured right at the other end of history, for his first appearance was in 1867, when with George Freeman he virtually started the great dynasty of Yorkshire bowlers. Tom was a host in himself, always ready with the unpredictable action and the irresistible *mot*.

It was he who, toiling with the rest of England's bowlers and as ineffectually as any of them, against the merciless menace of W.G., solemnly suggested the formation of a society to murder the Old Man and so give all good bowlers a fair chance; and 'Plum' Warner, whose coach Tom eventually was at Rugby, has penned an unforgettable picture of him: '. . . as though it were yesterday, striding across the Close, with his grey and well-shaped head, crowned by a Yorkshire cap, held high and his body as straight as the most ramrod sergeant on parade could desire.'

Eighteen sixty-seven, when Tom played his first full season for Yorkshire, was four years later than the actual formation of the County Club. This took place in Sheffield, and largely under the influence of Sheffield men, in 1863, and it is necessary to go back a little beyond that to see the history of the thing.

There were plenty of cricket clubs up and down the broad acres of Yorkshire in the early days; some of them well known, such as those at York[3] or Doncaster, plenty of others no doubt not so famous; and as far back as 1833 there was a 'Yorkshire v. Norfolk' match so called although as yet no real Yorkshire County Club existed.

This early game is interesting because Fuller Pilch, at that time the great star of Norfolk cricket, was by birth and early upbringing, a Sheffield man.

Sheffield, indeed, had for a long time established itself as the centre of Yorkshire cricketing interest and activities. Other teams there were, as we have seen, but Sheffield was by far and away the most important of them, and one has only got to consider the long series of Sheffield v. Nottinghamshire games stretching right from 1771 to 1860 to realise the truth of this statement.[4]

Sheffield has known three major cricket grounds. The first was opened in 1822 for the traditional 'derby' against Nottingham. This was the Darnall Lane Ground situated some three miles out of the town, along the Glossop road. Yorkshire usually considers that if a thing is worth doing it is worth doing well and that early ground at Darnall Lane was surprisingly well equipped both as to stand accommodation and seating.

No big games were played here after 1829, and indeed by that time it had already been superseded by the Hyde Park Ground, which was commenced in 1824 and ready for play two years later. This had several advantages; it was larger, the playing surface was better, and it was situated only half a mile from the smoky centre of Sheffield.

It was here in 1846 that 16,000 people crowded to see the mighty All England XI play, and beat, twenty men of Sheffield.

This second home of cricket in the city could not be judged a bad one by any standards, but in 1855 a move was made to yet a third, and a still more ambitious, setting – the ground in Bramall Lane, which as a home both of cricket and football has now for two generations been almost a household name.

---

[3]There was certainly a club at York in 1784; and they must have been keen players there, for there was a fine of 3d. for every member 'not within sight of the wickets each morning when the Minster clock struck five'!

[4]In this series of 'needle' matches T. Marsden, one of the best of the early Yorkshire batsmen, had the astonishingly good average score of 40 runs for each of 20 innings.

This property was first of all leased (for 99 years) from the Duke of Norfolk's Yorkshire estate, and later in 1898 security of tenure was assured when the Sheffield United Football Club bought the freehold of it for £10,000.

It was universally felt through the county that a worthy home having been acquired, a County Club should be brought into existence to occupy it, and consequently in 1863 it was proposed and carried to set about forming such a club which should be based on, and should operate in, not only Sheffield but several others towns in the county as well.

Of this Club the first President was Mr M.J. Ellison (he remained in office until 1898), a fine, full-bearded Victorian figure of the old school, looking remarkably like one of the more imposing figures out of the Old Testament.

The first subscription to the Club was the exceedingly modest one of 10s. 6d.,[5] but some of the people who paid even that unalarming sum may have regretted it in the first two years of the Club's existence, for 1865 and 1866 were made barren and unpleasant by strifes and dissensions not only in Yorkshire but in the cricketing world generally, and they were lean years at Bramall Lane.

Looking back for a moment it should be noted as a matter of historical interest that Yorkshire played their first county game at The Oval in June of 1863, in which Surrey made 315 and 60, Yorkshire replying with 257 in their first innings and not batting again as the game was abandoned for rain.

The bickering and backbitings that marred 1865 and 1866 eventually smoothed themselves out, as most human worries have a habit of doing; and in 1867 with Tom Emmett, a new arrival, and George Freeman at his best, Yorkshire had a great season, winning all seven matches that they played.

Several things should be borne in mind if we are to get even an approximately accurate picture of the Yorkshire cricket of those days.

First, it was as yet an entirely professional side; the age of the 'essential-to-have-an-amateur-captain' idea had not yet dawned, the amateurs were not yet good enough; second, there was as yet nothing resembling a County Championship as we understand it today, even the rudiments of this set-up did not appear until 1873; and third, although an

---

[5]Which was not altered until 1881, when it was doubled.

official 'County Club' now existed, a good deal of important cricket was still being organised in Yorkshire by bodies other than the Committee of the County Club.

Before we move on in time to see how these three points developed and changed during the years, let us glance for a moment at some isolated names and incidents of these early days of the Club.

George Freeman was the mainstay of the attack, and a most efficient mainstay he was; indeed, both W.G. himself and Richard Daft, two of the greatest authorities on cricket, concurred in holding him to be the best fast bowler they played against.

Eighteen seventy-two was memorable at Bramall Lane for the first appearance there of W.G. – his first appearance, that is, in a county game; he had been there once before in 1869.

This was the year that turnstiles were first introduced to the ground – perhaps to cope better with the crowd that W.G.'s visit might be expected to draw – and the Old Man did not disappoint the numbers who flocked to see him: he made a vigorous and aggressive 122.

Two other names that stand out from those early days are those of Ephraim Lockwood and George Ulyett. One can understand a certain reluctance to keep calling a companion Ephraim, and this may be the reason why Lockwood was given the odd nickname of 'Old Mary'. Whatever the reason, 'Old Mary' he was, but if the nickname be thought to imply any sort of old maidenishness about him it is singularly misleading, for, as a batsman, his defence was Yorkshire stubbornness in its most uncompromising form and when he wanted to score his cutting was near perfection. In fact Lord Hawke, a man from whom compliments were not in the habit of flowing, and who was chary of superlatives, always used to give it as his considered judgement that a particular innings of 208 played by 'Mary Ann' was the finest exhibition of cutting he ever saw. Ephraim had a strong streak of Yorkshire in him and it was never better illustrated than on the tour to American in 1878 (under Dicky Daft), when he and Pinder, the Yorkshire wicket-keeper, were gazing at the majestic and awe-inspiring sight of Niagara in thunderous mood.

After a moment or two Pinder enquired what his companion thought of the sight.

'Nowt,' Ephraim said. 'If this is Niagara, give me Sheffield any day.'

Big burly George Ulyett also went on that American tour. He began with Yorkshire as a bowler but soon developed into their most dependable bat. Lord Hawke thought a lot of him and often took his wise advice, and for upwards of twenty years he was one of the most noteworthy players in England. His record in touring teams was extraordinarily good, as witness his performance in Australia in 1881, for instance, when his Test match scores were 87, 23, 25, 67, 0, 23, 149 and 64.

It was not until 1873, the year in which the idea of a County Championship was first mooted, that there was really a complete centralisation of cricketing authority in Yorkshire, and it was not until ten years later, in 1883, that an undergraduate still at Cambridge was elected to the captaincy of the team.[6]

The undergraduate was the Hon. M.B. Hawke, and his position cannot have been an enviable one. He was a good deal younger than any other member of the team, and until that time it had always been an entirely professional concern. It is not difficult to imagine that the sudden advent into the hard-bitten Yorkshire ranks of someone whom they no doubt referred to as 'an amateur schoolboy' was not taken to very kindly at first.

But in the event, as all the world knows and as all Yorkshire came most gratefully and handsomely to acknowledge, that appointment was the most important single fact that ever happened in the county's cricketing history.

Lord Hawke (he succeeded to the title in 1887) made the Yorkshire county side. His cricketing ability was considerable; more than once he got Yorkshire and England out of a tight place. All told, in 'big cricket' he made 16,931 runs for an average of 20. But it was far exceeded by his qualities as a captain on the field, and as a leader generally.

He spoke with the voice of just and genial autocracy, and he was obeyed. He was obeyed because he was respected greatly, feared not a little, loved a lot. 'Now, boy, buck up,' was the extent of his reprimand on the field, and it was enough. Under his wise and enthusiastic guidance Yorkshire were built up by the Nineties into the formidable and almost legendary side that we know today.

It was in 1890 that F.S. Jackson first played for them. If there has ever been a keener, cleaner cricketer than 'Jacker' and one of more use to his side at a pinch, Yorkshire would like to see him – and wouldn't

---

[6]In the first season Tom Emmett acted as captain 'in the absence of a gentleman' until the University came down.

believe it if they did see him. His total figures were 790 wickets at 20.1 and 15,956 runs at 33.5.

Hawke had good material besides 'Jacker'; were not John Tunnicliffe ('Long John o' Pudsey') and John Brown there to strike dismay into the bowlers by their famous opening stands (a little matter, for instance, of 554 against Derbyshire in 1898); was not Schofield Haigh bowling; and was there not hard-hitting George Hirst, who could bowl as well as he could bat, and who in 1906 made 2000 runs and took 200 wickets? And in addition to these, was there not David Denton, who first played for the county in 1895 and who in the next twenty years was to score over 36,000 runs?

Yes, certainly Yorkshire now commenced to be great and long continued so. Figures, boring though an overdose of them may become, must sometimes speak loud and clear, and when we consider that from 1893 until 1946, including the lost war years, Yorkshire won the championship *twenty-two* times, there is little need to say more.

Under the keen eye of their captain, Yorkshire nearly always kept first and foremost in view the business of winning their matches, but just occasionally they let themselves revel in an orgy of scoring for scoring's sake, as, for instance, when they went to Edgbaston in 1896, encamped on a perfect wicket at 11.30 a.m. on Monday morning and were not dispossessed until late on Wednesday, by which time they had put together the appalling total of 887 runs. Lord Hawke was so pleased with this performance (he made 166 by the way) that he had the full 'card of the match' printed on satin and hung up in his study.

Three years later they made 681 against Sussex at Sheffield, of which Brown and Tunnicliffe put on 378 for the first wicket.

In 1897 there was a young man living at Kirkheaton whose father 'had no other thought than to make a cricketer of him'. How wonderfully that admirable parental ambition was achieved in Wilfrid Rhodes is now cricketing history. In his first season the newcomer averaged 21 runs and took 126 wickets for 13 runs each!

What a beginning to a career which was one long series of triumphs. In those early days Rhodes batted No. 11; thirteen years later, whilst still bowling almost as well as ever, he went in first for England and broke the record for a first-wicket stand in Test matches. He played in his last Test in 1926 when there were players in the English side who had not tasted mother's milk when he had first faced Australian bowling. F.S. Jackson, Wilfrid Rhodes (who in 1903 had a batting average of 44 and took 118 wickets at 12.79 each!), George Hirst – it is not easy to see how a county could hope for three better all-rounders than these.

The Headingley ground at Leeds had been opened in 1892, and eleven years later the focus of cricketing matters in the county had so shifted that the offices and headquarters of the County Club were transferred there from Sheffield.

A year after this move (in 1903) F.C. Toone became secretary of the Club and when in 1910 Lord Hawke resigned the captaincy which he had held for 28 years, a great era had come to a close.

Although the year previous (1909) had seen at least one Yorkshire disaster – the game against Surrey at the Oval when the scoreboard for Yorkshire's second innings read 26.10.0 – setbacks were only temporary and players of great promise kept arriving regularly from the various 'nurseries'.

Holmes first played in 1913, Herbert Sutcliffe was not to come until 1919. What can one say of this great opening pair, so watchful, so polished, so patient, so punishing to anything that merited punishment?

'Mr Warner, sir, I love a dog fight', 'Plum' reports Sutcliffe as having said when being complimented on some particularly dour piece of defence against an Australian attack venomous on a wicked pitch. It sums up the imperturbable, immaculately turned-out man, never to be hurried, never to be worried and never (many a bowler must have thought despairingly) to be got out.

The world rated him above his county partner, but all Yorkshire has always been firm in the opinion that 'one was as good as t'other', and that Percy Holmes was a neglected man as far as representative matches go.[7]

The old guard kept going, of course; 'youth will be served' is the cruellest but the most incontrovertable dictum in all sport. David Denton retired in 1920, Hirst in the next year. On the other hand Macaulay made his first appearance, and a player who had first been seen in the Yorkshire ranks as far back as 1899 made a welcome reappearance in 1922. This was E. Rockley Wilson, who having been out of county cricket for twelve years before the first world war, returned to bowl so well in the early twenties that for four years he stood high in the county averages.

In 1924 Yorkshire won the championship for the thirteenth time, and this in spite of a trouncing by Lancashire at Headingley – and the White

---

[7]Which surely illustrates the distracting difficulties of selectors pretty well, for if you have J.B. Hobbs available as an opening bat how can you choose anybody else? Nobody could bat *better* than Hobbs.

Rose doesn't take kindly to an event of that nature. In this game only 226 runs were scored altogether and Yorkshire were all out for 33 in their second innings, R. Tyldesley taking six of their wickets for three runs each.

As an offset to this meagre showing Percy Holmes put together the massive score of 315 not out against Middlesex at Lord's.

In the following year Yorkshire did not lose a single match, and Roy Kilner (who died so tragically three years later) and Waddington were bowling at the top of their form, whilst that broad-shouldered great-hearted left-hander, Maurice Leyland, was performing powerfully with the bat.

And so the long story of Yorkshire triumph goes on – in 1930 one of the indisputably great figures goes when Wilfrid Rhodes eventually retired, cricketing honours and history thick about him; but in the very same year an equally indisputably great bowler, Hedley Verity, made his first appearance. It will probably always be debated in the pavilions as to whether Verity was quite as good a bowler as Rhodes. Let it be argued; suffice it to say that he was in the company of really great bowlers and that for the best part of ten years, until his life was cut short by war, he was the spear-point of the best attack in county cricket.

In 1932 Herbert Sutcliffe scored 132 at Bradford against Gloucester, and so registered his one hundredth century in first-class cricket.

A.B. Sellars was captain in that year – Yorkshire won the championship, of course (for the seventeenth time) – and W.E. Bowes, whose fourth season it was, came third in the bowling averages, and to be third behind such bowlers as Verity and Macaulay was no mean feat, especially when you consider that in the Notts match of this year Verity took 10 wickets for 10 runs in the second innings!

In 1934, since even Herbert Sutcliffe could not go on for ever and it seemed advisable to find a successor to him before he finally retired, a young man called Hutton was given a trial and justified himself by scoring 196 against Worcestershire. As a student and protégé Hutton satisfied even the exacting standards of Sutcliffe, his mentor, and that here is an altogether worthy successor to the county's great line of opening batsmen has been amply demonstrated.

And so right down to the captaincy of Norman Yardley, the long successful story of Yorkshire cricket right back from Lord Hawke's day has continued.

Bramall Lane and Headingley are names known to cricketers all over the world. Here, they know, will be found informed and appreciative crowds, the keenest of keen cricket, and that sense of there being an 'edge' on the game which Yorkshiremen love and revel in.

MANCHESTER

R.C. Robertson-Glasgow

Unlike the apocryphal gentleman who took the railway ticket, I am fond of going to Manchester for cricket. Others may laugh or weep, according to their philosophy, knock Manchester about with slapstick and threadbare facetiousness – I know one who always takes two umbrellas to Old Trafford – but I like it, because it's ugly. Like the poetaster of A.A. Milne who gave an incomprehensible recital, Manchester, I feel, is ugly on purpose; as if it could be quite good-looking if it wanted to be, but was above all that sort of thing; knowing that it is the respectable thing to be plain.

It is silly to hurry on your way to the Test at Old Trafford; you should wander down its more solemn streets; wide, serious, and easy to be lost in; where the constables, when questioned, point out the way to more streets, obviously relations, even twins, of the first street; whose faces hide large, old-fashioned offices where business is done by some of the kindred if not of the house of Chuzzlewit, and a Mr Chuffey still shuffles about with tight little secrets and difficult papers, and there are partners whom nothing would shock except the news that a Lancashire batsman had gone mad, hit three consecutive sixes against Yorkshire, then been stumped by four yards and several seconds.

So, by decent stages, to Old Trafford, whose beautiful turf gains glory from its saturnine surroundings: at one end is the railway, where the engine-drivers seem perpetually to be shunting themselves into position to discern between the googly and the genuine off-break; at the other, at a quaint angle, the Press Box, which suggests that it might have been designed by Einstein immediately after a reunion dinner of mathematicians: eccentric perch of the critics. It is a ground which seems to have decided, none daring to contradict, that the beauties of the cricketing art are self-sufficient, and have no need of meretricious appurtenances; it is abrupt, like a rude and true remark from Carlyle or Sam Johnson; proclaiming disdain of the soft meadows and orchard lawns of the South, of 'bowery hollows crowned with summer sea'. If you want that sort of thing you can go and eat the Lotus in Kent, elbow through the trippers for a plate of whelks at Southend, or take a cheap ticket to the wonders of Blackpool.

I have not heard that John Bright or W.E. Gladstone ever played cricket, but, if they did, they should never have played away from Old Trafford, which, on a rainy day, is the nearest thing I know to an academic speech on Free Trade. It must have taught many a cricketer its own philosophy, batsmanship such as that of Harry Makepeace or, in his stubborn days, Charles Hallows, which seldom deviated into brilliance, but flowed on with a staid majesty like the lines of Milton or a leader of the great C.P. Scott, with scarcely the easement of a paragraph, without ever the hope of an anacoluthon! Indeed, I always consider that it was almost a rebuff to Nature that Lancashire permitted, I will not say encouraged, such batsmen as A.C. MacLaren, who refused to unlearn what Harrow and youth had taught him; R.H. Spooner, whose grace was of no one County or time; such masters of bowling and clowning as Johnny Briggs and Cecil Parkin. In more modern years Old Trafford has seen the 'mutiny' of Ernest Tyldesley, whose wickets were visible when you bowled, and who might use the pull-drive in the first over; of Eddie Paynter, who sometimes plays a stroke with neither foot on the ground; great heretics all.

If you talk to the older spectators at Old Trafford you will find that they most remember the Australian victory by three wickets in 1896 with the tremendous bowling of Ernest Jones and Tom Richardson, and the 154 not out by 'Ranji' in England's second innings, when others failed and he kept flicking Jones off his face to the leg boundary. One ball nicked his ear, and he remarked afterwards: 'It was very important to get the head well behind the ball to get a good sight of it'! The Australians needed only 125 to win, but it took them three hours and seven wickets, and Richardson bowled through those three hours for six of the wickets, having bowled 68 overs in the first innings. Talk of Alexander and Hercules!

Here in 1934 O'Reilly took three English wickets in one over, as it were in one flush – Walters and Hammond and Wyatt, and I can still revive the tremors of that shock. In the same match Pat Hendren made a century, flowering from the early and habitual stiffness of defence into the full warmth of extra-cover driving. Here, six years ago, Constantine and Martindale assailed D.R. Jardine with bounce and speed, and he quelled them and was caught in the end low at gully for 127, and the ground rose to him.

Manchester is a tough old nut, but when you crack it the kernel is sweet enough. Warm, even wild, are the hospitalities underneath the harsh exterior of reception; dinner parties such as only Test matches beget, and conversations that tire out the night before the talkers. But some, perhaps, have never learnt the way.

A CRICKET PILGRIMAGE

Richard Binns

I started from Farnham by road, a few days ago, and ended my pilgrimage at Hambledon, passing through a district which, without moving very much to one side or the other, contains more associations with the old cricketers than any other neighbourhood in England. Farnham and 30 miles round, William Beldham once said, reared all the best players up to about 1780, and the cricketers of the three parishes around Farnham itself at last beat the men of Hambledon. 'Surrey,' in the old scores, meant nothing more than the Farnham parishes.

Harry Hall, the gingerbread baker who taught Beldham to play cricket, was a Farnham man. At Ash, near by, Robert Robinson ('Three-fingered Jack'), who caused the first Law regulating the size of cricket bats to be made, was born. Beldham and 'Honest John' Wells were born at Wrecclesham, close to Farnham, where once there was an inn which boasted that it was 'the rendezvous of the celebrated cricketers Beldham and Wells'.

Beldham spent the greater part of his life at Tilford, a few miles from Farnham. For some time he kept an inn there, and there he died in 1862 at the ripe age of 96 years. 'From Farnham to Hambledon is 27 miles,' said Beldham to Pycroft, 'and we used to ride both ways in the same day, early and late.' They rode on horseback. When Beldham and Wells began to build a vehicle for the journey their enterprise was frustrated by the imposition of the Cart Tax. Thereafter, if no horse was available, they walked to their cricket. I followed the road by which they went.

The thought that I had never seen Tilford before touched me reproachfully when, rounding a right-angled bend in the road, the first glimpse of its Elysian cricket green came suddenly upon my sight from the first of the village's two quaint old bridges. Involuntarily I stopped, just to look. Across the stream, starred with white water-flowers, the venerable Tilford oak, now nearing its thousandth year, spread its shady branches, casting shadows on 'Silver Billy' Beldham's cottage behind. A few paces further a pretty inn, the 'Barley Mow'; and through the leaves of the oak the back of a white sight-screen, and the white chain-posts of the green itself came into view. Across the second bridge, the cottages of the village people, only a few steps away and age-coloured like mulled wine: trees as yet undusted, with friendly seats beneath them, and fresh green grass everywhere: ducks and swans lazily floating on the water of the Wey flowing coolingly beneath the arches: not a jarring note, the only sounds those of the birds and of the lesser winged creatures humming brief life away in the warmth of an English high summer's day.

A peacefulness that could be *felt* brooded over the place. Here, it seemed, was the very heart of England, held tenderly in a tree-lined basin, most gently sloping on every side down to that smooth piece of carefully-tended turf stretched across the foot of the hollow. As the soothe of it all wrapped me around I paid silent homage to the memory of Silver Billy, standing for a few moments on the very ground the grand old patriarch of cricket had himself so often walked.

As I turned towards the sandy road that hugs the green on two of its sides, to pass on, a weather-browned countryman, seventy summers limned in the creases of his honest face, came beside me and bade me time o' day. He carried his jacket on his arm, a straw hat of uncertain age on his grey head, and a pipe from which the mouthpiece had long since disappeared hung precariously from his toothless gums. He was doing a job of work, he said, with the soft suave accent of the speech of the neighbourhood, a bit of gardening, because he didn't like to be idle and a few shillings in the week 'eked out' his pension.

Had he ever head of Billy Beldham? He should think so. Why, his father *knew* Billy Beldham. 'The old gentleman was a bit of a criceter himself,' said the veteran, his eyes lighting at the recollection of his father's tales, 'and he said a lot about William Beldham and his cricket-playing. He held there never was such a cricketer as Silver Billy.' And they still play cricket on Tilford Green, so near to Beldham's cottage that what would be a lofted 'three' at The Oval or Lord's would go clean into the cottage garden or through one of its windows. The old man said there would be a match there the following Saturday, and that the onlookers from the villages near by would sit outside the Barley Mow, under the trees, on the grass, and by the wayside to watch the play; and 'proper cricket' it would be. To my infinite regret I was unable to stay until that

Saturday; but I made a mental vow that very soon I *must* see a cricket match on Tilford Green!

I passed up the hill away from Tilford reluctantly, taking the way that Cobbett knew, past the Pride of the Valley inn on the outskirts of Churt, and climbing steadily thence towards Hindhead, with its eerie Devil's Punch Bowl where the wind whispers ghostly tunes through the pine trees, and its Golden Valley, beloved of Barrie, dropping steeply away between adjacent ridges. Near the Punch Bowl were once the lands farmed by 'Old Everlasting' Tom Walker, classic stonewaller and father of the lob, and his brother Harry, among the first of the great cutters of the past, Hambledonians both, clubmates of Beldham, Nyren and Small. I followed still the way they used to go, through Petersfield, whence also old John Small travelled, to their history cricket matches out on the Downs. It is a longish way – eleven miles or so from Hindhead to Petersfield; and another half-dozen on to Broad Halfpenny: playing cricket at Hambledon required self-sacrifice from the men of Hindhead and Petersfield, as it did from those of the Farnham parishes.

But first I turned aside a little way to enjoy a pleasant halt at Haslemere: lovely old-fashioned spot with a name that one repeats over and over again, so agreeable it is to let the word roll off the tongue. Here lived James Saunders, brilliant left-hander who wrought great deeds for the Players against the Gentlemen in the 1820s:

> 'A fine flashy hitter, by few he's surpassed,
> And when he's well in gets his runs very fast.'

To the south-east, not far away, might almost be seen North Chapel, in Sussex, the home of swarthy agile Noah Mann, whose feats of skill on horseback used to entertain the cricketers and watchers on Broad Halfpenny, whither it was his pleasure to ride. Noah was the first recorded swerver of a cricket ball: his under-arm bowling, left-hand, had, said John Nyren, 'a peculiar curve the whole way'.

Back to the planned route again, beyond Hindhead, through flower-bestrewn lanes, in and out, crossing and re-crossing the Surrey–Hampshire–Sussex border: bearing south-west into Hampshire about leafy Grayshott, into Sussex immediately after Liphook, along the Sussex–Hampshire margin past Liss, where lived 'Doctor' Richard Purchase, the blacksmith, slow under-arm bowler of the Hambledon club, alongside the broad Rake Common and fully into Hampshire at Sheet, a mile before Petersfield. A journey this, full of summer glory and delight through country rich in character, holding much to please the eye and much to interest the mind. Unfamiliar names of families one saw on the roadside and remembered: Madquick and Minshull, Funnell and Furlonger, Puttick, Emm and Pew, Wedge and Cutbath, Fariminer and Friady; and there were inns that looked inviting and had well-sounding titles: Box and Pelican, Seven Thorns, Royal Anchor, Flying Bull, Jolly Drover and Half-Moon. The friendly folk of East Hampshire and those of the border spread good humour even among the names of their inns: besides the Jolly Drover I saw a Jolly Farmer, and a Jolly Sailor, too!

I would have lingered at the head of the rise between Liphook and Liss to look down that wide-sweeping and beautiful wooded valley into Sussex and towards Midhurst. But time pressed, and Petersfield claimed a major halt. This quaint, quiet market town must ever lay a spell of fascination upon the cricketer: a lukewarm lover of cricket he, indeed, whose imagination is not quickened by the humble churchyard mound where rest the mortal remains of John Small, maker of bats and balls, one of the first members of the Hambledon club, one of the greatest cricketers of his day, and one of the most notable characters in the whole picturesque history of the game – the man who first made a straight bat with shoulders on it, and who first elaborated the principles of defensive batsmanship into a science in the era of fast under-arm length bowling.

John Small was born in 1737 – not at Emsworth, near Havant, as I have seen stated, but at the village of Empshott, between Liss and the Selborne of Gilbert White, a few miles from Petersfield, to which he was brought as a child of six, and where he lived for the next 83 years, died and was buried. The centre of Petersfield now, as then, is the Square, a true open literally four-sided square, with narrow old-fashioned streets (in which are some very old houses) leading away from its corners. Today the Square serves as cattle market and motor-'bus stopping place. One side of it is bounded by the church of St. Peter; the directly opposite side by a group of shops and business buildings, midmost among them the neat, white-painted establishment of Mr Norman Burton, whom I had the good fortune to meet. Mr Burton's shop is built on the spot where Old Small's house and shop once stood. The Square now has a modern utilitarian surface, of necessity; but John Small used to walk from his front door across to the church (where he sang in the choir for 75 years) on grass, hence the former name of the church, 'St. Peter's-in-the-Field'.

Old John's painted sign, which he hung before his house, has been quoted innumerably in books and articles, usually in these terms:

'Here lives John Small,
Makes Bat and Ball,
Pitch a Wicket, Play at Cricket,
With any man in England.'

This, as Mr Altham very well says, 'was no idle boast, for indeed he was for years the first batsman in the land'. Mr E. Arden Minty, F.R.I.B.A, in his informative booklet on Petersfield history, gives another and somewhat curious version of the sign:

'John Small. Linen Draper, Silk Mercer, etc.
The said John Small
Wishes it to be known to all
That he doth make both bat and ball,
And will play any man in England
For Five Pounds a side.'

I have been unable to find any trustworthy evidence that the first Petersfield John Small was ever a draper and haberdasher. His son, John, and his grandson, John, both carried on that trade in the same shop and living in the same house wherein they were born; and Mr Burton to this day conducts a handsomely modernised form of the same business on the exact site. But Old John was originally a shoemaker, afterwards a game-keeper, and he won far more fame as a cricketer and a maker of bats and balls than he did in either of his other occupations. It has been somewhere asserted that Old John's tombstone was lost. That is not the case. There are several Small tombstones near the church porch, and another by the wall behind the East window. The graves outside the porch are those of Old John and his wife and three daughters who died young, his two sons, the two wives of the more famous son John, and a son and daughter of the latter. Ann, the wife of Old John, died in 1802 at the age of 65. Old John himself died in 1826, aged 89.

Their stone bears, besides their names and those of the young children, the inscription:–

'Praises on tombs are trifles vainly spent,
A man's good name is his own monument.'

The second John Small, friend of John Nyren, a cricketer truly as good as his father, and a member of the later Hambledon eleven at the age of 19, died in 1836 seventy years old.

Confusion about Old John's tombstone may well have arisen because

of the existence of another epitaph to him in a compilation called
'Death's Doings':

> 'Here lies, bowled out by death's unerring ball,
> A cricketer renowned, by name John Small.
> But though his name was Small, yet great his fame,
> For nobly did he play the noble game.
> His life was like his innings, long and good,
> Full many summers he had Death withstood.
> At length the ninetieth winter came, when
> (Fate not leaving him a solitary mate)
> This last of Hambledonians, old John Small,
> Gave up his bat and ball, his leather, wax and all.'

If these words were ever on a memorial stone in Petersfield churchyard
or elsewhere, it is that stone which has been lost, not the tombstone.

All three John Smalls were musicians of considerable local repute. Old
John played the tenor violin, and the Duke of Dorset once gave him an
instrument as a tribute to his cricket. It was in a field near Petersfield that
Old John, returning late from a musical party, is said to have turned the
wrath of an enraged bull into pacifism by playing to it on his violin! The
third John Small played the bass-viol, and was one of the last surviving
young players in Petersfield Church. The organ which displaced him he
called 'a box of whistles, the invention of the Devil'.

It was a cattle market morning when I arrived at Petersfield, and
the Square, bright and cheerful in the sunshine, was thronged with
interesting types – both human and bovine. Easy, agreeable, helpful folk
I found these people to be; thrifty and busy, but not too busy to chat
informatively to an inquiring stranger. One of them, a bronzed elderly
cattle-drover, locking the picture of health – they live long down here –
took an evident pride in telling me that he knew John Small the third,
and it was he who, laying his stick across the broad back of one of his
heifers, directed me to Mr Burton's shop across the way. Some students
of cricket history may not be aware of the existence of finer memorials
to Old John Small than tombstone and epitaph – a room, a stable and a
garden, Old John Small's very own – all hidden behind the white facade
of Mr Burton's emporium. I was privileged to spend an engrossing hour
examining their contents.

The living quarters in Mr Burton's haberdashery are mostly above
and behind the shop. One of these upper rooms a few years ago was

a children's play-room, possessing four just ordinary-looking walls. A chance domestic accident aroused the proprietor's curiosity, and he decided to cut one of the walls in two and pull part of it down. The discovery, among the debris, of a copy of *The London Telegraph,* dated 1803 (containing a doctor's advertisement for 'skulls and bones') prompted the entire demolition of that wall, the stripping of the other walls of age-old layers of paper, and the removal of level after level of floor coverings. There stood revealed *the room of Old John Small*! And what is more, it was found that the room had been occupied by previous tenants of the site in 1684 – nearly sixty years before Old Small's father brought his family to the house when John himself was six years old!

John Small's room, up the stairs, is an altogether delightful *pied à terre*. There is a floor of wide, heavy oak planks, irregular now with the warping of the years. Two of the walls are shortened by the long, steep slope of the roofing: on one slope a fanlight; on the wall below a low, wide window opening on to a pretty miniature roof-rockery overlooking the tiniest of yards – a little well brimming with wistaria bloom – from which a narrow shady alley leads to the Square. Truly John Small had an eye for a room! But pleasant as are the incidentals and externals of this charming retreat, its chief glory is the fireplace of old red brick with deep alcoves on either side each provided with a narrow window. This was uncovered by the demolition of the old wall. A great bent beam, a belly timber believed to have been brought from a broken-up 'wooden-wall' man-o'-war at Portsmouth, stretches its huge bulk right across the end of the room, welding fireplace and wall-structure together – the heart of a tree more patriarchal than Small himself and a grand sample of the old builder's mechanics.

Although, unfortunately, no personal relics of Old Small remain, the room has been thoughtfully and discreetly furnished with articles of his period. One association with Small, however, still stands, a striking witness to his thoughtfulness and consideration for others. If you step into one of the fireplace nooks, you will see a narrow ledge about the height of your shoulder. Touch it, and it will lift, disclosing a lidded guttering that passes right through the room from side to side behind the great beam and through the back of the chimney stack – a water channel, cunningly constructed in just that spot so that John Small's waste rainwater should not annoy his neighbours!

Further behind the shop and the room there is an ancient stable, the only other structural part of the original premises left. Beyond it is John Small's garden, a secluded well-proportioned plot scented with the true old English flowers. I trod reverently on the lawn in John Small's garden and looked at the lichen and moss-mellowed old wall that protects its privacy. John had made plain his individuality on his shop sign; and I found that he had emphasised it in his garden. Pushing a shrub aside here and there I saw a few bricks which had had limed facings. On one, the facing intact, I saw inscribed the name 'John Small' – 'his wall' – the implied purport. There appear to have been numerous such bricks in the wall. Time and unscrupulous souvenir-hunters have filched away most of the facings; only one or two remain. Every year, I was told as I left the place, a few of the townsmen, mindful of his life and fame, lay a wreath on Old Small's grave on the anniversary of his death.

On the road again from Petersfield to the south-west, up Butser Hill, with Tegdown Hill (a sheepland name) to the right just ahead, along the gap at the top cut clean through the limestone hill, and into the wide spaces and long curving sweeps of the Hampshire downs – bound for Hambledon. In imagination one saw Old Small and his wife alongside, Mistress Ann carrying the huge green umbrella which she used to take with her to the cricket matches, brandishing it excitedly while her good man was making his many runs! Happy wife she must have been on that occasion when, as we read, Mr Small 'fetched above seven score notches off his own bat!'

More treasures for the town-weary eye as one covered the next few miles: a windmill on a sugar-loaf hill with a thin ribbon of road curling down it; a flash of gold and scarlet from a field of ketlock and poppies; the village of Clanfield; a roadside duck-pond, thatched cottages, a bucket well with a covering of thatch; springy turf of the kind that helped to make cricket; shadows and grass ripples blown by the breeze like little waves across a hayfield.

A turn more sharply westward, a steep climb, and then – a surprise at the very crest of the hill, the historic Bat and Ball inn, headquarters of the old Hambledon Club, and the Cricket Memorial stone enclosed by plain wooden railings across the road in front of the inn on the extreme edge of Broad Halfpenny Down. The inn sign, on a tall post, bears two pictures: a portrait of John Nyren facing you as you mount the hill, and on the opposite side a painting of top-hatted, tight-trousered gentlemen playing cricket in the two-stump wicket days. The original sign went the way of firewood when the old Hambledon Club was disbanded, but the present one is worthy of the traditions of the inn which Nyren immortalised – a place where, he wrote, they sold 'ale that would flare like turpentine, genuine Boniface that would put the souls of three butchers into one weaver'!

Cricket is played in Broad Halfpenny again today, though for a time the field was allowed to lapse into ploughland after the ancient heroes had ceased their deeds upon it. One cannot but be moved by the singular simplicity of the things to be seen there now – a small wooden thatched 'tent', scarce to be called a pavilion, a homely roller and an inexpensive net, iron stanchions round the pitch – the *materia* of any village team. But, homely, though the visible tokens of the spot may be, and humble their monument of stone, the shades of the great men of Broad Halfpenny long past hold you here in thrall. Full summer afternoon once more – solitary save for a passing car, and an odd way-farer who went away as quickly as he came, and silent, save for the luscious velvety croon of wood-pigeons and the jewelled song of the larks, the sun blazing down from a cloudless vault of blue on to this famed field high up and away from noise and care – I sat for an hour and let the warm brooding peace of Broad Halfpenny, and its many memories, have their way.

The pilgrimage neared its end. 'Greatest of all Elevens,' I had to say in thought with Mitford, 'fare ye well.' Downhill next, two and a quarter miles between hedgerows abloom with campion, speedwell and dog-rose, to a quiet hollow – screened by hillside trees and flanked on the western side by Windmill Down, the second home of Hambledon Club – wherein the villagers of Hambledon pursue the even tenor of their present day. Scarcely a village within walking distance of Hambledon that cannot recall some old cricketer or other. There is Horndean, the home of William Barber, whose family, like the Nyrens, once kept the Bat and Ball; Catherington, where Brett the 'steam-engine' bowler, lived; and Southwick, the home of Hogsflesh – Hambledon players whom Andrew Lang named in his 'Ballads of Dead Cricketers': 'Ah, where be Beldham now, and Brett, Barber and Hogsflesh, where be they?'

It is a beautiful village, so far unspoiled. At the head of its narrow High Street there is the spick-and-span George Hotel, with a knightly sign, the former meeting-house of the cricket club, once kept by Richard Nyren, its secretary and captain, John Nyren's father. A few yards along stands the well-known New Inn and at the farther end of the street the Green Man, where 'Buck' Stewart was one-time cricketer-host. A team-sheet of the local club of today caught my eye as I passed one of the shops.

At the top of a steep cobbled street at right-angles to the High Street to the church, surrounded by the narrow grassy beds and lichened stones grey with weather and years beneath which the forefathers of the hamlet sleep – among them Tom Sueter, Edward Aburrow, George Leer ('Little George', the long-stop), and Buck Stewart, whose names in cricket 160 years ago were names to conjure with. Tom Sueter, 'the ladies' pet', the first great wicket-keeper and the first cricketer to step out of his crease to drive, sang in the choir. He was a builder, and his name, as such, is inscribed on a stone in the church tower.

The church on its hill benignly overlooks the village, and from the porch, beside which a grand old yew tree covers a group of gravestones with its drooping branches, one can see down into the High Street, across the thatched roofs of cottages and a cosy farmstead, and up the shady green rise on the opposite side: a wholesome, satisfying view for today and an appeasing reminder of the men who lived and worked and played in this calming sequestered vale long ago. A great peace come over my spirit as I stood and looked, leaning upon one of those grey old stones. 'Greatest of Elevens, fare ye well!'

Not far beyond Hambledon lies a hamlet with the quaint name of World's End; and so, indeed, it might literally seem to a cricket-lover leaving Hambledon behind him at the close of such a pilgrimage. A petrol machine cutting hay close to one of the farms strove to justify the intrusion of modernity upon the past oral scene, and I wondered what Old Small and John Nyren would have thought of that. But it seemed to me that the all-enveloping serenity of the landscape made the machine look insignificant. One may hope that it always will be so, and that neither this nor any other mechanical age will ever be allowed to lay impious hands upon such beauty or to efface such memories.

Chapter 7

COLLECTING

CRICKET TREASURES IN MY HOME MUSEUM

Ron Yeomans

The first essential for a cricket museum at home is to find a good-natured wife – or mother – according to circumstances. After all, your *cricketana* is going to overflow throughout the home, so without co-operation you are lost to begin with.

Infiltration of *cricketana*, because infiltration it will be, is rather like the story of the Trojan Horse. You have to get the pieces in without anyone really knowing, until someone looks up and says '*Hello, another piece?*'

In my boyhood days, Herbert Sutcliffe coached me at cricket, so did that great Lancastrian, Cecil Parkin. I knew Jack Hobbs. In fact, I got to know all the cricketers and have been meeting cricketers ever since.

Cricket was part of my life, but it was not until I had finished playing serious cricket that I began what has now become my cricket museum. My most treasured piece is a magnificent original Victorian oil painting showing an old man bowling – a no-ball, alas – to a small boy in a farmyard. It came to me via Sothebys a few years ago.

It was really this picture that put me right with my wife. She liked it. But she said if I had it hanging in the hall, I must have the hall re-papered. So I struck that bargain and then went one further! All right, I said, but could the paper be some cricketing wallpaper that Len Hutton had found me. So we struck bargain number two!

Now part of the hall, staircase and landing is papered with what I call my Griffin wallpaper, because a cricket scene is shown, but the bowler is bowling with a bent arm!

Something I love nearly as much as my picture is a recent acquisition – a six-inch brass cricketing ornament. It consists of a clock resting on two sets of stumps, complete with two bats and a ball. I picked this up in Edinburgh, the most unlikely place you might think for finding anything to do with cricket. But collectors *do* find things in the most unusual places!

I am as pleased with my collection of pottery and china as much as anything – china plates bearing the signatures in gold of touring cricket teams, a plate made to celebrate W.G. Grace's 100 centuries in 1895, scores of cricket figures and mugs – many of them bearing pictures of old-time cricketers in relief. Particularly nice is a Leeds Pottery jug.

Two silver figures, one of a batsman and one of a bowler, both about 100 years old, are treasures too. A more recent silver piece is a solid silver ash tray struck to commemorate the centenary of the first English team to tour Australia in 1861. Nearly 20 other cricketing ash trays I have, one of them in the shape of a cricket ball, are a gift from the makers. Each time a new one is turned out, I am sent a sample. A silver-plated toast rack, made up of wickets, bats and balls, is another curio.

Then there are cricketing medals and tokens, cricketing tiles, miniature bats – and glassware. The tumblers, engraved with cricketers' faces, I use regularly.

Most of the items are spread about the house. I keep my fingers crossed that no one will ever knock one over! Some items, of course, are in glass cabinets.

A large marquetry picture of a cricket match in Leeds on Boxing Day is in my porch, and close at hand is a colourful piece of stained glass, showing cricketers and cricket scenes. It is the only piece of cricketing stained glass I know of and now makes a panel in one of my doors.

I mentioned infiltration. My *cricketana* starts at the front gate, with a gate made up of three stumps used in a Test match, spreads into the porch, the hall, and two downstairs rooms, goes up the stairs (by way of pictures, prints and engravings) and into one bedroom. Two silk pictures are there – one of them of W.G. Grace in batting position.

You might ask, where do I find all these things? The answer is diligent, continual and systematic searching at every antique shop – yes, and junk shop too – that I see. Scores of people know that I collect *cricketana* and often write to me offering me a piece, or telling me where a piece is. So if *you* have a piece of *cricketana* you can spare, *do* write and tell me.

You think that I'm a cricket fanatic? All right, maybe I am, but there are plenty worse things than cricket to be mad about!

CRICKETANA

L. E. S. Gutteridge

This is in effect a Collector's Corner. It is not specifically called so, since I have a feeling that the term may have been used before. It is proposed to deal with items of exceptional interest at length, and to a lesser extent with such cricketana as changes hands from time to time, and may be worthy of note to the interested reader. It is also hoped to keep the reader interested.

That omnivorous collector the late E. Rockley Wilson possessed among many other fine things an exceptional collection of what might be called Cricket 'Bloods'. Such luscious titles as *Body-line Bill the Bowler* and *Cricketer-Cracksman* (run-scorer by day and safe-breaker by night) are fair enough examples. They consist of lurid paper-covered magazines of some 64–90 pages most ineffectively secured with a wire staple that rusts rapidly. They retailed at 4d each. These are a natural evolution of such collectors' delights as Varney the Vampire, Dick Turpin, Sexton Blake and The String of Pearls. They have a recurrent theme of the schoolboy's cricket hero, who, against the vilest jealousy and opposition of the relative of the county chairman, who happens to be captain, finally wins through to marry his beautiful and wealthy niece. He always plays for England and his deeds with bat and ball are only equalled by his phenomenal fielding. I have much appreciated the excuse that this article provides, to make time to read some of them.

One of particular interest is entitled *Captain of Claverhouse* and, according to its cover and its half-title, it is by 'Wally Hammond, England's Famous Test Cricketer'. It is a 'stunning yarn of School and Cricket'. It was published by the Amalgamated Press and was No. 293 of The Boys' Friend Library (New Series) and has 64 pages. 'Who "sacked" Barham? All Claverhouse is buzzing with that question from the moment that a housemaster is found tied hand and foot with a sack over his head. Then comes a still bigger sensation: the finger of suspicion points to Drummond Cloyne, the finest cricketer and the most popular captain Claverhouse has ever had.'

Does this whet your appetite? Alas it is long out of print and space-travel has usurped its place.

No. 680 of the Boys' Friend Library is also entitled *Captain of Claverhouse*, has a new and brighter cover, is dated 6 July 1939, and has no mention of any author's name. Then appeared a smaller publication with a newly designed cover. It is entitled *Captains of Claverhouse* (the plural is intentional) and the author is given as John Grey. It is No. 23 in the "Boys" Wonder Library'. The publisher is the same, but the price has fallen by half to twopence for 64 pages. How can a book with the same number of pages, but only half the number of words per page contain as much material as the 4d edition? The answer is that it cannot and does not. The problem of condensing a book has caused many an editor to frown and the manufacturers of blue pencils to rejoice. There exists a perfect method that has the hallmark of genius by virtue of its simplicity and speed. The editor's furrows disappear and the blue pencil manufacturers pay a more modest dividend on their first debentures. Simply remove alternate chapters. I assure you that this method was adopted in John Grey's *Captains of Claverhouse*. Doubtless the editor had the best interests of youth at heart and was intent on providing them with an opportunity to exercise their ingenuity and to develop their imagination, by filling in the gaps. I cannot feel that John Grey's edition, although at half price, was as good value as the original Wally Hammond at 4d. In any case, the Wally Hammond would be so much easier to swap.

Other titles are: *The Mystery Batsman* (Grand Story of Cricket and International Intrigue), *A Wizard at the Wicket*, *The Hypnotised Cricketer* and *The School Boy Test Match Player*. There are many others.

A BARGAIN

E. V. Lucas

Chancing to be one of those persons who have never been able to sell anything except for less than I gave for it, I received a staggering shock when, the other day, in a forgotten packing-case, I found a copy of a book for which, many years ago, I paid a few shillings, but which now, according to Mr Goldman's *Bibliography of Cricket*, is worth five pounds.

The title is *Some Recollections of Cricket*, and the author Lord Charles J.F. Russell. The tiny work was printed by Fisher at Woburn in 1879. Apart from intrinsic merit, it is so valuable because only twelve copies were issued.

Lord Charles Russell, a son of the Sixth Duke of Bedford, was born in 1807 and was President of the MCC in 1835. At the time of the publication of these *Recollections* and of his speech at the presentation to W.G., he was seventy-two.

Haygarth, the author of the biographies scattered about *Lillywhite*, wrote of Lord Charles (in 1860): – '(Lieutenant-Colonel) Lord Charles James Fox Russell (half-brother of Lord John Russell) played steadily and with a straight bat. His name will be found occasionally in this work for about a quarter of a century, and it is believed he never scored two noughts (or "a pair of spectacles") in any match. In the field he was generally middle-wicket-off. Is one of the Committee of the Marylebone Club, and is likewise a capital judge of play. Was born in Dublin, 10 February 1807. Height 5ft 9¾ in, and weight 10 stones 2lbs. Is Sergeant-at-Arms in the House of Commons.'

The present Mr Fisher of Woburn, a son of the printer of the little book, tells me that Lord Charles was also an author and an authority on hunting, and that he rode to hounds when over eighty. 'I remember,' Mr Fisher says, 'that Lord Charles wrote in a most undecipherable hand and sometimes when my father was stumped by some frightful hieroglyphics he would have to go to Crow Holt, where Lord Charles lived, to ask him what the word was. After donning his spectacles and much humming and clearing his throat, he would own himself beaten and call loudly for Runc (his house-keeper, Miss Runciman) who could usually put the matter right.' Lord Charles, I should add, lived on until 1894, when he was eighty-seven.

For the benefit of the considerable number of unfortunate people who (unlike myself) do not possess the book, let me describe it. To start with, it is dedicated to the Hon. Frederick Ponsonby and the Hon. Robert Grimston, 'once champions of cricket, now guardians of the game', followed by a quotation from the well-known Harrow poem, beginning: –

> Old Damon and old Pythias,
> They always found together,

but Lord Charles Russell, who was not an Harrovian, made the very natural mistake of changing the second line to: –

> Were always found together.

I say 'very natural' because, when quoting the same lines in a little book of my own, I (also not an Harrovian) committed the same error, and was properly chidden for it by no less an authority than the great Dr Butler, formerly Headmaster of Harrow and then Master of Trinity, who made me understand once and for all that, at Harrow, 'found' means shared.

Then comes Lord Charles's preparatory note; and then what he calls the over of four balls, together with a last ball added as an afterthought. The first of these balls is bowled by George Richmond, RA, reprinted from *Baily's Magazine*; the rest are Lord Charles's own, being 'Round-Arm Recollections'; 'Lord's and Prince's, 1872'; 'Bedfordshire Cricket, 1878'; and the text of the speech made by Lord Charles on the occasion of the presentation to W.G. Grace, at Lord's, on 22 July 1879, of a clock and a cheque.

Such is the little slender work, 39 pages, bound in red cloth.

I should like to quote practically all the book, for Lord Charles (or Miss Runciman) was a good writer, mellifluous, direct and convincing. But there is no room. Therefore I must give only a little, beginning with the reminiscences of George Richmond, RA, that fine painter, many of whose pictures were exhibited at Norwich last year, who numbered so many eminent men among his friends, from William Blake to Gladstone. Although in 1879 Richmond was only seventy, he signs himself 'Octogenarian': a pardonable error in the old. Like Lord Charles, he lived on to be eighty-seven.

Here is an enkindling passage: –

'How often have I watched the bowling of Lillywhite, that prince of bowlers, or, as he was called in Sussex, "The Nonpareil". It was a treat to see Fuller Pilch, when playing against him, reaching out and crushing ball after ball. Well might Lillywhite say, "Me bowling, Pilch batting, and Box behind the wicket, that's cricket." But it required such bowlers as Lillywhite or Cobbett to prevent Pilch from running away with a match, for he would punish any bowler tremendously who was an inch or two out of the wicket. To use Lillywhite's own words, "I supposes if I was to think every ball, they wouldn't get ever a run. Three balls out of four straight is what we calls mediogrity".'

Lord Charles also has something to tell us about the 'Non-pareil', remarking that the perfection to which he brought round-arm was said to be owing to some defect in his arm. 'Be that as it may, certain it is that his delivery in fielding was identical with that of his bowling. But, again, this may have resulted from his extreme jealousy of the cunning of his right hand, as he would often refuse a hard chance of c. and b. with the remark, "Ha, where would you be without my *bowling*?"' To this I may add, with relevance, that what I always think the best cricket story is that of 'The Nonpareil' stepping aside to let a terrific chance of a catch go to the boundary. 'You might, at any rate, have tried,' said his captain. 'No,' said Lilly, rhyming 'bowled' to 'howled', 'when I've bowled her I've done with her.' But let it never be forgotten that during his career his fingers were broken three times.

To return to George Richmond, he says of Harvey Fellows, the fast bowler:

'Then there came up a bowler, Mr Harvey Fellows, who, by his tremendous pace and spin, put all the play of the professionals to rout; they would not stand up to it. Talk of Mr Osbaldeston, or of Brown of Brighton, Mr Fellows was much faster than either of them. And yet I have seen the fragile-looking Lord Charles Russell playing that terriffic bowling with all the coolness imaginable, as if it was only medium-paced. It may be said that the players depended for their living upon not being maimed, and that if Lord Charles Russell had had a finger broken he would still have remained Sergeant-at-Arms, but for all that it was a fine display of the pluck of the English gentleman.'

It is Lord Charles Russell's eulogism on W.G., in 1879, that I finally quote: –

'I can say, with a clear conscience, that I have never seen a better field, and I have never seen any one approach him as a batter; but he might be the good bowler that he is, the fine field, and the grand batter, without being a thorough cricketer; more than manual dexterity and agility of limb are required to play Cricket; the game must be played with head and heart; and in that respect Mr Grace has been eminently prominent. I have often seen an England eleven playing an uphill game steadily and well; a sudden change had placed the game in their favour, and a change came over the field, such as there would be were the sun now to break out over our heads. Looking at Mr Grace's playing, I have never been able to tell whether that gentleman was playing a winning or a losing game. I have never seen the slightest lukewarmness or inertness in him in the field; should any want to know how he plays Cricket, let them look at him playing one ball; you all know the miserably tame effect of the ball hitting the bat instead of the bat hitting the ball, but whether acting on the defensive or offensive, in playing a ball Mr Grace puts every muscle into it, from the sole of his foot to the crown of his head; and just as he played one ball, so he played the game; he was heart and soul in it; I have never heard the bell ring for Cricketers to go into the field but he was the first into it; and that is a great matter in Cricket playing.' Noble words, I think.

The actual presentation was made by Lord Fitzhardinge. W.G. was then thirty-one and the reader naturally assumes that there may have been some idea that his cricketing days were over. On the contrary, he played on until 1908.

'PLEASE, SIR, WILL YOU SIGN?'

David Lemmon

R.E.S. Wyatt, captain of Warwickshire and England, was one of the great batsmen in the period between the wars, yet, for a personal and selfish reason, I disliked him. He had been a favourite, one of whom I was in awe when I first saw him at Lord's during the war, but then came the fatal day. He was playing for the Army or Sir Pelham Warner's XI in one of those marvellous games that brightened the darkness of the Forties. During the afternoon interval, autograph book in hand, eleven years old, I ambushed Bob Wyatt behind the pavilion a Lord's. The moment of closeness to greatness had arrived. 'Please, sir,' I stammered, 'could I have your autograph?' The voice that bellowed back in Dickensian authority still reverberates in my mind. 'No, I am going to have my tea.' I never forgave him, and now, thirty years on, my admiration of his ability is still grudging.

One coveted autograph of the time was gained at Lord's. An old man, virile and smiling, carefully but knowingly managed the steps at the side of the pavilion and willingly wrote 'Pelham Warner' in the book of an adoring youngster to whom he was a part of history, touched with Grace, Ranji and Hobbs, and for whom that final season of over twenty years before and the final match against Surrey was legendary reading.

Of course, the time comes when you become too old, too sophisticated, too self-conscious to ask cricketers to sign. Like all changes in life the lines of demarcation between when one did and when one didn't any longer are hazy, but, of course, your urge lives on or is reborn. Though I have not looked at it for several years, I have never quite been able to give up my old autograph book and it has survived the crises of National Service, youth, marriage, living abroad and children. It is through the children, of course, that one continues to collect vicariously, and the delight at one's sons' captures cannot always be disguised by the blasé attitude of age. Hutton and Compton on the same day at Harlow last year – what a day – and who was most excited? And, in any case, is not father invaluable? How else would they have known Jack Young outside the tavern at Lord's? And what warmth and encouragement have followed in subsequent meetings with that kind man, as warm a human being as he was fine a bowler. There is more than a name in an autograph.

There certainly was in Jim Sims'. He would drive the van round behind the pavilion at Lord's, put in the bags, and line up the Middlesex team to sign for the boys. His death was much lamented by many grateful youngsters. But even Jim's organisation could not compare with John Snow's. He climbs from his sports-car and within five seconds has turned a clambering rabble into an orderly line who depart gloriously happy – 'I've got John Snow' – within three minutes.

Rightly many cricketers will reject the scrap of paper and sign only books or pictures. Neatly arranged under counties or countries, they make attractive presentations. It is easy to classify Snow, Richards, Kanhai, but what of the greats of the past, such marvellous captures as Keith Miller – getting into his car. They have a special place at the back of the book where legendary characters tumble over each other. It is here that you will find D.B. Carr.

Donald Carr was accosted by my sons while strolling towards the gate at Lord's. When asked to sign he turned to them with a solemn twinkle and with affected pomposity, asked, 'Do you know who I am?'

'Yes, sir, you are Mr Carr. My father saw you play,' the elder said.

Donald Carr took the books smilingly, signed, and said, 'Your father must be very old, boy.'

But it is not just father who follows vicariously. Mother ambushed Alec Bedser at a back gate whilst crowds milled elsewhere and asked him to sign twice for her sons. She presented the signatures to them with the contemptuous grunt that she got them one of the greatest bowlers of all time while they panted vainly after lesser mortals.

Endurance is important. Two years ago, my younger son, then seven, chased Jim Laker up six flights of stairs to be rewarded at the top in recognition of perseverance and exhaustion. Will he remember, I wonder, when he looks at that famous name in years to come? Will the excitement be recalled, the momentary contact with greatness? For that, I suppose, is what collecting autographs is – a physical contact – with the idols of our youth in the greatest of games, and, however exhausting it may become, it places a responsibility on them as human beings who can give joy or pain to other human beings.

I shall never forget my first image of Robin Hobbs coming down the steps from the dressing room at Chesterfield after a long, hot, hard day in the field, with a glass of beer in one hand and fountain pen at the ready in the other, saying to a group of patient, apprehensive youngsters, 'OK lads, I'm ready now'. No wonder they love him. And then there was Alvin Kallicharran saying to my elder son, 'Yes, of course I'll sign. I watched you bat in the tea interval. You're a left-hander like me.' What a hero was made there. Nor can I forget the great international cricketer who, for four years, has been promising to sign 'tomorrow'.

All those pieces of paper and all those signatures and all that excitement that warms our winters and later memories. Please, sir, sign? Why? Because, as a great sportsman once said, the day to start worrying is when they don't ask you to sign any more.

CRICKET IN FICTION

Alan Gibson

The oppressing thing in writing about cricket is that so much has been written about it already: not just because it is so hard to say anything fresh, but because even when you *think* you have said something fresh, the chances are you haven't. In his novel, *A Season in Sinji*, J.L. Carr brings in two cricketers called Wood and Stone. As soon as I saw the names I knew we were going to have the ancient joke about Bishop Heber's hymn,

> The heathen, in his blindness.
> Bows down to wood and stone.

But then it struck me that he had had a Methodist upbringing and might well have thought of it himself. In *Wisden* for 1972, John Arlott mentions 67 items concerning cricket, published in 1971. How many books of any sort do you read? I have kept a list of my reading for many years, and I find it difficult to get much beyond two books a week, properly read: about a hundred books a year, a minuscule proportion. I see that last year I read seventeen cricket books. No doubt it was too many, even for one with a professional interest, but it leaves me a long, long way from being a well-read man even in terms of cricket. So these comments on fictional cricket are far from comprehensive.

Schooldays
I suppose I enjoyed my earliest reading of this kind as much as any since: the 'school stories' which were so popular in the first half of this century. If you can stand the social and moral assumptions, which did not trouble me in my youth, you will find some capital cricket in them. Hylton Cleaver, John Mowbray, Gunby Hadath were all very good. I still find gripping the climactic match in Cleaver's story *The Old Order*, and have kept my copy over many years. I like it better than the classics of the genre, *Tom Brown's Schooldays*, *The Hill*, and *Playing Fields* (I never

managed to finish *Playing Fields*). Of course, Hughes, Vachell and Parker were writing, or pretending to write, about real schools: Hughes even makes Tom Brown's last match end in a draw, as historically it did.

At the other extreme was Frank Richards, whose matches nearly always ended in a victory by one run or one wicket for Greyfriars (if he was writing in the *Magnet*) or St Jim's (if he was writing in the *Gem*). I believe that one of Richards's editors tried to make his cricket matches more realistic, but the master was wrathful and the experiment swiftly dropped. Talbot Baines Reed was an excellent writer of school stories, and his cricket matches hold your attention, though I doubt if he was a cricketer himself.

All these writers had one great advantage as writers of cricket fiction: they were writing of a world where cricket was a natural element. In the summer it commanded attention more than anything else in the school. Anyone reading these books would know that, and would expect some knowledge of the game on his part to be assumed. It was thus possible to write a novel (not to argue about the correct use of that word) in which cricket did not have to occupy the whole scene, *or* to be dragged in. It was there already, a familiar part of the setting. You could have as much or as little of it as the author liked.

This ceases to be true when the novelist is writing for adults, many of whom may not be interested in cricket, and is describing situations where cricket is not the main occupation of the summer, but peripheral to life.

Probably the most distinguished writer ever to take cricket as a main theme for a novel was P. G. Wodehouse. He wrote many school stories, and much about cricket in them, when he was young. But after writing *Mike*, a story about public school cricket, he followed Mike Jackson and his friend Psmith ('the P is silent, as in pneumatic') from the cricket fields to their adult pursuits – Wodehouse then allowed his heroes to grow older – and so we followed them to the city, and later to New York, and Psmith became the first great Wodehouse comic character.

Until Psmith took over, Wodehouse was only known as a writer of school stories and sentimental light novels. You could say that Wodehouse's future was won on the playing fields of Wrykyn and Sedleigh: *but*, except in passing, he never returned to writing about cricket. It had served its turn, and he put away childish things.

Adult categories
Cricket fiction intended for adults falls into two categories: (1) books which are dressed-out accounts of cricket matches; (2) books on other

subjects than cricket which contain passages about it, put in for colour or atmosphere, usually with humorous intent.

Category 1: I expect Hugh de Selincourt's *The Cricket Match* is still the best. Neither he himself in later efforts, nor his many imitators, equalled the simple beauty of that day in the life of Tillingfold. I would also like to commend (against some influential opinion) *Malleson at Melbourne*. This is an account of the tribulations of an English captain during an Australian tour. I have lost my copy, and cannot even remember the name of the author, and it built up to the last-Test last-over last-wicket finish, just like Frank Richards; but when Malleson at last won I was much moved.

Category 2: there are many examples, of which Dickens is still perhaps the best-known. Writers who bring in a cricket match, as part of the English scene, are liable to be tripped by technicalities. Dickens knew a bit about cricket, but All Muggleton *v* Dingley Dell would not read convincingly if you treated it as a serious account. Dorothy L. Sayers often watched cricket, but all the same there are some false notes in the match which occurs near the end of *Murder Must Advertise*. Wimsey would have had a sounder technique if he had really scored a hundred at Lord's for Eton. There is a similar occurrence in *The Berry Scene* (Dornford Yates) when Bertram Pleydell thus describes his efforts against the dreaded fast bowler of a neighbouring village: 'He played clean into my hands. He sent one down dead straight, which kept very low; and I let him have it straight back with every ounce that I'd got. He tried to get out of the way, but he hadn't time.'

The famous match in *England, Their England* rings true because A. G. Macdonell did not need to get the technical details right: he wrote as a young Scotsman playing for an eleven of English *litterateurs* (it was based on Sir John Squire's XI) and the more mysterious the proceedings were, the funnier. Yet this is not the account of an imaginary match which has made me laugh most. That I find in *Fate Cannot Harm Me*, by J. C. Masterman.

Serious thread

From time to time, attempts have been made to establish a third category of cricket fiction: a novel intended for adults, intending to say something serious, but with cricket one of its threads; and yet not *about* cricket. I have never read a satisfying one, if one calls *Mike* a school story. *Pip* (Ian Hay) and even *Raffles* (E. W. Hornung, a good writer) did not amount to much more than an extension of the *ethos* and characters of the public school story.

I doubt if it can be done. I doubt, even, if it is worth trying. J.L. Carr, in the book I mentioned at the beginning, had a good try (*A Season in Sinji*, £1.25, from the author, 27 Mill Dale Road, Kettering). That Mr Carr is a writer of talent was recognised in the success of his second novel, *The Harpole Report. A Season in Sinji*, as he engagingly puts it himself, 'sank almost at once without trace.' I dive after it only to this extent, that nothing a good writer publishes is negligible, and that I would have enjoyed it if he had left out the cricket.

He forces his analogies, he strains his language, to show that life is just a game of cricket, which is neither more nor less true than that life is just a bowl of cherries, some of them going bad, or a sack of potatoes, or – well, whatever analogy happens to come to you.

Mr Carr is very strong on breasts and lavatories, which I suppose is mandatory in the modern novel. Just as I was beginning to get interested in the bosoms, there was a piece about cricket; and just as I was beginning to get interested in the cricket, back came the bosoms, and the dirt, and the violence. No doubt life is like that: but since we all have to experience it anyway, I doubt if we have any *obligation* to read about it as well.

But this is a comment on the function of a novel, rather than the possibility of writing a *cricket* novel. I think anyone interested in cricket literature as a species, or in what happened in an RAF station in West Africa during the Second World War, or who does not worry about these learned thoughts but simply lets the story swing him along – I think it would give enjoyment to you, if you are one of these people. But read *Mike*, and *The Cricket Match*, and (I have just remembered it) *Mr Evans* first.

CRICKET HOWLERS

James Thorpe

Of the journalism of cricket, the chief examples have been *Cricket*, edited by C.W. Alcock (1882), and *The Cricket Field* (1892). Both are, alas, defunct, the latter being eventually merged into a lawn-tennis magazine: truly a sad ending! Their place has been recently filled by *The Cricketer*, which, under the able editorship of P.F. Warner, first appeared in 1921, has carefully played itself in, and is now going strong. H.S. Altham's *History of Cricket* first appeared in Vols. II, III, IV, V and VI, and was afterwards published in book form.

Magazine and newspaper articles and stories innumerable have appeared, and when written by cricketers are often worth a place in the scrap-book. The pitfalls for the writer who does not know the game are many, and one example is worthy, I think, to be passed on to the reader. The story deals with the time-worn theme of the cricket match for the hand of the beautiful daughter of the vicar of the village: the rivals, of course, being captains of the opposing sides. Extracts will convey, I fear, but a weak idea of the gripping power of the narrative; they may, however, serve as a warning to other budding non-cricketing authors.

Although the captains tossed in the pavilion 'the coin flew into the air with a merry click and next instant it lay on the grass,' presumably having rolled down the steps. The hero, strange to relate, wins the toss, and after seeing his best batsman stumped off the first ball of the match, he, 'with a grim set look, put on the pads, and strode out to the wicket,' having kept the fielders waiting some minutes. Having scored a four off the fourth ball, he 'snicked the last ball of the over for one'. 'Then it was my partner's turn.' But why? This batsman hit a four and one during the over, and our hero 'again faced the music', in spite of the fact that it was his partner's knock. However, he '*cut* the first ball to leg for three,' ran a bye and scored 'one from the last ball of the over'. *Again* his partner jumped his claim, but swift retribution was at his heels. He gave a 'chance to point, who missed it, but cover point caught it': note the virtue of backing up! Although his 'nervous apprehension returned with redoubled force', he 'did not lose his nerve', but next over 'carefully took the centre, and played the ball, sending it past the man in the slips for three runs' – evidently off the edge. In his next over he gave a chance.

The vice-captain of the fielding side bowled 'a full-length ball', and he 'went out to meet it', and again 'caught it on the edge of the bat', with the result that it went into 'the very hands of mid-on! Oh, the agony of that moment! Would he hold it? A thousand eyes were watching him' (evidently a good 'gate'), 'yes, he has it! Heavens, no! He drops it! Oh, the relief!' Although this escape had the effect of somewhat steadying him, he was bowled for 'only twenty-seven runs'. He then 'went into the pavilion *and washed*, and went to where Minnie was sitting'. Her consolation took the form of the cryptic utterance, 'You should have played more slips with the fast bowling.' The score reached a total of 123.

The hero, of course, started the bowling, and although he 'tried every imaginable kind of ball', fifty runs were up with no wicket down. He had visions of losing the match, leaving the country, and trying to forget Minnie. However, he decided to change the bowling and himself kept wicket, when, of course, he promptly stumped the aggressive batsman. A providential 'rot' set in and eight wickets were down for 118 and nine for 122!!! 'Then the temptation came. Satan entered into my heart. I must win at any cost, and if I could not win by fair means, I determined to do so by foul.' Which means that he flicked the bails off with his finger, and the last batsman was given out, bowled. Having married Minnie, he confessed in full to his rival, who, like a real sportsman, admitted that he had bribed our hero's star batsman for £20 to make less than ten runs. You may remember that he was stumped first ball, and so earned his money rather easily.

Perhaps some day, when he has nothing more serious on hand, Mr Ashley-Cooper will make for us a collection of these cricket howlers. It should make an interesting addition to the cricket library.

Chapter 8

THE FUNNY
SIDE

Graham White

Every age has it compensations, they say, but when, at the end of the last season, anno demanded that I put away my cricket gear once and for all, I confess I found the truth of it hard to appreciate.

Fortunately, it hasn't taken long to find at least one consolation in retirement. True, I still experience a nostalgic pang or two when I watch our opening pair making their way to the wickets: but as batsman after batsman wends his way back to the pavilion, melancholy gives way to a sense of overwhelming relief. Sad it may be that never again shall I be asked to go in, but how inexpressively sweet is the realisation that never again shall I have to come out.

And please do not confuse the act of getting out with that of coming out. The former process involved neither difficulty nor embarrassment, and there were times when coming out was as painless an exerience as an after-dinner stroll. When, with my score at 2, an ominous crash announced the fall of my wicket, I could negotiate the 70-odd yards to the pavilion with a nonchalance probably unequalled in club cricket. And if my latest failure were one of a long series, demanding avoidance of sympathetic glances, I could fix a passing sparrow with a look of rapt concentration such as even Mr Ludwig Koch would find it difficult to better.

But just how to comport myself when fortune smiled upon me, and the pavilion must inevitably rise to do me honour, was a problem to which, in 30 long years, I never found a satisfactory answer. It may be that in my youth I was more sensitive to these things than most; more alive to the dangers attendant upon an incorrect recognition of the pavilion's tribute. All too vividly was I aware that in the time it takes to cover those last 30 yards you are the cynosure of all eyes, your every action magnified a hundredfold. And how quick are the ancients to fasten upon any error of taste at such a time.

Lift your cap with too exaggerated a gesture, waggle your bat a trifle too energetically, and what is the impression you have created in the eyes of the watchers? 'Yes, my good sirs, you do well to applaud,' you seem to say. 'You'll be lucky to see another knock like that this season.' And immediately the whisper goes round that you cannot carry your corn, that you are a dashed sight too cocky by far.

And it is just as easy – and just as fatal – to err too much the other way. A perfunctory touch of the cap and a deadpan expression may spring from a natural modesty, but the man who has clapped his hands sore for your benefit will deem it a poor return for his efforts. And soon he will be voicing the opinion that you are a stuck-up, standoffish young puppy, and no mistake. In either case you will have earned yourself a reputation that will take a lot of living down.

That, at all events, was how I saw it, and the thing quickly became an obsession. So much so that on my frequent visits to Lord's and The Oval, I found myself paying less attention to the masters at the wicket than at the wicket gate. Practice makes perfect, I suppose, and oh! the grace and assurance with which the Hobbses, the Hearnes and the Woolleys of that distant age met the pavilion's rapturous ovations. How completely right was the lift of the cap, the waggle of the willow, how perfectly regulated to the volume of applause.

'Not too little – not too much – but just right!', as the well-known advertisement has it.

Before a mirror in my bedroom I strove to imitate their outgoings as assiduously as others copied their deportment at the wicket. My first model was none other than the great Archie MacLaren. There was majesty in his every movement, and when he received the crowd's homage it was in the manner of a monarch returning from a successful campaign.

Cold reason put an early end to that ambition, however, for obviously my performance would have to be all of a piece; and my best friend could not have described my batting as majestic. It wasn't even aristocratic. 'Laboured' would perhaps have been the best description, since my bat had so pronounced a tendency to Swing to the Left, as it were.

I turned then to another idol, one Patsy Hendren, who seemed to possess the perfect answer to the problem which beset me. For in success or failure Patsy greeted the massed ranks at Lord's with a smile so wide that only he can say how he got it through the pavilion gate without turning sideways. But, alas, it needed but one long look in the mirror to convince me that Smiling Through was an occupation best left to the Irish.

Why, you may be asking, did I overlook that simplest of expedients still much favoured by young and old alike today. The scalded cat technique. The approach is made with the bat at the trail and the eyes modestly downcast. Then, as the first ripple of applause breaks out, the bat is brought swiftly to the under-the-arm position and the batsman streaks for the changing room like a different kind of bat out of you-know-where.

Be assured that the idea did not escape me, but it was stifled as the result of a lamentable incident in my very first season with the club. We were playing the MCC, I remember, and young Robertson, having collected a handsome 47 against our redoubtable opponents, made his exit from the field in a manner which clearly anticipated jet propulsion.

Now there are doubtless many clubs who can say with The Bard: 'We have our exits and our entrances.' We have but one which must needs serve both purposes. And young Robertson entered just as Col. Bagshawe, Indian Army, Rtd, exited, gallantly bearing tea for five in the direction of the pavilion enclosure . . . A speed limit was subsequently set on incoming batsmen, and never since have meringues appeared on the tea menu.

To retail every single one of the stratagems I considered and discarded would take far more space than the Editor is likely to allow me. And, anyway, it really doesn't matter now. Gone for ever are those nightmare Friday nights when I turned and tossed in my bed, frantically searching for some fresh way of avoiding the possibility of irretrievable disaster. Yes, in very truth, every age brings its compensations. Not that I shan't find myself wondering occasionally just what I should have done – had the necessity ever arisen.

MEN, CRICKET, AND THINGS

R.C. Robertson-Glasgow

The other evening a very dull man introduced to me another man, even duller, and began talking of the dullest subject in the world, the dullness of modern cricket.

> 'They were not deep nor eloquent;'
They were the sort of men in whose presence
> 'Wit shoots in vain his momentary fires;'
at whose fell approach
> 'Fancy's gilded clouds decay.'
[A reader: Why all this d——d poetry?
Myself: I can please myself about that.]
On and on they creaked with
> 'Nonsense precipitate, like running lead,
> Which slipped through cracks and zigzags of the head –'
Until at last a silence, like that silence

'where no man can be'
fell, mercifully.
A regular opiate of an evening.

· · · • · · ·

And there was another evening, in the bar-parlour of the Pelican and
Vixen; there were several of us, and round the walls there looked down on
the company Fred Archer, a few effete athletes immortalised by Spy, and
the Fire Brigade of the days when fire was extinguished by hand. From
the thickest corner came a voice, peremptory at first, then, when none
answered, pleading: 'Tike Tite,' it said: it was the voice of Mr Candle, of
whom the village said that his largest sentence, in fact his only sentence
with a subject and a finite verb, had been 'I do,' when the vicar asked
him if he would consent to love and cherish Mrs Candle: and even that
had been under pressure – the sentence, not the wedding. And now he
was asking us to 'tike Tite'. Most of us took nothing, but two others and
I took Tate, reluctantly. We took him up and down the pitch, from leg to
off, from off to leg, we took his action, his feet, his averages, his father,
in fact a considerable liberty with him. Personally, I was all for him,
and was, it seemed, carrying the majority, but then Mr Candle spoke
his second sentence, 'Tite's dead.' 'As a bowler?' I said, 'or in person?'
But Mr Candle was back again in iron taciturnity, and his third pint.

A good evening, very.

· · · • · · ·

£25's WORTH.
By DON KIPPMAN.
[Exclusive Article by Cable.]
This Week: THE FORWARD STROKE.

Now this is a stroke that no cricketer should be without: in fact, it
might be termed as an essential part of his repertoire. I myself have
used it a great deal, notably at The Oval, when compiling 221 not out,
at Adelaide, and in many minor matches. It should first be noted that
this stroke is most useful for parrying a ball that is too far up to play
with the back stroke, without risk of hearing the crash of timber – that
fateful moment in the batsman's career – and yet not far enough up to
meet on the full pitch. There are four distinct uses for this stroke: – (a)
Defensive stroke back to the bowler; (b) Scoring stroke between mid-on
and mid-off; (c) Scoring stroke between mid-off and point; (d) Scoring
stroke between mid-on and square-leg. The essential point for the pupil

to bear in mind is that the bat should be swung perpendicularly, as far as possible from leg-stump towards the bowler's left shoulder; the left foot – or, in the case of a left-handed batsman, the right foot – should be as far as possible moved simultaneously and in conjunction with the blade of the bat. Daylight should hardly be observable between the leg and the bat. Of course, care should be taken to time the ball correctly, as much labour can be wasted through smothering the ball, and considerable exasperation may arise through being so late that the ball is missed altogether. The pupil also should be on the alert against hitting his wickets on the back swing: this is usually occasioned by standing too close to them during the strike, or else taking guard too far inside the crease. During the winter months, and, indeed, during summer, if the weather is wet, much useful practice can be obtained by swinging the bat in a straight line up and down a pre-arranged mark on the floor or carpet.

Next Week. – ALAN PONSFAX ON THE BACK STROKE.

[P.S. – I have endeavoured, without success, to persuade Mr George Hickling to write on the Assyrian Snootch or Delayed Glide. – ED.]

• • • • • • •

There is no doubt about it. Fast-medium bowling, with an occasional fast one thrown in, – some of us still get away with a few shrewd throws – is mere folly. In a dry summer it is death to the feet and jars the joints; in an English summer, bowled from a quagmire on to a slough, it is a shocking waste of time. I shall, therefore, give it up. I advise others to follow my example. I shall go into a shed this winter and practise leg-breaks and googlies, and top-spinners, until my power of bias is such that the ball will erode holes from the matting, and a casual passer-by will fancy he hears the sound of a steam laundry. I shall strive to imitate Grimmett, the great master, and to that end will drink oceans of strong tea, cultivate a thin, bronzed look of unplumbed cunning, and drop my arm to half-mast. But where to find a shed? Where *do* these self-made bowlers, of which we natural geniuses read, go to ground? Into what deep, romantic chasm did D.W. Carr, for instance, descend as a mere novice, to re-emerge the terror of the Umbrian, the terror of Tom Hayward? I have a few sheds in my mind's eye, but they are always so otherwise occupied: with logs of wood, apples, or forgotten bicycles rejoicing in perennial deflation; then there is the drill-hall, but the Girl Guides have that on the days when there is no Badminton. No matter: my purpose cannot be deflected: I shall 'find out some uncouth cell'

and, passing the winter with these magic rites, shall next year once again bowl – fast-medium.

• • • • • • •

We moderns live in a whirl. Two days ago I received a letter from a clergyman to tell me that, in an article on the 'History of Bowling', written two years ago, I had perpetually confused J.C. Shaw with Alfred Shaw; yesterday I wrote back to him and said no doubt but their names, he must admit, were very alike. And to-day is the cricket concert: where the doctor's wife is to reward our best batsman (average 6.3) with a false smile and an Imperial Driver, whereas our best bowler (average 6.2) will get the same smile but a short-handled bat. A concert will follow for those who sing. Personally, I am taking the bass part in 'Oh, Who Will O'er the Downs So Free,' and must shortly get away to run it up and down. Hence the whirl.

• • • • • • •

The same spirit of inquiry which led Mr Pecksniff to speculate on Mrs Todgers' views about legs has led me to wonder how Nero would have played cricket. I fancy he would have had his mother out on cold evenings and given her a sharp fielding-practice, and, when she took a low drive on the shins, or a high dropper on the points of the fingers, he would have laughed immoderately. In a set match, say Nero and Senate Selected v. The Equestrian Order, he would have scored freely, and his entry and exit alike would have met with thunders of suborned applause. His fielding would have been negligible; as a bowler, he would have answered his own appeals in person. At the close of the season he would have caused to be published a sort of Royal Wisden, with the letter N engraved on it in gold; the five best cricketers of the year would have been Nero, playing forward, Nero playing back, Nero playing to leg, Nero playing to off, and, finally, Nero rewarding an umpire with an Eastern Province.

• • • • • • •

I have played a great deal of cricket this summer with my small cousin John, on the sand by the sounding sea. He told me at once, in the strictest confidence, that he had 'changed his action', and he wanted me to change mine. I told him that I was past those kinds of pleasantry. A wonderful boy, John. He is one of a select few who can bowl an in-swinger with a star-fish.

• • • • • • •

Whoever goes to Australia in 1932, we must, at all costs, 'tike Tite'.

SOME HUMOURS OF CRICKET

A. Quaife

'Humour in Cricket?' said my American cousin, as we sat together on the Mound Stand watching a rather protracted duel between Sandham and Durston, 'I should say not. I like cricket. It soothes me. But funny? No, sir.'

'You don't see a lot on big county grounds,' I admitted, 'but come and see a few games in club and village cricket, and if you understand the game and possess a vestige of the sense of humour, you'll get all the laughs you want. For instance – '

And I tried to picture to him that the humble club cricketer does not derive all his delight in our great summer game from just batting, bowling and fielding.

. . . .

Three summers ago I was playing in a village match upon a ground which, although excellent in all other respects, sloped or rather dropped off sharply over a brow behind cover. I was seeing the ball nicely, and smote a half volley hard in the direction of extra cover. The ball disappeared over the brow, and we ran two before it was thrown in by an invisible hand. The bowler had commenced his run for the next delivery, when the game was held up by the appearance of the local curate, toiling up the slope.

'Oh – er – er – ' he said mildly, 'I – er – caught that last ball, you know.' And he beamed gently upon us all. The fielding captain turned to his umpire like a flash. 'How *was* it, George?' 'Out,' said George, and I had to go. I was bemused, but not so my partner. He lay down on the pitch and roared with ill-time mirth. I laughed too, afterwards. But a long time afterwards.

Another central figure in a humorous cricket episode who did not see it at the time was the skipper of a rather famous club in the South. He was a sound fellow and a good cricketer, but a little inclined to do himself very well at lunch. One afternoon he was fielding – very badly – at second slip. Balls kept ticking off the edge of the bat straight at him, only to be placed carefully on the floor. First slip got annoyed, and at the next likely looking one being delivered from the bowler, edged over to second slip, and as the ball shot off the bat, gently shoved his skipper to one side. He miscalculated, however, and the ball coming like a bullet, smote the skipper fairly in the centre of the forehead, knocking him head over heels, and bouncing off. First slip, without taking the smallest sort of notice of the stricken man, calmly caught the ball as it bounced off his face, and politely asked the umpire how it was. The batsman went, and so did the skipper, to re-appear some half an hour later with an enormous egg-like growth between his eyes. For several matches after that he was observed to be most temperate, and fielded in the deep.

I was once cast for the role of 'fons et origo mali' in a similar regrettable affair. I was keeping wicket – a position to which I had been called by the absence of a real stumper on the side – for the Old Boys match against my old school. The batsman was a master, and one who had been at the school in my time. We both cordially disliked each other, even after many years had had a chance to make our hearts grow fond. This gentleman's first ball beat him, and I gathered it. I tossed it back to the bowler, when, my hand slipping, and he moving slightly, it hit him upon the back of his shining bald head and bounced into the air. He turned to me fiercely.

'What the —— ' he said with heat, as I gazed dumbly upon his catastrophe. And then the ball, which had arisen off his head perfectly straight up into the air, returned in accordance with the laws of gravity, and cracked him sharply on the same place. It was too much for me, and the laws of gravity were suspended so far as I was concerned for a space. Of course I apologised humbly, but I have always been too busy to play in the Old Boys matches held since.

Some situations, of course, are humorous only to the onlooker. Under this category comes the episode of the two teams which visited each other – on the same Saturday afternoon. The secretaries had omitted to send the usual card at the beginning of the week, and the fixture card of one of the teams being misprinted, the home team sallied gaily off in a charabanc to visit the visitors. They actually passed each other on the way, without taking it in. Their feelings when the grisly truth dawned upon them I am unable to describe.

We had a skipper once, a studious sort of chap, and very keen. He read in an article by one of the 'game-going-to-dogs-sir' school that the true late cut is in these decadent days practically 'non est'. He took this quite seriously, and being tall above the average, and quick on his feet, set out to disprove the statement. It happened that we shortly after played a club who groaned (or ought to have) in the possession of a wicket-keeper, a fussy little brute about five feet high, who talked incessantly throughout the game. Two of our best bats had been 'talked out', and the skipper went in. The keeper was standing up to medium-paced bowling, and the bowler sent down a ball well off the off stump, and short. Our scientific captain waited with bat raised until the ball had passed his wicket, and the keeper moved to take it. Then, like avenging sword, the bat descended, caught the wretched keeper beside the head, and nearly cut him for four. The captain, who had not observed him in his concentration on the ball, was both surprised and annoyed.

'Damn you, sir,' said he, 'why can't you get out of the way?' And then the opposing umpire (village cricketers will understand me when I speak of 'opposing umpires') gave him out, without being asked, for obstruction. He always hooks short balls on the off now, especially when the wicket-keeper is short, too . . .

Sandham's bails shot up in a little explosion, and the batsman turned briskly to the pavilion, stripping his gloves. A ripple of applause ran round the sunlit stands, and deep mid-on sank gently on the grass below us.

'Um-y-e-es,' said my American cousin, politely, 'very funny.' He mused awhile, and then turned to me, the light of discovery in his eye.

'That parson fellah, now?' said he, 'I guess he never caught that goldarned ball at all, eh?'

THE AUTOCRAT OF THE CRICKET FIELD

A.S. Gardiner

No, this is not about Grace. It is about Traddles. Traddles has only lately brought his cricket season to an end. I am not quite sure why we called him Traddles, for he in no way resembles Dickens's genial creation, but Traddles he has always been, and the high-sounding name by which he will be known in after life is at present almost forgotten. From the statement that he recently finished the season it will be gathered that Traddles is an enthusiast at cricket. He is. When other players are thinking of putting their bats away for the winter, he is as keen as ever, showing no sign of the exhaustion which a long season is supposed to produce, and determined (with the reluctant assistance of his brothers and sisters) to go on pitching the wicket until rain finally puts the game out of the question. Despite his enthusiasm, however, he has not yet attained first-class county form. As a matter of fact, he is in his fifth year.

We have to play cricket under somewhat serious disadvantages. Our ground is a plot of grass at the back of the house, and, not only are the boundaries inconveniently narrow – rendering a toilsome journey over

the fences a frequent necessity – but some of the best strokes are spoiled
by the contiguity of fruit trees. However, the conditions are quite good
enough for Traddles, and whenever the opportunity arises he pounces
upon me and drags me off to the scene of operations. Sometimes we put
up the stumps; occasionally a wine case serves in their place. It is quite a
matter of indifference to him.

Traddles's methods and rules are somewhat arbitrary. He always
insists, for instance, that he is entitled to first innings, and usually
gets it. But it is when he actually starts batting that his superiority
over all laws and regulations becomes fully apparent. I am confident
that he knows nothing about the accomplished 'leg-play' which has
become a part of modern first-class cricket, but the genius of the
game is upon him, and he sturdily maintains his right to stand in
front of the wicket. His style of batting, too, is a never-ending source
of bitterness to the souls of his twin brothers, who are seasoned veterans
of nine.

Our procedure is generally something like this: I take up my position,
as bowler, at a spot indicated by Traddles, and regarded by him as the
most convenient for his own purposes. He holds the bat, with the fore-
finger of his right hand down the blade and his left hand hopelessly out
of place. 'Hayward' and 'Hobbs' – his brothers – put his hands right, and
try to enforce the necessity of keeping the left elbow well advanced. A
smile of contentment passes over the curl-framed face of Traddles, and
we make a start. I send the ball down slowly, and directly the young
rascal catches sight of it he throws all the principles of the game to the
winds, and prepares for a mighty 'slog'. If he misses the ball his legs are
conveniently in the way, so that the chances of bowling him are rather
unfairly reduced.

Nor is it easy to run him out. It is quite true he will start for the smallest
hit, but, as he decides when his run is completed, and that is always
just before the wicket is put down, he incurs no risks. Occasionally,
he astonishes himself so thoroughly by a particularly slashing hit that,
in following the course of the ball in silent admiration, he forgets to
run. When he recovers from his surprise, however, and appreciates the
situation, he calmly adds two or three to his total. We have never yet
unravelled the mysteries of his method of reckoning, but there can be
no doubt about its effectiveness, for his score rises with a rapidity that
would excite the envy of even Jessop.

It will be understood that it is not an easy thing to get rid of Traddles,
but nobody who has never had to bowl to him can quite understand

how difficult it is. Perhaps you catch him out. He drops the bat between his knees, claps his hands in the most generous fashion, calls out 'Well catched, sir,' and coolly takes up his position to play the ball again. Or, by a lucky chance, you clean bowl him. Even then he is not out. He emphatically decides that it was a trial ball, and that he is entitled to continue his innings. And so he goes on serenely pulling balls from the off-side to long-on. It should be added that he claims a privilege not usually granted in cricket; he lays down a strict rule as to the kind of bowling he is to receive, and trouble follows if a departure be made from this rule. A well-pitched ball is not adapted to his style of batting, and even a 'long-hop' is easily missed when one swings the bat round. Having discovered all this by experience, Traddles commands the delivery of 'grubs', which, as everybody knows, it is not difficult to sweep to the on.

All things, however, must come to an end at some time, and even Traddles's innings has eventually to be closed. Now and then he retires with a good grace, but occasionally he protests indignantly against the injustice that is being done when he is requested to leave after having been caught or bowled five or six times, and, when 'Hayward' or 'Hobbs' takes the bat, he throws himself at full length in the middle of the pitch. I explain to him that I intend to bowl my patent 'slow twists' to his successors, and that it will soon be his turn to bat again, but it is only after vast persuasion that he consents to let the game proceed. No, it is not an easy thing to dispose of Traddles as a batsman.

Like many other cricketers, he has a soul above fielding, and persistently declines to take an active interest in it. He spends the greater part of the time between his innings in the consumption of sweets and apples, but sometimes we seduce him from these delights of childhood, as being beneath the dignity of a cricketer, and it is the pleasantest part of our game to see him pursuing the ball – his little slippered feet toiling one over the other, and his curly head wagging from side to side. I am doubtful whether Traddles will ever become a batsman. He is too impetuous, and his defence is deplorably weak. On the other hand, he possesses a qualification which I have observed distinguishes most eminent cricketers, and that is a ready resource in discovering excuses for his own failure. In any case, I am quite sure that, whatever the future may have in store for me, it can bring no greater delight than I experience in bowling to Traddles.

TYPES OF AGGRAVATING CRICKETER

By the Author of Leaves from the Diary of an Old Free Forester

Most stories have a sequel, and to most full-figured cricketers arrives a period when the old bat is hung up, the old flannels put away – washed, too, beforehand, we will hope, by way of a new sensation – and the old bag, pads, gloves, and other paraphernalia distributed among the rising generation. Unfortunately in this particular case the veteran retained the feeling that the glory of having bowled out a belted earl had given him a distinct status in society. And so it came to pass that in an evil moment, while watching a match in which two of his sons were batting, he clapped a hot hand on the flannelled shoulder of a gentleman, who, having finished his own innings, was taking his ease in the pavilion.

'How's yourself, captain, and which of my two lads made that hit?'

He had selected his man badly. For the somewhat short-tempered individual thus suddenly addressed happened to have, beyond any other man of my acquaintance, an instinctive dislike to undergoing the process of being 'pawed'; furthermore, the enviable knack of saying, when wrathfully inclined, of intuition, and on the spur of the moment, the thing best calculated to annoy the person who had unnecessarily, though at the same time it may chance to be also unintentionally, annoyed him.

'Do you mind taking your hand off my shoulder? And if you want to know the score you had better ask the scorer. I don't know which hit it. At least, I don't know his name, but it was the dirtiest one of the two.'

And so the mystery remained unsolved.

If it has been my habit to regard individuals of the types already mentioned in previous chapters as the principal villains in that over-lengthy piece, my cricket career, I am afraid that it must not be supposed that among such alone have I ere now found fitting objects of wrathfulness. There are minor characters in every drama, in pretty well every cricket match some individual that will act as a petty irritant. The man who borrows my bat, for instance – how often have I wished that he had never been born. Let me begin by explaining that I am making no allusion whatever to the victim of an accident, the man, shall we say, who has been unfortunate enough to break the one or two bats that he may happen to have in his bag, or, again, through his own or a porter's carelessness, to lose his bag on a journey. Such a man, if I chance to know him, is welcome to the run of my bag. But the man I have in my eye for condemnation is the habitual bat-borrower, who never by any chance possesses a bat of his own, but arrives on the scene of action prepared to trade upon his neighbour's good nature.

> 'One man in his time plays many parts
> His Acts being seven ages.'

I am not in any way interested in the bat-borrower's earlier career, whether as 'mewling infant' or 'whining schoolboy', but here, briefly, are the five Acts which he plays in my presence.

1st. He roams round the pavilion, examines every cricket-bag in turn, pulls out a bat here and there, looks at the maker's name, does his level best to break the two or three that seem to take his fancy by weighing heavily on the handle and then executing a series of imaginary and idiotic strokes.

2nd. He finally selects one of mine, and having so done, proceeds to hurt both the bat's feelings and my own by calling that which is a much-prized friend, and an exceptionally good piece of wood, an 'old stick'.

'This don't look a bad old stick. A bit wobbly in the handle, but I think it will do for me.'

3rd. Having practically stolen and done his best to damage my property, he comes up to me and by way of establishing right of possession, announces his intention of using it.

'I say, old chap, I am going to try this old article of yours. You don't mind? It don't look up to much, but perhaps it will carry through all right.'

4th. He then proceeds to the wicket, and having mis-hit three balls and edged four more, he invites the sympathy of the field, who crowd round him and examine my bat as if it were either a dynamite bomb or a Japanese toy.

5th. By the mercy of Providence he is clean bowled, whereupon he walks out, informing deep cover-point in a voice clearly intended to reach my ears that 'a fellow can't be expected to play cricket with a lump of lead', enters the pavilion, takes no notice whatever of myself, but throws the bat down in a corner.

The final stages of such a man's career must be left to the reader's imagination. As a matter of fact, I seldom read the 'Police Reports' in my newspaper.

In the matter of cricket-bats the advice of Polonius should be rigidly followed.

'Neither a borrower nor a lender be
For loan oft loses both itself and friend.'

There are still left many minor offenders, who have been temporarily assigned to my black list, before being finally received into favour again. These must be dealt with seriatim and briefly, though not perhaps in strict order of merit.

With the man who runs me out, whether owing to my own slothfulness or inadvertence, or even when I travel at best speed in compliance with a not very discreet call, I have no quarrel of any kind whatsoever. There have not been wanting occasions when I have even preferred to be run out; for instance, when I have gone in last, when quite enough runs have been got, when there have lain before me the alternatives of being 'not out', 'run out 0', or even 'bowled 0'. For I count the possession of a possible ground for being aggrieved quite as possible as a single figure score where the issue of a match is not affected. Even with the partner whose habit it is never to call for a short run until he is absolutely sure that he can get home himself, I have seldom let the sun go down upon my wrath. For half an hour or so perhaps I may have been inclined to think that he ought to be put in a glass case, labelled 'selfish pig', and despatched to Erebus, but a little reflection has reminded me that I probably have been guilty in my time of the same offence.

But I have drawn the line very strongly at being run out by a partner because he neglects to articulate properly, and swallows an essential part of the King's English. The man, I mean, who, using three calls: 'Yes,' 'No,' 'Not yet,' proceeds to enunciate the last with a view to his own edification, instead of my instruction. Where 'No' is quite a clear prohibition, 'Not yet' sounds far too much like an invitation to come. Twice, on both occasions, too, when I fancied myself well set, I have been run out in this most aggravating way. Once the caller apologised to me afterwards.

'I forgot you were a bit deaf, old chap. I'll shout louder next time.'

But the other man, though I really had not posed as an aggrieved party, came up to me at the conclusion of an innings in which he had only just failed to carry his bat, and took me to task, curiously enough following the same line of defence as his predecessor in iniquity had adopted:

'What on the face of the earth made you come tearing up the pitch like that?'

'Because you called me.'

'Called you? I told you to wait. I said: 'Not yet!' quite distinctly. You're not stone deaf, are you?'

And just then the captain of the other side, an old ally, apt on occasion to be more plain-spoken than polite, and ungifted to a singular extent with the capacity of suffering fools gladly, put in his oar.

'Pity he wasn't! I am not stone deaf myself. But I was fielding mid-off and I could have sworn that you said "Yes," and I believe you did.'

The man who monopolises the bowling. Most of us have been accused of doing that in our time, but—

'Why do married men live longer than single?' I was once asked. I gave it up. 'They don't really, but it seems longer.'

Similarly only the very selfish cricketer wilfully monopolises the bowling in reality – excepted always those occasions when it is to the interest of the side that he should so do; but the batsman who flatters himself that he is in good form and then hardly seems to get a ball at all, is prone to wax impatient. Especially and justly impatient when time is a consideration, and the man in possession insists on playing back to half volleys. It rankles in my mind today that many years ago, on a ground where, for some extraordinary reason, the boundary hit counts three, I watched my partner play back to the last four balls of a match which two boundary hits would have won.

My own feeling about cricket is that it should be a comparatively silent game, and that conversation, at all events between two batsmen, can be conveniently reserved till they meet in the pavilion. This, no matter what form the conversation takes beyond the requisite calls about a run. I quite recognise that I am hopelessly behind the age, because in a Test match – which is, I believe, to be regarded as a rather exalted type of cricket – I have noticed that the batsmen have quite a lot to say to each other, and manage to kill quite a perceptible amount of time while they are talking. But as three-day matches are altogether beyond my standard, and as time is very precious in my sight, I neither relish being questioned in the course of an innings concerning the health of an aunt by marriage, nor do I care to be told that I have outraged the feelings either of the bowler or my partner by hitting a ball which ought to have been played.

'Do you know as that there ball would have bowled your middle stump right out of the ground?' inquired a very celebrated professional – I have heard him called Julia – who was evidently under the impression that I squinted.

'That is why I hit it.'

And the answer, delivered, in all innocence, quite put him off.

'Well, I never did!' he exclaimed, and with that he returned to his own end, and promptly got out himself.

'Hold your peace, sir!' said the Duke in *Old Mortality*, 'and keep your ain breath to cool your ain porridge. Ye'll find them scalding hot, I promise you!'

I can still see the expression of horror on poor 'Julia's' face as he walked back to his wicket, doubtless writing me down in his own mind as a wholly impossible fool, an opinion quite possibly shared with a young Harrovian, who had presented me with a wholly impossible conundrum two or three years before.

'Would you mind telling me,' inquired the wearer of a very hideous if serviceable straw hat, 'what I ought to have done with that ball of yours that bowled me?'

'Hit it out of the ground,' I replied, having not the remotest conception what manner of ball it was, but certain that if it had been hit out of the ground it would not have bowled him.

IMAGINARY INTERVIEWS: SECOND ROUND

'Henry'

1. – Mr F.T. Mann.
The large-bodied but beautifully proportioned Old Malvernian, Pembrokian, Cambridgian, was reclining on one of the ample seats of Lord's Pavilion, watching Harry White, the head groundsman, putting his staff through weed and worm-drill. 'May I ask you a question, Mr Mann?' I said. 'Certainly,' came the reply. 'Then will you kindly tell me whether you are going to retain the Championship this season?' 'Without a doubt,' replied Frank M., 'and for the following, amongst other reasons: Jack Hearne is his old self, Durston will be better than ever, Patsy Hendren has got all his confidence back, Nigel Haig will be great, and I hope to pop one clean over the pavilion or break the doggo record, whichever is the more necessary.' 'Thank you very much, sir,' I replied, 'but I have seen Mr Tennyson, Mr Calthorpe, and Mr Fender; they all expect to roll up on top, and I've little doubt that Messrs Geoffrey Wilson, Miles Kenyon, Carr, and John Daniell,

plus the rest, say precisely the same thing.' The old Light Blue Rugger forward smiled indulgently. 'Our reserves are large,' he said, and waved an ample hand. 'Yes,' I replied, 'I have heard of J.T. Hearne, Tarrant, Trott, and a few more. I know you have a wide area of selection.' 'Don't be silly,' remarked the ex-officer of the Brigade of Guards, 'they were all duly qualified.' 'Yes, we won't argue,' I replied, 'and in any event you're a fine sporting side, and I can only express the hope that the best team will win the Championship.'

•   •   •   •   •   •

2. – Mr J.W.H.T. Douglas.

Still cheerfully humming a tune – 'A Life on the Ocean Wave' – to the words of 'Johnny Won't Hit To-Day' – I entered the office of the great Old Felstedian, Amateur Middle-Weight Boxing ex-Champion, and England cricket and Association football player. 'May I respectfully be allowed to congratulate you, sir, on, firstly, the great part you have played in English sport, and, secondly, your doggedness in times of crisis?' 'Certainly,' replied J.W.H.T.D., 'and what's the damage?' 'Nothing,' I replied, 'but if England possessed some tens of thousands more of your kidney we should hear less from the clowns and half-wits who call us a C3 nation.' 'That's good of you,' said Johnny, 'but we do our best.' 'Being a Boy Scout Cub myself,' I replied, 'I am more than pleased to meet yer.'

   'How dare you call me a cub, you bear!' shouted Mr Douglas. 'Pity a poor blind man,' I wailed. 'Yes,' said he, 'I thought you were.' Rapidly disguising myself as the Rev. F.H. Gillingham, and making noises like Felsted School chapel bell, I managed to pacify him, and then, assuming my best Mormon manner, I said, 'Do you know, brother, what should be your favourite hymn?' 'No,' Douglas replied, all agrog – agog. 'Rock of Ages,' I answered, and left him to think it out.

•   •   •   •   •   •

3. – Mr A.E.R. Gilligan.

Having read in my *Daily Mail* last season, under the signature of a distinguished critic, that Mr Arthur Gilligan was the second long loose-limbed member of a famous long loose-limbed brotherhood of cricketers, it came as a considerable shock to me to find that he was only of medium height and extremely squarely built. Something was obviously wrong somewhere. 'I beg your pardon, sir,' I said, 'but surely I am addressing Mr A.E.R. Gilligan, of Dulwich, S.E.; Pembroke College, Cambridge; Cambridge University, Surrey, Sussex, and a one-time gymnast of merit, not to mention an erstwhile

Rugger Blue, or, very nearly, plus a dash of hockey in your old age?'

'Yes, my name's Gilligan all right,' replied the newly-appointed Sussex skipper, his blue eyes dancing and fair-hair waving in the balmy Brighton breeze. 'Then why aren't you long and loose-limbed, as stated by the distinguished critic of the *Daily Mail*?' I queried. 'He must have mixed me up with my little brother, A.H.H., who is inordinately long and reasonably loose-limbed for one so tall,' he remarked. 'Frank, my elder brother, who's married, is loosishly limbed, but not frightfully long,' he went on, 'so I cannot quite understand it.' 'Look at this,' I said, and produced my last season's *Mail*. There it was: 'A.E.R. Gilligan, the long loose-limbed member of . . .' 'Do you think he confused me with the Rev. F.H. Gillingham, who is long, but not very loose-limbed nowadays?' he ventured. 'I cannot say,' I replied, 'but it doesn't matter very much, if indeed at all, as the phrase has a sweet timbre.' And while we stood thus ruminating, o'er Mr Gilligan's face there broke a long loose-limbed smile.

· · · · · ·

4. – Mr Tom Webster.

Having temporarily renounced cricket, I had signed an important contract with the management of Ciro's, and was spending my customary evening at that famous rendezvous when who should seat himself at my table but Tom Webster, the famous sporting cartoonist. 'Bring me a devilled kidney and a small whisky and soda,' said the great wit and friend of Messrs Harry Preston and Jack Dempsey, and with alacrity I obeyed his behest.

'May I ask you a question, sir?' I ventured. 'Certainly,' was the ready answer, and his eyes shone with merriment under their extremely long and fair lashes. 'It's this way sir; you are always pulling people's legs in the *Daily Mail* – poor old Inman, for example. Would it amuse you to have yours pulled a bit?' 'I shouldn't care a Cochran or a cocktail either way,' he replied, laughing. 'May I suggest an Inman or an onion?' I countered. 'What about a Hayward or a haddock?' said he, entering into the spirit of the thing, and when I told him he'd won with a 'Fry or fried fish,' we were on the best possible terms. Momentarily forgetting my resolve to try and pull his leg, I asked, 'I expect, sir, you get hundreds of invitations to attend dinner and things in the hope that you will draw their ugly mugs – portraits?' I corrected.

Mr Webster nodded his fair, round head, and produce from the pocket of his elegantly cut dinner jacket a bundle of correspondence, the top letter of which read, 'From Wapping St. Giles Bowling Club'. I did not pursue the subject further. Suddenly the lights were dimmed, and in the centre of the dancing floor – cleared as by magic – appeared a sweet young lady and her partner. To a lilting strain they danced, perfect in time and rhythm. Up went the lights once more; I turned to Mr Webster – his seat was vacant. He had stolen away – and I had not pulled his leg. On his plate I found a note. I opened it and read 'Dear Waiter, – I have not left you a money tip, as I think this one will pay you better. If you are dealing with Tom Webster, the artist, or the horse of the same name, owner by Melbourne Inman, take my tip and – leave them alone.' I felt so ill that I must, I fear, have given a good imitation of Tishy, as drawn by T.W.

A DAY IN THE LIFE . . .

Peter Edwards, Secretary/General Manager, Essex CCC

All match days have one thing in common. You will go home with a headache. Let me take you through a typical day.

I aim to arrive at the ground by 8 a.m. and by that time a number of the staff will have been working for an hour or more. When I get to my reserved parking spot (one of the few privileges of the County Secretary) there is a member awaiting my arrival. He may be anxious to inquire after my health or to pass some urgent message to me. But, more likely, he will want to complain. And there is more than a good chance that his complaint will have nothing to do with my area of responsibility. It may be: (a) Why did Fletcher declare against Middlesex and lose by two wickets? (b) Why isn't Alan Lilley in the side? (c) Did I know that beer was 2p per pint cheaper at Bristol, Chesterfield and Southampton? (d) Why won't the BBC put the scores out at 1.45 on Saturday afternoons?

No, none of these today. He wants to know why he couldn't get his car into the car park at Worcester last Sunday. Ten minutes later, following a promise to telephone Worcester and to instigate reciprocal measures against any visiting supporters from the Midlands for the rest of the season, you escape to your office where your first cup of coffee of the day has got cold.

Then, in no particular order, things get worse. Any one of a number of problems will emerge, often in multiples of three or more.

(a) At least two stewards will telephone in to say they are sick. On a really bad day they go sick without telephoning in.

(b) The overnight ground clearance work has not been done and the whole ground looks like Southend beach after a Bank Holiday Monday.

(c) The rain has got under the covers.

(d) The captain is worried about the weather and has already been on the telephone. (That is if he has not already been on the 'phone at home earlier.)

(e) The cleaner hasn't cleaned the dressing rooms, Pavilion, Executive Suite or worse still, the Committee Room. And her car has broken down – again.

(f) Yesterday's umpires have returned to Somerset (all umpires come from Somerset) with the key to the umpires' room.

(g) There are no clean towels for the players.

(h) Someone has banked all the gatemen's floats.

With a little bit of luck

By 9 a.m. most of the initial problems have been solved and with a little luck the gates will be open and the car park manned. There is then time to have a few words with the catering manager (which gives a lie to the impression that he and I have never met!) and then one will be ready to greet the umpires and to listen to their tales of harsh treatment everywhere else. More coffee will be needed to settle their nerves while they examine the match balls, fill in their expense claim forms and tell you that cricket is not what it was when they played.

Nearer to 10 o'clock I have to welcome the visiting captain. This is hazardous business because unless you have been reading the papers you may not know who the visiting captain is or, worse still, you may approach the person who was the visiting captain last time you did read the papers.

Next comes the weather discussion with our captain. Am I sure that it will rain at 4 o'clock? Have I checked with all the local pundits? In fact, anyone who has rung the County Ground on the morning of a match will be asked what the weather is doing where they are ringing from so that we build up a complete meteorological survey of the whole South of England. All this is a complete waste of time because at a team meeting yesterday it had been decided that if we win the toss we will bat.

Now is the time for the big game. It is called 'getting the teams'. Neither captain will reveal his team in case either I or the girl who produces the scorecard reveal the information to the other captain.

Eventually you spot the captains throwing money around on the pitch so the assumption is that they now know who is playing but they seem keen to keep this information from the rest of us. I have to take my life in my hands to find out as neither captain returns to the Pavilion. One goes to continue practising slip catches and the other goes jogging around the ground.

In between a leaping Fletcher and Gooch I discover that 'Ackers' is out and 'Ponty' is in and that I can put them down to bat in any order I like. To get the visiting team I have to do two laps of the ground with the visiting captain. He says that the team is the same as played at Headingley yesterday except that 'Blue eyes' is in for 'Swinger' and 'Bedsocks' for 'Sleepy'. Now unless you have yesterday's paper or you are intimately familiar with the internal affairs of the visiting side this information is unlikely to solve your immediate problem. Eventually, after a further lap, you get a hazy idea of who will play, who has won the toss and who will bat.

You breathlessly return to the office, past a queue of grumbling members complaining about the lateness of the scorecards again, say a prayer that today will not be the day when the great god Gestetner decides to withdraw his patronage and, with a little luck, the scorecards will shortly be in the hands of the needy.

How did the game go, dear?
Thereafter the day runs smoothly. There will, of course, be the sponsor who is unhappy because our opening batsmen never seem to hit the balls into his advertising board. The players will inquire about lunch so that they can complain in advance. Also the players will be telling me that both the AA and I had better check our maps as the mileage to Birmingham was more than we think it is (how can the speedo on his Japanese sponsored car lie?). We shall issue the TCCB stipulated number of complimentary tickets to several different visiting players; children will lose their dads; wives will ring up with urgent messages for their husbands. Hopefully the dads and husbands are in the bar where they can't hear the public address system and are helping to swell the club profits.

After the day's play an hour or so is spent explaining cricket in a sponsor's box and when you get home at nine o'clock your wife will ask how the game went. You advise her to read the paper in the morning and then to let you know – you certainly won't have seen much of it.

NETS

R.C. Robertson-Glasgow

'On Monday last, with rain threatening, and the wind in the East – that Jarndyce v. Jarndyce feeling – I, the greater wading bird, led down my young wadelings to their baptism, some flapping their callow wings with eager and lively hope, some quacking faint but disregarded protest. For twenty minutes we swam about, then came the rain once more, and evening, and soon

> Universal darkness buried all.

And that, my boy, was our first day's practice at the nets.'

Thus, some weeks ago, with aquatic and ornithological metaphor, hitting his favourite quotations a customary crack *en passant*, wrote my old friend S—, who, after preliminary skirmishes, has year by year sent forth his juvenile troops to do battle on the green fields, in sun, hail, rain, wind; the left legs drilled to coverpoint, the insidious binocular stance exorcised with tempered abuse, the right foot, that strays too easily to square-leg, goaded into orthodoxy, every move in the field attempted, practised, repractised, bungled, ameliorated, almost perfected – the swift return with flick of wrist, the high swerving ballooner, the cruel kick of the 'half-half-volley' to ankles, till their

> 'Young skins became as leather, –'

And so he writes, in that study well-remembered, surrounded by the flannelled gladiators of his golden age, Sam Woods, Lionel Palairet, the great Doctor towering in bearded majesty – he always favours the heroes of the West – to tell me that he is doing it all over again, cursing the gathering momentum of youthful degeneracy, the soft hands, the dense heads, the all-too-tardy feet, telling me by letter what he once told me so unerringly by verbal precept, anxiously awaiting the first match, yet calm when its inevitable failures come, a noble workman in a noble craft.

• • • • • •

In those days the best net to be in was D—'s; for some years there was a hole, by tradition unrepaired, about three yards from the ground, little more than the size of a cricket-ball, in the line of extra-cover: to put a drive through it was the Mecca of D—'s pupils: for several reasons; æsthetically it was a greater triumph than finding a dedans guarded by Peter Latham at Tennis, so small and strait was that hole, and therefore called by some, irreverently I fear, the 'path to heaven': then, the ball, once through the celestial aperture, came to rest either among sweet-peas, which suitably enraged the gardener, or amid the raspberries, which rewarded the finder: again, it irritated D—, to whom any stroke that lifted the ball an inch, was according to the height of the parabola, a bad stroke.

Good Spartan D—! Long-suffering mentor! Stern and inflexible purist! None after you has so plumbed the *foundations* of the game, for ever crying out on the misdirected toe, curtly praising some stray freak of brilliance, never bowling till the bat was raised over the leg-stump, gazing resignedly through short-sighed glasses at your pupil, who scours the red-lipped fruitage for the erring ball, who feebly feigns victory in the search,

iam iam prensans

yet another raspberry, with the ball long since in his right trouser-pocket!

Behind D—'s net, a long carry for a boy, was a bank topped with pines, and beyond them – oh bliss! – the roof of the school laundry, on to which sometimes, on red-letter mornings, a young Thornton would crash the guileful delivery of D—, and scarcely suppress his shout of triumph as the slates rattled to the earth. One boy there was, everafter to me, though he now renounces such trumpery with elderly disdain, whom I watched hit three consecutive rockets, two from boys, the last from D— in person, on to that roof, high over the trees against the blue, and D—, almost angry, yet inwardly, I fancy, not wholly displeased, said 'dash it boy, dash it, fetch those balls, and don't *grin*, confound you!' Yes, he may renounce it, tinsel of infancy, but I can hear the death-rumble of those slates to-day.

At Greyfriars we were not popularly supposed to be skilful at cricket. That is as may be. But it was not for lack of practice. L—n, noble sward, was netted more accurately than the codfish on the Dogger Bank, and, in the halcyon days, we could burst forth from the sweat of Danish Steelyards and the prison of paradigms to the field where C—, an old professional of immemorial cunning, sparing yet accurate and benevolent in precept, was waiting with an inexhaustible supply of off-breaks pitched to a length: he bowled them without emotion, deviation or strain, a source of joy and wonder to the unspoilt eye of boyhood; and if he were not obtainable, what matter? Perish the cant which denies value to untutored play! Bradman picked up what passed for a bat, and, unseen of the critical and corrective coach, blossomed into the wonder of the modern world. A coach can guide, but never give: the supple wrist, the intuitive eye, the rhythmic abandon of stroke, these are the gifts of nature, not the learning of man: and if those untutored nets at Greyfriars were not always wholly serious, if, after half-an-hour, the time for experiment set in – monstrous swerves, unearthly googlies, late cuts off half-volleys of a Macartneyesque frivolity, what would you of four boys whose combined ages were scarce more than that of Wilfred Rhodes when he helped England to win back the Ashes and her sliding fame at the Oval in 1926?

Then, in two or three swift-gliding years, came the nets on Green: most beautiful of grounds, with the Hindhead hills in the distance, a glory of varying blue, and M—, true Yorkshireman, bowling away the sunny hours, and with him, the silent G—, left-handed machine, who spun them from leg with horny fingers even on that smooth dureness, and loved to pitch them where the guy-ropes cast a shadow, dire whim that recalls the figure of honest Lumpy seeking out a fair downhill trend for his shooters on the slopes of Broadhalfpenny Down.

Lastly, the nets at Oxford, in the Parks: over the High, past the Bodleian, into which there passes a bent old scholar in cap and gown, burdened with books, loving learning more than the sun: a river-party emerges into the light with cushions and laughter and cheering flagons: the smell of the trees in Parks Road, and soon the urchins at cricket under the trees, irrelevant perambulators, and Tom Hayward, reluctantly retrieving coups-de-vache from the longer and the wetter grass.

LADIES AND LORD'S:
HINTS ON WATCHING CRICKET

By E.V. Lucas

Beginning with dress, let me say that cricket matches should be attended only in your best clothes. The larger the hat, the better, because by impeding the view of the person behind you it will make him concentrate with more thoroughness on the game – and concentration is good.

If there is any sun, put up a parasol.

Remember, even at a cricket match nothing is more important to you than your health; and it is generally agreed by the medical profession that walking, being one of the best forms of exercise, is a promoter of health without a rival. Riding, of course, is good, but riding is elaborate: it means a horse, equipment, a groom, and the right conditions. Walking requires no preparation, and it can be done everywhere, but perhaps nowhere so suitably as at a cricket match. Such contests as those between Oxford and

Cambridge, and Eton and Harrow, afford perfect opportunities, for you can then enjoy both the pleasure of walking and the rapture of attracting attention. But for this steady locomotion while play is in progress many of your friends might miss you.

Waiting for the over to end before leaving one's seat has been recommended by certain cricket enthusiasts, but they are chiefly men; and you know what men are. Besides, you have your health to consider, and this is best served by obeying the impulse and walking whenever the mood takes you. Some of the most noticeable women at Lord's are hardly ever in their seats at all.

Don't be deterred by the knowledge that a great many toes have to be stepped on or stepped over. The best exercise comes from rough walking. When tired of moving about, there is no harm in stopping to talk to an acquaintance; but be careful to stand while doing so, for in this way you may spare a keen partisan the pain of seeing one of his side bowled or caught.

As to subjects of conversation, while it is permissible to ask now and then, 'Is Eton still in?' or 'Why don't the umpires ever bat?' the staple should be something that has no reference to the game whatever, for there is no doubt that too much cricket shop is talked. Hats are an excellent theme. Dress of all kinds is sound. Prospects for the summer holiday; recent luck at cards; new plays and other people's follies should not be neglected. But perhaps the best form of conversation consists in identifying friends, acquaintances, and even foes, as they pass, and retailing personal information about each. The louder the voice the better, because then others can hear too and have their minds distracted from the monotony of batting, bowling, and fielding.

CRICKET IN THE CAUCASUS
or
THE VOLGA BATMEN
(Translated from the Russian)

A.P. Herbert

'I tell you what it is, Andrey Andreyevitch,' said Stepan Pepushkin impatiently, 'if the cricket competition does not soon begin it will be dark before it is finished. And then, you know, we shall be hampered by the wolves.'

'What is the hurry?' replied the old man, chewing grass. 'I am too drunk to umpire yet. Natalya Popova cannot find the bats. And, besides, the young men have not yet settled the dispute about the teams.'

'Sometimes,' replied the other passionately, 'I think I see the stars in your old eyes, Andrey Andreyevitch; and sometimes I do not understand you.'

Stepan Pepushkin was a poet. He wore a peaked cap and black knickerbockers. He was eager for the new game, which would bring back poetry to the village, the Commissar had said. 'How can there be a dispute among brothers?' he cried.

'Well, you see, it is perfectly simple,' said the old umpire. 'I think I can stand now. I will get up. What a disgusting creature I am to be drunk on Wednesday! And Olga Merinin says the harvest will be late. What was I saying, Stepan Stepanovitch?'

'You were raving quietly,' replied the young man. 'There is Natalya, carrying the two bats like torches over her shoulders. How beautiful she is!'

'The young men are quarrelling. Boris Borisovitch has emptied the whitewash pail over Lopakhin; and now we shall have no crease. But all this is highly intelligible when you come to think of it.'

'If I were to kill Maria Andreyevna,' said the poet dreamily, 'would you marry again?'

'Excuse me, the trouble is that our village has been collectivised under the Decree. Everything is in common. We are all in common. We are all brothers. Naturally, therefore, say the young men, we cannot have two teams of brothers playing against each other, for there can be nothing brotherly in trying to get the better of one another. But the Commissar has a paper from Moscow. He says there must be two teams of eleven, each with a captain; but the young men will not have captains. It is all rather unpleasant. I think I shall lie down again.'

'Eleven is a beautiful number,' said the poet. 'Two ones. Two ones – two captains – two bats of forest wood. Some day, Andrey Andreyevitch, I shall go to London where this beautiful game was thought of.'

But the old man was asleep.

Stepan Pepushkin walked over to the debate of the young men. He went straight up to Natalya Popova and kissed her. 'Will you marry me?' he said loudly, because of the noise of the speakers, many of whom were talking in common. She had very brown eyes, like a small cow in springtime. She wore a Tartar skirt and knee-pads for the wicket.

'I think I am engaged to some of the others,' she said. 'Besides, you are a poet, Stepan, and there is no place for poetry now. We should have no food.'

'If I were to write in prose,' said the young man, 'would you love me?'

'Prose is more respectable, to be sure,' said Natalya Popova, 'but, excuse me, every one is active and vigorous now, ploughing and making grain for the State or combating the counter-revolutionaries. You are only a dreamer; Olga Merinin told me she found you feeding nightingales in the wood. What is the use of that when Russia is starving, Stepan Pepushkin? To-day, to take an example, the Committee will not let you take part in the batting. They have appointed you to count the runs. I tell you what is in my mind, Stepan; I am sorry I let you kiss me.'

Stepan smiled dumbly and listened to the speakers.

'Comrades,' shouted Serge Obolensky, the humane slaughterer, 'the solution is evident. We cannot have two hostile teams competing against each other, for this would be to play into the hands of the Capitalist Governments, which seek to divide the workers. But we can all play on the same side.'

'*Pravda!*' 'Well spoken, Serge!' '*Yashmak!*' cried the cricketers.

Big Lubov, the bearded schoolmaster, came to the rostrum carrying a stump. 'I have a proposition.'

'*Nitchevo!*' '*Chuchuk!*' 'A proposition!'

'My proposition is that all runs should be shared in common.'

'*Pravda! Yashmak!*' 'All runs to be shared in common!'

But Bortsov, the Commissar, stepped forward. 'I have a paper from Moscow. At Moscow they say that you are idle; the grain lies unreaped, the bins are empty.'

'*Tchai!*' '*Merovestia!*' cried the angry villagers.

'Moscow says that the will to compete and act energetically must be born again in you. Therefore they have given you this cricket which the English workers play. Therefore you must have two teams striving for victory, and therefore each worker shall keep his own runs, striving to gain more than his comrade.'

'Kill the Commissar!' cried everyone. 'Capitalism!' 'The counter-revolution!'

'I will kill the Commissar!' yelled Big Lubov the schoolmaster. 'Give me a bat, Natalya Popova,' he said in a softer voice; for Big Lubov loved Natalya.

'There are only two bats,' said the girl, 'and they must be restored to the Government after the game. It would be a pity to break them.'

'*Pravda!*' said Lubov; and he drove the sharp stump which he carried through the Commissar's heart.

'And now let us begin the game,' said the schoolmaster.

II

'Now that we have killed the Commissar,' Serge Obolensky was saying, 'we have no one who can explain the rules of cricket. But Russia is like that.'

'Who wants rules?' said young Nicolai Nicolaievitch. 'Rules were made for the bourgeois.'

'*Pravda*. True. But, excuse me, it would be convenient if we could come to some agreement about the method of our proceedings. To take an example, Nicolai Nicolaievitch, we know that there are two sets of stumps, for the Commissar told us so much; but where in the world are we to put them?'

'It is simple enough, Serge Obolensky. We will put one set here and the other over there.'

'Yes, Nicolai,' replied the older man patiently; 'but where?'

'There.'

'I recognise the energy of your mind, Nicolai – but how far away?'

'Give me the Commissar's paper. Twenty-two yards – that is versts. *Cuculin!*' said the young revolutionary in triumph.

'No one in the village can throw a leather ball so far. I tell you what, we will let each man bowl according to his capacity. The strong man shall throw from a great way off and the weak from a little distance. Thus we shall establish equality. Big Lubov, to take an example, must throw at the batsmen from the next field, and I shall throw from here.'

'But,' said the young cynical clerk of the bank, 'suppose that the strong man pretends to be weak, then he will have an advantage.'

'Then,' said Serge Obolensky simply, 'we shall kill him.'

III

Big Lubov and Natalya Popova were still batting. All the village had bowled the round ball at them, some from this place and some from that. None of the peasants had hit them. Big Lubov defended his body nimbly with his great bat. But the young men did not like to throw the ball at pretty Natalya. They threw it away from her, so that she could not strike it with her bat. So it came about that Lubov had gained seven runs, but pretty Natalya had made none.

Old Volodja's best cow lay in the shade watching the game. Dreamily, sitting on the cow, Stepan Pepushkin wrote the runs in his book. He thought that Natalya was like a tulip.

'Ho, Stepan!' Big Lubov cries, 'how goes the count?'

'Lubov – 9 runs,' answers the poet; 'Natalya Popova – 7 runs.'

'*Nitchevo!* How is this? Not once has Natalya struck the ball.'

'From time to time I give her a run,' said the poet, 'because she is so beautiful.'

'*Yashmak!*' At first Big Lubov was angry. But he loved Natalya and he shrugged with good temper. When Big Lubov shrugged it was like a storm on the hills. Trees fell down.

'Besides,' said Serge Obolensky cunningly, 'since all the runs are to be shared in common, Lubov Lubovinsky, the question has no significance. Strictly speaking, the count is Lubov – 8; Natalya – 8.'

'*Botsch!*' shouted the schoolmaster angrily. 'No man or woman shall take *my* runs!' For Lubov had begun to enjoy the cricket, and the will to win was in his great heart, which was shaped like a pear.

'You are a *molak*, Lubov!' cried Nicolai Nicolaievitch. 'Run-hog! *Menshevik!*'

'Bowl, thou,' replied the big man with a threatening motion, 'or I will bat thee.'

Presently Lubov had made 13. Stepan gave Natalya two more runs because of the pretty curve of her waist, which was like the prow of a small ship. Natalya Popova was 9.

Then Alexis the blacksmith took the ball.

Lubov cries out: 'Ho! blacksmith, you come too close! Stand yonder by Obolensky in the farther field!'

But Alexis throws the ball strong and low and strikes the schoolmaster in the stomach.

'*Yashmak!*' 'Hit!' 'Lubov is out!' cry the peasants.

'The blow was irregular,' cries the batsman angrily. 'He came too near. What is the verdict, Andrey Andreyevitch?'

All eyes turned to the aged umpire. But the umpire was still asleep.

'He is drunk,' said Serge Obolensky.

'I tell you what,' said Lubov, 'is it not a very extraordinary thing that all the time, while we have been playing this game the umpire was lying drunk at the place called square-leg, and none of us perceived it?'

'Russia is like that,' said Serge Obolensky. 'My father's sister kept beetles in her bedroom and fed them on sunflower seeds. Nobody knew.'

'Practically speaking,' the schoolmaster remarked logically, 'the game, so far, has not been happening, for the official, in a manner of speaking, was not present. It follows therefore that I am still batting.'

'In that case,' said the cunning Nicolai, 'you have not made 13 runs, but no runs.'

'*Pravda!*'

Lubov weakened. He thought that none of the peasants would make so many as 13 runs.

'Besides, as you will be the first to appreciate, Lubov Lubovinsky, this umpire is only a mouthpiece for the voice of the people. Indubitably he is incapable; but what of that? The voice of the people has said that you are out.'

'Out!' 'Out!' '*Slava!*'

Lubov with a bad grace gave up the bat, saying, 'As for you, Andrey Andreyevitch, to-night I will give you to the wolves'.

The old man woke. 'The queer thing is, brother,' he said, 'that I have forgotten your name.'

'Russia is like that,' said Serge Obolensky.

'I have just remembered,' said Big Lubov unpleasantly, 'that I have a pistol in my breeches pocket. If any brother or comrade makes more than 13 I will shoot him through the head.'

IV

All the peasants batted in turn and were thrown out. Boris Polunin was stunned. Michael Andrid ran away. Only Natalya Popova remained always at the stumps. Natalya had 11 runs; but Stepan would not give her any more now for fear of Big Lubov's pistol. Alexis the blacksmith had made 7. The others had made nothing. Meanwhile Big Lubov had become exceedingly dogmatic and unpopular. When the last man was out he said, 'Well, it must be evident to all of you that Lubov Lubovinski has gained the victory.'

The angry shouts of the villagers drowned his speech; and Alexis the blacksmith said 'Excuse me, the affair is not concluded. Stepan Pepushkin has not yet tried his skill.'

'*Pravda!*' 'Stepan!' 'Pepushkin the poet will put the schoolmaster down.'

They summoned Stepan to the stumps, and gave the ball to Nicolai

Nicolaievitch. The young poet was overjoyed to be batting with Natalya. On his way to the stumps he took her in his arms and kissed her.

'Your hair is like the wild jasmine which grows in the Caucasus,' he said. 'Now, Natalya, if I am not mistaken, you are going to see that I am not a dreamer only.'

Nicolai prepared to throw, but the poet stepped forward, lifting his hand. 'Excuse me, Nicolai Nicolaievitch,' he said, 'but, do you know, this is a highly significant moment? Here am I, a young man who never in his whole life has played with bat and ball before. I have never been clever with my hands. At carpentry and needlework I was the duffer of my school. I never could knit or tie up parcels. Truly, I don't know any one so clumsy with his fingers. I am always dropping my tea-cup, upsetting things, pushing things over. As you see, Nicolai, I am quite unable to tie my cravat in a presentable bow. The only tool I was ever able to use was a lead pencil. And yet—'

'Pardon my abruptness, Stepan Pepushkin,' said Nicolai, 'but if you are going to relate to us the history of your life it seems to me that the fieldsmen had better sit down.'

'That is as you please, Nicolai Nicolaievitch.' And all the peasants sat down on the grass.

'As I was saying,' the batsman continued, 'the extraordinary thing is that there I am with this really most unfamiliar instrument in my hands, and, do you know, I am superbly confident? I am absolutely convinced that I am going to succeed in the game, and gain more runs than this blustering schoolmaster. Is it not remarkable?'

'*Pravda*,' said the bowler, yawning slightly.

'The reason for all this is, I think, perfectly evident. It is Natalya – Natalya Popova, standing there with her Government bat like a torch of a new truth. Now that the Union of Soviet Republics has inscribed cricket upon its advancing banners I think you will agree that we shall conquer the world. Cricket was the one thing that Holy Russia lacked. Cricket will save Russia. Cricket—'

'Excuse me,' said Serge Obolensky, rising to his feet at mid-off; 'night is falling, Stepan Pepushkin; the grass is wet with dew, and I perceive that wolves are gathering at the borders of the field. It would be convenient to most of us if we could continue the game.'

'By all means,' answered the poet. 'But do you know, in spite of my confidence it has now occurred to me that men are but mortal and the future is uncertain? It is just possible that Nicolai Nicolaievitch will kill me with the ball. Permit me therefore to embrace Natalya Popova before we begin.'

'Naturally, Stepan Pepushkin.'

This ceremony concluded, the poet prepared to defend himself. Nicolaievitch threw the ball very hard at his head. Stepan put his bat before his face, and the ball, touching it, flew into the forest, scattering the wolves.

'Run, Natalya Popova!' cried the poet, and they ran.

Old Volodja, the long-stop, was fat and slow. They ran nine runs.

The ball was carried back at length, and Stepan, panting, faced Nicolaievitch again.

Big Lubov stepped forward. 'I tell you what,' he bellowed, 'I have just realized that all this business is simply a waste of time. When you come to think of it, there are crops to be garnered, cattle to be tended, cows to be milked. The moon is rising, and here we all are throwing a leather ball at Stepan Pepushkin. Is it not preposterous? What in the world does it matter, I ask myself, whether Stepan gains more runs than Lubov or not? Naturally it is most unlikely that he will overcome me; but will the State be any the better for it if he does? Andrey Andreyevitch is asleep again. Let us all go to the village and drink *tchai*.'

'What you say is extremely reasonable,' said Serge Obolensky, 'but, excuse me, you should have said it before. It is evident that Stepan Pepushkin has a talent for the game, and it would not surprise me if he were to overcome you.'

'*Pravda!*' '*Yashmak!*' cried the peasants, who hated the schoolmaster.

Nicolaievitch threw the ball at Pepushkin's face a second time. The poet struck the ball towards the wood.

'Run, Natalya!'

'I run, Stepan. Do thou run also!'

A big wolf runs out of the wood and takes the ball in its mouth.

'Run, Volodja! The wolf has the ball. Follow and help him, Boris Borisovitch!'

The wolf runs into the wood. Volodja runs after the wolf. Boris Borisovitch runs after Volodja. Serge Obolensky runs after Borisovitch. Alexis the blacksmith runs after Obolensky. Olga Merinin runs after Alexis. Nicolai Nicolaievitch runs after Olga Merinin. The other peasants follow; and last of all, Andrey Andreyevitch, waking up, totters into the wood, where the wolves devour him with the others.

Only Big Lubov remains in the field, watching with a sour smile while Stepan and Natalya run up and down, hand-in-hand, between the stumps. Stepan has made two-hundred-and-ninety-four. Out of breath, he pauses; Natalya folds her strong arms about him.

'You are a true man, Stepan Pepushkin,' she whispers. 'We will go to Moscow together and make fly-papers for the Government.'

But Big Lubov has picked up the Commissar's paper.

'It is all very well,' he says spitefully, 'but, do you know, Pepushkin, we were playing without the bails? Moscow says that without the bails the game does not exist.'

Natalya wept.

'After all, then, Stepan, I find that I do not love you.'

'Russia is like that,' said Stepan Pepushkin.

THE SEASON'S PROSPECTS

Herbert Farjeon

With the cricket season close at hand, and all the sporting experts busy writing articles on the prospects of the various first-class counties, it may interest you to receive, for once in a way, a little exclusive information on the forthcoming composition of less famous, but no less representative, teams.

After all, to be told under the heading 'Gloucestershire' that Wally Hammond is pretty sure to collect a tidy number of runs before the middle of September, or to be told under the heading 'Yorkshire' that Sutcliffe is a well-tried veteran, hardly makes inspiring reading. You don't really need much experience or inside information to be able to write that sort of thing. Even the references to promising colts may be criticised on the ground that these colts are nearly always dismissed as complete washouts long before the strawberries begin to swell.

Your attention, then, is invited for a change to the prospects of some of our best-known village, park, and nomadic blazer teams, beginning, since one must begin somewhere, with

Plympton-On-The-Plymp

'The prospects of Plympton-on-the-Plymp are, generally speaking, a good deal rosier than last year, and it is hoped that, for not a few of the matches, it may be possible to produce a full team without enlisting the services of the small boys in the long grass. The assiduous efforts of the secretary have happily reduced the number of cattle on the home ground by fifty per cent, three additional vice-presidents have been elected, and another figure 0 obtained for the telegraph board. Thanks to last year's heavy fixture list, the number of club pads has been increased from three to five.

As regards the composition of the team, George Hodge, who created such a favourable impression last year by scoring several runs on the off side, will still be available, while Bob Stubbins, the lightning bowler, may be relied on once more to find the dandelion with his accustomed accuracy.

We understand that Jim Cobley will be seen in an entirely new pair of braces. Sam Stubbs, who will again keep wicket, is said to be in better voice than ever. Master Ronald Verney, the colonel's son, will, as usual, join the team in August, and, thanks to his school training, may confidently be expected once more to raise the standard of the team's batting by playing forward to wides in the best manner.'

Primrose Hill Ruffians
'This formidable side is likely once again to prove the terror of the open spaces of North-West London, where for many years they have demonstrated such a marked superiority over their many rivals in seizing a pitch and holding it against all comers. Alf Atkins their captain, who set up a remarkable record last year by bowling unchanged throughout the season, will again go in first. It is estimated that, in the course of his career, he has made more runs after 9.30 p.m. than any other batsman on the Hill.

Mr Atkins will be assisted by a powerful side, including Bert Smith, who has now, we are happy to hear, completely recovered from his accident in last year's concluding match, when it will be remembered, he had the misfortune to be hit over the head with a stump. The team will also include Joe Brown, the celebrated long-stop, who has saved so many runs with his coat; and Tommy Robinson, because, of course, it's his bat.

'The ball is said to be in excellent condition, and it is expected that the other bail will be found again before the season opens.'

The Old Beans
'Impressive as it has been in the past, there are indications that this side will have even more side this year than last. The blazers of the new members include many calculated to turn Joseph's brethren, and even Joseph himself, green with envy, while some of the sweaters are so impressive that to miss a catch in them will be no disgrace at all. It will be merely laughable.

An entirely new cap has been designed in which, according to report, it is absolutely impossible to make a duck, and the size of the cricket-bags has now reached such proportions that many of the Old Beans actually go to bed in them while their pals are knocking up centuries.

'The Hon. Alastair Fitzmorency will again lead his gallant men on to the field, and several weeks of hard practice have been put in at trick tossing and catching, in order to impress and alarm opposing batsmen before they come in. It has been resolved by the Managing Committee that any Old Bean who neglects to have the bowling screen moved at least once in every innings shall be disqualified from membership, but no player is to be allowed in future to call for a drink from the pavilion before he has made at least ten runs, owing to the large number of drawn games played last year.'

THE RETURN MATCH WITH KENT

David J.M. Armstrong

The return match with Kent, at Norwich, will long be remembered by all who saw it; Norfolk, after a bad start, were making a fine recovery. In reply to a total of 314, they had lost three quick wickets, but Edrich and Clements had hit back with a great stand. Clements made 80, including two fine sixes, before being dismissed, and then J.M. Pearson joined Eric Edrich in a further profitable partnership. With only five runs needed for the lead, a sensational hold-up occurred. By the way of the main gate and pavilion steps, a large cow cantered on to the field and scattered batsmen, fielders, and umpires as she made merry round the square. Benches were overturned as in great haste the fair-sized crowd tried to find cover from this menace.

The scorebox was soon packed full of hysterical humanity as the cause of all the fuss ran a lonesome Grand National over the few benches which remained standing. Several drovers had by this time arrived, one mounted on a bicycle, and assisted by some brave persons in the enclosure, who from one of the cars had collected a length of rope, managed to trap the cow in a corner of the ground. However, being a freedom-loving animal, she soon contrived to escape once more, this time choosing the nearby allotments as her playground, and the game was able to continue after a break of nearly a quarter of an hour. Norfolk eventually ran up the fine total of 403. Pearson made 56, and Eric Edrich, when he at last ran of partners, had made 170 not out.

NOMINAL CRICKET

B.G. Whitfield

. . . the time is now 11.30 and we are about to take you over from the Studio to the County ground at Tunbury where our team of commentators will be describing the second day's play in the match between Hopshire and Southants. As listeners may be aware, the County Championship depends on this match which starts today at 11.30 and was left overnight in a particularly interesting position. Before we go over to Tunbury we will just give you the list of our commentators on this game; in view of its importance we have endeavoured to send our best team. It consists of Cholmondeley Hadge, de Beers Jorkins, Humbert Galbraith – who is also well known to many listeners for his critical analyses of secondary Victorian poetry – and Wotan Maloney. Over now to Tunbury where Chomondeley Hadge is at present at the microphone . . .

Well, here we are at Tunbury – for this vital match – and I think it is pretty generally agreed that it will be the first few overs that will count. It is really a most interesting position; I'll just recall to listeners the present state of the – but here are the players coming out, they are a few moments late perhaps, but here they are, coming out. It is a very warm day. They seem to be feeling the warmth a bit, don't you think. Humbert? You agree? They really do appear to be feeling the warmth – several of them seem to wiping the perspiration off their mouths already. It really is a pretty scene – the players and the umpires are all there. Do you think the umpires are all there, Wotan? You don't? Who are the umpires, Wotan, by the way? The fat one with the beard is Cuthbert and the other, of course, old Henry? Why 'of course'? And Cuthbert and Henry who? You aren't sure? Well, anyhow, listeners may take it that Cuthbert and old Henry are the umpires. In a moment or two, between the overs. I will read you the score-card, but we aren't in a position to do so for a few minutes as we haven't yet been able to find out the Christian names of two of the Hopshire side. Well, there's the wicket out there; do you think that the wicket is a little bit green, Humbert? Where's Humbert? Just gone to see about his lunch? Call after him and ask him, will you, Wotan? What does he say? 'It nearly always is'? Yes, of course, I see. Ah, now there's the bowler just going to bowl the vital first over; it really is an interesting position, most interesting. You see, Hopshire now need – just a moment, the bowler's picked up that ball now in his left hand. It is his left hand that he's picked up that ball with, isn't it, Wotan? You

agree? Now he has walked back and he is just coming up to bowl . . .
he's bowling, he's bowling, HE'S BOWLED? YES HE'S BOWLED!
Just a minute, we must apologise to listeners, but we have to put you
over to the Studio for a moment for an important announcement.

*This is the Studio speaking. The time is 11.37. You have just been
listening to the vital opening minutes of the County Championship match
at Tunbury between Hopshire and Southants. We have an important
announcement to make. Owing to an unfortunate error the Christian
name of one of the commentators was wrongly announced at the start
of this broadcast. It should not be de Beers Jorkins, but de Bors. Now
over to Tunbury again where Humbert Galbraith has taken over at the
microphone.*

. . . Here we are still at Tunbury for this vital match. It really is a very
pretty ground, very pretty indeed. It used to be even prettier, I believe,
before the local Council decided to build their new mortuary along
there on one side of the ground. But it is a fine building. Don't you
agree it is a fine building, Chomondeley? You do? What's that? And
so functional? Yes, I quite agree. It seems to be functioning, anyhow.
Well, here they are all playing, and there is, I may say, a pretty good
attendance today as you might expect. Yes, I do think the attendance is
pretty good; but I see, all the same, there's a wide space of empty seats
at the far end; it's funny about that vacant space. Do you understand it,
de Bors? Oh, it's just in front, you say, of the new Isolation Hospital?
I see. Yes, well here's the bowler just coming up to bowl again and
the situation is indeed tense. I'll just give you the – I say! There's
a one-armed fielder there! I've never heard of a one-armed cricketer
before. Have you, de Bors? Can you see him there? What do you
make of it? He has positively only one arm. What's that? You say
it's the bowler going off and that he has one arm inside his sweater?
Well, now, how silly of me, that really is very silly of me. Never mind.
Now, the new bowler has just got that ball in one hand, and he is going
to bowl it now. Yes, he's definitely coming up to bowl, here he comes
. . . he's come now. The score now is – what is the score, de Bors? Work
it out will you? Just at the moment there seems to be a bit of a hold-up
– they are all crowding round one of the umpires. What do you think
they are all crowding round the umpire for, de Bors? You can't make
it out? I can't either. I'll just put you over for a bit to Cholmondeley
Hadge, to see if he can tell you . . . over to you Cholmondeley.

. . . Thank you, Humbert. It really is very interesting, this. I just can't make it out. Can you make it out, Wotan? It is really rather like what happens at Twickenham sometimes: the umpire is quite hidden now. What's that, de Bors? You say you don't think it can be that? Well, I feel we must find out somehow. Perhaps you would go along and find out from someone, de Bors? Now they are playing again and I will hand you over to Wotan Maloney. We are all very glad to have him here for this vital match. I expect many listeners have read his powerful articles and remember his suggestion that our bowlers should not bowl over or round the wicket, but through it. Many cricketers think it might have made all the difference in Australia. What did Freddie Brown say might have happened, Wotan? He said, 'Quite a lot'? I'm not surprised. Well. I am just going to hand you over to Wotan. There's another batsman just coming in at this moment. Can you see who it is, Chomondeley? Oh, here's de Bors just come back. Did you find out about the umpire, de Bors? De Bors says the umpire had had a telegram. Something to do with form? I can't quite make out what de Bors means, but anyhow now I am handing you over to Wotan Maloney. His suggestion for the team for next year's Tests has made quite a big sensation as there were only eight men from the Oval in his list. Did you get many letters, Wotan? Mostly from Kennington, you say? Well, now I am turning listeners over to Wotan. Over to you, Wotan.

A FEW OVERTHROWS

James Thorpe

Much has been written of the great men of Cricket, its pioneers and heroes. Little or nothing has been said of those less-known but worthy people who, with small hope and less achievement of reward, contribute so much to the success of the game.

First and foremost stands our old friend the 'Rabbit', for whom I have the profoundest respect. The sponsors 'who gave him this name' are even now unknown, although the credit is often attributed to that great cricket character, Sam Woods, and I hope it is correct. A.A. Milne in *The Day's Play*, has immortalised one type of rabbit in delightful manner, but no one has paid him the full tribute of his due. The real rabbit does not jest about it: he takes his cricket rather more seriously than most of us. He is an enthusiast who lives on hope and his hero-worship of others. The story of Jimmy Herbert's day explains the type of man I mean. Apart from the name of the hero, it is a perfectly true story.

Jimmy Herbert was our 'bunniest' rabbit: he would have been the first to admit it. His one invaluable quality as a cricketer was an unlimited enthusiasm. He would go anywhere at the shortest notice to play cricket. When he wasn't playing cricket he was watching it. During the season you always knew where to find Jimmy – tucked in a corner of the enclosure at Lord's, almost in a line with the wickets. Cricket was his religion, and there was never a more fervent and devout disciple. His heroes were the real cricketers; he worshipped them, revelled in their reflected glory, and strove without avail to emulate their excellence. He was a slight, pathetic, little figure, with a rather sad expression, but keenly appreciative of the humour of life and the seriousness of cricket. As a music-hall actor, his profession gave him plenty of opportunity to follow the game.

It so happened, as alas it too often does, that the skipper was let down late at night for our match next day. The only course open was to wire first thing in the morning to Jimmy. We had to catch an early train, as our objective was a village in the distant wilds of Essex, two miles from the station, where a brake was to meet us. Jimmy arrived with a wild rush, just in time to see the tail of our train leaving the platform. Nothing daunted, he completed his interrupted breakfast in the refreshment room, and caught the next, about two hours later. By unusual good fortune, there was a cab at the station, and Jimmy and his bag were at length deposited in a lane and directed across two fields to the scene of the match. He found the 'ground' tenanted only by a few placid cows and returned somewhat sadly to the lane. The day was broiling hot: no one was in sight: and the bag was heavy. Jimmy sat down on the bag to rest and meditate.

In due course, an intelligent native appeared, who put him on the track of the real ground, rather more than a mile away. Gripping his bag, he trudged off hopefully. Hot and weary, he found that we had just gone to lunch at a neighbouring inn, where he joined us with evident relief, and profuse apologies for being late. It was a real pre-war country cricket lunch – such as old cricketers may still remember – and Jimmy, who felt that he had earned it, did himself particularly well. As he revived, he related his morning's adventures.

We still had three wickets to get, and Jimmy, who had slipped into his flannels and said a few words of thanks to his substitute, took up his position at cover. Although the three wickets were not long in falling, Jimmy managed in that short time to drop two real 'sitters'.

As a reward for his zeal, the skipper put him No. 6. He had never previously attained a higher eminence in the batting order than No. 10, and the honour was not lost on Jimmy, who began to strap on his pads soon after our first two had gone to the wicket. Things went so well that Jimmy recovered sufficient confidence to become reminiscent. He told us again of his two great innings: when he helped to put on 54 for the last wicket, his share being 21 not out, and when he kept his end up for three quarters of an hour for five, while the other man made 40, to win the match. 'Funny thing, though,' he concluded, 'the last three games I have been bowled first ball.'

After a long spell of excited anticipation, his turn came to bat: the great moment to which he had looked forward since he received the wire. Sure enough the first ball he had was a good one, and he was bowled 'all over the shop'. With a pathetic expression of disappointment and resignation he returned to our midst, in a quietude whose depths revealed our general sympathy. For the rest of the game he smoked his pipe in silence. When we had won the match, with a few wickets still in hand, he asked permission to catch the 5.40 back to town to start his day's work. The skipper readily agreed, with thanks for his sportsmanship in turning up, and Jimmy left with a glow of virtue if not of triumph.

We drew stumps at 6.30, and the brake took us down to catch the 7.28. As we crossed the bridge, we spied below a lone forlorn figure on an otherwise bare platform. It was Jimmy: by this time just a little depressed! Still, as he said, if he had caught his train he would have been very dreary, with no one to talk about Cricket. We left him perfectly happy at the other end, and had he been invited next day at equally short notice to risk repeating his experience, he would have responded eagerly.

Such is the fascination of Cricket; and there are thousands of these real unselfish sportsmen – hopeful and hopeless – but true lovers of the game.

Another rabbit of my acquaintance once lured some of us on to a small boat for a yachting cruise. We noticed that he showed a persistent tendency to hug the shore, which he scanned very closely. At last, after two or three days, we hove-to in a secluded creek on whose shore was a small but open strip of turf, and the skipper suddenly and furtively produced six stumps, two bats, and a disreputable ball. There was nothing for it: we were at his mercy and must humour him. One of his delusions was that he was a lob bowler, but hitherto he had had few chances of verifying this supposition. Now at last was his golden opportunity: he would show us. Having lost the toss, he opened the bowling, but was, unfortunately, unable to find a length. Long-hop after long-hop was despatched with increasing gusto to the square-leg boundary, which, unfortunately, in this case was the water's edge. Square-leg was for this occasion impersonated by the 'crew' – a hefty specimen of the Naval Rating on leave – and he soon found that it would be easier and more expeditious to field in the dinghy. I still have the score, but unfortunately the bowling analysis was not recorded. However, the skipper had his bowl, and the remainder of us much running exercise: and for the rest of the week we left the shore and 'made for the open sea'.

A certain enthusiastic major of whom I heard recently, was wont to bring a team every year to a Yorkshire home week. As became a Yorkshireman, he did the thing well: not only did he include several of the county eleven, but also brought his private band, which, in the intervals of cricket, he conducted. In return for all this well-meant generosity, the bowler was instructed to present the Major with a perfectly good half-volley. Unfortunately, it was straight and immediately proved fatal. 'Damn cricket,' he exploded, 'give me music,' and having removed his pads, he resumed the direction of the band.

The term 'rabbit' is generally considered generical, but there are degrees even in this classification. We were once trying some mild leg-pulling on our 'Number eleven'. 'After all,' he retorted, 'I'm not a rabbit, I'm a ferret: I go in after the rabbits.'

One parting word of advice to the rabbit on the question of 'colours'. Be content to wear a plain blazer, or at most, one of your club's colours. Don't wear anything too conspicuous unless you have earned it. A very young cricketer once turned out for us in an MCC tie, an I Zingari sash, and a Free Foresters' blazer, or very close imitations of them. It was too much to live up to!

Another cricket hero, whose sterling worth has never been properly valued, is the 'Hon. Sec.' If he is a cricketer, he may be said to derive some actual recompense for his work, and well does he deserve it. Often, though, he is not a player, or at best no more than a rabbit, and then his self-denial is truly heroic. Few cricketers who have not filled the post, realise in the slightest degree the large amount of work and the numerous duties of the 'Hon. Sec.' Even in a small club, the greater part of his spare time is sacrificed to the management of the club's affairs. Collecting teams is in itself enough to prematurely age any man, and many members add considerably to this work by slackness in replying to his polite communications, replete with the fullest information for their comfort and guidance. If every cricketer were compelled at some time to have practical experience of secretarial work, he would extend at least some measure of sympathy to the 'Hon. Sec.'

The success of a club in every way depends to a very great extent on the self-denying, enthusiastic labours of the 'Hon. Sec.' See to it, therefore, all ye real cricketers, that he is at least supported and assisted in every possible way. Answer his post-cards promptly, and always turn up to the match, even if it snows, unless he instructs you otherwise. So shall you spare him much unnecessary work and anxiety.

Other excellent people there are who work with unselfish enthusiasm in the wings, while the stage is set and the lime-light flashed on us unworthy heroes, the players. The ladies who supply us with tea, the diligent scorer who records our successes and ignores many of our failures, and many other willing helpers who minister to our comfort, and too often to our vanity; all these are worthy of grateful tribute from an abler pen than mine.

Chapter 9

MEMOIRS AND CONFESSIONS

Peter Roebuck

I can't remember when I fell in love with cricket. Though I lived most of my early years in Scarborough, I did not come from strong cricket stock. Oh, my mother breezily reflects upon her time as Oxford University's wicket-keeper (she also says she once danced in *Swan Lake*, and after a couple of sherries at Christmas she is the dying swan again) and my father remembers leaving his factory in Manchester at lunchtime if word spread that Washbrook was still in.

But these connections are slight. Certainly my parents did not drive me to cricket. My father cared not what I did so long as I did not become a ballet dancer! Nor was cricket an attractive profession in the early 1960s, years of small income, falling gates, repetitive three-day cricket – a game dying on its feet. No wonder, upon realising my enthusiasm, my parents sent me to Peter Wight's indoor school hoping that my interest would wane after a few knocks with a hard cricket ball!

Yet love conquers all. We moved to Bath in 1963 and my determination to be a cricketer grew. I'd watch the festival week on the Recreation Ground by the Avon (frequently under the Avon, as a matter of fact). In those days, Bath was a treacherous pitch. They used to come down a few days before the Festival with a scythe to cut the outfield and a decrepit roller to flatten the pitch, if they could find it. Locals said that Old Father Time at Lord's was Somerset groundsman Cecil Buttle to a 'T'.

Those were the years when, if you led by 50 in the first innings, you might well win by an innings (as happened against Worcester once, mind you, they had no batsmen, only Kenyon, Headley, Richardson, D'Oliveira and Graveney, if memory serves me well). In those days, there wasn't much point in waiting until the third day to watch the cricket, there wouldn't be any! No, I cannot pretend to be inspired as a youngster by watching cricket. The only game at Bath I can remember was against Derbyshire. For some reason the picture of Derek Morgan stoutly defending the superbly economical deliveries of Bill Alley has stayed in my mind.

My affection for cricket must have come from within. In Bath, I used to play in the garage yard behind our flat with my brother, if I could persuade him that bowling to me and fetching the ball constituted fun. Failing that, I'd play on my own with a plastic ball in the indoor area beneath the flat. I'd throw the ball against the wall and drive it all over the place, describing each ball as if I were John Arlott.

Just next to this space was a spiritualist's meeting place. I'm afraid my games were often mistaken for messages from someone's mother. As the medium was unravelling the knocks in a fever of excitement, they would hear my running commentary, 'Oh yes, and Butcher is bowled by that one . . .'

In the end, some lunatic burnt down the flats, a man obsessed with hatred for spiritualism, the police said (though what they told the spiritualists I never did hear!) My family and relations (14 in all) were in the flat at the time of the fire and escaped through a narrow window with a few minutes to spare. The building was gutted. I was at school, unaware of the drama. On my way home, I bought an *Evening Chronicle*, as was my wont. Splashed over the front page was news of my family's escape, and descriptions of the courageous firemen. I did not notice this. You see, the Bath Festival was on at the time so I walked home with my nose in the back page, reading details of Somerset's collapse. I climbed half way up the stairs, utterly oblivious of the ruins around me, and was only stopped by the kindly hand of some enormous policeman.

For a while, I had to settle for games of 'Owzat', but I never found this satisfactory, as unless I cheated I could easily score nought myself and it did strike me as ridiculous that Pocock and Underwood could score 86 and 72 (mainly in sixes I might add) whilst Sobers and Nurse and I might fall for nothing.

In all these games there would be a team invented by me. I had a squad of about 14 players to be selected by and led by me. Each had his own character; the unpredictable, the reliable, the difficult, the colourful and so on. As captain I was inspiring, as a bowler I'd heroically make vital break-throughs and as a batsman I stood up and thundered the ball like Ted Dexter (only harder and more often). I can't remember losing many games, though we had some narrow scrapes against the West Indies.

At 12 years of age, I applied for a scholarship to Millfield school deep in Somerset. I met R.J.O. Meyer the headmaster. It was an interesting meeting. I knocked on the door and noticed an orange flying towards me. I caught it. 'You're in,' said Meyer, 'But why didn't you throw it back?'

He watched me bat on a tennis court with a tennis racquet, facing my sister's bowling. I did not mention my sister earlier. She later rose to the heights of captaining a victorious Oxford Ladies Team, but this is much too embarrassing so I hush it up. Observers say that she bowled me out. I deny this absolutely (though Shakespeare warns us: 'The lad 'ee doth protest too much methinks')!

Almost anything could happen at Millfield. At any rate towards the end of term my flighted leg-breaks propelled me to the First XI. My captain, I discovered, was called 'Military Madness' (I never did find out where the 'Military' came from). He kept wicket inadequately. He could not pick my googly. I was instructed to brush my hair as I returned to my mark as a signal. Sometimes I forgot. And even when I did remember, 'Military Madness' would miss the signal unless I did an impersonation of Larry Grayson, by which time, of course, the batsman was alerted.

At the end of term I rose quickly from the Somerset under-15s to under-19s, leaving one Ian Botham in my wake. Bill Andrews, Somerset's coach, was responsible for this climb. Bill was a fine man, still is. One lunchtime, he stormed into our dressing room and berated the bowlers, being particularly severe on Y. Upon Y protesting, 'But Bill, I'm not playing,' Bill roared, 'Don't argue with me, son!'

For all his qualities, Bill was no organiser. Consequently, my introduction into the higher echelons of Somerset cricket was far from dull. On the under-19s' first away trip, we arrived at the prescribed bed and breakfast house. I said, you will observe, 'bed' not 'beds and breakfast'. There were two bedrooms in all. Undeterred, we piled in, some sleeping three to a bed, some on the floor and some on settees, driven on by Bill's invective.

A month later, I was selected to play for the Second XI in Devon. Bill mumbled something about meeting Bob Clapp outside such and such a pub at 8 p.m. Trouble is, I forgot the name. I told my startled parents that I had to be outside the something something, or was it the something and something, at 8 p.m. This didn't reduce the field much so we roamed around the town for 2½ hours, desperately hoping to bump into the mysterious Mr Clapp. Eventually, we found him outside The Crown and Sceptre at 10.30 p.m. We needn't have worried; Bob wasn't thinking of going anywhere until closing time anyhow.

We arrived in Devon at 1a.m., as the chords of the current number one 'In The Year 2525' signalled its gloomy predictions on the radio. I wouldn't worry about them though. There'll always be youngsters mad on cricket, ready for whatever falls their way.

CLUB CRICKET IN THE TWENTIES

Alec Waugh

I suppose that for the casual cricketer, someone like myself who had a couple of years in his school XI, and hoped when he went up to Oxford or to Cambridge – I did not go myself because of the war – to become an Authentic or a Crusader, the opening of the twentieth century was the golden era. The country house cricket that Raffles made his hunting ground flourished so amply then that P.F. Warner in 1913 lamented in the *Westminster Gazette* that he could no longer get amateurs for Middlesex in August because they were booked for country house weeks. 'Surely hosts and hostesses should realise that the county came first.'

By 1919 all that was over; Sir Julian Cahn had his tours and weeks but they were for first-class performers, or those approximating thereto. In 1930 when the MCC Western tour was sumptuously entertained during a two-day match against Sir John Power's side, a number of attractive females were included among the house guests. It was a very gay occasion, and the older members of the side said ruefully: 'Twenty years ago you had this kind of thing right through August.' It was the only time I ever had it. But in compensation there was during the Twenties an unlimited amount of varied club cricket in and around London, and I was fortunately placed to make the best of it.

At the time I had a flat in Kensington, and a part-time job in my father's publishing house. I went to his office on Mondays and on Fridays. I did no serious writing during the summer. That gave me five days for cricket, either watching or playing, and I took as full advantage of my good luck as the vagaries of the English climate permitted. Quite a number of other men were in the same position, men who seemed to do no work yet were able to afford four days' cricket every week. I suppose it was the last legacy of Victorian and Edwardian affluence. Are there many today? I question it. I read an article recently by Lord Kinross who in the Twenties was Mr Gossip of the *Sketch* and very much a playboy. 'One has to work today,' he said, 'there's no-one to do nothing with.' Playing cricket is, I suppose, doing nothing – and there was no lack of companionship in the Twenties.

Most regular club players had a home club such as Hampstead, Richmond, Hornsey, Ealing, or farther afield Byfleet, Reigate, Purley, and in addition a touring club like the Incogniti, the Cryptics, the Stoics, the Nondescripts, or the Wanderers. Most of these wandering sides ran tours; and most of the home sides ran 'a week'. There were also one or two specialist sides like the Thespids which drew mainly on the theatrical profession. They concentrated on Sunday cricket and C. Aubrey Smith often captained them. As a lay member I took the field with Owen Nares, Nigel Bruce, Dennis Noble, the O'Gorman brothers and Desmond Roberts, for whom Aubrey Smith found many 'bit parts' in Hollywood productions – either as a butler or a diplomat, roles that required British dignity and phlegm – so that he could display his skill upon 'a foreign field'.

There were also one or two amusing private sides, for which the only qualification was that you knew the captain. Francis Meynell, himself a considerable performer, ran such a side in Essex. I played for it once. John Strachey went in first. He made 20 or so with ease and elegance. I was surprised. 'I had no idea that you were so good,' I said. He laughed. 'I should have been in the Eton side. If I had, I might not have become a socialist.'

Cricket has always appealed to men of letters. Once J.M. Barrie ran a side: and before the first war Clifford Bax entertained a side for a week's cricket at his manor house in Broughton Gifford. After the war he organised 10-day tours, first from Newbury, later from Bath, calling his side the Old Broughtonians. His brother Arnold played for it, also Herbert Farjeon the dramatic critic, Walter O'Donnell who conducted the Royal Marines Band, Armstrong Gibbs the composer, Keith Falkner who now runs the Royal Academy of Music, K.L. Lindsay the politician, A.D. Peters the literary agent, and Eric Gillett the ubiquitous man of letters. We played quite good cricket too and beat, as often as not, the local Somerset and Wiltshire sides like Chippenham, Devizes, Melksham and Bath.

Chiltern Ramblers

I did not myself have a home side. I played for the Stoics, the Thespids and the Richmond half-day sides. I also played for, in addition to the Old Broughtonians, two highly individual sides, the Chiltern Ramblers and the Invalids. In retrospect those two sides seem more typical of the Twenties than any others. The Chiltern Ramblers started in 1923; at least they first took the field in 1923, but as they opened with a full fixture list, it must have been launched during the previous winter. I was invited to join by G.P. Glanfield, a law student in his last year at Oxford, with whom I had played in a number of matches for the Stoics. We played against a few schools, and some clubs mainly in Buckinghamshire. Later on, one of our chief features was a weekend in the West Country when we played

Clifton College on the Saturday and Downside on the Sunday.

We were launched so quickly that at our first annual dinner P.F. Warner was our guest of honour and became our President. Our colours were chocolate, pink and blue. The cap was arranged in the harlequin style. We had a team song, composed by that powerful left-handed smiter Pat Barrow. I can only remember the last lines of the chorus. It was delivered by the captain as he set his field, and concluded with

> 'And you in the box, I beg,
> While I go on at the gasworks end
> For the chocolate, pink and blue.'

I do not know how long the side continued to play. I turned out for it for the last time in 1929, and if I list some of its members, old timers will have an idea of the strength that we could muster. The captain, E.E. Carus-Wilson, a member of the bar, was at that time clerk to the governors of St Bart's, and a great friend of the famous Oxford-Australian, R.H. Bettington. Bettington was our spearhead, both with bat and ball. O.G. Battcock was the secretary. He was responsible, I suspect, for our link with Bucks. W.B. Franklin kept for us now and then, and usually when he played so, too, did P.W. Le Gros. Sir Henry Aubrey-Fletcher, who wrote detective stories under the name Henry Wade, also kept wicket for us. Perhaps through the Oxford Law School there was a sprinkling of lawyers – Frank Evershed and Walter Monckton, for example. Close links with Magdalen College, Oxford, produced the two Price brothers, V.R. and H.L., who were responsible for two old school fellows from Bishop Stortford – A.G. and J.H. Doggart. Do these names mean anything today? I am sure that to many old-stagers they will bring a reminiscent smile.

I can remember G.M. Louden – one of the best amateur bowlers of his day – toiling through a long, hot afternoon at Oxford against Magdalen. P.N. Durlacher was one of us; so was W.G. Lowndes. And I can remember Miles Dempsey, the famous general, then a captain in the Royal Berkshires, coming on the Clifton-Downside weekend. Anyone who turns the pages of *Wisden* for 1925 will recognise that we could put a formidable side into the field, many of whom have since achieved a considerable measure of success in public life. T.C. Hunt, for instance, another of our wicket-keepers, acquired a CBE for his services to medicine.

How was it that such a side could have been assembled so quickly, so effectively? It must have been entirely due to the personality of

Carus-Wilson. What put him on to it? Perhaps his friendship with Reg Bettington helped to form his resolve to get together a side of reasonable cricketers all of whom genuinely liked each other, who would play serious but light-hearted one-day cricket.

What was Carus-Wilson's own cricket history? Of his background I have no idea. He was on the edge of 30 in 1923. He must therefore have played some cricket before the war. He was tall, elegant, sandy-haired. He had charm. He was competent. He was someone you instinctively respected. He knew a lot about the game. He was a good captain. He *looked* a cricketer. He would walk to the wicket with a firm, confident stride. He would take guard, look round, settle his stance. Then as the bowler's arm went over, he would lift his bat; his leg would go down the wicket; his left elbow would face the bowler; his bat would follow his leg: a copybook forward stroke. But the ball would miss the bat. He usually went in number nine. He did not need to bat so very often for a side like the Ramblers, but I never saw him make a run. He once played for me in a match at Teddington. I put him in number five. He collected a magisterial cypher. The bowler was delighted, convinced that he had delivered a ball of unplayable length. The trouble was, I fancy, that Carus could not judge the speed of approaching objects. His blind spot was three feet wide and six feet long. He put himself to field at mid-on. I do not remember seeing him hold a catch.

For seven years the Ramblers flourished; then it subsided. It did not languish. It just died. I do not know how or why. Perhaps when Reg Bettington went back to Australia, Carus lost interest in the game. It seemed to me typical of club cricket in the Twenties that a man like Carus-Wilson should have built up a side like the Chiltern Ramblers.

The Invalids

The other side for which I played during those years was eminently eccentric. It was captained by the poet J.C. Squire, and it inspired the account of the village match in A.G. Macdonell's *England their England*. The various incidents were taken from several different matches on various grounds, from Bridge, from Ditchling, and from Fordcombe. But the account was not a caricature. Invalid matches were like that. Squire had got the idea of running the side during the last year of the war, when he was visiting a wounded friend in hospital. That is why it was called the Invalids. Its colours were hospital blue and orange; in broad stripes. A badge of crossed crutches was on the left-hand breast pocket. The stripes on the cap were arranged in the Harrow style. It suited men with a sallow complexion.

Unlike Carus-Wilson, Squire did not look a cricketer. He was very untidy. He was clumsy. He was short-sighted and wore powerful spectacles. He did not appear to have received any basic training. He did not stand at the wicket like a batsman. He did not run up to the popping-crease like a bowler. In the field it was a safe single every time the ball was patted in his direction. At one time he had an idea that he was an opening batsman. This was unfortunate for the other opener, who often happened to be myself, as he would convert the other man's twos into singles – one did one's best to score in boundaries – but whenever he hit the ball himself he started off to run. The opposition mercifully considered that it was unsporting to run out either himself or his partner. They did not believe that he would delay their attack for very long.

He had considerable faith in his own talents as a bowler. Macdonell's description of his action is photographic. He ambled up to the wicket and projected the ball into the sky. It had no spin on it. Certainly it had no swerve. It might pitch anywhere. But it was the kind of delivery that often broke up a partnership. He did not, however, when he had broken a partnership, recall his opening bowlers; he continued his attack!

As a captain he operated as Hitler did as a general, by the light of intuition. Once, opposed to a reasonable club side, he opened with his second and third change bowlers. At the end of the day – and it had been a long, hard day under a heavy sun – he explained his strategy. 'I thought I would get two or three cheap wickets, then loose my good bowlers when they were fresh against the tail.'

The qualifications for a Chiltern Rambler were reasonable ability on the field and friendship with one of the committee. The qualification for an Invalid was friendship with the captain. Squire, however, had a large heart and many interests. He described himself as a centipede with a foot in a hundred worlds. Some very strange performers appeared in orange and blue blazers, some of them not unlike the ragged victims of fortune with whom an earlier Sir John declined to march through Coventry. But they were all eminently companionable and some of them were cricketers of class.

The eleven that Macdonell portrayed was unknown to *Wisden*: the fat wicket-keeper was Cecil Palmer, the publisher; the fierce major was Reginald Berkeley, author of *The Lady with the Lamp*. I was disguised as Bobby Southcott. J.B. Morton (*Beachcomber* of the *Daily Express*) was the journalist who fell asleep in the outfield. But in his files there appeared a number of more than adequate players. Squire was related by marriage to C.T.A. Wilkinson, the Surrey captain. C.T.A. hit our first century for us. There were a number of Harlequins and Authentics like Arthur Barker, Howard Marshall, Louis Wharton, Walter Monckton. Anthony Bushell, the film actor, turned out sometimes. Most of Clifford Bax's Old Broughtonians played for him, including Bax himself. Squire could field a strong eleven but the essential feature about his matches was the way in which on the big occasion his men played above their form.

The staff work could not have been more casual. Old members will reminisce about sides that turned up late, that turned up short, when the taxi driver had to be requisitioned, of sides that were sent to the wrong ground: of mornings when Squire had not finished his weekly article for the *Observer*, and a third of the team had to wait for him downstairs along with the office boy who would hurry the manuscript down to Fleet Street. There were many such occasions and there were quite a few ignominious afternoons when we were hopelessly outclassed.

I remember a day against Highgate School when R.W.V. Robins was their captain. On that vast ground where you could run a nine, we were like an army in retreat, that had flung away its packs and rifles. But there were other days of shining glory. We once beat the RAOC at Aldershot; and our greatest match was at The Oval where we beat the Lords and Commons, and M.R.K. Burge, who wrote thrillers under the name of Milward Kennedy, made over 90. He had not made so many runs since he left Winchester; if he had ever made as many there. That was the thing about the Invalids: affection and loyalty made us feel that we had to save Jack's face for him. The Invalids went on playing through the Thirties. A few matches were played during the war; there were even some after it. But their heyday was in the Twenties. They, like the Chiltern Ramblers, were typical of the kind of cricket that made that decade so rich in memories.

ANOTHER SEASON, ANOTHER TIME

Bernard Hollowood

At the end of last season, after a string of exceptionally (for me) low scores,[1] I announced that I was retiring from cricket. This bombshell

---

[1] In detail they were 0, 3, 2, 0, 0 and 0; I usually manage something in the higher digits.

nearly took my colleagues by surprise; it was two or three seconds before they managed to swallow immediate emotion and comment on the effect of my decision on the club's future.

'You'll stand umpire, I hope?' said Marks, a fellow who would bowl all day and both ends if you would let him, and with me out of the way he might manage it.

'Give you ten bob for your pads,' said MacDooley, a big, tough, extramural type whose batting is contemptuous of either style or umpires' decisions.

'Well,' said Years, 'you've had a good run for your money, and I *mean* run.'

I put most of this banter down to the team's momentary uneasiness. After all, they had suddenly to face a future in which they had only one recognised opening bat and two pairs of batting gloves, and at the back of their minds was the question, 'Will this mean that his wife won't help with the teas?' I understood.

That was last September. In November the club held its annual jumble sale and my contribution to the rubble was carefully scrutinised. The books and magazines were swept aside in the rush to get at my cricketing props – the bat, gloves, pads and bag.

'So it's true,' said Marks, 'you're definitely packing it in?'

'I don't usually go back on my word,' I said.

'Well, you know best,' said MacDooley. 'If you're not up to it, you're not up to it. We ought to price your bat at five bob at least.'

'That's a bob for every run,' said Sanders.

'Rubbish,' said Marks, 'why, the edges alone are worth more than that. Remember that winning snick against Halbury?'

'It's worth 30 shillings of anybody's money,' I said.

In the end the whole job lot went for 25, including my cap. I was happy to see that a young fellow called Byers acquired them. A promising batsman, Byers. Too much right hand, of course, like most Old Carthusians, but *promising*. It was good to hand on the torch to such a likely lad.

In February the club held its annual dinner, and I attended with some embarrassment. I am not one who enjoys valedictory orations or sentimental encomiums, but I took the trouble to prepare a little speech of acknowledgment, a few words belittling my efforts for the club, and comparing my role with that of such tryers as Freddie Brown, Kenyon of Worcestershire, Simpson of Nottinghamshire, and Craig of Australia. Four speeches were delivered, all of them wordy and trite in the extreme, and there was no mention of changes in personnel. Then Marks (just elected vice-captain, Good Heaven!) got up to propose The Visitors. He had a word or two to say about all the chief guests, about their contribution to cricket, their renown, their scores and wickets and so on. Then he mentioned me:

'Finally,' he said, 'I have to mention our most recent "guest". The club will learn with regret that Mr H. had resigned from his position as deep square-leg or deep extra-cover (laughter) and will recall that he resigned from adjacent positions in 1956, 1957, 1958 and 1959. This year, it seems, his intentions are strictly honourable. He really does mean to keep out of the way. And so, gentlemen, I ask you to rise and drink a toast to our former opening bat, coupling with it the name of any club to which Mr H. may transfer his allegiance.'

As a matter of fact I had already decided in my own mind to seek pastures new. Whiteheath is not an ideal club: it is, I regret to say, torn by dissension and riddled with cliques. I have known the time when three players whose wives are not on the tea list have all been selected for the First XI in an important 'social' game – say the annual fixture with Winsley Green. And I happen to know that MacDooley (right-arm slow straight) was preferred to me (right-arm googly) several times last season merely because his car seats five – seven if you count the boot.

The club I had my eye on was none other than Winsley Green, a decent lot of chaps without an ounce of starch among them, and goodish cricketers into the bargain. I thought I should at last find cricketing happiness with them; happiness *and runs*, for it had become increasingly obvious that the difficult 'atmosphere' at Whiteheath was chiefly responsible for my moderate form with the bat.

In March I approached the Winsley secretary in the Bricklayer's Arms and my tentative overtures were warmly welcomed. 'Glad to have you, old chap,' said this fellow Taffs. 'Quite an exodus, isn't it?'

It turned out that young Byers, Marks and Years were also joining Winsley – possibly, I supposed, because there had been too many resignations at Whiteheath for the club to remain in the first flight of village clubs. Naturally enough I demanded some explanation from the boy Byers. I explained that I should never have allowed my equipment to go to a member of a rival club, that he was in honour bound to return it to the Whiteheath club. I offered him 25 shillings. Unfortunately he had already disposed of his loot. And at a decent profit, of that I was certain.

In a fortnight's time Whiteheath play their first game of the season, and I have decided to let my name go forward for selection. With Byers, Marks and Years out of the running I feel it my duty to stick by the old club one more season and see them out of trouble. Then I shall pack it in. I dare say I shall get used to the club tackle after a time. And it will be interesting to see what MacDooley makes of my bat, gloves, pads, bag and cap.

JEMMY DEAN

Rev. James Pycroft

Two veterans, Jemmy Dean and Pagden, both famed in Sussex, made a single-wicket match, in 1871, when too old and heavy to run. Jemmy was to run his own hits, but Pagden, weighing about eighteen stone, was allowed a deputy; still this could not prevent his exertion as bowler in saving short runs. Jemmy, though carrying a fair rotundity of belly, his watch-chain plumbing a perpendicular as he stood, made above fifty runs, and then knocked his own wicket down.

The amusing part was, that Jemmy had appeared at the wicket with two bats. 'What do you want with two bats?' we asked. 'Why, because I mean to stay in long enough to wear out one to be sure,' was the reply. Pagden was beaten in more senses than one – beaten physically as well as in a cricket sense.

Six months after, as I made inquiries, Dean said, 'I am sorry, sir, I played that match; I killed my man. Pagden was never well after it, and is now dead and buried.'

Jemmy Dean was a shrewd and amusing fellow, always in a good humour, and, like Ben Griffiths, most popular with the ring, at Lord's and elsewhere. His name will be found in the scores of all the great matches from about 1837 to 1860. Both as long-stop and bowler he was first-rate. His balls rose with a spin very abruptly when the ground favoured him. He was an awkward bat, but did good service frequently, when 'Go it, Jemmy!' was the cry from the men of pewter and of pipes. He once said, 'Sir, that ball was such a shave that with another coat of paint I should have had your wicket;' and when asked why the manufacturing counties were so strong at cricket he said, 'You see, sir, that cricket is a gift; and there is such a blessed lot of them up there to have the gift.' One reason for the pre-eminence of Yorkshire, Lancashire, and Nottingham is no doubt that those men can play not only enjoyably but profitably all the summer, and return to the factories in the winter; whereas in the agricultural counties cricket involves a sacrifice of employment, and we frequently see sad cases of used-up professionals. Even Pilch was in difficulties before he died; and not a few find that the usual resource of keeping a Bat and Ball public-house brings more temptations to drink than return for their little investment.

One more word of Jemmy Dean. One day we were discussing the decided superiority of Mr W.G. Grace over all the players we had ever known. 'No doubt, sir,' said Dean, 'Mr Grace stands in a class of his own; but as to his many runs you must take into account that there is no break in his practice; early and late in the cricket season, and perhaps before, Mr Grace is always playing. Now with most others there is a break and interruption; that takes the eye off the ball, and then the hand and eye do not act together. I have experienced this in my own case very often. You remember I used to keep my wicket up for hours even when I did not score much; and I do assure you, sir, that by the middle of the season my eye was so steady *I could see the stitches on the ball*.' He added judiciously, 'It is the calm and steady eye that does it – the eye that does not wink but follows the ball right up to the bat. Why, lots of gentlemen I have bowled to used regularly to shut their eyes when the ball pitched on the right spot, like bad shots when they pull the trigger.'

STAND AND DELIVER

Dennis Castle

After nearly forty years of after-dinner cricket speaking, it is time to hang up my bow-tie. I shall miss the old familiar faces of both team-mates and opponents who once stood lithely at creases but now, like me, have them etched round their eyes. I shall miss the busy winters when curtains were drawn against the blizzards outside while cricket went on stubbornly round dining tables, shining with silver cups and shields awaiting presentation. I shall miss the wit of fine speakers, the genial tedium of orators who went on too long and the end-of-season statistics as read out by captains of every eleven . . . 'Best batting performance, H. Gilks, 41 not out *v* Acme Biscuit Co., best bowling, Joe King, 4 for 186 *v* A Hovercraft XI . . .' I shall miss the pleasure of speaking in the august company of Test and county players – and the laughter in the bar afterwards.

But, above all, I shall miss the highwaymen and the pirates, those who write down your jokes on the back of the menu while you are speaking. Ironically, with the vanity of a twenty-year-old in the mid-Thirties, I ran my own wandering side, calling it 'The Footpads'. But it was not until I began speaking about the game that I actually met them.

Almost without exception there is one at every dinner. I recall Long John Silver Pencil who was a permanent 'guest' of clubs around south London. He belonged to none but apparently threatened nervous members with the Black Spot if he was not invited.

Long John Silver Pencil was not there for the meal or to enjoy himself but bent on plunder. Lean, ferret-faced and magpie-eyed, as a speaker rose that silver pencil would appear as if by sleight of hand. The menu would be reversed and when the speaker, apropos of some entirely irrelevant observation, added 'which reminds me of the story of . . .' Long John began to write. All that speaker's hard work in preparing his speech was ruthlessly transposed to the menu. The fact that someone was giving his services to the cause mattered not to Long John. He ruthlessly cached away each wise-crack.

Sometimes he would complain bitterly that I had made the same speech at Barclays Bank dinner as I had at Beddington or Spencer. 'Nothin' new from you,' he'd grumble. 'I wonder you don't get tired of it.'

But, as all public speakers know, if you have a format which works, you stick to it as long as possible, only changing it when you receive 'return' dates. So, as time went on, Long John would gaze at me contemptuously as I rose to speak, curl his lip and close his eyes. He had milked my speech dry by then. Then one night at a Mitcham dinner, seeing he was dreaming of the better loot he might have pilfered at the Cyphers dinner which was on the same night, I slipped in a new joke – not my invention but currently doing the rounds. Just a quick two-liner – but it brought the house down. Long John came to with a gasp – snatched up his pencil and stared wildly round him. 'What wassit?' he demanded of his neighbour – but the laughter went on. Long John was distraught. He gazed at me with hatred and for the rest of my speech he worried those on his sprig with nudges and whispers, trying to get them to repeat the gag.

I have no doubt he got it in the end.

In the North the anecdote buccaneer was Ballpoint Bert. Fat, heavily jowled, he sweated a good deal. He seemed to be a member of every cricket association north of Leicester and wore the appropriate tie for each occasion – all amazingly old, frayed and soup-stained by hundreds of dinners. He carried a pen of blood-red mica and was completely open about appropriating his loot. As you commenced an anecdote, he would lean back and begin to inscribe on the menu what appeared to be an illuminated address. The pale, pudding face would remain impassive, only his dewlaps swinging as he engrossed your joke. He was an artist to his light-finger tips.

Once I asked him: 'Am I going too fast for you?' always the evergreen 'ad lib' in these circumstances. The room laughed but his slitted eyes barely flickered. 'Heard the joke before,' he said, 'this is joost a reminder . . .'

In Scotland there was Angus McFilcher who, despite the request to wear a dark suit, would appear in a loud tweed hacking jacket, the heather in his lapel matching the mauve of his nose. I suspect he was a reporter, there on duty, under sufferance – but he, too, methodically committed all my anecdotes to the menu. He could throw a speaker because he would write round the edges, slowly turning the oblong card, seeming to end the joke in the middle like a scrawled maze. This produced a snake and rabbit fascination and many a speaker tailed off into petrified silence watching him. Actually he was using shorthand so I could never work the 'off the cuff' quip about going too fast . . .

The Midlands freebooter was Raffles. Always nattily dressed, evening shirt flounced, gold pen matching his teeth, he was extremely garrulous. At receptions, prior to the dinner, he would be at my elbow, greeting me as an old friend. There was a wheel-shaped badge in his lapel and I realised that, for the first time, I could see a motive for such plagiarism. I was always puzzled as to why Long John, Ballpoint Bert, McFilcher and others bothered with such plunder. None appeared likely to use the material themselves. Possibly they belonged to some speakers' thieves kitchen which fenced funny stories for pieces of eight – but Raffles was a raconteur himself.

But like them all he had no sense of shame about his joke sharping. 'I dined out all last winter on that polar bear gag of yours,' he'd say brightly. 'Hope you've got a few new ones tonight – I've got a ladies night in Birmingham next week . . .'

Raffles knew, as I knew, that no joke is copyright. But the use of other people's *anecdotes* is questionable and can, if badly misquoted, cause a slander action. My cricket speaking was constructed almost entirely from my own experiences gathered over years of playing for bizarre showbusiness cricket clubs like the Concert Artists and The Stage. My cricket in India also formed a part of the speech, again entirely peculiar to myself. Why Raffles, or indeed any other member of the pirate crew, ever wanted to adapt my personal cricket to themselves, or even in the third person, remains forever a mystery.

But Raffles regarded any use of my material by him as granting me an Order of Merit. As far as he was concerned I should be deeply honoured that he stood up, week after week, spouting *my* life story! But I never complained, as a friend of mine from that area had heard Raffles make a speech. Apparently while basic ingredients of mine were used, Raffles completely fogged them by elaborations of his own. Never known to raise a laugh, he was, sadly, the biggest bore on the circuit.

In north London there was Captain Hook. He possessed both hands but his nose gave me his name. Angularly tall, he would sit, stiff and upright like a moulting eagle in its eyrie, and he wielded a Swan pen. Besides using the reverse of the menu for my stories, he would also cross off each course as he consumed it. Hook was methodical. Leave your notes on the table when you went, during the interval, to the washroom, and he would swoop, eyes blazing with triumph and rifle through them. Not that my abbreviations could help him much but, having heard me before, he might be able to fill in some sections he had hitherto missed.

Again he seemed an eternal guest. I was told he was something to do with Cable and Wireless. So I had visions of him, heavily cloaked, slinking away from Brondesbury, Southgate or Mill Hill to a Hampstead attic to tap out my material at dead of night to a secret cricket agent in the Lofoten Islands.

The Red Shadow I so named because he was a toastmaster who wrote down every speech I made in his hearing. With a sheaf of notes in his white-gloved hands, he was ideally placed to purloin ideas. I fancy he was slightly deaf for I could hear – and feel – his heavy breathing on the nape of my neck when I was speaking. Sometimes when I raised a laugh, I'd hear him mutter exultantly: 'Useful, very useful.' In view of his job his contraband haul must have been massive. But where did he use it? Certainly it would be valueless at a toastmasters' convention for there cannot be any joke in existence that they have not heard.

Blackbeard in the West was a real swash-buckler. His bushy whiskers he used to cover his menu jottings – they also swept up the crumbs – locking his elbow round them to prevent his neighbour cribbing his work. In the East was Blind Pew. He did not start the evening sightless of course but, by the time the festivities were over, he was so drunk that he needed my lapels to hold himself upright. Pew was the least successful pirate I ever met. During the speeches he would gradually lose focus and by the end he could never read back his menu hieroglyphics. So, in the bar, he would grab me . . . 'Wha' wuz tha' you shaid 'bout Denish Com'pon? I didunt get the larsht bit . . .'

Then, like so many we all meet at such dinners, he'd become aggressively desirous of improving my own story repertoire. 'Here's one you can clean up for your speeches . . .' then ramble on about a situation entirely set in a public lavatory which relied upon a repulsive reference to sewage for the pay-off.

The highwaymen of cricket dinners were not such attractive rogues. Particularly unforgivable was Spring-heeled Jack who once stood up before my turn came and made my speech almost word for word. Visibly shaken, I had to make some drastic improvisations and managed to pass muster. Jack's rendering of my material had not been too successful but he defended himself in the bar afterwards on the grounds that nothing of mine was copyright. He refused to see any creativity or accept originality. Mulishly he arrogated that once I'd said anything in public it was anyone's meat . . . but as far as I know he never did it again. The truth was he had not expected me to be there.

Another was Dick Tapeworm, a particularly insidious plagiarist. He recorded your speech on tape ostensibly for his club's archives. Comedian Leslie Crowther and I were both victims of this when we appeared at a most reputable association's function. Their Tapeworm member resigned soon after and emigrated to another English-speaking country – taking the spools with him.

But all these freebooting types had one characteristic in common – they never laughed at any of the jokes they stole. They seemed to sail under the un-Jolly Roger. Yet evening after evening they would slink home clutching beneath their overcoats menus loaded with 'gems' for their secret treasure chests.

If you recognise any of them – many are in Davy Jones's locker by now – be kind.

SOME PASTIMES AND A FUNERAL

Lynn Doyle

Though I do not remember that life in the Ulster of my childhood was dull, looking back I can see that the range of our amusements was very limited.

Cricket was almost our only outdoor sport; and even cricket could hardly be said to flourish. When a man has followed a plough or a harrow all day, or mowed hay or pulled flax, his desire for open-air exercise has generally been satisfied. Then, time was an important factor. There was no talk of an eight-hour day for the farm labourer fifty years ago. 'Quitting-time' was six o'clock; and after that there were horses to be cleaned, and cattle fed, and supper eaten. It was well on to half-past seven before the country cricketer could take the field, which restricted his season to about eight weeks; and even in that period he finished most of his games in blind man's holiday. I have known us play till the bowler could hardly discern the wicket at which he was aiming, and remember Hughey Dixon splitting his bat with a mighty drive at a round stone rolled up by our humorist, Dick Murray.

I say, rolled up, because we practised only underhand bowling in our team, from necessity as much as from choice. We enjoyed no artificial creases of pampered turf, laid with a spirit level, and smoothed to billiard-table flatness. We esteemed ourselves well provided for with a few square yards of old lea, with the thistles cut, and the stones gathered off it. On such a pitch the young farmer or labourer stood up to fast bowling without either gloves or pads; and if his body suffered, his tongue seldom proclaimed the fact. But it was a Spartan pleasure, nevertheless; and though the pace was tempered to a small boy like myself I was always glad enough when, after I had suffered a few hard knocks, it fell to the wicket's turn.

It was not till I had been to boarding-school that I learned of such niceties of cricket as cuts and leg-glides, and forward and back play. There were but two methods of dealing with the ball, in our country team, 'blocking' and 'driving.' The same batsman seldom exhibited both strokes. Nature fixed his style. The 'blocker' was of a cautious temperament, and leaned to defence, safeguarding his wicket by the simple yet masterly plan of placing his bat in the block-hole and holding it there till danger was past. The 'driver' was of a sanguine habit of mind, and hit out at everything. It was by the latter that fame was won, and matches. Yet the life of such, though merry, was apt to be short; and in picking a team an admixture of blockers was necessary, to weary the bowlers and keep down mortality of wickets. Hughey Dixon, the blacksmith's assistant, was our most famous driver. His style was perhaps a trifle ponderous. He handled his bat very much as he used a sledge-hammer, and grunted as he smote. Too often he fell early to a wily one; but, as he was fond of saying, 'when he hit them he hit them.'

The opposite pole of fame was occupied by Thomas Hamilton, a sober-minded man, known even then to be saving. Thomas was the heart-break of bowlers, the Fabius Cunctator among batsmen of the County Down. Perhaps he was too cautious. I remember that he went in first against the K—— team, and carried his bat for three runs – but we won the match. I met Thomas not long ago. He has put on weight, and is more stolid than ever. But he brightened up hugely when I recalled our cricketing days, and reminded me of the time when he used to be called 'Six-hit Hamilton'.

The rules under which we played were not all made at Lord's, though we thought they were. In particular I remember our belief that a player was out for striking the ball with the wrong side of his bat; for when I first played cricket at boarding-school I claimed a wicket under that rule of ours, and was a long time living my blunder down. I am afraid we had another rule, unwritten, for inter-club matches, that the umpire should be very slow to give out a member of his own team; but seeing that our opponents usually played under the same code no great injustice was done.

This confession, I must admit, exhibits our club as a poor school of sportsmanship and fair play; yet we fostered some of the virtues. Toleration, that rare plant in the North East corner of Ireland, found a nursery among us. At that time the Gaelic League had not yet arisen to teach young Ireland that cricket was a Saxon and immoral game. Our membership was drawn from both sides. Our wicket-keeper, of outstanding skill in the district, and later found worthy to play for our county town, was a Nationalist, and one, too, inclined to set his light on a hill; yet though most of our players were Protestant, and even Orange, I cannot imagine Pat Heaney being superseded by an Orange butter-fingers. And we played for the game. No cups or medals adulterated our legitimate and primitive pleasure in triumphing over our enemies. We knew, too, the salutary levelling of a pastime pursued in common. Farmer and labourer, master and man, ranked at values derived from Nature. Jack was as good as his master, and sometimes a dozen runs or a couple of wickets better.

SYDNEY PAWLING

Arthur Waugh

Sydney Pawling was a man of many friends, and in the making and keeping of them his wife played no small part, for she was one of the gentlest, kindest, and most sympathetic women imaginable. She was the elder daughter of Aldam Heaton, the decorative artist, whose younger daughter, Monica, was married to Mr E.H. Ledward, a well-known solicitor, whose family were soon added to our own list of life-long friends. Immediately he was settled in Bedford Street Pawling asked me out to Hampstead, and his wife and I made friends at once. She was full of interest in young people who wanted to get married; she knew everything about ways and means; what could and what could not be done upon a small income; and, like the optimistic Harland, she was also convinced that it is better to starve together than apart. So we went to Hampstead, to be near her and her husband, and have lived in Hampstead ever since.

To be sure, our first home was not exactly the sort of place one associates with what topographers call 'the northern heights'; as a matter of fact, it was an upper part over a dairy, close to the Finchley Road station on the North London Railway. The dairy still stands on the same spot; though, in this age of absorption and amalgamation, it has changed proprietorship several times since then. But it has still the same row of sunny windows overlooking the Finchley Road, and the same little, dark, back entrance which served us for a front door; and I shouldn't wonder if the present inhabitants are still disturbed, as we were, on Sunday evenings by melancholy little girls, grasping empty jugs, and inquiring for ''alf-a-pint o' milk, please; we've run right out'. We could not help them, however; for all the milk was locked up in the cellars down below.

The building is indeed the same still, but all around is utterly changed; for in those days our row of shops, called Fitzjohn's Pavement, was the northern limit of the advancing bricks and mortar; and above the North London station, where now the maze of avenues, gardens, and roads is flanked with regiments of handsome villas, we could walk across the fields to the Heath, without encountering a building or a tradesman's cart until we emerged above Platts Lane, while the Finchley Road itself was almost as restful as a country thoroughfare, with a lonely mansion here and there, set in its green garden seclusion. Behind our back windows lay the Hampstead Cricket Ground, not yet built in by row after row of crowded houses, but overshadowed by what Pawling described at one of the club dinners as 'the glory of those umbrageous trees' – a phrase which so tickled the fancy of the unliterary sportsmen, that for months afterwards he was greeted with the inquiry, 'Hullo, Skipper; off to your umbrageous trees!' A simple-minded jest, befitting a simple-minded company; but on their native cricket-field those lusty gallants were by no means to be derided. For the Hampstead Cricket Club was a great power in those days, and Sydney Pardon, the editor of *Wisden's Almanack*, was speaking by the card when he described it as 'the nursery of Middlesex cricket'. There on a Saturday afternoon one might see A.E. Stoddart, Gregor McGregor, Dr G. Thornton, H.B. Hayman, and W.S. Hale, all members of the county side, and two of them notable internationals, yet not one of them so comfortably at home as on the Hampstead ground. And towering above them all, like an untiring eagle, was the great demon bowler of the Australian 'Eighties, F.R. Spofforth himself, still endowed with so much of the old 'devil' that he was taking, year after year, some 200 wickets in club games for less than half a dozen runs apiece, although he was over forty years old. Fast bowlers do not often last like that.

Pawling was a fast bowler, too, a very destructive ally in club cricket; and it was during our first summers in Hampstead that he also got his (rather belated) chance of appearing for the county. He always thought that he had had less than his share of luck on the cricket field, and his complaint was not unjustified. If the authorities had discovered him earlier he might have done great things. He bowled very fast, making good use of his height; but he was erratic, and had missed the advantage of professional coaching at the crucial stage, for he left Mill Hill for his uncle's office while still a young boy who had just got his school colours. In this summer of 1894 he was invited to play at Lord's for Middlesex Second XI v. Lancashire Second XI, and performed with deadly effect, his little son Claud and myself raising such a hullabaloo at the fall of each wicket that we had to be gently restrained by the mother and wife in charge of us.

But there was no need for restraint in our congratulations two nights later, when, after the arrival of the last post, the Pawlings suddenly came knocking at our door, to display an invitation from Mr A.J. Webbe, begging Sydney to play for the county in the next three matches, against Sussex, Surrey, and Kent. Then we filled a bumper to fortune and to sport; but perhaps we ought to have made it a triad. For that luck we invoked did not outlast the first of the three matches at Brighton, where 'the Skipper' scattered the Sussex men to the extent of eight for 120 (in the two innings); so that the more enthusiastic of his friends had visions of his getting a place against the Players, fast bowlers being then, as now, rare birds among the amateurs. But it was not to be. In the next two matches he only got a single wicket, and had to return to his weekly triumphs under 'the umbrageous trees'. There for many years to come he remained the most popular figure in a cheery crowd, and one of the best judges of the game that ever kept his team in a good temper, when things were going wrong, and the need of leadership was paramount.

CRICKETERS IN KHAKI

E.M. Wellings

It was no more than coincidence that, as the remaining Golden Age survivors were dropping out of the game, it became more defensive and dull in the Thirties. That was the subject of an inquiry by a commission chaired by Billy Findlay, former Lancashire stumper and MCC secretary. The Findlay Report of 1938 achieved what no other has since threatened to match. It galvanised the players, and the last two pre-war seasons were so scintillating that they dulled the memory of recent less satisfying summers.

Bradman was in England in 1938, blazing the revival trail. Hammond played one of his most majestic innings – 240 in the Test at Lord's. Hutton and Compton had arrived excitingly on the Test scene, the former hitting his marathon 364 at The Oval. Woolley played his last thrilling innings against Australian bowling at breakneck speed. Yorkshire, making light of lending leading players to England, no fewer than five at The Oval, again romped away with the Championship. And right at the top of the bill was a wonderful Test innings by Stan McCabe at Trent Bridge.

He made 232 out of 300 inside four hours, and his strokeplay was so dazzling that it drew a supreme compliment from Bradman. Most Australians were in their dressing room. The Don called them to the balcony because 'you'll never see anything like it again'. The climax was a last-wicket stand of 77 in 28 minutes with Fleetwood-Smith. McCabe's share was 72, mostly scored off Doug Wright, who had taken four wickets, and Ken Farnes, whom he hooked mercilessly. Jim Kilburn afterwards remarked, 'It all happened so fast that Hammond hardly had time to change the bowling.' Bradman was most surely right; none of us present has ever seen anything to match that innings. It was undoubtedly the greatest innings played since the Great War. Whether Gilbert Jessop's hurricane century against Australia at The Oval in 1902 matched it none can say. I doubt it.

McCabe was a curious cricketer. He had periods when he did very little for a batsman of his talents. During the remainder of that series he merely jogged along. His big scores were usually made when Australia were most in need of runs. He began the 1932–33 series by showing the other Australian batsmen how to deal with Larwood and Voce during a four-hour innings of 187. Again his hooking was a feature of fine strokeplay. In that series also he did comparatively little afterwards until making 73 in the final Test.

War put an end to cricket's exciting revival. It had long threatened, but its arrival was nonetheless a shock. It was inevitable long before the last ball was bowled in first-class cricket, and the West Indies team had already cut short their tour and sailed for home. The most unhappy match I can remember was between Kent and Yorkshire at Dover. It was played against the background din of military vehicles rumbling past the ground. Almost continuously a blackboard was carried round the boundary summoning men to report to various barracks and depots. We who were reporting the match were cut off by phone from London after lunch on each day. It was no disappointment that Yorkshire won with a day to spare.

We saw two fine players for the last time. Hedley Verity and Jerry Chalk fell in the war, but each gave us something special to remember. Chalk carried his bat for 115 through the Kent second innings of 215 while Verity was taking five for 48 for match figures of nine for 80. Chalk might well have developed into an England captain. He had the batting and fielding potential, and as their captain he hoisted Kent well up the Championship table. When war started he joined the Honourable Artillery Company, the same outfit as myself, though we were in different batteries. Soon he transferred to the RAF and won the DFC before being downed in 1943. A year later I lost my younger brother similarly. He won a DFC while bombing the enemy in a Blenheim before and during the Dunkirk evacuation.

I saw one more game in a dull stupor at Lord's while we awaited the inevitable. I cannot remember anything about it, not even who opposed Middlesex, and I have no wish to be reminded. Then on the Sunday war was declared.

'So great was the thing which started, for us, on September 3rd last year, so pervasive of our thoughts, homes, and even of our pastimes and sports, that to look back on the English cricket season of 1939 is like peeping through the wrong end of a telescope at a very small but very happy world. It is a short six months since Constantine gave the England bowlers such a cracking at The Oval, like a strong man suddenly gone mad at a fielding practice, but it might be six years, or sixteen; for we have jumped a dimension or two since then in both time and space.'

That was the first paragraph of 'Notes On The 1939 Season' by R.C. Robertson-Glasgow in the 1940 edition of *Wisden*, and a fine example of his writing. He wrote the notes because the then editor had fled London. The position fell to Norman Preston's father, Deafy Preston, who invited his close friend Crusoe to help him. Hubert Preston, deaf as could be and very good-natured, often sat next to him in the press box, where he enjoyed Crusoe's leg-pulling.

Six summers were to pass before the world was again safe for the playing of Championship and Test cricket. I am sure not more than a handful of Britons doubted that we should muddle through and eventually win the war. Even in the most depressing days, when the British Empire stood almost alone and scantily equipped against the Nazis and fascists, our confidence remained. Yet, looking back, I confess we had no justification for our belief. In the hateful name of political expedience – the cause of much disturbance in sport also during the Seventies and Eighties – our defences were shamefully neglected under Ramsay MacDonald and Stanley Baldwin, despite Churchill's many warnings. When it came to the point, moreover, our faults and mistakes were such that the stoutest heart might have wavered . . .

. . . Between times I bumped into cricketers to remind me of happier times. The first, apart from those in the HAC, was Bill Bowes when we were fellow cadets at OCTU at Llandrindod Wells. When my brother used to collect me from a satellite air-field not far from the Stiffkey firing camp to take me to his station at Upwood, Bill Edrich was among others on the station completing their training as bomber pilots. My brother between operational spells was an instructor, and he could touch down near Stiffkey while piloting young navigators whom he was instructing. Upwood also housed six WAAF officers, all particularly good-lookers. My brother married one, Bill another.

At Carlisle, Lancashire's Wilkinson, whose leg-break bowling was a war casualty, was a PT instructor, and in Gloucestershire I met Johnny Clay. He was probably second only to Tom Goddard among slow off-spin bowlers between the wars. His type was not much favoured by England selectors in that period. He played one Test only, Goddard and Vallance Jupp eight each. Left-arm and right-arm leg-spin was more in demand. It was generally believed that there was little profit in turning the ball into the good batsmen, that they were, generally speaking, vulnerable only to the ball leaving them. That was a theory which my experience tended to refute. I was quickly put on to bowl off-breaks when a left-hander began an innings, but I had more success against such batsmen when I managed to make the ball move into them. Moreover, Hutton was always more vulnerable to the off- than the leg-break. Several times in Test cricket he was tied down by off-spinners, including the South Africans Athol Rowan and Hugh Tayfield.

At the time I met Clay he had dropped a pip to become ADC to a Corps General as a lieutenant. They came to inspect a battery of the regiment in which I was adjutant. In the first gun pit visited the General took off his almost white raincoat and tossed it to Clay, who held it up and located a smear of paint. 'They always do some painting before an inspection, and the General always rubs some of it off,' was Clay's audible aside.

I met other cricketers soon after I was out of the fray and they were still in uniform or the equivalent. I played on the same side as Nichols, Morris to some of his friends and Stan to others. For Essex he did the all-rounder's double eight times, batting left-handed and bowling right-handed. He was 44 but still able to bowl fast and maintain his pace in that match at Imber Court. Before we took the field Morris told the skipper that he could bowl as long as he wanted, 'But don't take me off and ask me to come back for a second spell, for I can't.' He bowled non-stop from 11.30 until the lunch break two hours later, 21 overs of sustained speed which accounted for the early batsmen. He was a great-hearted cricketer with stamina which more modern players would regard as impossible. Three years after Yorkshire's opening pair, Holmes and Sutcliffe, had humbled Essex by making 555 for the first wicket, Nichols, with the aid of Hopper Read, avenged his county right royally. The two fast bowlers – some considered the tearaway Read the fastest bowler of the period – shot out the champions for 31, in less than an hour, and 99. Nichols took 11 for 54, the other nine going to Read for

62, and rubbed in his dominance with an innings of 146, 25 more than 11 Yorkshiremen managed in 22 innings.

On the other side of London I played against an army side captained by Tom Pearce and containing Charlie Harris of Nottinghamshire. He was a cricketer who belonged in the tradition of George Gunn, for in his various ways he was no less eccentric. Once, playing against Kent, he took out his dentures, laid them on the pitch and invited Doug Wright to bowl at them. Doug said that he could never afterwards bowl well at Harris because he remembered the incident and was put off by his suppressed laughter. Charlie's contribution to wartime cricket was mainly in a northern league, until he was chosen to play for the Army at Lord's. He declined the invitation and was summoned for interview by his CO, who explained that being chosen to play for the Army was an order, not an invitation, and asked why he did not wish to play.

'I go north each week-end to play League cricket and pick up 15 quid, Sir. Playing at Lord's I get only expenses, and Mr Warner is not too generous with them.'

Harris's explanation did not help him. His Colonel was sympathetic but insisted that he would have to play, adding 'Mr Warner tells me the public want to see you.'

So Charlie went to Lord's and dawdled along at around ten runs an hour during the morning, which did not please Plum. He tackled Harris during the lunch interval but got little change out of him.

'Mr Warner,' Charlie protested, 'You told my CO the public wanted to see me. I'm giving them a jolly good chance to do so.'

Afterwards he biffed a few fours, for he could play several roles as the mood moved him, and got out. The next week-end Sgt Harris was free to go north from the RA Depot at Woolwich to pick up his usual 15 quid in League cricket.

For me cricket had been a rare luxury in the earlier war years, four or five matches while at OCTU, a couple later in Gloucestershire and an invitation to play one in the Orkneys. Happily that was not an official match, and, the ground being perilously rough, I was able to decline. Now at the war's end I actually played more cricket than in any peacetime season since my Oxford days. I came in contact with several more recently arrived players. One I met with particular pleasure was Harold Gimblett, who in 1935 hit a century against Essex in 63 minutes in the first innings of his first match for Somerset. That remarkable knock won him the Lawrence Trophy for the season's fastest hundred. Now at Lord's, after Laurie Fishlock had scored a century for the Buccaneers, Harold did the same for the West of England. As a bowler I had a close view of him. He was, of course, a most attractive batsman, but it was as a splendid companion with whom to play cricket that I remember him particularly.

He did play Test cricket, but the war came at the worst time for him and he never enjoyed a Test tour. That was unfortunate, for he would have been an asset to any side. The six war years were fatal. He was chosen once afterwards to play for England, but he arrived on the eve of the match with a vast carbuncle on the back of his neck and was automatically ruled out. Even then, suffering as he was, Harold remained his usual cheerful self. He deserved other Test chances at that time, for while the 1946 team was being chosen he scored nearly 2000 runs and averaged almost 50. Somerset was a long way away and her players were apt to escape proper notice. They were not alone in suffering that fate. Of all our opening bowlers in the first twenty post-war years Les Jackson of Derbyshire was the most feared and respected by opposing opening batsmen. Yet he played only twice for England. Selectors, critics and all overlooked his claims, for which we really can put forward no excuse.

End-of-war cricket also gave me a match against the Australian Imperial Forces, captained by Lindsay Hassett, at the Saffrons in Eastbourne. That was my luckiest ground, and it was so that day, when the pitch lacked its benign peacetime character. It was a very low-scoring match, which the Australians won by a single wicket against our total of 128. Luck was certainly on my side that day, for I have clear recollection of playing and missing close outside the off-stump, particularly against Ces Pepper's leg-breaks and googlies. He cussed and cussed at his bad luck. Then at the lunch table he came and sat beside me, and his cricket complaints were cheerfully forgotten – until the afternoon session. The luck held, for Pepper in favourable circumstances gathered one wicket only, while my 47 was the highest score in the match. Curiously, I also enjoyed a good day while Gimblett was making his hundred at Lord's, for, after being dismissed for a duck at No. 3, that was one of the few post-war occasions when my bowling functioned well and I took five for 58. I recall that bowling particularly, for my first success was against Tom Barling, with whom I had played in the Surrey side. He was caught at second slip in my second over from an off-spinner which swung much to the off. With the new ball it was always good policy to spin a couple each over from the start. If the hand was turned sideways instead of being behind the ball, the result was often later and more appreciable away-swing than was achieved by other means. Sydney Barnes, of course, never used any other means to achieve swing.

While at OCTU Desmond Eagar was an opponent. He was skipper of the South Wales Borderers whom we visited. Desmond followed me into the Cheltenham College and Oxford sides, ten years or so behind me. Now the pair from the same stable were in opposition, and the scoresheets read:

Capt. E.D.R. Eagar b Wellings   0.
Cadet E.M. Wellings lbw b Eagar   0.

We remained good friends.

In one sense Desmond's cricket was a war casualty. In the Gloucestershire side he had been a spirited batsman with fine strokes and the urge to use them freely, to our considerable entertainment. At the war's end he joined Hampshire as captain-secretary. At the time the county were short of solid batting, and Eagar changed his methods to act as stuffing. His motives were excellent, but I always thought he was wrong to sacrifice his natural bent for attack. His bat served Hampshire well enough, but in his aggressive style he might have done even more. As secretary of a struggling county he was outstanding. Surely no county has had a secretary so devoted as Eagar was to his adopted Hampshire. By visiting all parts of the county night after night he increased the membership remarkably year after year. He worked like that for a salary few others would have accepted, for he knew Hampshire's shortages were not limited to solid batting.

Shortly before my time in the Army ended occurred the most bizarre event to underline the strange way in which Whitehall tackled war. One of our light AA detachments shot down a hedge-hopping plane over open sights with the Bofors gun, a fine achievement by the sergeant in command. Soon, however, 11 senior officers, oozing gold braid and red tabs, descended on the site to inquire why the Kerrison predictor had not been used. Some high-up – high-ups, perhaps – had an interest in that lovely firing-camp toy, which on active service was a useless liability, for the Germans flew either far above the modest range of the Bofors or very low at top speed. In that event they were not in sight long enough to allow the Kerrison to be brought into use. Only the top brass seemed ignorant of that fact.

I also saw blundering by the Navy and RAF. The Navy botched

arrangements for POWs I was to escort from Scapa Flow to Inverness. Confusion began with us finding that the Naval Intelligence Officer had not been told about the prisoners, which caused considerable delay. It proceeded with HMS *Shropshire* issuing a list of the prisoners on paper with the ship's name at the top, after insisting that the one fact which must at all costs be concealed was the ship from which we had collected them. If that news reached Germany their codes, which we knew, would have been changed for the area in which the *Shropshire* had been operating.

Security in the RAF could similarly err. One evening, while spending a week-end with my brother at Upwood, four of us visited a nearby fighter station at Wyton. We were driven by a Flight-Lieutenant Sowerby. At the entrance to Wyton he leaned out of the window and called 'Sowerby'. The corporal on guard stepped back and saluted. We proceeded inside, and I remarked to Sowerby that he seemed to be very well known there.

'No,' he said. 'I've never been here before.'

Would someone leaning out of a car window and calling 'Goering' with sufficient conviction and authority have been admitted?

Yet, scrambling through, we did win that war.

THE OBSESSIONS OF ENGLISHMEN

Margaret Campbell

A circular addressed to my husband trickled through the letter box along with bills and other unimportant literature. 'Butterflies C.C.,' I read in the top left-hand corner.

Curious to the point of dishonesty, I opened it to discover that 'Butterflies' not only play cricket against reputable old school clubs, but have a dinner and dance at a West End hotel for members and friends.

From my own experience of these masculine organisations, the very shadow of a woman reduces the whole thing to a level of absurdity. Imagination conjures up a vision of the mortal wife of one of these ephemeral creatures performing an arabesque with a Cabbage White of 53, whilst a Red Admiral of 70 cavorts gaily with the shy daughter of a Pale Clouded Yellow. The batchelor Butterfly, as usual, goes in search of any delectable greenfly that happen to be floating around.

It is recorded that, as long ago as 1865 the 'Butterflies', who were the first British club to visit Paris, were so lavishly entertained by the French that some members took their leave in so boisterous a manner that they were seized by the gendarmes and locked up. They were rescued after a satisfactory explanation had been given by the British Ambassador!

This was, however, not the only incident. That particular game was played at the Pelouse de Madrid in the Bois de Boulogne with Napoleon III and Eugénie occasionally watching the matches. It is said that when one of the players broke an arm while batting, it was only a direct appeal to the Emperor which saved the club from being closed by the police as a dangerous institution.

'Butterflies', of course, begin *in statu papilionis* so to speak, at Public School. And it was at Rugby that the 'Butterflies', who have just celebrated their centenary, had their origin.

It appears that in 1860, Rugby School formed a club called the 'Pantaloons', which was restricted to boys in the First XI. Had there been a Second XI club, no doubt they would have been called the 'Bloomers'. Two boys, Arthur Wilson and A.G. Guillemard in the Fourth XI, decided to form a club for boys who had not won their colours, and called it 'The Butterflies'.

At one of their earliest meetings in 1863, membership was extended to 'Gentlemen who had been educated at Charterhouse, Eton, Harrow, Westminster and Winchester.' In 1864, faced with these insuperable odds, the 'Pantaloons' gave way to the majority and joined forces.

Their colours of magenta, black and mauve were adopted in 1864, and Miss Anne Wilson, an aunt of the founder, designed them a blazer in white silk, gaily embroidered with butterflies.

The obsession which Englishmen have for appearing 'incognito' (not to be confused with 'Incogniti'), pervaded the Universities. At Cambridge, the trial match between the 'Perambulators' and the 'Etceteras' extended the variety of disguises to animal and mineral, since the 'Perambulators' team was drawn exclusively from 'Butterflies' schools.

No fewer than thirteen Butterflies have captained England, and in 1882–83 there were six in the team which brought back the Ashes from Australia. Among famous names which appear on the score sheets in the period between the two wars, is that of Lord Dunglass, better known today as the Earl of Home, Foreign Secretary.

In my youth I was partial to 'Wasps'; during my married life, 'Hawks' have swooped upon my husband and me from the darkest corners of hotels throughout Europe. Now, when I see an elderly 'Swallow-tail' flitting from flower to flower, I shall not be surprised when my husband shakes the pollen from his own wings and asks, 'Are you a Butterfly?'

EARLY DAYS AT BROADWAY –
BARRIE AND CRICKET

Mary Anderson de Navarro

We were a very merry little colony in Broadway: all friends – fencing, gardening, riding together. It became a joke among us that the many friends – artists, writers, musicians – who came to see us, all wanted houses in the village. Even society people and reigning London beauties, as well as several ambassadors and their wives, were equally keen, but no houses were to be had. I had a wood-carving class for men, and an embroidery-class for girls. Both did very well. Tony and I had two spiritual guilds, and tended to the wants of our poorer friends. I kept up the guitar and organ, delighting in Bach's glorious chorales, and began to sing, and I read favourite plays and sonnets of Shakespeare to intimate friends. And far above everything there was the 'little man' who had to be in everything; always occupied, always happy. Seeing Sir James Barrie (then J.M. Barrie) in London, we 'fixed up' a cricket match between his team, the Allahakbarries, and a team of artists and singers which he wished me to collect and captain . . .

    . . . The time for the great test match arrived. One lovely morning, Barrie (Captain), Owen Seaman, Augustine Birrell, Bernard Partridge, A.E.W. Mason, S. Pawling, W. Meredith,[1] Gilmour, H.T. Ford,[2] E.T. Reid, A.N. Other, three reserves and a bevy of their charming ladies, drove up to the village green, waving and cheering in the true holiday humour. We were in the road to welcome them, all like children out of school. My team included H. Plunket Greene, Kennerley Rumford, Hermann Herkomer, Frank Millet, Alfred Parsons, Tony, C. Turley Smith, C. Standring, etc., no reserves. With the exception of three or four, there were no real players. Barrie made a fascinating little book to give to the two teams; it was printed privately. Its title:

---

[1] Son of George Meredith.
[2] Member of the well-known cricketing family.

*The Allahakbarrie
Book
of
Broadway Cricket.*

dedicated

To our dear Enemy
Mary de Navarro

In my copy he has written
'With love and admiration
from the rival Captain,
J.M. Barrie.'

I cannot resist giving a few extracts from it. It is a whimsical forecast of the great Match.

'A perfect wicket, a little on the creamy side, had been prepared by the groundsmen, Millet and Navarro. . . . Barrie (Capt.) expects the wicket to play queerly.

The Broadway team took the field at 11.30; they look a gamey lot.

•   •   •   •   •   •   •

Seaman[3] is carrying his bat over his shoulder, which creates a favourable impression.

Gilmour is to take first over. He looks pale but determined.

In a strange silence Plunket Greene sends down the first ball. The next man in is Ford.

Ford stands seven feet in his stockings, and meets all balls in the middle of the pitch. . . . Ford has opened his account by pulling Greene beautifully all round the wicket for 3.

•   •   •   •   •   •   •

It is Seaman's turn to face the music. Seaman shapes very badly. I fear he will not be a stayer.

•   •   •   •   •   •   •

In lifting a ball to deep mid-off Seaman was smartly caught by Parsons standing at square leg; he had compiled a very stylish 9 in twelve and a half minutes. 13 for 2. It is still anybody's game.

Meredith is Ford's next partner. He is a graceful bat. 13 for 3.

Pawling is the next to wield the willow.

The score reads 13 for 4. It is Ford who is out.

---

[3]Sir Owen Seaman, then Editor of *Punch*.

Reed has joined Pawling, and from his third ball he gave a palpable chance to Herkomer at cover point, but it was not held. Profiting by this escape Reed fluked the ball finely through the slips for 2, and manipulated it to the on for a dainty single. He was then out l.b.w. The let-off has cost Broadway dear.

The next man in was Barrie (Capt.) On returning he received an ovation.

Partridge and Pawling now came together. Partridge is wearing his new pads. . . .

The long innings of Pawling has come to a close. He has scraped together 6. His wickets were spread-eagled by Navarro. Pawling retired much dissatisfied with the ruling of the umpire.

On Mason's joining Partridge the score stood thus: 22 for seven . . . Partridge opened by bagging a brace of lovely cuts, each for three and both off his pads.

Partridge has just despatched the sphere to the boundary. It was a glide off his pads. I am confident Partridge's pads will stand him in good stead today. . . .

Smith is bowling with his head. He has just sent down a very hot one, but Partridge opened his pads to it and four accrued.

The 50 is now up, and the scoring is terrific. Partridge has laid aside his bat and is kicking out. . . . With two threes and a beauty to the ropes for four Partridge has sent up the 60. All bowling is alike to him to-day. The 80 is now up. In a single over from Parsons, Partridge snicked him to mid-off, smashed him to leg, hurled him among the crowd, and twice lifted him in the air and banged him hard against the pavilion. This sent up the 100 amid loud applause.

There was an interval of a few minutes at this point to enable Partridge to be photographed. . . . On the game being resumed Mason appeared without his bat, and Partridge, who is much annoyed, appealed to the umpire. The decision was given against him, however, and Mason is trying to play Partridge's game. Partridge continues to give them beans. Off two overs he has scored three fours and four threes. The 130 is now up.

In winter Partridge is by profession an artist. He is on the ground staff of *Punch*. He is a modest unaffected fellow, and very popular among his brother pros. According to *Who's Who* he has yet published nothing, but contemplates a work to be entitled *A New Way to Play Old Cricket*. . . . His telegraphic address is 'Pads,' London. His position at the wicket is easy and alert. He plays with a very straight pad.

• • • • • • •

Mason[4] is out, caught and bowled, and has lent invaluable assistance, which must not be judged by the number of his runs. His full score stands thus: 1.

The remaining batsmen are Birrell and 'Tother. The end is now close at hand.

Herkomer is deputed to bowl. The first ball Birrell got went straight through him. The second, third, and fourth hit him on the chest. Herkomer has found the spot.

Birrell is out. 'Tother missed the first ball and ran, but he was given out. His has been a short but merry innings. The tenth wicket fell at 132. Partridge carried his pads for a superb 110.

• • • • • • •

It reads merrily enough, but the high nervous tension, even consternation we all experienced during the game was not at all merry.

It may seem suspicious, but I do not remember who won that year. I know one of my men, Herkomer, was carried off the field in triumph. So it looks as if *we* won. (I can only hope Barrie will not see this book.)

The next summer there was another match, Conan Doyle being on Barrie's side. It had come to my ears he had made 100 at Lords. I, therefore, wrote to Barrie before the match saying I hoped he would not bring crack players, and that he should be like unto me in having only 'amateurs' on his side, or words to that effect. I admit a 'centurion' made me nervous. I give his reply; it is a curious mixture of 'vitriol' and the milk of human kindness'.

DEAR LADY,

I am naturally greatly elated by your letter, and the kind things you insinuate rather than express. What particularly delights me is the note of uneasiness which you are at such pains to hide, but which bobs up repeatedly thro'out your bold defiance. The other day I showed my big dog to a child and he kept saying, to give himself confidence, 'He won't bite me; he won't bite me; I'm not afraid of his biting me,' and it is obvious to the Allahakbarries that even in this manner do you approach me. They see also a wistfulness on your face as if, after having lorded it over mankind, you had at last met your match. Not, they say, that it

---

[4]Author of *The Four Feathers*, etc.

will be your match. They read between the lines that in your heart you know it cannot be your match. Hence the wistfulness of your face as the summer draws near.

As one captain speaking to another, I would beg you not to let your team see that you are hopeless of their winning. It will only demoralize them *still further*. As for my score last year,[5] it was naturally a bitter pill to you, coming as it did somewhat unexpectedly, but it is unwise to let your mind brood on what I may do at our next engagement. As you say I may make five, but try to hope that by some accident I may not be in such superb form again.

I have no intention of changing my team this year. If I can get them I shall bring down last year's *winners* without alteration. That is, unless you, *as on another occasion*, get some of your musicians and artists from Oxford.

Also I offered last year not to put on Doyle and Pawling to bowl unless you put in your cracks, and when the fatal day arrives I am willing to make a similar offer again. I have always wanted the poorer players to have a chance, but your side would never agree.

Lastly, you say 'Be then like unto me.' If you would kindly tell me how it can be done, I shall proceed to do it right away.

Don't think by this that I mean I want to lure your players on to my side. I mean I want to be like you in your nobler moments. Teach me your fascinating ways. Teach me to grow your face. Teach me how you manage to be born anew every morning.

In short, I make you a sporting offer. Teach me all these things, and I will teach your team how to play cricket.

Awaiting your reply,
Yours ever,
J.M. BARRIE.

I believe (again I hope this book will escape him) Barrie was jealous of Tony's cricket. To have one of his best men 'spread-eagled' by a beginner – whose games were baseball, racquets, tennis – must have been a shattering blow to him. I may be wrong in this belief, but of one thing I am certain: the brilliant Barrie was not a shining light in the cricket field. I never saw him make a single run. His speciality seemed to be in *poultry*.

---

[5]It will be remembered that his score was a duck.

Often in passing by the old inglenook in the hall, I can still see the slight figure of Barrie sitting in it, smoking a long church-warden pipe, his limpid eyes looking as innocent as those of a baby, while, as I learned to my sorrow, he was planning murder to my team: serenely puffing away, and death to the Broadway team in his heart!

Never was there more chaff than between the teams and their captains. We were like happy children and, D.G., some of us are so still. Barrie is not tall, in the cricket days he was very slim; his pale face is lit up by large, kind grey eyes; a lovable, a fascinating friend.

'Was ever set so huge a heart
Within so small a frame?
So much of tenderness and grace
Confined in such a slender space?'[6]

THE FLOWER SHOW MATCH

Siegfried Sassoon

Butley Church clock was tolling twelve while our opponents were bearing down on us from the other side of the field, with William Dodd already half-way across to meet them. But the Rotherden men appeared to be in no great hurry to begin the game as they stopped to have a look at the wicket. Meanwhile Butley bells chimed sedately to the close of the mellow extra celebration which Providence allowed them every three hours without fail . . .

'I suppose they've got their best team?' I faltered to Dixon, whose keen gaze was identifying the still-distant stalwarts.

'You bet they have!' he replied with a grim smile.

Two of the tallest men had detached themselves from the others and were now pacing importantly down the pitch with Dodd between them. Dixon indicated this group. 'They've got Crump and Bishop, anyhow,' he remarked . . . Crump and Bishop! The names had a profound significance for me. For many years I had heard Dixon speak of them, and I had even watched them playing in a few Flower Show Matches. Heavily built men in dark blue caps, with large drooping moustaches,

[6]Harry Graham's *J. M. Barrie.*

one of them bowling vindictively at each end and Butley wickets falling fast; or else one of them batting at each end and Butley bowling being scored off with masterful severity.

But they had also produced a less localised effect on me. Rotherden was on the 'unhunted' side of our district; it was in a part of the county which I somehow associated with cherry-blossom and black-and-white timbered cottages. Also it had the charm of remoteness, and whenever I thought of Crump and Bishop, I comprehensively visualised the whole fourteen miles of more or less unfamiliar landscape which lay between Butley and Rotherden. For me the names meant certain lovely glimpses of the Weald, and the smell of mown hayfields, and the noise of a shallow river flowing under a bridge. Yet Crump was an ordinary auctioneer who sold sheep and cattle on market days, and Bishop kept the 'Rose and Crown' at Rotherden.

III

Butley had lost the toss. As we went on to the field I tightened the black and yellow scarf which I wore round my waist; the scarf proved that I had won a place in my House Eleven at school, and it was my sole credential as a cricketer. But today was more exciting and important than any 'House Match', and my sense of my own inferiority did not prevent me from observing every detail of the proceedings which I am now able to visualise so clearly across the intervening years.

The umpires in their long white coats have placed the bails on the stumps, each at his own end, and they are still satisfying themselves that the stumps are in the requisite state of exact uprightness. Tom Seamark, the Rotherden umpire, is a red-faced sporting publican who bulks as large as a lighthouse. As an umpire he has certain emphatic mannerisms. When appealed to he expresses a negative decision with a severe and stentorian 'NOT OUT': but when adjudicating that the batsman is out, he silently shoots his right arm toward the sky – an impressive and irrevocable gesture which effectively quells all adverse criticism. He is, of course, a tremendous judge of the game, and when not absorbed by his grave responsibilities he is one of the most jovial men you could meet with.

Bill Sutler, our umpire, is totally different. To begin with, he has a wooden leg. Nobody knows how he lost his leg; he does not deny the local tradition that he was once a soldier, but even in his cups he has never been heard to claim that he gave the limb for Queen and Country. It is, however, quite certain that he is now a cobbler (with a heavily waxed moustache) and Butley has ceased to deny that he is a grossly partisan umpire. In direct contrast to Tom Seamark he invariably signifies 'not out' by a sour shake of the head: when the answer is an affirmative one he bawls 'Hout' as if he'd been stung by a wasp. It is reputed that (after giving the enemy's last man out leg-before in a closely fought finish) he was once heard to add, in an exultant undertone – 'and I've won my five bob'. He has also been accused of making holes in the pitch with his wooden leg in order to facilitate the efforts of the Butley bowlers.

The umpires are in their places. But it is in the sunshine of my own clarified retrospection that they are wearing their white coats. While I was describing them I had forgotten that they have both of them been dead for many years. Nevertheless, their voices are distinctly audible to me. 'Same boundaries as usual, Bill?' shouts Seamark, as loudly as if he were talking to a deaf customer in his tap-room. 'Same *as* usual, Muster Seamark; three all round and four over the fence. Draw at six-thirty, and seven if there's anything in it,' says Sutler. And so, with an intensified detachment, I look around me at the Butley players, who are now safely distributed in the positions which an omniscient Dodd has decreed for them.

I see myself, an awkward overgrown boy, fielding anxiously at mid on. And there's Ned Noakes, the whiskered and one-eyed wicket-keeper, alert and active, though he's forty-five if he's a day. With his one eye (and a glass one) he sees more than most of us do, and his enthusiasm for the game is apparent in every attitude. Alongside of him lounges big Will Picksett, a taciturn good-natured young yokel; though over-deliberate in his movements, Will is a tower of strength in the team, and he sweeps half-volleys to the boundary with his enormous brown arms as though he were scything a hayfield. But there is no more time to describe the fielders, for Dodd has thrown a bright red ball to Frank Peckham, who is to begin the bowling from the top end. While Crump and Bishop are still on their way to the wickets I cannot help wondering whether, to modern eyes, the Butley team would not seem just a little unorthodox. William Dodd, for example, comfortably dressed in a pale pink shirt and grey trousers; and Peter Baitup, the ground-man (whose face is framed in a 'Newgate fringe'), wearing dingy white trousers with thin green stripes, and carrying his cap in his belt while he bowls his tempting left-hand slows. But things were different in those days.

In the meantime Bill Crump has taken his guard and is waiting with watchful ease to subjugate the first ball of the match, while Peckham, a stalwart fierce-browed farmer, takes a final look round the field. Peckham is a fast bowler with an eccentric style. Like most fast bowlers, he starts about fifteen paces from the wicket, but instead of *running* he *walks* the whole way to the crease, very much on his heels, and breaking his aggressive stride with a couple of systematic hops when about half-way to his destination. Now he is ready. Seamark pronounces the word 'Play!' And off he goes, walking for all he is worth, gripping the ball ferociously, and eyeing the batsman as if he intends to murder him if he can't bowl him neck and crop. On the ultimate stride his arm swings over, and a short-pitched ball pops up and whizzes alarmingly near Crump's magnificent moustache. Ned Noakes receives it rapturously with an adroit snap of his gauntlets. Unperturbed, and with immense deliberation, Crump strolls up the pitch and prods with his bat the spot where he has made up his mind that the ball hit the ground on its way toward his head. The ground-man scratches his nose apologetically. 'Don't drop 'em too short, Frank,' says Dodd mildly, with an expostulatory shake of his bristly grey cranium. Thus the match proceeds until, twenty-five years ago, it is lunch time, and Rotherden has made seventy runs with three wickets down. And since both Crump and Bishop have been got rid of, Butley thinks it hasn't done badly.

The Luncheon Tent stood on that part of the field where the Flower Show ended and the swings and roundabouts began. Although the meal was an informal affair, there was shy solemnity in the faces of most of the players as they filtered out of the bright sunshine into the sultry, half-lit interior, where the perspiring landlord of the 'Chequers' and his buxom wife were bustling about at the climax of their preparations. While the cricketers were shuffling themselves awkwardly into their places, the brawny barman (who seemed to take catering less seriously than his employers) sharpened the carving-knife on a steel prong with a rasping sound that set one's teeth on edge while predicting satisfactory slices of lamb and beef, to say nothing of veal and ham pie and a nice bit of gammon of bacon.

As soon as all were seated Dodd created silence by rapping the table; he then put on his churchwarden face and looked toward Parson Yalden, who was in readiness to take his cue. He enunciated the grace in slightly unparsonic tones, which implied that he was not only Rector of Rotherden, but also a full member of the MCC and first cousin once removed to Lord Chatwynd. Parson Yalden's parishioners occasionally complained that he paid more attention to cricket and pheasant shooting than was fit and proper. But as long as he could afford to keep a hard-working curate he rightly considered it his own affair if he chose to spend three days a week playing in club and country-house matches all over the county. His demeanour when keeping wicket for his own parish was both jaunty and magisterial, and he was renowned for the strident and obstreperous bellow to which he gave vent when he was trying to bluff a village umpire into giving a batsman out 'caught behind'. He was also known for his habit of genially engaging the batsman in conversation while the bowler was intent on getting him out, and I have heard of at least one occasion when he tried this little trick on the wrong man. The pestered batsman rounded on the rather foxy-faced clergyman with, 'I bin playing cricket nigh on thirty years, and parson or no parson, I take the liberty of telling you to hold your blasted gab.'

But I hurriedly dismissed this almost unthinkable anecdote when he turned his greenish eyes in my direction and hoped, in hearty and ingratiating tones, that I was 'going to show them a little crisp Ballboro' batting'.

The brisk clatter of knives and forks is now well started, and the barman is busy at his barrel. Conversation, however, is scanty, until Tom Seamark, who is always glad of a chance to favour the company with a sentiment, clears his throat impressively, elevates his tankard, fixes Jack Barchard with his gregarious regard, and remarks, 'I should like to say, sir, how very pleased and proud we all are to see you safe 'ome again in our midst.' Jack Barchard has recently returned from the Boer War where he served with the Yeomanry. The 'sentiment' is echoed from all parts of the table, and glasses are raised to him with a gruff 'Good 'ealth, sir,' or 'Right glad to see you back, Mr Barchard.' The returned warrior receives their congratulations with the utmost embarrassment. Taking a shy at my ginger-beer, I think how extraordinary it is to be sitting next to a man who has really been 'out in South Africa'. Barchard is a fair-haired young gentleman farmer. When the parson suggests that 'it must have been pretty tough work out there', he replies that he is thundering glad to be back among his fruit trees again, and this, apparently, is about all he has to say about the Boer War.

But when the meal was drawing to an end and I had finished my helping of cold cherry-tart, and the barman began to circulate with a wooden platter for collecting the half-crowns, I became agonisingly aware that I had come to the match without any money. I was getting into a panic while the plate came clinking along the table, but quiet Jack Barchard unconsciously saved the situation by putting down five shillings and saying, 'All right, old chap, I'll stump up for both.' Mumbling, 'Oh, that's jolly decent of you,' I wished I could have followed him up a hill in a 'forlorn hope' . . . He told me, later on, that he never set eyes on a Boer the whole time he was in South Africa.

• • • • • •

The clock struck three, and the Reverend Yalden's leg-stump had just been knocked out of the ground by a vicious yorker from Frank Peckham. 'Hundred and seventeen. Five. Nought,' shouted the Butley scorer, popping his head out of the little flat-roofed shanty which was known as 'the pavilion'. The battered tin number-plates were rattled on to their nails on the scoring-board by a zealous young hobble-dehoy who had undertaken the job for the day.

'*Wodger* say last man made?' he bawled, though the scorer was only a few feet away from him.

'Last man, *Blob*.'

The parson was unbuckling his pads on a bench nearby, and I was close enough to observe the unevangelical expression on his face as he looked up from under the brim of his panama hat with the MCC ribbon round it. Mr Yalden was not a popular character on the Butley ground, and the hobbledehoy had made the most of a heaven-sent opportunity.

From an undersized platform in front of the Horticultural Tent the Butley brass band now struck up 'The Soldiers of the Queen'. It's quite like playing in a county match, I thought, as I scanned the spectators, who were lining the fence on two sides of the field. Several easily recognisable figures from among the local gentry were already sauntering toward the Tea Tent, after a gossiping inspection of the Flower Show. I could see slow-moving Major Carmine, the best dressed man in Butley, with his white spats and a carnation in his buttonhole; and the enthusiastic curate, known as 'Hard Luck' on account of his habit of exclaiming, 'Oh, hard luck!' when watching or taking part in games of cricket, lawn tennis, or hockey. He was escorting the Miss Pattons, two elderly sisters who always dressed alike. And there was Aunt Evelyn, with her red sunshade up, walking between rosy faced old Captain Huxtable and his clucking, oddly dressed wife. It was quite a brilliant scene which the Butley Band was doing its utmost to sustain with experimental and unconvincing tootles and drum-beatings.

Soon afterwards, however, the Soldiers of the Queen were overwhelmed by the steam-organ which, after a warning hoot, began to accompany the revolving wooden horses of the gilded roundabout with a strident and blaring fanfaronade. For a minute or two the contest of cacophonies continued. But in spite of a tempestuous effort the band was completely outplayed by its automatic and unexhaustible adversary. The discord becoming intolerable, it seemed possible that the batsmen would 'appeal against the music' in the same way that they sometimes 'appeal against the light' when they consider it inadequate. But William Dodd was equal to the emergency; with an ample gesture he conveyed himself across the ground and prohibited the activity of the steam-organ until the match was finished. The flitting steeds now revolved and undulated noiselessly beneath their gilded canopy, while the Butley Band palavered peacefully onward into the unclouded jollity of the afternoon.

• • • • • •

The clock struck four. Rotherden were all out for 183 and Tom Dixon had finished the innings with a confident catch on the boundary off one of Dodd's artfully innocent lobs. No catches had come my way, so my part in the game had been an unobtrusive one. When Dodd and Picksett went out to open our innings it was a matter of general opinion in the Beer Tent that the home team had a sporting chance to make the runs by seven o'clock, although there were some misgivings about the wicket and it was anticipated that Crump and Bishop would make the ball fly about a bit when they got to work.

Having ascertained that I was last but one on the list in the scorebook, I made my way slowly round the field to have a look at the Flower Show. As I went along the boundary in front of the spectators who were leaning their elbows on the fence I felt quite an important public character. And as I shouldn't have to go in for a long while yet, there was no need to feel nervous. The batsmen, too, were shaping confidently, and there was a shout of 'Good ole Bill! That's the way to keep 'em on the carpet!' when Dodd brought off one of his celebrated square-cuts to the hedge off Bishop's easy-actioned fast bowling. Picksett followed this up with an audacious pull which sent a straight one from Crump skimming first bounce into the Tea Tent, where it missed the short-sighted doctor's new straw hat by half an inch and caused quite a flutter among the tea-sipping ladies.

'Twenty up,' announced the scorer, and the attendant hobbledehoy nearly fell over himself in his eagerness to get the numbers up on the board. A stupendous appeal for a catch at the wicket by the Reverend Yalden was countered by Sutler with his surliest shake of the head, and the peg-supported umpire was the most popular man on the field as he ferried himself to his square-leg location at the end of the over. Forty went up; then Dodd was clean bowled by Crump.

' 'Ow's *that*?' bawled a ribald Rotherden partisan from a cart in the road, as the rotund batsman retreated; warm but majestic, he acknowledged the applause of the onlookers by a slight lifting of his close-fitting little cap. Everybody was delighted that he had done so well, and it was agreed that he was (in the Beer Tent) 'a regular chronic old sport' and (in the Tea Tent) 'a wonderful man for his age'. Modest Jack Barchard then made his appearance and received a Boer War ovation.

Leaving the game in this prosperous condition, I plunged into the odoriferous twilight of the Horticultural Tent. I had no intention of staying there long, but I felt that I owed it to Aunt Evelyn to have a look at the sweet peas and vegetables at any rate. In the warm muffled air the delicate aroma of the elegant sweet peas was getting much the worst of it in an encounter with the more aggressive smell of highly polished onions. Except for a couple of bearded gardeners who were conferring in professional undertones, I had the tent to myself. Once I was inside I felt glad to be loitering in there, alone and away from the optical delirium of the cricket. The brass band had paused to take breath: now and again the brittle thud of a batsman's stroke seemed to intensify the quiescence of the floralised interior.

As I sniffed my way round I paid little attention to the card-inscribed names of the competitors (though I observed that the Miss Pattons had got second prize for a tasteful table-decoration): I found many of the flowers tedious and unpleasing – more especially the bulbous and freckled varieties with the unpronounceable names – the kind of flowers which my aunt always referred to as 'gardeners' green-houseries'. On the whole the fruit and vegetables gave me most enjoyment. The black cherries looked delicious and some of the green gooseberries were as large as small hen's eggs. The two gardeners were concentrating on Sam Bathwick's first-prize vegetables and as they seemed to grudge making way for me I contented myself with a glimpse of an immense marrow and some very pretty pink potatoes. As I passed, one of the gardeners was saying something about 'copped 'im a fair treat this time', and I absent-mindedly wondered who had been copped. When I emerged the home team had lost two more wickets and the condition of the game was causing grave anxiety. Reluctantly I drifted toward the Tea Tent for a period of social victimisation.

•　•　•　•　•

The Tea Tent was overcrowded and I found Aunt Evelyn sitting a little way outside it in comparative seclusion. She was in earnest communication with Miss Clara Maskall, a remarkable old lady who had been born in the year of the Battle of Waterloo and had been stone-deaf for more than sixty years.

My aunt was one of the few people in the neighbourhood who enjoyed meeting Miss Maskall. For the old lady had a way of forgetting that the rest of the world could hear better than she could, and her quavering comments on some of the local gentlefolk, made in their presence, were often too caustic to be easily forgotten. She was reputed to have been kissed by King George the Fourth. She was wearing a bunched-up black silk dress, and her delicately withered face was framed in a black poke-bonnet, tied under the chin with a white lace scarf. With her piercingly alert eyes and beaky nose she looked like some ancient and intelligent bird. Altogether she was an old person of great distinction, and I approached her with an awful timidity. She had old-fashioned ideas about education, and she usually inquired of me, in creaking tones, whether I had recently been flogged by my schoolmaster.

But the menace of Roman Catholicism was her most substantial and engrossing theme; and up to the age of ninety she continued to paste on the walls of her bedroom every article on the subject which she could find in *The Times* and the *Morning Post*. Aunt Evelyn told me that the walls were almost entirely papered with printed matter, and that she had more than once found Miss Maskall sitting on the top step of a library ladder reading some altitudinous article on this momentous question of 'the Scarlet Woman'. To the day of her death she never so much as trifled with a pair of spectacles. But she was still very much alive when I saw her at the Flower Show Match. Sitting bolt upright in a wicker-chair, she scrutinised me keenly and then favoured me with a friendly little nod without losing touch with what my aunt was engaged in telling her by 'finger-talk'.

'*What* is it the man has been doing, Evelyn?' she asked, her queer, uncontrolled voice quavering up to a bird-like shrillness. There was something rather frightening about her defective intonation.

'Write it down; write it down,' she screeched, clawing a tablet and pencil out of her lap and consigning them to Aunt Evelyn, who hurriedly scribbled two or three lines and returned the tablet for her to read aloud, 'such a dreadful thing, the judges have found out that Bathwick has been cheating with his prize vegetables'. She passed it back with a tremulous cackle.

'How did he do it?' More scribbling, and then she read out, 'He bought all the vegetables at Ashbridge. The judges suspected him, so they went to his garden in a pony trap and found that he has *no glass* –

not even a cucumber frame.' Miss Maskall chuckled delightedly at this, and said that he ought to be given a special prize.

'I call it downright dishonest. Almost as bad as embezzlement', wrote Aunt Evelyn who, as one of the judges, could scarcely be expected to treat the offence in a spirit of levity.

Miss Clara now insisted that she must herself inspect the fraudulent vegetables. Rising energetically from her chair, she grasped her ebony stick with an ivory knuckled hand, and shaped an uncompromising course for the Horticultural Tent with Aunt Evelyn and myself in tow. The villagers at the gate made way for her with alacrity, as though it had dawned on them that she was not only the most ancient, but by far the most interesting object to be seen at the Flower Show Match.

• • • • • •

Miss Maskall had made the game seem rather remote. She cared nothing for cricket, and had only come there for an afternoon spree. But she was taciturn during her tour of the Flower Show: when we tucked her into her shabby old victoria she leant back and closed her eyes. Years ago she must have had a lovely face. While we watched her carriage turn the corner I wondered what it felt like to be eighty-seven; but I did not connect such antiquity with my own future. Long before I was born she had seen gentlemen playing cricket in queer whiskers and tall hats.

Next moment I was safely back in the present, and craning my neck for a glimpse of the scoreboard as I hustled Aunt Evelyn along to the Tea Tent. There had been a Tea Interval during our absence, so we hadn't missed so very much. Five wickets were down for ninety and the shadows of the cricketers were growing longer in the warm glare which slanted down the field. A sense of my own share in the game invaded me and it was uncomfortable to imagine that I might soon be walking out into the middle to be bowled at by Crump and Bishop, who now seemed gigantic and forbidding. And then impetuous Ned Noakes must needs call Frank Peckham for an impossibly short run, and his partner retreated with a wrathful shake of his head. Everything now depended on Dixon who was always as cool as a cucumber in a crisis.

'Give 'em a bit of the long handle, Tom!' bawled someone from the Beer Tent, while he marched serenely toward the wicket, pausing for a confidential word with Noakes who was still looking a bit crest-fallen after the recent catastrophe. Dixon was a stylish left-hander and never worried much about playing himself in. Bishop was well aware of this, and he at once arranged an extra man in the outfield for him. Sure enough, the second ball he received was lifted straight into long-off's hands. But the sun was in the fielder's eyes and he misjudged the flight of the catch. The Beer Tent exulted vociferously. Dixon then set about the bowling and the score mounted merrily. He was energetically supported by Ned Noakes. But when their partnership had added over fifty, and they looked like knocking off the runs, Noakes was caught in the slips off a bumping ball and the situation instantly became serious again.

Realising that I was in next but one, I went off in a fluster to put my pads on, disregarding Aunt Evelyn's tremulous 'I do so hope you'll do well, dear.' By the time I had arrived on the other side of the ground, Amos Hickmott, the wheelwright's son, had already caused acute anxiety. After surviving a tigerish appeal for 'leg-before', he had as near as a toucher run Dixon out in a half-witted endeavour to escape from the bowling. My palsied fingers were still busy with straps and buckles when what sounded to me like a deafening crash warned me that it was all over with Hickmott. We still wanted seven runs to win when I wandered weakly in the direction of the wicket. But it was the end of an over, and Dixon had the bowling. When I arrived the Reverend Yalden was dawdling up the pitch in his usual duck-footed progress when crossing from one wicket to the other.

'Well, young man, you've got to look lively this time,' he observed with intimidating jocosity. But there seemed to be a twinkle of encouragement in Seamark's light blue eye as I established myself in his shadow.

Dixon played the first three balls carefully. The fourth he smote clean out of the ground. The hit was worth six, but 'three all round and four over' was an immemorial rule at Butley. Unfortunately, he tried to repeat the stroke, and the fifth ball shattered his stumps. In those days there were only five balls to an over.

Peter Baitup now rolled up with a wide grin on his fringed face, but it was no grinning moment for me at the bottom end when Sutler gave me 'middle-and-leg' and I confronted impending disaster from Crump with the sun in my eyes. The first ball (which I lost sight of) missed my wicket by 'a coat of varnish' and travelled swiftly to the boundary for two byes, leaving Mr Yalden with his huge gauntlets above his head in an attitude of aggrieved astonishment. The game was now a tie. Through some obscure psychological process my whole being now became clarified. I remembered Shrewsbury's century and became as bold as brass. There was the enormous auctioneer with the ball in his hand. And there I, calmly resolved to look lively and defeat his destructive aim. The ball hit my bat and trickled slowly up the pitch. 'Come on!' I shouted, and

Peter came gallantly on. Crump was so taken by surprise that we were safe home before he'd picked up the ball. And that was the end of the Flower Show Match.

Chapter 10

FICTION
DEPARTMENT

Sir Home Gordon

There were two things Paul longed for – to be married to Vanda and to play for Middlesex.

Whilst both families thoroughly approved of the engagement, they mutually agreed that as yet they were too young to marry. Lady Santall had been impressed with the rapidity of the war-marriages, and the almost equal rapidity with which some of them developed into failures. Paul's grandmother, being old-fashioned as well as old in years, described love as stuff and nonsense.

'I married your grandfather because my mother told me to, and it turned out well, as you can see by the inscription I put on his tombstone. Indeed, his only real fault was snoring, and that may have been due to adenoids, which were not discovered until after his time. Well, he married at thirty, and so did your father, Paul, and that will be time enough for you. The longer a marriage is postponed, the better the young couple know their own minds.'

In vain Paul and Vanda protested; but, as she was equally obdurate about not running away with a registry office certificate, he could only grumble that he was being sacrificed to eight prospective bridesmaids and some bishop as well as a bridal dress.

However, Vanda had the engaged girl's way of comforting her man, and they enjoyed plenty of freedom in going about together. The liberty accorded to the modern girl is positively disconcerting to old maids, who regret that their own opportune time has gone never to return. Chances missed are even more fatal in life than in cricket.

Paul's opportunity to represent Middlesex soon came. A county so dependent on its amateurs can rarely get it full strength for out-matches before August. So Paul was the recipient, at rather short notice, of a place in the county side against Somersetshire at Weston-super-Mare. Travelling from Paddington with the rest of the unpaid division, he was soon set at his ease. Some county sides indulge sociable cricket; others, off the field, are frankly bored with one another. The Middlesex amateurs prided themselves on being a happy family, and any colt was made welcome so long as he showed himself all right.

Somersetshire have invariably played the most sporting of games. Often their elevens seem gathered on the compulsory principle of somehow having to fill the three or four last places; but the finest traditions are always acted up to. At their best, they have upset the most uniformly successful opponents, whilst their history bristles with good finishes and unflagging efforts, often under circumstances that would have depressed other than their succession of great-hearted captains.

The ground, inside a park, at Weston-super-Mare is of a somewhat unconventional character; for the arrangements are not quite so complete as in other places, and the wicket possesses a tendency towards low-scoring diametrically contrary to pitches such as those at Leyton or Brighton.

Proceedings began with a day so wet that a perfunctory visit to the ground was almost superfluous. Still, both sides hung about in the listless fashion that is associated with waiting for play. Some told and others listened to cricket yarns, whilst a few engaged in a miniature form of batting in a dressing-room with a ball bowled at six yards. The proceedings were noisily amusing until abandoned because they grew tiresome. Luncheon became rather protracted since there was nothing to do. Then, whilst the home team scattered, four of the amateur visitors retired to bridge at the hotel, and the rest, including Paul, who did not play cards, patronised the local cinema.

Next morning, with a hot sun on the wet ground, it was evident that the bowlers would have complete command, though a drying wind foreshadowed improvement later. As a matter of fact, less than four hours finished off the whole match. The Middlesex captain took the risk that is so seldom justified of putting the other side in, and his first pair of bowlers were effective enough to dismiss the home team for 35. Indeed, had not one batsman hit out lustily, the score might have been a record in minimums. Middlesex could not do very much, but the batsmen who opened approached 30 before being parted, and the big tapper of the side hit six fours, which was the highest contribution of the day. Somerset, on again facing the original couple of bowlers, lost 5 wickets for as many runs, and though the wicket-keeper and a bowler played up with some resolution, they could not save the innings defeat.

Paul's contribution had been a couple of singles, and he had not been called on to bowl. His performance might have been no worse than that of more seasoned men on the side, but he could not tell whether he would be granted another trial or just be shunted for somebody else, to be given an opportunity under more favourable conditions.

With nothing said to him by anyone in authority, he returned to London to play for the Eton Ramblers against the Household Brigade at The Oval, since the charming ground of the soldiers at Burton's Court appears to be lost evermore owing to the war. Not only was the one-day match a jolly one, but Paul did well. Feeling familiar with his surroundings, from war-time associations, he took four wickets, and hit so freely that his share for the first wicket, when he was bowled, was 63, whilst Tommy Santall had made 18.

He dined that night with the King's Guard at St James's Palace, one of the pleasantest incidents that can befall a young man; the meal being superlatively good, even better than usual on that occasion, because the Gold-Stick-in-Waiting was one of the guests. The dignified room, with the fine portraits on the walls, the magnificent display of plate on sideboard and table, and the way the eight took their ease under the attentive care of the mess-servants formed a vivid contrast to many meals he had eaten 'Somewhere in France' in the previous years.

It must be confessed that Paul was bitterly disappointed when, in the next county match, there was no overture to include him in the Middlesex side, and perhaps he was not altogether regretful to find they had much the worst of the draw at Leyton. Owing to some obvious shortage of bowling, under the two-day conditions they were likely to play a tiresome preponderance of unfinished matches.

He went up to Lord's to see the start of their next match v. Kent, and directly he entered the pavilion he was hailed with:

'Ah, Rignold, the very man we want! Macbeth is too seedy to play, and we've been telephoning for you to fill his place.'

In an hour and a half before lunch Kent compiled 97 for 2, and then rain prevented any more play. Under the difficult conditions on the morrow, this proved highly advantageous. The hop county were out for 196; Paul being given an over when the last wicket was knocking up runs, and obtaining it by a catch at third man.

Somewhat to his chagrin, he found himself tenth in the batting order, and wondered what he was being played for, since his bowling was evidently disregarded. The whole side were sent back for 67, of which he made 5 not out. The wonderful length kept by a famous left-handed bowler, who brought his ball from behind his back with admirable delivery, was far too good for his opponents.

Following on drab cricket was displayed until, when only a quarter of an hour remained for play and only 2 wickets to fall, Middlesex still needed 23 runs to save defeat. Paul then came in, and, contrary to the poking methods adopted by his predecessors, hit out at everything. An obliging 'life' was accorded to him at deep-square leg incidentally, whilst he made 25 out of 27 and then was stumped rushing out to the last ball of the day and missing it.

'A refreshing knock that saved the situation,' said the venerable old man in the bath-chair who, sixty years before, would have played precisely in the same fashion.

This time there was no hesitation:

'You'll play for us against Yorkshire, I hope?'

Superfluous to add that the answer was affirmative.

In the history of cricket there have been few finer matches than that one, which will often be recalled when lovers of the game talk over great contests.

Both sides were at full strength, and on a perfect wicket runs were obtained at a great pace, which is not a characteristic of the modern professional who preponderates in the Tyke side. Winning the toss, the visitors made the average total of 259, the best contributions coming from the player who, going in first, exhibited an almost golf follow-through to his strokes, and a middle-aged fast bowler, the vigour of whose hitting delighted his supporters. Yorkshire are deservedly popular wherever they go, but nowhere do they possess more friends than at Lord's.

Paul, put on as fourth change, came out as well as any of his colleagues, for his analysis read 2 for 42. This time he was promoted to eighth in the batting, and arrived at the wicket an hour and a half to play and a mighty tapper at the other end. The crowd was beginning to stream away, but those who stayed witnessed a remarkable stand. The Yorkshire bowling is some of the most difficult and varied in England. Yet the colt and the hitter obtained such complete mastery that in an hour 112 runs were added. Neither was faultless; but it was a great effort, and the beautiful way in which Paul made his runs was sharply in contrast with the vigorous punching of his more experienced partner, who seemed shoulder-tied until he let out for a prodigious drive. When the latter was out, Paul seemed to redouble the pace of his run-getting. Nor did he slacken as he approached three figures. Just on the call of time, however, he mistimed one from a particularly crafty left-hander, and was bowled.

Ninety-two in an hour and a half against Yorkshire was a notable feather in the cap of the latest recruit, and not only justified his school reputation, but put him on an altogether different footing. It was characteristic of the sportmanship of Lord Hawke that he should come to the Middlesex dressing-room on purpose to congratulate warmly the young amateur who had done so well against his own county. Paul was perhaps more pleased at this than at anything thus far in his career.

'Well,' concluded the Yorkshire captain, 'if you have knocked my boys about, it's a comfort to think you've come from the old school. It's a lot of years since I played for Eton, and I wish I were as young as you are to-day. Now you are not to think me nasty, but I do just hope that you will not be quite so successful tomorrow, for you've tons of other matches in which to make scores.'

Whatever may be said against two-day first-class cricket – and not one soul objected to its obsequies at the end of that season – there were some days of mammoth scoring. Such a one was witnessed on that Saturday.

Yorkshire proceeded to make well over the third century, one of the older guard being responsible for a three-figure score, leaving Middlesex 279 to get in just over three hours. Such a total as this seemed out of the bounds of possibility. Neither did the methods of the captain, who could not get the ball away, nor those of his companion, a twice-wounded excellent bat of the slow order, seem to open the innings as if the side entertained any hopes of doing more than play out time. Nor, yet again, was this latter altogether a certainty when, after an hour and a half, four of the best men were out and only 129 were recorded.

Paul, in recognition of his success the previous evening, was then sent in, promoted to number six in the order. He had again captured two wickets, but, like all the other Middlesex bowlers, had been pretty ruthlessly maltreated. For the first time when batting for the county he did not feel nervous. He thought if he could again play pretty well, he might be sure of a place for the rest of the season, and he meant to do his best. Glancing up at the score-board he calculated that in ninety minutes 150 runs had to be made. That, Euclideanly, could be demonstrated as impossible against such bowling. Now was it? Preposterous as it might seem, he meant to have a try.

Three balls remained of the over from the fastest bowler, and Paul drove each of them very hard almost to the same spot on the boundary. The crowd were delighted. Playing in very easy style and using his wrists almost after the fashion of H.K. Foster, scoring was not fatiguing to him because of his perfect timing. Getting to the other end he had to deal with a left-handed slow bowler, and two late cuts, followed by an unblushing 'pull' right on to the canvas covering of Block B, fairly sent spectators roaring. They settled themselves down really to enjoy the methods of this new cricketer; yet they did not at first realise that not only was he knocking the bowling into smithereens, but also that he was making a bold bid for victory.

His off-side strokes seemed to be placed with uncanny precision. If a fieldsman was shifted, the next stroke appeared invariably to be directed where the man had been before. His off-drives 'simply ripped' to the boundary, and he varied this by putting two successive balls into the pavilion for six, the second hitting the balcony rail.

When Paul went in, a sedate and cautious partner at the other end seemed well set, and, so long as he was content with his natural game, proceedings were satisfactory. But he grew tired of seeing Paul knock the ball all over the field, and, lunging out at a short one, missed it. Before his foot was down again, the wicket-keeper had whipped off the bails, and sadly he walked back to the pavilion. The next man was out on a confident appeal for obstruction before he had troubled the scorers.

Then arrived the mighty tapper who, on the previous evening, had inspired Paul with such emulating confidence. It was a quarter to seven when applause greeted him. Nobody was leaving the ground, for at the pace which Paul was setting with such a collaborator a victory was becoming possible. Eighty-three to get in forty-five minutes, with the cunningest left-handed bowler in the world, backed up by well-varied changes to prevent the runs being scored! There was the chance, too, that in pressing for the runs, Middlesex might lose the match.

By now Paul saw the ball beautifully, and his partner had no nerves. Runs came at magical speed. A positive shiver went through the crowd when Paul played on, but so gently that the bails were not removed. One terrific skier towards the refreshment pavilion was dropped, though the fieldsman had judged it accurately; and the tapper chipped a ball to second slip, which the man from the North could not keep in his hands, in spite of three attempts. These things seemed to be hurdles in the steeplechase of the race against the clock.

Considering what risks both men were taking, the quality of the cricket they were playing was a remarkable as the pace of the run-getting. All the resources of the Yorkshire attack were in turn called upon, but none seemed to disturb the equanimity with which every type of bowling was hit. People held their breath as the daring strokes were made, and then shouted with appreciation of the consummate skill displayed. The clock was watched almost as anxiously as the performers.

With twenty minutes to go, 32 runs had still to be made. Then Paul was compelled to play a strictly defensive maiden to the famous left-hander, every ball needing all his skill to keep it out of his wicket. At the other end was a straight fast bowler. The tapper drove him for 4 and snicked him for 3. Paul, confronting him, banged him – it is the only accurate verb – for four successive boundaries, alternately to right and left of the wicket, all hard forcing shots.

Seven to win; and now spectators had a fresh problem. Paul was 95 not out. Would he attain the coveted three figures? This time the tapper had to face the left-hander, and he, too, had to submit to the restraint of another maiden. The Yorkshire captain then brought on a slow bowler. Three balls could not be scored off, after which Paul had a beautiful late cut that fairly raced to the ropes. A half-hearted appeal for leg-before was given in his favour, and then, wide of long-on, he smote for victory and century. Both were achieved, though the last run was made on the throw-in, and the batsman had to scramble to save being run out.

So the game was won by one of the most prodigious feats ever witnessed at Lord's. Late as was the hour, the crowd gathered in front of the pavilion, and would not cease clamouring until Paul twice, from the dressing-room balcony, acknowledged their frantic applause, after having received such a welcome on his return to the pavilion as he had never heard from the members. No wonder his eyes sparkled and his cheeks were flushed. In that match, he had 'made cricket history'.

THE LAST INNINGS

John Finnemore

Five wickets for sixty. Things looked well for Slapton, but no Slaptonian dared permit himself to rejoice. Some of the remaining wickets were weak. Kerrison was still his dreadful self, and if the five best wickets had made sixty, it did not at all follow that the five worst would make twenty, and win the match. Cricket is all too uncertain a game for that. There was but one hope in every Slapton heart. There at one end still stood the little marvel of the game. He had gone in to open the innings; he was still there unbeaten; and if he could only be supported, there was a feeling abroad that he could win the game off his own bat.

The support he had from the next man was good. He was Jimmy West, and the old Bat was, as ever, cool as a cucumber. Runs came very, very slowly, for the Hazlemere bowling and fielding were superb; but still by ones and twos they came, and a roar of joy hailed the seventy.

It was answered by a counter-shout from Hazlemere. A bailer of immense speed from Kerrison slipped over the shoulder of Jimmy's bat, flicked a bail fifty yards, and dashed on to the boundary.

Four wickets to fall and ten to win. It was the first ball of Kerrison's over; what would happen to the rabbits before the last ball had been sent whizzing down?

No. 1 of the four came in, had a plucky smack at the mighty fast man, and sent it somewhere – he had not the least idea where; but Frank howled, 'Come on!' and they ran two.

Inspired by that, he had a whang at the next ball, missed it, heard a frightful crash just at his back, and returned to the pavilion.

No. 2 of the rabbits came in all of a shiver, for, though a splendid fieldsman and a useful change bowler, he was only a moderate bat, and knew it, and was full of foreboding. His gloomy anticipations were correct. He had one of Kerrison's best yorkers, and missed it by a mile or less. 'Ta-ta!' murmured the wicket-keeper, a facetious person whose love of a little joke conquered his good manners.

Rabbit No. 3 arrived with a red face and a stout heart. He too wasn't much of a bat, but he had any amount of pluck, and he made a lucky slam at a rising ball, and sent it somewhere, anywhere, into the air. It was pure luck that it fell into an empty part of the field, and the batsmen ran two before it was fielded. Six to win, and Kerrison with one ball left of his over.

The great fast bowler did not waste it. He bowled a beautiful break-back and spread-eagled the stumps in great style.

All Hazlemere snapped their fingers in vexation. Here came the last man, and Kerrison's over was finished! Oh, if he had but just one more ball! Slapton were still six runs from victory, and one of Kerrison's balls would surely give his side the win.

It was hard lines on Hazlemere, or so Hazlemere thought. For there was that little demon who had carried his bat right through the innings, waiting calmly to take up the batting. Suppose he smacked up six in the coming over? Whew! the thought of it made the blood run cold in the veins of Hazlemere supporters.

As for seeing his dismissal, they had but slight hopes of that. He had not stood through all the stress of the great battle to crack up at the last moment. He was not one of that sort.

The over was watched with interest so deep as to be almost painful. The first ball proved the soundness of little Sandys's wicket judgment. He put it neatly through the slips and stood still to watch it.

'Run, Sandys, run!' roared a hundred voices. Sandys did not stir a peg. He turned and waved his companion back, and the knowing ones gave him a hearty cheer. 'Good man!' they said. 'It's only one, and a rather risky one. He's sticking to the batting. Great head on that kid!'

The second ball he turned to leg. They ran two, though it would have been quite possible to run three. But Frank pulled up at the batting end, and the last man, much relieved, stayed where he was. He was a stunning good man at cover, but a mere stick of a batsman, and he knew very well that a good ball would make an end of him and the match at the same moment.

Four to win! The tension was tremendous. Every eye was glued on the pitch, and every Slapton heart was longing to see the fine little bat whip one to the boundary, and thus make the winning hit.

But the bowler was doing his utmost, and his utmost was very good. Frank dared not hit. There was no ball which, either in length or in direction, was hittable. And so it came to the last ball of the cover.

As the bowler began to run the silence was profound. If this ball produced no runs, then Kerrison would be let loose upon the unlucky last man, and it was a million to one that Hazlemere would snatch a victory at the last moment.

Crack! There was a roar from Slapton throats, as the impact of bat upon ball rang across the meadow. 'Boundary! Our match!' they yelled. Then the cry was checked, as they saw a fieldsman come tearing across, field the ball splendidly, and return it like lightning.

Frank was leisurely trotting down the pitch, and made his ground good as the wicket-keeper put the ball to the stumps. He had got the batting at any rate, and that was all to the good.

Kerrison took up the ball, with a do or die look on his face, and went at his work with tremendous power. He sent down a trimmer, pitched on the off stump, and Frank played it back to him. He sent another a little shorter and a little wide of the stump, and Frank appeared to feel for it.

Kerrison's eye lighted up. If the little beggar was going to feel for his off-balls, there would soon be a chance in the slips. But it was diamond cut diamond. Frank had pretended to feel for the off-ball to draw Kerrison on, and as the ball was sent down he saw that he had succeeded in deceiving the fast bowler.

The ball was pitched a good foot from the off stump, and was rising sharply – just the ball for a man to touch and send into the slips.

But Frank was ready for it. Rising to the whole of his very modest height, he got over it, and brought his bat down with a terrific slash.

The cut scarcely needed strength so much as direction. The tremendous speed of the ball gave it pace, and it flashed past cover and was shooting across a clear field towards the ropes before a hand could be stretched towards it.

How all Slapton rose to that tremendous last smite! The winning hit! Victory, after all! A victory, which had been trembling on the very verge of defeat, had been secured for the old school by the marvellous little cricketer.

One shout of 'Sandys! Sandys!' filled the air, and a rush was made for the little, scurrying figure.

No sooner did Frank see that the four was a dead certainty than he fled from the wicket straight for the pavilion. But his comrades were not to be denied. They pounced upon him half-way, and swung him up and carried him in in triumph. Then upon the very steps of the pavilion there was a striking scene.

On the top step stood Teddy Lester, captain of cricket, his eyes shining with delight for the fine victory which his little new recruit had gained. And as the procession marched up the steps, carrying Frank Sandys on high, Teddy stepped forward, took his own First Eleven cap from his head, and placed it on Frank's bare head, thus giving him the coveted dignity of a First Eleven cap in public, and with the greatest honour possible.

This striking scene was hailed with a fresh outburst of cheers, and the Hazlemere Eleven, good sportsmen all, clapped heartily in honour of their game and clever little opponent.

A VILLAGE MATCH AND AFTER

M.D. Lyon

The ground was only half a mile or so away from the house: and at half-past ten, summertime, we all set out. Our bags had been sent on ahead on the back of the old Ford lorry.

As we went along a shilling sweepstake was organised on who would be top score. I drew myself; the first out of the hat. But although this augured well, no one wanted to buy my ticket.

Several local supporters were already clustered round the old oak tree that served as a telegraph board. Eight nails formed up three-two-three, like a rugger scrum, were used to hold up the figures, but it was an almost unknown event for the whole of the bottom row to be occupied, except when facetious boys took delight in putting up some wholly impossible score.

Robert Judd, the visiting captain, had arrived; he was a bookmaker; his pink braces, canvas boots and dulcet voice proclaimed him as such; and he had been one long enough to purchase Glevenham Hall.

Sir William won the toss, his opponent calling ' 'eads', and the lucky crown – kept for the occasion – falling 'tails'.

After a committee meeting lasting fifteen minutes, during which the weather forecasts were carefully considered and the time of the tides accurately noted, our skipper decided to bat first.

The 'Ghosts' took their stand just before twelve o'clock, and Johnson, the gardener, and Sir George Markham went out to bat. The former wore the brown leg-guard that belonged to the club, but the latter disdained the use of any kind of pad, and strode to the wicket fearlessly, armed only with his bat, which was an old and time-honoured weapon covered with black binding from the bottom to the shoulder.

Johnson took first ball from young Judd, who was the Glevenham champion, and bowled rather fast right hand round-arm. The first over was a remarkable one in some ways, for Johnson had evidently decided to attack the bowling. He ran up the pitch to meet the first three balls, and drove them hard for four a-piece. He also ran out to meet the next two, but missed them, and the visiting wicket-keeper was jeered at even by his own supporters for not stumping him. Not to be outdone, and in order not to do anything so obvious as standing up close to the wicket, the stumper again stood back, but began to steal towards the wicket as the bowler began his run. When the ball was delivered, he still was two yards from the wicket, so he jumped this distance; but unluckily the ball 'popped' a bit, and hit him full in the mouth. And then there were ten.

I sat with Mary, and although I was to go in No. 7, I had got my pads on, because somehow my side did not inspire so much confidence as they ought to have done.

Sir George at the other end dealt with the first over quite successfully, although he did not score. He is naturally rather a careful player; in fact, the year before, he had gone in first and had carried his bat for a faultless three, not out.

Four or five overs passed with no further score, and then our captain, thinking of the moral effect on the enemy if no one got out before lunch, ran out and instructed our opening pair to bide there at all costs. Johnson's method of carrying out these instructions was a curious one. He took guard again, making quite sure that he was covering the middle stump, and then simply held his bat in the block hole with a square face towards the bowler, and kept it quite still, so leaving a very small target, which, as luck would have it, young Judd was unable to hit.

Some of the fielding side got rather fed up with these digging-in operations, and after seventy-five minutes out in the hot sun I overheard old Judd call out to a rather plump old fellow with a grey beard, who was at short-leg, ' 'Ave you any suggestion about the bowling? 'Oo shall we put on?'

The rather caustic reply was, 'I should put the clock on.'

At the other end Sir George was as firm as a rock, so that when the time arrived to take lunch our score was twelve runs for no wickets. It is true that the play must have been rather dull for the spectators, because they had to watch eighty-nine minutes' batting without a run being scored, but the fury shown by the Glevenham bowlers, while they raged like an angry sea against the Johnson breakwater, doubtless compensated them for any lack of excitement in other directions.

But after lunch, which on account of the free flow of cider-cup and beer would probably be described by Frank Trent as a 'bit wet', things began to go wrong.

Sir George, in playing back to a high slow full toss, sat on his wicket; Johnson ran out to drive but slipped and fell, and, the ball having hit him in the chest while he was lying flat on his back, was quite properly given out leg before wicket.

There followed in quick procession to and from the wicket Sir William and two of his sons, all of whom were dismissed without scoring. Five down for twelve. It seemed that my dream might come true. I breathed on my glasses and rubbed them hastily on my shirt sleeve and picked up my hat.

'Now's your chance,' Mary whispered.

I ground my teeth and walked out to the wicket.

'Don't let 'em knock your castle over first ball, old man,' Jim called out after me.

I reached the crease. My heart was beating more loudly than it should have done, and I hoped the bowler couldn't hear it.

'A little towards you, sir,' said Wilkes, 'that covers the two. Three to come.'

Young Judd was bowling, and there was a great difference between his state of mind and mine. He had his tail up; I had the wind up. The first one was very fast and pitched on the off stump. I threw my wrists at it – thinking of MacLaren – and the ball sailed high over slip's head for four.

The next one pitched outside the off stump and broke back sharply. I lunged forward and just got a touch, the ball hurrying between my legs and the wicket to the long-leg boundary. The last ball of the over young Judd let slip out of his hand, and it went very slowly towards cover. I ran out after it, reached it just before it stopped, and clipped it past extra-cover for four.

There was considerable excitement, and Wilkes signalled a boundary and called out, 'Wide and the ball is over.'

Frank Trent was in the other end. He is a great stylist and is still at Eton. He played forward in the classic style, but the ball rose abruptly from the pitch and moved the peak of his cap round over his right ear. He laughed, rather hollowly I thought. At the next ball he again played a copy-book forward shot, but it hit him hard on the fingers.

The third and fourth balls both made him duck hurriedly, and it seemed that some of his style was deserting him.

He turned his back on the fifth ball, which did not jump as the others had done, but struck him sharply on the seat of his trousers, and the last ball of the over, a slow full-toss, knocked his off-stump down while he was half-way towards the square-leg umpire.

Welham, the cowman, then joined me, and, as he has the reputation of being a forcing batsman, I decided to try and stay, without worrying about the runs.

Now my partner had one favourite shot just in front of square-leg, a shot which he seems to have modelled upon the stroke he employs when he is cutting down the nettles that grow in odd corners of his pastures. But on the Butley ground this shot was a particularly fruitful one, for, the first time he brought it into play, he sent the ball into the branches of a high chestnut tree in full leaf, and while it was slowly descending to earth, jolting first on one branch and then on another, we ran four.

This shot he repeated twice in spite of the fact that the square-leg fielder had been placed underneath the tree, and each time the ball finally dropped safely to earth on the opposite side of the trunk to that occupied by the expectant fieldsman. However, when he again faced the bowling, their captain sent out four men to wait underneath the tree, and although Welham hit the ball thrice more, accurately into the topmast branches, his luck deserted him and he was rather easily caught by one of the square-legs waiting in the shade, after a good deal of shouting, such as, 'There she comes, Bill,' and 'Look out your side, Fred,' and 'Now you've got him,' and so on. But his twenty runs were invaluable, our score only having reached forty-four with seven men out.

Philip Markham came in next, and he and I managed to put on a few runs, although it is true that the ball when played by me did not always travel in the direction pre-determined by the batsman. But it was half an hour of what the Press would call 'crowded life', and we added fifty runs before he was caught off his glove by the wicket-keeper standing back.

Our last two batsmen were soon dismissed, but I carried my bat for thirty-eight, and our total in the end reached ninety-seven.

All our supporters gave me a great reception on my return to the pavilion, but the Glevenham side were rather ungenerous and said my innings was a lucky one. Perhaps this was because they had missed me seven times, and Judd had twice hit my leg stump without removing the bails. I felt very proud, especially when Mary congratulated me; but although I sat next to young Markham at tea and waited hopefully, he didn't say anything about a trial for Middlesex: so I thought that it might have been that my quick-scoring was quite unfit for county cricket. After all, Sir George may be right when he says that the atmosphere of being in church that prevails in all first-class cricket must be preserved.

And so it came about that at half-past four on a May afternoon, under an English sun, on an English field, near English trees, Glevenham went out to bat.

The pink and white chestnuts were in full bloom, their blossoms banked tier upon tier like the crowd in the Coliseum at Rome, while a glance at the blue sky through the transparent new leaves of the copper beech left me wondering whether Japan with all her cherry trees must not take second place to England.

Every cricketer knows what it's like to go out to field in the evening, when the hot tea brings out the sweat on one's brow, to be followed, soon after, by a cool refreshed feeling. The new ball flashed red as it was thrown gaily from one to another amid merry jest and laughter.

Glevenham's innings was more or less without incident during the first hour – they had two hours to get the ninety-eight runs necessary for victory, and so they naturally adopted leisurely methods.

I was fielding in the country and several times had to run hard up and down the sloping furrows to retrieve a good hit, and after a particularly lively run, during which my white sun-hat fell off, I suddenly felt rather sea-sick. But Mary luckily had some Mothersill with her, and I made a rapid recovery.

It was almost six o'clock, when seven of their side were out for eighty, that things began to happen. Old Judd came in and hit two fours, but was then well caught by the Padre, standing waist-deep in the pond at long-on. Young Judd followed in and excitement was rising, for, with only two wickets to fall, they still needed ten runs to win. His very first ball he hit past me at extra-cover on to the road that leads straight down a sharp incline to the village. All runs on this side of the ground are run out, and it looked as if they might get seven or eight off this one, but I sprang on a push-bike that had been left on the grass at the side of the road and pedalled hard after the ball, which was trickling down the hill, thus saving two or three runs.

It was at this stage, when they wanted five to win with fifteen minutes to go, that Welham was called away to attend a red-poll that was calving down in a neighbouring field; and as luck would have it, no substitute came to field for him. For twelve tense minutes there was no score except one leg bye, but the breathlessness of these minutes has rather dimmed my memory, and all I can tell you is that when the last over came their last man was in and their score was ninety-four.

That over, however, remains vividly within my memory and forced me to set this match on record even more than the exciting events that happened afterwards.

The first two balls missed the wicket by a coat of paint, each time to the accompaniment of a gasp from all those watching. The third ball was hit high in the air and would have fallen in the middle of the wicket. Four eager fielders rush at it and all meet in a fierce collision and the ball falls safely to earth after hitting an upturned face a cruel blow on the nose.

When the fifth ball is delivered, I am filled with horror, for it is hit hard and comes sailing towards me but rather over my head. I shuffle slowly backwards down a slope; but, just as the ball is dropping into my upstretched hand, I trip up and fall over backwards, and an old Berkshire sow, who was peacefully sleeping with her litter round her, gets up, grunting loudly, angry at being disturbed. Very red in the face I return the ball to the bowler, but they have run two.

The world seems to be standing still. One ball to go, one run to tie, two to win, and Johnson bowling his fastest. All seems in suspense. Johnson takes off his suspenders. It is clear he means to give them socks. Not a sound disturbs the peace except the cawing of some tired rooks on their homeward journey. The ball is bowled and is driven towards the gate where Welham had gone fifteen minutes before. He is seen on his way back. 'Come on, Welham,' we all shout. 'Catch it! Catch it!' He dashes up, vaults on to the gate, and, sitting on it with both legs inside the ground, makes a safe catch.

'How's that?' everyone appeals. Wilkes's finger goes up; but the Glevenham umpire calls loudly, 'Not out.' Immediately there is pandemonium and a dozen good fights are started in different corners of the ground.

The two umpires held a heated argument with their faces less than an inch apart; and then Wilkes gave his colleague of the white coat a push. The push was returned – rather more strenuously – so Wilkes gave him a shove, which was again returned with interest. Wilkes threw his antagonist violently to the ground, but the latter quickly took off his coat of office and kicked Wilkes in the stomach. Wilkes bit him on the popping crease . . . and so on. Some of our supporters had 'chaired' Welham and were carrying him up and down in front of the pavilion with shouts of triumph.

•   •   •   •   •   •   •

But tragedy trod hard on the heels of comedy. For the disorder on the far side of the ground gradually ceased as four excited stable lads bustled towards us, exchanging jerky remarks as they ran. I saw Sir William go up to them. He gave them some brief instructions, and then came over to where Jim and I were standing.

'I want you to come back to the Hall at once,' he said. 'I shall be in the library. Please don't be long.'

It was clear that something serious had happened.

The crowd had become strangely quiet, except for muttered conversation. But they were not discussing the match. I beckoned to Johnson and asked him what had happened.

'It's Master Hugh, sir,' he said. 'He was riding "Beeswing" up on the mile gallop close to the big wood, and all I can make out yet is that he has been kidnapped and the colt stolen.'

Jim screwed his eyeglass farther into his eye.

'Get Philip Markham,' he said to me, 'we must go back at once.'

HOW JEMBU PLAYED
FOR CAMBRIDGE

Lord Dunsany

The next time that Murcote brought me again to his Club we arrived a little late. Lunch was over, and nine or ten of them were gathered before that fireplace they have; and that talk of theirs had commenced, the charm of which was that there was no way of predicting upon what topics it would touch. It all depended upon who was there, and who was leading the talk, and what his mood was; and of course on all manner of irrelevant things besides, such as whisky, and the day's news or rumour.

But today they had evidently all been talking of cricket, and the reason of that was clearer than men usually seem to think such reasons are. I seemed to see it almost the moment that I sat down; and nobody told it me, but the air seemed heavy with it. The reason that they talked about cricket was that there was a group there that day that were out of sympathy with Mr Jorkens; bored perhaps by his long reminiscences, irritated by his lies, or disgusted by the untidy mess that intemperance made of his tie. Whatever it was it was clear enough that they were talking vigorously of cricket because they felt sure that that topic if well adhered to must keep the old fellow away from the trackless lands and the jungles, and that, if he must talk of Africa, it could only be of some tidy trim well-ordered civilised part of it that he could get from the subject of cricket. They felt so sure of this.

They had evidently been talking of cricket for some time, and were resolute to keep on it, when shortly after I sat down amongst them one turned to Jorkens himself and said, 'Are you going to watch the match at Lord's?'

'No, no,' said Jorkens sadly. 'I never watch cricket now.'

'But you used to a good deal, didn't you?' said another, determined not to let Jorkens get away from cricket.

'Oh, yes,' said Jorkens, 'once; right up to that time when Cambridge beat Surrey by one run.' He sighed heavily and continued: 'You remember that?'

'Yes,' said someone. 'But tell us about it.'

They thought they were on safe ground there. And so they started Jorkens upon a story, thinking they had him far from the cactus jungles. But that old wanderer was not kept so easily in English fields, his imagination to-day or his memory or whatever you call it, any more than his body had been in the old days, of which he so often told.

'It's a long story,' said Jorkens. 'You remember Jembu?'

'Of course,' said the cricketers.

'You remember his winning hit,' said Jorkens.

'Yes, a two, wasn't it?' said someone.

'Yes,' said Jorkens, 'it was. And you remember how he got it?'

That was too much for the cricketers. None quite remembered. And then Murcote spoke. 'Didn't he put it through the slips with his knee?' he said.

'Exactly,' said Jorkens. 'Exactly. That's what he did. Put it through the slips with his knee. And only a leg-bye. He never hit it. Only a leg bye.' And his voice dropped into mumbles.

'What did you say?' said one of the ruthless cricketers, determined to keep him to cricket.

'Only a leg bye,' said Jorkens. 'He never hit it.'

'Well, he won the match all right,' said one, 'with that couple of runs. It didn't matter how he got them.'

'Didn't it!' said Jorkens. 'Didn't it!'

And in the silence that followed the solemnity of his emphasis he looked from face to face. Nobody had any answer. Jorkens had got them.

'I'll tell you whether it mattered or not, that couple of leg byes,' said Jorkens then. And in the silence he told this story:

'I knew Jembu at Cambridge. He was younger than me, of course, but I used to go back to Cambridge after to see those towers and the flat fen country, and so I came to know Jembu. He was no cricketer. No, no, Jembu was no cricketer. He dressed as white men dress and spoke perfect English, but they could not teach him cricket. He used to play golf and things like that. And sometimes in the evening he would go right away by himself and sit down on the grass and sing. He was like that all his first year. And then one day they seem to have got him to play a bit, and then he got interested, probably because he saw the admiration they had for his marvellous fielding. But as for batting, as for making a run, well, his average was less than one in something like ten innings.

'And then he came by the ambition to play for Cambridge. You never know with these natives what on earth they will set their hearts on. And I suppose that if he had not fulfilled his ambition he would have died or committed murder or something. But, as you know, he played for Cambridge at the end of his second year.'

'Yes,' said someone.

'Yes, but do you know how?' said Jorkens.

'Why, by being the best bat of his time I suppose,' said Murcote.

'He never made more than fifty,' said Jorkens, with a certain sly look in his eye, as it seemed to me.

'No,' said Murcote, 'but within one or two of it, whenever he went to the wickets, for something like two years.'

'One doesn't want more than that,' said another.

'No,' said Jorkens. 'But he did the day that they played Surrey. Well, I'll tell you how he came to play for Cambridge.'

'Yes, do,' they said.

'When Jembu decided that he must play for Cambridge he practised at the nets for a fortnight, then broke his bat over his knee and disappeared.'

'Where did he go to?' said someone a little incredulously.

'He went home,' said Jorkens.

'Home?' they said.

'I was on the same boat with him,' said Jorkens, drawing himself up at the sound of doubt in their voices.

'You were going to tell us how Jembu played for Cambridge,' said one called Terbut, a lawyer, who seemed as much out of sympathy with Jorkens and his ways as any of them.

'Wait a moment,' said Jorkens. 'I told you he could not bat. Now, when one of these African natives wants to do something that he can't, you know what he always does? He goes to a witch doctor. And when Jembu made up his mind to play for Cambridge he put the whole force of his personality into that one object, every atom of will he had inherited from all his ferocious ancestors. He gave up reading divinity, and everything, and just practised at the nets as I told you, all day long for a fortnight.'

'Not an easy thing to break a bat over his knee,' said Terbut.

'His strength was enormous,' said Jorkens. 'I was more interested in cricket in those days than in anything else. I visited Jembu in his rooms just at that time. Into the room where we sat he had put the last touches of tidiness: I never saw anything so neat: all his divinity books put away trim in their shelves – he must have had over a hundred of them – and everything in the room with that air about it that a dog would recognise as foreboding a going away.

'"I am going home," he said.

'"What, giving up cricket?" I asked.

'"No," he answered and his gaze looked beyond me as though concerned with some far-off contentment. "No, but I must make runs."'

'"You want practice," I said.

'"I want prayer," he answered.

'"But you can pray here," I said.

"He shook his head.

'"No, no," he answered with that far-away look again.

'Well, I only cared for cricket. Nothing else interested me then. And I wanted to see how he would do it. I suppose I shouldn't trouble about it nowadays. But the memory of his perfect fielding, and his keenness for the one thing I cared about, and his tremendous ambition, as it seemed to me then, to play cricket for Cambridge, made the whole thing a quest that I must see the end of.

'"Where will you pray?" I said.

'"There's a man that is very good at all that sort of thing," he answered.

'"Where does he live?" I said.

'"Home."

'Well, it turned out he had taken a cabin on one of the Union Castle line. And I decided to go with him. I booked my passage on the same boat; and, when we got into the Mediterranean, deck cricket began, and Jembu was always bowled in the first few balls even at that. I am no cricketer, I worshipped the great players all the more for that; I don't pretend to have been a cricketer; but I stayed at the wickets longer than Jembu every time, all through the Mediterranean till we got to the Red Sea, and it became too hot to play cricket, or even to think of it for more than a minute or two on end. The equator felt cool and refreshing after that. And then one day we came into Killindini. Jembu had two ponies to meet us there and twenty or thirty men.'

'Wired to them I suppose,' said Terbut.

'No,' said Jorkens. 'He had wired to some sort of a missionary who was in touch with Jembu's people. Jembu, you know, was a pretty important chieftain, and when anyone got word to his people that Jembu wanted them, they had to come. They had tents for us, and mattresses, and they put them on their heads and carried them away through Africa, while we rode. It was before the days of the railway, and it was a long trek, and uphill all the way. We rose eight thousand feet in two hundred miles. We went on day after day into the interior of Africa: you know the country?'

'We have heard you tell of it,' said someone.

'Yes, yes,' said Jorkens, cutting out, as I thought, a good deal of local colour that he had intended to give us. 'And one day Kenya came in sight like a head between two great shoulders; and then Jembu turned northwards. Yes, he turned northwards as far as I could make out; and travelled much more quickly; and we came to nine thousand feet, and forests of cedar. And every evening Jembu and I used to play stump cricket, and I always bowled him out in an over or two; and then the sun would set and we lit our fires.'

'Was it cold?' said Terbut.

'To keep off lions,' said Jorkens.

　　　．　　．　　．　　．　　．

'You bowled out Jembu?' said another incredulously, urged to speech by an honest doubt, or else to turn Jorkens away from one of his interminable lion-stories.

'A hundred times,' said Jorkens, 'if I have done it once.'

'Jembu!' some of us muttered almost involuntarily, for the fame of his batting lived on, as indeed it does still.

'Wait till I tell you,' said Jorkens. 'In a day or two we began to leave the high ground: bamboos took the place of cedars; trees I knew nothing of took the place of bamboos; and we came in sight of hideous forests of cactus; when we burned their trunks in our camp-fires, mobs of great insects rushed out of the shrivelling bark. And one day we came in sight of hills that Jembu knew, with a forest lying dark in the valleys and folds of them, and Jembu's own honey-pots tied to the upper branches.

'These honey-pots were the principal source, I fancy, of Jembu's wealth: narrow wooden pots about three feet long, in which the wild bees lived, and guarded by men that you never see, waiting with bows and arrows. It was the harvest of these in a hundred square miles of forest that sent Jembu to Cambridge to study divinity, and learn our ways and our language. Of course he had cattle, too, and plenty of ivory came his way, and raw gold now and then; and, in a quiet way, I should fancy, a good many slaves.

'Jembu's face lighted up when he saw his honey-pots, and the forest that was his home, dark under those hills that were all flashing in sunlight. But no thought of his home or his honey-pots made him forget for a single instant his ambition to play for Cambridge, and that night at the edge of the forest he was handling a bat still, and I was still bowling him out.

'Next day we came to the huts of Jembu's people. Queer people. I should have liked to have shown you a photograph of them. I had a small camera with me. But whenever I put it up they all ran away.

'We came to their odd reed huts.

'Undergrowth had been cleared and the earth stamped hard by bare feet, but they did not ever seem to have thinned the trees, and their huts were in and out among the great trunks. My tent was set up a little way from the huts, while Jembu went to his people. Men came and offered me milk and fruit and chickens, and went away. And in the evening Jembu came to me.

'"I am going to pray now," he said.

'I thought he meant there and then, and rose to leave the tent to him.

'"No," he said, "one can't pray by oneself."

'Then I gathered that by 'pray' he meant some kind of worship, and that the man he had told me of in his rooms at Cambridge would be somewhere near now. I was so keen on cricket in those days that anything affecting it always seemed to me of paramount importance, and I said "May I come, too?"

'Jembu merely beckoned with his hand and walked on.

'We went through the dark of the forest for some few minutes, and saw in the shade a great building standing alone. A sort of cathedral of thatch. Inside, a great space seemed bare. The walls near to the ground were of reed and ivory: above, it was all a darkness of rafters and thatch. The long thin reeds were vertical, and every foot or so a great tusk of an elephant stood upright in the wall. Nuggets of gold here and there were fastened against the tusks by thin strands of copper. Presently I could make out that a thin line of brushwood was laid in a wide circle on the floor. Inside it Jembu sat down on the hard mud. And I went far away from it and sat in a corner, though not too near to the reeds, because, if anything would make a good home for a cobra, they would. And Jembu said never a word; and I waited.

'Then a man stepped through the reeds in the wall that Jembu was facing, dressed in a girdle of feathers hanging down from his hips, wing feathers, they seemed to be, as in a crane. He went to some sort of iron pot that stood on the floor, that I had not noticed before, and lifted the lid and took fire from it, and lit the thin line of brushwood that ran round Jembu. Then he began to dance. He must have been twelve or fifteen feet from Jembu when he began to dance, and he danced round him in circles, or leapt is a better word, for it was too fierce for a dance. He took no notice of me. After he had been dancing some time I saw that his circles were narrowing; and presently he came to the line of brushwood at a point that the fire had not reached, and leapt through it and danced on round Jembu. Jembu sat perfectly still, with his eyes fixed. The weirdest shadows were galloping now round the walls from the waving flames of the brushwood; and any man such as us must have been sick and giddy from the frightful pace of those now narrow circles that he was making round Jembu, but he leapt nimbly on. He was within a few feet of my friend now. What would he do, I was wondering, when he reached him?

Still Jembu never stirred, either hand or eyelid. Stray leaves drifting up from the dancing savage's feet were already settling on Jembu. And all of a sudden the black dancer fainted.

'He lay on the ground before Jembu, his feet a yard from him, and one arm flung out away from him, so that that hand lay in the brushwood. The flames were near to the hand, but Jembu never stirred. They reached it and scorched it: Jembu never lifted a finger, and the heathen dancer neither moved nor flinched. I knew then that this swoon that he had gone into was a real swoon, whatever was happening. The flames died down round the hand, died down round the whole circle; till only a glow remained, and the shadow of Jembu was as still on the wall as a black bronze image of Buddha.

'I began to get up then, with the idea of doing something for the unconscious man, but Jembu caught the movement, slight as it was, although he was not looking at me; and, still without giving me a glance of his eye, waved me sharply away with a jerk of his left hand. So I left the man lying there, as silent as Jembu. And there I sat, while Jembu seemed not to be breathing, and the embers went out and the place seemed dimmer than ever for the light of the fire that was gone. And then the dancing man came to, and got up and bent over Jembu, and spoke to him, and turned; and all at once he was gone through the slit in the reeds by which he had entered the temple. Then Jembu turned his head, and I looked at him.

'"He has promised," he said.

'"Who?" I asked.

'"Mungo," said Jembu.

'"Was that Mungo?" I asked.

'"He? No! Only his servant."

'"Who is Mungo?" I asked.

'"We don't know," said Jembu, with so much finality that I said no more of that.

'But I asked what he had promised.

'"Fifty runs," replied Jembu.

'"In one innings?" I asked.

'"Whenever I bat," said Jembu.

'"Whenever you bat!" I said. "Why! That will get you into any eleven. Once or twice would attract notice, but a steady average of fifty, and always to be relied on – it mayn't be spectacular, but you'd be the prop of any eleven."

'He seemed so sure of it that I was quite excited; I could not imagine a more valuable man to have in a team than one who could always do that, day after day, against any kind of bowling, on a good wicket or bad.

'"But I must never make more," said Jembu.

'"You'll hardly want to," I said.

'"Not a run more," said Jembu, gazing straight at the wall.

'"What will happen if you do?" I asked.

'"You never know with Mungo," Jembu replied.

'"Don't you?" I said.

'"No man knows that," said Jembu.

'"You'll be able to play for Cambridge now," I said.

'Jembu got up from the floor and we came away.

•　•　•　•　•　•　•

'He spoke to his people that evening in the fire-light. Told them he was going back to Cambridge again, told them what he was going to do there, I suppose; though what they made of it, or what they thought Cambridge was, Mungo only knows. But I saw from his face, and from theirs, that he made that higher civilisation, to which he was going back, very beautiful to them, a sort of landmark far far on ahead of them, to which I suppose they thought that they would one day come themselves. Fancy them playing cricket!

'Well, next day we turned round and started back again, hundreds of miles to the sea. The lions . . .'

'We've heard about them,' said Terbut.

'Oh, well,' said Jorkens.

But if they wouldn't hear his lion-stories they wanted to hear how Jembu played for Cambridge: it was the glamour of Jembu's name after all these years that was holding them. And soon he was back with his story of the long trek to the sea from somewhere North of a line between Kenya and the great lake.

He told us of birds that to me seemed quite incredible, birds with horny faces, and voices like organ-notes; and he told us of the cactus forests again, speaking of cactus as though it could grow to the size of trees; and he told us of the falls of the Guaso Nyero, going down past a forest trailing grey beards of moss. There may be such falls as he told of above some such forest, but we thought more likely he had picked up tales of some queer foreign paradise, and was giving us them as geography, or else that he had smoked opium or some such drug, and had dreamed of them. One never knew with Jorkens.

He told us how they came to the coast again; and apparently there are trees at Mombasa with enormous scarlet flowers that I have often seen made out of linen in the windows of drapers' shops, but according to him they are real:

Well, I will let him tell his own story.

'We had to wait in that oven' (he meant Mombasa) 'for several days before we could get a ship, and when we got home the cricket season was over. It was an odd thing, but Jembu went to the nets at once, and began hitting about, as he had been doing in the Red Sea; and there was no doubt about it that he was an unmistakable batsman. And he always stopped before there was any possibility that he could by any means be supposed to have made fifty.

'I talked to him about Mungo now and then, but could get nothing much out of him: he became too serious for that, whenever one mentioned Mungo, and of the dancing man in the temple I got barely a word; indeed I never even knew his name. He read divinity still, but not with the old zest, so far as I could gather whenever I went to see him, and I think that his thoughts were far away with Mungo.

'And as soon as May came round he was back at cricket; and sure enough, as you know, he played for Cambridge. That was the year he played first; and you have only to look at old score books to see that he never made less than forty-six all that year. He always got very shy when he neared fifty: he was too afraid of a four if he passed forty-six, and that was why he always approached it so gingerly, often stopping at forty-seven, though what he liked to do was to get to forty-six and then to hit a four and hear them applauding his fifty. For he was very fond of the good opinion of Englishmen, though the whole of our civilisation was really as nothing to him, compared with the fear of Mungo.

'Well, his average was magnificent; considering how often he was not out, it must have been nearly eighty. And then next year was the year he played against Surrey. All through May and June he went on with his forty-seven, forty-eight, forty-nine and fifty; and Cambridge played Surrey early in July. I needn't tell you of that match; after Oxford v. Cambridge in 1870, and Eton v. Harrow in 1910, I suppose it's the best-remembered match in history. You remember how Cambridge had two runs to win and Jembu was in with Halket, the last wicket. Halket was their wicket-keeper and hardly able to deal with this situation; at least Jembu thought not, for he had obviously been getting the bowling all to himself for some time. But now he had made fifty. With the whole ground roaring applause at Jembu's fifty, and two runs still to win I laid a pretty large bet at two to one against Cambridge. Most of them knew his peculiarity of not passing fifty, but I was the only man on the ground that knew of his fear of Mungo. I alone had seen his face when the dancing man went round him, I alone knew the terms. The bet was a good deal more than I could afford. A good deal more. Well, Jembu had the bowling; two to win; and the first ball he stopped very carefully; and then one came a little outside the off stump; and Jembu put his leg across the wicket and played the ball neatly through the slips with his knee. They ran two, and the game was over. Jembu's score, of course, stayed at fifty: no leg byes could affect that, as anyone knows who has ever heard of cricket. How could anyone think otherwise? But that damned African spirit knew nothing of cricket. How should he know, if you come to think of it? Born probably ages ago in some tropical marsh, from which he had risen to hang over African villages, haunting old women and travellers lost in the forest, or blessing or cursing the crops with moods that changed with each wind, what should he know of the feelings or rules of a sportsman? Spirits like that keep their word as far as I've known: it was nothing but honest ignorance; and he had credited poor Jembu with fifty-two, though not a ball that had touched his bat that day had had any share in more than fifty runs.

'And I've learned this of life, that you must abide by the mistakes of your superiors. Your own you may sometimes atone for, but with the mistakes of your superiors, so far as they affect you, there is nothing to do but to suffer for them.

'There was no appeal for Jembu against Mungo's mistake. Who would have listened to him? Certainly no-one here: certainly no-one in Africa. Jembu went back to see what Mungo had done, as soon as he found out the view that Mungo had taken. He found out that soon enough, by dropping back to his old score of one and nothing in three consecutive innings. The Cambridge captain assured him that that might happen to anybody, and that he mustn't think of giving up cricket. But Jembu knew. And he went back to his forest beyond Mount Kenya, to see what Mungo had done.

• • • • • •

'And only a few years later I came on Jembu again, in a small hotel in Marseilles, where they give you excellent fish. They have them in a little tank of water, swimming about alive, and you choose your fish and they cook it. I went there only three or four years after that match against Surrey, being in Marseilles for a day; and a black waiter led me to the glass tank, and I looked up from the fishes, and it was Jembu. And we had a long talk, and he told me all that had happened because of those two leg-byes that had never been near his bat.

'It seems that a tribe that had never liked Jembu's people had broken into his forest and raided his honey-pots. They had taken his ivory, and burnt his cathedral of thatch, and driven off all his slaves. I knew from speeches that he had made at Cambridge that Jembu in principle was entirely opposed to slavery; but it is altogether another matter to have one's slaves driven away, and not know where they have gone to or whether they will be well cared for. It was that that broke his heart as much as the loss of his honey-pots; and they got his wives, too. His people were scattered, and all his cattle gone; there was nothing after that raid left for Jembu in Africa.

'He wandered down to the coast; he tried many jobs; but Mungo was always against him. He drifted to Port Said as a stowaway, to Marseilles as a sailor, and there deserted, and was many things more, before he rose to the position of waiter; and I question if Mungo had even done with him then. A certain fatalistic feeling he had, which he called resignation, seemed to bear him up and to comfort him. The word resignation, I think, came out of his books of divinity; but the feeling came from far back, out of old dark forests of Africa. And, wherever it came from, it cheered him awhile at his work in that inn of Marseilles, and caused him to leave gravy, just where it fell, on the starched shirt-front that he wore all day. He was not unhappy, but he looked for nothing better; after all, he had won that match for Cambridge against Surrey: I don't see what more he could want; and many a man has less. But when I said good-bye to him I felt sure that Mungo would never alter his mind, either to understand, or to pardon, those two leg-byes.'

'Did you ask him,' said Terbut, 'how Mungo knew that he got those two leg byes?'

'No,' said Jorkens, 'I didn't ask him that.'

THE CLERKS ALL OUT

Dennis Castle

Mookerjee approached the pavilion almost treading on the hem of his white coat.

' 'Tis time to recommence, colonel sahib,' he piped, doffing his panama. 'Our battin' men are refreshed from appetisin' food an' have kep' free from alcoholic beverages.'

'Thikai,' sighed the colonel, awakening in a deck chair.

'Ah, a little baby,' crooned Mookerjee over the pram.

'God, you keep away from him!' boomed the colonel, now bolt upright.

'He is yours?'

'Me grandson.'

'He is *white*, too . . . a foreign child!'

Mookerjee knew how to hurt the British. The colonel lay back speechless with rage.

Courtney limped over. Without solids for lunch, he felt much better after the whisky, very much better.

'You consult me before you decide when the game re-starts,' he told Mookerjee as he struggled into his coat.

'Allow me to assist in view of your leg . . .'

'I don't put me coat on me leg! Keep away . . . I don't trust yer . . . you'd probably pick me pocket and steal me six stones . . .'

Mookerjee sighed as he watched his fellow umpire light up another pipe, now in the likeness of Gladstone. All that smokin' an' drinkin' – this man would be joinin' his ancestors very soon – which made Mookerjee very sorry for the ancestors.

'And you, Bandmaster Rowbottom,' yelled Courtney, 'stop that infernal row . . . we're startin' . . .'

Higginbottom cut off 'Tit-Willow' in its prime and staggered blindly into the pavillion. First he'd had to stop his band while the British listened to records of Judy Garland, Bing Crosby dreaming of a white Christmas and Vera Lynn singing 'Yours'. Then, some damned half-chat girl had requested 'Onward Christian Soldiers' so that she could sing about trams . . . now he'd been called 'Rowbottom' and they'd buggered up his *Mikado*. As Akkar Singh passed him a new bottle, the Punjabi bandsmen produced leaf-enfolded food from within the scores of 'West-end Musical Successes' and slid from their chairs to the more natural comfort of the grass.

The crowd had increased round Glenbourn. Word had gone through the bazaar that the bara sahibs were in trouble and, in the trees, was an ever-swelling throng of dark-skinned figures, agog with excitement.

'They're massin',' said McBurn apprehensively, 'there's native unrest in yon trees.'

The Governor had not made his appearance when the Army took the field again. The officers were heavier of foot than the four NCOs, who, rationed to one bottle of Solan beer each, still retained a spritely light-infantry step. With this situation in mind, the colonel threw the ball to Sinker for the first time.

Sinker had bowled in the East Riding League. Sharrabuddin, he observed, had only one stroke, a one-handed lob. This Sinker immediately exploited and a stomach-high full toss was hit back tamely into his hands, first ball after lunch. Gopi Mukta scratched one run and was then l.b.w. to Sinker, Courtney's finger going up a split second before the appeal.

For one who had wanted to call his side 'The Tigers', Bannerjee's attitude at the wicket was surprisingly mouse-like. Shrinivassen looked pained as he watched his number eight draw away from the first ball from Sinker, head averted, eyes shut, shouting 'Ooh!' as it just missed the off stump. He also drew away from the last ball, ending up hiding behind Innes-Whiffen as the wicket-keeper took the ball.

It was, however, after Shrinivassen had scored a single off the fourth ball of Wood's next over, that Bannerjee really complicated the field.

'Oi,' said Courtney, ready to give guard. 'You were a right-hander down this end. Now you're battin' *left*-handed!'

'I know,' said Bannerjee, 'but now bowlin' ish from other end . . .'

'This man,' said the colonel firmly, 'must make up his mind which way round he is goin' to bat . . .'

'He is left-hander,' said Mookerjee. 'He has his rights as left-hander.'

'But when he gets down this end again,' said Courtney, 'will he change his ruddy mind?'

Bannerjee now looked mutinous.

'I am holdin' bat with both left an' right handsh,' he argued. 'What more ish it you want?'

'He hasn't a clue,' sighed Innes-Whiffen.

'I do have clue,' snapped Bannerjee, 'an' my clue ish you are all tryin' to confushe me into battin' bewilderment with your Army quick-march, left right, leftsh, double-croshin' me with double-dutsch. I no longer wish to partishipate in such criminal procheedin'sh.'

So, in left-handed stance, he backed away to allow Wood's full toss to clip his off stump.

'Am not rishkin' wind an' limb,' he shouted as he walked away. 'I am for pashive reshistanch. I jusht did not try – sho there!'

An embarrassed Shrinivassen apologised profusely to the colonel.

'We are but a scratched side. Our committee had only unsolicitated testimonials of our players to work upon and we were not able to check, verify and investigate each trumpet-blown claim of cricket skill.'

'I malum thoroughly,' smiled the colonel. Three wickets down for a mere three runs – a great after-lunch transformation. This would please the Governor . . . when he turned up.

But the arrival at the wicket of Torkham Wazir brought a sudden atmosphere of evil over Glenbourn. Except for old tennis shoes, his was the costume of his tribe, the long grey flapping shirt, open jurgi waistcoat and gilt basket-style turban wound with lengths of loose white cotton. Without pads on his baggy blue shalvar trousers, he gazed round malevolently from kohl-rimmed eyes.

'Did anyone rub a lamp?' asked Mott.

If Shrinivassen looked uneasy, the colonel was thunderstruck.

'A Pathan!' he breathed. 'An' I can't remember a word o' Pushto . . .'

'I see, Torkham Wazir,' said Mookerjee, 'that you are for ignorin' pads an' gloves. The British bowl fast an' wild, man . . .'

'I, too, am fast and wild,' said Torkham Wazir.

Major McBurn repressed a shudder.

'Takes me back,' he muttered to Baker-Stewart. 'These blighters half-decimated the battalion in '29 . . .'

Mookerjee loathed Torkham Wazir but enjoyed the effect he was having on the British.

'Do you require guard?' he asked.

'I can guard myself.'

Torkham Wazir's only sport had been 'bushkrashi' on horseback but he had studied his team batting with the purposeful observation for which his race was famous. Now he crouched correctly as Wood bowled, fast and short, a fraction outside the leg stump. The bat blade flicked like a darting cobra tongue but the ball beat it for pace – and met the Pathan's shin with an ugly, pistol-shot crack.

As one man, all on the field gasped, participating in the excruciating agony. Even Courtney clutched at his own stiff leg before limping impulsively to help the batsman. But the Pathan stood, fierce and indignant.

'Do we not run?' he asked . . . and galloped down the matting.

'Go back, man,' moaned Shrinivassen, his eyes watering in telepathic pain. 'The ball has mercifully gone for four leg byes. Are you not mortally hurt?'

'Hurt – by the British?' The Pathan bared long pointed teeth. 'Never!'

At the sound of the terrifying impact of ball on bone, Baker-Stewart had called, with his famed clarity of diction, 'Doctor Grahame! Man hurt!' and a cursing, dishevelled 'twelfth man' had unwound himself from Nancy to dash from behind the pavilion. Grahame possessed no colourful cricket blazer and he despised the British officers' fetish of wearing mufti at every possible off-duty moment. Rather than stain a perfectly good 'civvy' jacket of his own, he preferred to spill beer down the King's uniform – so he appeared on his khaki tunic, belt flapping and brass buttons lustreless. Uncertain of the victim, he turned over the first prone figure he saw.

'Where are you hurt, colonel?'

'I'm not . . . jus' restin' . . . it's that Pathan wallah . . . ball on shin.'

Grahame hurried towards Torkham Wazir who eyed the approach of the hated British uniform with smouldering fury.

'Take care, mon,' shouted McBurn, 'he's a hillman . . .'

'Well, he's certainly not a Morris Cowley,' said Mott.

'Remain melancholy, Mott,' warned Grahame, 'or you may be the next victim . . . kicked in the dingle dongles for bad jokes.'

'Stand back, Englisher,' said Torkham Wazir menacingly as he dropped his bat.

The Australian obeyed this inappropriate order instantly – for the Pathan was now holding a long thin dagger.

'D'you know,' said Innes-Whiffen, tapping his gloves together, 'I don't believe I'm really here.'

'Hurl the next missile,' stormed Torkham Wazir, pointing the blade at Sergeant Wood.

'Put that bloody pig-sticker away first,' stuttered the grey-faced bowler.

'Give it to the umpire to hold, old man,' said Mott.

'He's not givin' it to me,' screeched Courtney. 'I'm not bein' paid any danger money to stand in this game. And you can appeal till you're all blue in the face but that fuzzy-wuzzy won't be given out from my end . . .'

Mookerjee, however, stamped over and snatched away the knife.

'Pathan butcher!' he shrilled. 'Charity Red-Cross match is not for blood-lettin'. Let Australian doctor see your injury . . .'

But gradually, a strange, surprised look crossed Torkham Wazir's dark face. He put a shaking hand to his brow, heaved convulsively – then slowly keeled over, crumpling to the mat.

'My leg!' he gasped in sudden shock.

Grahame knelt beside him and, taking the knife from Mookerjee, split the ankle band of the shalvar trousers.

'Whew, what a crack! Must get him to hospital for an X-ray . . .'

'No,' grunted Torkham Wazir. 'I bat on . . .'

'You're crazy, you can't even stand on that . . .'

'I have breath in my body – I fight on . . .'

Gently, Grahame moved the Pathan's knee, testing reaction.

'Now,' he enquired, 'how's that?'

'Out!' cried Mookerjee. 'Leg before W! Why did you Army take so long to appeal?'

'Dear Mookerjee,' whispered Shrinivassen gratefully, 'you are indeed man of tact. This is most astute way of overcoming disaster.'

Torkham Wazir slumped again and Grahame laid him flat, folding his own tunic under the lolling head. Having loosened the long white gauze pugree from the Pathan's turban, he began to bind both legs together.

'You are making a mummy of him already?' asked Mookerjee coldly. 'While he still breathes . . .?'

'If you had ever been a boy scout, Mookerjee,' said Grahame, his long fingers busy, 'you'd know I was usin' his one good leg as a splint for the other . . .'

'His leg is broken snapped?' enquired Shrinivassen mournfully.

'Well, I'd say it was certainly fractured . . . anyway, they'll know at the hospital.'

'Anything I can do, Jack?' Mott enquired.

'Yes, get some soft material I can bind his legs with. Not rope . . . but old shirts, say . . .'

'Old shirts?'

'The Crusaders never wear old shirts,' said Innes-Whiffen.

'Lend us yer stuffed ones, then,' said Grahame impatiently.

Mott trotted off to the pavilion calling, 'Any old clothes!'

Barkside-Twist sank on the grass beside his captain.

'Damn nearly a frontier incident, that, Eddgers . . .'

'Who appealed, Twisty? That Pathan was given out . . . hardly sportin' . . .'

'It was Grahame . . .'

'But he's not even *playin*'! Really, these Australians . . .'

'It's a good job he's here, Eddgers. Best thing to give that hillman out, knife and all. Otherwise 'retired hurt' on the score-sheet might make more newspaper trouble for us.'

The colonel turned his anguished face to the clear blue sky.

'Not likely to be any rain, either,' he sighed.

Mott returned from the pavilion carrying a rather meagre assortment of bandage material. His request of 'old clothes' had deeply offended the British deck chairs. Heads had been averted, so Mott had to improvise with Akkar Singh's glass cloths, a frayed Altruist tie and a yellowing flannel shirt from the deep recesses of his own cricket bag, a chiffon scarf which Nancy pressed on him with strict instructions to tell 'Doctah Jack' she had sent it – and a pair of silk stockings.

To Mott's amazement, Muriel Barkside-Twist had beckoned him from behind the pavilion. Putting her hand on his shoulder for support, she had whispered: 'I wouldn't do this for anyone but you, Basil,' and, fumbling feverishly under her skirt, had, tantalisingly, drawn the stockings down her sturdy legs. 'They're still warm,' she said as she draped the stockings over his arm. Then she kissed him and scampered away, her face a bright pink.

Dazed by her daring, Mott tottered back on to the field with his miscellaneous collection. 'Any rags, bottles or bones!' called Harrison derisively.

'Call this "totting"?' replied Mott. 'Feel these stockings . . . they're still warm.'

Harrison gaped in amazement. There was jus' no stoppin' this sex-maniac captain.

Mott dumped the assortment on the matting and Grahame immediately reinforced the Pathan's ankles with the Altruist tie. He ripped the shirt up the back and Mott sighed in sadness to see this relic of his English cricket days so ruthlessly dismembered.

'That's Nancy's scarf,' he said loyally as Grahame bound Torkham Wazir's knees together.

'Keep his legs straight, Motty . . .' Grahame turned to binding the Pathan's thigh . . . 'Whose stockin's are these, for God's sake?'

'Spotty Backside's . . .'

'You took 'em by force, you Weybridge werewolf . . .'

'No, honestly . . . she shed 'em in my presence, quite voluntarily. Frankly, she shook me rigid. I saw right up her suspender belt . . .'

'I know the symptoms. She wants you, Motty. Your American reputation is payin' off . . . get under her mozzy net to-night an' clear up her complexion like a good, randy citizen . . .'

Mott turned away. Grahame was only echoing a thought which had entered his mind behind the pavilion. But fancy bedding down the

daughter of an MCC member! Yet, let's face it, she had a good figure
. . .

'Eh, Grahame,' said the figure of her father suddenly beside them,
'don't leave the ground, will you? Colonel's orders. If anything violent
happens, we must think of the womenfolk.'

'Mott was doin' jus' that,' said Grahame. 'Right, I'll stay on tap to
staunch the blood.'

Hazel returned from the green bell-tent marked 'Ladies (British)
Only' to see Grahame and the four NCOs carrying Torkham Wazir,
stiff and flat, on a bench to the trees.

'What's goin' on, Desai?' she snorted. 'Leave you a moment an'
somethin' happens.'

'Most tragic dismissal of Torkham Wazir.' Desai was shaking. 'Leg-
before-wicket minus pad to Sergeant Wood – for zero runs.'

'A duck, eh?' Eagerly she filled in the details.

'There was also four leg byes . . .'

'Dash it, that makes another seven-ball over Mookerjee's given . . .
really, as a clerk you'd think he'd be able to count, even if anythin' over
ten meant he had to take his boots off.'

Desai had only recorded six balls to that over, but said nothing. To
draw her attention to it only meant she would lean over again, touching
his shoulder with her almost visible breasts as she studied his book.

'Private Evans!' she yelled. 'The score is 98-8-nought.'

Nancy hung up the plates, her hair sprouting with grass cuttings, a
seraphic smile on her face. If Jack hadn't been called away jus' then –
oh dearah, he'd been very nearly thereah! That chiffon scarf had been
sent out as a reminder not to be long . . .

'Really, Major Grahame does lead her on, so,' muttered Hazel,
swatting at a persistent wasp with a folded newspaper.

'No, please,' said Desai urgently, 'never kill God's creatures.'

'Rubbish. They sting God's creatures too . . . get *off*!' She smashed
again at the wheeling wasp. Desai, who habitually shook his bedding
gently every morning to release any inadvertently trapped insect, sighed.
No wonder Jain priests averred that women were evil.

The NCOs had returned to the field of play after helping Grahame
strap Torkham Wazir into a rickshaw to avoid any body weight on the
trussed legs. The Indians were stunned to silence. If the British could do
this to their most warlike player, what chance did lesser mortals stand?
As Grahame scribbled a note to the hospital, Swarmi approached him
quivering with fury.

'You have assaulted and batterised our best player ... I demand damages ... I am manager ...'

'You're jus' the man I want then, Fatso. Go with this Thief o' Baghdad an' give this chitty to the duty doctor at the hospital. An X-ray is wanted – an' there's no bloody phone here at Glenbourn.'

'Ah, it is an out-moded place you British choose for your cricket. Why don't you, as doctor, travel with the dying man?'

'Because I'm "twelfth man" an' the only doctor on the ground. Anyway, this chap'll live. He shouldn't've batted without pads ... after all the trouble Captain Mott took to get 'em for you from St Hayward's School, too. However, treat him gently in that rickshaw. He's in a state o' shock, so give him some hot, sweet tea ...'

The major left to find Nancy, and Swarmi stared after him shrugging his fleshy shoulders contemptuously.

'Who will volunteer?' he demanded of the team.

'The doctor sahib said you were to go,' said Narna Bag, 'we shall be bowlin' and fieldin' soon ...'

'I am manager, cannot leave post,' said Swarmi imperiously. 'Here you, coolie ...' He passed Grahame's note to the rickshaw leader. 'Hospital jaldi karo. Torkham Wazir zakhum. Duty doctor sahib ko yea khut doo.'

'Pundra rupee ...'

'Fifteen? You thieving badmush!' Swarmi shook his head, gave him the fare, making a note in his managerial notebook of another twenty rupees expenses. The rickshaw jerked away up the incline, Torkham Wazir's head lying inert against the folded hood. The clerks did not watch him go – they preferred to ignore failure.

Back on the field, the Army watched Futti Pant waddle to the wicket. The rotund little man in his Gandhi cap was not wearing the schoolboy pads of his team-mates but a pair designed for a much larger man. The top of the right pad flopped over at the knee, obviously weakened by years of unorthodoxy.

'My verd,' he cried as he took guard, 'that Pathan von't bat vith no leg-pads no more, I am tellin' you – hey, vat is ideah?'

Barkside-Twist had, with a purposeful thrust, turned back the top of the drooping pad. Marked in red ink was the name 'ffoliot'!

'The wing-commander's pads,' cried the major hoarsely. 'I knew I recognised them!'

Futti Pant stared down at him indignantly.

'He is my cousin from Ahmednager ...'

'You are a lying fellow,' said Barkside-Twist. 'Wing-Commander ffoliot comes from Harrogate.'

Shrinivassen hung his head in horror. So much for the fate of the RAF cricket gear when they left Tophar, sold off by their servants instead of being faithfully packed . . .

'Dear old Folly's pads!' stormed the colonel. 'Got forty for us once in those . . .'

'Forty-three,' amended McBurn precisely, 'against the Literary Society. Fancy the wing-commander bein' so lax – do hope he kept the Crusader colours safe . . .'

The colonel's heart missed a beat – the hanging blazer – and the face of this new little Indian batsman was just like a melon.

'I buy these pads in bazaar, secon' han',' said Futti Pant sullenly. 'The ving-commandah mus' have pawned them . . .'

'Pawned 'em? Old Folly?' Nupp-Jevons laughed hollowly. 'He had private means . . . his old mother owns acres of Norfolk . . .'

'Never mind that now,' said Mookerjee, 'time is wastin' for no man. Futti Pant is innocent of RAF pad-stealin' treachery. He is honest clerk in *Army* Surplus Department . . .'

'Terrible pads anyvays,' said Futti Pant, 'von is all broke . . .'

'Play on,' said the colonel jadedly. 'We'll sort it out later.'

The Army's hopes of getting the last two wickets cheaply now received a tantalising set-back. Futti Pant and Shrinivassen edged runs all round the wicket against the fumed heads and leaden feet of the commissioned men, all of whom, save Mott, fielded far too close to the wicket. Futti Pant, realising this, became the artful dodger, much to the hysterical delight of the Indian spectators. Mott's slow spinners gave him particular pleasure. He gambolled down the wicket, swiping and sometimes swatting overarm, always hitting the ball past the inner ring but never as far as the outfielders.

Short singles were now more fascination than boundaries. The Indians in the trees chanted, inciting Futti Pant to even greater risks. He waved his bat to them and again war-danced down the mat as Mott came up to bowl. Twice he had stopped in his run and thrown the ball past the advancing Futti Pant, but each time Mookerjee called 'no ball'.

As the four NCOs ranged round the boundary became incensed by their officers' lethargic display, 'overthrows' became another attraction. The batsmen scampered extra runs from wild throws aided by complete lack of backing-up ability by the officers. Shrinivassen was disquieted. The sahibs were getting rattled. It was, after all, just a friendly game. If only the Governor would come . . . 'God Save The King' always calmed the British . . .

' 'Tis my success in Poonah all ovah again, Shriniwassen!' Futti Pant called between the overs. 'I am in vondah form. Have got all soldiah bowlahs at sea, I am tellin' you.'

Then the little man hit one from Baker-Stewart, now reduced to a gasping half-pace, straight along the ground to the colonel at mid-off.

'Vun run to the colonel sahib as always,' he carolled as he ran.

The outraged colonel had stooped, but anger and inertia retarded him. The ball jogged on between his legs.

'Again, again!' screamed Mookerjee. 'The colonel has missed it! Gone through like a croquet hoop, it has . . . run, run!'

'This isn't a cricket match,' howled Courtney, 'it's a bloody congress meetin'!'

At 138 for eight, the colonel, who had been confident his officers could mop up the tail-enders, was forced much against his will to hand the ball to Sinker again. Such a batsman as Futti Pant would not have lasted five minutes in Yorkshire, and the corporal cunningly gave away two runs, drawing Futti Pant down the wicket with a gentle half-volley. He watched the fat batsman's smile of anticipation – then released the next ball from well behind his shoulders. The oncoming Futti Pant realised too late that it was sailing high over his head. With a cry of alarm, he tried a tremendous over-arm smash with one hand . . . but the ball was already behind his squat figure. He fell on his face as Innes-Whiffen whipped off the bails.

'Fool, Futti Pant!' screamed Mookerjee. 'Look where you are, inert on the mattin'. I have no alternative . . . you are out stumped, miles from your unoccupied crease!'

Futti Pant slowly levered himself up, scowling furiously.

' 'Tis svindlin', bowlin' too high,' he bleated. 'I am but five feet vun in my bare socks. Never had such hoodvinkin' bowlin' like that in Poonah. Not even from vite men . . .'

He could not have offended the Army more deeply.

'How dare he say that,' muttered Barkside-Twist. 'I remember R.H. Bettington bowling that ball for the MCC.'

The Indian crowd gave their little bandy hero a thunderous reception for his 31, but shook their fists at the field of play. Their clown was out . . . those bloody British again!

'Ought to report that fellar to the Conference,' snorted Nupp-Jevons, whose average had suffered by Futti Pant's tactics.

'Don't know what you're all grousin' about,' said Courtney, limping past. 'It wasn't out really . . . Whiffey took it in front of the wicket . . . but I'd have given it too, had it been my end . . . me bladder's near burstin'.'

'I must pump ship too,' said McBurn. 'That damned sherry's run straight through me.'

Within a minute, only the four NCOs remained on the field.

'We have one player to come,' screamed Mookerjee, waving his rule book. 'Eleven men to bat . . . that is the law!'

'I made no gesture of declaration – I hope,' said a worried Shrinivassen as they hurried to the pavilion together. Higginbottom, in a vague haze, saw the field clearing, and struck up 'In a Persian Market'.

Grahame told Mookerjee where the Army officers were.

'Ah,' said the umpire, clicking his tongue in remonstration. 'That is what alcohol does for you, doctor. To look on the wine when red is to play jackanapes with the kidneys . . .'

'You have a point there, Chatterjee,' said Grahame.

'My name,' came the haughty reply, 'is Mookerjee.'

'It ought to be Chatterjee . . .'

The little umpire was struck dumb with anger.

The colonel apologised to Shrinivassen when he returned with his more comfortable officers. Courtney had snatched another nip, filled a likeness of Lloyd George with tobacco and felt really well again. With a shriek that echoed to the Himalayas, Hazel silenced the band and, as Akkar Singh steered Higginbottom back to his bottle, the Army returned to the attack. The Governor had not yet appeared . . .

Sashi Bokaneer was waiting at the wicket and, around him, the four British NCOs were doubled up with laughter. The batsman had an abdominal protector between his legs, but strapped *outside* his trousers.

' 'E's got 'is bollock box showin'!' howled Sinker, doubled up.

The colonel reeled and held Mott's shoulder for support.

'Tell him, someone, for God's sake . . . there's womenfolk in the pav . . . it's disgustin' . . .'

'What is trouble afoot now?' asked Mookerjee.

'Tell your batsman,' barked Baker-Stewart, 'to turn his back and put his 'box' on *inside* his trousers . . .'

'But,' said Mookerjee, 'he is only clerk beside Jalim Singh to posses such a cricket appendage . . . naturally he is proud to reveal it . . .'

'It goes inside,' said Innes-Whiffen, tapping his trousers hollowly with his gloves, 'as I'm wearin' mine now . . .'

'Steady, Whiffy,' said the colonel. 'No need to lower the tone . . .'

'The box is not then,' said Mookerjee, 'worn like a Scottish sporran . . .?'

Mott forced McBurn away.

But Shrinivassen had already taken action. The protesting Bokaneer was turned about to face the Himalayas as the NCOs readjusted his unique acquisition, much to his embarrassment.

'I wonder,' said Mott, 'if there's an RAF name in that box . . .'

'That we shall not investigate,' snapped the colonel.

From the ringside point of view, it would have been better if the British had allowed Bokaneer to keep his box exposed. But now he fidgeted, rubbed his thigh and kept peering down the top of his trousers, grumbling that he was 'bein' rubbed raw like sandpapah!' The British ladies became fascinated as he clutched and fumbled with himself . . . and several deck chairs collapsed through undue restlessness, while Hazel broke two pencils.

But Bokaneer batted better than a number eleven. Though Mookerjee insisted he was primarily 'magnificent bowler of collosus stamina', he also possessed a keen eye. The Army reeled again under this unexpected attack as Bokaneer hit at everything. He also shouted as he smote the ball, a deep baying sound caused by the chafing box, and the Army dropped three catches in the echoes. But at last he was caught on the ropes by Harrison for 28, to give Mott his only wicket. The All-India Civilian XI were all out for 179, Shrinivassen being undefeated for 26.

The players trooped off as Higginbottom, now conducting what appeared to him to be double his usual band strength, drew forth 'The Fishermen of England'.

'It's terrible . . . terrible,' said the colonel, shaking his head.

'Oh, sir, 180 is gettable,' said Baker-Stewart.

'No, not that,' rasped the colonel. 'Dear old Folly's pads . . . he must miss 'em terribly.'

UNEXPECTED CONCLUSION OF A
CRICKET MATCH

Dorothy L. Sayers

The party from Pym's filled a large charabanc; in addition, a number of people attended in their own Austins. It was a two-innings match, starting at 10 a.m., and Mr Pym liked to see it well attended. A skeleton staff was left to hold the fort at the office during the Saturday morning, and it was expected that as many of them as possible would trundle down to Romford by the afternoon train. Mr Death Bredon, escorted by Lady Mary and Chief-Inspector Parker, was one of the last to scramble into the charabanc.

The firm of Brotherhood believed in ideal conditions for their staff. It was their pet form of practical Christianity; in addition to which, it looked very well in their advertising literature and was a formidable weapon against the trade unions. Not, of course, that Brotherhood's had the slightest objection to trade unions as such. They had merely discovered that comfortable and well-fed people are constitutionally disinclined for united action of any sort – a fact which explains the asinine meekness of the income-tax payer.

In Brotherhood's régime of bread and circuses, organised games naturally played a large part. From the pavilion overlooking the spacious cricket-field floated superbly a crimson flag, embroidered with the Brotherhood trade-mark of two clasped hands. The same device adorned the crimson blazers and caps of Brotherhood's cricket eleven. By contrast, the eleven advertising cricketers were but a poor advertisement for themselves. Mr Bredon was, indeed, a bright spot on the landscape, for his flannels were faultless, while his Balliol blazer, though ancient, carried with it an air of authenticity. Mr Ingleby also was correct, though a trifle shabby. Mr Hankin, beautifully laundered, had rather spoilt his general effect by a brown felt hat, while Mr Tallboy, irreproachable in other respects, had an unfortunate tendency to come apart at the waist, for which his tailor and shirt-maker were, no doubt, jointly responsible. The dress of the remainder varied in combining white flannels with brown shoes, white shoes with the wrong sort of shirt, tweed coat with white linen hats, down to the disgraceful exhibition of Mr Miller who, disdaining to put himself out for a mere game, affronted the sight in grey flannel trousers, a striped shirt and braces.

The day began badly with Mr Tallboy's having lost his lucky half-crown and with Mr Copley's observing, offensively, that perhaps Mr Tallboy would prefer to toss with a pound-note. This flustered Mr Tallboy. Brotherhood's won the toss and elected to go in first. Mr Tallboy still flustered, arranged his field, forgetting in his agitation Mr Hankin's preference for mid on and placing him at cover point. By the time this error was remedied, it was discovered that Mr Haagedorn had omitted to bring his wicket-keeper's gloves, and a pair had to be borrowed from the pavilion. Mr Tallboy then realised that he had put on his two fast bowlers together. He remedied this by recalling Mr Wedderburn from the deep field to bowl his slow 'spinners', and dismissing Mr Barrow in favour of Mr Beeseley. This offended Mr Barrow, who retired in dudgeon to the remotest part of the field and appeared to go to sleep.

'What's all the delay about?' demanded Mr Copley.

Mr Willis said he thought Mr Tallboy must have got a little confused about the bowling order.

'Lack of organisation,' said Mr Copley. 'He should make out a list and stick to it.'

The first Brotherhood innings passed off rather uneventfully. Mr Miller missed two easy catches and Mr Barrow, to show his resentment at the placing of the field, let a really quite ordinary ball go to the boundary instead of running after it. The eldest Mr Brotherhood, a spry old gentleman of seventy-five, came doddering cheerfully round from the pavilion and sat down to make himself agreeable to Mr Armstrong. He did this by indulging in reminiscences of all the big cricket matches he had ever seen in a long life, and as he had been devoted to the game since his boyhood, and had never missed a game of any importance, this took him some time and was excessively wearisome to Mr Armstrong, who thought cricket a bore and only attended the staff match out of compliment to Mr Pym's prejudices. Mr Pym, whose enthusiasm was only equalled by his ignorance of the game, applauded bad strokes and good strokes indifferently.

Eventually the Brotherhoods were dismissed for 155, and the Pym Eleven gathered themselves together from the four corners of the field; Messrs Garrett and Barrow, both rather ill-tempered, to buckle on their pads, and the remainder of the team to mingle with the spectators. Mr Bredon, languid in movement but cheerful, laid himself down at Miss Meteyard's feet, while Mr Tallboy was collared by the aged Mr Brotherhood, thus releasing Mr Armstrong, who promptly accepted the invitation of a younger Brotherhood to inspect a new piece of machinery.

The innings opened briskly. Mr Barrow, who was rather a showy bat, though temperamental, took the bowling at the factory end of the pitch and cheered the spirits of his side by producing a couple of twos in the first over. Mr Garrett, canny and cautious, stonewalled perseveringly through five balls of the following over and then cut the leather through the slips for a useful three. A single off the next ball brought the bowling back to Mr Barrow, who, having started favourably, exhibited a happy superiority complex and settled down to make runs. Mr Tallboy breathed a sigh of relief. Mr Barrow, confident and successful, could always be relied upon for some good work; Mr Barrow, put off his stroke by a narrowly missed catch, or the sun in his eyes, or a figure crossing the screens, was apt to become defeatist and unreliable. The score mounted blithely to thirty. At this point, Brotherhood's captain, seeing that the batsmen had taken the measure of the bowling, took off the man at the factory end and substituted a short, pugnacious-looking person with a scowl, at sight of whom Mr Tallboy quaked again.

'They're putting on Simmonds very early,' he said. 'I only hope nobody gets hurt.'

'Is this their demon bowler?' inquired Bredon, seeing the wicket-keeper hurriedly retire to a respectful distance from the wicket.

Tallboy nodded. The ferocious Simmonds wetted his fingers greedily, pulled his cap fiercely over his eyes, set his teeth in a snarl of hatred, charged like a bull and released the ball with the velocity of a 9-inch shell in Mr Barrow's direction.

Like most fast bowlers, Simmonds was a little erratic in the matter of length. His first missile pitched short, rocketed up like a pheasant, whizzed past Mr Barrow's ear and was adroitly fielded by long-stop, a man with a phlegmatic countenance and hands of leather. The next two went wide. The fourth was pitched straight and with a good length. Mr Barrow tackled it courageously. The impact affected him like an electric shock; he blinked and shook his fingers, as though not quite sure whether his bones were still intact. The fifth was more manageable; he smote it good and hard and ran.

'Again!' yelled Mr Garrett, already half-way down the pitch for the second time. Mr Barrow accordingly ran and once again stood ready for the onslaught. It came; it ran up his bat like a squirrel, caught him viciously on the knuckle and glanced off sharply, offering a chance to point, who, very fortunately, fumbled it. The field crossed over, and Mr Barrow was able to stand aside and nurse his injuries.

Mr Garrett, pursuing a policy of dogged-does-it, proceeded systemati-cally to wear down the bowling by blocking the first four balls of the next over. The fifth produced two runs; the sixth, which was of much the same calibre, he contented himself with blocking again.

'I don't like this slow-motion cricket,' complained the aged Mr Brotherhood. 'When I was a young man—'

Mr Tallboy shook his head. He knew very well that Mr Garrett suffered from a certain timidity when facing fast bowling. He knew, too, that Garrett had some justification, because he wore spectacles. But he knew equally well what Mr Barrow would think about it.

Mr Barrow, irritated, faced the redoubtable Simmonds with a sense of injury. The first ball was harmless and useless; the second was a stinger, but the third he could hit and did. He whacked it away lustily to the boundary for four, amid loud cheers. The next kept out of the wicket only by the grace of God, but the sixth he contrived to hook round to leg for a single. After which, he adopted Mr Garrett's tactics, stonewalled through an entire over, and left Mr Garrett to face the demon.

Mr Garrett did his best. But the first ball rose perpendicularly under his chin and unnerved him. The second came to earth about half-way down the pitch and bumped perilously over his head. The third, pitched rather longer, seemed to shriek as it rushed for him. He stepped out, lost heart, flinched and was bowled as clean as a whistle.

'Dear, dear!' said Mr Hankin. 'It seems that it is up to me.' He adjusted his pads and blinked a little. Mr Garrett retired gloomily to the pavilion. Mr Hankin, with exasperating slowness, minced his way to the crease. He had his own methods of dealing with demon bowlers and was not alarmed. He patted the turf lengthily, asked three times for middle and off, adjusted his hat, requested that a screen might be shifted, asked for middle and off again and faced Mr Simmonds with an agreeable smile and a very straight bat, left elbow well forward and his feet correctly placed. The result was that Simmonds, made nervous, bowled an atrocious wide, which went to the boundary, and followed it up by two mild balls of poor length, which Mr Hankin very properly punished. This behaviour cheered Mr Barrow and steadied him. He hit out with confidence, and the score mounted to fifty. The applause had scarcely subsided when Mr Hankin, stepping briskly across the wicket to a slow and inoffensive-looking ball pitched rather wide to the off, found it unaccountably twist from under his bat and strike him on the left thigh. The wicket-keeper flung up his hands in appeal.

'Out!' said the umpire.

Mr Hankin withered him with a look and stalked very slowly and stiffly from the field, to be greeted by a chorus of: 'Bad luck, indeed, sir!'

'It *was* bad luck,' replied Mr Hankin. 'I am surprised at Mr Grimbold.' (Mr Grimbold was the umpire, an elderly and impassive man from Pym's Outdoor Publicity Department.) 'The ball was an atrocious wide. It could never have come anywhere near the wicket.'

'It had a bit of a break on it,' suggested Mr Tallboy.

'It certainly had a break on it,' admitted Mr Hankin, 'but it would have gone wide nevertheless. I don't think anybody can accuse me of being unsporting, and if I *had* been leg before, I should be the first to admit it. Did you see it, Mr Brotherhood?'

'Oh, I saw it all right,' said the old gentleman, with a chuckle.

'I put it to you,' said Mr Hankin, 'whether I was l.b.w. or not.'

'Of course not,' said Mr Brotherhood. 'Nobody ever is. I have attended cricket matches now for sixty years, for sixty years, my dear sir, and that goes back to a time before you were born or thought of, and I've never yet known anybody to be really out l.b.w. – according to himself, that is.' He chuckled again. 'I remember in 1892 . . .'

'Well, sir,' said Mr Hankin, 'I must defer to your experienced judgment. I think I will have a pipe.' He wandered away and sat down by Mr Pym.

'Poor old Brotherhood,' he said, 'is getting very old and doddery. Very doddery indeed. I doubt if we shall see him here another year. That was a very unfortunate decision of Grimbold's. Of course it is easy to be deceived in these matters, but you could see for yourself that I was no more l.b.w. than he was himself. Very vexing, when I had just settled down nicely.'

'Shocking luck,' agreed Mr Pym, cheerfully. 'There's Ingleby going in. I always like to watch him. He puts up a very good show, doesn't he, as a rule?'

'No style,' said Mr Hankin, morosely.

'Hasn't he?' said Mr Pym, placidly. 'You know best about that, Hankin. But he always hits out. I like to see a batsman hitting out, you know. There! Good shot! Good shot! Oh, dear!'

For Mr Ingleby, hitting out a little too vigorously, was caught at cover point and came galloping out rather faster than he had gone in.

'Quack, quack,' said Mr Bredon.

Mr Ingleby threw his bat at Mr Bredon, and Mr Tallboy, hurriedly muttering, 'Bad luck!' went to take his place.

'What a nuisance,' said Miss Rossiter, soothingly. 'I think it was very brave of you to hit it at all. It was a frightfully fast one.'

'Um!' said Mr Ingleby.

The dismissal of Mr Ingleby had been the redoubtable Simmonds' swan-song. Having exhausted himself by his own ferocity, he lost his pace and became more erratic than usual, and was taken off, after an expensive over, in favour of a gentleman who bowled leg-breaks. To him, Mr Barrow fell a victim, and retired covered with glory, with a score of twenty-seven. His place was taken by Mr Pinchley, who departed, waving a jubilant hand and declaring his intention of whacking hell out of them.

Mr Pinchley indulged in no antics of crease-patting or taking middle. He strode vigorously to his post, raised his bat shoulder-high and stood four-square to whatever it might please Heaven to send him. Four times did he loft the ball sky-high to the boundary. Then he fell into the hands of the Philistine with the leg-break and lofted the ball into the greedy hands of the wicket-keeper.

'Short and sweet,' said Mr Pinchley, returning with his ruddy face all grins.

'Four fours are very useful,' said Mr Bredon, kindly.

'Well, that's what I say,' said Mr Pinchley. 'Make 'em quick and keep things going, that's my idea of cricket. I can't stand all this pottering and poking about.'

This observation was directed at Mr Miller, whose cricket was of the painstaking sort. A tedious period followed, during which the score slowly mounted to 83, when Mr Tallboy, stepping back a little inconsiderately to a full-pitch, slipped on the dry turf and sat down on his wicket.

Within the next five minutes Mr Miller, lumbering heavily down the pitch in gallant response to an impossible call by Mr Beeseley, was run out, after compiling a laborious 12. Mr Bredon, pacing serenely to the wicket, took counsel with himself. He reminded himself that he was still, in the eyes of Pym's and Brotherhood's at any rate, Mr Death Bredon of Pym's. A quiet and unobtrusive mediocrity, he decided, must be his aim. Nothing that could recall the Peter Wimsey of twenty years back, making two centuries in successive innings for Oxford. No fancy cuts. Nothing remarkable. On the other hand, he had claimed to be a cricketer. He must not make a public exhibition of incompetence. He decided to make twenty runs, not more and, if possible, not less.

He might have made his mind easy; the opportunity was not vouchsafed him. Before he had collected more than two threes and a couple of demure singles, Mr Beeseley had paid the penalty of rashness and been caught at mid-on. Mr Haagedorn, with no pretensions to being a batsman, survived one over and was then spread-eagled without remorse or question. Mr Wedderburn, essaying to cut a twisty one which he would have done well to leave alone, tipped the ball into wicket-keeper's gloves and Pym's were disposed of for 99, Mr Bredon having the satisfaction of carrying out his bat for 14.

'Well played all,' said Mr Pym. 'One or two people had bad luck, but of course, that's all in the game. We must try and do better after lunch.'

'There's one thing,' observed Mr Armstrong, confidently to Mr Miller, 'they always do one very well. Best of the day, to my thinking.'

Mr Ingleby made much the same remark to Mr Bredon. 'By the way,' he added, 'Tallboy's looking pretty rotten.'

'Yes, and he's got a flask with him,' put in Mr Garrett, who sat beside them.

'He's all right,' said Ingleby. 'I will say for Tallboy, he can carry his load. He's much better off with a flask than with this foul Sparkling Pomayne. All wind. For God's sake, you fellows, leave it alone.'

'Something's making Tallboy bad-tempered, though,' said Garrett. 'I don't understand him; he seems to have gone all to pieces lately, ever since that imbecile row with Copley.'

Mr Bredon said nothing to all this. His mind was not easy. He felt as though thunder was piling up somewhere and was not quite sure whether he was fated to feel or to ride the storm. He turned to Simmonds the demon bowler, who was seated on his left, and plunged into cricket talk.

'What's the matter with our Miss Meteyard to-day?' inquired Mrs Johnson, archly, across the visitors' table. 'You're very silent.'

'I've got a headache. It's very hot. I think it's going to thunder.'

'Surely not,' said Miss Parton. 'It's a beautiful clear day.'

'*I* believe,' asserted Mrs Johnson, following Miss Meteyard's gloomy gaze, '*I* believe she's more interested in the *other* table. Now, Miss Meteyard, confess, who is it? Mr Ingleby? I hope it's not my favourite Mr Bredon. I simply *can't* have anybody coming between us, you know.'

The joke about Mr Bredon's reputed passion for Mrs Johnson had become a little stale, and Miss Meteyard received it coldly.

'She's offended,' declared Mrs Johnson. 'I believe it *is* Mr Bredon. She's blushing! When are we to offer our congratulations, Miss Meteyard?'

'Do you,' demanded Miss Meteyard, in a suddenly harsh and resonant voice, 'recollect the old lady's advice to the bright young man?'

'Why, I can't say that I do. What was it?'

'Some people can be funny without being vulgar, and some can be both funny and vulgar. I should recommend you to be either the one or the other.'

'Oh, really?' said Mrs Johnson, vaguely. After a moment's reflection she gathered the sense of the ancient gibe and said, 'Oh, really!' again, with a heightened colour. 'Dear me, how rude we can be when we try. I do hate a person who can't take a joke.'

. . . .

Brotherhood's second innings brought some balm to the feelings of the Pymmites. Whether it was the Sparkling Pomayne, or whether it was the heat ('I do believe you were right about the thunder,' remarked Miss Parton), more than one of their batsmen found his eye a little out and his energy less than it had been. Only one man ever looked really dangerous, and this was a tall, dour-faced person with whipcord wrists and a Yorkshire accent, whom no bowling seemed to daunt, and who had a nasty knack of driving extremely hard through gaps in the field. This infuriating man settled down grimly and knockd up a score of 58, amid the frenzied applause of his side. It was not only his actual score that was formidable, but the extreme exhaustion induced in the field.

'I've had – too much – gas,' panted Ingleby, returning past Garrett after a mad gallop to the boundary, 'and this blighter looks like staying till Christmas.'

'Look here, Tallboy,' said Mr Bredon, as they crossed at the next over. 'Keep your eye on the little fat fellow at the other end. He's getting pumped. If this Yorkshire tyke works him like this, something will happen.'

It did happen in the next over. The slogger smote a vigorous ball from the factory end, a little too high for a safe boundary, but an almost certain three. He galloped and the fat man galloped. The ball was racing over the grass, and Tallboy racing to intercept it, as they galloped back.

'Come on!' cried the Yorkshireman, already half-way down the pitch for the third time. But Fatty was winded; a glance behind showed him Tallboy stooping to the ball. He gasped 'No!' and abode, like Dan, in his breaches. The other saw what was happening and turned in his tracks. Tallboy, disregarding the frantic signals of Haagedorn and Garrett, became inspired. He threw from where he stood, not to Garrett, but point-blank at the open wicket. The ball sang through the air and spread-eagled the Yorkshireman's stumps while he was still a yard from the crease, while the batsman, making a frantic attempt to cover himself, flung his bat from his hand and fell prostrate.

'Oh, pretty!' exulted old Mr Brotherhood. 'Oh, well played, sir, well played!'

'He must have taken marvellous aim,' said Miss Parton.

'What's the matter with you, Bredon?' asked Ingleby, as the team lolled thankfully on the pitch to await the next man in. 'You're looking very white. Touch of the sun?'

'Too much light in my eyes,' said Mr Bredon.

'Well, take it easy,' advised Mr Ingleby. 'We shan't have much trouble with them now. Tallboy's a hero. Good luck to him.'

Mr Bredon experienced a slight qualm of nausea.

• • • • •

The remainder of the Brotherhood combination achieved nothing very remarkable, and the side was eventually got out for 114. At 4 o'clock, on a fiery wicket, Mr Tallboy again sent out his batsmen, faced with the formidable task of making 171 to win.

At 5.30, the thing still looked almost feasible, four wickets having fallen for 79. Then Mr Tallboy, endeavouring to squeeze a run where there was no run to be got, was run out for 7, and immediately afterwards, the brawny Mr Pinchley, disregarding his captain's frantic appeals for care, chopped his first ball neatly into the hands of point. The rot had set in. Mr Miller, having conscientiously blocked through two overs, while Mr Beeseley added a hard-won 6 to the score, lost his off stump to the gentleman with the leg-break. With the score at 92 by the addition of a couple of byes, and three men to bat, including the well-meaning but inadequate Mr Haagedorn, defeat appeared to be unavoidable.

'Well,' said Mr Copley, morosely, 'it's better than last year. They beat us then by about seven wickets. Am I right, Mr Tallboy?'

'No,' said Mr Tallboy.

'I beg your pardon, I'm sure,' said Mr Copley, 'perhaps it was the year before. You should know, for I believe you were the captain on both occasions.'

Mr Tallboy vouchsafed no statistics, merely saying to Mr Bredon:

'They draw stumps at 6.30; try and stick it out till then if you can.'

Mr Bredon nodded. The advice suited him excellently. A nice, quiet, defensive game was exactly the game least characteristic of Peter Wimsey. He sauntered tediously to the crease, expended some valuable moments in arranging himself, and faced the bowling with an expression of bland expectation.

All would probably have gone according to calculation, but for the circumstance that the bowler at the garden end of the field was a man with an idiosyncrasy. He started his run from a point in the dim, blue distance, accelerated furiously to within a yard of the wicket, stopped, hopped, and with an action suggestive of a Catherine-wheel, delivered a medium-length, medium-paced, sound straight ball of uninspired but irreproachable accuracy. In executing this manoeuvre for the twenty-second time, his foot slipped round about the stop-and-hop period, he staggered, performed a sort of splits and rose, limping and massaging his leg. As a result, he was taken off, and in his place Simmonds, the fast bowler, was put on.

The pitch was by this time not only fast, but bumpy. Mr Simmonds's third delivery rose wickedly from a patch of bare earth and smote Mr Bredon violently upon the elbow.

Nothing makes a man see red like a sharp rap over the funny-bone, and it was at this moment that Mr Death Bredon suddenly and regrettably forgot himself. He forgot his caution and his rôle, and Mr Miller's braces, and saw only the green turf and The Oval on a sunny day and the squat majesty of the gas-works. The next ball was another of Simmonds' murderous short-pitched bumpers, and Lord Peter Wimsey, opening up wrathful shoulders, strode out of his crease like the spirit of vengeance and whacked it to the wide. The next he clouted to leg for three, nearly braining square-leg and so flummoxing deep-field that he flung it back wildly to the wrong end, giving the Pymmites a fourth for an overthrow. Mr Simmonds's last ball he treated with the contempt it deserved, snicking it as it whizzed past half a yard wide to leg and running a single.

He was now faced by the merchant with the off-break. The first two balls he treated carefully, then drove the third over the boundary for six. The fourth rose awkwardly and he killed it dead, but the fifth and sixth followed number three. A shout went up, headed by a shrill shriek of admiration from Miss Parton. Lord Peter grinned amiably and settled down to hit the bowling all round the wicket.

As Mr Haagedorn panted in full career down the pitch, his lips moved in prayer. 'Oh, Lord, oh, Lord! don't let me make a fool of myself!' A four was signalled and the field crossed over. He planted his bat grimly, determined to defend his wicket if he died for it. The ball came, pitched, rose, and he hammered it down remorselessly. One. If only he could stick out the other five. He dealt with another the same way. A measure of confidence came to him. He pulled the third ball round to leg and, to his own surprise, found himself running. As the batsmen passed in mid-career, he heard his colleague call: 'Good man! Leave 'em to me now.'

Mr Haagedorn asked nothing better. He would run till he burst, or stand still till he hardened into marble, if only he could keep this miracle from coming to an end. He was a poor bat, but a cricketer. Wimsey ended the over with a well-placed three, which left him still in possession of the bowling. He walked down the pitch and Haagedorn came to meet him.

'I'll take everything I can,' said Wimsey, 'but if anything comes to you, block it. Don't bother about runs. I'll see to them.'

'Yes, sir,' said Mr Haagedorn, fervently. 'I'll do anything you say. Keep it up, sir, only keep it up.'

'All right,' said Wimsey. 'We'll beat the b—s yet. Don't be afraid of them. You're doing exactly right.'

Six balls later, Mr Simmonds, having been hit to the boundary four times running, was removed, as being too expensive a luxury. He was replaced by a gentleman who was known at Brotherhood's as 'Spinner'. Wimsey received him with enthusiasm, cutting him consistently and successfully to the off, till Brotherhood's captain moved up his fieldsmen and concentrated them about the off-side of the wicket. Wimsey looked at this grouping with an indulgent smile, and placed the next six balls consistently and successfully to leg. When, in despair, they drew a close net of fielders all round him, he drove everything that was drivable straight down the pitch. The score mounted to 150.

The aged Mr Brotherhood was bouncing in his seat. He was in an ecstasy. 'Oh, pretty, sir! Again! Oh, well played, indeed, sir!' His white whiskers fluttered like flags. 'Why on earth, Mr Tallboy,' he asked, severely, 'did you send this man in ninth? He's a cricketer. He's the only cricketer among the whole damned lot of you. Oh, well placed!' as the ball skimmed neatly between two agitated fielders who nearly knocked their heads together in the effort to retrieve it. 'Look at that! I'm always telling these lads that placing is nine-tenths of the game. This man knows it. Who is he?'

'He's a new member of the staff,' said Tallboy, 'he's a public-school man and he said he'd done a good deal of country-house cricket, but I hadn't an idea he could play like that. Great Scott!' He paused to applaud a particularly elegant cut, 'I never saw anything like it.'

'Didn't you?' said the old gentleman with asperity. 'Well, now, I've been watching cricket, man and boy, for sixty years, and I've seen something very like it. Let me see, now. Before the War, that would be. Dear, dear – I sometimes think my memory for names isn't what it was, but I fancy that in the 'varsity match of 1910, or it might be 1911 – no, not 1910, that was the year in which—'

His tinkling voice was drowned in a yell as the 170 appeared on the scoreboard.

'One more to win!' gasped Miss Rossiter. 'Oh!' For at that moment, Mr Haagedorn, left for an unfortunate moment to face the bowling, succumbed to a really nasty and almost unplayable ball which curled round his feet like a playful kitten and skittled his leg-stump.

Mr Haagedorn came back almost in tears, and Mr Wedderburn, quivering with nervousness, strode forward into the breach. He had nothing to do but to survive four balls and then, except for a miracle, the game was won. The first ball rose temptingly, a little short; he stepped out, missed it, and scuttled back to his crease only just in time. 'Oh, be careful! Be careful!' moaned Miss Rossiter, and old Mr Brotherhood swore. The next ball, Mr Wedderburn contrived to poke a little way down the pitch. He wiped his forehead. The next was a spinner and, in trying to block it, he tipped it almost perpendicularly into the air. For a moment that seemed like hours the spectators saw the spinning ball – the outstretched hand – then the ball dropped, missed by a hair.

'I'm going to scream,' announced Mrs Johnson to nobody in particular. Mr Wedderburn, now thoroughly unnerved, wiped his forehead again. Fortunately, the bowler was also unnerved. The ball slipped in his sweating fingers and went down short and rather wide.

'Leave it alone! Leave it alone!' shrieked Mr Brotherhood, hammering with his stick. 'Leave it alone, you numbskull! You imbecile! You—'

Mr Wedderburn, who had lost his head completely, stepped across to it, raised his bat, made a wild swipe, which missed its object altogether, heard the smack of the leather as the ball went into the wicket-keeper's gloves, and did the only possible thing. He hurled himself bodily back and sat down on the crease, and as he fell he heard the snick of the flying bails.

'How's that?'

'Not out.'

'The nincompoop! The fat-headed, thick-witted booby!' yelled Mr Brotherhood. He danced with fury. 'Might have thrown the match away! Thrown it away! That man's a fool. I say he's a fool. He's a fool, I tell you.'

'Well, it's all right, Mr Brotherhood,' said Mr Hankin, soothingly. 'At least, it's all wrong for your side, I'm afraid.'

'Our side be damned,' ejaculated Mr Brotherhood. 'I'm here to see cricket played, not tiddlywinks. I don't care who wins or who loses, sir, provided they play the game. Now, then!'

With five minutes to go, Wimsey watched the first ball of the over come skimming down towards him. It was a beauty. It was jam. He smote it as Saul smote the Philistines. It soared away in a splendid parabola, struck the pavilion roof with a noise like the crack of doom, rattled down the galvanised iron roofing, bounced into the enclosure where the scorers were sitting and broke a bottle of lemonade. The match was won.

• • • • • • •

Mr Bredon, lolloping back to the pavilion at 6.30 with 83 runs to his credit, found himself caught and cornered by the ancient Mr Brotherhood.

'Beautifully played, sir, beautifully played indeed,' said the old gentleman. 'Pardon me – the name has just come to my recollection. Aren't you Wimsey of Balliol?'

Wimsey saw Tallboy, who was just ahead of them, falter in his stride and look round, with a face like death. He shook his head.

'My name's Bredon,' he said.

'Bredon?' Mr Brotherhood was plainly puzzled. 'Bredon? I don't remember ever hearing the name. But didn't I see you play for Oxford in 1911? You have a late cut which is exceedingly characteristic, and I could have taken my oath that the last time I saw you play it was at Lords in 1911, when you made 112. But I thought the name was Wimsey – Peter Wimsey of Balliol – Lord Peter Wimsey – and, now I come to think of it—'

At this very awkward moment an interruption occurred. Two men in police uniform were seen coming across the field, led by another man in mufti. They pushed their way through the crowd of cricketers and guests, and advanced upon the little group by the pavilion fence. One of the uniformed men touched Lord Peter on the arm.

'Are you Mr Death Bredon?'

'I am,' said Wimsey, in some astonishment.

'Then you'll have to come along with us. You're wanted on a charge of murder, and it is my duty to warn you that anything you say may be taken down and used in evidence.'

'Murder?' ejaculated Wimsey. The policeman had spoken in unnecessarily loud and penetrating tones, and the whole crowd had frozen into fascinated attention. 'Whose murder?'

'The murder of Miss Dian de Momerie.'

'Good God!' said Wimsey. He looked round and saw that the man in mufti was Chief-Inspector Parker, who gave a nod of confirmation.

'All right,' said Wimsey. 'I'll come with you, but I don't know a thing about it. You'd better come with me while I change.'

He walked away between the two officers. Mr Brotherhood detained Parker as he was about to follow them.

'You say that man's called Bredon?'

'Yes, sir,' replied Parker, with emphasis. 'Bredon is his name. Mister Death Bredon.'

'And you want him for murder?'

'For murder of a young woman, sir. Very brutal business.'

'Well,' said the old gentleman, 'you surprise me. Are you sure you've got the right man?'

'Dead sure, sir. Well known to the police.'

Mr Brotherhood shook his head.

'Well,' he said again, 'his name may be Bredon. But he's innocent. Innocent as day, my good fellow. Did you see him play? He's a damned fine cricketer and he'd no more commit a murder than I would.'

'That's as may be, sir,' said Inspector Parker, stolidly.

• • • • • •

'Just fancy that!' exclaimed Miss Rossiter. 'I always *knew* there was *something*. Murder! Only think! We might all have had our throats cut! What do you think, Miss Meteyard? Were you surprised?'

'Yes, I was,' said Miss Meteyard. 'I was never so surprised in my life. Never!'

SOURCES AND ACKNOWLEDGEMENTS

1 GREAT MATCHES

A. A. THOMSON, 'Hundreds and Thousands' (*The Cricketer*, 1957).

NEVILLE CARDUS, 'Oval Test Match' (*Good Days*, Jonathan Cape, 1934).

MIHIR BOSE, 'The Cup from the Pru' (*All in a Day, Great Matches in Cup Cricket*, Robin Clark, 1983).

ROBERT LYND, 'Verity's Test Match' (*Both Sides of the Road*, Methuen, 1934).

RICHARD STREETON, 'The Fastest Hundred' (*P. G. H. Fender*, Faber, 1981).

PELHAM WARNER, 'The Greatest Game I Ever Played In' (*The Book of Cricket*, J. M. Dent & Sons Ltd, 1911, this edition Sporting Handbooks, 1945).

JIM LAKER, 'A Great One-Day Match' (*One-Day Cricket*, Batsford, 1977).

2 GREAT CHAMPIONS

ALAN HILL, 'The Legacy of the "Little Wonder" ' (*The Cricketer*, 1984).

MAJOR C. H. B. PRIDHAM, 'A "W.G." Story' (*The Cricketer*, 1942).

RALPH BARKER, 'Denis Compton' (*Ten Great Innings*, Chatto & Windus, 1964).

G. D. MARINEAU, 'The First Off-spinner: Lamborn "the Little Farmer" ' (*The Cricketer*, 1946).

HENRY BLOFELD, 'Godfrey Evans' (*Cricket Heroes*, Essays by Members of the Cricket Writers Club, Queen Anne Press, 1984).

NEVILLE CARDUS, 'J. T. Tyldesley' (*Days in the Sun*, Grant Richards, 1924).

MAJOR C. H. B. PRIDHAM, 'Harold Gimblett' (*The Cricketer*, 1936).

'Five Cricketers of the Year: William Harold Ponsford' (*Wisden's Almanack*, 1935).

'Other Deaths in 1919: Caffyn, William' (*Wisden's Almanack*, 1920).

FRANK KEATING, 'Tom Graveney' (*Cricket Heroes*, Essays by Members of the Cricket Writers Club, Queen Anne Press, 1984).

RICHARD DAFT, 'County Cricket from 1860 to 1871' (*Kings of Cricket*, J. W. Arrowsmith, 1893).

GORDON STRONG, ' "The Bishop" – a Great Edwardian Eccentric' (*The Cricketer*, 1983).

PATRICK MURPHY, 'Zaheer Abbas' (*The Centurions*, J. M. Dent & Sons Ltd, 1983).

H.B.H., 'W. G. Quaife' (*The Cricketer*, 1945).

ALAN GIBSON, ' 'Endren, 'Earne and 'Aig' (*The Cricketer*, 1980).

R. D. WOODALL, 'The "Demon Bowler" of Notts' (*The Cricketer*, 1984).

W. A. BETTESWORTH, 'Mr C. I. Thornton' (*Chats on the Cricket Field*, Merritt & Hatcher, 1910).

ERIC PRICHARD, 'Hesketh Prichard' (*Hesketh Prichard – A Memoir*, E. P. Dutton, 1924).

ALAN GIBSON, 'Jackson' (*Jackson's Year*, Cassell, 1965).

IVO TENNANT, 'The "Three Ws" ' (*Frank Worrell: A Biography*, Lutterworth Press, 1987).

BRIAN STATHAM, 'The Truth About Trueman' (*Flying Bails*, Stanley Paul, 1961).

3 FAR PAVILIONS

'A *Country Vicar*', 'Cricket in Corfu' (reprinted in *The Cricketer*, 1977).

R. A. FITZGERALD, 'London' (*Wickets in the West*, Tinsley Brothers, 1873).

BRIGADIER G. P. L. WESTON, 'In Darkest Burma' (*The Cricketer*, 1946).

P. A. SNOW, /*Sydney Referee*. 'Seventh Match: Bau v. Queensland' (*The Cricket in the Fiji Islands*, Whitcombe & Tombs, New Zealand, 1949).

R. WILKINSON, 'Cricket in India' (*The Cricketer*, 1922).

CECIL HEADLAM, 'European Cricket in India' (*Ten Thousand Miles through India & Burma*, J. M. Dent, 1903).

J. H. FINGLETON, 'Arabs East of Suez' (*The Cricketer*, 1969).

HUBERT MARTINEAU, 'Water Martins in Egypt' (*My Life in Sport*, Water Martin Press, 1970).

4 CRICKET WATCHING

ROBERT LYND, 'The Gentlemen of England Batting' (*Irish and English Portraits and Impressions*, Francis Griffiths 1908).
PETER ROEBUCK, 'Something Fell from Heaven' (*The Cricketer*, 1981).
GEOFFREY GREEN, 'AWOL from Old Trafford' (*The Cricketer*, 1978).
CYRIL P. FOLEY, 'Alletson's Innings (*Autumn Foliage*, Methuen & Co., 1934).
EDMUND BLUNDEN, 'The Village Game' (*Cricket Country*, Collins, 1944).
W. PETT RIDGE, 'Taking Holiday' (*I Like to Remember*, Hodder & Stoughton, 1925).
TERENCE RATTIGAN, 'Wanted for Murder' (*The Cricketer*, 1964).
'Avon', 'Three Years Ago' (*The Cricketer*, 1941).
B. BENNISON, 'Cricket' (*Giants on Parade*, Rich and Cowan, 1936).
C. H. FREAME, 'How's That?' (*The Cricketer*, 1933).
'Taverner', 'The Aside of Cricket' (*The Cricketer*, 1944).
'A Country Vicar', 'Place aux Dames' (*The Cricketer*, 1931).
G. D. MARTINEAU, 'One Day – A Memory' (*The Cricketer*, 1939).

5 TECHNICAL MYSTERIES

'Gryllus', 'Captaincy Technological' (*Homage to Cricket*, Desmond Harmsworth, 1933).
LORD GRANVILLE GORDON, 'Playing the Game' (*Sporting Reminiscences*, Grant Richards, 1902).
A. C. MACLAREN, 'Three Types of Batsmen' (*Cricket*, Anthony Treherne & Co., 1906).
SIR PELHAM WARNER, 'Wicket-keeping' (*The Book of Cricket*, J. M. Dent & Sons, 1911, this edition by Sporting Handbooks, 1945).
MAJOR PHILIP TREVOR, 'Average Keeping' (*The Problems of Cricket*, Sampson Low, Marston & Co., 1907).
R. C. ROBERTSON-GLASGOW, 'The Day When Neither Umpire Knew *Who* Was Out' and 'A New Thing' (*The Cricketer*, 1965 and 1933).
R. W. V. ROBINS, 'On Making A Pair – Or, Rather, Four!' (*The Cricketer*, 1967).
CECIL HEADLAM, 'Masters of a Fading Art' (*The Cricketer*, Annual 1922-33).
J. BARTON KING, 'The Angler' (*A Century of Philadelphia Cricket*, ed. J. A. Lester, University of Pennsylvania Press, 1951).

6 CRICKET GROUNDS

J. C. SQUIRE, 'Broad Halfpenny Down' (*Sunday Mornings*, Heinemann, 1930).
GERALD BRODRIBB, 'Big Hits at Canterbury' (*The Cricketer*, 1962).
TREVOR BAILEY, 'Lord's' (*Wickets, Catches and the Odd Run*, Collins Willow, 1986).
GRAHAM WHITE, 'The New Pavilion' (*The Cricketer*, 1942).
A. A. THOMSON, 'See You at Scarborough' (*The Cricketer*, 1967).
FRANK KEATING, 'The Charm of Cheltenham' (*The Cricketer*, 1978).
H. H. MONTGOMERY, 'Kennington Oval' (*History of Kennington*, H. Stacey Gold and Hamilton Adams, & Co., 1889).
LAURENCE MEYNELL, 'Yorkshire' (*Famous Cricket Grounds*, Phoenix House, 1951).
R. C. ROBERTSON-GLASGOW, 'Manchester' (*Cricket Prints*, T. Werner Laurie, 1943).
RICHARD BINNS, 'A Cricket Pilgrimage' (*The Cricketer*, 1936).

7 COLLECTING

RON YEOMANS, 'Cricket Treasures in my Home Museum' (*The Cricketer*, Winter Annual, 1967-68).
L. E. S. GUTTERIDGE, 'Cricketana' (*The Cricketer*, 1959).
E. V. LUCAS, 'A Bargain' (*The Cricketer*, 1938).
DAVID LEMMON, 'Please, Sir, Will You Sign?' (*The Cricketer*, 1974).

ALAN GIBSON. 'Cricket in Fiction' (*The Cricketer*, 1973).

JAMES THORPE. 'Cricket Howlers' (*A Cricket Bag*, Wells Gardner, Darton & Co. Ltd, 1929).

8 A FUNNY GAME

GRAHAM WHITE. 'On Coming Out' (*The Cricketer*, 1957).

R. C. ROBERTSON-GLASGOW. 'Men, Cricket and Things' (*The Cricketer* Annual, 1931-32).

A. QUAIFE. 'Some Humours of Cricket' (*The Cricketer*, 1927).

A. S. GARDINER. 'The Autocrat of the Cricket Field' (published with 'The Old Crocks' from The Office, 24 Park Lane, 1917).

'*The Author of Leaves from the Diary of an Old Free Forester*', 'Types of Aggravating Cricketer' (*The Cricketer*, 1922).

'Henry'. 'Imaginary Interviews: Second Round' (*The Cricketer*, 1922).

PETER EDWARDS, 'A Day in the Life . . .' (*The Cricketer*, 1981).

R. C. ROBERTSON-GLASGOW. 'Nets' (*The Cricketer*, 1932).

E. V. LUCAS. 'Ladies and Lord's: Hints on Watching Cricket' (*The Cricketer* Annual, 1922-1923).

A. P. HERBERT. 'Cricket in the Caucasus' (*Mild and Bitter*, Methuen, 1936).

HERBERT FARJEON. 'The Season's Prospects' (*Cricket Bag*, Macdonald & Co., 1946).

DAVID M. ARMSTRONG. 'The Return Match with Kent' (*A Short History of Norfolk County Cricket*, Ranchi House, Holt, 1958).

B. G. WHITFIELD. 'Nominal Cricket' (*The Cricketer* Spring Annual, 1952).

JAMES THORPE. 'A Few Overthows' (*A Cricket Bag*, Wells Gardner, Darton & Co. Ltd, 1929).

9 MEMOIRS AND CONFESSIONS

PETER ROEBUCK. 'Little Acorns' (*The Cricketer*, 1982).

ALEC WAUGH. 'Club Cricket in the Twenties' (*The Cricketer*, Winter Annual 1969-70).

BERNARD HOLLOWOOD. 'Another Season, Another Time' (*The Cricketer*, 1960, reproduced by kind permission of *Punch*).

REV. JAMES PYCROFT. 'Jemmy Dean' (*Oxford Memories*, Richard Bentley & Son, 1886).

DENNIS CASTLE. 'Stand and Deliver' (*The Cricketer*, 1978).

LYNN DOYLE. 'Some Pastimes and a Funeral' (*Not Too Serious*, Duckworth, 1946).

ARTHUR WAUGH. 'Sydney Pawling' (*One Man's Road*, Chapman & Hall, 1931).

E. M. WELLINGS. 'Cricketers in Khaki' (*Vintage Cricketers*, George Allen & Unwin, 1983).

MARGARET CAMPBELL. 'The Obsessions of Englishmen' (*The Cricketer*, 1963).

MARY ANDERSON DE NAVARRO. 'Early Days at Broadway – Barrie and Cricket' (*A Few More Memories*, Hutchinson & Co., 1936).

SIEGFRIED SASSOON. 'The Flower Show Match' (*Memoirs of a Fox-hunting Man*, Faber, 1928).

10 FICTION DEPARTMENT

SIR HOME GORDON. 'County Cricket' (*That Test Match*, Duckworth & Co., 1921).

JOHN FINNEMORE. 'The Last Innings' (*Teddy Lester. Captain of Cricket*, W. & R. Chambers, 1916).

M. D. LYON. Chapter III (*A Village Match and After*, Eveleigh, Nash & Grayson, 1929).

LORD DUNSANY. 'How Jembu Played for Cambridge' (from *Best Sporting Stories*, chosen by J. Wentworth Day, Faber and Faber, 1942).

DENNIS CASTLE. 'The Clerks All Out' (*Run Out the Raj*, Joanna Productions, 1974).

DOROTHY L. SAYERS. 'Unexpected Conclusion of a Cricket Match' (*Murder Must Advertise*, Victor Gollanez Ltd, 1933).

The editors acknowledge with gratitude those who have given permission for the use of copyright material. Every effort has been made to trace all copyright holders and the editors apologise to anyone who has not been found or properly acknowledged. Subsequent editions will include any corrections or omissions notified to the editors.